LEGAL CASES FOR TEACHERS

LEGAL CASES FOR TEACHERS

G. R. BARRELL
B.Sc (Econ.), F.C.P., F.R.S.A.

Headmaster, Sir John Cass's Foundation and
Red Coat Church of England Secondary School, London

LONDON
METHUEN & CO LTD
11 NEW FETTER LANE EC4

217408

By the same author:

TEACHERS AND THE LAW

Distributed in the USA
by Barnes & Noble Inc

First published in 1970

© 1970 G. R. Barrell

SBN 416 19280 7

Printed in Great Britain by
Richard Clay (The Chaucer Press) Ltd,
Bungay, Suffolk

PREFACE

This book contains a wide variety of cases concerned with education in general
and schools in particular, and it is hoped that readers who are used to traditional case-books will not find distracting the inclusion of a number of
reports outside the scope of those normally included in such a work. Although
the book is sufficiently comprehensive to be of value to administrators,
professional associations, and others concerned with educational law, it was
primarily prepared to help practising teachers. Consequently it seemed
desirable to include as wide a variety as possible of situations which have
given rise to actions before the courts, even though some of the cases were
heard by inferior courts and, therefore, do not form precedents. For the non-
legal reader such cases may serve as illustrations of the way in which the
principles laid down in the superior courts may be applied.

Whilst this book was in the press, two important decisions were reported.
In *Crump* v. *Gilmore* (*The Times*, November 5, 1969) the Divisional Court of
the Queen's Bench Division held that the Education Act 1944, s. 39 (1),
created an absolute offence, and it is unnecessary to show any knowledge by
parents of absences or neglect to ensure that a child attends school regularly.
In *Butt* v. *Cambridgeshire and Isle of Ely County Council* (*The Times*, November 27, 1969) the Court of Appeal held that when children of nine or ten are
using pointed scissors it is not necessary to wait until after a lesson, or to
make sure the rest of the class put their scissors down, before giving individual attention to one child.

Permission to reproduce material from the reports has been granted by the
Incorporated Council of Law Reporting for England and Wales (*Law Reports*
and *Weekly Law Reports*), the Scottish Council of Law Reporting (*Sessions
Cases*), the Controller of Her Majesty's Stationery Office (*Inland Revenue
Tax Cases*), Butterworths (*All England Law Reports* and *Justice of the Peace
Reports*), Sweet and Maxwell (*Law Times Reports* and *Law Journal Reports*),
Charles Knight & Co., Ltd (*Local Government Reports*, the Solicitors' Law
Stationery Society (*Solicitors' Journal*), Times Newspapers Ltd (*The Times*
and the *Times Law Reports*), the Councils and Education Press, Ltd (*Education*), and the proprietors of *The Guardian*, the *Yorkshire Post*, the *Western
Morning News*, and the *Kentish Gazette*. Permission has also been granted by
the Trustees of the British Museum to make use of material obtained by
means of the Museum's Rapid Copy service. To all who have granted these
consents I am most grateful; as I am to my son, Douglas, for his assistance
in the preparation of the tables and the index.

G.R.B.

6 *December* 1969

CONTENTS

VII DEFAMATION OF TEACHERS

TABLE OF CASES

TABLE OF STATUTES

ABBREVIATIONS

1 Law Reports

A.C.	Law Reports (Appeal Cases), 1891–
All E.R.	All England Reports, 1936–
All E.R. Rep.	All England Reports Reprint
App. Cas.	Law Reports (Appeal Cases), 1875–90
Ark.	Arkyns (Chancery), 1736–54
B. & Ad.	Barnewall & Adolphus (King's Bench), 1830–34
B. & S.	Best & Smith (King's Bench), 1861–70
Barn. K.B.	Barnardiston (King's Bench), 1726–34
Bing. N.C.	Bingham's New Cases (Common Pleas), 1834–40
C. & P.	Carrington & Payne (Nisi Prius), 1823–41
Ch.	Law Reports (Chancery Division), 1891–
Ch. App.	Law Reports (Chancery Appeal Cases), 1865–75
Ch. D.	Law Reports (Chancery Division), 1875–90.
Com. Cas.	Commercial Cases (Commercial Court), 1895–1941
Cox C.C.	Cox's Criminal Cases, 1843–1941
Cr. M. & R.	Crompton, Meeson & Roscoe (Exchequer), 1834–36
Cunn.	Cunningham (King's Bench), 1734–36
D.	Session Cases, 2nd series [Dunlop], 1838–62
E.R.	English Reports (reprints of reports before 1865).
Esp.	Espinasse (Nisi Prius), 1793–1807
Ex.	Law Reports (Exchequer Division), 1865–75
F. & F.	Foster & Finlason (Nisi Prius), 1856–67
Gow	Gow (Nisi Prius), 1818–20
H. & C.	Hurlstone & Coltman (Exchequer), 1862–66
H. & N.	Hurlstone & Norman (Exchequer), 1856–62
Holt N.P.	Holt (Nisi Prius), 1815–17
I.R.	Irish Reports, 1838–
I.T.R.	Industrial Tribunal Reports, 1966–
J.P.	Justice of the Peace Reports, 1837–
Jur.	Jurist Reports, 1837–54
Jur. (N.S.)	Jurist Reports, New Series, 1855–66.
K.B. (Q.B.)	Law Reports (King's (Queen's) Bench Division), 1891–
K.I.R.	Knight's Industrial Reports, 1966–
L.G.R.	Knight's Local Government Reports, 1903–
L.J.Ch.	Law Journal (Chancery Section), 1831–1946
L.J.Eccl.	Law Journal (Ecclesiastical Section), 1866–75
L.J.Ex.	Law Journal (Exchequer Section), 1831–75
L.J.K.B. (L.J.Q.B.)	Law Journal (King's (Queen's) Bench Section), 1831–1946
L.J.M.C.	Law Journal (Magistrates' Courts Section), 1831–1896
L.J.P.C.	Law Journal (Privy Council Section), 1865–1946
L.J.Q.B. (L.J.K.B.)	Law Journal (Queen's (King's) Bench Section), 1831–1946
L.J.R.	Law Journal Reports, 1947–49
L.R.A. & E.	Law Reports (Admiralty and Ecclesiastical), 1865–75
L.T.	Law Times Reports, New Series, 1859–1947.
L.T.(O.S.)	Law Times Reports, Old Series, 1843–59
Ll.LR.	Lloyd's List Law Reports, 1919–50
Lloyd's Rep.	Lloyd's List Law Reports, 1951–
Macq.	Macqueen's Scottish Appeals (House of Lords), 1851–65
M. & S.	Moore & Scott (Common Pleas), 1831–34
P.D.	Law Reports (Probate Division), 1875–90
Peake, Add. Cas.	Peake's Additional Cases (Nisi Prius), 1795–1812
Q.B. (K.B.)	Law Reports (Queen's (King's) Bench Division), 1891–
Q.B.D.	Law Reports (Queen's Bench Division), 1875–90

R.	Session Cases, 4th Series [Rettie], 1873–1898
R.R.	Revised Reports, 1785–1866
Russ.	Russell (Chancery Appeals), 1823–29
S.C.	Sessions Cases, 1906–
S.L.T.	Scots Law Times, 1893–
S.J.	Solicitors' Journal, 1857–
Stark.	Starkie (Nisi Prius), 1814–23
Stra.	Strange (King's Bench), 1716–49
Tax Cas.	Tax Cases, 1875–
T.L.R.	Times Law Reports, 1884–1952
Tyr.	Tyrwhitt (Exchequer), 1830–35
Ves.	Vesey Junior (Chancery), 1789–1817. (The first two volumes of Vesey Junior's reports are cited as Ves. Jun.)
W.L.R.	Weekly Law Reports, 1953–
W.R.	Weekly Reporter, 1853–1906

2 Miscellaneous

Att.-Gen.	Attorney-General
B.	Baron [of the Exchequer]—an obsolete title for a judge of the Court of Exchequer: now superseded by the judges of the Queen's Bench Division
C.A.	Court of Appeal
C.B.	Chief Baron [of the Exchequer]—the principal judge of the former Court of Exchequer: now superseded by the Lord Chief Justice of England
C.J.	Chief Justice—formerly the principal judge of the Courts of King's Bench and of Common Pleas: now superseded by the Lord Chief Justice of England, who is the President of the Queen's Bench Division
D.C.	Divisional Court
H.L.	House of Lords
I.L.E.A.	Inner London Education Authority
J.	Justice
JJ.	Justices
K.C.	King's Counsel
L.C.C.	London County Council—the local education authority for London from 1902 until 1964, when it was superseded by the Inner London Education Authority
L.C.	Lord Chancellor—the head of the judiciary
L.C.J.	Lord Chief Justice of England—the presiding judge of the Queen's Bench Division and, in the Lord Chancellor's absence, the President of the High Court: also an *ex-officio* member of the Court of Appeal.
L.J.	Lord Justice of Appeal—a member of the Court of Appeal
L.JJ.	Lords Justices of Appeal
M.R.	Master of the Rolls—formerly a judge of the Court of Chancery and keeper of all patents and grants which pass the Great Seal: now a member of the Court of Appeal, over a Division of which he normally presides
N.P.	Nisi Prius
Orse	Otherwise
P.	President of the Probate, Divorce and Admiralty Division
P.C.	Judicial Committee of the Privy Council
P.D.	Probate Division
Q.C.	Queen's Counsel
R.	The King (or Queen)
s.	Section (of a statute)
v.	Against (in criminal cases); and (in civil cases)
V.-C.	Vice-Chancellor—a subordinate judge of the former Court of Chancery: the title is now used only in the Chancery Court of Lancaster

INTRODUCTION

1 Purpose of the Book

During the past few years there has been an increasing interest in the legal rights and responsibilities of teachers, a development which has stressed the need for a collection of forensic cases concerned with education. With two exceptions[1] those presented in the following pages still, at the time of writing, have an effect on educational matters which fall to be decided by the courts.

Since the book is primarily designed for the use of teachers it does not follow exactly the usual pattern of a case book intended for law students. Teachers are frequently concerned with situations which may lead to court proceedings, and their need is for guidance in such a form that they may so order their professional lives as to avoid conflict with the law. They are often, though not always, less concerned with a minute consideration of the details in the argument of a judgment. For this reason the facts are frequently set out more fully than in a lawyer's case book, and the report of the judgment is generally restricted to the *ratio decidendi*. The reader who wishes to follow the judges' reasoning in more detail is referred to the appropriate law reports, which may be consulted in the principal public libraries.

A second difference lies in the way in which the cases have been selected. Traditional case books usually include only leading cases, the decisions in which are binding in accordance with the principles explained below. It is hoped that the important principles concerned with the profession of teaching have all been included, but it will be found that a number of cases are set out in which the principle has been followed rather than stated. In some of the examples the decision may have been made by a court whose decision is not binding on other courts. The reason for this arrangement is that teachers, in their everyday professional lives, start in practice with the situation rather than with the legal principle.

There are few common-law principles concerned exclusively with education, and cases in this field are decided in accordance with the general rules of, say, trespass, negligence, or defamation. Consequently many of the basic principles are to be found in cases which have nothing to do with education. An excellent example is to be found in *Donoghue* v. *Stevenson*[2] where Lord Atkin, dealing with the general principle of negligence, defined the duty of care as a duty not to injure one's neighbour. He continued: "Who then, in

1. *R.* v. *Cockerton*, page 30; *Dyer* v. *London School Board*, page 36, *infra*.
2. [1932] A.C. 562.

law, is my neighbour? The answer seems to be persons who are so closely and directly affected by my act that I ought reasonably to have them in contemplation as being so affected when I am directing my mind to the acts or omissions which are called in question." This case was concerned with the marketing of soft drinks, but Lord Atkin's dictum has been commended with approval in a vast range of subsequent cases concerned with negligence, including those alleging negligence by a schoolmaster. Similarly, the same rules will be applied in considering questions of corporal punishment as are applied generally to cases of trespass against the person, although they are modified by the status of the schoolmaster *in loco parentis*.

In order to illustrate the application of binding principles of this kind to educational matters by the lower courts whose decisions are not to be regarded as established precedents, it has been decided to include one or two such cases.

For the benefit of readers without any legal training it has been thought helpful to include an introduction to the study of case law, and also to annotate some of the cases.

Terms marked with an asterisk are explained in the glossary at the end of the book.

2 Common and Statute Law

The meaning of the expression "common law" varies according to the context in which it is used. With the development of a strong central monarchy after the Norman Conquest local customs and local courts gave way gradually to a common justice administered to the whole country by the royal courts. The law so administered was frequently based on ancient English usages, but it is not surprising that there was an accretion of Norman law. The important point, however, is that this law was common to the whole realm. Sometimes it was enshrined in charters such as Magna Carta (1215), sometimes in statutes such as the Statute of Westminster I (1275) promulgated by the king with the advice of his council. The main stream of development, however, is to be found in the application of legal principles to facts proved in the courts. Before the days of systematic law reporting it was inevitable that different courts would apply the common law differently. Nevertheless, a means of standardisation was found in the county and central courts presided over by the king's officers. New patterns of fact called for fresh applications of the ancient legal principles by means of new decisions, or even new remedies, based on a reconsideration of the law, and these decisions and remedies gradually became part of the common law of the realm which, with every new decision, became more precise and certain in its application.

This is the basic definition of the common law: the law universally accepted throughout the kingdom. In his *Commentaries* (1765), Blackstone defined the term as "the ancient unwritten law of this kingdom," thus restricting the use to the law stated in judicial decisions as opposed to statute law. "The common

law," it was said, "is in the bosom of the judges." Various other expressions
have been used in an attempt to distinguish this particular aspect of the law,
and it is sometimes referred to as "case law" or "judge made law." The judges
have always been careful to state that they do not make law. There is, it is
said, in the common law of the realm everything which is necessary to enable
them to pronounce on any facts which might be argued before the courts, and
the function of the judges is to declare the law applicable to the cases they are
called upon to decide. Perhaps the most acceptable term for this form of law
is "declaratory law," although it frequently appears that a chain of decisions
moulds the law to such an extent that it is considerably changed over a period of
time, and gives the appearance of having been made by the judges. As will be
seen later, this impression is heightened by the binding force of precedent
which has the effect of preventing the reversal of certain judicial interpretations
save by Act of Parliament.

Uniformity in the administration of the common law was secured by the
development of the royal courts at Westminster. At different times the Court
of Exchequer, the Court of Common Pleas, and the Court of King's Bench
were separated from the King's Council (the *Curia Regis*), and began separate
existences which lasted until the Judicature Acts of 1873–75. It was the function of these courts to administer the common law, and sheriffs were ordered
to bring all men empanelled as jurors in any civil action in their counties to
Westminster on a certain date unless first (*nisi prius*) the itinerant justices of
assize had visited the county concerned. The *nisi prius* courts also formed part
of the common-law system, and civil actions were bound by the strict rules
of the Forms of Action. This meant that a plaintiff had to find a writ within
the four corners of which he could bring his action; if he made a mistake his
action failed and he had to start again, or abandon his cause.

The effect of this excessive formalism was that plaintiffs were sometimes
prevented from succeeding in a manifestly just action; sometimes it was
equally apparent that a suitor should not, in natural justice, be allowed to
enforce a judgment to which he was entitled at law. In such cases it was open
to the party aggrieved to refer the matter to the king, praying that justice
might be done "for conscience sake." Such petitions were referred to the
Chancellor who, in those days, was not only the principal Secretary of State
but also, until the sixteenth century, a dignitary of the Church and the keeper
of the king's conscience. The Chancellor was in no way bound by the rules
of the common-law courts, and was free to decide each issue equitably in
accordance with the principles of natural justice. Inevitably there was a con-
considerable degree of inconsistency between the decisions of different Chancellors, and even between successive rulings of the same Chancellor. There
was a great deal of truth in the jibe that "Equity is as long as the Chancellor's
boot." In time there grew up a body of equitable principles which were largely
rationalised during the eighteenth century. Although it was not considered
the function of equity to override the common law, but rather to remedy its
imperfections, there developed a distinction between the formalism of the

common law and the flexibility of equity, which forms the basis of a further differentiation in the use of the term "common law."

The term "common law" is also employed to distinguish between the municipal law of England and those systems of law (including the canon law of the Church) which are derived from Roman civil law. By an extension of this usage, countries whose legal systems are based on the English model are often referred to as "common-law countries."

The supreme court of the land is the High Court of Parliament. From the time of the Norman Conquest statutes were promulgated by the sovereign by and with the advice of the Great Council of the realm. In Tudor times the number of statutes began to increase. The heightening complexity of modern life, coupled with the extension of governmental activity into many departments of public and private affairs, has seen a mediaeval stream swell to a modern torrent of legislation. No court can override an Act of Parliament; but a statute may reverse completely the course of a branch of the common law as it has developed in the courts, sweeping aside and nullifying for the future what would otherwise be binding judgments. Statutes may break new ground and extend the range of governmental action into new spheres; they may consolidate the law in a particular subject, or they may amend or repeal previous common or statute law. Yet no statute is so perfectly drawn that it may be applied to every conceivable situation; Acts of Parliament deal in general principles, they do not envisage every particular situation. The courts must apply them to the cases they hear. Furthermore, even the Parliamentary drafting counsel may nod, and allow uncertainties to be enacted. Here, again, it is for the courts to determine, in accordance with established rules, what was the will of Parliament and, having determined the law, they must apply it. In dealing with statutes, as with the common law, it is still the function of the courts to declare the law in the circumstances of any case referred to them.

3 Civil and Criminal Law

It is, perhaps, a curious glamour which has given rise to the popular fallacy that criminal work forms the major activity of the courts. In fact, the reverse is true, and by far the greater proportion of the time of the courts is devoted to the adjudication of cases concerning the rights of citizens.

In a civil case the plaintiff brings an action against the defendant by which the former makes a claim or asks that his rights should be declared by the court, and that he should be granted any appropriate remedy which may be available in the circumstances. Essentially it is a dispute between two private citizens in which the plaintiff invokes the aid of the state to enforce his supposed rights. The plaintiff may, for example, ask for the enforcement of a contract, or he may seek to recover damage he claims to have suffered at the hands of the defendant; he may pray that his marriage be dissolved, or seek the direction of the court concerning a disputed will.

Some matters, however, are regarded as being so serious that society needs to be protected from the law-breaker. In criminal cases the alleged offender is prosecuted in the name, or on behalf, of the Queen, and if he is found guilty he is liable to punishment. Criminal offences range from the old common-law felonies such as treason, murder and arson to modern statutory offences such as failing to sign a driving licence. The ancient division was between felonies, which involved forfeiture of land and goods, and misdemeanours, which were generally punished by fine or imprisonment. The Forfeiture Act 1870, s. 1, abolished forfeiture for treason and felony, and the distinction has thus become somewhat blurred. The tendency today is to distinguish between indictable and non-indictable offences. Indictable offences are triable before a jury at quarter sessions or assizes, the indictment being a statement of the charge preferred. Non-indictable, or summary, offences are tried before lay or professionally qualified stipendiary magistrates, the statement of the alleged offence being contained in an information laid by a complainant who may be a police officer, an officer of a local authority, or even a private citizen.

This distinction does not end the matter. Some offences are triable either summarily or on indictment. In certain cases the accused may elect to be tried before a jury, accepting the possibility that if he is found guilty the sentence is likely to be heavier than that which the magistrates have power to impose. Again, if the magistrates find a case proved in summary proceedings, but feel that they have not power to impose a sufficiently heavy penalty, they may record the conviction and send the defendant to quarter sessions for sentence.

There are also certain matters which may form the basis either of a civil action or of a criminal prosecution, or of both. Some of these are of particular interest to the teaching profession. Trespass against the person, including false imprisonment as well as the varying degrees of assault, is normally dealt with as a criminal matter. Thus, a schoolmaster who is alleged to have administered unreasonable corporal punishment is usually charged with assault, assault and battery, or a more serious offence if the circumstances appear to warrant it. It is by no means unknown, however, for a civil action for damages arising from the alleged assault to be brought.

On the other hand, cases arising from defamation are generally the subject of civil actions for damages arising from the tort. From time to time, nevertheless, there are instances where the situation arises from so flagrant a disregard of responsibility that it is arguable that there has been an offence against society. In these circumstances it is possible to charge the alleged offender with criminal libel. Similarly, matters of negligence are normally dealt with by civil process, but a gross breach of the duty of care may lead to a prosecution for criminal negligence.

4 The Hierarchy of the Courts

In order to understand the doctrine of the binding force of precedent it is necessary to understand the hierarchy and jurisdiction of the courts. The present system of English courts is as follows:

A   The High Court of Parliament
(*a*) *The House of Lords*—The Committee of Privileges determines all disputed claims to peerages, and disputes concerned with the privileges of the House. Theoretically, the House can still try those impeached before it by the House of Commons, but the practice has fallen into disuse since *Lord Melville's Case* in 1805. The right of peers to be tried by their House for treason and felony was abolished by the Criminal Justice Act 1948. The House still hears appeals from the English Court of Appeal, the Court of Appeal of Northern Ireland (except in constitutional matters), and the Scottish Court of Session. Lay peers do not participate in the jurisdiction of the House as a court; this is exercised by the Lord Chancellor and not more than nine Lords of Appeal in Ordinary. Former Lord Chancellors and peers who have held high judicial office may sit if they wish.

(*b*) *The House of Commons*—The jurisdiction of the House of Commons is confined to matters touching its own privileges.

B   The Supreme Court of Judicature
(*a*) *The Court of Appeal*—Since 1966 this court has consisted of the Civil and Criminal Divisions, and is staffed by Lords Justices of Appeal, augmented when necessary by puisne* judges of the High Court. The Master of the Rolls presides over the Civil Division, the Lord Chief Justice of England over the Criminal Division. The Court of Criminal Appeal, which existed from 1907 to 1966 did not form part of the Supreme Court of Judicature, although it exercised an analogous appellate jurisdiction in criminal matters.

(*b*) *The High Court of Justice*
   (*i*) *The Queen's Bench Division*—Any Division of the High Court has power to try any action. In practice, however, the Queen's Bench Division has taken over the work of the former Courts of Queen's Bench, Common Pleas, and Exchequer. Thus it deals with cases arising out of breach of contract, torts, and the recovery of land; and it exercises a supervisory jurisdiction to prevent abuse of power by public officials, authorities, and even the central executive. All assize courts form a part of the Division. Appeals from magistrates' courts on points of law by way of case stated are heard by a Queen's Bench Divisional Court, normally consisting of three, sometimes two, judges.
   (*ii*) *The Chancery Division*—The jurisdiction of the Chancery Division is largely concerned with trusts, the administration of estates, partnerships, the wardship of infants and the care of their estates, company law, and bankruptcy. A Chancery Divisional Court may hear bankruptcy appeals from the county courts.
   (*iii*) *The Probate, Divorce and Admiralty Division*—The reason for assigning three jurisdictions, apparently so diverse, to one Division is largely historical. Testamentary and matrimonial matters were long dealt with by

the ecclesiastical courts. Canon law was considerably influenced by Roman law in the Middle Ages, and this influence was not lost during the Reformation. Similarly, maritime law was based on the international customs enshrined in the Laws of Oléron which were also rooted in Roman law. Hence the jurisdiction of this Division represents that part of the law which owes more to civil than to common law. A Divisional Court may hear matrimonial appeals from the magistrates' courts.

C   The Judicial Committee of the Privy Council

The Judicial Committee of the Privy Council consists of all Privy Councillors who hold, or have held, high judicial office. This term includes High Court judges, Lords Justices of Appeal, and the Lords of Appeal in Ordinary. Eminent Commonwealth judges who are Privy Councillors may be called on to sit. Until the passing of the Statute of Westminster 1931, the Committee was the final court of appeal for all the Dominions and Colonies. Under that Act, however, the self-governing Dominions were permitted to abolish such appeals and many of them have done so. The Committee also hears appeals from the ecclesiastical courts, the Prize Court, the courts of the Channel Islands and the Isle of Man, and from the Disciplinary Committees of the General Medical Council and the General Dental Council. The Committee's findings take the form of advice to the Queen, but if it is a majority finding this is not indicated, and no dissenting judgment is delivered.

D   Quarter Sessions

Quarter sessions are general sittings of all the magistrates of a county, although in practice the jurisdiction is now usually exercised by a legally qualified chairman or deputy chairman. Borough quarter sessions are held before the Recorder, who must be legally qualified. The jurisdiction is considerable, and extends to all indictable offences not punishable by death, by imprisonment for life on a first conviction, or cases of an "unusually grave or difficult nature." Quarter sessions have a limited civil jurisdiction, and may hear appeals from the magistrates' courts. The hearing of such appeals takes the form of a re-trial.

E   County Courts

The modern county court is in no way descended from the medieval sheriffs' court, but is the creation of a nineteenth-century statute. These courts deal purely with civil matters, and to a considerable extent their jurisdiction is concurrent with that of the High Court in common law, equity, admiralty, and probate. There are, however, limitations of consent, class, or amount. The county courts, which are presided over by a legally qualified judge, also exercise a special jurisdiction under certain statutes.

F   Magistrates' Courts

Formerly known as petty sessions, the magistrates' courts consist of the magistrates of a division of a county sitting to deal with summary (non-indictable) offences arising within their division. Mostly they are not professionally qualified, and are therefore collectively described as "lay." In certain urban areas the jurisdiction is exercised by a legally-qualified stipendiary magistrate, who may sit alone. Except in certain strictly limited matters two magistrates form a quorum in courts not presided over by a stipendiary. A person accused of a petty offence which carries a maximum penalty of more than three months' imprisonment may elect to be tried by a jury at quarter sessions; alternatively, some indictable offences may be tried summarily. Three magistrates, selected from a specially nominated panel, and sitting in a different place or at a different time from the ordinary court, form a juvenile court for trying persons under seventeen. Magistrates' courts have a limited civil jurisdiction: they may make affiliation orders, and orders for judicial separation and maintenance. Justices of the peace also act as examining magistrates in indictable offences: unless they determine that a prima facie* case has been made out, an accused person cannot be sent for trial. Magistrates' courts still undertake certain administrative functions, including the issue of licences for the sale of intoxicants and, in some areas, of licences for stage plays, music, and dancing.

This summary of the jurisdiction of the courts is not intended to be complete, but it is adequate for an understanding of the cases included in the book. Consequently, no account has been taken of the coroners' courts, of the complex structure of the ecclesiastical courts, or of the vast range of tribunals which has developed in recent years. The reader anxious to complete his knowledge of English courts will find these described in text books on the English legal system or on constitutional law.

5 Appeals

During the course of English legal history a procedure has developed by which any person who feels himself aggrieved by a decision in the courts may, with certain limitations, appeal against that decision. Such appeals may be based on a number of grounds.

A person convicted of a criminal offence may appeal either against the conviction or against the sentence. An appeal against conviction embraces an appeal against sentence since, if the conviction is quashed, no sentence can be imposed. An appeal against sentence, however, accepts the verdict of the court, but seeks to establish that the sentence, having regard to all the facts, was too heavy.

An appeal may lie on a matter of fact or a matter of law. If an appeal is made on a matter of fact, the appellant alleges the court was in error in holding as proved the facts which led to its decision; if the appeal be on a point of law it is pleaded that the court found the facts correctly, but was at fault in applying the law to them.

A summary of the appellate system is given below.

A From Magistrates' Courts

(a) *To quarter sessions*—This course is open only to the defence, and is one of the few appellate procedures which involves a complete rehearing of the case. All the evidence is re-heard, with the effect that questions both of fact and law are reviewed. Appeals to quarter sessions in boroughs having a recorder are heard by the Recorder alone, although he sits with two juvenile-court magistrates as assessors when hearing appeals by persons under the age of seventeen. Quarter sessions may also hear appeals against sentence.

(b) *To the Queen's Bench Division*—Either the prosecution or the defence may appeal to a Divisional Court of the Queen's Bench Division, which normally consists of three judges. Such an appeal is by way of case stated, and is possible only on questions of law. The appellant requires the magistrates to state a case, that is, to prepare a statement of the facts as found at the trial and of the legal problem involved. Since the facts are not in dispute they are not argued in the Divisional Court, but are accepted as proved. The Divisional Court may affirm the conviction or acquittal; if, however, it is decided that the magistrates were wrong in law, the Divisional Court does not of itself set aside the magistrates' decision. The case is remitted to the court which heard it, with a direction to reverse its verdict. This procedure may be employed either directly from the magistrates' court, or following an appeal to quarter sessions.

B From County Courts

(a) *In bankruptcy matters*—Appeal lies to a Divisional Court of the Chancery Division.

(b) *In all other matters*—Appeal lies to the Civil Division of the Court of Appeal (see below).

C From Quarter Sessions

(a) *To the Queen's Bench Division*—The procedure is as outlined above for appeals from magistrates' courts. Quarter sessions may be asked to state a case in matters concerned either with their original or with their appellate jurisdiction.

(b) *To the Court for Crown Cases Reserved (1884-1907)*—The power of convicted persons to challenge verdicts was very restricted under the common law, and was limited to errors appearing on the record. A new trial might be ordered where there had been a miscarriage of justice during the trial of a misdemeanour, but this was not extended to felonies. The judges, however, developed a practice of reserving their judgments in difficult cases for discussion with their colleagues. This procedure was given statutory sanction in 1884 by the establishment of the Court for Crown Cases Reserved to which any judge of assize or chairman of quarter sessions could refer a difficult point of law. The Court consisted of an uneven number of judges, being not less than three nor more than thirteen. Reference to the Court, however, was

B

entirely at the discretion of the trial judge, so that the Court scarcely merits
more than a mention in a description of the appellate system.

(c) *To the Court of Criminal Appeal (1907–66)*—Mounting dissatisfaction,
centred round the miscarriage of justice in the trial of Adolf Beck, led to the
establishment of the Court of Criminal Appeal, of which all judges of the
Queen's Bench Division, together with the Lord Chief Justice, were members.
Appeals were heard by three judges. Any persons convicted on indictment had
an absolute right of appeal to the Court against conviction on a question of
law. On a question of fact, or of mixed law and fact it was necessary to obtain
a certificate from the trial judge, or leave of the Court of Criminal Appeal.
Leave of the Court was necessary for an appeal against sentence. The Court
was empowered to interfere with a verdict if it appeared that "on any ground
there was a miscarriage of justice," but this provision was strictly interpreted
and the Court would not interfere where the issue was purely one of disputed
evidence. Appeal against sentence carried the risk that the sentence would be
increased if the Court thought fit. The Court of Criminal Appeal did not form
part of the High Court of Judicature.

(d) *To the Court of Appeal—Criminal Division (from September 1966)*—The
Criminal Appeal Act 1966 abolished the Court of Criminal Appeal, establishing in its place a Criminal Division of the Court of Appeal as part of the
Supreme Court of Judicature. Judges of the Queen's Bench Division may sit
at the request of the Lord Chief Justice. The Criminal Division has already
developed the practice of sitting in three divisions. Of these one, including the
Lord Chief Justice and a Lord of Appeal, hears appeals; the other divisions,
each consisting of one Lord Justice and two puisne judges,★ hear applications.
The Court may quash a verdict which is "under all the circumstances of the
case unsafe or unsatisfactory," and the power to increase sentences has been
removed. The Court of Criminal Appeal had no power to hear new evidence
unless it was not available at the trial, and did not normally admit evidence
referring to events after the trial. The Criminal Division is required to hear
evidence, provided it is relevant and appears to be credible, if satisfied that it
was not given at the trial and there is a reasonable explanation for the failure.

D   *From the High Court*
(a) *Criminal matters*—Appeals from the criminal side of the assizes have
always been on the same footing as appeals from quarter sessions described in
the three preceding subsections. The Administration of Justice Act 1960 provides that appeals against the judgment of a Divisional Court of the Queen's
Bench Division may be made under a procedure similar to that governing
appeals from the Court of Appeal (Criminal Division) as described below.

(b) *Civil matters*—Unless the parties agree not to appeal, an appeal lies from
all divisions of the High Court to the Court of Appeal (Civil Division). Leave
is necessary when an appeal is taken from a Divisional Court. The Court of

Appeal consists of any three of the permanent judges of the Court; if there is considerable pressure of work a puisne judge of the High Court may be asked to sit. The Court has power to hear witnesses, but seldom does so, and does not in any case re-hear evidence given at the trial. The decision of the Court is given, if necessary, by a majority. It is open to an appellant to apply for a new trial, but this is an expensive procedure which has been employed rarely since judges in civil actions have tended to sit without juries.

E   From the Court of Appeal

(a) *Criminal matters*—Appeal lies to the House of Lords from the Criminal Division of the Court of Appeal. It also lay from the Court of Criminal Appeal between 1907 and 1966. Such an appeal may be lodged either by the Crown or by the convicted person, but it cannot be heard except by leave of the Court of Appeal (Criminal Division) or of the House itself. The Administration of Justice Act 1960 provided that such leave should be granted only if the Court of Criminal Appeal (now the Criminal Division of the Court of Appeal) certifies that a point of law of general importance is involved, and that it appeared to the Court of Criminal Appeal or the House of Lords that the point should be considered by the House. The same Act provided, subject to similar safeguards, for appeals from a Divisional Court of the Queen's Bench Division to the House of Lords, where judgments are delivered in the form of speeches which are put to the vote of the qualified members of the House who are in attendance.

(b) *Civil matters*—Appeal also lies from the Civil Division of the Court of Appeal to the House of Lords. As in criminal cases it is necessary to obtain leave either from the Court of Appeal or the House of Lords. About two-thirds of the applications are refused; rarely is the decision of the Court of Appeal reversed. Appeals are usually confined to points of law rather than matters of fact.

6   The Binding Force of Precedent

It is important that law should be predictable and ascertainable. As has already been shown, decisions made in the courts have two effects. In the first place they decide an issue between the parties in the case; secondly they declare the law applicable to the facts in issue. It is a common fallacy that every judgment not successfully appealed against, becomes a precedent for the future. The extent to which any judgment is to be regarded as binding depends upon the hierarchy of the courts already described. Decisions made in the inferior courts, *i.e.* those below the High Court, are not binding, and it must be remembered that, within its jurisdiction, a superior court may overrule the finding of the court below.

From time to time the courts find themselves in some difficulty in dealing with existing precedents. In such cases they may well find some slight difference of fact which enables them to distinguish the case before them from the precedent. Unless this can be done the precedent must be followed if it is binding on the court concerned.

The effect of the doctrine of the binding force of precedent is as follows:

The House of Lords, traditionally, binds itself as well as all lower courts. However, in 1967, the Lord Chancellor indicated publicly that in future it must not necessarily regard itself as absolutely bound by its own decisions. Decisions of the House in Scottish cases are treated as authoritative in England, unless the law on the subject is different from English law. Once the House has pronounced judgment on a given point of law the only means to effect a change is by legislation, although this statement will need qualification if the House follows the Lord Chancellor's advice referred to above.

The Judicial Committee of the Privy Council does not bind other courts; neither is it bound by its own decisions. Although not binding on courts in this country, the advice tendered to the Queen by the Judicial Committee is regarded by other courts with great respect, and has high persuasive value, but this may vary with the personal authority of the members of the Committee and does not rest on the binding effect of precedent.

The Court of Appeal (Civil Division) binds all lower courts, and is generally bound by its own decisions.

The Court of Criminal Appeal (1907–66) was not bound by decisions of the Court of Appeal (now the Civil Division). This court was always sensible of the fact that it was dealing with matters in which the liberty of the subject was at stake and, for this reason, it was not unusual for it to depart from one of its own previous decisions where this appeared faulty.

The Court of Appeal (Criminal Division) may be expected to follow a policy similar to that of the Court of Criminal Appeal.

A Divisional Court is not strictly bound by the decisions of the Court of Appeal, but the two Courts have taken care in recent years to keep their decisions in harmony in cases where their jurisdiction is not mutually exclusive. A Divisional Court of the Queen's Bench Division is probably bound by decisions of the Court of Appeal (Criminal Division), and was probably bound similarly by the Court of Criminal Appeal.

High Court judges are bound by all courts superior to them, but not by each other at first instance, *i.e.* when trying cases alone or with a jury. Nevertheless a judge will often incline to follow another unless convinced that he was wrong; much depends, naturally, on the persuasive authority of the judge in question.

County court judges are bound by all superior courts. The correctly reported decision of a county court judge may have considerable persuasive authority, even in the Court of Appeal, as evidence of county court practice.

The Scottish Court of Session is regarded with great respect, even in the Court of Appeal, on points where English and Scottish law are identical.

Magistrates are bound by the decisions of all superior courts, but their decisions do not bind each other.

7 *Ratio Decidendi* and *Obiter Dicta*

The name *ratio decidendi* is given to those parts of the reasoning of a judgment which are relevant to the point in issue and, strictly speaking, it is only the *ratio decidendi* which is binding on future decisions. Any statements made by the judge on matters which are not necessary to the decision of the point, or points, in issue are known as *obiter dicta*.[3] The dividing line is not clearly marked and, if counsel have argued the point before the court, a ruling given is usually accepted as a precedent, even when it goes beyond the facts of the case. Where there are several judges and differing opinions, only the majority decision is regarded as binding; nevertheless, within the scope of that decision more than one binding reason may be assigned for reaching it. *Obiter dicta* have an authority which depends largely on the reputation of the judge from whom they fall.

It is only in the superior courts that the court itself seeks all the binding cases relevant to the facts in question. In the inferior courts it is much more usual to rely on counsel to refer to these during the course of their argument. As a result it occasionally happens that a court comes to a decision different from that in the leading case simply because its attention was not called to the precedent. Such an inconsistent ruling is not binding and is said to be *per incuriam*.

Judgments are frequently given immediately after the completion of evidence and argument. Sometimes, however, the court decides to take time to consider its findings. Such judgments, distinguished in the Law Reports by the words *curia advisari vult* are generally regarded as more persuasive.

8 Law Reports and Citation

The practice of law reporting has a long history, but it is only in comparatively recent times that it has achieved a consistently high standard of reliability. The earliest records are the *Year Books* which cover most of the period from 1289 to 1535, and are chiefly concerned with real property. They are notes on methods of pleading rather than reports of evidence or the trial of issues.

From the end of the sixteenth century there began a collection of cases both in common law and equity. For the modern lawyer their value varies enormously. In some cases they consisted of posthumous editions of the trial notes of eminent judges, in others they were glossed and elaborated to such an extent that it is difficult to separate the report from editorial comment. The fullest exposition of common-law principles belonging to this period is to be found in the reports of Lord Chief Justice Coke during the reign of James I. Indeed, so great is the esteem in which they are held that they are frequently referred to as *The Reports*, and are cited as "Rep."

The year 1785 saw the establishment, for the first time, of a contemporary series known as the *Term Reports*. These were prepared by regular reporters,

3. Literally, "sayings by the way." The singular is *obiter dictum*.

and included an outline of the pleadings, details of the facts, the arguments of counsel, and the judgment. Judgments of the House of Lords were not included before 1800, and at no time were the decisions of single judges on assize reported.

The present series of reports began with the establishment of the semi-official Council of Law Reporting in 1865. All the courts are covered by the *Law Reports*, the annual volumes of which appear in monthly parts. The reports include a headnote giving a summary of the points in issue, a summary of the case and the findings, a statement of the facts, the arguments of counsel, the judgments, and the decision of the court. The reports are prepared from the transcripts, and the judges have an opportunity to verify the accuracy of the report. The volumes are:

Chancery Division	Ch.
Probate, Divorce and Admiralty Division	P.
Queen's Bench Division, Volume 1	1 Q.B.
Queen's Bench Division, Volume 2	2 Q.B.
Appeal Cases[4]	A.C.

A precedent is binding from the moment of judgment, but it is clearly not possible to prepare the full report immediately and publish it in the full form of the *Law Reports*. In order to reduce the delay in making decisions available the Council commenced publication in 1953 of the *Weekly Law Reports*. Three annual volumes are issued in weekly parts. The arguments of counsel are not given, but the judgments are reported in full. Opportunity is also taken to include cases which will not be included in the *Law Reports*, and also to include decisions of importance on assize, in the Restrictive Practices Court, in diocesan consistory courts, and elsewhere. The cases of lesser importance, which will not receive fuller treatment, are printed in Volume 1; those which it is intended to include in the *Law Reports* appear in Volumes 2 and 3.

In addition to the semi-official *Law Reports* there are several proprietary series of which the most important is, perhaps, the *All England Reports* which first appeared in 1936.

Recognised abbreviations are used in referring to cases which have appeared in these reports. In citing a case it is customary to begin with the year-date of the volume in which the report is to be found (which is not necessarily the year of the hearing). If the date is an essential part of the reference it is placed in square brackets; if not it is in round brackets. The date is followed by the initials of the series, preceded by the volume number. Then comes a page number. This is the first page of the report of the case cited; it may be followed by another number preceded by the word "at" which refers to the exact page to which reference is being made. Thus:

Munson v. *British Railways Board and Others* [1966] 1 Q.B. 813.
This refers to a case actually heard on July 8 and 9, 1965, but which was not

4. House of Lords and Judicial Committee of the Privy Council.

reported in the *Law Reports* until a year later. The report begins on page 813 of Volume 1 of the Queen's Bench Division reports. As has been seen, the Appeal Cases reports are confined to the House of Lords and the Judicial Committee of the Privy Council. Therefore, although this case was heard in the Court of Appeal, it is included in the Queen's Bench cases since it began in that Division.

Murphy v. *Verati* [1967] 1 W.L.R. 641 at 644.
This was an appeal to the Queen's Bench Division by way of case stated, and was heard on February 7, 1967. The reader is being referred to a part of the judgment appearing on page 644, the actual report commencing on page 641. As it appears in Volume 1 of the *Weekly Law Reports* it is unlikely to appear in the *Law Reports* themselves.

9 Overseas Cases

Cases heard overseas, *e.g.* in the Dominions or in other common-law countries such as the United States of America, may be cited in English courts if the law is manifestly the same in the two countries. The respect accorded to any particular decision depends on the persuasive force of the court which heard the case, and no English court is bound by such judgments. *The English and Empire Digest* presents a conspectus of many such cases.

I

THE ADMINISTRATION
OF EDUCATION

(A) CENTRAL ADMINISTRATION:
POWER OF COURTS

1 Board of Education v. Rice [1911] A.C. 179

HOUSE OF LORDS

It is the duty of the Board of Education to determine questions arising between the local education authority and the managers of a voluntary school. In the event of failure by the Board there is a remedy by way of mandamus* and certiorari.*

Facts: The managers of a non-provided school* in Swansea alleged that the Swansea Borough Council were failing to "maintain and keep efficient" the school on the ground that the salaries paid to the teachers were insufficient, being lower than those paid by the authority to teachers in similar provided schools.* The Board of Education did not adopt the findings of a public inquiry which were favourable to the managers, the Board giving its decision in a document which failed to deal with the matters in issue.

The managers obtained a writ of certiorari from a Divisional Court of the King's Bench Division,[1] for the purpose of quashing the decision, and also a writ of mandamus directing the Board to determine the question. The Board of Education appealed to the Court of Appeal, which affirmed the decision of the Divisional Court.[2] The Board appealed further to the House of Lords, which affirmed the decision of the Court of Appeal.

Extract from Speeches

LORD LOREBURN L.C.: . . . I proceed now to consider what is the statutory duty laid upon the Board of Education in regard to disputes of this kind.

Their duties, so far as concerns the present litigation, are twofold. In the first place they are required by section 7 (3) of the Act of 1902 to determine a certain class of questions. The words of the subsection run as follows: "If any

1. *Rice v. Board of Education* [1909] 2 K.B. 1045.
2. *R. v. Board of Education* [1910] 2 K.B. 165.

16

question arises under this section between the local education authority and the managers of a school not provided by the authority, that question shall be determined by the Board of Education. . . ."

Comparatively recent statutes have extended, if they have not originated, the practice of imposing upon departments or officers of state the duty of deciding or determining questions of various kinds. In the present instance, as in many others, what comes for determination is sometimes a matter to be settled by discretion, involving no law. It will, I suppose, usually be of an administrative kind; but sometimes it will involve matter of law as well as matter of fact, or even depend upon matter of law alone. . . . I need not add that in doing either they must act in good faith and listen fairly to both sides, for that is a duty lying upon everyone who decides anything. But I do not think they are bound to treat such a question as though it were a trial. They have no power to administer an oath, and need not examine witnesses. They can obtain information in any way they think best, always giving a fair opportunity to those who are parties in the controversy for correcting or contradicting any relevant statement prejudicial to their view. Provided this is done, there is no appeal from the determination of the Board under section 7 (3) of this Act. The Board have, of course, no jurisdiction to decide abstract questions of law, but only to determine actual concrete differences that may arise, and as they arise, between the managers and the local education authority. The Board is in the nature of the arbitral tribunal, and a court of law has no jurisdiction to hear appeals from the determination either upon law or upon fact. But if the court is satisfied either that the Board have not acted judicially in the way I have described or have not determined the question which they are required by the Act to determine, then there is a remedy by mandamus and certiorari.

In the second place the Board are authorised, by section 16 of the Act of 1902, to make such order as they think necessary or proper for the purpose of compelling the local education authority to fulfil its duty, if after holding a public inquiry they think it has failed to fulfil any of its duties under the Act of 1902. . . .

Such being the duties of the Board of Education, I next inquire what it is that they have done. They have purported to determine a question under section 7 (3) of the Act which I do not think was really that which arose between the parties. . . .

In my opinion the questions which the Board of Education were required by section 7 (3) of the Act of 1902 to determine in this case are accurately stated at the end of Mr Eden's letter of February 3, 1908, on behalf of the managers in the following terms: (1) Whether the local education authority have in fixing and paying the salaries of the teachers fulfilled their duty under subsection (1) of section 7 of the Act. (2) Whether the salaries inserted in the teachers' present agreements are reasonable in amount and ought to be paid by the authority, or what salaries the authority ought to pay.

I am of opinion that the Education Board have not really determined these questions in the document of December 17, 1908, which purports to be their decision. I think there has been a confusion between the points that were to be decided and the arguments of either side, and perhaps also a confusion between the Board's duty under section 7 (3) and their duty under section 16. The managers were entitled to an explicit determination of the questions which they raised. This they have not obtained, and though in the mass of mixed argument and assertion which lasted over years, and was complicated by other disputes which have now been settled, there may have been room for misunderstanding, the true questions were those formulated in Mr Eden's letter of February 3, 1908, which I have already quoted. That suffices to dipose of the case, and I move your Lordships to dismiss this appeal with costs.

Appeal dismissed

[NOTE: The facts on which this case was based are no longer likely to give rise to a similar dispute, since the salaries payable to teachers in all maintained schools are now determined in accordance with the Remuneration of Teachers Act 1965 and the Burnham scales are binding on all local education authorities. But section 7 (3) of the Education Act 1902 was re-enacted as section 29 (9) of the Education Act 1921 and the current provision for the determination of disputes is contained in section 67 (1) of the Education Act 1944, which gives the Secretary of State similar powers to determine disputes between a local education authority and the managers or governors of county, as well as voluntary, schools. To the Secretary of State's exercise of those powers the principles laid down in the present case would apply.]

2 Gillingham Corporation *v.* Kent County Council [1952] 2 All E.R. 1107; [1953] Ch. 37

CHANCERY DIVISION
The courts have no jurisdiction to entertain an action to question a decision by the Minister of Education upon a matter which has been referred to him under statutory provisions.

Facts: By the Education Act 1921, s. 3 (1)(*b*), the council of a non-county borough with a population of more than ten thousand according to the census of 1901 were the local education authority for elementary education, and the county council were the authority for higher education by virtue of section 3(2) (*a*).

In 1937 the Gillingham Borough Council leased the Gillingham Technical Institute to the Kent County Council for the purposes of higher education. The Education Act 1944, s. 6 (1), as read with Schedule IX, made the county council the local education authority for all purposes and, by section 6 (3), provided that all property held by a county district for their functions relating to education immediately prior to April 1, 1945, should be transferred to the local education authority for the county.

The Gillingham Borough Council issued a writ for a declaration that the technical institute had not been transferred to the county council by virtue of the Education Act 1944, s. 6 (1). The county council sought to have the service of the writ set aside on the ground that the question fell to be determined by the Minister of Education under section 96 (2) of the 1944 Act.

Section 96 (2) provides:

> "Where any question arises as to whether any officers, property, rights, or liabilities, have been transferred by virtue of this Act from a former authority to a local education authority, that question shall be determined by the Minister."

Extract from Judgment

DANCKWERTS J.: . . . The Gillingham Technical Institute was not used by the borough council for elementary education, but was leased by them to the county council for the purposes of higher education, and, therefore, it is contended by the corporation that the borough council were not a local education authority in respect of the property and that the matter is not determinable by the Minister under section 96 (2) of the Act of 1944. It is, however, plain that the borough council were a local education authority for some purposes. If the clear effect of section 96 (2) is to refer the dispute to the decision of the Minister, there is authority that the jurisdiction of the court is ousted and is transferred to the tribunal provided for by the statute: see *Crisp* v. *Bunbury*,[1] which was decided in 1832 and approved by the Court of Appeal in *Joseph Crosfield & Sons Ltd* v. *Manchester Ship Canal Co.*[2] There is no doubt that the principle has often been recognised, but it is argued on behalf of the borough council that I ought to have regard to the purpose of this statutory provision and the nature of the council with which it is concerned and that it cannot have been intended to give the Minister power to decide what is really a question of the construction of section 6 (3), and, therefore, a matter of law. But if I am satisfied on the precise terms of section 96 (2) of the Act of 1944 that the question is referred to the Minister for decision, it seems to me that I have no choice in the matter.

It is plain that the dispute concerns property and whether or not that property has been transferred to the county council by section 6 (3) of the Act of 1944. In my opinion, a local education authority for the purposes of the provisions of former Acts is "a former authority" for the purposes of the Act of 1944 even though under the former Acts the council was only a local education authority for certain purposes, and, therefore, the borough council is a "former authority" within the meaning of section 96 (2) of the Act of 1944. It seems to me that the words of section 96 (2) are perfectly plain and that this is a matter which is not open to consideration by this court because by that subsection it must be referred to the decision of the Minister. Accordingly, it seems to me that this motion succeeds and that I should set aside the service of the writ.

Order accordingly

1. (1832) 8 Bing. 394; 1 L.J.C.P. 112; 131 E.R. 445.
2. [1904] 2 Ch. 123; on appeal [1905] A.C. 421, H.L.

3 Blencowe v. Northamptonshire County Council [1907] 1 Ch. 504

CHANCERY DIVISION

The courts have no jurisdiction to deal with a question arising between the managers of a voluntary school and the local education authority where statute has provided that the central administration shall determine that question.

Facts: The buildings of Marston St Lawrence public elementary school had been erected about 1847 by the owners, who permitted their use by a body of managers as a national school in connexion with the Church of England. In 1877 the school was put under government inspection, and became a public elementary school. The owners continued to allow the use of the school premises voluntarily and without rent for the purposes of such a school.

On ordinary days the register was marked at 9.45 a.m., and was closed at the end of the religious instruction period at 10 a.m. The children were taken to church at 11 a.m. on saints' days and holy days and, to meet the requirement that there should be two hours' consecutive secular instruction, the registers were marked at 9 a.m. on these occasions from about February 1893. The time-table showing these arrangements was from time to time approved by His Majesty's Inspectors, one such approval being given on February 4, 1904.

Section 7 of the Elementary Education Act, so far as it was material, provided:

"Every elementary school which is conducted in accordance with the following regulations shall be a public elementary school within the meaning of this Act; and every public elementary school shall be conducted in accordance with the following regulations (a copy of which regulations shall be conspicuously put up in every such school) namely . . ."

Then followed subsection (1), commonly known as the conscience clause, and subsection (2) which is the important one in this case:

"The time or times during which any religious observance is practised or instruction in religious subjects is given at any meeting of the school shall be either at the beginning or at the end or at the beginning and the end of such meeting, and shall be inserted in a time-table to be approved by the Education Department, and to be kept permanently and conspicuously affixed in every schoolroom; and any scholar may be withdrawn by his parent from such observance or instruction, without forfeiting any of the other benefits of the school. . . ."

In September 1904 the local education authority issued Circular 45N, which included the following regulations:

"(2) Time of Religious Instruction.—Secular instruction in all schools shall commence not later than 9.45 a.m., and occupy the school hours for the rest of the day.

(3) Holidays of Observance.—District sub-committees are empowered to allow the closing of any school in their district for a number of days not exceeding ten in any one year, in addition to the fixed holidays defined by the education committee. This regulation will, it is hoped, meet the wishes of each locality, as, for instance, in the case of difficulties arising from the feast-week in villages, and in the case of days of observance which have in some places been uniformly accompanied by a holiday.

(4) Place of Religious Instruction.—In consideration of the answer given in the House of Commons by Sir W. Anson to Mr Halsey on Friday, June 10 last, religious instruction of children attending an elementary school shall not be given in any place other than the school during the hours in which the school is open, unless it be in connection with the withdrawal of children under the conscience clause."

Contending that these directions were an interference with their rights and duties, and that the local education authority had no power to give directions as to religious instruction in non-provided schools, the managers took all children not claiming exemption under the conscience clause to church at 11 a.m. on All Saints' Day, St Andrew's Day, and St Thomas's Day (November 1, November 30, and December 21), 1904. On Ash Wednesday, March 8, 1905, one teacher was left behind with certain children, and the premises were kept open. Secular instruction on these days commenced at 9 a.m., and was broken off at 11 o'clock when the children went to church, thus breaking the requirement that it should continue for "the rest of the day."

On December 16, 1904, the local education authority wrote to the correspondent of the managers of the school in the following terms:

"I am to inform you that the education committee must insist upon the observance of the regulations as to religious instruction (see Circular 45N) and that the time-table must be revised and submitted to His Majesty's Inspector for signature upon his next visit."

On January 19, 1905, His Majesty's sub-inspector visited the school and, finding the time-table had not been altered, put his pen through the note "On saints' days and holy days registers are marked at 9 a.m.," signing the alteration: "Cancelled for His Majesty's inspector, Thomas Harrison, sub-inspector."

In view of the fact that the children were again taken to church on Ash Wednesday, the local education authority wrote to the managers informing them that all financial assistance had been withdrawn as from March 1, later amending the date of withdrawal to March 25.

On March 27 the local education authority's inspector visited the school and informed pupils and teachers that, in view of the withdrawal of the local education authority's support, the school was closed. The staff were allowed to choose new schools from a list of provided schools submitted to them, and the children were told that they must attend a neighbouring school. The inspector made the following entry in the log book:

"27th March 1905: The school was closed this morning, the Northants Education Committee having transferred the teachers.—D. Elliott."

The inspector then went to the vicarage and informed the vicar of what had taken place, after which both returned to the school. The inspector repeated his previous statement, and the vicar protested. On the same day the managers appealed to the Board of Education which, on April 14, confirmed the action of the local education authority. In the meanwhile the managers found sufficient funds to reopen the school with new teachers.

The managers brought an action against the local education authority claiming:

(1) a declaration that they were entitled to have the school maintained from March 25, 1905;

(2) payment of the sum necessary for the maintenance of the school from that date;

(3) damages for trespass and for certain illegal acts in closing the school and for inducing or procuring the teachers to break their contracts.

Extracts from Judgment

WARRINGTON J.: . . . By refusing to take steps to get the time-table altered the managers, in my opinion, committed a further breach of a direction as to secular education, a direction which was impliedly contained in direction No. 2,[1] because without an alteration of the time-table that direction could not be carried into effect, and was expressly contained in the Board's letter of December 16, 1904, which I have just read, and to which I have said I attach very great importance. That being so, I think the question, whether regarded as one with reference to the time of secular instruction or as one with reference to the time-table, must be considered as one wholly arising under section 7 of the Act of 1902. If that be so, the matter was one which under subsection (3) was to be settled by the Board of Education, and the Court has no jurisdiction to deal with it. I do not forget that the expressed object of the local education authority was to prevent the children from being taken away from the school for religious instruction during school hours; but it seems to me that if this object was attained by a direction which they were competent to give under section 7, their motive is immaterial, and it certainly cannot affect the question of jurisdiction. Having come to this conclusion with reference to the question raised by direction No. 2 in Circular 45N, it is unnecessary for me to express any opinion as to No. 4, namely, whether No. 4 is *ultra vires* or not, and, being unnecessary, I think it is undesirable to do so.

As to the other causes of action, the first head of claim is trespass. . . . I have since the arguments carefully looked at the pleadings again, and I do not find that the plaintiffs allege that his [Mr Elliott's] entry was a trespass. They

1 Of Circular 45N; see page 20, *supra*.

tacitly admit that he entered properly as inspector of the local education authority. . . .

Now the plaintiffs' case on this head is this: They contend that, assuming Mr Elliott's entry was originally lawful, his subsequent conduct was an abuse of the authority he possessed as inspector and rendered his entry a trespass *ab initio*, for which they are entitled to recover damages. I think the question which lies at the root of this claim is whether the managers were in possession of the school so as to entitle them to maintain an action for trespass. . . . Putting it shortly, therefore, the only allegation of possession upon the pleadings is such possession, if any, as the managers have by virtue of their position as managers under the Act of 1902. [His Lordship read sections 6 (2) and 7 (1) and (2) of the Act.] The effect of those provisions of the Act of 1902 seems to me to be that the Act assumes the provision of the school and says nothing about the ownership; and I think that the true conclusion to be drawn from the provisions is that the managers have merely certain statutory rights over such school-house as is provided by the owner, whether under a trust deed or, as in the present case, a private owner, who voluntarily, to use the expression in the statement of claim, allows it to be used for the purposes of the school. They merely have certain statutory rights over the building and only such rights over the building while devoted by the owner to the purposes of the school as will enable them to perform their statutory duties. Possession, in the strict legal sense, such as is required to maintain an action for trespass, is not, in my opinion, necessary in order to enable them to perform those duties, and remains in the owner; for example, have they such possession under the Act that they could exclude the owner? I can see nothing whatever in the Act which would enable them to treat the owner as a trespasser, if, for some purpose of his own, he desired to, and did in fact, visit the school. In my opinion, therefore, on this statement of claim the plaintiffs have not alleged or proved a possession sufficient to support an action of trespass. . . .

As to the claim for damages for inducing the teachers to break their contracts, I find on the facts that there was no such inducement held out. Realising the loss that the teachers would suffer if employment was not found for them, the local education authority offered them places elsewhere. In this, I think, they were reasonably justified, though, as I have already said, I think Mr Elliott too hastily assumed that the school would not continue.

The result is that the action fails, and there must be judgment for the defendants, with costs.

Judgment accordingly

4 Lee and others *v.* Secretary of State for Education and Science (1968) 66 L.G.R. 211[1]

1. The reader who wishes to study the actions leading to this case should first read *Bradbury and others* v. *London Borough of Enfield* [1967] 1 W.L.R. 1311, page 39, *infra*; and *Lee and another* v. *London Borough of Enfield* (1968) 66 L.G.R. 195, page 46, *infra*.

VACATION COURT

When the Secretary of State proposes to make an order under section 17 of the Education Act 1944 varying the articles of government of a secondary school, he must allow a reasonable time for interested parties to make representations under section 111 of the Act.

Facts: On August 23, 1967, the Vacation Court of Appeal (Lord Denning M.R.; Danckwerts and Diplock L.JJ.) granted an interim injunction restraining the Enfield Borough Council from ceasing to maintain eight schools, including Enfield Grammar School and Chace Secondary Modern School, unless the Secretary of State had previously given approval under the Education Act 1944, s. 13.[2] The Court held that to admit pupils to Enfield Grammar School only after they had spent some years in the "lower school" at Chace was so fundamental a change as to amount to ceasing to maintain the school. On August 31, the education committee approved a revised scheme for admissions, providing for the admission of pupils to Enfield Grammar School at the age of eleven-plus, but without reference to their suitability for a grammar school. On September 13 Donaldson J. granted an injunction restraining the local education authority from acting on the revised scheme of admissions, holding it to be incompatible with articles 9 and 11 of the school's articles of government.[3]

On the same day the governors of the school met and asked the Secretary of State for Education and Science to amend the articles of government to permit an unselective entry of pupils. By article 17 the Minister had power to make changes in the instrument of government or articles of government if it seemed to him just and expedient. On the next day, September 14, being Thursday, the Secretary of State informed the governors and the headmaster that he proposed to make the changes requested by the governors, and that he would allow until noon on Monday, September 18 for representations to be made.

Mr E. M. Lee, a foundation governor and old boy of the school; Mr R. P. St John, the father of a pupil at the school; and Mr K. O. Lane, an assistant master at the school, sought alternative declarations under the Education Act 1944, ss. 17 and 111, which empowered the making and variation of articles of government after an opportunity had been given for representations to be made.

The Vacation Court of the Queen's Bench Division was convened on Saturday, September 16, in view of the urgency of the matter since the schools had opened on the previous Monday, but the new intakes had not been admitted. Permission was given for trial before issue of the writ on the understanding that it would be issued on Monday, September 18.

Geoffrey Howe Q.C. (for the plaintiffs): The local education authority has a

2. *Bradbury v. London Borough of Enfield* [1967] 1 W.L.R. 1311; see page 39, *infra.*
3. *Lee v. London Borough of Enfield* (1968) 66 L.G.R. 195; see page 46, *infra.*

wide discretion in carrying out its duties under the Act. Unreasonable conduct by a local education authority was to be controlled by the Secretary of
State, and if he acted unreasonably, or allowed the authority to act unreasonably, the courts could not interfere. But the constitution, frail though it may
be, provides that the Minister can be controlled by the courts if he is proposing
to act contrary to the rule of law. The Secretary of State is not conforming to
the rules of natural justice and fair play which the courts have developed over
the years, and he has predetermined the case so as to reduce to a farce his duty
to act quasi-judicially in hearing representations. To expect the foundation
governors to formulate their representations and consider their position within
a long weekend was absurd and unrealistic. The plaintiffs sought a declaration
that the Secretary of State had not afforded people concerned with the
management of the school a proper and sufficient opportunity to make representations.

Nigel Bridge Q.C. (for the defendant): The Minister's duty to afford an opportunity to make representations means a real opportunity, not an elusive one,
but there is no vestige of evidence that the Minister's mind is not open. A
decision one way or the other is a matter of urgency. The letter did not indicate
that any reasoned application for extension of time would be refused.

Extract from Judgment

DONALDSON J.: . . . The plaintiffs make these contentions: first, they say
that the Secretary of State, in varying the articles of government, is performing a quasi-judicial function and is bound to act in accordance with the rules
of natural justice: and they have elaborated that to some extent. Secondly,
they say that the class of persons concerned with the government of the
school, within the meaning of section 17 (5), is at least wide enough to include
the parents of boys at the school and the parents of younger children who may
be affected hereafter, and they go so far as to say it may include the inhabitants
of the parish of Enfield. Thirdly, they say that the time allowed so far by the
Secretary of State for representations has been far too short. Fourthly, they
say that the Secretary of State has or appears to have predetermined the issue
of whether nor not there should be a variation.

Mr Bridge, for the Secretary of State, joins issue upon all these contentions.
As to the class of persons dealt with in section 17 (5), he says that it is limited
to the governors and the headmaster only. He concedes—and it may be that
this is an important concession; I will be corrected if I have it wrong, but I
understand him to concede—that the view of parents must be considered by
the Secretary of State by force of section 76 of the Act, if and in so far as they
are known to him; but he says that section 17 (5) does not require the Secretary of State to give the parents an opportunity to make representations. It
would follow, I suppose, from that concession that if parents chose to make
representations and they came to the notice of the Secretary of State he would
be bound to consider them.

I am not prepared to find that the Secretary of State has predetermined this issue of whether there shall be a variation of the articles. I am told by Mr Bridge for the Secretary of State that he has not, and there is no evidence at all which in any way displaces that assurance that he gives me.

I am not prepared to determine whether the Secretary of State, in relation to a variation of articles of government, is acting in a quasi-judicial capacity, because I consider it unnecessary to decide precisely what those words mean and whether they are apt to describe the Secretary of State's functions in this respect. Those functions are in my judgment sufficiently clearly defined in section 17 (5), provided that one reads into that section, as Mr Bridge concedes that I should, an obligation to give a real and not an illusory opportunity to make representations.

I am not prepared to define exhaustively which are the classes of persons to whom the Secretary of State is bound to give an opportunity to make representations. The words in the section 17 (5) are "concerned with," and I think they are much more restrictive than "concerned at" or "concerned by" or "interested in." I incline to the view that the class described is limited to those who have an active part to play in the government of the school. I am therefore prepared to assume that Mr Bridge is right in his submission that in the case of this school those who fall within the class are limited to the governors and the headmaster.

That leaves the question of time. Mr Bridge says that the urgency of the matter is such that the time at present allowed is sufficient. He also says that the issue is a simple one and has been the subject of debate for a long time.

First of all, as to urgency. The urgency arises from two attempts by the local education authority to put into effect unlawful schemes which would have affected the school and their failure to admit boys to the school in accordance with the existing articles of government. By "the existing articles of government" I mean, of course, those which exist unless and until varied by the Secretary of State. Urgency undoubtedly exists—that is why we are all here today when we would not normally be here—but this urgency which arises in this way does not, in my judgment, justify any abridgement of the time which legitimate objectors should have in which to formulate their objections.

Next, as to the simplicity of the issue. I agree that this issue can be simply stated, but I am not at all convinced that it is a matter upon which representations can be made with simplicity. The ramifications of it may be, and from what I have heard in the previous action probably are, very complex. What is currently under consideration, or indeed may be said to have been decided upon, subject to the Secretary of State making variations in the articles of government, is the transformation of this school into a three-form entry comprehensive school. As I made clear earlier on, contrary to what I said by inadvertence during the argument, it is only two weeks and not six weeks since that proposal first saw the light of day, and it is a proposal which is wholly different in kind, apart altogether from the details, from the original proposal, which was to turn this school into a comprehensive school serving an age group of fourteen to eighteen and having a seven-form entry.

I say it is wholly different because I found myself (as Mr Bridge conceded I was entitled to do) not upon evidence which has been given in this action but upon evidence which was given in the last action, *Lee* v. *London Borough of Enfield*,[4] and given by the chief education officer, who is also the clerk to the governors of Enfield Grammar School. He made it perfectly clear to me that a three-form comprehensive school is open to very grave objections if it is to be adopted as anything other than a temporary measure. There may be others, of course, who disagree with him and feel that it is a perfectly viable proposition. But at all events it is clear that there are very unusual features about what is now proposed, and no one other than those in the education office of the local education authority has had any opportunity of considering them before August 31 of this year. No one, of course, outside the education office knew until Tuesday of this week that such objections as there might be to the scheme were wholly or partly supported by the chief education officer himself.

It is clear that those objections which relate solely to a three-form entry comprehensive school, or in so far as they do only relate to a three-form entry comprehensive school, may disappear when the Court of Appeal injunction in *Bradfield* v. *London Borough of Enfield*[5] is discharged—as it will be discharged—when the conditions which attach to it, which relate to the giving of notices and a decision by the Secretary of State, are fulfilled.

But in my judgment the time so far allowed by the Secretary of State is wholly unreasonable, in the circumstances of this case, and amounts to a denial to the persons named in section 17 (5) of the rights conferred upon them by that subsection.

If I am asked to decide—and there have been times when I thought I was asked to decide this and times when I was not so sure about it—I should say that bearing in mind the fact that the scheme for a three-form entry was first mentioned on August 31, the fact that what is proposed goes to the whole character of the grammar school as it has been known for 400 years, the fact that the governors or groups of governors may wish to consult together and formulate a collective view as to what is best for the school, and, lastly, the fact that this is the holiday period—taking those factors into consideration, I consider that the period of four weeks from September 14 would be reasonable but that a shorter period, or at any rate any substantially shorter period, would not be reasonable and would not comply with section 17 (5).

I was not impressed by the argument that that would keep the boys away from school. So far as I can ascertain, the school can go on as a selective school until the proper steps have been taken to change its character.

Now it is clear from what I have said that I do not accede in whole to either of the alternative forms of declaration which are sought in the draft or proposed writ, and it may be that it will be thought more convenient in this particular

4. (1968) 66 L.G.R. 195.
5. *Sic.* This should read *Bradbury* v. *London Borough of Enfield* [1967] 1 W.L.R. 1311; [1967] 3 All E. R. 434; 66 L.G.R. 115, C.A.

case to leave the question of settling what the actual form of declaration should be until counsel have had the opportunity of considering it. It does emerge from the judgment that it is entirely a question of paper work hereafter. I am quite ready to listen to argument about it, but I should have thought this was the most convenient way of dealing with the matter.

[NOTE: Donaldson J. intimated that an appeal could be heard after the writ had been issued on Monday, September 18. An hour after the court adjourned the Secretary of State announced that he would not appeal. On September 18 a further announcement stated that the time allowed for making representations would be extended until October 16, *i.e.* a total of four-and-a-half weeks. The articles of government were amended in due course, and in December 1967 a Bill was introduced to provide that a school should not be regarded as discontinued or newly established by

(1) a change in the age-range of pupils in a primary school, or in a secondary school;
(2) a change to or from co-education;
(3) enlargement of the premises.

The Bill, which became law early in 1968, provided that any significant change in character or size, a change from a selective school to a comprehensive school, or a change to or from co-educational organisation should be regarded as a major change requiring the issue of notices under the Education Act 1944, s. 13. Objections to a proposed change in the articles of government of a voluntary secondary school are, under the Act, to be taken at the same time as section 13 objections. Provision was also made to legalise all changes since 1954 made without the application of the section 13 procedure. On December 7 1967, the Enfield Parents Joint Emergency Committee announced that it had decided not to press its action to trial.

The Enfield group of cases demonstrates clearly the determination of the courts that Ministers of the Crown and public authorities are answerable to the rule of law, and may not cut legal corners for administrative convenience. Within a matter of months legislative action was taken to make possible the achievement of the intentions of the Enfield local education authority and of H.M. Government. Until then, however, both had to act in compliance with the intentions of the legislature as at that time embodied in statutory form.]

(B) LOCAL ADMINISTRATION: DELEGATION OF POWERS

5 Young *v.* Cuthbert [1906] 1 Ch. 451

CHANCERY DIVISION
Where a local education authority statutorily delegates any of its powers to an education committee, such committee is, in respect of the powers so delegated, the local education authority.

Facts: The plaintiff was appointed on July 5, 1900, as headmistress of St John's Home School, Clewes, Berkshire, under an agreement which provided that the employment might be determined by either party giving the other three calendar months' written notice at any time. On November 30, 1905, the defendants, as managers of the school, gave notice of the termination of the agreement from the next day, and enclosed a cheque for three months' salary in lieu of notice. The letter stated that the approval of the Berkshire Education Committee had been obtained.[1]

On December 2, 1905, the plaintiff wrote to the managers saying she had been advised that the notice was invalid and inoperative. By the Education Act 1902, s. 7 (2), the consent of the authority was required to the dismissal of a teacher by the managers of a non-provided school, unless the dismissal was on grounds connected with the giving of religious instruction. On December 18, the plaintiff issued a writ for an injunction to restrain the defendants from acting on the notice of dismissal until the consent of the local education authority had been obtained and she had had an opportunity of defending herself.

The motion came on for hearing on January 19, 1906, and, on hearing that the education committee were to meet the following day, it was directed to stand over until January 24. It was then apparent that the education committee had consented to the dismissal. The question before the court was whether the notice was invalid because the education committee *had not* previously given its consent.

Extract from Judgment

BUCKLEY J.: ... The facts as to what had been done are as follows: The Education Act came into force in this district on August 30, 1903. In October 1905 no charges or complaints had been brought against Miss Young by the managers, but they had come to the conclusion that the teacher was out of harmony with the managers and that this was detrimental to the best interests of the school. Under these circumstances, on October 17, 1905, there was a meeting of the managers, at which the plaintiff attended, and a resolution was passed that, "in view of the evident friction with which the school was being conducted," the lady should be asked to resign, and that, if she refused, notice should be sent to the Berkshire Education Committee that the managers desired to terminate their agreement with her. The lady did not resign, and accordingly a letter was written by the managers to the Berkshire Education Committee, which evoked a reply of November 28, 1905. That reply stated that "the committee will approve the notice given by your managers to Miss Young to terminate her engagement."

Acting upon that letter, the notice of dismissal was given on November 30. The authority for the letter of November 30 was this: The Berkshire County Council had, pursuant to section 17 of the Act of 1902, delegated their powers to an education committee, and that committee, in exercise of the power given by Schedule I, A (6) of the Act, had appointed a sub-committee to deal with, amongst other things, the appointment and dismissal of teachers. The sub-committee appointed a section to deal with the details surrounding the

1. It should be remembered that it is the county council or county borough council which is the local education authority. The authority was, and is, statutorily obliged to appoint an education committee to which it may delegate any or all of its powers with the exception of borrowing money or raising a rate.

dismissal of teachers and to make recommendations to the sub-committee. On November 25 the section gave its consent. This was the consent referred to in the letter of November 28. On December 9 the sub-committee approved and adopted the action of the section. The writ was issued, as I have stated, on December 18. Subsequently, on January 20, the consent of the education committee itself was given, as I have before stated.

In my judgment, the education committee, having regard to section 17 of the Act, could exercise all the powers of the local education authority. The education committee was for this purpose the original authority. Further, having regard to Schedule I, A (6), the sub-committee was, I think, a body which could determine, and not merely report to the committee upon, a question such as this consent. But I do not think that the "section" was other than a subordinate body. Its duty was to consider and recommend to the sub-committee. Its action required, I think, approval by the sub-committee.

Under these circumstances it seems to me that on November 30, 1905, the consent of the authority had not been obtained. But in my judgment this is not a matter upon which the plaintiff can rely as invalidating the notice which was given her. This matter of consent was, as I have said, a matter arising only as between the authority and the managers. It was not a condition precedent to a good notice of dismissal. A subsequent consent by the authority to that which the managers had done under a provisional consent given by their subordinate section refers back, I think, and ratifies the act which the managers did, if any such ratification was required. Moreover, on December 9, being before the issue of the writ, the sub-committee had approved the action of the section. Further, and as a separate point, absence of consent, if there was such absence at the relevant date, is not, I think, a matter which the plaintiff can set up. It gives her no right. It is a matter which would have no consequences except as between the school and the education authority. In my opinion the action fails and I dismiss it, and, if the defendants ask for costs, it must be dismissed with costs.

Judgment for defendants with costs

(C) LOCAL ADMINISTRATION: *ULTRA VIRES**

6 R. *v.* Cockerton, *ex p.* Hamilton [1901] 1 K.B. 726

COURT OF APPEAL
It is not within the power of a school board to provide at the expense of the ratepayers science and art schools or classes in day schools.[1]

Facts: The Education Act 1870 provided for the establishment of school boards for the purpose of providing sufficient "public school accommodation"

1. This case is included for its great historical importance although, in so far as it was decided on the precise facts before the court, it is now obsolete. The reader is referred to the note at the end of the judgment.

in those areas where there was a deficiency of public elementary schools. The boards received grants from the Lords of the Committee of the Privy Council on Education, sometimes known as the Education Department or the Whitehall Department. The syllabus of conditions under which the grants were made was called the "Code," which implemented in detail section 2 of the Act which defined an elementary school as "a school or department at which elementary education is the principal part of the Education there given." The Code of 1870 provided for no instruction beyond the three R's, but in 1875 grammar, geography, and history were added, together with a list of "specific" subjects, proficiency in which would attract grant. These included mathematics, Latin, French, German, mechanics, animal physiology, physical geography, botany, and domestic economy. Drawing appeared in 1885 as an optional class subject; in 1886 it was made obligatory; in 1887 it was dropped altogether; in 1890 it was restored as an optional subject for boys in infants' schools or classes; in 1890 it became an obligatory subject for boys in schools for older scholars. It was included in the Code in 1898, having previously been the responsibility of the Science and Art Department.

Side by side with the Education Department existed another committee of the Privy Council commonly known as the Science and Art Department, or the Kensington Department. Its function was "for the promotion of science and art," and its grant conditions were issued in a "Directory." Although there was some overlap between the Code and the Directory, the former included many subjects not to be found in the Directory; while subjects common to each were taken to much greater depth by the Science and Art Department, including higher mathematics, chemistry of a very advanced character, hygiene, geology and physiography, all to a university level.

From 1875 onwards a number of school boards introduced science and art classes in their elementary schools, and the School Board for London began this practice in 1885 for children who had passed out of the standards. During the audit of the London School Board's accounts for the half-year ending September 29, 1898, the District Auditor disallowed seven test items as being payments illegally made out of the funds of the Board, and surcharged them on members of the Board. Three of these items were surcharged on Mr William Hamilton, Mr J. Scott Lidgett, and Mr G. S. Warmington, who applied to the Queen's Bench Division for an order of certiorari* to bring up and quash the auditors' certificate in respect of the following items:

(1) a sum of £32 6s. 10d. paid to Mr A. W. F. Langman for salary as drawing instructor;

(2) a sum of £4 paid to Mr H. H. Crick for special instruction in chemistry at Medburn Street evening continuation schools;

(3) a sum of £58 paid to the Polytechnic for science and art papers, and as remuneration for the secretary of the Polytechnic in conducting science and art examinations.

The question to be decided was whether the School Board for London could lawfully pay the expenses of schools and classes for teaching subjects prescribed by the South Kensington Directory.

The Queen's Bench Divisional Court (*per* Wills J.) held that it could not, but that such educational work might be carried on by the school board provided the whole of the funds required for it were furnished from sources other than contributions from the rates. Assuming the impossibility of apportioning the items which had been disallowed between legitimate and illegitimate expenditure, the disallowances were properly made.

Rule discharged
Appeal to the Court of Appeal

Extracts from Judgment

A. L. SMITH M. R.: My brothers Wills and Kennedy in the Queen's Bench Division have upheld certain disallowances and surcharges made by an auditor upon the accounts of the School Board of London in respect of payments made by that board out of moneys obtained from ratepayers towards the cost of certain education. The learned judges have held that no Act has authorised these payments, and the School Board of London appeals. . . . It is now sufficient for me to say that the South Kensington Department and the Whitehall Department have always been, and are, separate and distinct institutions. They have a different registration of scholars, different examiners, different grants, and different inspectors; and the South Kensington Department deals by means of its Directory with a high and very advanced system of education, while the Whitehall Department, by means of its Code, deals with an education of a lower and of a much less pretentious character. I may say, without going through the details of the South Kensington Directory, that no effort of imagination can describe the system of education therein set forth as elementary education; and for the purposes of this case, but only for this case, it is to be taken by admission of the Attorney-General that the education prescribed by the Whitehall Code is elementary education within the meaning of the Act of 1870. I am not asked in this case to say whether the Code embraces more than elementary education, but I may say it appears to me to embrace elementary education up to its high-water mark.

. . . It is beyond dispute that if the School Board of London, or, indeed, any other school board (they are all corporations created by statute), is to justify the payment of the expense of education out of the money of the ratepayers, this must be done by producing some Act of Parliament, or Order in Council having the force of an Act of Parliament, which enacts that the ratepayers' money shall be levied and applied to that purpose. Neither a Code nor a Directory has any such force. . . . That the recipients of the education mentioned in the Act are children, and children only, cannot be denied, for I would ask who else can be found pointed at throughout the Act, to receive the education the Act prescribes, other than children. I now take the definition in section 3 of the Act of 1870 of the term "elementary school." It is as follows: "In this Act the term 'elementary school' means a school or department of a school at which elementary education is the principal part of the education there given, and does not include any school or department of a school at which the ordinary payments in respect of the instruction, from each scholar, exceed ninepence a week." It is argued for the school board that this definition constitutes a statutory enactment whereby a board school or a department of a board school is empowered to give the highest and most advanced education of the South Kensington Directory at the ratepayers' expense, if the principal part of the education given in such school or department of such school is elementary. As to this contention the first observation to be made is that this definition of the term "elementary school" is not an enactment providing for the giving of any education at all, and much less an enactment that a school board in a public elementary school is thereby empowered to give the education prescribed by the Directory of South Kensington at the expense of the ratepayers. This seems to me to be an answer to the school board's contention. But, if the contention really be that it is a statutory enactment such as the board contends for, what is the meaning of the last part of the definition "and does not include any school or department of a school at which the ordinary payments in respect of the instruction from each scholar exceed ninepence a week"? I heard no reason given as to this by the learned counsel for the school board. It is common knowledge that prior to the Act of 1870 there was in this country a vast amount of education of all descriptions, elementary and non-elementary, carried on by schools supported by voluntary contributions, and, indeed, at the present day there still exists a considerable amount of such education. These schools have come to be known as voluntary schools. It was not the object of Mr Forster's Act to destroy these voluntary schools and thus cast upon the rates their enormous cost, which was being provided for by voluntary contributions. What Mr Forster's Act enacted was that the school board should supply and the ratepayer should pay for the elementary education of children if, taking into consideration every school, whether public elementary or not, and whether situated in the school district or not (s. 8), the elementary education which was then being provided was not sufficient. The object and meaning of the definition clause in my judgment is that, inasmuch as all kinds of education were then being taught in these voluntary schools, those outside schools only should come within the Act, and derive the benefits by way of grants and otherwise conferred by the Act, at which elementary education was the principal part of the education therein given; and, in addition, that only those outside voluntary schools should come within the Act if they were schools at which the ordinary payments therein in respect of the instruction, from each scholar, did not exceed ninepence a week apiece. . . .

I now come to the next Education Act which was passed—namely, the Elementary Education Act 1873, by section 2 of which it is enacted that: 'This Act shall be construed as one with the principal Act" (that is, of 1870), "and the expression 'this Act' in the principal Act shall be construed to include this Act." In other words, the Act of 1873 is made part and parcel of the Act of

1870, which Act is to be read as if the Act of 1873 had been contained therein. Now what do we find in this Act of 1873? Section 13, in my opinion, is decidedly of importance. It enacts, "A school board shall be able and be deemed always to have been able to be constituted trustees for any educational endowment or charity for purposes connected with education, . . . and to have and always to have had power to accept any real or personal property given to them as an educational endowment or upon trust for any purposes connected with education; provided that (1) Nothing in this section shall enable a school board to be trustees for or accept any educational endowment, charity, or trust the purposes of which are inconsistent with the principles on which the school board are required by section 14 of the principal Act to conduct schools provided by them." That is the section relating to the non-teaching of religion distinctive of any particular denomination. "And (2) every school connected with such endowment, charity, or trust shall be deemed to be a school provided by the school board, except that nothing in this section shall authorise the school board to expend any money out of the local rate for any purpose other than elementary education." Here in this section, as it seems to me, is an emphatic declaration by the Legislature, which, be it remembered, forms part and parcel of the Act of 1870, that the school board is not to expend any money out of a local rate for any purpose other than elementary education. In fact, it enacts in short and positive terms that which is the whole tenor of the Act of 1870, as I have above endeavoured to show. In my opinion, the many Acts which were subsequently passed down to and including the year 1891 have no real bearing on the point I have to decide, except that they show that the Legislature was throughout dealing with the elementary education of children and nothing else. . . . There is one other Act to which I must make reference, for it was much relied upon by the school board. It was not one of the Elementary Education Acts of 1870 to 1891, which form a Code of themselves, but is one of the Technical Education Acts 1889 to 1891, which form a distinct Code of themselves. The Act is called the Technical Instruction Act 1889 (52 & 53 Vict. c. 76). It is an Act to facilitate the provision of technical instruction. It is said that this Act contains a legislative recognition that the higher education of South Kensington, and not merely the elementary education provided by the Code, can be taught by school boards and be paid for out of rates. This Act, by section 1, enacts that a local authority (this is not a school board, but a town or county council) may out of a local rate (this is not an education rate) supply or aid technical or manual instruction, but shall not out of the local rate supply the same to scholars receiving instruction at an elementary school in the obligatory or standard subjects prescribed by the minutes of the Education Department, Whitehall. The reason for this seems pretty obvious, because to the scholars in those standards the Education Department might well give elementary technical or manual instruction—that the local and school board authorities were not to clash. Then comes a provision about making a local rate, by a local authority, which has nothing to do with a school board. It is there provided, section 1 (g), that the rate to be raised in any one year by a local authority is not to exceed 1d. in the pound, and yet, according to the argument of the school board, it may levy for technical and manual instruction a rate to any amount it may require, Section 1 (3) enacts: "Nothing in this Act shall be construed so as to interfere with any existing powers of school boards with respect to the provision of technical and manual instruction." As before stated, it seems to me that there may well be technical and manual instruction of an elementary kind which the school board may well teach as being elementary education. Then comes this—the conditions on which parliamentary grants may be made in aid of technical and manual instruction—*i.e.*, to the local authority—shall be those contained in the minutes of the Department of Science and Art, the Department, as before shown, with which the Elementary Education Act of 1870 has nothing to do.

I have gone far enough in this Act to show that it has nothing to do with the true construction of Mr Forster's Act of 1870, and with just a reference to the novelty of the attempt to interpret one Act by another Act passed nineteen years afterwards, upon another and different subject-matter, I will conclude by saying that the Act of 1889 is not a legislative recognition of the right of the school board to teach the Directory education and make the ratepayers pay for it.

I now answer the questions put to me, but I will answer (1) and (2) together. (1 and 2) I say it was not within the powers of a board as a statutory corporation to provide science and art schools or classes of the kind referred to in this case, either in the day schools or in evening continuation schools, out of the school board rate or school fund. (3) That the rule nisi should not be made absolute in regard to any of the disallowances and surcharges, for in my judgment, for the reasons above given, they were correctly made by the auditor. I may add that, if the school board is to have the powers it seeks, these must be obtained by legislation, for the powers it desires to have do not exist in any statute or its equivalent already passed. This appeal must be dismissed.

Appeal dismissed

[NOTE: The Cockerton judgment had a remarkable and swift influence on the development of education in England and Wales. Prior to the case the London Technical Education Board had applied to become the authority for secondary education, and had secured the support of the county council. Sir John Gorst, the Vice-President of the Education Department, decided in favour of the Technical Education Board, and asked its secretary to raise the question of illegal expenditure by the School Board for London with Mr T. B. Cockerton, the District Auditor.

Following the judgment a special Act was passed to legalise the work of the School Board pending the preparation of the Education Act 1902. The 1902 Act abolished the school boards, and made the councils of counties and county boroughs the local education authorities for elementary and secondary education; except that non-county boroughs with a population of more than ten thousand at the 1901 census became the authorities for elementary education.

The case has been included for two reasons:

(1) as an example of the way in which Parliament may take legislative action to quash a decision of the courts which, although strictly in accordance with the law, is out of harmony with the spirit of the times;

(2) to illustrate the fact that a body (be it, for example, school board or local education authority) created by statute and clothed with statutory powers may have its acts condemned by the courts should it do anything which is *ultra vires** those powers.

The following case, *Dyer* v. *London School Board*, refers, and the *Enfield* case (see page 23) is a further example of the control of the executive by the courts.]

7 Dyer *v.* London School Board [1902] 2 Ch. 768

COURT OF APPEAL

It is not within the powers of a school board to expend money raised by local rate upon any education other than elementary.[1]

Facts: In his audit of the accounts of the London School Board for the half-year ended Michaelmas, 1901, the auditor, Mr T. B. Cockerton, disallowed the sum of £27 10s. 11d. as a payment illegally made out of the funds of the school board for lithographing bills of quantities in reference to the erection of a pupil teachers' centre in Hilldrop Road, Islington.

The reasons given for the disallowance were (1) because the said sum was not paid in respect of the erection of a public elementary school within the meaning of the Elementary Education Acts; (2) because school boards are not legally entitled to erect at the cost of the school fund schools or other buildings for the instruction of pupil teachers exclusively; (3) because the said sum was not expended in the provision of accommodation in public elementary schools for the district of the said school board within the meaning of section 5 of the Elementary Education Act 1870, or any of the Acts amending the same; (4) because the said sum was paid in respect of the erection of a building for the provision of education in subjects not allowed, provided for, or recognised by the Education Code; (5) because the said sum was paid in reference to the erection of a building for the provision of instruction of teachers, pupil teachers, or other persons who do not form part of the educational staff of a public elementary school within the meaning of the Elementary Education Acts; (6) because the said school board had not any authority in law to pay the said sum and to charge the same in their accounts as aforesaid. Despite the auditor's certificate, the school board proceeded with the erection of the pupil teachers' centre on the site above mentioned.

Three ratepayers, of whom one was Joseph Dyer, applied to the Chancery Division for an injuction to restrain the school board from proceeding with the scheme until judgment or further order. It was said for the board that they intended to apply to the King's Bench Division for an order of certiorari* to remove the auditor's certificate into the court and quash it. Farwell L.J. granted the injunction. The board appealed.

1. As in *R.* v. *Cockerton* (page 30, *supra*) this judgment is now obsolete, but is included to illustrate the sequence of events leading to the Education Act 1902. It is still, of course, *ultra vires* for a local education authority to spend money on the exercise of functions not assigned to it by statute.

Extract from judgment

VAUGHAN WILLIAMS L.J.: . . . Now, speaking for myself, I am not disposed to question the proposition that, in an elementary school, such an education may be given to pupil teachers under the agreement with pupil teachers as cannot properly be described in itself as being merely elementary education. I do not so far dissent from the argument based upon the fifth clause of the agreement, but I see nothing in that agreement to lead me to suppose that that education which is undertaken by the managers to be given to the pupil teacher should not be given in the public elementary school itself, as had been the usual practice; in fact, I gathered from what Mr Jenkins said that, so far from denying it, he affirmed the practice, saying that where it was done an extra payment was made to the certificated or qualified teacher who, in the school, gave that instruction. But although he makes that admission, he asks us to say that, as a necessary consequence of the agreement the form of which is recognised by the Code for the employment and instruction of pupil teachers—and which, as he says, is not allowed by the Code to be in any way departed from—the school board have the power to establish a separate school for the purpose of giving this instruction to pupil teachers, and to charge the cost of carrying on that separate school, and of the building of that separate school, upon the local rates.

I cannot agree with that in the slightest degree. It seems to me that so to hold would be entirely inconsistent with the judgment in the *Cockerton* case.[2] The judgment in the *Cockerton* case in substance decides that the only schools which are to be paid for out of the rates, whether in respect of buildings or instruction or anything else, are elementary schools which are devoted to the elementary education of children; and it seems to me that whatever instruction may be given in those schools to pupil teachers beyond the mere elementary instruction is a mere accessory of the public elementary schools, and that it is not right to draw an inference from the kind of education to be given to pupil teachers in the public elementary schools that the school board have a right to establish a school for the purpose of giving education that cannot be described as elementary education—a school which it is admitted cannot be properly described as a public elementary education school. The force of what I have been saying is very much increased when you come to consider what is in fact done at a school for pupil teachers. It is a school at which the average age of the scholars ranges between fourteen and twenty-four: it is a school apparently to which scholars may come from, not a limited district, but any part whatsoever from which they choose to come to get their education at the school, an education which is obviously higher education and not elementary education. It seems to me impossible to say, consistently with the *Cockerton* case,[3] that the Education Act of 1870 authorises the charging of the rates with the expense of the establishment and conduct of such a school—a school which

2. [1901] 1 K.B. 726; see page 30, *supra*.
3. [1901] 1 K.B. 726; see page 30, *supra*.

is not an elementary school, and not intended for the giving of an elementary education.

Appeal dismissed

On behalf of the School Board, Jenkins K.C. then asked that the injunction might be suspended with a view to appeal to the House of Lords.

VAUGHAN WILLIAMS L.J.: Certainly not. We disapprove of your being allowed to go on at all making payments that are unjustifiable.

Several days later a further application was made that the injunction should not apply to payments to the contractor in respect of work actually executed by him and certified before the judgment was pronounced. Great harm would be done to the contractor if he were not paid for what he had done.

Application refused

[NOTE: The climate of opinion prevailing in some quarters at the time of this case is illustrated in the following letter to the editor of *The Times*, published on January 7, 1901:

"Sir, Having been one of the many victims who have suffered at the hands of the School Board for London in its efforts to acquire, under compulsory powers, valuable properties in the midst of quiet residential neighbourhoods, where no Board-school accommodation is required, to be used for the erection of so-called 'Pupil Teachers' Centres,' I have been not a little interested in your report of the decision in the case of '*The Queen* v. *Cockerton*'; and I can only hope that my neighbours and myself who are ratepayers will be benefited thereby, notwithstanding the protestations of some of your correspondents who seem to think that ratepayers ought to be still further taxed to provide education for the children of persons who are perfectly well able to afford to pay for it themselves, and who ought to be left to do so. In my own case compulsory powers have been obtained by the School Board enabling it to acquire a site in such a neighbourhood as I have mentioned, to the great detriment of my own and my neighbours' properties (amounting to upwards of £20,000) and of the quiet and peaceable enjoyment of our houses; and it was avowedly admitted by the School Board experts that amongst the purposes for which the property was required was the provision for lawn tennis and such-like recreations for the pupils. I should like to know if this is elementary education and a proper application of the ratepayers' moneys. No one need wonder that when the Elementary Education Acts are administered in this way the rates should be upwards of 1s. in the pound, instead of the original assurance (upon the faith of which the Act of 1870 was passed) that by no possible means could they ever exceed 3d. in the pound. I therefore welcome the decision of the Court, for I think it is high time that some limit should be placed on the schemes of the School Board, not the worst of which is this system of providing out of the rates higher-class education for adults, many of whom do not, and never intend to become teachers, and who thus obtain a good education at the public expense. I believe that it is the intention of the School Board to provide on the site in question chemistry laboratories and other such-like expensive accessories for the higher education of persons who are not really children and who certainly do not fall within the reasonable definition of children in whose interest alone the Elementary Education Acts were passed.

Yours obediently,

N. CLAYDEN"

27, Hilldrop-road, N., Jan. 1.

For the political results of this case, see the note to *R.* v. *Cockerton, ex p. Hamilton*, page 30, *supra*.]

8   Bradbury and others *v.* London Borough of Enfield [1967]
1 W.L.R. 1311

VACATION COURT OF APPEAL

Changes in the curricula, size of form entry or the method of selection of pupils do not necessarily constitute "ceasing to maintain" an existing school, but changes in the age range and sex of pupils are so fundamental as to make a school a different institution and so amount to "ceasing to maintain" an existing school.

Facts: The plaintiffs were ratepayers, and all but one were parents of children attending schools in the London Borough of Enfield. The defendants were the local education authority and were required by section 31 of the London Government Act 1963 to prepare a revised development plan by April 1, 1966, a date later extended to April 1, 1967.

A sub-committee was established in February 1965, and there were various meetings and consultations until in July of that year the Secretary of State for Education and Science issued Circular 10/65. This declared the Government's intention to end selection at eleven-plus, and to eliminate separatism in secondary education. Following the issue of the circular there were meetings of the education committee and of the sub-committee, and letters were sent to parents stating that the defendants proposed to change to a comprehensive system of education.

A revised development plan was prepared and submitted to the Secretary of State on June 1, 1966. Protests made by parents and teachers were not laid before the committee until after this date. On December 13, 1966, the Secretary of State accepted the proposals generally in relation to certain schools, but stated that in other cases they required further examination or they were not acceptable in their present form. Further recommendations were adopted by the education committee on December 22, 1966, and a revised plan was submitted to the Secretary of State on January 18, 1967.

By the end of that month the Secretary of State had approved the plan, subject to compliance with section 13 of the Education Act 1944, with the exception of the Roman Catholic schools and the Latymer School. The defendants thereupon advertised for, and engaged teaching staff. In some cases the appointments were provisional under section 13, in others firm appointments were made.

On May 19, 1967, the Secretary of State approved the proposals for the establishment and discontinuance of schools under section 13, but stated that he attached importance to the chief education officer's assurance that staff movements would be kept to a minimum, and would cease by September 1969. The authority proceeded with its scheme, proposing that the reorganisation should take effect in September 1967 for all but one of the twenty-eight secondary schools in the borough.

The plaintiffs issued a writ making three general and three specific complaints:

(1) that the proposed reorgansation was *ultra vires** because it was being embarked upon before the revision of the Development Plan required by section 31 of the London Government Act 1963;

(2) that the defendants failed to consider the adverse effects of their scheme on the educational standards of the borough—the character of each comprehensive unit—whether they would have the appropriate staff available—appropriate accommodation—and sufficiency of cash, remembering all the time sections 8 and 76 of the Education Act 1944;

(3) that the defendants, in exercising their discretion, failed to regard considerations by which they ought to have been guided, and were guided by aims and objects by which they ought not to have been.

The plaintiffs moved for interlocutory relief,* asking for an interim injunction to restrain the defendants from doing anything further to implement the scheme pending trial of the action. For the plaintiffs it was urged that, in the event of their contentions being upheld at the trial, either the court would grant the relief asked (which would cause the council incomparably greater inconvenience than now); or, if no relief were granted, the plaintiffs would be left without a remedy to which they were entitled. On the balance of convenience it would be better to grant an injunction now.

An affidavit by the chief education officer stated that, if the injunctions claimed were granted, complete chaos would ensue. Headmasters designate had been preparing for months for the reorganisation in September. If the reorganisation did not take place, new arrangements would have to be made before the beginning of the new term. It could not be done when the schools were closed and the staff dispersed. Furthermore the authority had entered into binding commitments to teachers, 265 of whom had been accorded increased salary and status under the new scheme. About 120 teachers from outside Enfield had been appointed, some to posts which would disappear if the injunctions were granted. To place a body of seven hundred teachers in professional uncertainty, and in some cases in jeopardy, would be disastrous in its consequences for the borough and its children. It would attract a reputation to the authority which would make the recruitment of teachers more difficult.

Even more disastrous would be the effect on the 2,917 children due to transfer to secondary schools in September. If the injunctions were granted, it was not known what would be done about them. A selective admission for September could not now be arranged.

To delay the proposed reorganisation would utterly disrupt education in Enfield and would be an educational disaster for the children affected.

Goff J. held that the authority had acted unlawfully in failing to give notice of their intention to cease to maintain eight schools, and that about eight other schools would not conform with the building regulations governing accommodation when they became comprehensive. The three general complaints failed:

"On the question of the balance of convenience in the granting of any interlocutory relief, injury to the defendants would be grave. The chief education officer has said that complete chaos would ensue and that seems, prima facie to be substantially accurate. Moreover, it would be an injury affecting third parties; namely some at least of the teaching staff and certainly a considerable number of children due to proceed to secondary school in September.

Except for one point there would be no doubt that, on the balance of convenience, the Court's discretion ought not to be exercised to interfere by way of interlocutory relief pending trial. That point has given me much concern. It is that the breach of duty under section 10 might well be irremediable, for the chief education officer had said in his affidavit that in a number of respects accommodation would be less than that laid down by the Standards for School Premises Regulations 1959.[1]

Even so, the Court has power to suspend an injunction and it is probable that the trial judge would exercise the power to enable the 'egg to be unscrambled' with care, and with a minimum of injury to all.

It is not a case, therefore, in which interlocutory relief ought to be granted pending the trial."

Injunction refused

The plaintiffs appealed.

Extracts from Judgment

LORD DENNING M.R.: . . . The crucial question is as to the meaning of the words "maintain" a "school" in these statutes. The definitions do not help much; but reading them in the light of the various sections, it appears to me that a "school" is an institution which exists independently of the buildings in which it is housed for the time being. Many a school retained its identity during the war even though it was evacuated to a place 200 miles away. A school is an institution with a character of its own. If an education authority is under a duty to "maintain" a school, it must see that it retains its fundamental character. If the education authority makes a change of a fundamental nature, so much so that anyone would say it was a different school altogether, then it "ceases to maintain" the existing school and "establishes a new school." That is, I think, the effect of the decision of *Wilford* v. *West Riding of Yorkshire County Council.*[2]* The question there arose under the Education Act 1902, under which the local education authority was under a duty to "maintain" and keep efficient all public elementary schools within their area. There was at Garforth a public elementary school for children of all standards from one to seven. The county council gave a direction saying that it was to be confined

1. S.I. 1959 No. 890.
2. [1908] 1 K.B. 685; 24 T.L.R. 286; 6 L.G.R. 244.

C

to children in standards one to three. The result was that in future the school was to be turned into an infants' school, and that the older children were to go elsewhere. Channel J.[3] held that the effect of the direction was "to alter the whole character of the school," and that it was not legitimate for the authority to give such a direction. He said that: "The result of the defendants' action is, however, a thing which I must look at, and that result seems to me clearly to be to alter the fundamental character of the school."

Applying this test, I do not think that the change in the curriculum of a school necessarily alters its fundamental character. Suppose a local education authority change the curriculum from a secondary modern curriculum to a comprehensive curriculum, or even from a grammar school curriculum to a comprehensive curriculum. There may be a difference in the range of subjects which are taught, and in the emphasis given to them, but those differences may not be so extensive as to alter the fundamental character of a school. Nor do I think that a change in the method of entry necessarily alters its fundamental character. Suppose a local education authority change the method from selection by examination to selection by interview, or allocate places to pupils according to the preferences of parents, they may get a different intake of pupils, but those differences may not be so extensive as to alter the fundamental character of a school.

But I do think that a change in the age group of pupils may be a fundamental change, just as it was in *Wilford* v. *West Riding County Council*.[4] A change from a senior school to an infants' school would alter its character altogether. So do I think a change from a boys' school to a girls' school would be a fundamental change. It would be a complete change in character.

This brings me to consideration of the specific proposals in regard to these eight schools.

The first proposal concerns two of the existing schools, the Enfield Grammar School for Boys (749 boys) and the Chace Secondary Modern School for Boys (526 boys). These two schools are over a mile apart. It is proposed to combine these two schools into a comprehensive school for boys, using the existing buildings. The premises at present used by the Enfield Grammar School are to house an Upper School for boys from fourteen to eighteen years with its own head teacher. The buildings of the Chace Modern Secondary School are to house a lower school for boys from eleven to fourteen years with its own head teacher. In my opinion the change in each case is of a fundamental character. It comes to this: the education authority intend to "cease to maintain" the existing Enfield Grammar School and to establish a new school in the existing buildings for senior boys; and they intend to "cease to maintain" the existing Chace Secondary Boys School and establish a new school there for junior boys.

The second proposal concerns three of the existing schools, namely, the Mandeville Mixed Secondary Modern (262 pupils), the Eldon Mixed Second-

3. [1908] 1 K.B. 685.
4. [1908] 1 K.B. 685; 24 T.L.R. 286; 6 L.G.R. 244.

ary Modern (267 pupils), and the Houndsfield Mixed Secondary Modern (261 pupils). It is proposed to combine these three schools into a mixed comprehensive school, using the existing buildings. One building is to house an upper school for pupils from fourteen to eighteen, with its own head teacher. The other buildings are to house two lower schools (pupils eleven to fourteen) each with its own head teacher. These changes are, in my opinion, of a fundamental character, so much so that the education authority intend to "cease to maintain" the existing secondary modern schools and establish new upper and lower schools.

The third proposal concerns three more of the existing schools, namely, Higher Grade (Mixed Selection) (308 pupils), Hazelbury Girls' Secondary Modern (347 girls), and Raynham Mixed Secondary Modern (259 pupils). It is proposed to combine these three schools into a mixed comprehensive school, using the existing buildings, with an upper school for fourteen to eighteen years and two lower schools for eleven to fourteen years. These changes are fundamental, just as in the previous cases, but with the addition of the change of Hazelbury from a girls' school into a mixed school for boys and girls.

So much for the eight schools. I need not say anything about the other existing schools which are to be changed to comprehensive schools, because the education authority admits that in most cases their proposals mean that they will "cease to maintain" the existing schools and establish new schools. They have issued public notices accordingly. But I must say that I see no differences between these cases and the eight. They all fulfil the test of a "change in fundamental character." Take, for instance, the Albany Boys (Secondary Modern) (469 boys), and the Albany Girls (Secondary Modern) (460 girls). It is proposed to combine these into a mixed comprehensive school using the existing buildings with one head teacher. It is admitted that, on this being done, the council will "cease to maintain" the existing schools. I see no difference between such cases and the eight schools. The fact that there is one head teacher cannot make all the difference.

I hold, therefore, in agreement with the judge, that in regard to the eight schools, the education authority intend to "cease to maintain" them and "to establish new" schools within section 13 of the Act of 1944. They ought, therefore, to have given public notices of their proposals, so that people could object. On objection being lodged, the Minister would have to consider them. Not till then could the Minister give his approval. Mr Francis[5] submitted to us that the Minister's approval would be good, even though public notices were not served, nor objections considered. I cannot agree. It is implicit in section 13 (3) and (4) that the Minister cannot approve unless he has considered all objections submitted to him.

Mr Francis also submitted that the Minister could dispense with the public notices and so forth, by giving "leave" under section 13 (5) of the Act of 1944. I do not think he can do so. I think that section 13 (5) must be read subject to

5. Counsel for the defendants.

the last part of section 13 (8). The Enfield London Borough Council were under a duty to "maintain" these eight schools: and they were not at liberty to "cease to maintain" them until the Minister had given his approval under section 13 (4); and that involves public notices and considering objections.

I hold, therefore, that the council have not fulfilled the statutory requirements of section 13 (3) and (4) in regard to the eight schools. They must continue to maintain them and must not cease to maintain them until the statutory requirements are fulfilled.

I turn now to the second point. It concerns the standard of the buildings and accommodation in the new schools. This point concerns all the new schools, not merely the eight schools (where the public notices were not given) but also the remaining schools (where public notices were given, objections considered, and approval given). It is said that the education authority were not authorised "to establish a new school" unless it conformed to the regulations which prescribe the standards for school premises.

This contention rests on section 13 (6) and (7) of the Act of 1944. Those subsections show that, when an education authority propose to establish a new school, and have obtained (after public notice) the Minister's approval to this proposal, they must submit to the Minister specifications and plans of the school premises. If the Minister is satisfied that they come up to the prescribed standards, he will approve them; and the education authority must then carry them out.

Mr Howe[6] submitted to us that, on the true construction of those sections, the council were not at liberty to proceed with the establishment of any of the new schools (even those which were to be established in existing buildings) unless the school premises had been brought up to the prescribed standards. He urged that there was a great deal of evidence that in many of these cases the premises did not come up to the prescribed standards. Mr Howe admitted that if this failure had been due to shortage of labour or materials, the Minister might have granted exemption from the duty to conform: see section 7 (2) (b) of the Education (Miscellaneous Provisions) Act 1948. He said that there is no ground for exemption here, because there is no shortage of labour or materials, at most a shortage of money, which is no ground for exemption.

Looking at the Acts of 1944 and of 1948, it seems to me that Parliament did intend that before a new school is established, the local education authority should see that the school premises come up to the prescribed standards unless they are excused owing to shortage of labour or materials. But the question is: What is the remedy? Can those who are dissatisfied come to the courts and stop the new school being established? I think not. I think the only remedy is to complain to the Minister under section 99 of the Act of 1944. The Minister can then give such directions as to the school premises as he thinks expedient. If he does not think it expedient to make the education authority conform to the prescribed standards—or if he thinks it expedient to grant them further

6. Counsel for the appellants.

time in which to conform—that is the end of the matter. The courts cannot compel him to act, any more than they could in *Watt* v. *Kesteven County Council.*[7]

I am confirmed in this view by reference to section 13 (5). That prohibits the education authority from doing anything until the Minister has duly given his approval to the establishment of a new school. The courts of law can enforce that statutory prohibition. But once the public notices have been served and he has duly given his approval, the statutory prohibition ends, and the power of the court ceases. Thenceforward the duty in regard to the school premises is enforceable by the Minister and not by the courts. It is for the Minister to see that the new schools come up to the prescribed standards.

I come now to the last point. Ought an injunction to be granted against the council? It has been suggested by the chief education officer that, if an injunction is granted, chaos will supervene. All the arrangements have been made for the next term, the teachers appointed to the new comprehensive schools, the pupils allotted their places, and so forth. It would be next to impossible, he says, to reverse all these arrangements without complete chaos and damage to teachers, pupils, and the public.

I must say this: If a local authority does not fulfil the requirements of the law, this court will see that it does fulfil them. It will not listen readily to suggestions of "chaos." The Department of Education and the local education authority are subject to the rule of law and must comply with it, just like everyone else. Even if chaos should result, still the law must be obeyed. But I do not think that chaos will result. The evidence convinces me that the "chaos" is much over-stated. If an injunction is granted now, there will be much less chaos than if it were sought to reverse the situation in a year or so. After all, the injunction will only go as to the eight schools, and not as to the remaining twenty or so schools in the borough.

And in regard to these eight schools, it will only affect the new intake coming in at the bottom forms. I see no reason why the position should not be restored, so that the eight schools retain their previous character until the statutory requirements are fulfilled. I can well see that there may be a considerable upset for a number of people, but I think it far more important to uphold the rule of law. Parliament has laid down these requirements so as to ensure that the electors can make their objections and have them properly considered. We must see that their rights are upheld.

I have only to add this: It is still open to the education authority to fulfil the statutory requirements, that is, to give the public notices so that objections can be submitted to and considered by the Minister. I will not venture to predict what the results will be, but that is the least that must be done in order that the law should be observed.

I would therefore vary the judge's order and grant an injunction in respect of the eight schools.

7. [1955] 1 Q.B. 408; [1955] 2 W.L.R. 499; [1955] 1 All E.R. 473, C.A.; see page 136, *infra.*

DANCKWERTS L. J.: I agree with the judgment of Lord Denning M.R. I only wish to add that, in my opinion, in cases of this kind, it is imperative that the procedure laid down in the relevant statutes should be properly observed. The provisions of the statutes in this respect are supposed to provide safeguards for Her Majesty's subjects. Public bodies and Ministers must be compelled to observe the law; and it is essential that bureaucracy should be kept in its place. I also would allow the appeal in the manner which has been mentioned by the Master of the Rolls.

Appeal allowed
Injunction accordingly

9 Lee and another *v.* London Borough of Enfield (1968) 66 L.G.R. 195

VACATION COURT

For a local education authority to implement a scheme of admission to a school that contravenes the articles of government of that school is an act of malfeasance and, as such, is justiciable in the courts.

Facts: In the summer of 1966 the Enfield Borough Council, being the local education authority for the London Borough of Enfield, produced an educational development plan. The plan proposed the reorganisation of secondary education so that children would no longer be selected for admission to grammar schools or secondary modern schools by reference to, *inter alia* their suitability for a particular kind of education. Under the plan Chace School was to become a junior comprehensive school for boys between eleven and fourteen years of age; the former grammar school was to be a senior comprehensive school for boys from fourteen to eighteen.

On August 23, 1967 the vacation Court of Appeal granted an interim injunction to a group of parents, restraining the local education authority from ceasing to maintain eight schools, including Enfield Grammar School and Chace School, unless the Secretary of State had previously given approval under the Education Act 1944, s. 13.[1]

In the face of the injunction the chief education officer prepared a revised scheme for admissions. This provided for the entry of boys at eleven-plus to both schools in September 1967, but without regard to their suitability for a particular kind of education. This scheme was approved by the education committee on August 31. A number of parents objected, and the forty-four assistant staff at the grammar school signed a memorandum condemning the scheme on educational grounds.

A writ claiming an injunction to restrain the local education authority from replacing a selective intake at Enfield Grammar School by a "mixed entry" as being contrary to the school's articles of government was issued on Septem-

1. *Bradbury and others* v. *London Borough of Enfield* [1967] 1 W.L.R. 1311; see page 39, *supra.*

ber 7. The plaintiffs were Mr Edgar Morton Lee, a foundation governor and old boy of the school, and Mr Alan Ross McWhirter, a ratepayer. Donaldson J. granted an injunction *ex parte* on the same day, and the action came to trial without formal pleadings on September 11 in the Queen's Bench Division.

Geoffrey Howe Q.C. (for the plaintiffs): Enfield Grammar School has had to face a greater variety of threats in the four hundred or so days since the London Borough of Enfield decided to reorganise education than in the four hundred or so years since its foundation. It was less than three weeks since the Court of Appeal had observed in the other action which was still proceeding that public bodies must be compelled to observe the law. The question was whether the borough council was going to maintain the school in accordance not merely with the order of the Court of Appeal, but with the school's articles of government. The borough council had not taken into account the wishes of the parents of 177 children who were being arbitrarily divided between the grammar school and Chace Secondary Modern School. The scheme did not comply with article 11 of the school's articles of government in that it took no account of the records or other information that might be available or the more general matter of the general type of education most suitable for the particular pupil or of the views of the headmaster as to the admission of the pupil to the school. It is really a plan to turn the two schools into an educational transit camp for a short period.

In evidence the headmaster said that recently he had had an opportunity of studying the records of the eighty-nine pupils allocated to his school. Twenty or twenty-two were suitable by grammar school criteria. Some were clearly remedial pupils for whom the school had no facilities.

Millett (for the defendants): Under the Education Act 1944 and the articles of government, the admission of pupils was under the sole control of the governors. If there had been a breach, the plaintiffs had chosen the wrong defendants; and the remedy was not by proceedings at law against the governors, *a fortiori* not against the council, but by complaint under the Education Act 1944, ss. 68 or 99, to the Minister by any parent aggrieved.

Cur. adv. vult

Extract from Judgment

DONALDSON J.: . . . The local education authority was convinced that this new scheme was in the best interests of the children at Enfield. A group of parents was equally convinced that it was not. That is a political matter and not one which concerns the courts. The concern of the courts is to ensure that nothing is done by the local education authority, the school governors or the parents which is contrary to law. . . .

The plaintiffs contend that the revised scheme does not comply with the provisions of article 11 in the following respects: (a) It takes no account of the wishes of the parents. (b) It does not take into account the records and other information which may be available or the related matter of the general type of education most suitable for the particular pupil. (c) It does not take into account the views of the headmaster as to the admission of the pupil to the school.

The defendants contend as follows: (1) the matters complained of are matters reserved to the Secretary of State under section 99 of the Education Act 1944 and cannot be considered by a court. The basis of this contention is that what is here complained of is nonfeasance and not malfeasance. (2) The Enfield Borough Council is not the proper defendant since it does not admit pupils to Enfield Grammar School or implement the scheme of admission. If there has been any breach of duty in this case, it is a breach of duty by the governing body of Enfield Grammar School. The sole duties of the local education authority are to determine the general educational character of the school and its place in the educational system, to agree with the governors upon arrangements for the admission of pupils and to determine which candidates for admission to the school are qualified by reason of their having attained a sufficient educational standard. These things they have done, they say. . . . (3) The plaintiffs have no *locus standi*. . . . (4) The revised scheme in fact complies with article 11 of the articles of government. . . .

The plaintiffs say that defect [omission to take account of the wishes of the parents] involves a breach of article 11 and also of section 76 of the Education Act 1944. . . .

In my judgment the plaintiffs succeed on this point. The preferences expressed in the summer of 1967 were in relation to a different scheme, and were preferences for the Enfield Grammar/Chace Boys Group of comprehensive schools. No parent has ever been asked to express a preference between Enfield Grammar School and Chace School. . . .

The plaintiffs' second contention under article 11 was that the scheme does not take into account the records or other information which may be available or the related matter of the general type of education most suitable to the particular pupil. . . .

The question therefore arises whether this part of article 11 is to be ignored or whether it requires amendment before the school can adopt a non-selective scheme of admission. In this connection I should refer to article 9 (1) of the articles of government [which provided for the authority to determine the general educational character of the school].

At the time when the articles were made, and at all times after they were made and prior to July 1967, the general educational character of the school was that of a grammar school. . . . It was tacitly accepted and is recorded in the Middlesex development plan which preceded the making of the articles. . . .

In any event, what is now proposed is a three-form entry comprehensive school for boys aged eleven to eighteen. No other determination, so far as I can see, has been made expressly under article 9 (1) and the plaintiffs therefore submit that the grammar school status of Enfield Grammar School continues to exist. . . . This is a very difficult point, and it may well be that article 9 (1) does not permit the local education authority to alter its determination once made as to the general educational character of the school in the absence of the

words "from time to time" in the article after the words "shall determine." . . .
I express no view upon this point.

I am, however, clear that it is quite impossible for the local education
authority and the governing body to agree upon a non-selective scheme of
entry, that is to say, one not based upon the academic ability of the candidates,
unless and until article 11 is amended by deleting the words: "any school
records and other information which may be available, the general type of
education most suitable for the particular pupil."

Those words are apt only in relation to a selective system of entry. The local
education authority cannot, in my judgment, render them ineffective by
determining under article 9 that the school shall be a comprehensive school. . . .

The plaintiffs' third contention under article 11 was that the scheme does
not take into account the views of the headmaster as to the admission of particular pupils to the school or of a particular pupil in the singular. The scheme
itself clearly does not provide for the views of the headmaster to be taken into
account. The defendants, however, contend that the headmaster was in fact
invited to express his views at the meeting of the governing body on September 8. I do not think this is an answer to the plaintiffs' contention, because it is
the "arrangements" which must be such as to take account of the headmaster's
views. . . .

I therefore conclude that the revised arrangements for the admission of
pupils to the Enfield Grammar School do not accord with article 11 . . . first,
they are not of such a character as to take account of the wishes of the parents;
secondly, they are not of such a nature as to take account of any school records
and other information which may be available; and thirdly, they are not of
such a nature as to take account of the views of the headmaster as to the
admission of the particular pupil to the school.

I have been asked to express a view on what can be done, since the children
must go to school and do so as soon as possible. Application can no doubt be
made to the Secretary of State to amend article 11, and possibly also article 9.
Meanwhile, the wishes of the parents of at least the eighty-nine boys provisionally allocated should be sought, and the records of those boys studied
and the views of the headmaster considered. If and in so far as the result is not
to admit any of the eighty-nine boys, the process can be repeated with other
boys. The result should be that any boys admitted will be such as will benefit
from the education provided by Enfield Grammar School. . . .

The implementation of a scheme of admissions which contravenes article
11 . . . is clearly an act of malfeasance and as such is justiciable in this court.

Accordingly, I hold that the plaintiffs succeed on all points and are entitled
to an injunction substantially in the terms claimed in the writ, although the
precise wording can no doubt be agreed between the parties.

[On an application for a stay, pending a possible appeal]: All I have held is
that you are not entitled under the articles of the grammar school to admit
boys to that school on a non-selective basis. There is nothing in my injunction
that keeps any boy out of school for one day.

Millet (for the defendants): The whole purpose of my application for a stay was in order to get these children into school as quickly as possible.

DONALDSON J.: It was in order to get these children into the school in accordance with the system your clients favour.

Millet: It may possibly be right.

DONALDSON J.: I am not prepared to assist in that.

Injunction granted; stay refused;
Defendants to pay costs

[NOTE: Later in the same day (September 14) on which Donaldson J. granted an injunction and delivered the judgment reported above, the governors of the grammar school passed a resolution asking the Secretary of State to make an order changing the articles of government to permit the school to take a "mixed ability" entry. The Secretary of State informed the governors and headmaster immediately that he proposed to accede to the request, and would allow until noon on Monday, September 18 for the governors and headmaster to make representations. A further action was then brought by a governor, a parent and an assistant master at the school: *Lee and others* v. *Secretary of State for Education and Science* (1968) 66 L.G.R. 211; see page 23, *supra.*]

(D) LOCAL ADMINISTRATION:
PROVISION OF TRANSPORT

10 Surrey County Council *v.* Ministry of Education
[1953] 1 All E.R. 705

QUEEN'S BENCH DIVISION
When a pupil attending a secondary school lives more than three miles from the school, the local education authority must provide transport for the whole distance.

Facts: The Surrey County Council adopted a scheme by which the full cost of transport to and from secondary schools by public conveyance of children living more than three miles from their schools should no longer be paid by the council. Payment was to be so limited to partial payment of fares that no child had to travel more than three miles in either direction unaided by public funds. The Surrey Council asked the court to decide the validity of its action: (1) Whether on the true construction of section 55 (2) of the Education Act 1944 (as amended by the Education (Miscellaneous Provisions) Act 1948), the council was authorised to make such arrangements as those described, and (2) whether it was a question of fact in each individual case whether such arrangements were suitable arrangements, within the meaning of section 39 (2) (c) of the Act, for the transport of a child to and from the school at which he was a registered pupil.

Extract from Judgment

LYNSKEY, J.:.... The answer to the questions put to me depends entirely on the construction of section 55 of the Education Act 1944, as amended by the Education (Miscellaneous Provisions) Act 1948, s. 11 and Schedule I, Part I, and that of section 39 of the Act of 1944, and, in addition, the general scheme of the latter Act as indicated by its terms. As I follow the Act, it imposes on an education authority the obligation to provide education of different standards. I am concerned here particularly with primary education, the council having to provide primary education within the confines of its juris-diction. That is a mandatory obligation imposed on the local education authority.... There is an equal duty imposed on parents to see that their children take advantage of the educational facilities provided.... Then provi-sion is made by section 37, if the child is not at school, for the making of a school attendance order, and then there is imposed on the parent the obliga-tion of sending the child to the school of which such school attendance order requires him to be a registered pupil.

Section 39 deals with the question of the obligation of the parent to send his child to school.... After mentioning prevention of attendance by reason of sickness and non-attendance on religious holidays, section 39 (2) continues:

"(c) if the parent proves that the school at which the child is a registered pupil is not within walking distance of the child's home, and that no suitable arrangements have been made by the local education authority either for his transport to and from the school or for boarding accommodation for him at or near the school or for enabling him to become a registered pupil at a school nearer to his home."

Then by section 39 (5) "walking distance" is defined:

" ... the expression 'walking distance' means, in relation to a child who has not attained the age of eight years two miles, and in the case of any other child three miles, measured by the nearest available route."

So that, on the face of section 39, if a parent did not send his child to school, and the child lived outside the three-miles' radius of the school and no trans-port was provided for him, the parent would be excused for the child's non-attendance.

It is said on behalf of the county council that their obligation is imposed by section 55 and not by section 39. Section 55 as amended runs:

"(1) A local education authority shall make such arrangements for the provision of transport and otherwise as they consider necessary or as the Minister may direct for the purpose of facilitating the attendance of pupils at schools or county colleges or at any course or class provided in pursuance of a scheme of further education in force in their area, and any transport provided in pursuance of such arrangements shall be provided free of charge. (2) A local education authority may pay the whole or any part, as the authority think fit, of the reasonable travelling expenses of any pupil in attendance at any school or county college or at any such course or class as aforesaid for whose transport no arrangements are made under this section." . . .

The county council are saying, in effect, that they have a discretion as to what they shall pay. They have to make arrangements for facilitating the attendance of pupils at school, and the argument on behalf of the council is that by their scheme they are providing payment in respect of the child's transport which will enable the child to reach the school by walking less than three miles. It will be taken from outside the three miles' area, or will go into the three miles' area and join some form of public transport there. . . . The case put forward on behalf of the Minister is that, if section 55 stood alone and apart from anything else in the Act, that is a possible construction and a possible view, but, it is argued, if that view is adopted, one will get a scheme which will not prevent the parent taking advantage of the provisions of section 39 (2) (c) if proceedings are taken against him for "truancy," and, says, the Minister: "If you are going to provide a scheme for making arrangements of that sort, that is obviously not a suitable arrangement within the words of section 39 (2) (c)." . . .

In my view, this case turns on the interpretation of section 39 (2) (c) and section 39 (5). The question is: Has the council made suitable arrangements for the transport to and from school of a child who lives more than three miles from the school—and "to and from school" in that context means to and from the child's home to the school. I should have thought that could have only one meaning because the English of it is too clear. Provision has to be made, if the child lives more than three miles distant from his school, for transport to and from the school and the home. It seems to me to suggest that transport to a point three miles away from the school—which would mean not transport to the school, but transport part of the way to the school—cannot be read into these words. In this case the scheme is to provide a substitute for transport by payment, but, in my view, the reasoning applicable to the provision of transport must apply equally to the reason for payment as a substitute for transport. If, in fact, the obligation is to provide transport to and from the school when the child is resident more than three miles away from the school, then equally I am satisfied that the substitute for transport in the shape of payment for public transport must be of the same character and must provide for payment of the sum which will cover the cost of taking the child by public transport from a point reasonably near his home to a point reasonably near the school—I do not say to the school door, but reasonably near thereto. In those circumstances, on my view of the law, the answer I must give to the first question is "No." In my opinion, on the true construction of section 55 of the Education Act 1944, as amended by the Act of 1948, the council are not authorised to make such arrangements as they propose. On the second question, I accept the answer which has been suggested to me by counsel for the Ministry that the proposed arrangements as a matter of law are not "suitable arrangements" within the meaning of section 39 (2) (*c*).

Declaration accordingly

11   Shrimpton *v.* Hertfordshire County Council (1911) 104 L.T. 145

HOUSE OF LORDS

A local education authority which provides transport for the conveyance of children to and from school may be held negligent for injury to a child who uses it only by permission or consent, and who has no legal claim to the use.

Facts: The Hertfordshire County Council entered into a contract for the conveyance of children in a brake between their homes at Chandler's Cross and the school at Croxley Green, more than two miles away. As there was room, the school attendance officer allowed the two Shrimpton children, who lived only about a mile from the school, to use the brake. As the children were alighting one day in March 1909, someone called out, "All right!" and the horses moved on. Florence Shrimpton fell from the step on to the road. Two doctors believed that only a successful operation could prevent permanent brain injury, but two others could not discover evidence of permanent damage. The plaintiff alleged that, having provided the vehicle and having permitted her to ride in it, the county council was legally bound to exercise reasonable care, and should have provided a conductor. For the defence it was contended that, if there were any negligence, it was on the part of the jobmaster and his servant, and also that there was contributory negligence on the part of the girl.

A special jury at Hertford Assizes, on February 10, 1910, found for the plaintiff for £27 3s. 6d. special damages (doctors' fees) and £250 general damages. Channell J. said that he was reluctant to enter judgment for the plaintiff as he did not think she had a good case in law. On May 28, 1910, the Court of Appeal (Vaughan Williams, Fletcher Moulton, and Buckley L.JJ.) set aside the judgment. The plaintiff appealed to the House of Lords. The question before the House was whether the local education authority owed a positive duty of care to a child whom it was under no legal duty to convey.

Extract from speech

LORD LOREBURN L.C.: . . . Really two questions are raised upon this state of facts. The first is whether the child was driven on the occasion in question in this conveyance by the consent or licence of the county council? It was the business of the attendance officer to communicate with the parents as to what children should ride. He did authorise this child to ride. He did not tell the child's parents that there was any difference between the position of this child

in the conveyance and that of any of the other children, and it was reasonable
that the parents should suppose, as I have no doubt that they did suppose, that
the only education officer whom they saw was acting by the authority of
the education committee, who were themselves acting by the authority of the
county council. I think, therefore, that when he sanctioned or permitted the
conveyance of this child in this vehicle he thereby bound the county council.
The next question was, Did the child enter, and was she conveyed in this
vehicle on the terms of using it *tale quale*,* such as it was, and was the only
duty of the county council a negative duty, not to lay what is called a trap for
the children who used the vehicle? It was argued that their only duty was not
to lay a trap, because there was no obligation on them to take this child, she
living within one mile of the school, and not being able to be excused from
attendance by reason of the distance of her home from the school. Let us see
how this vehicle came to be provided. There is a duty on the part of the county
council to carry out the Education Act, including as one object, at all events,
the procuring of children to come to school. There may be an excuse on the
part of those children arising from the distance of their homes from the school,
and accordingly the county council have the power of providing, if they think
fit, a vehicle for children living more than two miles away from the school, and
also of providing out of the rates a vehicle for the service of children living not
more than two miles away, but within a mile, if they do so within the fair
discretion given to them under this statute. I agree with the learned counsel
for the respondents that here there was no duty or obligation whatever on the
county council to provide for the carriage of this child, but if they did agree to
do so, and did provide a vehicle, then it is clear to my mind that their duty was
also to provide a reasonably safe mode of conveyance. This was not done
according to the findings of the jury. They have found that it was not a reasonable and proper way for the county council to convey children to school in this
vehicle without a conductor or some adult person to take care of them. It is
said that there is no evidence in support of this finding. To my mind it is a
question which any man of the world can answer by the exercise of his own
common sense and his knowledge of life. It appeared to the learned counsel for
the respondents a very perverse view to take of things. I am sorry to say that
I take the same view myself, when you have little children, five, six, or seven
years of age, up to ten or twelve, and send them in a conveyance such as has
been described, without anyone to look after them, I must say that I should be
very much disposed, if I were on the jury myself, to say that it was not a
reasonable or proper way of conveying them to school. However, that does not
matter. The jury said so. They are the judges, and my opinion on the subject is
of no importance. I am content to place upon that ground the advice which I
would respectfully offer to your Lordships—upon the ground that if the
county council did through their representative agree to provide a vehicle for
this child, it was their duty to provide a reasonably safe mode of conveyance,
and in the opinion of the jury they did not do so. I do not think that it is
necessary to enter upon the larger question whether the county council would

or would not be responsible for the negligence of the driver. I shall, therefore, respectfully advise your Lordships to allow this appeal.

Order appealed from reversed, and appeal allowed with costs in the courts below, and such costs as are usual in pauper cases in this House

(E) VOLUNTARY SCHOOLS: DUTY TO PROVIDE SERVICES AND EQUIPMENT, ETC.

12 Trowbridge Water Co. *v.* Wiltshire County Council [1909] 1 K.B. 824

KING'S BENCH DIVISION

As part of its duty to maintain a school a local education authority is bound to provide a supply of water.

Facts: Prior to the passing of the Education Act 1902, the plaintiffs supplied the managers of the Trowbridge British School* (otherwise Adcroft School) with water, payment being made by the managers. Under the Act the school became a non-provided school, and the water which was necessary for the maintenance of the school was supplied as before. There was no contract for the supply between the Water Company and the local education authority except as might be implied from the fact of the supply, the purpose for which the water was supplied, the course of dealing, and the circumstances under which the water had previously been supplied.

The Water Company continued to send their demand note to the managers and, after the Act, the managers included the amount in their quarterly accounts of expenditure which they sent to the local education authority. The local education authority paid the Water Company direct, and a receipt was given by the Water Company to the authority.

For a considerable time the local education authority continued to pay the demand notes, but in respect of a certain period they refused, contending that they were not, but the managers were, legally liable for the supply of water to the school. In an action by the Water Company against the local education authority, the county court judge gave judgment for the plaintiffs for £13 4s. 10d.

The defendants appealed.

*Cur. adv. vult**

Extract from Judgment

WALTON J.: . . . The main contention before the county court judge appears to have been that the local education authority have no power to enter into contracts for the supply of water or anything else which may be required for the maintenance of a non-provided school, and, therefore, that the defendants had no power to enter into a contract for the supply of water to the Adcroft School. . . .

Section 7,[1] in so far as its provisions are material to the present case, is as follows: "(1) The local education authority shall maintain and keep efficient all public elementary schools within their area which are necessary, and have the control of all expenditure required for that purpose, other than expenditure for which, under this Act, provision is to be made by the managers; but, in the case of a school not provided by them, only so long as the following conditions and provisions are complied with." The expenditure for which provision is to be made, not by the local education authority, but by the managers, is that required for providing and keeping in repair the school house, as described in section 7, subsection (1) (d). Subject therefore, to this exception, the Act of 1902 imposes upon the local education authority the obligation of maintaining and keeping efficient all non-provided schools in their district, which are public elementary schools and are necessary within the meaning of the Act. Before the Act of 1902 was passed there was, under the earlier Education Act, no obligation upon any one to maintain or keep efficient any voluntary school.

It seems quite plain that there is, under the Act of 1902, no obligation upon the managers of the Adcroft School to make themselves personally responsible for the expenditure required for the maintenance of the school. The managers might, of course, have entered into a contract for the supply of water which by its terms might have made them liable to the water company. In the present case there was no express contract. Water was supplied. The bills for the water rate were sent in quarterly by the water company to the managers of the school, were paid to the water company direct by the county council as the local education authority, and receipts for the payments were given by the water company to the county council. This was the course of business followed from the time when the Act of 1902 came into operation until the question arose which led to the present action.

Upon these facts the learned county court judge has held that the Wilts County Council are the persons liable to the water company for the water supplied. Having regard to the fact that the county council were, in the words of the Act, bound to maintain the school, and therefore to provide a supply of water, and had control of the expenditure necessary for that purpose, we think that the county council had power under the Act of 1902 to make themselves liable to the water company for the water supplied, and we think that there was evidence upon which the learned county court judge might properly find that the county council were the persons with whom the contract for the supply of water in question was made. We see no reason for thinking that his finding was wrong in law. . . .

It was argued by the defendants that, inasmuch as the obligation of the local education authority to maintain the school ceases upon the breach by the managers of any of the conditions prescribed in section 7, subsection (1), practical difficulties will arise in the working of the Act if the local education authority are directly responsible for the cost of maintenance. We think that

1. Of the Education Act 1902.

such difficulties may easily be foreseen and provided against.

This appeal must be dimissed with costs.

Appeal dismissed

[NOTE: The present duties of a local education authority for the maintenance of a voluntary school are laid down in the Education Act 1944, section 15 (3). The expression "maintain" is defined in section 14 (2) of that Act.]

13 R. *v.* Easton, *ex p.* Oulton [1913] 2 K.B. 60

COURT OF APPEAL

A local education authority has power to provide and pay for the new furniture of a school provided by persons other than the local education authority.

Facts: In 1908 notice was given by the promoters of their intention to provide two new public elementary schools in Liverpool to be called St Sebastian's and St Hugh's, plans of which were approved by the Board of Education, and no appeal was made with regard to either school. The schools were erected, St Sebastian's being opened on May 3, 1909, and St Hugh's on September 6, 1909. When St Sebastian's was opened, it was supplied by the managers with certain furniture, school apparatus, and desks. No furniture was supplied by the managers of St Hugh's School. The Board of Education placed both of them on the Parliamentary grant list as from the dates of their opening respectively. The managers applied to the local education authority to furnish St Hugh's School.

The local education authority not being satisfied with the character of the furniture in St Sebastian's School (which had then been used as a school for some months) took it out, and then furnished both St Sebastian's and St Hugh's Schools with desks and cupboards. The sums paid for this purpose by the local education authority were surcharged by the auditor on the ground that they had no power to pay them.

A rule nisi* for certiorari* directed to George Easton, an auditor of the Local Government Board was obtained to remove into the King's Bench Division certain disallowances and surcharges made by him, amounting in the aggregate to £403 6s. 7d., on his audit of the accounts of the Liverpool Local Education Authority for the year ended March 31, 1910.

The rule was moved on behalf of one of the members surcharged.

The Divisional Court held (Darling J. dissenting) that the duty to maintain and keep efficient a public elementary school imposed on a local education authority by section 7, subsection (1), of the Education Act 1902, included the duty of providing with desks, cupboards, and other school furniture necessary to its being carried on as a public elementary school, a new non-provided school coming into existence since the "appointed day" under the Act and provided by persons other than the local education authority, if it had been erected under the provision of section 8, subsection (1), of that Act and there had been no appeal or an unsuccessful appeal against it under that section. The Divisional Court therefore made the rule absolute.

The auditor appealed.

Extract from Judgment

LORD ALVERSTONE C.J.: . . . In my judgment the decision of the Divisional Court was right and this appeal ought to be dismissed. . . .

On behalf of the appellant Mr Buckmaster contended that obligation did not arise till they can be started as equipped schools. We must be guided by such light as the statute throws upon the question as to who is to bear the burden of equipping the schools, and in my judgment there are certain considerations which point to the fact that the statute does not contemplate any part of the burden of equipment being borne by the managers. . . . I think section 7 (1) (*d*) goes a long way to help us to decide this question. It says: "The managers of the school shall provide the school house free of any charge, except for the teacher's dwelling-house (if any), to the local education authority for use as a public elementary school, and shall, out of funds provided by them, keep the school house in good repair, and make such alterations and improvements in the buildings as may be reasonably required by the local education authority." It is not suggested that under these words any obligation is cast upon the managers to equip the school, put in the furniture, maps, and so on. . . . There is, in my judgment, an important distinction between the obligation to provide the buildings . . . on the one hand and the obligation to provide the cost of equipment on the other hand. . . . In my judgment the language of clause (*d*) of section 7, subsection (1), clearly indicates that the only responsibility placed upon the managers when they come into existence is the obligation to provide and to improve the school house from time to time. . . . It is not denied that furniture must be provided before it becomes a public elementary school. . . .

All we have to decide is whether the Divisional Court was wrong in holding that there is nothing in the Education Act 1902 which prohibits the local education authority from providing the furniture, and in my opinion the language of section 7 of the Act of 1902 indicates that the provision of and making the building fit for a public elementary school and maintaining the building as a public elementary school is thrown upon the managers, the provision of the equipment falls upon the local education authority, and the expenditure of the necessary money is expenditure "other than expenditure for which, under this Act, provision is to be made by the managers." It is not suggested that there is any provision in the Act for the expenditure of this money by the managers, and in my judgment that omission points to the fact that the local education authority are to be responsible for the equipment of the school as distinguished from the building. Clause 14 of the Second Schedule to the Act of 1902 confirms my view. . . .

In my judgment there is no ground for holding that it was *ultra vires** of the

local education authority to spend this money upon the furniture, and I think
the view taken by the majority of the Divisional Court—by all three judges, so
far as one school was concerned—is correct. The rule must therefore be
discharged.

Farwell L.J. delivered a concurring judgment.

EVANS, P.: (*dissenting*) ... I regret to say that I cannot come to the same
conclusion as my learned brethren. ...

The point is, in my judgment, the same in the case of St Sebastian's school
as of St Hugh's. ... The question is whether the local education authority had
the right to use public money for the purpose of supplying furniture which
was requisite for the adequate and suitable equipment of an elementary school
in a building which was proposed to be provided by persons other than the
education authority as a public elementary school. ... The expenditure of
money must be exactly coterminous with the obligations which are cast upon
them by the statute.

... The sole question before us, in my judgment, is whether the buildings
handed over as bare buildings were public elementary schools provided by
these donors or not. Now the local education authority might themselves have
stepped in in each and said "This school is necessary and we will provide it."
Then they would have erected the building; and suppose they had gone to the
Board of Education and said, "This is a building erected in accordance with
the plans you approved, and as we do not propose to do any more, nobody can
find the furniture and we do not propose to," it is impossible to suppose that
the Board of Education would regard that as a public elementary school. If it
is not a public elementary school when it is provided by the local education
authority how can it be a public elementary school—left in that state—when
it is provided by a private individual? ...

In my view, putting it shortly, four walls without desks and cupboards—
the articles of furniture in question in this case—are not a public elementary
school. ... I think those who undertook to provide these schools ought to have
been able to say to the local education authority: "We have provided for you
not only four walls but a building in which we have put the necessary
apparatus—a building which is adequately and suitably equipped for you to
take over and to conduct as a public elementary school." ...

Appeal allowed

[NOTE: The present law on this subject is contained in the Education Act 1944,
s. 15 (3), as amended:

"The managers or governors of a controlled school shall not be responsible for any
of the expenses of maintaining the school, but the following provisions shall have
effect with respect to the maintenance of aided schools and special agreement
schools:

(*a*) the following expenses shall be payable by the managers or governors of the
school, that is to say, the expenses of discharging any liability incurred by them
or on their behalf or by or on behalf of any former managers or governors of the
school or any trustees thereof in connection with the provision of premises or equipment for the purposes of the school, and expenses incurred in effecting such

alterations to the school buildings as may be required by the local education authority for the purpose of securing that the school premises should conform to the prescribed standards, and any expenses incurred in effecting repairs to the school buildings not being repairs which are excluded from their responsibility by the following paragraph:

(b) the managers or governors of the school shall not be responsible for repairs to the interior of the school buildings, or for repairs to those buildings necessary in consequence of the use of the school premises, in pursuance of any direction or requirement of the authority, for purposes other than those of the school."]

14 Gillow and others v. Durham County Council [1913] A.C. 54

HOUSE OF LORDS
The managers of a non-provided school are entitled to appoint caretaking and cleaning staff, and to have their salaries paid by the local education authority.

Facts: The appellants were the foundation managers and the trustees of St Patrick's Roman Catholic non-provided* public elementary schools at Consett, who asked for a declaration that the managers were entitled to appoint a caretaker and cleaner, and to have their wages paid by the local education authority.

On April 1, 1904, when the Education Act 1902 came into force as regards non-provided schools, the employment of William McGuinness and Margaret Kane, as caretaker and cleaner respectively, was continued, and the local education authority paid their wages. In 1909, claiming to have the power of appointment under regulations which they had made in 1904, the authority gave notice terminating the appointments. On May 31, 1909 they purported to appoint Margaret Kane as caretaker and cleaner. The managers objected, and issued a writ on October 21, 1909.

Hamilton J. declared (1) that the managers were entitled to cause the schools to be properly cleaned, cared for, and attended to, and that the respondents, the local education authority were not entitled to interfere with the managers in the performance of their duties in this respect, and (2) that the managers were entitled to have their reasonable expense of cleaning, caring for, and attending to the schools paid by the respondents as part of the maintenance of the schools.

The Court of Appeal (Fletcher Moulton and Farwell L.JJ.; Vaughan Williams L.J. dissenting) reversed the decision of Hamilton J.

The plaintiffs appealed to the House of Lords.

Cur. adv. vult

Extract from Speech
VISCOUNT HALDANE L.C.: . . . The question is whether the appellants or the respondents are entitled to appoint the caretakers and cleaners of the school. . . .

. . The Act of 1870 had for one of its main purposes a large increase in the supply of public elementary schools. The existing supply was to be supplemented by the addition of schools of a new class to be provided by school boards, and to be supplied with money, partly out of national funds and partly out of the rates. And the existing voluntary schools, or such of them as chose to conform to conditions laid down by the Act, were also to be used and assisted. These voluntary schools were to have no aid from the rates, but, provided that they complied with the provisions of section 7, which defined a public elementary school, and with those of section 97, which laid down the conditions under which a public elementary school could obtain a parliamentary grant, they were to be in as good a position as regards aid from such a grant as a school provided by a school board. Under the Act of 1870 the managers of a non-provided school were left in control of their school, and could manage the school just as they pleased, provided that those managers who wished to earn it observed the conditions requisite for the earning of the parliamentary grant. . . .

The new principle which the Act of 1902 introduced was that of entitling them to rate aid from the local education authorities, which the Act substituted for the old school boards, and the extent to which these authorities were permitted to interfere in their management can be found only in the Act itself. . . .

The real question appears to be, What powers of interference with this management are conferred on the authority? Those that are not in terms conferred on that body remain where they were. The relationship between the two bodies concerned was not that of principal and agent, but one of co-ordinate authorities, between which powers are distributed. I cannot agree with Farwell L.J. in his view that with certain exceptions the whole of the duties and powers under the Act have been committed to the local authority, and that the object is, in words which I have already quoted from his judgment, to supplement them by giving the authority the assistance of managers, "leaving the former the masters of the situation, just as a great landowner appoints an agent to manage his estates." This appears to me to be a misconception of the scheme of the statute, which was to give the bodies of managers, who were in existence when the Act began to operate, a title to aid from the rates similar to that of a provided school, while denying to the authority, as their paymaster, any but a limited title to interfere with powers of management. I think that those powers continue to include that of general management, and, as part of this, the responsibility for looking after the school and appointing the necessary caretakers and cleaners. I am therefore of opinion that the judgment of the Court of Appeal should be reversed and that of Hamilton J. restored, and that the respondents should pay the costs of this appeal and in the courts below.

Appeal allowed

[NOTE: The present provision is contained in the Education Act 1944, s. 22 (4): "At any controlled school or special agreement school the persons employed for the purposes of the care and maintenance of the school premises shall be appointed and dismissed by the local education authority, and the local education authority may give directions to the managers or governors of an aided school as to the number and conditions of service of persons employed at the school for such purpose." By section 114 (2) (*a*) of the same Act the local education authority is under a duty to defray all the expenses of maintaining a school except, in the case of an aided school or a special agreement school, any expenses payable by the managers or governors under section 15 (3) (*a*). The cost of caretaking does not fall within the expenses for which the managers or governors are liable.]

(F) MANAGERS OR GOVERNORS: LIMITATION OF ACTIONS

15 Greenwood *v*. Atherton [1939] 1 K.B. 388

COURT OF APPEAL

The managers of a non-provided voluntary school are a public body acting in pursuance of a statutory duty.

Facts: The plaintiff, a schoolchild, was injured during break-time on April 8, 1937, in the playground of this school, being a non-provided voluntary school. On November 10, 1937, a writ was issued against the head teacher and the managers of the school, alleging that the plaintiff's injury was caused by the defendants' negligence in failing to take care of the infant plaintiff while in attendance at the school. The school was a non-provided voluntary school, and both the school and its body of managers were in existence before the passing of the Education Act 1921. Under that Act, however, the school received a grant towards the cost of education.

The defendants pleaded the Public Authorities Protection Act 1893, section 1 of which limits the time within which any action can be commenced against any person for any act done in pursuance, or execution, or intended execution of any Act of Parliament, or of any public duty or authority, or in respect of any alleged neglect or default in the execution of any such Act, duty, or authority, to six months after the act, neglect, or default complained of.

The point with regard to the Public Authorities Protection Act 1893 was argued before Lewis J. as a preliminary point without the actual facts of the case being gone into. Lewis J. held that the Act of 1893 applied and, as the action has not been commenced within six months of the occurrence, the case could not be pursued.

The plaintiff appealed. The question before the court was whether the managers of a public elementary school were a "public authority."

Extracts from Judgments

MACKINNON, L.J.: . . . The Public Authorities Protection Act 1893, s. 1, provides: "Where, after the commencement of this Act any action, prosecution, or other proceeding is commenced in the United Kingdom against any person for any act done in pursuance or execution, or intended execution of any Act of Parliament"—then the action must be taken within the limited period. I think it is manifest that within the clearest meaning of those words these defendants, the managers as managing the school—managing a public elementary school governed by the Education Act of 1921—were providing and controlling this playground where the accident happened in pursuance, or execution, or intended execution of an Act of Parliament—namely, the statute of 1921. And that being so, it follows that any suit brought against them in respect of such an act must be commenced within the six months limited by the Act. This action not having been commenced within the time limited by the Act of 1893, the resulting penalty under that Act applies, with the result that I think this case was quite rightly decided by Lewis, J. and that this appeal must fail.

GODDARD L.J.: These foundation managers are acting in pursuance of a public duty. It seems to me really quite unarguable to say that they are not a public authority and not acting in pursuance of a statutory duty, and although it may be they could not be compelled to keep the school in existence, so long as they are in receipt of a grant from public funds I do not see how it can be said that they are not public authorities, and for that reason I agree that this appeal must fail.

Appeal dismissed

[NOTE: The special protection given to public authorities was removed by the Law Reform (Limitation of Actions, etc.) Act 1954, which repealed the Public Authorities Protection Act 1893, as amended by the Limitation Act 1939. Actions against a public authority, as against a private person, must now be commenced within three years.]

(G) MANAGERS OR GOVERNORS: LIABILITY FOR NEGLIGENCE

16 Griffiths *v*. St Clement's School, Liverpool (Managers) and Liverpool Church of England Schools Society [1939] 2 All E.R. 76

COURT OF APPEAL

sub nom. Griffiths *v*. Smith [1941] 1 All E.R. 66; [1941] A.C. 170

HOUSE OF LORDS

The managers of a school holding an exhibition of pupils' work are performing part of their function as managers of the school.

Facts: The plaintiffs were the parents of a boy who, at the material time, was a pupil at St Clement's School, Liverpool. The female plaintiff was invited to attend an exhibition of work by the pupils, the invitation being issued by the headmaster with the authority of the managers. The female plaintiff attended, and was injured when a floor collapsed through want of repair.

In an action for damages, it was contended on behalf of the managers that they were in occupation only as the agents of the general committee of the Liverpool Church of England Schools Society; and that in holding the gathering in question the managers were not acting in pursuance of any public duty, or in execution of any Act of Parliament, but were performing a purely voluntary act. The defendants claimed further that they were protected by the Public Authorities Protection Act 1893, s. 1, as the action was commenced more than six months after the act or default complained of. Tucker J. and the Court of Appeal held they were so protected. The plaintiff appealed to the House of Lords. The question to be decided by the House was whether the managers, in authorising the display, were acting in accordance with their function as managers, and therefore protected by the Act.

Extract from Speech

LORD SIMON L.C.: . . . Mrs Griffiths, whose son was a pupil at the school, was one of those invited by the headmaster, with the authority of the managers, to attend an exhibition on the premises of work done by the boys. There were also to be songs during the evening which the pupils had learned while attending the school. While this display was going on, the first floor of the school premises collapsed. Many persons, including Mrs Griffiths, suffered serious injuries, and two persons were killed. There is no dispute that the floor was in a dangerous condition. . . .

The duty of keeping the school house in good repair rests upon the managers (Education Act 1921, s. 29 (s) (d)). . . .

The body of managers constituted for a non-provided public elementary school* is the creation of the statute and the statutory provision is now to be found in the Education Act 1921, s. 30 (2). . . .

Counsel for the appellants put their claim on the basis that the managers had invited Mrs Griffiths to come upon premises which the managers occupied and controlled without warning her of their dangerous condition and without putting them in a proper state of repair. So stated, the claim is to enforce a common law liability . . . [and the managers must be regarded as occupiers]. Apart from the defence raised under the Public Authorities Protection Act 1893, both the courts below would have decided in favour of the present appellants. I entirely concur, and entertain no doubt that, if Mr and Mrs Griffiths had issued their writ more promptly, they would have had an effective cause of action against the managers. . . . However, the writ was issued on October 12, 1936, twenty-two months after the accident, and the managers thus have the opportunity of pleading that they were protected by the Public Authorities Protection Act 1893. The sole question in the appeal is whether this plea should prevail. . . .

There are . . . two questions to be decided as to the application of the Public Authorities Protection Act 1893 in the present case. First, are the managers a public authority? Secondly, was the neglect or default proved against them neglect or default in the execution of their statutory duty or authority? In my opinion, both these questions should be answered in the affirmative. . . . The

Court of Appeal has already held in *Greenwood* v. *Atherton*[1] that the managers of a non-provided school are a public authority within the protection of the Act, and it appears to me that this view is right.

Lastly, was the action of the managers in authorising the invitations to this school display an act done in the execution of their statutory duty or authority? It was strenuously contended for the appellants that this action was "voluntary" in the sense in which the sale of coke in *Bradford Corporation* v. *Myers*[2] was voluntary. It is true that St Clement's school could have been carried on without arranging to hold this display, but that is not the true test. The real question is whether the managers, in authorising the issue of invitations to the display on the school premises after school hours, should be regarded as exercising their function of managing the school. . . . It would be within the discretion of the managers to decide whether they would approve such a display or whether they would not. The point is, however, that they did approve it, and that they did so in the course of carrying on this public elementary school and of exercising the powers of management conferred upon them by the Education Act. There is, in my opinion, no ground whatever for saying that the invitations issued to this display were issued for some extraneous purpose unconnected with the management of the school. I am of opinion, therefore, that the managers can avail themselves of the protection of the Act. If they are discharged from liability, it is not disputed that the other defendants are also entitled to succeed, and I need not discuss whether in any event they could be held liable. I move that this appeal be dimissed.

Appeal dismissed

[NOTE: See Note to *Greenwood* v. *Atherton*, page 62, *supra*.]

17 Woodward *v*. Mayor of Hastings [1944]
2 All E.R. 565; [1945] K.B. 17

COURT OF APPEAL

If a caretaker is entrusted with the performance of a duty incumbent upon the governors, the governors are liable for his negligence, even though he is not their servant.

Facts: The plaintiff was a pupil at Hastings Grammar School, an endowed secondary school within the provisions of the Endowed Schools Acts, 1869–89. The Mayor of Hastings and the chairman of the borough's education committee were *ex-officio** members of the governing body which consisted of fourteen persons, of whom eight were appointed by a public authority.

Owing to the war the school was removed to St Albans in July 1940 and was accommodated in premises belonging to the Congregational Church. In January 1942 the steps to these premises were covered with frozen snow over

1. [1939] 1 K.B. 388; see page 62, *supra*.
2. [1916] 1 A.A. 242; 85 L.J.K.B. 146; 114 L.T. 83.

which was a layer of loose snow. The caretaker who usually did the cleaning for the Congregational Church swept the loose snow, but did not remove that which was frozen. No ashes or sand were placed on the frozen snow, and no warning was given of the danger. The steps were badly worn, and sloped steeply down.

While leaving the premises on the instructions of his teacher, the plaintiff slipped on the steps and sustained serious injuries. The defendants claimed that they were only licensees in occupation, and that the woman who swept the step was not in their employment, under their orders, or in any way their servant or agent. They denied negligence or breach of duty, and pleaded contributory negligence by the plaintiff or, alternatively that the accident was entirely due to his negligence. They pleaded that they were a public authority, and that the claim was barred because it was not issued within the time allowed by the Limitation Act 1939, s. 21 (1).[1]

Hallett J. said that the Congregational Church authorities were undoubtedly the caretaker's employer, but he did not think that the step was as safe for the scholars as reasonable care and skill could make it, that the governors continued to be responsible for the state of the premises although the school had moved, and that the action would have succeeded had it not been statute-barred. He held that the action failed on the ground that the defendants were acting in pursuance of a public duty and the writ was not issued within the time allowed.

The plaintiffs appealed on the finding that the defendants were a public authority, and the defendants cross-appealed on the finding of negligence.

Extract from Judgment
DU PARCQ L.J.: . . . The managers of a non-provided voluntary school undoubtedly act "in pursuance of an Act of Parliament" and of "a public duty," in the course of carrying on the management of that school. The governors of the school with which we are here concerned were in a very different position. They were administering a charitable trust, and the fact that it is in the public interest that they should do so does not make them a public authority, or their work a "public duty" within the Limitation Act 1939, s. 21. . . . On the facts of this case we have no doubt that the woman, who was admittedly negligent, had been entrusted by the defendants with the necessary work of cleaning the premises which they occupied. They had secured, by contract, the benefit of her services for that purpose. It may be, though we think it improbable, that the defendants expected the headmaster to supervise her work. If they did, he does not appear to have done what was expected of him. If they did not, then they left the care of the premises to the cleaner. It is idle to suggest that she was not authorised to brush snow from the step. It was clearly part of her duty to do so, and no one in her position would have been likely to omit that task. Negligence having been established against her, it follows that the defendants are responsible for their agent's failure to take reasonable care for the safety

1. See note to *Greenwood* v. *Atherton*, page 63, *supra*.

of their invitee. It does not avail them to say that they did not know of the danger. . . .

It is said by counsel for the defendants that the cleaner was not the servant of the defendants but of the diaconate of the Congregational Church, whose premises were occupied by the defendants. We do not accept this as the true view of her position. . . . Even if the cleaner was not temporarily under the control of the defendants, and thus for the time being their servant, they are liable on the ground that they delegated to her the performance of the duty which was incumbent on them. . . .

The craft of the charwoman may have its mysteries, but there is no esoteric quality in the nature of the work which the cleaning of a snow-covered step demands.

For these reasons we are of opinion that the judge would have been right to give judgment for the plaintiffs, as he would have done had he not come to an erroneous conclusion with regard to the plea of the statute. The appeal accordingly succeeds. The judgment for the defendants will be set aside, and a new trial ordered as to damages. The plaintiffs will have the costs of the hearing before Hallett J., and of the appeal.

Appeal allowed, cross-appeal dismissed
Order for new trial as to damages

[NOTE: This case may be compared with *Griffiths* v. *St Clement's School, Liverpool* [1941] A.C. 170, page 63, *supra*, in which it was held that the managers of a maintained voluntary school are a public body.]

II

CONDITIONS OF SERVICE

(A) APPOINTMENT: IMPROPER COMMUNICATION

18 Powell *v.* Lee and others (1908) 99 L.T. 284

KING'S BENCH DIVISION
An appointment improperly communicated to a candidate is not binding.

Facts: The plaintiff applied for appointment as headmaster of Cranford School, Middlesex. The managers hoped to appoint a man and his wife as headmaster and assistant mistress. The plaintiff was not married, but proposed that, if appointed, he would immediately marry a lady with the necessary qualifications for appointment as assistant mistress. There were three candidates on the short list, and at a meeting of the managers on March 26, 1908, three managers voted for the plaintiff, two for a candidate named Parker, and the chairman, who was the rector of Cranford, did not vote.

One of the managers, a Mr Dismore, who was acting in a quasi-secretarial capacity, was instructed to send a telegram to Mr Parker informing him that he had not been appointed. There was no evidence that he was instructed to communicate with the successful candidate.

On the following day the plaintiff went to see the rector, Mr Lee, and, as he later deposed, he was told that the rector had refused to give his casting vote and there was therefore no appointment. On April 1 the plaintiff received a telegram from Mr Dismore saying that he had been appointed.

The rector then called a further meeting of the managers with a view to appointing Mr Parker. The managers who had proposed and seconded that the plaintiff be appointed, one of whom was Mr Dismore, refused to attend. The resolution passed at the previous meeting was rescinded, and those present unanimously appointed Mr Parker as headmaster, and Mrs Parker as assistant mistress.

The plaintiff claimed that a valid contract had been made by the communication to him by Mr Dismore of the fact of his appointment, of which the subsequent resolution was a breach entitling him to damages. The county court judge at Uxbridge held that Mr Dismore's communication was unauthorised, and that the plaintiff had therefore established no contract to employ. Judgment was entered for the defendants.

The plaintiff appealed.

Extract from Judgment:

CHANNEL J.: . . . In my opinion the case depends on this, that where, as in this case, a body of six people, acting not as a corporation or a board of directors, but as six persons having the power to appoint to a post, vote on the question and resolve to appoint someone, they do not make a concluded contract then and there. There must be something more. There must be a communication made by the body of persons to the selected candidate. In this case the managers authorised a communication to Mr Parker to the effect that he had not been elected; but they did not authorise a communication to Mr Powell to the effect that he had been elected. To my mind, that implies that they reserved the power to consider the matter. Then one of the parties desired to reopen the matter, and he told the plaintiff that there was a difficulty. Later, another party, Mr Dismore, told the plaintiff that he had been elected on the 26th March. I think Mr Dismore made that communication to the plaintiff acting as an individual, and not for the body of the managers. If the mere knowledge of what happened at the meeting was sufficient to complete the contract, as, for instance, if the result of the voting was overheard at the door, the matter would rest upon a different footing. But I do not think that is sufficient to complete the contract. There must be notice of acceptance from the contracting party in some way, and the mere fact that the managers did not authorise such a communication, which is the usual course adopted, implies that they meant to reserve the power to reconsider the decision at which they had arrived. On these grounds, and on the grounds stated by the learned county court judge, I think his decision was right, and the appeal must be dismissed.

Appeal dismissed

(B) VOLUNTARY SCHOOLS: PRIVITY OF CONTRACT

19 Crocker *v*. Mayor and Corporation of Plymouth [1906] 1 K.B. 494

KING'S BENCH DIVISION
There is no privity of contract between a teacher in a non-provided* school and the local education authority, notwithstanding the fact that the teacher is paid directly by the local education authority.

Facts: The plaintiff, Mrs Lillie Crocker, was a mistress at Compton National School, a non-provided* school, maintained by the Plymouth Corporation. She brought an action in the Plymouth County Court claiming arrears of salary amounting to £32 8s. 4d. from the Corporation.

By agreement in writing dated March 22, 1899, the plaintiff, then Lillie Stone, a certificated teacher, was employed by the managers of the Compton National School, which was a public elementary school, as assistant mistress of such school at a salary of £50 a year, rising by yearly increments of £5 to a maximum of £80 a year payable monthly, and subject to three calendar months' notice to terminate the agreement either side.

On April 1, 1903, the Education Act 1902 came into operation. By virtue of section 1 the defendants became the local education authority for the borough of Plymouth, and by section 7 the duty of maintaining and keeping efficient all public elementary schools and controlling all expenditure required for that purpose was thrown on the defendants. The plaintiff continued to act as such assistant mistress, and so acted down to the commencement of the action. No express contract was entered into between the plaintiff and the defendants, and no written or verbal proposal for any such contract passed between the parties. The defendants continued from time to time to pay the plaintiff's salary to the plaintiff directly in the amounts and at the times stipulated for in the agreement down to November 30, 1904. The plaintiff gave receipts for the same to the defendants.

The plaintiff, on August 9, 1904, married William Crocker.

On or about November 30, 1904, the plaintiff received a letter from Mr Cook, the secretary to the education authority, informing her as follows: "That the three months' notice to which under the regulations your marriage was equivalent having now expired, the salary sent herewith will be your final payment as a teacher on the staff of the Compton Mixed School."

It was proved that on August 4, 1903, the following resolution was passed by the defendants: "That the marriage of principal and assistant mistresses in provided and non-provided schools shall be equivalent to three months' notice to terminate the engagement." On August 11, 1903, the following letter was written on behalf of the defendants to a manager of the Compton School: "I beg to inform you that the authority have decided that the marriage of principal and assistant mistresses in future shall be equivalent to three months' notice to determine the engagement." No notice to terminate the plaintiff's employment was ever given to the plaintiff either by the defendants or by the managers, nor was any such regulation or resolution ever communicated to the plaintiff. There was no evidence that the contents of the letter of August 11, 1903, were brought to the plaintiff's notice. The plaintiff, however, admitted that she heard of the "regulation" from various sources outside the school.

On December 12, 1904, Mr Berry, the chairman, and a manager of the Compton School, wrote to the defendant council's secretary a letter pointing out that the resolution of August 10, 1903, was not a direction to the managers; and asking if it was not the proper course to direct them to give the plaintiff notice to determine the agreement. No answer was put in, nor was any copy of a letter by the defendant council's secretary to the Board of Education put in evidence. Nothing further was done until the action was commenced to recover salary from November 1, 1904, to April 30, 1905.

By section 7 (a) of the Education Act 1902, "the managers ... shall carry out any direction of the local education authority ... including any directions with respect to the number and educational qualifications of the teachers to be employed for such instruction, and for the dismissal of any teacher on educational grounds; and if the managers fail to carry out any such direction the local education authority shall have the power themselves to carry out the direction in question as if they were managers and by clause (*c*) the consent of the local authority shall be required to the appointment of teachers, but shall not be withheld except on educational grounds, and it shall also be required for the dismissal of a teacher, except such dismissal be on grounds relating to religious instruction. By subsection (3), if any question arises under this section between the local education authority and the managers of a school not provided by the authority, that question shall be determined by the Board of Education.

Section 16 provides: "If the local authority fail to fulfil any of their duties under the Elementary Education Acts 1870 to 1900 or this Act . . . the Board of Education may, after holding a public inquiry, make such order as they think necessary or proper for the purpose of compelling the authority to fulfil their duty, and any such order may be enforced by mandamus."*

The county court judge was of opinion that, having regard to the evidence, at any rate after the first payment by the defendants to the plaintiff of her salary, there was a novation, the new contract being the terms of the original contract, except in so far as they were altered by the Education Act 1902 with a substitution as debtors of the defendants in lieu of the managers. He saw no reason why the ordinary implication arising from payment of salary in such circumstances should not apply to the defendants. He thought that, having so paid it, the defendants were precluded from denying that, so long as the plaintiff's employment continued, they were liable for salary earned. He therefore gave judgment for the plaintiff.

The defendants appealed, the question being whether the teacher was the servant of the local education authority.

Extract from Judgment
LORD ALVERSTONE L.C.J.: . . . Is the effect of section 7 of the Education Act 1902 to make a personal contract between the local education authority and the teacher, so that the education authority can be sued by the teacher for salary? . . .

I do not wish to attach too much importance to the practice that contracts with teachers are made by the managers; but it is the fact that they are so made, and it seems to me that the statute recognises bargains so made by the managers which will involve agreements to pay salaries, control by the managers of the duties of the teachers, and dismissal of teachers by the managers—in other words, there is a recognition by the statute that the ordinary contractual relations between managers and teachers remain as before. Then, do the words "The local education authority . . . shall have the control of all expenditure required for the purpose of paying the teachers"—I add these latter words—make it necessary that a contract should be implied between the teacher and the local education authority? In my opinion such a contract cannot be implied from the words used. The language points clearly to the provision by the local education authority of funds to meet the demands

of the managers under clause (*a*); they are the paymasters of the manager. . . .
It is not, therefore, correct to say that the Act imposes a duty on the local
education authority to pay salaries which can be enforced by action by individual teachers. There is no privity of contract between the teacher and the
local education authority; the mere fact of payment of the teachers' salaries
direct by the local education authority, which is consistent with the duty the
local education authority have to discharge, does not constitute privity of
contract between the teacher and the local education authority. The appeal
must therefore be allowed.

Appeal allowed

[NOTE: Taylor and Saunders, *The New Law of Education* (Butterworth, 6th ed., 1965)
raises a question as to whether the position as stated in this case has been modified by
the Education Act 1944, s. 24. The section provides clearly that teachers in controlled
and special agreement schools are to be appointed and dismissed by the local education
authority. In such voluntary schools, therefore, the teachers are the employees of the
authority. The proviso to the section enacts that teachers in aided schools shall, subject
to certain rights vested in the authority, be appointed by the managers or governors.
Nevertheless, even in aided schools, the rules of management or articles of government
must provide that the authority may prohibit the dismissal of teachers without the
authority's consent except for reasons for which the managers or governors have power
to dismiss (*i.e.* on religious grounds). The authority may also require the dismissal of
any teacher. Formerly the authority could require this only on educational grounds;
it appears that it may now require this on grounds not connected with the giving of
religious instruction. Taylor and Saunders suggest that the Act of 1944 supersedes this
case and *Young* v. *Cuthbert* [1906] 1 Ch. 451 (page 28, *supra*) so far as the dismissal of
teachers is concerned, as "there must be such a degree of privity of contract between
the authority and the teacher as is necessary to enable the dismissal to be made by the
authority." For all other practical purposes, however, the teacher is regarded as the
servant of the managers or governors.]

(C) MEMBERSHIP OF PUBLIC BODIES

20 Lamb *v.* Jeffries [1956] 1 Q.B. 431

QUEEN'S BENCH DIVISION
*Where a master is appointed to the service of a local education authority by the
governors of a school, and the appointment must be confirmed by a council which
is the divisional executive of an excepted district, he is disqualified from sitting on
that council.*

Facts: Raymond William Lamb pleaded guilty at Lowestoft Magistrates'
Court to a summons alleging that he acted as a member of Lowestoft Town
Council, being at the time disqualified for so acting, contrary to section 84 of
the Local Government Act 1933.

The Lowestoft Town Council had made a scheme of divisional administration which came into force on December 6, 1945. Pursuant to that scheme the
county council had made an instrument and articles of government relating to

county secondary schools within the borough. The articles provided *inter alia**
that the appointment of assistant masters by governors should be confirmed
by the town council acting as the divisional education executive.

The Local Government Act 1933, s. 59 (1), provides " . . . a person shall be
disqualified from being elected or being a member of a local authority if he—(*a*)
holds any paid office or other place of profit . . . in the gift or disposal of the
local authority or of any committee thereof." For the prosecution it was contended that the ratification of appointments by the town council acting as the
divisional executive had the effect of placing such appointments in the gift or
disposal of the local authority.

The defendant, who was fined £5 and ordered to pay £10 10s. costs,
appealed by way of case stated to the Divisional Court of the Queen's Bench
Division. The question was whether a master whose appointment must be
confirmed by a town council which is the divisional executive of an excepted
district is disqualified from membership of that town council because his
appointment is in the gift or disposal of the council.

Extracts from Judgments
LORD GODDARD C.J.: . . . I regret that [the justices] thought it necessary to
impose a fine of £5 in addition to costs in a case in which it is quite obvious
that the defendant had no intention of breaking or evading the law or acting
otherwise than in good faith. The case is one of considerable difficulty and
raises the question whether the defendant offended against section 59 (1) of
the Local Government Act 1933. I should have thought that it would have
been quite sufficient if the justices, having decided against him, had imposed
a nominal penalty merely to mark the fact that they thought a breach had been
committed. . . .

It is clear both from the scheme of divisional administration and from the
articles of government that an assistant master is chosen in the first place by
the governors in consultation with the head master, but his appointment is not
effective until confirmed by the divisional executive, which is the town
council.

. . . It seems to me that the local authority can either assent or dissent to the
appointment and, for that reason, the office is at their disposal because until
they have confirmed it the appointment is not a valid appointment.

I have come to this conclusion after considerable hesitation and with some
regret, but my duty is simply to construe the words of this statute. I regret
particularly that this matter has been brought in the form in which it has
because a point of this sort is of great importance to assistant masters. . . . It
would have been much better if it could have been fought out in the High
Court. . . . The justices came to a right decision in point of law.

STABLE J. (*dissenting*): . . . The only control that the borough council had
over the matter was to refuse to put forward the nominee of the governors. . . .
Was this an office in the gift or disposal of the Lowestoft Borough Council?

D

In my view, it was not. It certainly was not in their gift, and the mere fact that they had a right of veto and virtually nothing else would not, in my view, make that an office of which they had the disposal. . . .

It appears to me to be a matter of considerable public importance because the effect of this decision is that a large number of schoolmasters . . . will be debarred from taking part in many branches of local government.

Ashworth J. agreed with the Lord Chief Justice.

Appeal dismissed

[NOTE: This case should be compared with the following case *Boyd* v. *Easington Rural District Council*. The note on page 75, *infra*, sets out the reasons for the apparent variance of the judgments in the two cases.]

21 Boyd *v.* Easington Rural District Council [1963]
3 All E.R. 747

CHANCERY DIVISION

Where the headmaster of a school in an excepted district is appointed by a joint committee consisting as to one half of governors and as to the other half of borough and district members, he is not debarred from being a member of the district council.

Facts: The applicant, Mr William Boyd, was headmaster of Heselden County Mixed Primary School, and a member of the Easington Rural District Council. On April 1, 1963, Easington became an excepted district, operating its own scheme of divisional administration for educational purposes.

Under this scheme the appointment of headmasters and headmistresses was placed in the hands of a joint committee consisting, in each case, as to one half of governors or managers and as to the other half of equal members of borough and district members.

The Local Government Act 1933, s. 59 (1) (a), provides that "a person shall be disqualified from being elected or being a member of a local authority if he holds any paid office or other place of profit (other than that of mayor, chairman, or sheriff) in the gift of the local authority or any committees thereof." Under section 122 a person may not be employed by a local authority or appointed to a paid office (other than those named above) while he is a member, or if he has been a member within the previous twelve months.

On May 30, 1963, the Easington Rural District Council, relying on the decision in *Lamb* v. *Jeffries*,[1] declared that the applicant was the holder of a paid office in the gift, or at the disposal, of the Council, and that he was therefore disqualified from membership under the Local Government Act 1933, s. 59 (1) (a).

The applicant sought a declaration that he was still a member of the Coun-

1. [1956] 1 All E.R. 317; [1956] 1 Q.B. 431; see page 72, *supra*.

cil, and that he did not hold a paid office in the gift, or at the disposal, of the Council.

Cur. adv. vult

Extract from Judgment

CROSS J.: . . . The Council has not made out, to my satisfaction, that on the coming into force of this scheme Mr Boyd automatically forfeited his seat, and I will make a declaration that he remains a member of the Council.

Whether or not this is in accordance with what public policy requires, I do not know. On the one hand it may be desirable that experienced teachers should be able to take part in the administration of education in their neighbourhood by becoming members of the bodies which administer the service. On the other hand, it is clearly undesirable that anybody should be a member of the council or committee which will frequently have to consider matters which affect him personally. It is a question of where to draw the line.

I do, however, venture to suggest that the Minister of Education, having decided where to draw the line, would do well to embody the result in a section of an Education Act dealing specifically with teachers and stating clearly the sort of councils, committees or joint committees to which teachers may or may not belong. . . .

Declaration accordingly

[NOTE: The apparent inconsistency between this decision and that in *Lamb* v. *Jeffries* flows from the construction of the Lowestoft and Easington schemes. In the former it is specifically provided that consent of the town council is required to the appointment of teaching staff, and Lord Goddard C.J. held that this brought the office of teacher within "the gift or disposal" of the town council, thereby preventing teachers in the borough from being members of the town council. As stated in the facts above, the appointment of teachers in Easington does not require the consent of the district council, and the court held that the office of teacher is not, therefore, in the gift or disposal of the council. At the time of writing (September 1969) no proposals have been put forward for implementing the suggestion made by Cross J. that legislative action should be taken to achieve consistency.]

(D) SICKNESS: DEFINITION

22 Davies *v.* Ebbw Vale Urban District Council (1911) 75 J.P. 533

KING'S BENCH DIVISION

"Absence through illness" includes absence reasonably caused through illness, and covers the period of convalescence and also absence occasioned by approaching illness.

Facts: The plaintiff, Mrs Frances Jones, was appointed headmistress of the Rassaw Infants' School in 1900 by the Llangynider School Board at a salary of £60 a year, which subsequently rose to £120, no formal contract being entered into between the parties. In 1901, she was married; and in June 1902 her first child was born and she was absent from her duties for a month on full pay, during which time no substitute was provided by her. In 1903 a second child was born, and the plaintiff upon that occasion sent a substitute to take her place.

In 1904 the defendants became the local education authority, and the plaintiff retained her position as headmistress without any formal contract being entered into. On August 4, 1906, the plaintiff had a third child but, as it was born during the holiday time, no question arose concerning her absence on that occasion.

In September 1910 she was expecting another child, and on the 5th of that month she received a letter from the defendants asking her to retire from her duties in consequence of her approaching illness. She accordingly remained away during the months of September, October, November, and December 1910, being paid her salary for the month of September and one month's salary in addition. Her child was born on January 5, and on February 5 she returned to her duties. According to the plaintiff's evidence, she was fully capable of performing her duties up to Christmas, and it was in respect of her salary to that time that the present action was brought, the £10 paid by the defendants being allocated to the month of January.

The question to be decided was whether absence—at the request of the local education authority—during pregnancy, is absence due to approaching illness. The court held that it is not.

Extract from Judgment

CHANNELL J.: . . . I do not think that absence through illness is confined to the period of absence during actual illness, but includes absence reasonably caused through illness, and covers the period of convalescence and also absence occasioned by approaching illness. . . .

The remaining question is whether the absence was one through illness when, in the view of the employers, it was not desirable that the older children in the school should see the plaintiff in the condition in which she was. Can I say that absence on that ground was absence reasonably arising in consequence of approaching illness? I really do not think I can. It is one of the matters which the committee might quite reasonably have provided for in their rules, and I am informed that in the future they are providing against the difficulty by ceasing to employ married women as teachers, but as matters stand the case had not been provided for, and I do not think, upon a fair reading of the words "absence through illness," that this lady was so absent in the months of October and November. She was, in fact, absent because the defendants requested her to withdraw for the reason mentioned, and it seems to me that if they chose to ask her to absent herself they must pay her for the time during which she was absent. That being so, there must be judgment for the amount claimed.

Judgment for the plaintiff

(E) FITNESS FOR DUTY

**23 Watts *v.* Monmouthshire County Council and another (1968)
66 L.G.R. 171**

COURT OF APPEAL

(1) *The acceptance of a short-service gratuity by a teacher on the ground
that he has become permanently incapable of further efficient contributory
service frustrates and automatically determines his contract of service without
the need for notice.*

(2) *A local education authority is under no duty to reveal to a teacher the
contents of a medical report made to enable the authority to decide whether
to employ the teacher.*

(3) *A local education authority is not necessarily unreasonable in failing to
close a school when the temperature falls below the standard prescribed by the
Schools Premises Regulations 1955, without causing undue hardship.*

(4) *If a doctor's certificate reports a teacher as fit for duty it is not negligent
to employ him for duties which are not particularly onerous.*

Facts: The plaintiff, Mr Haydn Thomas Watts, previously employed by the
Berkshire County Council, was interviewed for a post at Llantarnam
Secondary School, Monmouthshire, on July 3, 1962. After the meeting he
was told by the headmaster, Mr A. V. Pavord, that his application had been
successful, but the formal offer (subject to medical examination) was not made
until August 1. The plaintiff accepted the appointment by letter dated
August 6, and underwent a medical examination at Heatherwood Hospital,
an orthopaedic unit at Ascot, during the same month.

The examination revealed that he was suffering from ankylosing-spondy-
litis, and that he required treatment by drugs. The report was sent to the
Chief Education Officer, and was forwarded by him to the County Medical
Officer. Neither the plaintiff nor the headmaster was told of its contents.

The plaintiff commenced duty in September 1962, and during the following
month he had the first of three accidents which he sustained while a member
of the school staff. On this occasion two boys collided with him while he was
doing playground duty; his hips became locked, but were freed by one day's
treatment with drugs. During the spring term, 1963, he had three days'
absence for rheumatism, and a week for bronchitis.

In November 1963, Dr Kotarski, the plaintiff's doctor, gave him a medical
certificate stating that he could not work for a short period because of
ankylosing-spondylitis. From this time the headmaster knew of the plaintiff's
disability. During February 1964, the school boiler broke down and could not
be repaired until the following month. As a result the temperature in the
school did not rise above fifty-five degrees, seven degrees below that required
by the Standards for School Premises Regulations 1959.

The second accident occurred in June of the same year when one or two girls accidentally bumped into the plaintiff in a corridor. On July 31, Dr Hill of a hospital in Bath wrote to the headmaster as follows:

"Dear Mr Pavord,

I am taking the liberty of writing to you to put you in the picture with regard to a young member of your staff, Mr Haydn Watts, who has from time to time in the last few years been under my care.

As you know, he suffers from one of the chronic locomotor diseases, ankylosing-spondylitis, a rare condition affecting the spine, and to a less extent the other joints, which strangely enough seems to have a curious predilection for the teaching profession—certainly I can think of many schoolmasters who have been presented with it. It can be a very painful, disabling disease, and is liable of course to produce undue fatigue and stress.

Unfortunately, on this occasion, Mr Watts also produced some gastric symptoms and an X-ray of his stomach showed him to have a small gastric ulcer. This appeared to be responding very well to treatment when he left. Finally, to cap it all, he has obviously had an inflammatory condition of his lungs in the past which has left him with a moderately diminished vital capacity. All in all, therefore, he has a considerable burden to carry and I think that he does very well. I thought that I would let you know these facts since I feel it is extremely important that he should carry on with a worth-while job which he enjoys, but at the same time he can only do so if he has a fairly generous background of rest."

The headmaster received the letter at the beginning of the autumn term, and took it to Mr Davies, the authority's assistant education officer. Mr Davies retained the letter, it having been decided to do nothing about it. It seems that the letter was never acknowledged, and that the plaintiff continued to do the same amount of duty as everyone else. His teaching, however, was confined to one or two classrooms.

The third accident occurred within a few weeks. At that time milk was distributed to the pupils about eleven o'clock in the morning. Milk was provided for 390 of the 650 pupils, but not all of them took it every day. About half was distributed in the main corridor, which ran from the south end of the main block to the assembly hall at the north end. The corridor, which was about a hundred feet long, and almost fifteen feet wide, had cloakrooms on one side. The remainder of the milk was distributed in the classroom corridor which, apart from the fact that it had one radiator less, was much the same as the main corridor. The crates containing the milk bottles were placed by boys between the radiators and, at morning break, the pupils helped themselves.

The staff of each house were responsible for milk duty one week in four. At one time all seven members of the house staff were on duty together, but this seemed to have been changed at a staff meeting when it was decided that half the house staff were to be on duty in the two corridors while milk was drunk. The duty, which was purely supervisory, lasted from five to ten minutes, and the plaintiff said that he was always in the main corridor with two other teachers, neither of whom was there on September 24, 1964.

On that day, while the plaintiff was on duty alone, there were, according to his evidence, about three hundred children in the corridor, a number which the trial judge felt to be wrong. The milk arrived late, and the plaintiff was jostled. Attracted by some noise, he turned round to deal with it at the moment the milk arrived. Thirty or forty boys rushed forward and crashed into him.

The headmaster sent an accident report to the county council, stating that the accident occurred at 11 a.m. in the back of the main corridor when the plaintiff was "reported to have been bumped by the boys when getting milk at the break period." On the day the accident occurred, the plaintiff wrote to the headmaster:

> "This morning whilst doing milk duty in main block, the milk was late arriving. When Powell, Bodenham and the other boys brought the milk there was a bit of a rush to grab for milk. In getting the senior boys under control, I was rather heavily jostled.
>
> At about 11.30 a.m. I started suffering with severe pains in my head and back and broke out in a clammy perspiration. After lying down all afternoon, I visited Dr Kotarski this evening and as you can see he has advised me to stay at home.
>
> I wish this to be regarded as an official report as this is the second occasion in which I have had to miss school because of carrying out normal school duties."

Dr Kotarski gave a series of medical certificates certifying that the plaintiff's ankylosing-spondylitis had been exacerbated by jostling by the boys, and that he was thereby unfit to work. Dr Kotarski explained that the disease itself was not made worse by the accident, and the exacerbation referred purely to the amount of pain suffered. These certificates continued until February 1965, on the 16th of which the plaintiff was admitted to the Royal National Hospital for Rheumatic Diseases at Bath.

During this period the plaintiff began a correspondence which led to the award of a short service gratuity. He first wrote on November 17, 1964, less than two months after the accident, to the Department of Education and Science. On December 28, he wrote again:

> "Further to my letter of November 17, 1964, which so far has brought forth no results, I am now writing to inform you that the worsening of my condition has rendered me incapable of carrying out the profession for which I was trained and have faithfully served for the past eighteen years. During that time I forfeited several more lucrative opportunities. Besides suffering severe pains in my head and back, I am now unable to raise my arms above shoulder height without considerable effort and great pain. This will prevent me writing on the blackboard which occupies a large percentage of my subject work—English and mathematics. My back is so weakened

that in simple operations like rising from a chair, putting on my coat, bending slightly forward and even when walking, I collapse to my knees. There is also an increase in the number of times I get a locking sensation in my groin.

I maintain that my present position has been brought about by the adverse working conditions and culminating in the two accidents mentioned in my previous letter. . . . I now wish to be examined as soon as possible by a doctor nominated by your department. If my opinion is confirmed, I intend to apply for an enforced retirement pension. My employers have denied all liabilities for the two accidents, against the terms of my tenure of appointment and despite the fact that both accidents have been classified as industrial injuries by the Ministry of Pensions and National Insurance. I intend taking action to sue them for loss of earning power and pension rights."

The plaintiff wrote to the Prime Minister, complaining about his treatment, on January 11, 1965. On January 12, the Department of Education and Science replied:

"I am sorry to learn of the worsening of your condition. This letter is the first intimation we have had that you wish to apply for infirmity benefits under the Teachers' (Superannuation) Act 1925, as we have been unable to trace receipt of your earlier letter of November 17, 1964.[1] A form, giving instructions for medical examination, on which you may apply for a short service gratuity is enclosed."

The plaintiff completed the first page of the form applying for the grant of superannuation allowances or a

"short service gratuity under the Teachers' (Superannuation) Acts 1925–1956, on the ground that I have become permanently incapable through infirmity of serving efficiently as a teacher in contributory service *brought about by adverse working conditions and culminating in two accidents in school.*"[2]

The plaintiff dated the form January 21, 1965, and attached a medical certificate from Dr Kotarski. The form was completed by the local education authority who gave March 22, 1965, as the "inclusive date to which salary has been or will be paid," *i.e.* six months from the date of the accident.

On February 9, 1965, the Department notified the plaintiff that, in view of the medical report dated January 19, 1965, he had been deemed permanently incapable of serving efficiently in contributory service, and that no absence on sick leave after the date of the report could be treated as contributory service. Confirmation of this information was sent to the local education authority,

---

1. The Department had, in fact, acknowledged this letter by postcard.
2. The words in italics were added by the plaintiff to the printed form. By the time the form reached the court, the alternative application for superannuation allowances had been crossed through, but the plaintiff said that he did not do so.

with a request for intimation of the agreed date for cessation of salary. After getting in touch with the plaintiff, the authority notified the Department that the agreed date would be March 21, 1965, and this was later amended to March 26.

On March 11, 1965, the Department of Education and Science sent the plaintiff a payable order for a short-service gratuity amounting to £617 14s. 10d.

The plaintiff was discharged from hospital on March 12, 1965.

On August 16, the local education authority sent the plaintiff a cheque for £108 18s. 6d. in payment of the balance of his full salary from September 25, 1964, for a period of six months. There followed some correspondence between the plaintiff's solicitors and the authority on the basis that acceptance of the cheque might prejudice a claim for salary in lieu of notice if the authority would not also pay half salary for a further period of six months. The cheque was eventually accepted in November on the basis that such a claim would not be vitiated thereby.

On May 6, 1966, the plaintiff was medically examined by Dr Kotarski and Mr Dillwyn Evans, who expressed the view that he was capable of teaching; although Dr Kotarski added a proviso that he would have to teach sitting down, and must not engage in any activity which might lead to further bumping or jarring. Mr Dillwyn Evans said he would have expected the increased pain to wear off after a few weeks, but this would depend on the patient and the nature of the jarring. Dr Kotarski said he thought that the increased pain continued until the end of February 1965, but that it had disappeared by the time of the patient's discharge from hospital on March 12. The doctors stated that the accident had caused no further progression of the disease; although there had been some deterioration in the plaintiff's condition between 1962 and 1964, there had been none between 1964 and 1966.

By an action against the Monmouthshire County Council and the headmaster, the plaintiff claimed damages for

1. breach of contract in not paying him his full salary after payment of the short-service gratuity, and

2. negligence and/or breach of statutory duty in

(*a*) not passing to him the report of the medical examination made on him prior to his employment;

(*b*) requiring him to teach in a classroom when the room temperature was below 62 degrees at a time when the outside temperature was 32 degrees Fahrenheit in breach of paragraph 53 (3) of the Standards for School Premises Regulations 1959; and

(*c*) failing to supervise adequately the pupils while he was on milk duty, alternatively failing to excuse him from milk duty.

The case was heard at Monmouth Assizes, Browne J. rejecting all heads of the plaintiff's claims. The Court of Appeal dismissed the plaintiff's appeal, adopting the judgment given at the Assizes. The principal judgment cited, therefore, is that of the Assize Court.

Extracts from Judgment (*Monmouth Assizes*)

BROWNE J.: . . . The first point which I think that I should consider is whether Mr Pavord, the second defendant, was a party to the contract of employment. The plaintiff alleges in his further and better particulars of the statement of claim, that there was an oral contract between him and the head-master, having been made on the evening of July 3, 1962, at the school, when there was a meeting of the board of management. It appears from the evidence of Mr Vernon Lawrence, the clerk to the council, and of the headmaster him-self that he, the headmaster, would have had no authority to have entered into such a contract. I accept the headmaster's evidence that he was only present on July 3 in an advisory capacity.

The letter of August 1, offering the plaintiff employment and acceptance of August 6 and the minutes make it perfectly clear, in my judgment, that the plaintiff's contract was with the Monmouthshire County Council and with no one else and I am satisfied that the headmaster was not a party to it. . . .

After this accident[3] there was considerable controversy between the plaintiff and the county council as to whether or not this accident arose out of or in the course of the plaintiff's employment and whether he was entitled to full salary under the relevant regulations regarding tenure. I am bound to say that the county council seem to have been entirely wrong in this controversy, but it was eventually put right—not until a year later—and the plaintiff has been paid his full salary for six months from September 26, 1964, and no questions on this point now arise in this action.

I come now to the plaintiff's claim for damages for breach of contract. He claims that his service was terminated on March 22, 1965, and that if he had been given proper notice, it should have terminated on August 31, 1965. It is common ground that in fact no notice was ever given. Under the regulations regarding tenure, three months' notice is required if service is terminated on August 31, whereas if it is terminated at either of the other two terms, two months' notice is enough. The plaintiff says that the defendants could not on March 22 have given notice in time to terminate his employment on April 30, and, therefore, they could have given no less than three months' notice to terminate at the end of August.

The defendants plead that the contract between the plaintiff and themselves was frustrated, and that that was recognised by the plaintiff when he accepted a short-service gratuity. [His Lordship read the correspondence leading to the award of the gratuity as outlined in the statement of facts *supra*, and con-tinued:]

Having regard to the correspondence, I now come to the question of whether there was frustration of this contract. It is quite clear, in my view, that the mere inability of the plaintiff to perform his duties by reason of illness or accident does not in itself amount to frustration of the contract. The regula-

3. This was the accident on September 24, 1964, *i.e.* the third accident which the plaintiff suffered at the school.

tions regarding tenure clearly contemplate that, even if the teacher does become ill or suffers an accident, the contract shall continue in existence in spite of that. But as a matter of common sense it seems to me that application for and acceptance by the plaintiff of a gratuity on the basis that he had become permanently incapable of serving efficiently as a teacher is wholly inconsistent with the continued existence of a contract by the county council to employ him as a teacher and by him to serve the county council as a teacher. . . .

I consider that it is plain that the whole basis of this gratuity is that the teacher has become permanently incapable of serving efficiently as a teacher. In my judgment, it is impossible for the plaintiff at the same time to accept a gratuity on the basis that he is permanently incapable of serving as a teacher and also to continue to serve as such. Having accepted this gratuity, the plaintiff was not, in my view, eligible to return to the service of the county council. In my view, the foundation of the contract was destroyed when the plaintiff accepted the gratuity and the contract then came to an end by frustration. If there is frustration, there is no need for either party to give any notice terminating the date of it. The determination is automatic. It is true that a letter written by the defendants seems to contemplate that some resignation by the plaintiff would be necessary to terminate the contract, but I was told that it was the usual practice to write such letters in the circumstances of this case as a matter of consideration for the teacher. In my judgment, it does not affect the legal position. The fact that Dr Kotarski and Mr Dillwyn Evans expressed the view that the plaintiff is not now incapable of teaching cannot, in my view, resuscitate the contract. Even if I am wrong on this and notice should have been given, the point, in my view, is academic. Under the relevant regulations the only right which the plaintiff had was to receive full salary for six months from September 24, 1964, and that he received. Even if the defence ought to have given notice of expiry on April 30 (which they could have done up to the end of February) or August 31, 1965, as the plaintiff claims, he would not have been entitled as of right to be paid anything by the county council after March 24, to which date he has now, in fact, been paid full salary. He could only receive more if the county council decided in the exercise of their discretion to pay half salary.

In accordance with the principle recently applied by the Court of Appeal in *Lavarack* v. *Woods of Colchester Ltd.*,[4] it must I think, be assumed in assessing damages for breach of contract that the defence would have performed their contract in the cheapest way for themselves and, therefore, that they would have exercised their discretion by deciding not to pay half salary after the expiry of six months. In fact, in the present case the county council decided in the exercise of their discretion not to allow half salary after the expiry of the six months full salary (see minutes of the education sub-committee on October 13, 1965, and the education committee on November 3, 1965, and the letter of November 3, 1965, from the clerk of the council to the

4. [1967] 1 Q.B. 278; 1 K.I.R. 312.

plaintiff's solicitors). I am satisfied that the phrase used in the minute and the
letter that the claim "be not entertained" is simply official jargon for "the
claim is refused." In my judgment, the plaintiff's claim in contract must,
therefore, fail.

I come now to his claims in negligence which are under three headings.

First, the plaintiff alleges that the defendants were negligent in failing to
pass on to him a report from the Ascot Hospital in September 1962. He says
that by reason of such negligence his hip became locked in October or
November 1962, because he had not had treatment, and was not informed of
the need for drugs. In my judgment, there are two answers to the plaintiff's
claim. First, this report was a confidential report from the hospital to the
defendants for the purpose of enabling them to decide whether or not they
would employ the plaintiff. In my judgment, there was no obligation on them
to pass it on to the plaintiff. Secondly, the plaintiff knew the effect of the
report, even though it was not passed on to him. When he first saw Dr
Kotarski in October, he told Dr Kotarski that he was suffering from ankylosing-spondylitis and this had been the diagnosis when he went to Ascot in
August. The plaintiff also said that Dr Brearley, whom he had seen in July,
told him he would need treatment, and Dr Arden told him that he would have
to do exercises, and Dr Arden and Dr Ansell who were doctors at Ascot, told
him that he was in need of treatment by drugs and exercises. It seems he was
put on drugs although they did not tell him. In my judgment, the plaintiff was
really in the same position as if that report had been passed to him.

I have also to consider whether the defendants were negligent in not passing
on the report to the headmaster of the school, so that he would have known
what the plaintiff's condition was. He did know in November 1963, before the
important accident in this case took place, that the plaintiff was suffering from
this disease, and, in my judgment, he would not have known any more even
if the report had been passed on to him. . . . In my judgment, there is no
ground for this allegation of negligence.

The second ground on which the plaintiff bases his claim is that the defendants were negligent in January 1963 and in February and March 1964 in
exposing him to undue cold, by reason of the very cold spell in January 1963
and the breakdown of a boiler-stoker in February and March 1964. He alleges
alternatively either that the defendants should have closed the school or that
they should have excused the plaintiff from duty during those periods. On this
part of the case the plaintiff places great reliance on paragraph 53 (3) of the
Standards for School Premises Regulations 1959. That paragraph provides:

"The heating system in every school and in all boarding accommodation
shall be such as to secure, that, when the outside temperature is 32 degrees
Fahrenheit and when the heating system is heating air at the rate specified in
this paragraph, the temperature at a height of not more than three feet from
the floor, shall be the temperature specified in this regulation as appropriate
to the type of room or other space, or as near as may be thereto."

The figure for teaching rooms is 62 degrees. That regulation, it will be observed, is dealing with the heating system to be installed. In my judgment, it does not mean that a school must be closed every time the temperature in a classroom falls below 62 degrees. Still less, in my view, does it mean that any individual has a right of action against the local education authority if the temperature does fall below 62 degrees. As to the allegation that the defendants were negligent in not closing the school, it follows from the finding of fact I have already made that they were not guilty of negligence on either occasion in deciding not to close the school.

As to the other allegation that they ought to have excused the plaintiff from duty, it seems to me that, if they had done anything, they would have had to excuse the plaintiff from *all* duties during the period of the cold spell or the breakdown of the boiler. The headmaster took the view that he was under no obligation to excuse the plaintiff on medical grounds unless he had a medical certificate. Mr Parnall[5] suggests, and I am disposed to agree with him, that in fact the headmaster would have had no power to do so without a medical certificate. The plaintiff said in evidence that he probably could have persuaded his doctor to excuse him, but that, if he had done so, it would have used up more of his entitlement to sick relief and he would have had to go on half pay at some stage during the year. In my judgment, it cannot be said that the defendants were negligent in not excusing the plaintiff during these periods when he did not ask to be excused or bring a medical certificate entitling him to be excused.

I come now to what I think is the most difficult and serious part of this case, that is, the accident on September 24, 1964. There had been two previous accidents in which the plaintiff was involved, one on October 12, 1962, while he was on playground duty, and the other on June 24, 1964, when two girls collided with him as he was coming along the corridor when he was not on duty, but simply coming out after class. The plaintiff does not suggest that there was any negligence which caused these two first collisions, but he does say they made the risk of his having a further collision foreseeable by the defendants. So far as the accident on September 24 is concerned, the plaintiff says, first, that the defendants were negligent in that there was inadequate supervision, and further, or alternatively, that he should have been excused milk duty and that the defendants were negligent in not so excusing him.

On this part of the case the decision of the House of Lords in *Paris* v. *Stepney Borough Council*[6] is of great importance. I think that the facts are sufficiently stated in the headnote in the Law Reports:

"A workman employed as a garage hand had, to the knowledge of his employers, only one good eye. In working on the back axle of a vehicle to remove a U-bolt, which had rusted in, he struck it with a hammer, and a metal chip flew off seriously injuring his good eye. He was not wearing

5. Counsel for the defendants.
6. [1951] A.C. 367; 49 L.G.R. 293.

goggles. He claimed damages against his employers in respect of that injury on the ground that they were negligent in failing to provide and require the use of goggles as part of the system of work.

Held, that, in the case of a workman suffering, to the employer's knowledge, from a disability which, though it did not increase the risk of an accident occurring, did increase the risk of serious injury if an accident should befall him, the special risk of injury is a relevant consideration in determining the precautions which the employer should take in the fulfilment of the duty of care which he owes to the workman."

. . . . I am quite satisfied that the principle of the *Paris* case applies to the plaintiff here. Indeed, the headmaster very frankly accepted that position. He said in the course of his evidence to me that:

"the consequence of an accident to the plaintiff might well be more serious than the consequence of the same accident to the ordinary teacher."

It seems to me, however, that when I am dealing with the two heads of negligence on this part of the case, first, inadequate supervision and, secondly, failure to excuse the plaintiff, *Paris's* case really relates to the second head of claim rather than the first. It seems to me that the defendants could not reasonably be expected to have a different system of supervision for milk duty when the plaintiff was on duty from the system they had when he was not on duty. So far as supervision is concerned, the plaintiff says that it was the duty of the defendants to provide adequate supervision for milk duty. It obviously was. This duty is recognised by the education committee's minute on responsibility and supervision of accidents dated April 1964. In the course of that document, which I need not read in full, it is stated that "a satisfactory system of work must be carried out." The plaintiff says that Mr Constance and Mrs Rosie (two other teachers) should have been on duty with him on September 24 but were not, as I have found that they were not. He also says that, if Mr Constance had been on duty that day in the main corridor, the accident would not have happened because Mr Constance would have prevented the pupils from rushing forward when the milk appeared. As I have already said, the system contemplated in the school routine was that on some days only three teachers would be on duty in two corridors, and so necessarily there would on those days, or rather in those weeks, be only one teacher in one corridor. The headmaster expressed the view that the essential minimum of supervision was to provide one person on duty in each corridor at any one time. He said that the school routine had been approved by the staff meeting, he thought either at the end of the spring term or the beginning of the summer term in 1964. The plaintiff relied on the Ministry of Education's circular No. 349, 1959, the appendix to which states in paragraph 3: "The minimum requirement for the supervision of dinners is two teachers in one room." But I do not find that this provision really helps me because it is plainly not based on safety considerations, and I am not satisfied that it necessarily applied to milk duty, which is a very much simpler operation than dinner duty. The milk duty consisted of the teacher standing or walking up and down for five or ten minutes exercising general supervision while the pupils took their milk out of the crates. In fact the number of pupils at any one time in the main corridor on the evidence before me might well not have been much more than 150. The number of bottles of milk provided in September 1964 was 390 a day, not all of which were taken on any one day and rather more than half of which were taken in the classroom corridor. All the evidence here is that there never had been any real trouble about milk duty, although there was sometimes horse-play among the children and there could be jostling among them. The only evidence from any witness of any previous accident during milk duty was that there had been one accident when a pupil hit or bumped his knee on a crate. I think that the headmaster and the deputy headmaster both spoke about one accident to one pupil, but I understood them to be speaking of the same accident. The plaintiff himself said in his evidence that, although he had a fear of any form of collision at any time, he had not before September 24 any specific fear of an accident on milk duty. He said that he considered his dis-cipline good enough to prevent such a collision, although he did add, "if the other teachers were there as well." Mr Pavord said that before September 24, 1965, he never appreciated there was any risk about milk duties. Mr Edwards, who was an assistant master at Llantarnam where he had been for twelve years and who had been teaching for eleven years before that, said that he had never come across an accident on milk duty. Some horseplay among children was natural, but there was never anything serious. He had never heard of a pupil or teacher being injured. He expressed the view that there was no undue risk to a teacher on milk duty and no more than there was in the classroom. He said he had never known of a teacher being bumped into on milk duty. It is fair to say that in expressing his view on risk he was speaking of a fit and normal teacher. In the case of the plaintiff he thought it would be right to assume that there might be some injury to him if he was bumped into. The deputy headmaster said that in his view there was no greater risk on milk duty than on any other duty—playground duty, assembly duty or dismissal duty. Mr Constance said he never had any trouble on milk duty, but added: "Not really." I asked him what he meant by "not really." He said:

"The children are high-spirited. The teachers sometimes have to prevent them from what they were doing in the way of carrying milk or drinking it. It could very easily happen that children might jostle."

That is the evidence before me. I am not satisfied on that that there was any negligence in the defendants' system under which one teacher—even the plaintiff with his known disability—would be on milk duty by himself in a corridor. But even if it was negligence to cause or allow the plaintiff to be on duty by himself in the main corridor on September 24, 1965, I am not satisfied that this caused the injury to him. From the description of the accident given by Mr Powell and Mr Cousins, the whole incident happened so quickly that I am not satisfied that it could have been prevented even if Mr Constance or Mrs Rosie or both had been on duty. Mrs Rosie's usual position was at the far end of the corridor from the entrance where the milk was brought in on this day; and Mr Constance had no fixed position in the corridor when he was there. Even if Mr Constance had been standing near the plaintiff, I very much doubt if he could have prevented this accident.

I come to the point which has caused me the greatest anxiety in this case, and that is whether the defendants were negligent in failing to excuse the plaintiff from milk duty. The headmaster knew before this accident happened that the plaintiff had ankylosing-spondylitis, and he agreed, in the passage in his evidence to which I have already referred, that he knew the consequences of an accident to the plaintiff might well be more serious than the consequences of a similar accident to the ordinary teacher. He knew of the accident of June 26, 1964, and its consequences to the plaintiff. He had had Dr Hill's letter of July 31. After the accident he wrote a letter dated September 30, to which I have not yet referred, addressed to the Director of Education.

"Dear Sir,
On the afternoon of June 26, 1964, when Mr Watts was going out through the classroom corridor two middle-school girls (thirteen years old) accidentally bumped into Mr Watts, dislodging his spectacles. He was absent (after refresher course) for two more days, July 6 and 7. A medical certificate was sent in explaining that his complaint (spondylitis) had been aggravated.

Mr Watts is small of stature and build and of the same height as middle-school boys. He is at present absent (since September 24) because he again was bumped into during milk duty. The M.C. which has been sent in with T.S.B. form states 'Exacerbation of Spondylitis.'

I should be glad to receive your advice with regard to the problems involved in view of this teacher's complaint."

The headmaster explained to me that by the word "complaint" he meant "illness." In his evidence he said this about that letter:

"I wrote this letter because I felt as an accident had been reported there might be some move in the future to consider some form of rest as outlined in Dr Hill's letter." . . .

The plaintiff relies on various regulations and circulars laying down that duties other than actual teaching should not impose undue or unreasonable burdens on teachers or should not be such as adversely to affect the quality of their teaching. . . . They are: regulation 14 (c) of the Provision of Milk and Meals Regulations 1945; Ministry of Education Circular 349 of 1959, paragraphs 3, 5, and the appendix; and Ministry of Education (Welsh Department) Circular 5/63 of 1963, especially paragraph 3 (iii). In my view, these provisions really add nothing to the defendants' common-law duty, which was to take reasonable care for the plaintiff's safety, having regard to their knowledge of his peculiar susceptibility to injury from collision or jostling.

In the light of after events, I think it is a pity that Mr Pavord and Mr Davies decided to take no action on Dr Hill's letter of July 31. They could at least have taken further medical advice either from Dr Hill or some other doctor. But I do not know what advice they would have received if they had done so. Dr Hill's letter was referring to the effect produced by the plaintiff's disease, the ankylosing-spondylitis, in undue fatigue and stress, and the final sentence of the letter is saying that Mr Watts needs a fairly generous background of rest. If the defendants had asked Dr Hill about the risk of collisions, I cannot tell what answer they would have received. It may be they would have received an answer on the same lines as Dr Hill's letter to the plaintiff of October 1 where he wrote this:

"I was sorry indeed to hear you are having difficulties in regard to your work; it is the more disappointing that you cannot get a more satisfactory background to your life, in view of the fact that the activity of your spinal disease diminished considerably while you were in hospital, and the situation in your blood was most satisfactory when you left. Obviously the rigidity of the spine makes you very liable to stress if and when you fall or are buffeted around, but I am afraid that is one of the hazards you must be prepared to meet."

If the defendants had asked for the advice of Mr Dillwyn Evans, they would presumably have received advice in accordance with his opinion expressed in his evidence here, namely, that it is important that people suffering from the plaintiff's condition should live a full and active life and get on with their own work. As he himself put it, trauma is not a risk he would bear in mind when sending someone back to his ordinary work. He gave as an example that some people who had this complaint work as bus conductors, and he said he tried to encourage them to go back to their ordinary occupation and accept the risk. If Dr Kotarski had been asked, I suppose that he might well have given his advice and his opinion as he gave it in his evidence. He said that the plaintiff's condition had not deteriorated since April or May 1964 and that the plaintiff could now teach, though only if he sat down and discontinued any activity in which he could be bumped or jarred again.

In my judgment, the defendants ought to have forseen the risk that pupils might jostle or bump into the plaintiff during milk duty, and that any such collision would have had more serious effects for the plaintiff than it would have had for other teachers and would exacerbate the pain caused by his condition. But, in my view, the risk of such a collision or jostling on milk duty was very small, and anyhow was no greater than the same risk on other duties to which the plaintiff was exposed—for example, there was his accident on the playground on October 12, 1962, and his risk existed even when he was going about the corridors when off duty, as on September 24, 1964[7], although the

7. [*Sic*] The reference appears to be to the accident in June 1964, referred to on page 85, *supra*, as having happened on June 24, and on page 88 as taking place on June 26.

plaintiff did say he minimised this latter risk by staying in his classroom. It seems to me that, if the defendants ought to have excused the plaintiff from milk duty, they ought to have excused him from all duties other than actual teaching. And any such exemption would have had to be permanent, not merely temporary. Mr Pavord's attitude can, I think, be summarised in what he said at one point:

> "If the doctor's certificate reports a teacher as fit for duty and the duties are not particularly onerous, I would not regard it as necessary to excuse him from duty unless he made a specific request."

Does that amount to negligence, having regard to Mr Pavord's knowledge of the susceptibility of the plaintiff to injury?

. . . After much hesitation, I have come to the conclusion that I should not be justified in holding the defendants were negligent in failing to excuse the plaintiff from milk duty. Accordingly, the plaintiff's claim fails and must be dismissed.

Judgment for the defendants

The plaintiff appealed.

Judgments (*Court of Appeal*)

SELLERS L.J.: The plaintiff has conducted this appeal in person with the utmost courtesy, moderation, fairness and ability. He appeals against a judgment of Browne J., dismissing his claims for damages against both the defendants. The judge gave this case the fullest consideration, and has investigated all the issues most carefully and thoroughly. His judgment deals with all the issues so admirably that I am content to adopt it as my own. The appeal is accordingly dismissed.

DANCKWERTS L.J.: I agree.

SACHS L.J.: I agree.

Appeal dismissed

(F) INCOME TAX: RESIDENTIAL EMOLUMENTS

24 Machon *v.* McLoughlin (1926) 11 Tax Cas. 83[1]

COURT OF APPEAL

An emolument which cannot be converted into money is not assessable for taxation.

Facts: The respondent, James McLoughlin, was employed at the County Asylum, Prestwich, at a salary commencing at £30 per annum with board, lodging, washing, and uniform. On April 15, 1920, the Lancashire Asylums Board resolved that no further allowances "in kind" (with the exception of

---

1. This is not an educational case, but is included because the staff of independent schools are sometimes appointed at a salary "together with residential emoluments during term time."

uniform, not including boots) be made to any member of the male or female staff, and that the remuneration of such staff be on a cash basis. The respondent contended that he was not assessable for tax on the amounts included in the Asylum scale of charges, as these were not perquisites which could be turned by the recipient into money. The Commissioners of Inland Revenue found that the respondent had not entered into any new contract of service, and allowed the appeal. At the request of the Inspector of Taxes they stated a case for the opinion of the High Court.

In the King's Bench Division, the appeal was allowed, and this decision was affirmed by the Court of Appeal. The respondent, in fact, was resident in the Asylum, but if he had had permission to live out he would not have had the charges deducted. On the matter of the assessability of emoluments Rowlatt J. said in the King's Bench Division:

"If a person is paid a wage with some advantage thrown in, you cannot add the advantage to the wage for the purpose of taxation unless that advantage can be turned into money. That is one proposition. But when you have a person paid a wage with the necessity—the contractual necessity if you like—to expend that wage in a particular way, then he must pay tax upon the gross wage, and no question of alienability or inalienability arises."

(G) SALARIES: ARBITRATION

25 Baron *v*. Sunderland Corporation [1966] 2 Q.B. 56

COURT OF APPEAL
Submission of a dispute to the Burnham Reference Committee does not constitute submission to arbitration.

Facts: The plaintiff, Frederick Baron, a diplomé of the Royal College of Teachers of the Blind, was employed in a special school by the Sunderland Corporation. He taught deaf and partially deaf children.

In paragraph 2 (*b*) of the Burnham report, which provides for the structure of salaries to be paid to teachers in maintained schools in England and Wales, there is a provision that teachers in special schools who hold specialist qualifications shall be paid an increment of £60 per annum. The report does not state that the increment may be awarded to teachers only if they are teaching the category of children for which they hold a specialist qualification.

Mr Baron sued the Corporation for £135 arrears of salary, claiming that, as the holder of a specialist qualification, he was entitled to be paid the increment provided by paragraph 2 (*b*). The defendants sought to stay the action in the Sunderland County Court on the ground that section V of the Burnham report set up a joint committee of reference for the determination of any question

relating to the interpretation of the provisions of the report, and the reference
of a question to this committee amounted to arbitration.

The registrar refused the defendants' application but Sharp J., sitting at
Sunderland County Court on June 17, 1965, stayed the action on the ground
that there had been a valid submission to arbitration within the meaning of
section 4 of the Arbitration Act 1950, which reads:

> "If any party to an arbitration agreement . . . commences any legal pro-
> ceedings in any court against any other party to the agreement . . . in respect
> of any matter agreed to be referred, any party to those legal proceedings
> may at any time after appearance, and before delivering any pleadings or
> taking any other steps in the proceedings, apply to that court to stay the
> proceedings, and that court or judge thereof, if satisfied that there is no
> sufficient reason why the matter should not be referred in accordance with
> the agreement . . . may make an order staying the proceedings."

The effect of this section is to oust the jurisdiction of the courts where arbitration is provided, and the local education authority rested its case on section
V of the Burnham report which, after determining the constitution of the
committee of reference, continues:

> " . . . any question relating to the interpretation of the provisions of this
> report brought forward by a local education authority acting through the
> authorities' panel or by any association of teachers acting through the
> teachers' panel or by consent of the Chairman of the Burnham Committee
> shall be considered and determined by the joint committee."

The local education authority contended that this amounted to an arbitration clause to which both teacher and authority were parties, and by which
they were bound. The authority promised to bring the matter before the joint
committee. At the time of the hearing of the appeal, six months after the
action had been stayed, this had not been done.

Extract from Judgment
DAVIES L.J.: . . . It seems to me that this is about as unlike an arbitration
clause as anything one could imagine. It is necessary in an arbitration clause
that each party shall agree to refer disputes to arbitration; and it is an essential
ingredient of an arbitration clause that either party may, in the event of a dispute arising, refer it, in the provided manner, to arbitration. In other words,
the clause must give bilateral rights of reference. The present clause, as I see
it, does nothing of the kind. It provides that the local education authority,
acting through the authorities' panel, may "bring forward" (to use the words
in the report) the question, or the association of teachers, acting through the
teachers' panel, may do so, or, alternatively, by consent of the chairman,
someone else may do so. In the present case we do not know whether the
teacher is a member of the union or whether the teachers' panel would be

prepared to bring forward his contention. We do not know whether the chairman would consent to the matter being brought forward. As I say, there is a complete lack of mutuality in this matter. Quite apart from that, I cannot, for myself, see that this committee of twenty-two really resembles anything like an arbitrator or arbitrators plus an umpire. . . .

He [Counsel for the Corporation] said that section V . . . amounted to a statutory ouster of the jurisdiction of the courts to decide any dispute between schoolmasters and the local education authorities who employ them, if such a dispute involved any question of the interpretation of the Burnham report. I do not so read section V of the report. It does not say that any question arising between a school-teacher and his employers, the local education authority, shall be referred. What it says is, " . . . any question relating to the interpretation of the provisions of this report brought forward . . . " It seems to me that the application of that clause in the report is dependent upon the question having been "brought forward," which it has not been in the present case.

Secondly, I would observe that there is nothing in section V remotely resembling the provisions which one has seen in other legislation such as that which provides that no action shall be brought, or that the decision of the committee shall be final and conclusive and shall not be challenged in any legal proceeding, or anything of that kind. . . .

I think that there is a great deal to be said for the submission made in opening by Mr McKinnon that really this is not primarily designed to deal with individual claims at all, although I suppose they might be brought with the consent of the Chairman of the Burnham Committee. What it is really meant to deal with is a question brought up by the teachers' side on the one side or the local authorities' body on the other in order to obtain a decision on a broad question of interpretation which may affect a large number of teachers up and down the country. This, I think, is no such case. This is a simple common-law claim by an employed person for salary which he claims to be due to him under his contract of service. And I can see nothing . . . which would justify the court in interfering with the normal process of this action.

SALMON, L.J.: For my part, I think that section V does not come within measurable distance of taking away the ordinary common-law right. I do not think that this section has any reference to litigation at all. The purpose of this section, as I see it, is an excellent one. It was designed to prevent disputes arising between teachers' associations and local authorities. . . . A dispute between those two bodies is something quite different from an individual teacher seeking to enforce what he conceives to be his common-law rights against his employers. This section does not make any reference at all to the case of a teacher suing his employers. To my mind, it would be quite impossible, since it makes no provision for such a case, to construe it as taking away the common-law rights of the teacher. . . .

Judgment for the plaintiff with costs in the Court of Appeal and below

(H) REORGANISATION OF SCHOOLS: SAFEGUARDING AND REDUNDANCY

26 Stott *v.* **Oldham Corporation.** See Appendix, *infra.*

27 Taylor *v.* **Kent County Council.** See Appendix, *infra.*

(I) PART-TIME TEACHERS: NATIONAL INSURANCE

28 Argent *v.* **Minister of Social Security (1968)** *The Times Educational Supplement,* **August 2**

QUEEN'S BENCH DIVISION

For the purposes of the National Insurance Acts a part-time teacher not employed under a contract of service, and with a great deal of latitude and freedom in the way he does his work, is a self-employed person.

Facts: The appellant, Mr Albert Edward Argent, was a part-time teacher at the Guildhall School of Music and Drama. He was paid on an hourly basis, and there was no written contract. He was allowed to leave the school in order to undertake professional engagements, and was given a great deal of latitude in the way in which he performed his duties. He had no administrative or disciplinary functions.

Under the National Insurance Act 1965, the appellant was required to pay contributions. The Act defines two classes of employed contributor: (a) those who are "employed persons" under a contract of service, and (b) "self-employed" persons who are gainfully employed, but not under a contract of service. Different rates of contribution and, to some extent, benefit, are applicable to each category.

The Minister of Social Security determined that the appellant was self-employed, and Mr Argent appealed.

Extract from Judgment

ROSKILL J.: The question is whether on the facts found the appellant is an employed person within section 1 (2) (*a*) or a self-employed person within section 1 (2) (*b*). It is a case of general importance affecting a large number of persons who teach part-time at the Guildhall school as well as other schools.

Such problems have come before the courts since the inception of social legislation and there is a considerable body of case law on the approach which should be adopted. It is axiomatic that every case turns on its own facts; no one factor is determinative, and all must be taken into account. The right approach is to refer to the facts and then, in the light of the facts, to apply well-established principles.

The appellant was employed from time to time on a part-time basis as a teacher of drama at the school. There was no written contract. He was paid on an hourly basis. He was allowed to leave the school and work with the

Royal Shakespeare Company and at the Mermaid Theatre. It is clear that he was given a great deal of freedom and latitude in the way he did the work he was paid to do by the Corporation of London, the owners of the school. It is relevant that he had no administrative or disciplinary duties at the school.

If one studies the cases, a number of tests are propounded. In the early cases the most important test was control by the employer over the alleged servant. Over the past fifteen or twenty years the emphasis has shifted, and although control is still an important factor, it is wrong to say that it is always decisive.

When one looks at all the facts it would be unreal to say that the appellant was employed on a contract of service. It is difficult to see, if it were otherwise, why barristers teaching part-time at a university at weekends would not be employed by the university and so be employed persons, whereas every practising barrister is self-employed. That is just one example.

The appellant was not employed under a contract of service; at all times he is self-employed. The appeal will be dismissed.

Appeal dismissed

(J) DISMISSAL

29 Watts *v.* London County Council (1932) *The Times*, December 9[1]

KING'S BENCH DIVISION
A local education authority may dismiss a teacher whose appointment is based on a false application.

Facts: The plaintiff, Miss Annie Mary Watts, was science mistress at Shoreditch Central (Mixed) School, from which post she was dismissed summarily on May 14, 1929. She claimed damages for wrongful dismissal.

The defendants pleaded justification on the ground that the particulars furnished by her when applying for appointment in July, 1922, were false within her knowledge, and that there were wilful omissions and suppressions of material facts. Further, the plaintiff was guilty of gross misconduct and serious irregularities with regard to examination papers of her class, proof of her date of birth, and the furnishing of particulars of her salary. Further, she had attached to her application form what purported to be a true copy of a testimonial given by the principal of New Cross and Camberwell Day Continuation School, whereas it was not given by the principal, but was signed "G. A. Wood, deputy principal," and the plaintiff had altered it by omitting the word "deputy."

For the plaintiff it was said that she now knew she was born on November 26, 1886; previously she had believed her uncle, who had written on a slip of paper that she was born on May 6, 1882. In 1917 she became a certificated

1. This is the date of the issue recording the judgment. The earlier part of the hearing is reported in *The Times* of December 3, 6, 7, and 8, 1932.

teacher, and in the following year she taught at Lower Sandhurst School at Farnborough. She had not mentioned her employment at this school in her application.

In the autumn of 1928 the headmaster of Shoreditch Central School made complaints against her. The plaintiff said that the investigation by the managers lasted seven hours, and that she had wanted to say a great deal, but she was not allowed to do so.

The managers passed three resolutions: that Miss Watts had given incorrect details as to age and appointments; that friction existed between her and other members of the staff; and that the charges of irregularity with regard to examination papers had been established.

In April 1929, the teaching staff sub-committee considered the matter for a day and a half, and the plaintiff was represented by counsel. In cross-examination the plaintiff said that at this inquiry the Lower Sandhurst School was referred to by a name different from that by which she knew it, and she therefore denied all knowledge of it. She spent about five months there, and it was one of her worst experiences.

The plaintiff agreed that she had included the Senior Cambridge Examination among the qualifications set out in her application in 1922, but that she had not, in fact, passed.

Evidence was given that the alteration of the name "Watt" to "Watts" on her birth certificate was by the writer of the body of the certificate, and was not in the plaintiff's hand.

One of the managers, Miss Amelia Hensher, described the managers' meeting: The managers were given the impression that the testimonial purporting to have been given by Miss Wood was forged. It was very disgraceful that they should have been given that impression because it led them to come to a wrong conclusion. It was supposed to be a managers' meeting, but they were dominated by the inspectors. The plaintiff's character was taken away completely, and the managers thought if a mistress forged a testimonial she was not fit to teach children. She did not remember what Mr Fitzgerald[2] said, but he emphasised the point that Miss Wood had no recollection of giving the testimonial. They afterwards regretted that they had come to a too hasty decision. At the end of the long sitting they were tired out through listening to piffle from the headmaster. For five or six hours they had to listen to a lot of rubbish. Friction was caused by the headmaster, who was determined to get rid of Miss Watts. They were never told that Miss Wood had recognised the testimonial as having been given by her.

Monier Williams (for the defendants): The courts of law will not interfere with the findings of a domestic tribunal unless there has been a departure from the laws of natural justice. . . . Where a term of the contract is submission to a domestic tribunal one would have to go far for the courts to interfere.

MCCARDIE J.: They must give notice of charges, give a fair hearing, and be honest in their decision.

2. One of the local education authority's inspectors.

Monier Williams: My proposition is that where a complaint has been made against a teacher and the matter has been properly investigated according to the regulations laid down in the red book[3] that is an end of the matter.

MCCARDIE J.: Even though the whole of the charges are in fact absolutely unfounded? Once dismissed on the finding of a local tribunal do you say that a teacher can never appeal to a court of law?

Monier Williams: That seems to be the law, however hard it may be.

MCCARDIE J.: Is there any statement here that the teacher shall abide by the decision of the L.C.C. staff sub-committee?

Monier Williams: I don't think so; it is not necessary. . . .

MCCARDIE J.: I shall reserve the point with regard to the power of the L.C.C. to dismiss summarily a teacher without the latter having recourse to a court of justice. It must be argued before me.

Mr Felix Hotchkiss, formerly headmaster of Shoredith Central School said that in November 1928 a parent complained that his daughter had received no science examination marks. The girl was marked "absent" on the report, but "present" in the attendance register. On November 1 he asked Miss Watts for the papers and, when she said they were at home, he asked her to bring them the next day. When she did so, there was no paper for the girl in question, and he asked for all the science papers at that examination. They were not produced until November 8, and he locked them away until November 23 when he discovered that there were no third-year papers among them. Miss Watts said she would look for them, but on November 30 she told him that they were lost. As the reports had been sent to parents, he did not accept her suggestion that they should be done again.

He had discovered on November 23 that some classes had had two examinations as the original papers had been lost. The marking of the examination was very carelessly done and distinctly unfair. One question asked the density of an object of given weight and volume, and the plaintiff had given seven marks out of ten for an accurately worked answer expressed in centimetres. Another paper which was hopelessly wrong was marked "right" and given seven marks. Mistakes were apparently unnoticed, and were therefore unpenalised. He informed Dr Spencer, the chief inspector of the L.C.C. He had had to call attention to Miss Watts' carelessness as far back as 1926.

It was he, not Miss Watts, who had been bullied at the managers' meeting. Some of the managers appeared to be biased in Miss Watts' favour, probably because she was a woman.

She did not get on well with other members of the staff, but he did not question her ability. A first-year paper was handed to the judge.

MCCARDIE J.: Do you say that little girls of eleven and twelve answer these papers?

Witness: Yes.

MCCARDIE J.: We are getting on with education, certainly.

3. *General Information with Reference to Teachers, Instructors and Instructresses in London Public Elementary Schools*, London County Council, June 1928.

In 1927 Dr Spencer, the chief inspector, had spoken rather seriously to Miss Watts and warned her, telling her that her work was not what it should be.

Extract from Summing-up

MCCARDIE J.: ... The case is of importance, and I am not sorry that so many points have been discussed, because it is in the public interest that they should be argued. Counsel for the plaintiff has referred to some public bodies as being bureaucratic and tyrannical, but all those great bodies exist to safe-guard the interests of the public and to advance public welfare. The question for the jury is whether or not the London County Council have acted rightly in dismissing Miss Watts from their service. According to the terms of the plaintiff's employment she was subject to a month's notice and therefore could in no case recover as damages a larger sum than £21. I assume, however, that the action has been brought not merely for the recovery of a month's salary, but that the plaintiff might if possible vindicate her character in respect of the charges made against her. Her pension rights remain, although they will not accrue until she reaches the age of sixty, whenever that may be. ... Even now we do not know her real age within four years.

No suggestion has been made of any lack of mental capacity on the part of Miss Watts. Even her late headmaster admitted that she was efficient. With regard to the testimonial which was given to the plaintiff by Miss Wood in June or July 1922, a copy of which was sent by Miss Watts to the defendants, it is not now suggested that the plaintiff forged it. If that charge had remained it would have been a most grave one. The part of the teaching staff sub-committee's report which concerned Miss Watt's conduct, was most unfortu-nately worded, because it might lead one to suspect that the testimonial had been wholly forged.

In considering the important issues which arose in the case you must re-member that the London County Council are a powerful body and the guardians of the educational interests of a vast number of children, the pro-gress and development of whom involves something more than the teaching of science. It has to do with moral training, and the Council are perfectly right in requiring from the teachers in their schools high moral standards, because unless they possess them the children under their care would be bound to suffer. If a teacher were dishonest in her statements how could it be suggested that she had the moral standard which would satisfy the just requirements of the L.C.C.? ...

[After dealing with the various charges made against the plaintiff]: If those charges or the substance of them are proved, the defendants as an educational authority were justified in not retaining her in their service.

[After an hour's retirement the jury returned to ask if they would be in order in returning a verdict for the defendants that the plaintiff's dismissal was justified, but not summary dismissal.]

MCCARDIE J.: I can understand you asking such a question but I must point out that if you think that the facts show that the defendants were justified in dismissing the plaintiff, it means that summary dismissal was justified. You must not be afraid of the consequences of your verdict. It is quite open to you to say that, although you thought that the defendants were entitled to dismiss Miss Watts summarily, it would have been more charitable in the circumstances to have given her a month's notice.

Foreman of the Jury: I and my colleagues have weighed the evidence very carefully, and we are of opinion that the defendants were justified in dismissing the plaintiff. We think, however, that the summary dismissal was based on one point only; otherwise Miss Watts would have been dismissed with a month's notice. We are of opinion that in the early stages the Council were very much misled by statements which had since been disproved.

[After a further retirement of an hour and three-quarters the jury returned a verdict for the London County Council. They expressed the opinion that the Council's methods and conduct of the inquiry in the case left much to be desired, and that there had been considerable laxity in checking their teachers' testimonials.]

Judgment for the defendants

30 Brown *v.* Dagenham Urban District Council [1929] 1 K.B. 737[1]

KING'S BENCH DIVISION
A public servant may be dismissed at pleasure notwithstanding the fact that there may be an agreed period of notice.

Facts: The plaintiff, Mr W. H. Brown, brought an action against the Dagenham Urban District Council to recover damages for alleged wrongful dismissal from his post as assistant overseer and clerk to the Council. He contended that members of the Council had conspired to oust him because he had stood for law and order during the general strike of 1926, in that he refused to help a member of the Council who acted as a dispatch rider for the strikers.

For the defendants it was alleged that the plaintiff had resigned his office of clerk to the Council, and was dismissed from the office of assistant overseer for dereliction of duty.

Cur. adv. vult

Extract from Judgment
MCCARDIE J.: . . . No actual resolution was passed, no letter of dismissal was sent, but the attitude and the acts of the defendants were unmistakable and in my view constituted a dismissal. . . . Hence the plaintiff claims damages for wrongful dismissal, and he alleges that he was entitled to three months' notice

1. This is not an educational case, but a brief report is included as the legal position of the plaintiff is on all fours with that of teachers employed "during pleasure" by local education authorities.

by virtue of the minute of his appointment on April 9, 1926. . . . There can be no doubt, and indeed it is not disputed, that the contract between the plaintiff and the defendants was, as shown by the minute, that the plaintiff should give three months' notice before he left the defendants' service and that the defendants should give the plaintiff three months' notice before they terminated his employment. The minute itself is ample evidence of the bargain. . . . The defendants, however, submit, and this is a grave matter for all clerks and other officials to local councils, that the minute is destitute of legal value on the point at issue and that no contract, whether verbal or written and whether under seal or not, is valid which provides that a clerk or the like official shall be engaged for a definite period or be entitled to notice before dismissal. It is asserted that the council can dismiss at any time, whether cause for dismissal exists or not, that the council is bound by no contract as to service, and that their powers, if bona fide* exercised, are absolute, despotic and uncontrolled with respect to a person in the position of the plaintiff. . . .

The question then is whether section 189 of the Public Health Act 1875 has conferred upon district councils a power of dismissal similar to that possessed by the Crown and a power of dismissal, moreover, which cannot be negatived or impaired by any contract of service whether under seal or not. I confess that I should myself have thought that the basis on which the powers of the Crown might be rested was a basis somewhat inapplicable to local corporate bodies such as the present defendants, but yet the Legislature inserted the words "at their pleasure" in section 189 and these words represent no more than those ordinarily used to describe the powers of the Crown as to dismissal. It would seem that, if those words are to receive their full effect, it must follow that any contract which cuts down the right of dismissal would be inconsistent with the words and the apparent policy of the section and, therefore, void. This, I fear, would be the case even though a person might have agreed to accept a low salary on the express bargain and for the express reason that in consideration thereof he should be engaged for a definite period of service. . . .

It results from what I have said that the plaintiff's claim for damages for wrongful dismissal and for the declaration he asks must fail. . . .

Another series of questions of fact and another series of questions of law have been raised with respect to the dismissal of the plaintiff from the post of assistant overseer.

The first question, then, is whether the defendants could, under the words of section 5 (1) of the Local Government Act 1894, "revoke" the plaintiff's appointment as assistant overseer at their will. . . . No such words as "at their pleasure," which appear in section 189 of the Public Health Act 1875, appear in section 5 (1) of the Local Government Act 1894, but the power of revocation again is given in the widest terms and no limitation is placed upon it. . . . All the text-books take the view that an assistant overseer can be dismissed at any time without cause given and without notice. In my opinion, the text-books are correct in the view they take. . . . I must, therefore, hold that the defendants could dismiss the plaintiff at any time without notice and without cause from his post as assistant overseer, subject, of course, to the question of bona fides. . . .

Judgment accordingly

31 Williams *v*. Glamorgan County Council (1916) 14 L.G.R. 741

CHANCERY DIVISION

A head teacher appointed during the pleasure of a county council and subject to their regulations may be dismissed for non-compliance with a regulation that teachers should live within a specified distance of their schools.

Facts: The plaintiff was appointed head teacher of Wern Boys' School, Ystalyfera on June 3, 1913, the appointment to date from July 1, in the same year, and the letter of appointment stated that he was to hold office during the pleasure of the local education authority and subject to their regulations and to clause (*a*) (1) of section 15 of the Code of regulations for public elementary schools in Wales. This clause provided that

"The teacher shall not be required to perform any duties except such as are connected with the work of a public elementary school, or to abstain outside the school hours from any occupation which does not interfere with the due performance of his duties as teacher of a public elementary school."

In June 1913 the local education authority made new regulations, one of which provided:

"The committee have made it a condition of the engagement of all recently appointed head teachers that he or she shall reside in the neighbourhood of his or her school, and all future appointments are subject to it."

The plaintiff lived four and a half miles from his school, and on January 22, 1915, he received a letter requiring him to take up residence in the immediate neighbourhood of his school in accordance with his promise given on appointment. In reply he wrote that he had given no such promise. On February 29, 1916, the plaintiff received three months' notice of dismissal to run from March 1.

In a letter dated April 18, the defendants offered to withdraw the notice if the plaintiff gave an undertaking to comply with their requirements immediately on his release from the army. The undertaking was not given, and a motion was brought to restrain the defendants from acting on the notice until trial of the action or further order.

The plaintiff stated that, travelling by train, he took only eighteen minutes to reach the school from home, and that he was usually in school a quarter of an hour before it opened. It was not possible to obtain a house within a mile

of the school. It was contended on his behalf that the requirement was contrary to the Code as it interfered with the plaintiff's occupations outside school
hours.

On behalf of the defendants it was argued that the introduction to the Code
stated that teachers should enlist, as far as possible, the interest and co-
operation of the parents and the home in a united effort to influence the children for good. It would be absurd to say that an education authority must
appoint a teacher even if he lived twenty miles from the school. Furthermore,
the defendants had the right to dismiss a teacher at pleasure.

Extract from Judgment

PETERSON J.: . . . As will have been observed, the letter of employment
which I read is expressly an employment during pleasure, subject to their
regulations and to clause (*a*) (1) section 15. That, in my view, is an employment during pleasure subject to the regulations, which include the one about
residing within the neighbourhood, because that had been passed and had
become a regulation though not published, and to this clause (*a*) (1) of section
15 of the Code of 1912.

The case that is put is this: that in substance this is a prohibition against the
dismissal of a head teacher for failure to comply with the requirements, which
requirements are in fact prohibited by section 15 (*a*) (1), inasmuch as that
clause has been incorporated into the agreement that has been entered into.
Now I cannot regard it as such. I am not satisfied, in the first instance, that
this clause relates to any such thing as the requirement in question. To my
mind, if a requirement to reside within a specified area is a requirement to perform a duty, I think it is very difficult to say that such a duty as is contemplated, the duty of residing with the object of having easy intercourse with
the parents of the children of the public elementary school, with a view of
assisting the work of the public elementary school being carried out more
efficiently, is not a duty which is connected with the work of a public elementary school; but assume that it were not so, then it seems to me the position
must necessarily be this: there is an employment at pleasure, one of the terms
of the agreement is that the teacher shall not be required to do anything,
putting it shortly, that is not connected with the work of a public elementary
school—he is told that is part of the terms of the agreement—it is not a prohibition by statute, but it is part of the agreement—and it is a term which
operates so long as the teacher remains in the employment under the agreement; but that, to my mind, does not prevent the employer, the council, from
acting on the power which the council has under the agreement, namely, to
cancel the employment at pleasure. Section 15 (*a*) (1) appears therefore to me,
assuming it to apply at all in such a case as the present, to apply only during
the continuance of the agreement, but does not prevent the determination of
the agreement; and, as the council have thought fit to terminate the agreement,
it seems to me, for the purpose of this motion, at any rate, that they have
acted within their power; and I am not able, on this motion, at any rate, to

restrain them from acting upon the notices which they have given to the three separate plaintiffs.

Judgment for the defendants

32 Gill *v*. Leyton Corporation (1933) *Education*, April 14

KING'S BENCH DIVISION

The courts will not interfere to prevent a local education authority from acting on a notice of dismissal unless there is evidence of corruption or bad faith.

Facts: The plaintiff, Horace Herbert Gill, was headmaster of Trumpington Road School, Leyton. At Stratford Police Court on March 2, 1932, he was bound over under the Probation of Offenders Act, and ordered to pay two guineas costs, on a summons following the corporal punishment of a boy. The justice stated expressly that there had been very great provocation, but that the punishment was excessive. The plaintiff's appeal to quarter sessions against the conviction was allowed with costs.

An inquiry, originally limited to matters concerned with the summons, was, the plaintiff said, enlarged to cover everything he had done, so far as it could be discovered, during the thirty years of his scholastic career. The plaintiff was suspended from duty, and the local education authority subsequently offered him a subordinate position. He refused this offer, and was then sent three months' salary in lieu of notice.

Claiming that the local education authority were not exercising a proper discretion, the plaintiff sought a declaration that the notice of May 6, 1932, was invalid and inoperative and that his contract of service with the council was still subsisting. He also sought an injunction to restrain the council from acting on the notice of dismissal, and claimed damages.

Extract from Judgment

CLAUSON J.: The Leyton Education Committee considered the position of Mr Gill, and whether the education machine would operate more satisfactorily if the plaintiff ceased to be in their employ. Rightly or wrongly, and it is only fair to say that there was a difference of opinion, they came to the conclusion that they would not be discharging their duties properly as an educational authority if they continued Mr Gill in their employment as headmaster of that school. Mr Gill's position as regards the Corporation of Leyton was that he was a servant of the Corporation, a servant whom his master was entitled, if he chose, to cease to employ. The question I had to decide was whether the motives of the Leyton Corporation in giving the notice which had terminated the employment of Mr Gill were corrupt, or *mala fide*,* or otherwise alien to the objects for which the Corporation as an education authority was created. If a jury was sitting there I am sure it would be my duty to direct the jury that on the materials placed before them there was no evidence upon which they could come to the conclusion that the motives of the Council were corrupt, *mala fide* or otherwise alien to the powers of an education authority. Sitting alone, I am the jury and I find it quite impossible to see any evidence whatever of that character. In that matter in law the Council were themselves judges unless there was an element present of corruption or of bad faith. The discretion and judgment in the matter was left in the hands of the Council and with that judgment I cannot interfere, except upon very narrow grounds. There was no suggestion whatever of corruption in any shape or form, and I have been unable to see any suggestion of bad faith.

Judgment for the defendants

[NOTE: This case illustrates very clearly the distinction between the penalties attaching to an offence at law on the one hand, and disciplinary action by a local education authority on the other. The plaintiff's conviction was quashed by the Essex Quarter Sessions and he was, therefore, guilty of no offence. Nevertheless, the authority decided to take drastic disciplinary action which was originally based on the incident giving rise to the action in the police court, even if it was extended, as the plaintiff claimed, to other matters. Provided there is no malice, the authority may discipline a teacher, even to the point of exercising its discretion to dismiss him, even though he has not broken the law.]

33 Harries *v.* Crawfurd and others [1919] A.C. 717

HOUSE OF LORDS
Notice of dismissal given to a teacher by a body of managers is not invalid by reason of a defect in the appointment of individual managers.

Facts: The plaintiff was headmaster of Sonning Boys' Elementary School in Berkshire. On March 13, 1917, the Reverend R. W. H. Acworth, an assistant diocesan inspector of schools, held a voluntary inspection, when the following questions were put to children between ten and thirteen years of age:

"1. Write out the answers in the Church Catechism to the following questions:—(*a*) 'Which be they?' (*b*) 'What meanest thou by this word sacrament?'

2. Who spoke the following words, whom to, when, and where?: (*a*) 'Do not lie unto thine handmaid'; (*b*) 'What said these men? and from whence came they unto thee?' (*c*) 'Lord, Lord, open to us'; (*d*) 'Put up again thy sword into his place'; (*e*) 'Trouble not yourselves, for his life is in him'; (*f*) 'I will hear thee when thine accusers are also come.'

3. What are the first words that our Lord is recorded to have spoken after he rose from the dead?

4. State, shortly, what you know of Abana, Rab-shakeh, Darius, Shushan, Caiaphas, Arimathea, Demetrius, Mnason, Euroclydon.

5. On what days are Proper Prefaces appointed to be said? What is sung or said immediately after each Preface?"

In the report of the examiners it was stated that the boys of the lower classes "answered well as far as they could", but the written answers of the higher classes were "much below the average and distinctly poor." The following letter, signed by all the staff of the boys' and the girls' schools was sent to the inspector:

"Dear Mr Acworth,—We teachers are very disappointed and hurt over your Scripture reports. Strive as hard as we can, you never give us any praise or encouragement, but instead we get such vague and ambiguous expressions as 'this school has great possibilities,' 'the children answered as well as they were able,' and so on.

As a consequence we regret to say we have lost faith in you and your methods of inspection, and instead of welcoming you to the schools as we should like, your visits and reports only upset and discourage us.

We cannot help feeling that your little differences of opinion with our vicar (which are apparent to us and which we cannot help) do influence you in writing these reports. We honestly believe that you inspect and report conscientiously and to the best of your ability, but unconsciously, perhaps your opinions are affected by these differences.

Under the circumstances we beg to propose that some arrangement will be made whereby you will be relieved of the necessity of writing these reports, which must be as painful to you to write as they are for us to read. Failing some mutually satisfactory arrangement, we teachers in justice to ourselves propose to lay the matter before the Bishop of Oxford."

On May 16, 1917, the plaintiff received a letter from the Reverend Gibbs Payne Crawfurd, the vicar of Sonning. This document suspended the head-master, informed him that his letter to the inspector was of a most insubordinate character, and went on to say that his conduct would be reported to the Berkshire Education Committee with a view to his dismissal.

On May 21 the plaintiff withdrew his protest. On May 22 the managers resolved to dismiss the plaintiff, and formal notice was given on May 23. On June 20 the plaintiff asked to be allowed to explain matters to the defendants. On June 25 the plaintiff and Miss Connelly, the headmistress of the girls' school, met the defendants with the result that the latter were still resolved to part with the plaintiff, but they withdrew Miss Connelly's notice of dismissal.

The plaintiff sought an injunction to restrain the managers from dismissing him until his engagement was duly and lawfully determined and until the consent of the local education authority had been obtained, and from acting on a resolution of May 22, 1917, purporting to dismiss him. He alleged that he was not informed of the charges against him until May 25, 1917, and that up to the issue of the writ he had had no opportunity of meeting the managers as required by regulation 56 of the Regulations and Instructions to Managers and Teachers of Public Elementary Schools 1913.

In the Chancery Division, Peterson J. said that it might be that another tribunal would have come to the conclusion that having regard to the plain-tiff's long service as headmaster, and to the fact that Mr Acworth had accepted his apology, the indiscretion might properly have been visited with an ad-monition and that the penalty of dismissal was an unnecessary severity. But

E

he had only to determine whether the defendants had power to do that which they had done. He found for the defendants and dismissed the action with costs.

The Court of Appeal (Lord Cozens Hardy M.R., Warrington and Duke L.JJ.) dismissed the plaintiff's appeal.[1] The plaintiff appealed further to the House of Lords.

Extract from Speech

VISCOUNT BIRKENHEAD L.C.: . . . My Lords, there remains a further point which was argued before us this morning with great ingenuity by Mr Maugham, and the contention which is advanced on this part of the case is that the managers who reached the decision, first to suspend and then to dismiss the appellant, were illegally constituted. Your Lordships were referred in great detail to such evidence as was available to the Courts below upon this point, and the attention of your Lordships was directed to the schedule of the Act and to the forms which were appropriate for the circumstances which have arisen. I do not think it necessary to examine that material in any detail for this reason, that I am willing to assume, and I do assume, for the purpose of the conclusion which I have reached, that three of the managers had not been legally elected.

Now, my Lords, what follows from that circumstance? It is contended by Mr Maugham that the circumstances of their election were so completely defective and that the degree of irregularity had been so extreme, and so protracted, that the section, to which I will shortly direct your Lordships' attention, has no application, and therefore, he says, the decision and the action which the managers purported to take have no effect at all.

There would have been much to be said for this view if it had not been for the actual words of the statutory provision. Your Lordships will recollect that under the first schedule to the Act of 1902, and under clause B, there are two or three rules which are highly relevant to this contention. The first rule of the second paragraph contains a proviso which is as follows: "Provided that the quorum shall not be less than three, or one-third of the whole number of managers, whichever is the greater." For the reason which I will presently give, I agree with the learned Lords Justices who dealt with this matter that that proviso is not without its relevance and importance. Rule 3 is as follows: "The proceedings of a body of managers shall not be invalidated by any vacancy in their number, or by any defect in the election, appointment or qualification of any manager"; and rule 11 is as follows: "Until the contrary is proved, a body of managers shall be deemed to be duly constituted and to have power to deal with the matters referred to in their minutes."

Now, my Lords, it is contended on behalf of the respondents, and it has been decided by the Court of Appeal, that the irregularities, to which I have drawn your Lordships' attention, and which for the purpose of my decision I am assuming, are met by the express language of the third rule: "The pro-

1. [1918] 2 Ch. 158.

ceedings of a body of managers shall not be invalidated by any vacancy in their number, or by any defect in the election, appointment or qualification of any manager." Mr Maugham replies to that in various ways; I do not examine them all or in detail, but I was not convinced by any of them and, indeed, his difficulties involved him in the necessity of contending that when the rule says "any defect," it must not be construed as "any fundamental defect" but must be considered to deal with some more trivial defect. My Lords, I cannot so construe these words. In my view the object of Parliament was this: to make sure that where a body of managers had acted, their transactions should not be impeached thereafter by persons, whether they were teachers or whether they were tradesmen or whoever they might be, who desired to raise the objection that an individual manager had not been properly appointed. A moment's reflection would show how many cases might arise in which great annoyance, inconvenience and expense might be entailed by a controversy of this kind without any gain of any kind to the public interest. I think therefore that Parliament, in order to avoid such actions and objections, determined to use language of a singular wideness. It would be difficult to discover language wider than that which the Legislature employed in this rule 3. Parliament has said that any defect in the election, any defect in the appointment, any defect in the qualification of any manager, shall not invalidate its proceedings.

Now, my Lords, my own assumption here is that there were defects in the election, defects in the appointment, and defects in the qualification of these three managers. What then is the effect of such a conclusion? The effect of it must be that which the rule says, that their proceedings in spite of those circumstances shall not be invalidated.

My Lords, their Lordships in the Court of Appeal, I think unanimously, thought that it was a relevant circumstance that there were present at that meeting three members whose qualifications were not in question. I also think that observation a relevant one, and for this reason; that I think the true meaning of rule 3 is that the proceedings shall not be invalidated for the reasons stated there; but I am still of opinion that the proviso to rule 1 remains, and that the proceedings, although they may not be invalidated by defect in the election, appointment or qualification of a manager, must depend upon the presence of a quorum as provided by the proviso to rule 1. Therefore I think it was a relevant circumstance, as their Lordships thought in the Court of Appeal, that there were three qualified members present.

My Lords, I have only one further observation to make and that is upon the contention which Mr Maugham very persuasively developed before your Lordships upon the language of rule 11. Rule 11 is in the following terms: "Until the contrary is proved, a body of managers shall be deemed to be duly constituted and to have power to deal with the matters referred to in their minutes." Mr Maugham contends upon that while rule 3 is to be constructed in the manner in which he attempts to construe it, it is to be read side by side with rule 11, and that the result is that while there shall be a presumption that the body of managers has been duly appointed that is a rebuttable presumption, and he claims that he is entitled to demonstrate the contrary to-day as he has attempted to do. My Lords, It is sufficient for me to say that so far as I am concerned I cannot reconcile such a construction of rule 11 with rule 3, nor is it credible to me that rule 3 should have been worded as it is worded if the true view of rule 11 had been that for which Mr Maugham contended. As I attempted to point out in the course of the debate, it is not necessary that one should do such violence to a joint construction of rule 3 and rule 11 as Mr Maugham invites us to do, because there are many legitimate occasions which can be conceived in which a useful meaning can be given to rule 11. For instance, rule 3 has in no way protected the proceedings of a body of managers excepting in the matter of a defect in their selection, appointment or qualifications; it does not interfere in my judgment, for the reason I have given, with the requirements of the proviso as to a quorum, and a proper operation can be found for rule 11 in the circumstance where a body of managers has not been duly constituted, because there has not been the regular and necessary quorum in attendance.

For these reasons, my Lords, I am of opinion that the defect to which attention has been directed is effectively met by the terms of rule 3. The conclusion follows that this appeal must be dismissed with costs, and I move your Lordships accordingly.

Appeal dismissed with costs

34 Richardson *v.* Abertillery Urban District Council; Thomas *v.* Abertillery Urban District Council (1928) 138 L.T. 688

CHANCERY DIVISION

A local education authority may delegate their powers of dismissing teachers to a finance sub-committee.

Facts: The plaintiffs were teachers employed by the Abertillery Urban District Council at salaries payable in accordance with Standard Scale III of the Burnham report. These engagements were determinable by one calendar month's notice to end on the last day of the month.

At the end of 1927 the Council was in serious financial difficulties, and applied for the consent of the Ministry of Health to the writing of a loan by way of overdraft. So heavy was the existing indebtedness of the Council that the Ministry insisted on strict measures of economy, and the Council appointed three of its members as a sub-committee with plenary powers to act. On January 13, 1928, this committee resolved "that the requisite notice be given to all head teachers, assistant teachers . . . and the two attendance officers to terminate their appointments." On January 16 the education committee handed over its powers to make economies to the sub-committee of three, and on January 30 the notices of dismissal were sent to the teachers. The defendants claimed that they had acted bona fide* in what they conceived to be the best interests of the district and the ratepayers, and in the main with a view to a readjustment of the terms of service entered into by teachers, and not with any object of permanently discharging teachers from the employment of the Council, save in so far as, on a reorganisation of arrangements, it might be possible to reduce the total numbers employed.

The plaintiffs sought an interlocutory injunction to restrain the defendants, their servants and agents, from acting on the notices of dismissal until judgment or further order.

Extract from Judgment

EVE J.: . . . What is asked would, in fact, be granting an injunction as a step to specific performance of a contract of service, which the court never does. But it is said that this is not a contract between a servant and an individual employer but between a servant and a public body, and that the law is not the same in the case of such a contract of employment. To what extent does it differ? In *Short* v. *Poole Corporation* Warrington L.J. (as he then was) said:[1]

"Is the position of a public body . . . different from that of an individual? In my opinion it is different only in this, that being established by statute for certain limited purposes, no act purporting to be that of the public body can have any operation as such, if the individuals purporting to exercise the functions of the public body have, in performing the act in question transcended the limits of the authority conferred upon it." . . .

It is said in the first place that the authority here, in determining to serve this notice, was not acting in pursuance of the statutory obligation, but as a mere matter of finance outside the duties imposed on it. . . . I can take judicial notice that the amount spent on education until the attention of the authority had been directed to see if it could be reduced was so far as regarded teachers the highest scale of the Burnham award. I am quite satisfied that in considering this question the defendants were acting in the fulfilment of their statutory obligations and if they do not succeed in this action there is no evidence which could possibly satisfy any tribunal that they were not so discharging their duties. So far, therefore, as the attempt to impugn the notice on the ground of motive is concerned, I cannot possibly entertain it.

It is then said that the formalities adopted were such as to make the notice totally irregular. The education authority had passed a resolution delegating all its powers to the education committee. That would not sterilise the authority, for a principal has always concurrent powers with his agent. . . .

It seems to me that the giving of notices is well within the powers of that sub-committee. The appointment and dismissal of teachers is clearly within the powers of the education authority, and on January 16 the education committee resolved that its powers with regard to economy should be delegated. The conclusion is irresistible that, both on behalf of the authority and the education committee, the sub-committee was invested with the power and duty of deciding how economy was to be effected both in the general work of the council and in education. It cannot be doubted that the education

1. [1926] Ch., at page 90.

authority has authority to delegate its powers. The education committee has statutory powers of delegation under section 4 (5).

I am clear that it was open either to the council or the education committee to ratify what was done, and by the position which it had taken in this action the council had ratified it.

On both grounds therefore the plaintiffs fail, and I propose to make no order on the motions.

Order refused

35 Jones *v.* University of London (1922) *The Times*, March 21 and 22

KING'S BENCH DIVISION

The provost of a university college has a discretion to dismiss a member of the academic staff for conduct incompatible with his position.

Facts: The plaintiff was a full-time assistant in the Department of Chemistry at University College, London. During the Foundation Week 1920 dance he took an eighteen-year-old girl student to a dark lecture theatre where they discussed hats. He then put his arm round her waist, squeezed her, and kissed her. In evidence the girl said that she then got up and tried to get out, but the bench was in the way and the plaintiff was between her and the door. She said, "Let me go," and, when he asked her to let him kiss her again, she said "No!" He then got up and left the lecture theatre. The student, "put out" about it, told a friend who told the vice-president of the union.

The matter came to the attention of the provost, Sir Gregory Foster, who interviewed the plaintiff. The provost understood that the plaintiff was willing to resign, and expected a letter in those terms the next morning. The plaintiff said that he told the provost he would not resign as he did not consider the matter serious enough to require such action. The provost later wrote to the plaintiff, requesting him to hand in his keys and to leave in the evening. This he did.

The plaintiff claimed £125 as salary due or, alternatively, as damages for wrongful dismissal.

Extract from Judgment

GREER J.: . . . This is an action for wrongful dismissal. No general rule of law can be laid down on the question what conduct would justify the immediate dismissal of a servant, but it is clear that it might be conduct either within his duties or outside them if it showed a character incompatible with the due discharge of those duties. The defendants relied on two defences: (1) that the plaintiff had in fact resigned, and that there was therefore no question of dismissal; and (2) that if they had dismissed the plaintiff his conduct was such as to justify them in doing so.

I am satisfied that the plaintiff did not resign. Sir Gregory Foster was under the impression that the plaintiff, at their interview, was willing to resign, and he expected to receive a letter of resignation next morning which he could have accepted. But no such letter was sent, and a mere expression of willingness to resign, or even a promise to resign was not an effective resignation.

As to the other defence, the plaintiff was engaged under an agreement as assistant in the Chemistry Department. His duties were, under the direction of the two professors, to lecture, to take tutorial classes, to assist in practical demonstrations, and to conduct private research himself. That obviously was a position which would bring him into close touch with the students—who were both male and female—in his department, and it was obvious that a person holding such a post would be required to have such a character as would enable him to maintain his authority and exert a good influence on the students to whom he was lecturer, tutor, and assistant demonstrator.

But the matter did not stop there. The agreement stated that the plaintiff was required to take an interest and play his part in all the activities of the college. Among those activities were social activities intended to provide the students with reasonable and healthy enjoyment of a kind proper to them with the sanction and approval of the authorities. One of those social activities was this dance in Foundation Week, which was given as part of the college festivities by the two unions which existed among the students and staff with the approval of the authorities. I do not suppose that the plaintiff analysed his feelings whether he was going there to enjoy himself or to carry out his agreement; but he went there as a member of the staff, and had no other right to be there. Then in the course of the evening he took a girl student, Miss Brown, to a dark lecture room, right away from the ballroom. She might have thought that she was quite capable of taking care of herself, and she did not object to going there. The plaintiff said that they discussed hats; on his own account, and still more on hers, nothing passed which would entitle him to think that he might take the slightest of liberties with her. Yet he took her to this dark room, put his arm round her waist, squeezed her and kissed her. This came to the knowledge of the provost, Sir Gregory Foster, and he was justified in coming to the conclusion that such conduct on the part of a lecturer was incompatible with his position. He was therefore entitled to dismiss the plaintiff, and there must be judgment for the defendants, with costs.

Appeal dismissed

36 Smith *v.* Macnally (1912) 10 L.G.R. 434

CHANCERY DIVISION

The fact that a teacher in a Church of England school appears to the managers to be no longer a member of the Church of England will not of itself support dismissal on grounds "connected with the giving of religious instruction in the school."

Facts: The plaintiff, then a spinster, was appointed a supplementary teacher at Hartwell Church of England School, Northamptonshire, in 1900. In 1906, her appointment was made subject to an agreement with the managers. Having married in 1908, she absented herself from school on August 18, 1911, on the account of her approaching confinement.

On August 31, 1911, she received from the defendant, the Reverend C. R. Macnally, who was the correspondent of the school managers, the following notice purporting to terminate her agreement: "The managers of the Hartwell Church of England School hereby give you notice that the agreement between themselves and you will be terminated on September 30, 1911, as they do not desire any longer to retain the services of a married woman teacher." On October 17, 1911, she received the following further letter:

"The local education authority have notified to the managers that the notice terminating the agreement between you and the managers which was handed to you on September 30, 1911, is not valid, and that, therefore, the local education authority are unable to give their consent to the termination of the agreement. The managers, therefore, give you the alternative of either (a) resigning your post as teacher, or (b) having your agreement terminated under section 7, clause (c) of the Education Act 1902, under which clause the consent of the local education authority is not necessary."

On October 21 the plaintiff replied to that letter, and on October 28 she received the following reply:

"At a meeting of the managers held on October 27 the following resolution was entered on the minutes and the correspondent was desired to forward a copy to you: 'That Mrs A. M. Smith be given notice that the agreement between the managers of Hartwell Church of England School and herself be terminated on November 30, 1911, on grounds connected with the giving of religious instruction in the school, the reason for the termination of the agreement being that the managers are not satisfied with the religious instruction given by Mrs A. M. Smith in the school.' "

Until that notice was given no fault had been found or complaint made, either by inspectors or managers, with regard to the religious instruction given by the plaintiff.

On November 30, 1911, that notice expired and the plaintiff left. Attempts were made by the local education authority to obtain reinstatement of the plaintiff, but they ended in failure.

The plaintiff sought an injunction restraining the managers from acting, or purporting to act, upon the notice of dismissal.

Extract from Judgment
WARRINGTON J.: . . . . The plaintiff's case is that the notice of October 28 was not a valid notice terminating her employment under the provisions either of the agreement or of the statute, and, further, that by reason of the statute she is not in the position of a servant contracting with a master, but has a *status*

given to her by statute, which she is entitled to ask the court to maintain on her behalf. Now the material provisions of the statute are these:

Section 7 (1) (*c*) of the Education Act 1902 provides that "the consent of the local education authority shall be required to the appointment of teachers, but that consent shall not be withheld except on educational grounds; and the consent of the authority shall also be required to the dismissal of a teacher unless the dismissal be on grounds connected with the giving of religious instruction in the school." By subsection (6) "Religious instruction given in a public elementary school not provided by the local education authority shall, as regards its character, be in accordance with the provisions (if any) of the trust relating thereto, and shall be under the control of the managers." And by subsection (7) "The managers of a school maintained but not provided by the local education authority shall have all powers of management required for the purpose of carrying out this Act, and shall (subject to the powers of the local education authority under this section) have the exclusive power of appointing and dismissing teachers." . . .

The defendant Macnally has in an affidavit filed in opposition to this motion stated what was the real ground throughout. He says the ground expressed in the first letter that she was a married woman was not the real ground, but that they had avoided stating the real ground until they found they could not obtain her dismissal by any other means. The real ground was this. The affidavit of the vicar stated that the plaintiff at the time of her appointment

"was a member of the Church of England, and up to about the middle of the year 1910 continued to be a regular and consistent attendant at the ordinary Church services, and also a regular attendant at Holy Communion at the Parish Church of Hartwell. From and after that time the plaintiff became and has continued an active supporter of the Wesleyan Methodist Society at Hartwell. She is a regular attendant at their meeting house, and has played the organ there . . . she could not properly have been appointed a teacher in the said schools had she been a supporter of the Wesleyan Methodist Society in the year 1900 when she was appointed. The principal difference between the tenets of the Established Church and that of the Wesleyan Methodists is that the latter do not believe in Confirmation and hold different doctrines about baptism, both of which are essential points of the doctrines of the Church of England, and as such should be introduced into the ordinary religious teaching of a Church of England school. In the opinion of the managers the plaintiff by her conduct proved that she had ceased to be a member of the Established Church of England, and they were on that ground desirous of terminating her engagement as teacher."

I need not read any more.

The ground expressed in the first letter was not the real ground. The ground expressed in their final letter, namely, that the managers were not satisfied with the religious instruction given by the plaintiff was not the real ground. The real ground was that in their opinion she had ceased to be a member of the

Church of England. She has, it would appear, attended some services at a Wesleyan Chapel, because, as she stated, the services as conducted at the parish church were not such as she approved of. What the particular reason is is immaterial. She has on certain occasions played the organ at the Wesleyan Chapel at the request of the regular organist. Now, is that, according to the true construction of the statute and of the agreement, a ground "connected with the giving of religious instruction"? It is really a ground connected with a religious belief, and a religious practice of the person in question.

In my judgment it is necessary in order to render a dismissal without the consent of the local education authority a valid dismissal not merely that managers should in their own minds consider that the ground is one "connected with the giving of religious instruction," but there must be, in fact, such a ground. Now is the ground alleged in this case a ground "connected with the giving of religious instruction" within the meaning of the statute? In my opinion it is not. I think the statute has, by the expressions it has used, carefully avoided inquiring into the religious belief and the religious practices of a teacher either on the occasion of his or her appointment, or on the occasion of his or her dismissal. On the one hand the consent of the local education authority is required to the appointment of teachers and it is provided that that consent shall not be withheld except on educational grounds. That is to say, that with regard to the appointment of a teacher it shall not be open to the local education authority to question the appointment on any ground connected with the religious opinion or religious practices of the candidates for the post. It is to be on educational grounds only that the consent of the local education authority can be withheld.

On the other hand, with regard to dismissal of teachers, it appears to me that the meaning of the section is that the managers are to be entitled to dismiss a teacher without the consent of the local education authority if they dismiss him on educational grounds, namely on grounds connected with the particular branch and form of education which in the statute is called "the giving of religious instruction."

It seems to me the use of that expression "The giving of religious instruction" is intended to exclude from consideration the religious belief or the religious practices of the person in question. It is intended, I think, that the ground for dismissal without the consent of the local education authority shall be really and in truth connected with the giving of religious instruction. In the present case, as appears from what I have read, it is not pretended that the religious instruction given by the plaintiff was either not efficient or not in accordance with the doctrines of the Church of England. I accept the defendant Macnally's statement as to the real ground but at the same time I think he had most unwisely been attempting to obtain the dismissal on other grounds. In my judgment, however, the real ground so stated is not a sufficient one for dismissal without the consent of the local education authority. In my opinion therefore the notice was invalid and notwithstanding that notice the plaintiff was entitled to be treated as continuing in her position as a teacher in this school under the statutory provisions as well as under the agreement. Under the circumstances what ought I to do? The notice expired on November 30. Attempts have been made through the Board of Education and through the local education authority without resorting to the court to obtain the reinstatement of the plaintiff. Those attempts have failed and meanwhile, I believe, though it is not in evidence, steps have been taken to fill up her place by the appointment of a temporary teacher. I am told that I ought to allow things to remain as they are at the present moment, that is in this condition—that the plaintiff is not a teacher in the school, that she has to depend upon her possible right to recover damages against somebody. It is not quite clear who the master or employer is whom she might sue, but, it is said, I ought to allow that state of things to continue until the trial when the matter can be more thoroughly thrashed out. The object of an interlocutory injunction is to maintain what is sometimes called the *status quo*, and I think I shall best be maintaining that in this case by granting the injunction asked for. I, therefore, grant an injunction and make a declaration in the terms of the notice of motion.

Injunction granted

37 Mitchell *v.* East Sussex County Council (1913) 109 L.T. 778

COURT OF APPEAL

The statutory relations which exist between a local education authority and a body of managers confer no rights on teachers.

Facts: The plaintiff was appointed headmaster of Pyecombe non-provided public elementary school in 1888. Following an adverse report on the school by His Majesty's Inspector in March 1912, the local education authority directed the managers to dismiss the headmaster on educational grounds. By the Education Act 1902, s. 7, the authority was bound to maintain and keep efficient all public elementary schools, so long as the managers of non-provided schools should carry out the instructions of the authority as to the secular instruction, including any "directions for the dismissal of any teacher on educational grounds."

The managers declined, and the local education authority then gave three months' notice to the headmaster "on educational grounds," purporting to act in accordance with the Education Act 1902, which provided that, if the managers failed to obey their direction, the authority should have power "themselves to carry out the direction in question as if they were the managers."

The managers appealed to the Board of Education, and the plaintiff moved for an injunction to restrain the local education authority from acting on the notice of dismissal pending the decision of the Board. Eve J. dismissed the motion, being of the opinion that the evidence did not disclose that the grounds of dismissal, as stated, were not the true grounds. The plaintiff appealed.

Extracts from Judgment

SWINFEN EADY L.J.: . . . This is an appeal from an order of Eve J. refusing to grant an injunction to the plaintiff, Frederick Sharp Mitchell, who is a teacher at the Pyecombe non-provided* school in East Sussex. On appeal the plaintiff asks for an order to restrain the defendants, the East Sussex County Council, who are the local education authority, from acting or purporting to act on a notice, dated May 17, 1913, to terminate the plaintiff's engagement as headmaster of the Pyecombe school.

It appears that the plaintiff has been headmaster of the school for a considerable number of years. He was appointed as far back as the year 1888. But on March 21, 1912, he entered into a written agreement with regard to his continuing in the position as teacher. A few days before that agreement was entered into—namely, on March 15—there was a report from Mr Freeland, His Majesty's inspector of schools, commenting adversely upon the school. He refers to the want of method and management, and that many of the children received but little benefit from the instruction. He further said: "The children who have almost concluded a year's work in the lower division are in reading and numbering backward, even when judged by the standard applied to elder infants."

That report was communicated to the school managers, and they wrote on March 30 saying that the plaintiff was "fully conscious of the necessity of improvement in method, and the managers feel sure that, given a little time, better results will be manifest." Then the local education authority were not satisfied with the position, and on April 19, 1912, they passed a resolution: "That with regard to the unsatisfactory reports on the work of Pyecombe School, the education committee be recommended to direct the managers to take the necessary steps to terminate the engagement of the headmaster, Mr Frederick Mitchell, on educational grounds." Then, on May 11, formal notice was given by the managers to the plaintiff to terminate his engagement. Then after that date an application was made to the local education authority, and they determined to give further time, and it was suggested there might be an improvement in the school. But on May 24 they wrote refusing to withdraw their instructions for the dismissal of the head master, although agreeing that there should be a suspension. . . .

On August 27, 1912, there was an adverse report upon the school by the inspector. It says that: "The attainments of the children in the three R's are certainly very low, and the older children, who study other subjects mainly by themselves, are not at present deriving much benefit from their work. The arithmetic is at present in a condition of chaos." Then on September 17 that report was considered by the local education authority and they withdrew their suspension. It was resolved: "That the managers be now instructed to give the head teacher, Mr Mitchell, the necessary notice to terminate his engagement on educational grounds, as the sub-committee cannot regard the report of His Majesty's inspector as sufficiently satisfactory to justify a longer suspension of the operation of their previous instructions." Then there was an application to the local education authority to reconsider the matter. They refused to modify the view that they had taken, and on December 18 there was an application by the local education authority to the Board of Education saying that a dispute had arisen under the section to which I will presently refer [section 7 (3) of the Education Act 1902], and asking the board to determine it. There was no decision from the board.

It appeared that the board were not informed of the fact that the suspension had been withdrawn and that the notice was now operative. . . . Then on March 7, 1913, the present year, the local education authority again directed that the managers should dismiss the plaintiff on educational grounds. The managers declined, and on May 17, 1913, the local education authority themselves gave the plaintiff three months' notice. That notice was given on May 17, 1913, to expire on August 17. While the notice was current the plaintiff issued his writ in the present action asking for an injunction.

Under the provisions of the Education Act 1902 the local education authority are responsible for the secular instruction under section 5; and then by section 7 (1) (*a*), it is provided as follows: "The managers of the school shall carry out any directions of the local education authority as to the secular instruction to be given in the school, including any directions with respect to the number and educational qualifications of the teachers to be employed for such instruction, and for the dismissal of any teacher on educational grounds, and if the managers fail to carry out any such direction the local education authority shall, in addition to their other powers, have power themselves to carry out the direction in question as if they were the managers." . . . It is under that power that the local education authority have given the notice. Then subsection (3) of section 7 provides that: "If any question arises under this section between the local education authority and the managers of a school not provided by the authority, that question shall be determined by the Board of Education."

While the notice was current, that is to say on June 28, 1913, there was an appeal by the managers to the Board of Education alleging that a dispute had arisen between them and the local education authority with regard to the dismissal of the head teacher and asking the Board of Education to determine that matter. The plaintiff does not in the evidence in support of the motion deny the existence of educational grounds, nor does he give any evidence or even suggest that the notice of dismissal given by the local education authority was given on other than "educational grounds." . . .

Under those circumstances it seems to me that the plaintiff has made out no case whatever for the interference of the court. The notice of dismissal has been given and has expired. The defendants in their evidence put forward the view that if there is a dispute between them and the managers as to whether there are sufficient "educational grounds" for giving notice to the plaintiff, it is for the local education authority to determine that and not for the Board of Education. . . . I do not propose to say whether that is right or wrong or to comment upon it. We have not the managers before us, and it is outside any question that we have to consider. The existence of educational grounds for the notice is not impeached or challenged on this motion, and under those circumstances I am of opinion that notice to terminate the plaintiff's engagement having been given and having expired the plaintiff has not made out any case for the interference of the court.

Appeal dismissed

38 Blanchard *v.* Dunlop [1917] 1 Ch. 165

COURT OF APPEAL
The requirement that notice of dismissal by a body of managers requires the consent of the local education authorities does not give the teacher any right to be heard by the authority.

Facts: The plaintiff, Mrs Blanchard, was appointed as a teacher at Albourne Church of England School on May 16, 1901. The agreement provided that the contract could be terminated by three months' notice on either side and that, where such notice required the consent of the local education authority, confirmation by the authority should be sufficient. On March 30, 1916, the plaintiff received a notice of termination of her appointment which did not state the grounds for dismissal. The dismissal was not on grounds connected with the giving of religious instruction, and on June 6 the plaintiff received a letter from the local education authority saying that, in view of the decision in *Young* v. *Cuthbert*[1] they were of opinion that they had no power to interfere.

The plaintiff sought an injunction to restrain the managers from acting upon their notice of dismissal until the consent of the local education authority had been obtained, and she had an opportunity of being heard. Astbury J. ordered the matter to stand over for a fortnight, and then refused the motion as the local education authority had then confirmed the dismissal on the ground that the parties were bound by their agreement to accept confirmation by the local education authority. Neither the agreement nor the Act gave the plaintiff a right to be heard by the authority.

The plaintiff appealed.

LORD COZENS-HARDY M.R.: . . . It is said that the education authority were in a judicial or quasi-judicial position and had no power to give their prior consent or subsequent confirmation without acting in a judicial character, or at least having the plaintiff before them and hearing what she had to say. This is not a case in which any complaint is made against this lady. We do not

1. [1906] 1 Ch. 451; see page 28, *supra.*

know what it is, but nobody suggests misconduct against her; a word of that kind is not breathed anywhere. If a few of the managers—or I will assume if the managers unanimously—said "We do not think it is in the interest of the school that this lady should be continued," not because of misconduct, but, suppose, on account of her age, or anything which is not misconduct, I myself see no ground for saying that there is any obligation on the education authority to consider the grounds upon which the managers have acted, and if that is done and the education authority then give their prior consent or their subsequent confirmation, all that the law requires from them has been complied with.

In my opinion the view of the position of the schoolmistress in this non-provided school which has been taken by the learned counsel for the appellant is one for which there is no foundation, assuming, as I do, good faith on the part of the managers and on the part of the education authority; and good faith has not been challenged, and could not be challenged, here. For these reasons I see no ground for the plaintiff's contention; she has the protection of the Act of Parliament which she is entitled to have, and I think this appeal should be dismissed.

PICKFORD L.J.: . . . It seems to me that, although the provisions of the section[2] may operate as a protection to the master or mistress, it is pretty clear, looking at the statute, that they were not inserted with a view to the teacher's interests; they were inserted with a view to the interests, if I may call them so, of the education authority. . . . I can see nothing to make them a judicial body: they are not investigating charges against the lady; they are only seeing that the interests of the education which is provided by them shall not be interfered with without their consent. I can see nothing judicial in those functions, and no provision pointing in favour of the teacher which requires a hearing of him or her by the education authority before they give their consent. . . .

Appeal dismissed

39 Perry v. Pardoe and others (1906) 50 S.J. 742

VACATION COURT

It is not incumbent on the managers or governors of a school to give a teacher an opportunity of stating a view as to how notice of dismissal should, or should not, be given.

Facts: The plaintiff, Mrs Perry, was appointed headmistress of Old Alresford National School, Southampton, in 1901. Upon the coming into force of the Education Act 1902, she entered into an agreement with the managers which stipulated, *inter alia*:

"(6) This agreement may be terminated at any time by either of the parties

2. Education Act 1902, s. 7 (1) (c).

hereto giving to the other of them three calendar months' previous notice in writing to that effect, and, if such notice is given by the managers it shall be given in accordance with the decision of a meeting convened by notice sent to every manager four days at least before the meeting, stating that the termination of the agreement with the teacher will form part of the business of the meeting. (7) Where such notice is given by the managers ... on grounds connected with the giving of religious instruction those grounds shall appear on the face of the notice."

From 1901 to 1905 the reports of the diocesan inspectors were very favourable to the plaintiff. In May 1906 it was stated that the results were not so good as in 1905, and that the lessons of life were not being brought home to the children.

On April 19, 1906, before this report was made, the Reverend George Owen Pardoe told the plaintiff that the managers wished her to resign, but she refused. On April 21 there was a meeting of the managers, and written notice was sent to her. It was admitted that this notice was bad, and on June 11 a further notice, terminating on September 11, was sent. This read as follows:

"To Mrs Perry,—The managers of the Old Alresford National School held a meeting last Monday, the 14th of June, at which the report of the diocesan inspector was read, showing the results in Division I to be not so good as last year, and intimating that lessons for life were not brought home to the children. The rector reported that he had been present at the inspection and that he confirmed this opinion of the inspector, and added that the answering in Division I on the Creed was very unsatisfactory. Upon this, it was proposed and seconded, that having for some time felt that the unsatisfactory tone of the school must be the result of imperfect training in religious matters, the managers hereby resolve to terminate the engagement with the head teacher. ... "

The plaintiff sought an interim injunction to restrain the managers from acting on the notice on the ground that there was no evidence that the religious teaching was defective as the managers very rarely visited the school and that, even assuming in discipline and roughness in the children, there was nothing to connect that with defective religious teaching more than with defective secular teaching. The grounds were not bona fide* but only to avoid getting the consent of the local education authority under section 7 (1) (c) of the Act.[1] Further, the managers, exercising semi-judicial functions, had no right to dismiss the plaintiff without giving her a hearing.

The defendants admitted that the plaintiff was a very good secular teacher, and that the managers had formed their opinion of what went on inside the school on the basis of their own observation of the conduct of the children outside, as well as on reports of what went on inside.

1. See also *Smith* v. *Macnally* (1912) 10 L.G.R. 434, page 111, *supra*.

Extract from Judgment

SUTTON J.: . . . In giving the notice under clause (6) of the agreement the managers were acting as such in the exercise of their discretion, and not in any judicial capacity, and the conclusion I have arrived at is that it was by no means incumbent on them as a question of law to give the plaintiff an opportunity of stating her view as to the way the notice should or should not be given. I think it is apparent on the face of the notice that it was given on grounds certainly connected with religious instruction. . . .

Injunction refused

III

PARENTS

(A) DEFINITION

40 London School Board *v.* Jackson (1881) 7 Q.B.D. 502

QUEEN'S BENCH DIVISION

The term "guardian and every person who is liable to maintain, or has the actual custody of any child" does not affect the primary liability of the parent, if there is one.

Facts: On June 16, 1880, Mr Hosack, a metropolitan police magistrate made an order requiring Caroline Jackson to cause her daughter of between thirteen and fourteen years of age to attend Hanover Street Board School, Islington, a certified efficient school selected by the defendant.

On November 4, 1880, the defendant was summoned for neglecting to comply with the order. She pleaded that she was very poor, and as she could not maintain the child she had sent her to live with an aunt in Fulham.

The magistrate dismissed the summons, holding that section 3 of the Education Act 1870, in defining the term "parent" as including "guardian and every person who is liable to maintain or has the actual custody of any child" did not contemplate that both the parent and the person having the actual custody of the child should be simultaneously liable to conviction. In his view the primary liability rested on the person having the actual custody. The school board appealed by way of case stated to the Divisional Court of the Queen's Bench Division.

Jeune for the School Board for London contended that the order had been made on the mother: she was bound to obey it, and could not discharge herself from that obligation by permitting her child to leave her house. The aunt could not be summoned for disobedience to an order made upon somebody else. The mother was liable to maintain the child and had the right to her custody, although she might be living with an aunt in another house.

Extract from Judgment

LORD COLERIDGE C.J.: . . . It was intended by the Education Act that the children of England should be educated, and it was intended to impose the responsibility of sending them to school upon definite persons where those

definite persons exist. . . . In certain specified cases the parent is exempted
from this responsibility, but the present is not one of those cases. This is the
case of a parent within the meaning of the interpretation clause who has had
an order made against her which is not obeyed, and she ought to be convicted. . . . The fact that the word "parent" includes by the interpretation
clause other persons, guardians, persons liable to maintain, and persons who
have the actual custody, if there be any such, does not appear to me to prevent
the operation of the word "parent" in its primary and obvious sense, where
there is a person who comes under that description.

Case remitted to the magistrate

41 London County Council *v.* Stansell (1935) 154 L.T. 241

KING'S BENCH DIVISION
*Where a father, mother and child are living together, the term "parent" refers
only to the father, and does not include the mother.*[1]

Facts: The appellants, the London County Council, appealed by way of case
stated against the dismissal of an information that the respondent, Florence
Stansell, being the parent of Alfred Stansell, a child attending a public
elementary school, whose person or clothing had been cleansed by the Council,
had allowed the child to get into such a condition that it was again necessary
to proceed under section 87 of the Education Act 1921.

It was proved before the justices sitting at Catford, that on November 14,
1934, the person and clothing of the child were examined and found to be
infested with vermin. The respondent failed to comply with a notice requiring
her to cleanse the person and clothing, and on December 4, 1934, the child
was removed from the school and cleansed. On February 19, 1935, a further
examination revealed that the child was again infested.

The respondent was the child's mother, living with the father who was her
husband, and the child lived in the same household.

The justices, on the authority of *Hance* v. *Burnett*[2] and *Woodward* v. *Oldfield*[3] held that the parent who has the *de facto** custody and control of the
child is the person to be charged for offences against certain sections of the
Education Acts and that, where the father is not absent, he is the proper
person to be charged.

The local education authority appealed to the Divisional Court of the King's
Bench Division.

Extract from Judgment
LORD HEWART C.J.: The justices were clearly right. They came to the
conclusion that the "parent" referred to in section 87 of the Education Act
1921, where the father and mother were living together and the child was

1. See note at the end of this case.
2. (1880) 45 J.P. 54; see page 124, *infra.*
3. [1928] 1 K.B. 204; see page 126, *infra.*

living with both of them, was the father. They have set out their reasons for their decision, and I think that they have come to the right conclusion for the reasons which they have given.

Appeal dismissed

[NOTE: The decision was unanimous, Goddard and Singleton L.J.J. concurring with the Lord Chief Justice. Later, as Lord Chief Justice, Lord Goddard in *Plunkett* v. *Alker* ([1954] 1 Q.B. 421.) expressed considerable misgiving as to the correctness of the decision in this case. See below on this page.]

42 Hance *v*. Burnett (1880) 45 J.P. 54

QUEEN'S BENCH DIVISION
The mother of a child having its actual custody and control is liable for neglecting to cause the child to attend school while her husband is at sea, whether he is the father of the child or not.

Facts: Mrs Burnett, the mother of a boy under the age of thirteen, was charged with neglecting to cause the boy to attend school. The child was living with her, and under her control, while her husband was at sea. It was not stated that the husband was the father of the child.

The Liverpool justices doubted whether a married woman could be convicted, and dismissed the information.

Held: The justices were wrong. The mother had the actual custody of the child, and ought to have been convicted.

Case remitted to justices with direction to convict

[NOTE: See, also, the *dicta* of Lord Goddard C.J. in *Plunkett* v. *Alker, infra.*]

43 Plunkett *v*. Alker [1954] 1Q.B. 421; [1954] 1 All E.R. 396

QUEEN'S BENCH DIVISION
Where the verminous condition of a child is due to the neglect of the mother, the term "parent" includes the mother.

Facts: Mrs Catherine Plunkett was convicted by the Liverpool stipendiary magistrate of sending her child to school with his head in a verminous condition contrary to the Education Act 1944, s. 54 (6). She was fined five shillings.

The defendant appealed to the Divisional Court of the Queen's Bench Division by way of cases stated on the ground that her husband was the parent responsible under the section. It was stated that the father was a maker of lolly ices.

LORD GODDARD C.J.: A man like a commercial traveller might be away from home for some little time. If his child is neglected then the person neglecting him is the mother.

Collinson (for the appellant): The father is the head of the family.

LORD GODDARD C.J.: In theory.

Extract from Judgment

LORD GODDARD C.J.: . . . Section 54 (6) provides If, after the cleansing of the person or clothing of any pupil has been carried out under this section, his person or clothing is again found to be infested with vermin or in a foul condition at any time while he is in attendance at a school maintained by a local education authority or at a county college, and it is proved that the condition of his person or clothing is due to neglect on the part of his parent, or in the case of a pupil in attendance at a county college to his own neglect, the parent or the pupil, as the case may be, shall be liable on summary conviction to a fine not exceeding twenty shillings. The word "parent" is defined in section 114 (1) of the Act of 1944 as follows: " 'Parent' in relation to any child or young person, includes a guardian and every person who has the actual custody of the child or young person." That section does not say that the mother is not a parent. It states whom the word "parent" includes, and I take it that under that section if a child is living with, say, an aunt, or grandparent so that that person has the actual custody of the child, she might be answerable under section 54 (6). It is at least a reasonable interpretation of the words in the definition section to assume that the legislature is drawing a distinction between actual custody and legal custody. The words used are "actual custody," which seems to indicate a person who at the time of the summons has the child in his or her custody. I think that the word "actual" is put in for that purpose. It must also be remembered that unless the contrary intention appears, the Interpretation Act 1889 requires us to read the singular as including the plural. Therefore the word "parent" must be construed as "parents" unless the contrary intention appears. . . .

The appellant was found to be responsible for the condition of the child and was fined, but it was argued that this court is bound by the decision in *London County Council* v. *Stansell*,[1] which was a decision under section 87 of the Education Act 1921. . . .

In *Stansell's* case the mother was summoned, and the justices, on the authority of *Hance* v. *Burnett*[2] and *Woodward* v. *Oldfield*,[3] held that the father was the person who ought to have been summoned, and not the mother; and on appeal this court, of which I was a member, held that the justices came to a right decision. Lord Hewart C.J., giving judgment, said "The justices were clearly right. They came to the conclusion that the 'parent' referred to in section 87 of the Education Act 1921, where the father and mother were living together and the child was living with both of them, was the father. They have set out their reasons for their decision, and I think they have come to the right conclusion for the reasons which they have given." Both Singleton J. and I agreed.

It is said that *Stansell's* case is binding on us and that we must give effect to it and hold that the father alone can be summoned. I say at once that, having

1. (1935) 154 L.T. 241; 34 L.G.R. 52; see page 123, *supra.*
2. (1880) 45 J.P. 54; see page 124, *supra.*
3. [1928] 1 K.B. 204; 25 L.G.R. 296; see page 126, *infra.*

further considered that case, I feel great doubt whether the decision was right. The Interpretation Act 1889 does not seem to have been brought to the attention of the court or the court did not remind itself of that Act. . . . If the condition of the child is due to the neglect of the mother, who is undoubtedly a parent, and is not excluded by the definition section of the Act from being a parent, I have great difficulty in seeing why the mother does not commit the offence which is mentioned in the section. . . . I have great doubt whether *London County Council* v. *Stansell*[4] was rightly decided, but as there is now another Act which contains other words, I think we can treat this case as *res integra** and put our own construction on the words of the section.

In the present case, therefore, it can be said that the magistrate having found as a question of fact—and it is not being suggested there was not evidence on which he could so find—that the condition of the child's head was due to neglect of the mother, she is answerable under this section. . . .

Appeal dismissed; conviction affirmed

44 Woodward *v.* Oldfield [1928] 1 K.B. 204

KING'S BENCH DIVISION
Where the father of a child is serving a term of penal servitude and the child resides with the mother, the mother is the parent whose consent is required for the admission of a defective child to a special school within reach of the child's residence.

Facts: The appellant, Marion Ann Woodward of Burnham-on-Sea, was ordered by the justices to comply with a requirement by the Somerset local education authority to send her daughter, Marion Lilian Woodward, to a special boarding school at Sandhill Park, Bishop's Lydeard, being a school certified as suitable for mentally defective children.

The girl, who was twelve years old, was at all material times residing with her mother, who was stone deaf. The consent in writing of the father was not obtained as he was serving a sentence of penal servitude, and was not released from Maidstone Gaol until the last week of April 1927.

The respondent, Norman Oldfield, who was deputy clerk of the county council had laid a complaint on October 11, 1926, and the justices ordered that the girl be sent to the special school.

The mother appealed, and her medical advisor stated that in his opinion the girl was incapable of benefiting by instruction at the special school. The child was of an emotional temperament, and her interests would best be served if she remained at home in her mother's care as it would be more beneficial for her to associate with normal persons than with other defective children.

Extracts from Judgment
LORD HEWART, C.J.: . . . Upon those materials two points have been

4. (1935) 154 L.T. 241; 34 L.G.R. 52; see page 123, *supra*.

urged on behalf of the appellant. The first is that there was no evidence upon which the justices could reasonably arrive at the finding of fact that the appellant withheld her consent to the child being sent to the certified school unreasonably and not with the bona fide intention of benefiting the child. With regard to that submission it appears to me that the evidence upon the one side and upon the other, which is fairly and clearly summarised in the case, was before the justices, and that it is clear that the justices upon that competing evidence came to a conclusion as to which it is only necessary to say that it was a conclusion of fact to which they were entitled to come. . . .

The second contention, which raises the real point of substance in this case, is that, notwithstanding that the father was at all material times serving a sentence of penal servitude in Maidstone Prison, he was nevertheless within the meaning of the Act,[1] the "parent" of the child; that nothing had happened to impose upon him any disability in relation at any rate to this matter; and that, as his consent had neither been asked nor received, the condition precedent had not been fulfilled, which required that before the local education authority made the order referred to here the consent of the parent must first be obtained or in the alternative unreasonably withheld. Is it true to say that within the meaning of the term in Part V of the Act the father in such circumstances as those of the present case continues to be the "parent," whose consent, whether given or withheld, is the material consent? That question depends upon the terms of this Act and not upon the use of like terms in some other Acts. . . . It was not denied in the argument on behalf of the appellant that, at the time when the father was detained in prison and the child was in the actual custody of the mother, it was the mother who would have been liable if there had been neglect of the duty imposed on the parent by section 42. . . . [His Lordship read section 54]. To apply that section to the circumstances of a case such as the present, if the father of the child, by reason merely of the fact that he remains the father, is to be regarded as the "parent" referred to in the section, notwithstanding that he is in prison serving a sentence of penal servitude, the consequences become a little grotesque. The local education authority must then satisfy themselves after consultation with the person undergoing penal servitude that he, being in that place and in those circumstances, is not making suitable provision for the child's education. The local education authority must then require the convict undergoing penal servitude to send the child to a certified class or school suitable for the child; and it is only if the convict fails without reasonable excuse to do so that they may by complaint apply to a court of summary jurisdiction for an order against him. If the father was the "parent" referred to, what more reasonable excuse could he offer to express his regret that he was not in a place where it was possible for him to comply with the requirement? The result would thus be that as he had a reasonable excuse for not sending the defective child to a special school, the child would be neglected until the period of penal servitude,

1. Education Act, 1921.

whatever it might happen to be, came to an end, because only on its expiration would he be deprived of a reasonable excuse.

... That is not to say that in other circumstances and under the provisions of other statutes the father in such circumstances may not retain the rights of a paternal parent. ...

In these circumstances, it appears to me that the justices were entitled to come to the conclusion of fact to which they came, and that in the interpretation which they put upon the law they were right. I think, therefore, that this appeal ought to be dismissed.

Appeal dismissed

(B) DUTIES IN RESPECT OF CHILDREN

45 *Re* Agar-Ellis, Agar-Ellis *v.* Lascelles (1883) 24 Ch. D. 317

COURT OF APPEAL
The father has the control over the person, education, and conduct of his children until they are twenty-one years of age.

Facts: On the marriage of the Hon. Leopold Agar-Ellis, a Protestant, to the Hon. Harriet Stonor, a Roman Catholic, in 1864, the husband promised his wife that all the children should be brought up as Roman Catholics, but he changed his mind shortly after the birth of his first child. One child died in 1872, but Mrs Agar-Ellis secretly indoctrinated the children with Roman Catholic views so that in 1878 they refused to go to a protestant place of worship with their father.

In June 1878, the father sought to make the children wards of court, and took out a summons for directions as to their education. The Court of Appeal restrained the mother from taking the children to confession or to Roman Catholic places of worship, and left the father free to do what he thought best for the children. He placed the children with various persons, and in 1883 the second daughter asked to be allowed to spend some time with her mother. Pearson J. refused the petition on the ground that, in the absence of fault on the part of the father, the court had no jurisdiction to interfere with the legal right of the father to control the custody and education of his children, and to decide upon where they should reside.

The petitioner appealed.

Extract from Judgment
BRETT M.R.: ... He refuses, therefore, to allow his daughter to pay a visit to her mother; he refuses to allow his daughter to see her mother more than once a month; he refuses to allow his daughter and her mother to correspond, except upon the condition that the letters are shown to himself or third parties. And we are told that this is done for fear that the affection of his daughter towards him should be altered. However, the petition is brought

before the court, and it has been argued on behalf of the mother and daughter that because the daughter is now more than sixteen, the father has no right to the control or custody over her; that she is emancipated from his control; and that the court ought so to declare. In support of that argument it was said that the authorities show that where a girl over sixteen is absent from her father and with other people, the court, upon a habeas corpus sued out by the father, will see the girl who is above sixteen and ascertain her view of the position, and if she is content to remain where she is, will not grant to the father upon the habeas corpus a return of the child into his custody. And it is said that that shows that the law is that when a girl is over sixteen her father has no longer any control over her. It was said further, that this was shown to be the law, because the court in the case of a testamentary guardian will, if necessary, interfere with regard to his mode of exercising the control which is given to him by law. Now I cannot accede to the argument thus put forward. It seems to me to be directly contrary to the law of England, which is, that the father has the control over the person, education and conduct of his children until they are twenty-one years of age. That is the law. . . .

Appeal dismissed

46 Hodges *v.* Hodges (1796) Peake Add. Cas. 79

GUILDHALL

A father is bound by every social tie to give his children an education suitable to their rank.

Facts: The plaintiff was the son of the defendant. The defendant and his wife living very uncomfortably together, and he having frequently struck her, she left his house, took several of her children with her, and went to live at the house of the plaintiff.

The plaintiff brought an action for the board of his mother and the money expended in educating the children.

Lord Kenyon, at *Nisi Prius** recommended the parties to settle out of court.

LORD KENYON: . . . if a husband turned his wife out of doors he sent a credit with her; and I am inclined to go further than I believe any other judge has gone before me. I am inclined to say, that if he behaved in such a way as to render it unsafe and dangerous for her to reside with him, that in that case the plaintiff would be entitled to recover for the board of his wife; further I cannot go, for the wife might apply to the Spiritual Court for a divorce.[1]

As to the children, they do not appear to have been driven from the defendant's house; and at all events nothing can be recovered on account of the money paid for their education. A father is bound by every social tie to

1. Until the middle of the nineteenth century the ecclesiastical courts exercised an exclusive jurisdiction in matrimonial matters.

give his children an education suitable to their rank, but it is a duty of imperfect obligation, and cannot be enforced in a court of law. The richest man
in the kingdom might say to his heir apparent, "Go and earn your daily bread
by your daily labour," and the law could not interfere. There is no further
obligation than that which nature has implanted in his breast. The law obliges
him to nothing but nurture, which duty expires when the child reaches the
age of seven.

[NOTE: A father's legal duty with regard to the education of his children is now, of
course, defined by the Education Acts, which require him to ensure that his child
receives full-time education suitable to his age, ability, and aptitude.]

47 London County Council *v.* Hearn (1909) 78 L.J.K.B. 414

KING'S BENCH DIVISION

*The duty of a parent to cause his child to receive efficient education is an absolute
duty unless the parent can show one of the statutory excuses. Truancy is not a
reasonable excuse.*

Facts: Dennis Hearn, the father of a twelve-year-old boy, was charged that
he did "on March 20, 1908, and other days, notwithstanding due warning,
unlawfully and habitually and without reasonable cause, neglect to provide
efficient elementary instruction for Thomas Hearn." Between March 9 and
March 27 the boy attended Blackstock Road Elementary School four times
out of a possible thirty.

The mother said that she had sent Thomas to school, but that he did not
like school, and would not go, and that his irregular attendance was his fault
and not that of his father. The magistrate Mr Mead, held that enrolling the
boy at school, coupled with his subsequent attendance was a sufficient compliance by the defendant, and that proof of irregular attendance was not
sufficient evidence of neglect on the part of the parent.

The London County Council appealed by way of cases stated.

Bodkin, for the appellants, said that he was asking for a school attendance
order, not for a penalty. The magistrates' finding that the enrolling of the
child was sufficient compliance was directly contrary to section 4[1] which said
"It shall be the duty of the parent of every child to cause such child to receive
efficient elementary instruction."

Extract from Judgment

LORD ALVERSTONE C.J.: In our opinion this order ought to have been made.
The importance of an attendance order is that it enables the education
authorities to control the instruction of the child. It seems to me that section 4
of the Elementary Education Act 1876 has been misunderstood. Under that
section the obligation imposed is that of causing the child to be taught, and
the section has nothing to do with the way in which the instruction is to be

1. Elementary Education Act 1876.

provided. Section 11 provides that it shall be the duty of the local authority, if the parent, habitually and without reasonable excuse, neglects to provide such instruction, to apply to a court of summary jurisdiction for an order compelling the child's attendance at an efficient school. In the same section certain things are specified which are to be a reasonable excuse for the non-attendance of the child at school. . . . I express no opinion as to what might be the proper answer of a parent summoned under section 12 (1) who desires to prove that he has made all reasonable efforts to secure his child's attendance at school in compliance with the order.

In my judgment, where a child is absent from school in such a manner as to show an habitual neglect by the parent to provide efficient elementary instruction within the meaning of section 11, the magistrate ought to make an attendance order.

In the present case the child only attended school on four days out of a possible thirty, and that is ample evidence of habitual neglect. I accept the magistrate's view that the respondent believed his wife's statement that the child did not like school, and would not attend. But that is the very state of things which was intended to be remedied by the proceedings subsequent to the granting of the order. They will be the means of forcing the child to receive instruction. We are not dealing here with a case under the by-laws, which, it may be, were made for the purpose of bringing pressure to bear on parents and of keeping them up to the mark; and the cases cited are quite consistent with the view we are expressing. The child is not in fact attending school, although the parent may, as far as his personal conduct is concerned, have a satisfactory answer in explanation of its non-attendance. This appeal must be allowed.

WALTON J.: I agree. I do not think that section 11 is satisfied by the parent entering the child's name in the books of the school, and starting him to go there. It seems to me that under that section the parent's duty is to provide that the child does attend, and if the child fails habitually to do so the parent has not fulfilled his duty, unless the non-attendance is accounted for by one of the reasonable excuses set out in the latter part of the section. . . .

Appeal allowed

48 Collins *v*. Cory (1901) 17 T.L.R. 242

KING'S BENCH DIVISION

A wife who by her husband's conduct is forced to live separately from him has an implied authority to pledge his credit for the education of the children who are in her custody.

Facts: Ivan R. Cory and Cyril N. Cory were placed by their mother as pupils at a private school owned by the plaintiff, Mr W. E. W. Collins at Slough. The plaintiff sued Mr Cory for £312 os. 8d. in respect of fees for instructing and boarding the boys during the autumn term, 1899, and the spring term, 1900.

During this period divorce proceedings were pending, and the mother had custody of the boys. The decree absolute was pronounced on March 27, 1900.

For the defence it was alleged that Mrs Cory had no authority to pledge her husband's credit by placing her sons at the defendant's school, and that education was not a "necessary" within the meaning of the rule of law which gives a wife forced to live apart from her husband the authority to pledge his credit.

Extract from Judgment
PHILLIMORE J.: . . . Although older authorities, e.g. *Anstey* v. *Manners*[1] and *Hodges* v. *Hodges*[2] might tend to show that the law was formerly that education was not a necessary, at the present day education of the children is a necessary.
Judgment for plaintiff

49 R. *v.* De Crespigny, *ex p.* Carter (1912) *The Times*, May 21

KING'S BENCH DIVISION
It is a matter of fact in each case whether refusal to consent to the performance of an operation on a child amounts to cruelty.

Facts: The applicant, a Northamptonshire quarryman was the father of a girl attending a public elementary school. The school authorities found the greatest difficulty in teaching her, and the medical officer was of the opinion that her imperfect articulation was due to a cleft palate. The father was urged to allow a simple operation and later, on the father's refusal, reported the matter to the Society for the Prevention of Cruelty to Children.

An information was laid, and the justices convicted the father, holding that on the evidence the operation would be beneficial for the child.

The father applied for a writ of certiorari* to remove the case into the Divisional Court of the Queen's Bench Division and to quash the conviction.

The proceedings had been commenced under section 12 of the Children Act 1908 by which it was an offence amounting to cruelty to neglect to provide medical aid for a child. For the father it was argued that the local education authority had really initiated the proceedings and that by section 3 of the Local Education Authorities (Medical Treatment) Act 1909 there was no obligation on a parent to submit his child to medical inspection or treatment under section 13 of the Education (Administrative Provisions) Act 1907. In reply to a question by Avory J., counsel for the father, said that section 3 amounted to an indemnity against prosecution in such a case, and therefore the justices had no power to convict. *Clarke Hall* said the prosecution had nothing to do with the authority.

1. (1818) Gow 10.
2. (1796) Peake Add. Cas 79; see page 129, *supra*.

Extracts from Judgments

LORD ALVERSTONE C.J.: . . . The question before the justices was simply one of fact, namely, whether the applicant had neglected to provide medical aid for the child. The question on the merits might be properly raised in another proceeding; but I am clear that certiorari will not lie in such a case. The rule will be discharged.

PICKFORD J.: I am of the same opinion, and only desire to add this—that we do not in any way decide the merits against the father of the child to whom it would be perfectly open to raise the question in any further proceeding.

AVORY J. concurred.

Rule discharged. Judgment for respondent

[NOTE: The father had appealed to the Divisional Court of the King's Bench Division. Such an appeal can lie only on a point of law, and not a matter of fact. The Court decided that the issue was one of fact, and therefore there was no jurisdiction to deal with it.

Section 12 of the Children Act 1908 is now incorporated in section 1 of the Children and Young Persons Act 1933: "(1) If any person who has attained the age of sixteen years, and has the custody, charge, or care of any child or young person under that age, wilfully neglects . . . him . . . in a manner likely to cause him unnecessary suffering or injury to health (including injury or loss of . . . organ of the body . . .), the person shall be guilty of a misdemeanour. . . . (2) For the purposes of this section—(*a*) a parent or other person legally liable to maintain a child or young person shall be deemed to have neglected him in a manner likely to cause injury to his health if he has failed to provide adequate . . . medical aid . . . or if, having been unable otherwise to provide such . . . medical aid, . . . he has failed to take steps to procure it to be provided under the enactments provided in that behalf . . . "

By the Education Act 1944, s. 48, a parent may be compelled to submit his child to medical inspection (but not treatment). Failure to do so makes him liable on summary conviction to a fine not exceeding five pounds.

In *Oakey* v. *Jackson* [1914] 1 K.B. 216; 78 J.P. 87, Darling J. said: "The justices in deciding whether there was wilful neglect must consider in each case the nature of the operation and reasonableness of the refusal to have it performed."]

(C) FATHER'S RIGHTS: CHILD'S NAME

50 *Re* T. (*Orse.** H.) (*An Infant*) [1963] Ch. 238

CHANCERY DIVISION

Where a divorced mother has the custody of a child of the marriage, she may not deprive the child of the father's surname without the consent of the natural father.

Facts: The parents of the child in this application were married in 1949, and the child was born on August 26, 1952. The mother petitioned for divorce and, in undefended proceedings, a decree nisi* was granted on September 9, 1959, and made absolute on December 10, 1959. The mother was granted custody of the child. No provision was made for the father to have access to the child, but in fact he had access from time to time.

The father remarried in July 1960 and the mother in October 1960. In August 1961 the mother, purporting to act as the child's legal guardian, executed a deed poll abandoning and renouncing the child's former surname and substituting the mother's new surname. The father was not informed or consulted before this was done, but the mother wrote to him on September 14, 1961, telling him of her action.

A summons was issued making the child a ward of court, and the father asked that the deed poll be cancelled and declared of no effect. The case was heard in chambers, judgment being given in open court.

Extract from Judgment

BUCKLEY J.: It is, of course, well known that a person's surname is a conventional name and forms no part of his true legal name. An adult can change his or her surname at any time by assuming a new name by any means as a result of which he or she becomes customarily addressed by the new name. There is no magic in a deed poll. The effect of a deed poll when changing a name is merely to record the change in solemn form which will tend to perpetuate the evidence of the change of name. But a change of name on the part of an adult must, in my judgment, involve a conscious decision on the part of the adult that he wishes to change his name and be generally known by his new name. An infant, and certainly not an infant of the age of the infant with whom I am concerned in the present case, is not competent to make such a decision. Certainly an infant of tender years cannot of its own motion change his or her surname. What I have to consider is whether any other person can change it for the infant, and, if so, who can do so?

There appears to be no authority on this point at all, but in *The Encyclopaedia of Forms and Precedents*, 3rd. ed., vol. XI, p. 8, there is a precedent for changing an infant's name by deed poll to be executed by the guardian of the infant. It is perhaps worth observing that by rule 8 of the Enrolment of Deeds Poll (Change of Name) Regulations 1949 . . . , which are regulations made by the Master of the Rolls under the Supreme Court of Judicature (Consolidation) Act 1925, section 218, it is provided that "in the case of an infant the application"—that is to say, the application to enrol—"must be made by the parent or legal guardian of the infant." If the infant is over sixteen years of age his or her signed "consent must be endorsed on the deed and duly witnessed."

As I understand it, these rules have no statutory force. They are merely practice rules of the registration department in respect of deeds poll for changing names. But that fact does give some support to the view that it may be competent for a parent or legal guardian to change the name of an infant. If there is such a right or power it is one which, in my judgment, resides primarily in the infant's father as the natural guardian of the person of the infant. It may be that if an infant has no father living or if for some reason the father is not available such power may reside in whoever is the legal guardian of the infant. In the present case the deed was executed without the consent of the infant's father and indeed without his knowledge at all; it was executed by the mother of the infant who was the person to whom the custody of the infant had been given by the order of the Divorce Court. An order for custody is as its name implies, an order which gives the person in whose favour it is made the right to the custody of the child and the right to bring up the child subject, of course, to any direction which the court may think right to make from time to time under its jurisdiction in relation to any matter. It does not deprive the father, who is not given the custody of the child, of all his rights and obligations in respect of his child. He remains, subject to the rights conferred upon the person to whom custody is given by the court, the natural guardian of the child and among the residual rights which remain to him are any rights which he may have at law with regard to the name of the child. In my judgment, the deed which the mother has executed with regard to the child is one which she had no power to execute so as to have any effect on the infant. In any case, as I have already observed, the deed poll does no more than provide evidence of the kind I have mentioned. The most effective way in which this child's name has in fact been changed is in the school register. In the day-to-day contact in her school, her name having been altered, she is now known by her mother's present surname. That was done, of course, in September last year. In my judgment the infant's mother had no status, which entitled her to take any step on behalf of the infant which would result in her being known by some surname other than the surname of her father, and I can find nothing in the facts of this case which would make it desirable that the infant should be known by any name except that of her father.

One can imagine cases in which it might be in the interests of a child to cease to be known by a particular name, perhaps because of some particularly unhappy association which that name might have acquired or possibly in order to comply with some condition contained in some trust document. But in the present case there seems to have been no reason at all for this change of name, except that the mother conceived that it was embarrassing to the child to be called by one surname while she herself was called by a different surname as a result of her having remarried. The mother in her evidence indeed suggests that the child herself asked that she might be called by the same name as her mother.

In the case of a divided family of this sort it is always one of the aims of the court to maintain the child's contact, respect and affection with and for both of its parents so far as the circumstances will permit. But to deprive the child of her father's surname, in my judgment, is something which is not in the best interests of the child because, I think, it is injurious to the link between the father and the child to suggest to the child that there is some reason why it is desirable that she should be called by some name other than her father's name. The fact that there has been a divorce and that the father was the person against whom the decree was granted is an insufficient ground for such a view. For these reasons, in my judgment, not only was the infant's mother incompetent to take a step on behalf of the infant which was of a kind calculated to have quite far reaching effects upon the child, but also, in my view, it was a step which was not in the interests of the infant and one which the court ought not to assist in any way. In these circumstances, I shall declare that the deed poll of August 24, 1961, was ineffective to change the name of the infant, and I shall direct the infant's mother, who is the appropriate person, to take such steps as are necessary to ensure that the infant is called by her proper surname as before this deed.

Order accordingly

[NOTE: Although this is not an educational case, it has been included since it deals with a problem which sometimes faces teachers, either when parents seek their advice or when a request is made for the change of a child's name in the school records.]

(D) PARENTS' RIGHTS: CHOICE OF SCHOOL

51 Watt *v.* Kesteven County Council [1955] 1 Q.B. 408; [1955] 1 All E.R. 473

COURT OF APPEAL

Although it is the duty of a local education authority to have regard to the general principle that children are to be educated in accordance with the wishes of their parents, this is not an absolute obligation and an authority is not bound to have regard exclusively to those wishes.

Facts: The plaintiff, Thomas Edward Leo Watt, claimed that, by virtue of the Education Act 1944, s. 76, he had the right to have his twin sons educated at an independent secondary school of his own choice. The boys passed an examination entitling them to a grammar school education. As there was no county school in that part of Lincolnshire, the county council arranged for them to go as day boys to an independent school, Stamford School, the fees of £60 10s. a year being paid by the local education authority.

Stamford School is a Church of England foundation, but the father wished the boys to go to a Roman Catholic boarding school, and arranged for their admission to a preparatory school owned by the Dominican Order, Blackfriars School, Llanarth, Raglan, Monmouthshire. The fees at this school were £120, of which £50 was for tuition and £70 for boarding. In 1952 the boys were transferred to Blackfriars School at Laxton in Northamptonshire, where the tuition fees were £61 a year. The local education authority agreed to make grants of £31 for the elder boy and £31 for the younger for the school year 1952–53. The father claimed assistance with combined boarding and tuition fees, and denied the right of the authority to base a grant towards tuition fees on an income scale.

Section 76 of the Education Act 1944 provides:

"In the exercise and performance of all powers and duties conferred and imposed on them by this Act the Minister and the local education authorities shall have regard to the general principle that, so far as is compatible with the provision of efficient instruction and training and the avoidance of unreasonable public expenditure, pupils are to be educated in accordance with the wishes of their parents."

Ormerod J. dismissed the claim.
The plaintiff appealed.

Cur. adv. vult

Extract from Judgment

DENNING L.J.: . . . The short answer to the father's argument is, I think, this: Whilst education is free in this country, it is only free at the schools which the county council make available. I can find nothing in the Act which compels the county council to pay the fees at any school which the father chooses. The duty of the county council is plain. They must make schools available for all the pupils in their area. But they can fulfil this duty, not only by maintaining schools themselves, but also by making arrangements with certain other schools. . . . At all the schools which the county council maintain themselves, no fees are payable. At the other schools with which they make arrangements, they must provide free places or pay the fees in full. Once they have fulfilled their duty in one or other of these ways—either by maintaining schools themselves, or by making arrangements with certain other schools—there is no more which they are bound to do. If a father wishes his child to go to yet another school of his own choice, with which the council has no arrangements, then he cannot claim as of right that the county council shall pay the fees. He can then only expect assistance according to his means. Regulations have been made which empower the county council to pay the whole or any part of the fees in any case where it would involve financial hardship on the father to pay them.

I think that the position is clearly as I have stated it: but it was urged before us that independent schools stand in a special position. If the county council have no school of their own, or no grant-aided school to which to send the boys, but have to send them to an independent school, then it was said that the father has a right to choose which independent school they should go to; and, corresponding to that right, that the county council are bound to pay the fees in full.

This argument was based on section 76 of the Act. It is obvious that that section cannot stand by itself. It only applies in the exercise of some other power or duty contained in the Act. In this case it was said to apply in the exercise of section 8. It was said that, when there is no maintained or grant-aided school, the county council have a duty under section 8 to make available an independent school and to pay the fees in full: and that, in exercising that duty, they must under section 76 have regard to the general principle that pupils are to be educated in accordance with the wishes of their parents. Hence if there are two independent schools, one in Stamford and the other far away,

F

both of which are efficient and charge the same tuition fees, the pupil should be educated at the one desired by the parents. All the more so when the school chosen by the parents is the cheaper.

I think that that argument is mistaken. It assumes that the duty of the county council under section 8 is to make available for the pupils any of the independent schools over the length and breadth of the country. That is not correct. Their duty is only to make available the particular independent school with which they have made arrangements. They must make arrangements for an efficient independent school to take the pupils from their area. They must get the Minister's approval to these arrangements: and they must then offer this school to the parents. . . .

Section 76 does not say that pupils must in all cases be educated in accordance with the wishes of their parents. It only lays down a general principle to which the county council must have regard. This leaves it open to the county council to have regard to other things as well, and also to make exceptions to the general principle if it thinks fit to do so. It cannot therefore be said that a county council is at fault simply because it does not see fit to comply with the parent's wishes. And that is all that the father's complaint comes to in this case.

In any case I cannot myself see any evidence to suggest that the county council in this case did not have regard to the general principle. The correspondence which passed on the matter showed that it was specifically brought to their attention and nevertheless they thought that "they would place themselves in an impossible position *vis-à-vis* parents in other parts of the county if they were to do what has been asked of them."

I can well see what they mean. If they paid the full fees in this case, it would mean that every other parent in the county, who sent his boys to boarding school, could come and ask the county council to pay the tuition fees, no matter how rich he was. The father in this case is asking for preferential treatment for himself over and above the other parents who send their children to boarding schools. The county council only helps those other parents according to their means. They cannot reasonably be expected to do more for the plaintiff. They cannot pay his fees irrespective of his means when they do not do it for others.

This being so, the appeal must be dismissed: and there is no need to consider the question, which was much debated before us, whether a breach of section 76 gives rise to a cause of action for damages. It could not itself do so, but only in connexion with the exercise of some other power or duty in which the general principle was not observed. In view of *Gateshead Union* v. *Durham County Council*,[1] I would not like to say that there can be no cases under the Act in which an action would lie, but I do not think that an action lies in this case. It is plain to me that the duty under section 8 (to make schools available) can only be enforced by the Minister under section 99 of the Act and not by

1. [1918] 1 Ch. 146; see page 175, *infra*.

action at law. That being so, a breach of section 76 in the exercise of section 8 can also be enforced by the Minister and not by action at law. . . .

Appeal dismissed. Leave to appeal to the House of Lords

[NOTE: The plaintiff decided not to appeal to the House of Lords, and the matter was dropped at this point.]

52 Darling *v.* Minister of Education; Jones *v.* Minister of Education
(1962) *The Times*, April 7

QUEEN'S BENCH DIVISION

A decision by a local education authority and the Minister of Education[1] that a school is overcrowded cannot be challenged in the courts by a parent who wishes his child to attend that school, and who claims to base his right on the Education Act 1944, s. 76.

Facts: Mrs P. Darling and Mrs E. Jones of Green Wood Avenue, Bury Green, Cheshunt, wished their children, aged six, to attend Bonnygrove Primary School, situated one hundred yards from their homes. The Hertfordshire local education authority said that this school was overcrowded, and that the children must go to Burleigh Primary School which was a mile away and on on the other side of the Great Cambridge Road (A.10).

The mothers claimed that this was a breach of the authority's duty under section 76 of the Education Act 1944, which provides that: "in the exercise of all powers and duties conferred, and imposed upon them, by this Act the Minister and local education authorities shall have regard to the general principle that, so far as is compatible with the provision of efficient instruction and training and the avoidance of unreasonable public expenditure pupils are to be educated in accordance with the wishes of their parents."

The fathers signed papers making the mothers the temporary legal guardians of the children, who were then kept at home in defiance of the Minister's confirmation of the local education authority's decision. In November 1961, each mother was fined ten shillings for failing to cause her child to attend school.

They then applied to a Divisional Court of the Queen's Bench Division for leave to apply out of time for an order of certiorari to remove the matter into the Queen's Bench and to quash the order of the Minister.

Brown Q.C. (for the applicants): The journey to the Burleigh Primary School involved dangerous traffic conditions, while the Bonnygrove School was near the children's homes. The question involves the children's welfare. The parents, being conscientious, had made temporary provisions for the children's education—namely, three hours' tuition in a week—but the local authority did not regard that as sufficient. Under section 76 of the Education Act 1944, the local authority must have regard to the wishes of the parents.

1. Now the Secretary of State for Education and Science.

Admittedly, section 76 (3) provides for the Minister to determine the school for a child where the local authority considered the child unsuitable for the school chosen by the parent or that unreasonable expense would be involved. The legal point involved is that, under section 37 (3) of the Act of 1944, overcrowding is not a ground on which the local authority can ask the Minister for a determination. The Minister's order was invalid because it was made on the ground of overcrowding.

LORD PARKER C.J.: What should the Minister do if the nearest school is overcrowded?

Brown Q.C.: The matter is an administrative one to be dealt with by the local authority, and it should be perfectly easy to readjust their pupils' list so that children could be moved to another school.

Cumming Bruce (for the defendants): The Minister's concern was for the welfare of the children. The parents were under a legal duty to send the children to school or make other arrangements. Three hours a week were not regarded as satisfactory. The children should have started school on September 9, 1961. The Minister can make a determination under section 37 (3) if the attendance of children at a school involved unnecessary expenditure. In this case it would involve such expenditure if additional accommodation had to be provided at the Bonnygrove School. The court should not give leave unless the applicants would undertake to make satisfactory arrangements for the children's education pending proceedings.

Brown Q.C.: The applicants are prepared to ensure that the children would get the necessary education by consultation with the local authority. This case does not involve a purely legal principle. The applicants would make such undertakings as the court thought fit to impose.

Extension of time granted. Leave to apply for order of certiorari refused

(E) PARENTS' RIGHTS: EDUCATION OTHERWISE THAN AT SCHOOL

53 R. *v.* West Riding of Yorkshire Justices, *ex p.* Broadbent[1] [1910] 2 K.B. 192

KING'S BENCH DIVISION

A parent is entitled to call evidence for the purpose of showing that he is providing efficient education for his child at home.

Facts: The applicant, Mr J. W. Broadbent, had been a public elementary school teacher for twenty-five years. He was summoned before the justices of the Morley Division of the West Riding of Yorkshire under the Elementary Education Act 1876, s. 12, for failing to send two of his children to school in

---

1. In some reports this case is referred to as *R. v. Morris, etc., West Riding JJ. ,ex p. Broadbent*.

accordance with the terms of an attendance order. The section provided that where an attendance order is not complied with, without reasonable excuse the court might impose penalties upon the parent and order the child to be sent to an industrial school.

The order had been made under section 11 of the Act which provided that if the parent of any child above the age of five years habitually and without reasonable cause neglected to provide efficient elementary education for his child, a court of summary jurisdiction might, upon the complaint of the local authority, order the child to attend some certified efficient school.

The Elementary Education Act 1870 provided that the fact that the child was under efficient instruction in some other manner afforded a "reasonable excuse" for non-compliance with the requirements of the Act. Section 48 of the Act of 1876 provided that the terms in that Act should, so far as they were consistent with the tenor thereof, have the same meaning as in the Elementary Education Acts 1870 and 1873.

At the hearing of the summons Mr Broadbent attended with six witnesses to prove that he had a "reasonable excuse," in that he provided efficient instruction in some other manner. The magistrate refused to hear the evidence on the ground that, having made the attendance order, all they had to do was to see that it was complied with.

The defendant obtained a rule nisi for a writ of certiorari to remove the case into the court, and for a rule nisi for a mandamus directing the justices to hear and determine the case. On his behalf it was contended that it was open to the defendant, on the hearing of a summons, to prove facts which would constitute a reasonable excuse. This the magistrates had refused to allow.

Extracts from Judgment

LORD ALVERSTONE C.J.: In this case two rules were obtained, one for a writ of certiorari to bring up two convictions of the applicant for non-obedience to attendance orders, and the other for an order directing the justices to hear and determine two informations preferred against the applicant for non-obedience to the attendance orders. The ground upon which the rules were obtained was that the justices refused to hear evidence of a reasonable excuse within the meaning of the Elementary Education Act 1876 for non-compliance with the attendance orders, which the applicant endeavoured to set up as an answer to the informations. The case is one of difficulty and the material sections are obscure. I am not certain that it is possible to give very clear reasons for the construction which I put upon the sections we have to consider, but I have come to the conclusion that it was not intended by section 12 of the Elementary Education Act 1876 to limit the reasonable excuses that might be set up, in answer to a summons for non-obedience to an attendance order, to the two reasonable excuses mentioned in section 11 of that Act. The provisions of section 11 relate to a child being ordered to attend school, and section 12 has reference to the proceedings to be taken if an attendance order is not obeyed. Under section 11 there is, apart from the reasons given by that section as constituting reasonable excuses, a preliminary question to be decided, namely, whether the parent has habitually neglected to provide efficient elementary instruction for the child. It is admitted that if a parent, in answer to proceedings taken against him under section 11 for unlawfully "habitually and without reasonable excuse" neglecting to provide efficient elementary instruction for his child, shows that he is providing that which the justices consider to be efficient elementary instruction for the child at home, such evidence affords a complete answer to the summons, and the question whether the parent has a "reasonable excuse" under the section does not arise. Therefore on the hearing of a summons under section 11 an inquiry takes place as to whether the parent has habitually neglected to provide efficient elementary instruction for the child, and, if so, whether he has a reasonable excuse. The effect of the two reasons being expressly mentioned in section 11, either of which is a reasonable excuse, is that, although a parent has not provided efficient elementary education for the child, an attendance order cannot be made if there is not a public elementary school within two miles which the child can attend, or the child has been absent by reason of sickness or any unavoidable cause. If an attendance order is made under section 11 it remains effective subject to certain questions of removal or alteration in the circumstances.

As to the construction of section 12 of the Elementary Education Act 1876, it would be a very strong thing to wholly deprive the parent of the right to give efficient elementary instruction to his own child during the whole period of the operation of an attendance order, and I think that it would require clearer language than the section contains to deprive him of that right. Having regard to the general nature of the Elementary Education Act 1876, the language used in section 12 seems to imply that that which would have been an answer to a summons issued under section 11 with a view to an attendance order being made might be an answer to a summons for a breach of the attendance order. I very much doubt whether the reasonable excuses mentioned in section 11 are meant to be exhaustive. If they are not meant to be exhaustive, the words in section 12, "any reasonable excuse within the meaning of this Act," must have a wider meaning than the expression "reasonable excuse" as defined under the two heads in section 11. Section 48 of the Elementary Education Act 1876 provides that terms in that Act shall so far as is consistent with the tenor thereof have the same meaning as in the Elementary Education Acts 1870 and 1873. We are therefore thrown back to section 74 of the Elementary Education Act 1870, which provided that the fact that the child was under efficient instruction in some other manner afforded a reasonable excuse for non-compliance with the requirements of that Act. It is therefore, to say the least, doubtful whether the two reasons mentioned in section 11 of the Act of 1876 are meant to be exhaustive, and it is not unreasonable to hold that the words "any reasonable excuse within the meaning of this Act" contained in section 12 are at least as wide as the words "reasonable excuse" in section 74 of the Act of 1870. The authorities appear to support that view.

The decision in *Belper School Attendance Committee* v. *Bailey*[2] dealt with a by-law respecting attendance, and therefore the mischief aimed at by the provisions which were in question in that case was of the same kind as that aimed at by the provisions which we are now considering. The by-law contained in substance the same reasonable excuses as those mentioned in the Elementary Education Act 1870, and it was held that there might be other reasonable excuses within the meaning of the by-law besides the three reasons therein specified. In *London School Board* v. *Duggan*,[3] where the question again arose under a by-law which provided that any of the following reasons should be a reasonable excuse for non-attendance, namely, that the child was under efficient instruction in some other manner, that the child had been prevented from attending school by sickness or any unavoidable cause, or that there was no public elementary school open, which the child could attend, within two miles from the child's residence, it was shown that non-attendance was caused by the child, a girl aged twelve, with fair elementary instruction having been in respectable employment, earning wages, which she gave to her parents, who were poor, industrious, and respectable people and applied them to the support of their other children, whom otherwise the parents from no fault of their own would have been unable sufficiently to support, and it was held that these facts constituted a reasonable excuse for non-attendance. In my judgment that decision supports the contention that it was open to the applicant in the present case to give evidence before the justices that he was efficiently educating the child at home, and that a person is not deprived of the right of complying with the statute in a way other than that mentioned in an attendance order because in a certain state of circumstances the attendance order was made against him.

Rules absolute

[NOTE: The Education Act 1944, s. 36, provides: "It shall be the duty of the parent of every child of compulsory school age to cause him to receive efficient full-time education suitable to his age, ability, and aptitude, either by regular attendance at school or otherwise." The term "reasonable excuse" does not appear in the 1944 Act, section 39 of which sets out three statutory defences. Section 36 permits a child to be educated otherwise than by attendance at school, and in accordance with the decision in this case the parent may bring witnesses to prove that he is fulfilling his duty under the section.]

(F) PARENTS' RIGHTS: EDUCATIONAL SYSTEM

54 Wood and Others *v.* Ealing London Borough Council [1967] Ch. 364

CHANCERY DIVISION
The statutory requirement that children are to be educated in accordance with the wishes of their parents means no more than that the local education authority must take into account the general principle; it does not inhibit the authority from

2. (1882) 9 Q.B.D. 259.
3. (1884) 13 Q.B.D. 176.

*modifying the development plan for the area, not from changing the fundamental
character of the schools by introducing a system of comprehensive education.*

Facts: On September 1, 1965, the schools sub-committee of the London
Borough of Ealing decided to proceed with a scheme for the introduction of
comprehensive education, and instructed a working party to work out the
details. The scheme envisaged that most of the borough would be covered by
five-year comprehensive schools with sixth-form colleges for pupils over the
age of sixteen, but that in some parts there would be single tier schools catering
for all pupils of secondary school age.

There was considerable opposition within the borough, led by the Joint
Parents' Committee of the Ealing Grammar Schools, and during the summer
of 1966 this was focused most strongly on the proposals for Acton County
Grammar School, Twyford Secondary Modern School, and Faraday Secondary Modern School. These were all schools provided for secondary education
in the development plan approved by the then Minister of Education under
the Education Act 1944. As a result of the operation of the London Government Act 1963, they were now under the control of the new London Borough
of Ealing.

Following the adoption of the scheme in September 1965, the local education authority called meetings of parents to explain the scheme and to receive
comments and questions. Parents were limited to one question only and, with
one exception, were not allowed to vote. The parents were told that they would
have a right to object when the scheme went to the Minister, but such a right
lies only under section 13 of the 1944 Act which refers to the establishment or
discontinuance of schools. The parents' meetings continued until May 1966,
by which time the scheme had been sent to the Secretary of State (April 6) and
he had given his approval (April 25).

The scheme provided, *inter alia,** for the establishment of "through" comprehensive schools in the former boroughs of Acton and Southall. Only the
Acton proposals were complete, and the Secretary of State concurred with the
authority's proposal to admit an unselected intake to the three Acton schools
named above. The long-term proposal was for six forms of entry at Acton, and
eight forms at Twyford and Faraday. This would necessitate additions to the
Acton building, which would have to remain at four forms of entry until further
building became possible. Parents and headmaster said that a four-form entry
school was not viable as a comprehensive unit, and a petition to this effect was
presented to the Secretary of State. On July 8, 1966, the authority decided
that there were not sufficient pupils for the complete implementation of the
plan, and settled on five forms at Acton and Twyford, with six at Faraday.
This seems to have been the only point at which the parents' wishes were
taken into account.

On July 8, the authority also decided, subject to the approval of the Secretary of State, to amend article 13 of the articles of government for the three
schools as follows: "The admission of pupils to each of the schools shall be

in accordance with arrangements made by the council which will be based primarily upon the age of the pupils, the wishes of the parents and the views of the headmaster." At the same time arrangements were made to increase Acton by one form of entry, and to engage staff to teach children who would not, under previous conditions, have been admitted to a grammar school.

The officers of the Parents' Committee, said to represent some ten thousand parents, had meanwhile issued a writ dated July 6, 1966, which claimed:

"(1) a declaration that the local education authority had no power to alter the existing scheme of secondary education by substituting a mixed scheme of single-sex and co-educational comprehensive schools;

(2) an injunction to restrain the defendants, their officers, servants and agents from introducing the scheme in substitution for that approved by the Minister of Education under the 1944 Act for the former Borough of Acton;

(3) an injunction to restrain the introduction of the Acton scheme in September 1966."

Two days later, on the day when the authority decided to amend the articles of government, the plaintiffs moved for an order to restrain the local education authority from introducing the Acton scheme, or from doing any further act preparatory to such introduction. The action was adjourned for fourteen days, and was heard before Goff J. in the Chancery Division on July 22, 25, 26 and 27.

Extract from Judgment

GOFF J.: . . . The first ground relied upon cannot be regarded as an independent head of claim, since the only operation of section 76 is to qualify the powers and duties of the local education authority, and indeed of the Minister, and one must consider it in relation to some power or duty in connection with which it is shown that the provisions of section 76 have not been observed. . . .

There is, in my judgment, no prima facie* case of a breach of section 76, since in administrative matters the obligation means "no more than that the authority must take into account the general principle, weighing it in the balance together with and against other considerations."[1] . . . The views of the parents were communicated to the working party on December 13, 1965, and March 14, 1966. Moreover, I cannot find anywhere in the Act any obligation on the local education authority to consult parents on the revision of the development plan. . . .

Then the plaintiffs rely on the development plan, but here they disclaim any reliance on section 76. It is conceded by counsel for the defendants that the proposals as to the three schools depart from the plan, but it is submitted that there is nothing in the Act to prevent this and that, on the contrary, section 11 (5) of the Act of 1944 in terms or effect authorises it. In my judgment, this

1. *Watt* v. *Kesteven County Council* [1955] 1 Q.B. 408, *per* Parker L.J.; see page 136, *supra*.

contention is well founded. That subsection empowers the Minister to impose duties on the education authority for the purpose of securing that effect will be given to the plan, those duties to be imposed by the local education order to be made under section 12. As I have already observed, and notwithstanding that the latter section is mandatory, no orders have been made as a matter of policy to keep the development plan flexible. . . . Section 12 is mandatory as o certain matters only, and neither section 11 (5) nor section 12 itself requires him to impose duties to ensure that effect shall be given to the approved plan. In my judgment, therefore, the plaintiffs cannot succeed on this ground.

I pass to the third ground which is based on section 8 either alone or in concert with section 76. Taking section 8 alone, it is said that the proposals as to the three schools are merely part of a plan to make all schools in the borough comprehensive, and if that be done they will not be sufficient in character within the meaning of section 8 (1) (b) and particularly within the description or definition in the latter part of that subsection which I read earlier in this judgment. Taking section 8 in conjunction with section 76, it is said that in making all schools comprehensive the defendants have not regarded the statutory general principle because on the evidence it is clear that they con-ceived they had the right to do this without ascertaining or regardless of the views of the parents and, . . . whilst generally speaking the evidence is that the parents do not object to the comprehensive principle, they are not satisfied that the right scheme has been adopted or will be properly carried out in detail, and because some five deponents have stated specifically that they object to comprehensive schools. The significance of this last point is that Sir Andrew Clark, for the defendants, has argued that on its true construction the general principle is confined to the wishes of particular parents in respect of their own particular children and does not refer to the wishes of parents generally. . . . I accept Sir Andrew's construction. . . . This alone, however, is not enough to answer the plaintiffs in view of the five deponents to whom I have referred and the allegations as to change of character. In my judgment, education in section 76 must refer to the curriculum, and whether it includes any, and if so what, religious instruction, and whether co-educational or single-sex, and matters of that sort, and not to the size of the school or the conditions of entry.

It is to be observed that the Act nowhere provides for grammar school edu-cation, or secondary modern education as distinct from grammar. . . . I am bound to accept the evidence of Mr Ayres, who says in paragraph 14 of his affidavit:

"The existing curricula will continue to be provided at all three schools. I am satisfied that the accommodation and teaching facilities will be adequate in each school and the quality of teaching thereat for all pupils (including the more able children) will be in no way inferior to that now pertaining. . . . "

Even if I were wrong on this, it seems to me that any breach of section 8 . . .

can only result in a failure to discharge the statutory duty of providing sufficient schools, and the only remedy for that, apart possibly from the case of an
individual plaintiff able to show that he or she had suffered damage (which is
not the case before me), is by complaint to the Minister under section 99. . . .

Sir Andrew Clark has contended that [all the defendants are doing is to
alter the articles of government] and that there is nothing *ultra vires* about
that. He points out that it requires the approval of the Minister under sections
17 and 111, and that if there be any breach of section 76 the time to attack it
will, so the argument runs, be when the order has become effective by his
approval and the Minister will then be a necessary party. . . .

In essence, I felt throughout that the plaintiffs were in this difficulty, that
though their counsel disclaimed this, they were in reality trying to establish
a general right to be consulted as to the revision of the development plan being
carried out pursuant to section 31 (2) of the 1963 Act,[2] and I still feel that that
is the real nature of their case. I can find no support for it in the Act, and
section 11 as a whole appears to me to negative any such right.

On this general ground and for the other reasons which I have given, I must
dismiss this motion, but I should add that had I taken a different view I
would, on the balance of convenience, have felt it right to preserve the
status quo.

> *By consent, the trial of the motion was treated as the trial*
> *of the action. Action dismissed with costs*

2. London Government Act 1963.

IV

THE ADMINISTRATION OF SCHOOLS

(A) DELEGATION OF PARENTAL AUTHORITY

55 Fitzgerald v. Northcote and another (1865) 4 F.& F. 656

COURT OF QUEEN'S BENCH

A parent, when he places his child with a schoolmaster, delegates to him all his own authority so far as is necessary for the welfare of the child.

Facts: The plaintiff, David Fitzgerald, was the son of the Right Hon. Mr Justice Fitzgerald and a pupil at the Roman Catholic College at Oscott, near Birmingham, where the defendants, the Reverend S. Northcote and the Reverend W. Stone were the heads.

At Christmas, 1864, he passed the matriculation examination of the University of London, and it was arranged that he should remain at Oscott until he went up for the examination for his B.A. degree. Dr Northcote pointed out to the father, who was an Irish judge, that the lad would be in an "exceptional position," but would remain *in statu pupillari.*

In February 1865, David Fitzgerald was guilty of several breaches of discipline, and eventually he was warned that he would be expelled for his next offence. There was a good deal of animosity between the lay-students, whose fees were paid by their parents, and the clerical students who were destined for the priesthood and paid for by funds provided for presentations to the college. Early in March 1865, a master found a notebook containing entries in the plaintiff's handwriting referring to the clerical students, *e.g.* "Uncle or brother keeps a small grocery establishment at Wednesfield Heath; father a general inspector of canal locks, Authority Honorary Secretary A.B.C. N.B. Examine Henry Walter of Trea, about Casell, of Dudley."

The letters A.B.C. referred to the "Anti-Bunker Confederacy," the word "bunker" meaning a clerical student.

The matter was reported to the President of the College, and on March 13 the co-defendant, Stone, went to Fitzgerald's room and demanded the pocket-book. When Fitzgerald refused, Stone took the book from his pocket. Fitzgerald was then taken before the President and told that, if the pocket-book supported the account given of it, he would be expelled. In his defence Fitzgerald said it was all nonsense and amusement, and had no serious object or design. The lad was then locked in his room for two or three hours until a conveyance was procured to take him to Birmingham.

On the same day the defendant Northcote wrote to Fitzgerald's father, stating the causes of expulsion, and complaining of the boy's behaviour during the previous six months. In response to an inquiry by the father, the Principal enumerated some of his other complaints about the boy:

(1) smuggling into college a bottle of spirits and entertaining his friends, two of whom drank to excess;

(2) borrowing a pass-key, and taking a rubbing and wax impression from it;

(3) going to an inn when he was already under discipline;

(4) breaking a penance, and enticing a friend into the plantations to shoot there;

(5) equivocation to the principal, and preferring a complaint against a master to forestall complaints against himself.

The plaintiff sued for assault and imprisonment, and for the conversion of the pocket-book.

COCKBURN C.J.: I hold that there is an implied contract between the parent and the preceptor—that the latter will continue to educate the child so long as his conduct does not warrant his expulsion from the school. And when we consider the serious consequences to a child of his being so expelled, it is the more essential that his implied contract should not be broken. . . .

Extract from Summing-up

COCKBURN C.J.: . . . As to there having been a legal assault, there could be no doubt, and the great question would be, whether it was justified. . . .

Now, as to this, I have to tell you, that the authority of the schoolmaster is, while it exists, the same as that of the parent. A parent, when he places his child with a schoolmaster, delegates to him all his own authority, so far as it is necessary for the welfare of the child. So that the question comes to this, whether, supposing a parent had reason to believe that a child was doing something that was wrong, and the evidence of it was in a book in his pocket, the parent would not, and rightly, think himself justified in demanding it, and if it were withheld, then (supposing the child under the age of an adult) taking it from him. . . .

It is a pity that Dr Northcote did not extend his inquiries a little further than the mere papers, and did not inquire whether there had been any actual annoyance to the clerical students—any outward manifestation of that which was supposed to be the real object of the society, instead of being, as the youth all along alleged, a mere piece of idle amusement. And, under the circumstances, it would have been far wiser had Dr Northcote simply sent for the youth and remonstrated with him. In the absence of any evidence of practical annoyance to the clerical students, and of anything to show that the supposed society was seriously mischievous, it did seem monstrous publicly and ignominiously to expel the youth from the College. I think that the authorities acted far too hastily in the matter; and, although the expulsion is not made a ground of action, it is material, in this way, with reference to the imprisonment. . . .

It is a case of great importance; for, on the one hand, it is for the general benefit of society, and especially of its youth, that the authority of those charged with the care of great scholastic establishments should be maintained; and, on the other hand, it is of equal importance that it should not be exercised arbitrarily. That it has been exercised honestly in this case there can, I think, be no doubt. The question is, whether it has been exercised reasonably or unreasonably, and according to your view upon that question, your verdict for the plaintiff or defendant must in the main depend. . . .

Findings of the jury: That there was an assault and imprisonment; that the plaintiff was a pupil in the College under the care and governance of the defendants; that there was not such a society as stated; that the circumstances were not such as to justify the assault or imprisonment.

Verdict for the plaintiff. Damages £5

56 Shepherd v. Essex County Council and Linch (1913) 29 T.L.R. 303

KING'S BENCH DIVISION

The duty of a schoolmaster in relation to his pupils is that of a careful father.

Facts: The plaintiff, Cyril Frederick Shepherd, was a fifteen-year-old pupil at Ilford County School. The defendant, Linch, was the chemistry master at the school.

On February 21, 1912, the chemistry class, which consisted of about twenty-eight boys, were told that they were going to do an experiment on ozone and that they were to go to the desk for some phosphorus. The plaintiff took a piece back to his desk but, seeing other boys with larger pieces, he and his partner decided to get some more. The partner fetched a larger piece, and the plaintiff put the old piece in the left pocket of his trousers. Shortly afterwards, experiencing a pricking sensation, he pulled the pocket inside out. The phosphorus was alight, and his trousers were burning.

The master told the boys to throw water on him, but before they could do so other boys wrapped him in a blanket. The fire appeared to be out, but burst out again when the blanket was removed. Water was thrown on the plaintiff until the fire went out. The master told the boys to rub in carron oil. This made things worse, and a doctor ordered him to be sent to hospital, where he spent five weeks in bed followed by eleven weeks in bed at home.

The plaintiff brought an action for damages for negligence against the local education authority and the chemistry master, alleging that the defendants ought to have seen that it was impossible for boys to take away dangerous chemicals, and that a special warning as to the nature of phosphorus ought to have been given. The defence contended that the plaintiff took the phosphorus when the master's attention was occupied with the object of carrying it home to amuse himself with it out of school; that he knew he was doing wrong; that any injury he might have suffered he had brought on himself by his own wrongful act; and that any boy who at the time of the accident had had as much previous instruction in chemistry as the plaintiff must have known of the dangerous nature of phosphorus.

Extract from Summing-up

DARLING J.: . . . It is not necessary for the defendants to disprove the plaintiff's case; the plaintiff must make it out himself. The only negligence relied on is an alleged failure to warn the boys; but there is evidence that warning was given two days before. The boy knew the phosphorus was always kept in a jar of water, and if he had thought at all must have known why. He has admitted that the year before another master had warned him particularly as to the danger of phosphorus, but he said he had quite forgotten that. The boy who worked with the plaintiff on the day of the accident told them that the plaintiff said to him, "You go and get another bit for the experiment; I want this for myself"; and it can be inferred that the plaintiff wanted to take the bit he had got home to play with.

Verdict and judgment for the defendants

(B) DUTY TO SECURE ATTENDANCE

57 Fox v. Burgess (1922) 86 J.P. 66

KING'S BENCH DIVISION

A parent who sends his child to school in circumstances in which he knows the child will be refused admittance has not caused the child to attend school.

Facts: The appellant, Mr George Charles Fox, was the father of a twelve-year-old girl who was a pupil at Portland Elementary School, Hove, until September 1921. In April of that year the child had refused to submit to a medical examination. An attendance order was obtained, but the child refused again in June and September. When the doctor put his hand on her shoulder she moved away, which was taken as indicating an intention to offer physical refusal. The medical examination was discontinued, and the child was expelled for persistent insubordination.

The appellant continued to send the girl to school from time to time, but she was refused admission, and a school attendance officer took out a summons for non-compliance with the school attendance order. The magistrates convicted the father, who appealed by way of case stated to the King's Bench Division.

Wedderburn (for the appellant): . . . Insubordination means a state of mind showing a disposition to refuse to submit to orders. Even if it was insubordination there was no power to expel the child. It was a very dangerous thing to extend too far the power of education authorities to use this roundabout method of compelling parents to do this, that, and the other thing. If too much latitude is given, a child who was idle over arithmetic might be expelled for persistent idleness, if not insubordination, and the education authority might say: "Until you whip your child sufficiently to make it industrious, we shall exclude it, and summon you for not sending it to school."

Extract from Judgment
AVORY J.: . . . Now it has been held in numerous cases that a parent who sends his child to a particular school, when he knows that in the circumstances the child will be refused admittance to that school, is not causing that child to attend school, and has no reasonable excuse for the child's non-attendance. The question in this case is whether the parent knew that in the circumstances the child would be refused admittance, and whether he had any reasonable excuse for the child's non-attendance.

It is quite clear in the facts found that he knew that the child had been reported for persistent insubordination and the child had been excluded from that school on the ground of persistent insubordination; and the child was refused admission on that ground. Therefore the parent knew quite well that it would be refused admission on that ground.

The remaining question is whether the child had been properly excluded from the school on that ground. Of course, if it can be shown that the child had not been properly excluded, then it cannot be said that the parent was guilty of not causing the child to attend when he sent it there. The insubordination for which the child had been reported was a refusal on the part of the child to allow itself to be examined by the medical officer under section 122 of the Children Act 1908. . . . The case finds that that was done under the guidance if not by the actual instructions of her father, the appellant.

Now it has been argued before us, and very ably argued, by Mr Wedderburn that although section 122 authorises the local education authority to direct the medical officer to make an examination for the purpose of discovering whether the child is dirty or in a verminous condition, this does not import or involve any obligation on the part of the child to submit to such an examination. . . . He suggests that the remedy, if a child refuses to submit, or if the parents instruct it not to submit, is for the school authorities to exercise their disciplinary powers upon the child so as to compel it to submit, and that that is the only remedy. Now, in my opinion, that would put upon the school authorities a responsibility which was never intended by this Act of Parliament. It would lead to scenes, possibly of violence and disorder in the school, and most probably to summonses in the police court, in every case where such disciplinary powers were attempted to be exercised alleging that an assault had been committed on the child. Such summonses are all too frequent at present when ordinary corrective discipline is applied in these schools. In my opinion, section 122 does import an obligation on the child to submit to that examination. And if a child refuses to submit under the instructions or guidance of its father, the father becomes responsible for the refusal. The child becomes insubordinate, and for this insubordination the father is himself responsible. If the child is excluded from the school in consequence of that insubordination, and the father knows that it is so excluded for the insubordination for which he is responsible, then, I think, he fails to cause the child to attend the school within the meaning of the statute, if he takes no steps to put the child in proper condition to be received into the school, and the only way in which he can put the child into a proper condition to be received into the school, is by removing his objection, and the child's objection to the examination: in other words, by allowing it to be examined by the medical officer, and, until he does that, he is himself preventing the proper attendance of the child at the school: in other words he is not causing it to attend within the meaning of the authorities. . . .

It might be sufficient to say that I concur in the judgment and their reasons, which were expressed very clearly by the justices, and are recorded in the special case. I see nothing in it to dissent from, and, for the reasons that I have given, I agree that judgment was right and the appeal ought to be dismissed.

SALTER J.: . . . I think that section 122 of the Children Act 1908 imposes . . . a duty to submit to the salutary examination which is there authorised. . . . This child had repeatedly and persistently refused to obey the lawful instructions of those in authority. It is quite unnecessary, I think, to consider whether the child's teacher or the medical officer or their representatives would have been authorised by law to overcome the child's resistance by force. Nor is it necessary now to consider whether the medical inspection and treatment, which are provided by education authorities in pursuance of the duty imposed upon them by section 13 of the Education (Administrative Provisions) Act 1907 is obligatory either upon the children or upon their parents. The material facts seem to me to be that this child had persistently refused to obey a lawful order with the result that she was a possible danger to the other scholars. . . . By proper use of his parental authority and control he [the father] could have induced her to obey the order given to her. If so, the effect is that the appellant sends the child instructed to disobey and to persist in disobedience to a lawful order. The question is whether in the circumstances the charge is made out that the order had unlawfully not been complied with without reasonable excuse. In my opinion it had. I do not propose to review the authorities which have been cited to us, but they appear to me to show that the law requires of parents of children who attend public elementary schools what I will venture to call a reasonable co-operation.

Judgment for the respondents

58 Chapman and others v. Essex County Council (1957) 55 L.G.R. 28

QUEEN'S BENCH DIVISION
Parents who neglect to perform their duty under section 36 of the Education Act 1944 have no right of action against the local education authority for failing to take steps under section 37 (1) to enforce the performance of that duty.

Facts: The infant plaintiff, Andrew Chapman, was born on February 14, 1947. The second and third plaintiffs were his father and mother.

In August 1951, the mother informed the South Essex divisional education office that she would like her son to attend an infants' school near his home from September 3. In the spring of the following year arrangements were made for the boy to be admitted to South Ockendon Infants' School on April 28, 1952, earlier admission being impossible because of overcrowding. The school was a mile or a mile and a quarter from the parents' home, and they asked for transport to be provided as the mother was suffering from poliomyelitis. This was not possible in the case of children who lived less than two miles from the school, but the divisional education officer, Mr Frost, devised a means of getting the boy to school.

The plaintiff was admitted on May 20, 1952, and attended regularly. Ten days later the headmistress, Miss Bush, was asked to ascertain how many of the children attending her school would wish to be transferred to the new Mardyke school which was to open on September 9 in the road in which the Chapmans lived. There was no evidence that Mr and Mrs Chapman were consulted, but their son's name was included in the transfer list, possibly because he lived so near to the new school.

On July 8, 1952, Andrew Chapman was knocked down after alighting from the school coach, and remained in hospital for eleven days. He was then discharged by his mother against the advice of the hospital authorities. In the meantime the parents made a claim against the Essex County Council, apparently on the ground that the boy should have been escorted across the road by the matron who accompanied the children on the coach. When collecting her son from the hospital, Mrs Chapman was accompanied by a neighbour with the idea that he should appear as her legal representative. The mother later alleged that the hospital authorities turned out her son as they did not wish to be involved in the action against the local education authority.

Dr Levy, advising the parents, thought that the boy would not be fit to return to school until the following Easter; but Dr Norris, on behalf of the insurance company, thought that he had probably been fit to go to school by November 1952.

At the beginning of the autumn term, 1952, Andrew Chapman's name was removed from the register of South Ockendon Infants' School as the headmistress thought that he would be transferred to Mardyke. The parents denied receiving a circular letter giving details of the opening of Mardyke

School, and also that they had received three visits from the school inquiry officer. The parents took no steps to secure the boy's admission to any school, and the local education authority took no steps to secure his attendance.

In or about May 1955, the father complained to a Member of Parliament that his son had been denied education by the defendants. The matter was taken up with the Ministry of Education and with the local education authority and on July 15, 1955, a school inquiry officer told the mother that her son should be presented at Mardyke school on the following Monday. The mother referred the officer to her solicitors, and on August 16, 1955, commenced an action against the local education authority. The boy had not been presented at any school since the date of the accident in July 1952.

By their action the parents claimed that the boy's education had been retarded, that the father had suffered expense in connection with educating the boy at home, and that the mother had lost earnings by remaining at home in order to provide such education. They alleged that the local education authority were under a statutory duty to provide suitable full-time education for children of school age and that, since Easter 1953, they had neglected and refused to do so.

The mother who was academically qualified had endeavoured to educate the child at home with such assistance as she could get from the British Broadcasting Corporation, and in August 1956, two months before the action came to trial, the boy was sent to live with a lady in Sussex.

Cur. adv. vult

Extracts from Judgment

HALLETT J.: The plaintiffs in this case claim damages against the defendants, the Essex County Council, by way of compensation for damage which they allege to have been caused to them by reason of a breach of statutory duty on the part of the defendants. . . .

By paragraph 2 of the statement of claim the plaintiffs allege that as such educational authority the defendants are under a statutory duty to provide for children, who have attained the age of five years and are resident in their county, full-time education suitable to their requirements. In response to a request for particulars showing how the alleged statutory duty arises, the plaintiffs alleged that it arises under section 8 (1), section 37 (1), section 61 (1) and section 76 of the Education Act 1944 (7 & Geo. 6, c. 31).

Section 8 (1) provides: "It shall be the duty of every local education authority to secure that there shall be available for their area sufficient schools (*a*) for providing primary education, that is to say, full-time education suitable to the requirements of junior pupils." This section was considered in the case of *Watt* v. *Kesteven County Council*,[1] where it was pointed out by Denning L.J. at pages 425 and 258, that the duty under that section is to make schools available, and by Parker L.J. at pp. 430 and 262, that the duty is merely to secure that facilities are available. It is therefore quite plain that the section

1. [1955] 1 Q.B. 408; 53 L.G.R. 254; see page 136, *supra*.

does not impose the duty alleged in paragraph 2 of the statement of claim. Moreover, it is quite plain from the same decision that, in so far as the plaintiffs sought to rely upon that section, their action for damages was unsustainable having regard to section 99 of the Act. It is therefore not surprising that counsel for the plaintiffs during the hearing stated and reiterated that he did not any longer rely upon section 8 to support the plaintiffs' case.

Section 61 (1) merely provides that the local education authority must not make a charge in respect of admission to any school maintained by it or in respect of the education provided in any such school. If as in the case of *Gateshead Union* v. *Durham County Council*,[2] a local education authority refused to allow children resident in their district to attend their public elementary school unless payment towards the expenses of maintaining the school in connection with the teaching of the children is made by the guardians or parents of the children, it may be that a claim for a declaration that the requirement of payment is not justified and for an injunction restraining the defendants from excluding the children would be sustainable, but no question of payment arises in the present case and section 61, therefore, affords no support whatever for the allegation contained in paragraph 2 of the statement of claim. It merely provides that the facilities afforded under section 8 must be afforded without charge, but it does nothing to make the local education authority provide more than free facilities.

Section 76 provides that pupils are to be educated in accordance with the wishes of their parents. Mr Gardiner has told me that in his experience this section has not proved to be of much practical assistance to parents, and he no doubt had particularly in mind his failure to profit from it in the case of *Watt* v. *Kesteven County Council*[3] already cited. The only relevance of this section for present purposes is as supporting the assertion made by the father and mother that they were entitled to educate their son at home if they chose to do so and could do so efficiently.

The plaintiffs can therefore only rely upon section 37 (1) as giving rise to the alleged statutory duty. They have not pleaded and cannot seek to rely upon section 37 (2), which is the only statutory provision under which the local education authority can serve a "school attendance order."

In my judgment, the whole of the plaintiffs' case is misconceived inasmuch as it ignores the provisions of section 36 of the Act and seeks to infer from section 37 (1) a duty which is not imposed by that subsection.

By section 36 it is made the duty of the parent of every child of compulsory school age to cause him to receive full-time education suitable to his age, ability, and aptitude, either by attendance at school or otherwise. The parent can discharge that obligation by sending the child to a school other than a school provided by the local education authority, or by arranging for the education of the child at home or by other private tuition; whereas the whole

2. [1918] 1 Ch. 146; see page 175, *infra*.
3. [1955] 1 Q.B. 408; see page 111, *supra*.

gist of the complaint here made on behalf of the father and mother is that the defendants did not take steps to compel the child to attend a school provided by the defendants.

In paragraph 3 of the statement of claim it is alleged that the infant plaintiff was at all material times ready, able and willing to receive the education referred to in paragraph 2.

I have been unable to find any evidence whatever that this is true of the infant plaintiff. Some children are undoubtedly willing to attend school, either because they like learning or because they enjoy the recreations at school or because they like the companionship of other children, but other children notoriously do not like to go to school. There is no evidence before me to show to which category the infant plaintiff belonged.

The case made for the father and mother, although not pleaded, has really been that their son was able to attend one of the defendants' schools and that they were ready and willing that he should do so.

The breach of statutory duty alleged in paragraph 3 of the statement of claim is that the defendants have since Easter 1953, failed, neglected and refused to provide the education specified in paragraph 2. There is no allegation that the defendants did not provide facilities for such education, and overwhelming evidence to the contrary. The only complaint in support of which there has been any evidence is that the defendants failed to take steps to compel the father and mother to avail themselves of those facilities.

I am quite satisfied, as will appear from my examination of the evidence, that in truth the father and mother, knowing quite well that such facilities were available, deliberately decided not to avail themselves of them; and I am far from satisfied that the defendants could have compelled them to do so. . . .

It is the fact that the defendants took no steps to compel the parents to send the boy to school and this is substantially the only relevant fact which the plaintiffs have succeeded in proving to my satisfaction. No section has been pleaded which, in my judgment, imposes upon a local education authority an obligation to compel children to attend one of their schools. The section which deals with the service of "a school attendance order," namely, section 37 (2), is, as already noted, not mentioned in the further and better particulars under paragraph 2 of the statement of claim; and I do not consider that the plaintiffs are entitled now to rely on it. In any case it only becomes applicable after (*a*) a notice has been served upon the parent under section 37 (1); (*b*) the parent has failed to satisfy the authority that the child is receiving the education specified in the notice; and (*c*) the authority is of the opinion that it is expedient that the child should attend school. I emphasise that even if the first two requirements are satisfied, it is still left to the authority to decide whether it is expedient that the child should attend school.

Where a discretion is left for any authority by a relevant statutory provision, it seems to me to be out of the question that any action for damages should lie against the authority for exercising the discretion in a particular way, provided always that the exercise has been made in good faith. The complaint made by the plaintiffs therefore resolves itself into a complaint of failure on the part of the defendants to serve a notice under section 37 (1).

It will be observed that at this stage the argument, and the only argument, for the plaintiffs appears to have travelled a very long way from the complaint and the only complaint made in the statement of claim, namely, that the defendants failed, neglected and refused to provide education for the infant plaintiff.

The decision whether an individual has a right to damages in respect of a breach of statutory duty depends on whether, upon a consideration of all the relevant indications, it appears that Parliament intended to give such a right. I shall discuss later the cases upon this subject, but I can say at once that it appears to me to be quite obvious that Parliament cannot have intended to confer on a parent who has deliberately failed to perform the duty imposed upon him by section 36, a right to sue the local education authority for damages on the ground that the local education authority has not taken steps whereby he might have been compelled to perform that duty.

I recognise, however, that preposterous as such a claim by the parents would be, in this case the boy affected is also a plaintiff and his rights must be separately and most carefully considered.

Apart from complaints which deserve no further attention, the first complaint made on behalf of the plaintiffs against the conduct of the defendants is that the boy's name was in substance marked off the South Ockendon School register before it was actually entered on the Mardyke School register. Regulation 4 of the Pupils Registration Regulations 1948[4] prescribes the grounds on which the name of a pupil is to be deleted from the admission register and it is not suggested on behalf of the defendants that any one of those grounds other than (a) (iii) existed for deleting the boy's name from the South Ockendon School register.

The defendants, however, rely upon section 80 (1) of the Act and the definition of "proprietor" contained in section 114 (1) as showing that responsibility for the due keeping of the admission register does not rest upon them. The definition of "proprietor" is that it means the person or body responsible for the management of the school. By section 80 (1) it is the proprietor of every school (that is to say, in the case of a county school or voluntary school the managers or governors thereof) who is required to keep, in accordance with regulations made by the Minister, a register containing the required particulars of all persons of compulsory age who are pupils of the school.

Both the South Ockendon School and the Mardyke School had managers and I do not accept as correct the contention of Mr Marlowe that as regards the keeping of the admission registers and other records relating to the children attending those schools the managers were servants or agents of the defendants. Accordingly, if it was wrong of Miss Bush to make the entry in

4. S.I. 1948 No. 2097.

the South Ockendon register that the boy had been transferred to Mardyke School, I am of opinion that this fact did not give any cause of action against the defendants. Miss Bush in fact sent the boy's record to Miss Flower, the headmistress of Mardyke School, and not unnaturally assumed that he would in fact be presented for registration at that school.

There would have been no possible complaint if the parents had presented the boy for registration at Mardyke School in time for the Autumn term, 1952, as they were asked to do or had so presented him at any subsequent time, as they knew perfectly well that they ought to have done, when he was again fit to attend school, unless they were discharging their duty under section 36 in some other manner. . . .

There are two methods which are usually employed for investigating the absence of children from school. If a school inquiry officer sees a child of apparent school age outside school during school hours, he may challenge the child; and it was through doing this in the case of Andrew Chapman that the senior school inquiry officer for the area, Mr Bartlett, exposed himself to the utterly scandalous and untrue allegations contained in a letter of September 19, 1955, written by the plaintiff's solicitors, of course on their instructions. The ordinary method, however, is for the headmistress to tell the school inquiry officer who attends at her school the names of absentee children about whom she thinks he should inquire; and, if any blame attaches to anybody for not causing Mr Turner to make inquiries about the boy, I think that it rests upon Miss Flower, although, having regard to the information which she had received, I do not think that she was in truth blameworthy.

I should point out that school inquiry officers have to exercise tact in performing their functions. If a parent claims that he or she is efficiently educating the child at home and asserts a right to do so and appears to be the sort of person who may well be doing so, the school inquiry officer may not feel it necessary or wise to challenge the claim.

Mr Marlowe, however, contends (*a*) that action should have been taken by the defendants under section 37 (1); and (*b*) that, if it had been taken, the defendants would have been able to serve a school attendance order under section 37 (2); and (*c*) that their failure to do so means that they were failing to provide education for the boy as alleged in the statement of claim.

In my judgment all these three propositions are ill-founded. Under section 36 it is the duty of the parent to cause the child to receive proper education. Under section 37 (1), if it appears to a local education authority that a parent is failing to perform that duty, it becomes the duty of the authority to serve the notice there specified.

The period complained of in the particulars under paragraph 3 (*b*) of the statement of claim is between Easter 1953, and July 1955. There is no evidence to satisfy me that it did appear to the defendants at any material time during that period that the parents were failing to perform the duty imposed on them by section 36.

Mr Marlowe contends that if the defendants had made appropriate inquiries

the necessity for a notice under section 37 (1) would have appeared to them;
but I am by no means satisfied that this is the case, nor am I satisfied that, if
such a notice had been served, the parents would have failed to satisfy the
authority in accordance with the requirements of that notice.

The father stated in evidence that his wife "is academically qualified" and
I myself formed the opinion that, whatever her record may have been, she is
a very intelligent and apparently well-educated woman. The steps taken by her
in connection with the child's education appear from correspondence with the
British Broadcasting Corporation; and it is only right that I should say that, so
far as I can judge, she was doing her best to give the child efficient full-time
education suitable to his age, ability and aptitude. The education provided by
parents need not be as good as the education which would be provided at a
public elementary school, provided that it is efficient (see *Bevan* v. *Shears.*[5])

In my judgment, no breach of the duty imposed upon the defendants by
section 37 (1) has been established.

Assuming I am wrong in holding that the alleged statutory duty of the
defendants has not been established and that I am also wrong in holding that
the alleged breach of that duty has not been established, the question next
arises as to what damages, if any, have been thereby caused to each of the
plaintiffs. I have already mentioned that the mother, whilst remaining a party
to the action, has expressly abandoned any claim to damages. As regards the
father, the claim which was originally £75 9s. but was reduced in the further
and better particulars to £62 2s. 4d., is in respect of expenses which he is
alleged to have incurred by reason of his son not attending school, and, since
that non-attendance, on the facts as I find them, was due either to the fault
of the parents in failing to send the child to school or to the parents electing
to educate the child at home, it is clear that these items cannot be recovered
by way of damages from the defendants.

As regards the infant plaintiff, the case made is that his education has been
retarded and his future prospects thereby impaired by the alleged breach of
duty on the part of the defendants. I have carefully considered the medical
evidence and the evidence of the lady with whom he is now living. It seems
that the boy is undoubtedly below average as regards reading, but it is
notorious that some children have more aptitude for reading than others and
take to it at an earlier age. On the other hand, his "general knowledge" is above
the average and he does not seem to have been markedly backward in other
subjects. Moreover, there is evidence that his mother, except for the purpose
of this case, regarded his standard of education as satisfactory. In her evidence,
she told me that she made every effort that she possibly could to see that the
boy was kept up to standard and that her efforts in fact kept the child up to
a fair standard. The nature of those efforts, as I have already said, appears
from the correspondence.

I think that what the boy really has lacked hitherto has been not so much
education in the narrow sense of learning the three Rs, as the companionship

5. [1911] 2 K.B. 936.

with other children which would have been so very desirable. His parents' conduct made him far too dependent on his mother. In this connection, it is only fair to mention that the mother did cause the boy to join a Cub pack, although his attendance there was discontinued when she made scurrilous allegations with regard to money collected by the lady who ran the pack. I have already said that I approve of the steps which have now been taken to educate him down in Sussex, which are involving no expense to his parents, and I have no reason for supposing that those steps will not result in his complete recovery from such ill effects as he may have sustained from the conduct of his parents in withholding him from school.

There remains the final question whether in any event an action for damages can be sustained for the alleged breach of the alleged statutory duty. I have recognised throughout that, if the answer to this question be in the negative, it would be sufficient by itself to dispose of this action; but, having regard to the fact that the defendants are a public authority, who have been vehemently attacked by the parents, I was clearly of opinion that it would be undesirable and, indeed, unfair for me to refrain from investigating and stating in my judgment the merits of the complaints made against the defendants.

The cases upon the question whether an action for damages lies in respect of a breach of statutory duty are very numerous, but they have been reviewed and the principles applicable authoritatively stated so very recently that counsel have rightly not thought it necessary to call my attention to more than a few of them.

It is customary in such cases to begin by referring to the general principle laid down in 1831 in *Doe d. Rochester* v. *Bridges*[6] at page 859, which is as follows: "Where an Act creates an obligation, and enforces the performance in a specified manner, we take it to be a general rule that performance cannot be enforced in any other manner." . . .

In the present case, a remedy for a failure by a local educational authority to discharge any duty imposed by the Act is provided in section 99 (1), and it would seem to be a most effective remedy.

As I have already mentioned, the parents did in fact make a complaint to the Minister, and the Minister took the action with regard to it which is revealed by the correspondence.

Another indication is whether it appears from the nature and terms of the statute as a whole that the duty in question is imposed for the benefit of particular persons, although it may be imposed for the benefit of the community in general.

Earlier and later examples of an affirmative answer are to be found in the cases of *Groves* v. *Lord Wimborne*[7] and *Monk* v. *Warbey*.[8] . . .

Finally, there is *Watt* v. *Kesteven County Council*.[9] In that case the plaintiff,

6. (1831) 1 B. & Ad. 847.
7. [1898] 2 Q.B. 402.
8. [1935] 1 K.B. 75.
9. [1955] 1 Q.B. 408; 53 L.G.R. 254, see page 136, *supra*.

a Roman Catholic, sought a declaration that the defendants were under a statutory obligation to provide secondary grammar school education at certain schools for his twin sons and an order of mandamus directing them to carry out their duty and repayment to him of sums paid by him in tuition fees. Once more the decisions, starting with *Doe d. Rochester* v. *Bridges*[10] were reviewed by my brother Ormerod at first instance and on appeal by Denning L.J. and Parker L.J. with whose judgments Birkett L.J. agreed. The Court of Appeal decided that the duty alleged did not exist and Denning L.J. at pages 425 and 258 added: "In view of *Gateshead Union* v. *Durham County Council*[11] I would not like to say that there can be no cases under the Act in which an action would lie, but I do not think an action lies in this case. It is plain to me that the duty under section 8 (to make schools available) can only be enforced by the Minister under section 99 and not by action at law." Parker L.J. said at pages 430 and 262: "If, as I think, the duty under section 8 is merely to secure that facilities are available, the only remedy for a breach of that duty would be by action by the Minister on complaint to the Minister under section 99."

If this be the position as regards a failure to secure that the facilities are available, I can see no reason why there should be a different position as regards a failure to take the administrative steps laid down in section 37 (1).

To summarise, I have come to the conclusion that the plaintiffs have failed to establish either, (*a*) the existence of the alleged duty; or (*b*) the commission of alleged breach of duty; or (*c*) that they or any of them have suffered the alleged or any damages as a result of such breach; or (*d*) that a right of action for damages in respect of such breach exists having regard to the nature of such breach and the provisions of the relevant statute. For each of these four reasons, which are cumulative, I have come to the conclusion that this action must fail and that there should be judgment for the defendants.

Judgment for the defendants

59 Jones v. Rowland (1899) 80 L.T. 630

QUEEN'S BENCH DIVISION
Offering a child for attendance at a school when it is known that admittance will be refused does not constitute an attendance by the child, nor does it constitute a reasonable defence to a charge of failing to cause the child to receive statutory education.

Facts: The appellant was the father of a ten-year-old child who, up to May 1898, had attended St Giles' School, Shrewsbury, which was a voluntary public elementary school. The managers had then refused further attendance and this refusal had been confirmed by the Education Department. The father was given notice of the managers' refusal, and was informed by the Shrews-

10. (1831) 1 B. & Ad. 847.
11. [1918] 1 Ch. 146; see page 175, *infra*.

bury School Board that he must send his child to another school under a by-
law which provided that every child of not less than five nor more than
fourteen years of age must attend school unless there was a reasonable cause
for non-attendance. The school board notified the father of other schools
within two miles of his home which would receive the child.

The appellant declined to send his child to any other school, and between
May and September he sent his child on several occasions to St Giles' School,
where admittance was refused. The respondent laid an information against the
parent for failing to observe the by-laws.

Before the justices the defendant contended that, as the child had been
offered and refused at St Giles' School, such offering amounted to an attendance, and was a good defence; and further that, until the matter had been
fully considered by the Education Department, the father had a reasonable
excuse.

For the authority it was alleged that the offering of the child did not
constitute an attendance, that the matter had been fully considered by the
Education Department, that the defendant had not caused his child to attend
any certified efficient school, and that he had no reasonable excuse.

The justices held that the defendant knew that the child would be refused,
that mere offering did not constitute an attendance, and that no reasonable
excuse had been proved. They accordingly convicted.

The father appealed to the Divisional Court of the Queen's Bench Division
by way of case stated.

Extract from Judgment
DARLING J.: This appeal must be dismissed. The justices were quite right.
No doubt they thought the man quite honest, and so the penalty was small.

Appeal dismissed

60 Walker v. Cummings (1912) 107 L.T. 304

KING'S BENCH DIVISION
*A parent knowingly sending a child to school in such condition that admission will
be refused has not caused the child to attend school.*

Facts: The father of Ivy Cummings, a child under the age of thirteen, was
charged before the Andover justices for failing to cause his daughter to attend
school without reasonable excuse.

On September 27, 1911, the child was refused admission by the headmistress on the ground that there were vermin in the child's hair. She was
examined on six occasions between July 21, 1910, and October 16, 1911, by
the applicant, an assistant county medical officer of health and a school
attendance officer, and on each occasion her head was infested with live vermin
or the eggs thereof. She was refused admission on these occasions, and it was
stated that the means of redressing the situation were within the parents'

reach, *i.e.* in a week by the use of soap, paraffin, and water or, if the hair were cut short, within twenty-four hours. The parent contended that, since the child was presented for school on the day named, he could not be convicted.

The magistrates held that some attempt had been made to cleanse the child, but the means employed were not the best and were not sustained. They believed that the child's condition on September 27, 1911, was not such as to prevent it from receiving instruction, nor to prevent other children from receiving instruction in her company although it was undesirable that she should be in contact with clean children. They were of opinion that the refusal to admit prevented them from convicting.

The informant appealed. The point in issue was whether an unavoidable cause, which it was within the power of the parent to remove, was an unavoidable cause within the by-laws made under the Education Acts 1870 to 1902.

Extract from Judgment

LORD ALVERSTONE C.J.: In our opinion this case is covered by the authority of the cases which have been cited. If I had thought that it must be taken that the parent did not know of the child's verminous condition I should have doubted whether we ought to have interfered; but the case states that the respondent had used some means, but not the best, to cleanse the child and the attempts were not sustained as they might have been, and were never entirely successful, and the justices also say that the condition could have been cured by the methods advocated by the appellant.

It seems to me that that establishes two things: first, that the respondent knew that the child had been refused admission to the school because of its verminous condition; and, secondly, that the parent had ineffectually tried to cure it.

I am of opinion that if a parent sends a child to school in a verminous condition when he is able to cleanse it, that is not causing it to attend school within the meaning of the by-laws. The words "cause such child to attend school" have reference to the child's receiving instruction; and I am glad that it is recognised that there is no obligation on the teacher to admit a verminous child to the school, because of the anxiety that would be caused thereby to the parents of clean children attending the school. If a parent sends a child in such a condition that the child will be refused admission, the fact that the child is refused admission does not amount to the child's being prevented from attending school by an unavoidable cause. The cases cited show that sending the child to school in such a condition that the child will not be capable of receiving instruction, or in such a condition that it will not be admitted, is not causing the child to attend school.

I think, therefore, that the magistrates ought to have entertained this case, and that the case must go back to them to be dealt with.

Appeal allowed. Case remitted to the justices with a
direction to convict

61 Spiers *v*. Warrington Corporation [1954] 1 Q.B. 61

QUEEN'S BENCH DIVISION

Sending a child to school dressed in such a way that it is known that admission will be refused as a matter of discipline constitutes failure to attend school.

Facts: Eva Spiers, then aged 13, was a registered pupil of Richard Fairclough Girls' Secondary Modern School, Warrington. She had had attacks of rheumatic fever in 1948 and 1950. On medical advice that she should be kept warm, the parent sent her to school in slacks. The headmistress considered slacks unseemly and unhygienic for girls, particularly adolescent girls. Nevertheless, the girl was told that the school rule against slacks would be waived in her case if she produced a medical certificate that they were necessary. Alternatively the girl could be examined by the school medical officer. No medical note was produced, and the girl was not sent to the school clinic. Thereafter, on each occasion that she appeared at school wearing slacks, she was sent home.

The father was convicted under the Education Act 1944, s. 39 (1), in that his daughter failed to attend school regularly between October 13 and December 3, 1952. He was fined ten shillings by the Warrington Justices, but the conviction was quashed by the West Derby Quarter Sessions Appeal Committee. The Corporation appealed, by way of case stated, to the Divisional Court of the Queen's Bench Division.

Extract from Judgment

LORD GODDARD C.J.: . . . The case now comes before us really upon a point of law whether or not the parents had the right to say that they were not going to send the child dressed in a particular way or whether the headmistress was entitled to say she was not going to admit the child in that way, and if she did, what was the effect upon her.

Referring first to the old authorities which are firmly established, *Saunders* v. *Richardson*[1] and *Fox* v. *Burgess*[2] decided that if a parent sent a child to school in circumstances when he knew that the child would not be admitted, he was committing an offence because he was not causing the child to attend school regularly. . . .

We are not deciding this case as a social matter; it is simply a point of law. [His Lordship read section 17 (1) and (3) and continued:] Obviously a head teacher must be responsible for the discipline of the school and, indeed, in this particular case the articles provide that the headmistress "shall control the internal organisation, management and discipline of the school . . . shall exercise supervision over the teaching and non-teaching staff, and shall have the power of suspending pupils from attendance for any cause which she

1. (1881) 7 Q.B.D. 388.
2. [1922] 1 K.B. 623, see page 151, *supra*.

considers adequate, but on suspending any pupil she shall forthwith report the case to the governors, who shall consult the local education authority." I quote the last part about the time of suspension simply because quarter sessions seem to have thought that the headmistress in this case was suspending the girl and ought to have reported it to the governors, who should then consult the local education authority. In point of fact, I think that that is a false point. The headmistress did not suspend this child at all. She was always perfectly willing to take her in; all that she wanted was that she should be properly dressed. Suspending is refusing to admit to the school; in this case the headmistress was perfectly willing to admit the girl but was insisting that she be properly dressed.

The next thing to which I must call attention—and this is where I think that quarter sessions have really been misled and have gone wrong—is section 39 of the Education Act of 1944, which is now the governing provision. [His Lordship read section 39 (1) and (2) and continued:] In 1929 *London County Council* v. *Maher*,[3] a case under the then Education Act, the Education Act 1921 was decided. By section 49 of the Act of 1921: "Any of the following reasons shall be a reasonable excuse for the purposes of this Act and the bye-laws made thereunder, namely: – (a) That the child had been prevented from attending school by sickness or any unavoidable cause; (b) That there is no public elementary school open which the child can attend within such distance, not exceeding three miles, measured according to the nearest road from the residence of the child, as the byelaws may prescribe; (c) In the case of non-compliance with a byelaw requiring a parent to cause his child to attend school, that the child is under efficient instruction in some other manner." In *London County Council* v. *Maher*[4] the parents set up as an excuse for not sending the child to school a matter which was not covered by either sub-paragraphs (a) (b) or (c), and the justices who heard the summons found that the excuse which the father had set up was a reasonable one. When the matter came up on case stated, the court pointed out that section 49 did not appear to be, if I may put it compendiously, exhaustive: it gave three excuses which the court must accept as defences, but it left it open to a parent to show other causes which the court might consider reasonable or not. It was held that if the justices below had found that the excuse was reasonable the court could not go behind that finding. That is in accordance with the well-known rule of law on which this court always proceeds, that the facts are not for us. We are bound by the facts found by the justices, and they held that under the then law it was open to the justices to find any matters as a reasonable excuse if they liked.

I think that quarter sessions approached this case bearing in mind *Maher's* case,[4] but the law has been altered, and the Education Act of 1944, be it noted, is not a consolidating Act. The long title to the Act is: "An Act to reform the law relating to education in England and Wales," and one of the changes

3. [1929] 2 K.B. 97.
4. [1929] 2 K.B. 97.

which have been made is that section 39 of the Act of 1944 has been substituted for section 49 of the Act of 1921. It appears to the court highly probable that the reason for that was that it was considered desirable to abolish the decision in *Maher's* case[4] and to substitute for it a new section which would not leave it open to justices to find any reasonable excuse parents might set up, but to confine the excuses for not sending a child to school to the reasons set out in subsection (2) (*a*), (*b*) and (*c*). That is the only construction which this court feels able to put upon section 39 (2).

We were reminded of *Jenkins* v. *Howells*,[5] which was heard in 1949, and in which I was sitting with Oliver and Cassels JJ. I do not hesitate to say that if it had been open to us there to find that there was a reasonable excuse for not sending the child to school, we would have found it. It was a very hard case, but we felt that the statute was too strong; we could not go into the question of reasonableness.

Quarter sessions came to the conclusion that the defendant and his wife were acting reasonably in that they were acting in the interest of their child, whose health and life they were seeking to safeguard, and that the case was not made out. They have attached to the case a note of their judgment, from which it is perfectly obvious that they thought that the headmistress was acting reasonably in insisting on uniformity of dress among the girl pupils of the school, but we are not here to balance which is the more reasonable or which is the more desirable. The headmistress obviously has the right and the power to prescribe the discipline for the school, and in saying that a girl must come to school not wearing a particular costume unless there is a compelling reason of health, surely she is only acting in a matter of discipline, and a matter which must be within the competence of the headmaster or headmistress of any school, whether it is one of the great public schools or a county secondary or county primary school. There must be somebody to keep discipline, and of course that person is the headmistress.

If it was a matter of whether parents reasonably believed that it was in the interests of the child to wear some particular dress, as I pointed out in the course of the argument, not in the least wanting to treat this matter as anything but perfectly serious, there are people in this country who believe, and honestly believe, that at any rate in the summer it is desirable in the interests of their children that they should wear no clothes at all except what the barest necessities of decency require. One sees in London squares and certainly in the country little children running about with no clothes except bathing slips, and one cannot suppose that a headmistress or headmaster would be obliged to admit children to school wearing no clothes at all. Yet if this view put forward to quarter sessions were right, provided that the parents honestly held that belief and one could not say that it was unreasonable for the health of the child to be exposed to sunlight or wear no clothes in the summer, the headmaster or headmistress would be obliged to take any little boy or

5. [1949] 2 K.B. 218; 65 T.L.R. 305; [1949] 1 All E.R. 942; see page 168, *infra*.

girl who came to school with no clothes: it would be a perfectly absurd position.

In my opinion the reason why we must reverse the decision of quarter sessions and restore the decision of the justices is because quarter sessions approached this matter from the wrong angle. They thought, perhaps following Maher's case,[6] that it was simply a question whether the parents had a reasonable ground for doing what they did. On the other hand, that is not the question. The question is: was the headmistress in communicating her refusal to allow the girl to come to school in this way acting within her rights? We hold that she was not only within her rights, but that it was her duty; and the parent, knowing that the child would not be admitted, and insisting on her being dressed in this way, brought himself within the reasoning in Saunders v. Richardson[7] and accordingly committed an offence.

For these reasons I would allow the appeal.

Appeal allowed; conviction restored

[NOTE: This is now generally recognised as the leading case where children are presented for school dressed in such a way that admission is refused as a matter of discipline. The Times of July 8, 1966, reported a conviction by the Ascot justices of the parent of a boy who was refused admission because of his long hair. The parents were told that the length of his hair prevented the boy from taking part in many school activities. Imposing the maximum fine of £1, the chairman told the defendant: "The headmaster depends on discipline and would be a laughing stock if he did not exercise his rights. We think you as a father should exercise more control over this boy in future at home."

It is interesting to note the distinction drawn by the Lord Chief Justice between suspending a pupil (in which case the matter is reported to the managers or governors) and excluding a child whilst still being willing to receive it if a reasonable and lawful condition is fulfilled (in which case, his Lordship implied, it is not necessary to report the matter to the managers or governors.)]

62 Jenkins v. Howells [1949] 2 K.B. 218

KING'S BENCH DIVISION
"*Unavoidable cause*" of failure to attend school must, like sickness, be in relation to the child.

Facts: The appellant was a school attendance officer, who appealed, by way of case stated, against the dismissal of an information by the Carmarthenshire justices sitting at Newcastle Emligh.

The justices had dismissed a charge brought against Mrs Hannah Howells because her fourteen-year-old daughter had failed to attend Newcastle Emligh Voluntary Primary School regularly between July 15 and 27, 1948, contrary to the Education Act 1944, s. 39. Between September 6, 1947, and July 31, 1948, the child missed 225 out of 390 sessions. The school was two-and-a-half miles from her home.

6. [1929] 2 K.B. 97.
7. (1881) 7 Q.B.D. 388.

Mrs Howells had been suffering from chronic heart disease for some years. She had been forbidden by her doctor to perform household duties. At the date of the hearing of the information she was awaiting admission to hospital for an eye operation. She had a farm of 260 acres worked by three unmarried sons. There was no one on the farm to do household duties except Mrs Howells and her daughter, and Mrs Howells had tried, without success, to obtain domestic help.

It was contended for Mrs Howells that no offence had in the circumstances been committed.

The justices held that the facts proved constituted an "unavoidable cause" within the meaning of section 39 (2) (*a*) of the Education Act 1944.

Extract from Judgment

LORD GODDARD C.J.: I do not wonder that the justices felt considerable sympathy with the respondent in this case. They dismissed the information because they came to the conclusion that the child had not attended the school by reason of "an unavoidable cause," within the meaning of section 39 (2) (*a*) of the Education Act 1944. This court feels that they are bound to say that there was no evidence on which the justices could so find, because the child had been continuously away from school. Out of 390 attendances she had missed 225. We think that the words "unavoidable cause" must be construed in relation to the child. By section 39 (2) (*a*), it is a defence to a prosecution under that section that the child only failed to attend school "by reason of sickness or any unavoidable cause." In my opinion, "sickness" in that paragraph must mean the sickness of the child. An "unavoidable cause" must be an unavoidable cause which actually affects the child. The alleged "unavoidable cause" in the present case was one which really affected the mother and not the child.

Parliament has not seen fit to provide that what may be called "family responsibilities" or "duties" can be relied on as an excuse for a child not attending school. If we allowed the distressing facts of the present case to afford a defence to a prosecution under section 39, it would mean that this child would not go to school at all and that the mother would keep the child at home all the time. I think that we are bound to hold that an "unavoidable cause" within the meaning of subsection (2) (*a*) of section 39 must mean an unavoidable cause which actually affects the child's attendance, such as sudden serious illness or some emergency of that kind. If her parents' house were burnt down that would be properly regarded, at any rate for a day or two, as an "unavoidable cause." But I think "unavoidable cause" must be read in the present context as meaning something in the nature of an emergency. In the present circumstances I think that we are bound to hold that there was no evidence of an "unavoidable cause" within the meaning of section 39 (2) (*a*), and that the case must therefore go back to the justices with a direction that the offence was proved.

Appeal allowed. Case remitted to the justices

G

63 Neave v. Hills (1919) 121 L.T. 225

KING'S BENCH DIVISION

Keeping a child at home to look after younger children during the mother's absence at work does not constitute a reasonable excuse for failure to attend school.

Facts: The appellant, John Neave, had been convicted by the justices for that, being the parent of William Neave, aged twelve, he unlawfully neglected to cause the child to attend a public elementary school, without reasonable excuse and after the expiration of due notice.

On appeal, by way of case stated, it was proved or admitted that the child was a registered pupil at Henny public elementary school in the county of Essex, and that the school was within two miles of his home. He was absent from school on November 15, 1918, the date of expiry of the notice, and on other subsequent days.

The appellant was an agricultural labourer earning 38s. a week, and had seven children of whom the eldest, a boy of fourteen, earned 14s. a week. None of the other children was earning, or capable of earning anything. The appellant's rent was 2s. 6d. a week, and he paid over three pounds a week for food, clothing, etc. In order to supplement the family's earnings the mother worked on the land, and William Neave was kept at home to look after the younger children in his mother's absence.

The father's solicitor contended before the justices that the facts constituted a reasonable excuse within the terms of the by-law, and the decisions in *Mather* v. *Lawrence*[1] and in *London School Board* v. *Duggan.*[2] The by-law provided that the following should be deemed reasonable excuses for failure to attend school:

(a) that the child was under efficient instruction in some other manner;

(b) that the child had been attending school by sickness or any unavoidable cause;

(c) that there was no public elementary school open which the child could attend within two miles measured according to the nearest road, from the residence of such child.

The justices accepted the mother's evidence as to the weekly earnings and expenditure of the family, but held that the facts did not constitute in law a reasonable excuse. They convicted the appellant and fined him 10s.

On appeal it was contended for the appellant that the child was prevented from attending school by unavoidable cause. In *London School Board* v. *Duggan*[3] it had been held a reasonable excuse that a boy was earning money when his parents were unable to maintain the other children without that assistance.

1. [1899] 1 Q.B. 1000.
2. (1884) 13 Q.B.D. 176.
3. (1884) 13 Q.B.D. 176.

Judgment

BRAY J.: In this case justices have convicted the appellant of not causing his boy, aged twelve, to attend a public elementary school without reasonable excuse. The appellant's answer to the charge was that he had a reasonable excuse, and I entirely agree that there may be other reasonable excuses within the meaning of the by-law besides the three reasons therein specified. The question the justices ask is whether, upon the statements of fact in the case, they came to a correct decision in point of law. The appellant's contention before the justices was that the facts disclosed in the evidence before them constituted a reasonable excuse, and *Mather* v. *Lawrence*[4] and *London School Board* v. *Duggan*[5] were cited in support of it. *Mather* v. *Lawrence*,[6] however, was a decision upon section 6 of the Elementary Education Act 1876 relating to the employment of a child by parents for purposes of gain, and is hardly in point here. It seems to me, however, that there is nothing in the case before us to show that it was necessary for this boy to be kept at home to look after the younger children, or that the parents could not have got someone else to do so. This apparently was the view taken by the justices, notwithstanding their acceptance of the evidence of the appellant's wife as to weekly earnings and expenditure on the family. I cannot say that the justices, holding as they did—namely, that upon the evidence before them the facts did not in law constitute a reasonable excuse—were wrong in law, and, in my opinion, the appeal must be dismissed.

Appeal dismissed

64   Osborne *v.* Martin (1927) 138 L.T. 268

KING'S BENCH DIVISION
A parent may not withdraw his child from school for one hour a week to attend private lessons.

Facts: Hilda Martin was a twelve-year-old pupil at Merle Common Council School, Oxted, Surrey. By-law 2 of the by-laws made by the Surrey Education Committee provided that:

"The parent of every child of not less than five nor more than fourteen years of age shall cause such child to attend school unless there be a reasonable excuse for non-attendance. Any of the following reasons shall be a reasonable excuse—namely: (*a*) that the child is under efficient instruction in some other manner. . . . "

The morning session at the school began at 9 a.m. and ended at 12 noon, the time from 9 a.m. to 9.40 a.m. being devoted to scripture, and the remainder to secular subjects. The girl's father was in the habit of withdrawing her at

4. [1899] 1 Q.B. 1000.
5. (1884) 13 Q.B.D. 176.
6. [1899] 1 Q.B. 1000.

11 a.m. on Thursdays for a pianoforte lesson from a private teacher about five miles away. It was hoped that the child would ultimately become a professional musician. There was no music teacher at Merle Common able to give the girl music lessons out of school hours. The lessons she missed were English and class singing, which were subjects approved by the Board of Education; pianoforte playing was not so approved.

On March 24, 1927, the headmistress issued a certificate that Hilda Martin attended school 170 times out of 185 from October 11, 1926, to March 24, 1927, and that she was absent on the morning of Thursday March 24, 1927. As the girl had not completed two hours' secular instruction, the attendance mark was cancelled in accordance with the regulations when she was withdrawn at 11 a.m.

The father was summoned by the local education authority, but the justices dismissed the information. The local education authority appealed by way of case stated, contending that instruction in pianoforte playing was not "efficient instruction in some other manner." The respondent claimed that it was.

Extract from Judgment

LORD HEWART C.J.: This is a very clear case. The words "under efficient instruction in some other manner" mean that the whole instruction of the child is being given in some other manner. It was never intended that a child attending the school might be withdrawn for this or that hour to attend a lesson thought by the parent to be more useful or possibly in the long run more remunerative. The time-table and discipline of a school could be reduced to chaos if that were permissible. In my opinion the justices misdirected themselves. They evidently decided as they did because they thought it a good thing that this child should have music lessons, but upon the facts of this case there was no evidence upon which they could decide that she was under efficient instruction in some other manner.

Appeal allowed. Case remitted to justices
with direction to convict

(C) WHAT CONSTITUTES FULL-TIME ATTENDANCE
65 Hinchley v. Rankin [1961] 1 All E.R. 692

QUEEN'S BENCH DIVISION

The regular attendance of a child at school is regular attendance for the times prescribed by the local education authority charged with the duty of providing the education. Absence at the time that the register is closed is a failure in regular attendance.

Facts: The father of Stephen Hinchley, aged six, was convicted and fined ten shillings by the Birmingham justices for that the boy had failed to attend school regularly, contrary to the Education Act 1944, ss. 39 (1) and 40 (1).

The defendant appealed to quarter sessions under section 39 (2) (*a*) of the 1944 Act which provides that no proceedings shall be taken if a child is prevented from attending school by sickness or other unavoidable cause. On behalf of the corporation it was said that in a period of six weeks the boy had been present twenty-seven times and absent twenty-nine. To be recorded as present a child must be in school by 9.45 a.m., and a certificate was put in showing the attendance record, and signed by the head of the school.

CRIPPS, Q.C. (*Assistant Recorder*): What would happen if a child arrived at ten o'clock every day for a month?

Witness: He would be marked absent for those sessions.

CRIPPS: Do you know—and it may well be that you do not know—of any statutory regulation that entitles a particular school to decide on a time for closing the register?

Witness: No, but technically the register should be closed at the time of the school assembly.

CRIPPS: The certificate relates to a non-existent section of the Act. It is headed as being issued under the Education Act 1944, s. 95 (*c*). Presumably what is meant is section 95, subsection (2) (*c*). When a certificate is issued under a section of the Act and may be accepted in court as evidence, it is, to say the least, undesirable that it should be expressed in terms of a section of the Act which does not exist. It does not pre-dispose the court to think that the certificate has any great value. . . .

When this certificate says "weekly attendances," it means in fact "weekly attendances by 9.45 a.m." I don't know if there is any authority under the Act whereby a local education authority is entitled to limit weekly attendances by failure to attend by a certain time. . . . From the evidence of the certificate, supplemented by the oral evidence (which in fact qualifies the certificate) it seems to me that the present position is that unless there is any authority under the Act to limit attendances to attendances by a certain time the first point of this case—failure to attend school—has not been established.

In view of the evidence of Mr Macknell,[1] there is not sufficient evidence before the court of non-attendance to require an answer from the appellant. What there is, is evidence of failure to attend punctually. It might well be that on each of the occasions when there was failure to attend punctually, there was no attendance at all. I am giving my decision on a purely technical point, without going into the merits of the case at all.

This certificate ought clearly not to be used more often than is necessary without correction of the misprint, and it ought not to be used before a court on the system on which it is at present being used. This certificate sets out to show a fact which I now know is not the fact at all. Used in its present form, without an explanation by an education officer, it is positively deceptive, and a dangerous document, one which I should have thought it quite improper for

1. The Welfare and School Attendance Officer.

the education committee to put forward in a court. It is in my view dangerous to have a certificate which purports to show one thing, and which will be accepted as evidence, unless there is oral evidence to establish that the certificate actually sets out what it sets out to prove.

The Assistant Recorder allowed the appeal without calling on the appellant. The Corporation appealed, by way of case stated, to a Divisional Court of the Queen's Bench Division.

Extracts from Judgment

LORD PARKER C.J.: The facts are in a very short compass. It appeared that before the assistant recorder a certificate was put in, which is evidence under section 95 (2) (c) of the Education Act 1944, showing that during the six weeks from February 15 to March 25, 1960, this boy Stephen was present twenty-seven times and absent twenty-nine times. He should have been there on each day by 9.15 a.m. which was the morning session laid down by the said school.

Before the assistant recorder, however, Albert William Macknell a school attendance and welfare officer, who handed in the certificate, gave it in evidence that the attendance register is closed at 9.45 a.m., and that pupils arriving on any day after that time would be marked absent, and shown as non-attendants for those sessions. The assistant recorder took the point that the certificate was no evidence at all of non-attendance, but might merely be evidence of unpunctuality—in other words that on all the twenty-nine times when the boy had been absent he might have arrived at 9.46 a.m. The assistant recorder took this point of his own motion; having come to the conclusion that the certificate was no evidence at all he held that no prima facie case had been made out, and he allowed the appeal.

For my part, I feel that that certificate, even on the view taken by the assistant recorder, was at any rate some evidence which called for an answer, but the real point for decision in this court is whether the construction which the assistant recorder put on the words of section 39 (1) "fails to attend regularly" was correct. It is to be observed that under the scheme laid down in the Act, it is the local authority whose duty it is to provide secular instruction, and for that purpose, as is laid down in section 23 (3), they have the power to determine the times at which the school sessions shall begin and end on any day, to determine the times at which the school term shall begin and end, and so on. Pursuant to their powers, 9.15 a.m. apparently was fixed as the commencement of the morning session. . . .

It seems to me that counsel for the appellant's argument must be right, and that when the Education Act 1944 is providing for full-time education and regular attendance for that purpose, it must be attendance for the periods prescribed by the person on whom the duty to provide the education is laid. Looked at in that way, even if this boy had regularly arrived only a minute or two late, albeit he was only a few minutes after 9.45 a.m., there would be a failure to attend regularly within the meaning of the Act. I used the word "late" to mean after the time when the attendance register was closed at 9.45 a.m. because the boy should have been there by 9.15 a.m.

It follows that the assistant recorder was wrong in saying that there was no prima facie case to be answered. The case should go back to him with an intimation that he should hear the evidence for the father and boy, who of course have a right to challenge the accuracy of the attendance register, and who have the right to put forward the various excuses open to them under the Act.

Appeal allowed: case remitted to quarter sessions to hear defendant's evidence and determine

[NOTE: The re-hearing took place before the Recorder of Birmingham, Mr Joseph Grieves. The defendant intimated that he was now not appealing against the conviction, but against the sentence. The Recorder said that the fine must stand but, as the defendant was unemployed, it should be paid at the rate of one shilling a week.]

(D) REFUSAL OF ADMISSION: REASONABLE GROUNDS

66 Gateshead Union v. Durham County Council [1918] 1 Ch. 146

COURT OF APPEAL

A pupil shall not be refused admission to a school on other than reasonable grounds. Education is to be available for children resident in the area without distinction.

Facts: The Durham County Council, with the consent of the Board of Education, refused to admit boarded-out poor law children to attend a public elementary school unless the poor law guardians made a contribution towards the maintenance of the school. By the Education Acts 1870–1903 and the Code (which had parliamentary sanction) the authority was obliged to provide and maintain efficient public elementary schools in their district. The Code provided that no child should be refused admission on other than reasonable grounds, and also that any question which arose in the interpretation of the Code, or as to the fulfilment of any of its conditions, should be finally determined by the Board.[1]

The Education Act 1870, s. 3, provided that the term "parent" should include "guardian and every person who is liable to maintain or has the actual

1. The current position is defined in the Education Act 1944, s. 8: "It shall be the duty of every local education authority to secure that there shall be available for their area sufficient schools . . . and the schools available for an area shall not be deemed sufficient unless they are sufficient in number, character, and equipment . . . "; and in the Schools Regulations 1959, No. 7: "A pupil shall not be refused admission to or excluded from a school on other than reasonable grounds."

custody of any child."[2] By the Elementary Education Act 1900, s. 2, power was given to poor law guardians to "contribute towards such of the expenses of providing, enlarging, or maintaining, any public elementary schools as are certified by the Board of Education to have been incurred wholly or partly in respect of scholars taught at the school, who are ... boarded out by the guardians."[3]

The guardians owned eighteen cottages at Medomsley Edge, and from 1900 to 1910 the children in the cottages who were between five and fourteen attended the public elementary schools at Benfieldside. In 1910 the defendants opened Medomsley Edge Council School and from then until 1915 the children in these cottage homes attended the new school, being more than half the total average number of scholars.

In January 1915, the defendants asked the guardians to make a payment of one pound a child per annum on the ground that Medomsley Edge School was provided largely to relieve overcrowding at other schools caused by the children from the cottages. The guardians refused, and pointed out that they were considerable rate payers, whereupon the local education authority obtained the opinion of the Board of Education. This was to the effect that, in view of section 2 of the Act of 1900 quoted above, it would not be unreasonable to exclude children in respect of whom a contribution was not made.

The guardians persisted in their refusal to pay, and in October 1915 the local education authority notified them that unless an agreement for a special payment was arrived at before December 31, 1915, the children from the cottages would be excluded.

The guardians sought a declaration that the children were entitled to attend Medomsley Edge Council School, a declaration that the defendants could not exclude these children from school, and an injunction against the defendants accordingly. Neville J. dismissed the action on the ground that there was no obligation imposed on a local education authority beyond the obligation to fulfil the conditions of the Code. The fulfilment of this was expressly to be determined by the Board of Education, and the jurisdiction of the court was excluded.

The plaintiffs appealed.

Extract from Judgment

SWINFEN EADY L.J.: This appeal raises the important question whether parents, who under the provisions of the Elementary Education Acts are bound to cause their children to attend school under a penalty enforceable by fine and imprisonment, have a corresponding right to the free education of their children at school. The defendants, who are the local education authority,

2. Currently, "parent" in relation to any child or young person, includes a guardian and every person who has the actual custody of the child or young person: Education Act 1944, s. 114 (1).

3. There is no equivalent provision today.

deny that they are under any legal obligation to give free education; where they consider that the parent is of sufficient ability to pay, or where for other reasons they consider that a payment ought to be made, they claim the right to require a money payment or contribution, and to refuse to receive a child if this payment is not made. . . .

No question is raised in these proceedings with regard to order or cleanliness as regards the children, or any disciplinary measures. The sole question is whether the defendants can refuse to receive the children unless payment is made for them—in other words, whether "parents" have any right to the free education of their children under the provisions of the Elementary Education Acts now in force. . . .

By the Elementary Education Act 1870, s. 3, "parent" includes "guardian and every person who is liable to maintain or has the actual custody of any child." The plaintiffs respectively are, therefore, "parents" within the meaning of the Act. . . .

I am of opinion that the Acts which require a parent to cause his children to attend school give him the right to comply with their provisions and enable him to insist that the child which he tenders shall be permitted to "attend" school—that is, to be and remain at the school—during school hours and receive the instruction which similar children receive, and that the defendants have not any right to refuse to receive his child unless they receive some payment or money contribution. He is entitled to free education for his child—that is, education without making any payment whatever. The accommodation in the school cannot be said to have been made "available" for children if they are refused admission unless and until their parents comply with some request to pay money which the statutes do not confer upon the local education authority any right to demand. . . .

If a parent has a legal right to free education for his child at a public elementary school, the Board of Education cannot, nor can the local education authority, take it away. The statute does not confer upon the Board any power to determine the legal right as between a parent and the school authority. The decision of the Board is only expressed to be final for the purposes of the Code. The Board may determine whether a child has been refused admission to a public elementary school, on other than reasonable grounds, for the purpose of deciding whether the conditions to obtain an annual grant have been fulfilled by the school or education authority, but not for the purpose of determining the legal rights of the parent. Compliance with the Code is a condition of earning the grant.

In my judgment the plaintiffs are entitled to the declaration for which they ask—namely a declaration that the plaintiffs are entitled to send the children in the statement of claim mentioned to any public elementary school within the district in which the children reside, if there is room for them, unless there is some reasonable ground for excluding them not inconsistent with the right of the parents to the free education of the same children.

Appeal allowed

(E) DAYS OF OBLIGATION

67 Marshall *v.* Graham; Bell *v.* Graham [1907] 2 K.B. 112

KING'S BENCH DIVISION
Ascension Day is a day exclusively set apart for religious observance by the Church of England within the meaning of the Education Acts.

Facts: The appellants in these cases, the appeals in which were heard together, were convicted and fined by the justices for that they, being the parents of children aged not less than five not more than fourteen years of age, did wilfully neglect to cause such children to attend school without lawful excuse for the whole time required under regulations made by the West Riding County Council under powers conferred by the Education Act 1902.

John Marshall was a pupil of eleven-and-a-half, attending Darfield Mixed School. On May 24, 1906, being Ascension Day, he attended church in accordance with his parents' wish in the morning, and returned to school in the afternoon. The father belonged to the religious body of the Church of England.

Mary Anne Bell was a nine-year-old girl, and a pupil at the Low Valley School. On Ascension Day 1906 she was wholly absent from school, both morning and afternoon. Before the justices the father stated that he was a member of the Church of England. Until 1895 he had attended church regularly, but since that date had been on only two occasions, one being his wedding in 1897. It was not proved that he had ever attended the communion of the Church of England, or that he had attended the worship of any other religious body. He did not know what place of worship his children attended: it might be the Wesleyan chapel, but he wished them to go to church that day.

The regulations of the local education authority provided, *inter alia*

"(2) The parent of every child of not less than five not more than fourteen years of age shall cause the child to attend school, unless there be a reasonable excuse for non-attendance. (3) The time during which every child shall attend school shall be the whole time for which the school selected shall be open for the instruction of children of similar age. (4) Provided that nothing in these by-laws . . . (*b*) shall require any child to attend school on any day exclusively set apart for religious observance by the religious body to which its parent belongs."

The information was laid by Thomas Graham, an officer of the county council appointed to enforce the compulsory school attendance of children in the area of the Ardsley and District Education Sub-Committee of the West Riding County Council.

The justices held that May 24, 1906, was not a day exclusively set apart for religious observance by the Church of England in the sense contemplated by the by-laws and the provisions of the Elementary Education Act. In the case of Bell they were not satisfied on the evidence that he bona fide belonged to, or was a member of, the Church of England, or that he belonged to that Church and a religious body in the sense contemplated by the by-law and the Education Acts.

The defendants appealed by way of case stated to the Divisional Court of the Queen's Bench Division, and the questions for the court were (1) whether the justices were warranted in not being satisfied that Bell belonged to the Church of England; (2) whether they came to a correct decision in point of law in respect of their conclusions in respect of their conclusions in both cases and, if not, what should be done in the premises.

The appellants relied largely on the statute 5 & 6 Edward 6,[1] c. 3, s. 1, and canon 13 of the Canons of 1603.

It was contended on behalf of the respondent, that the statute 5 & 6 Edward 6, c. 3, was not an ordinance of a religious body, but was a general public statute equally binding on all the subjects of the realm, of whatever religious views at the time it was enacted. Therefore, the days enumerated in the statute (including Ascension Day) could not be said to be days set apart for religious observance by a religious body.

It was further contended, with respect to the Canons of 1603 that the power of the Church of England with regard to the making of such canons was limited by Article 20 of the Articles of Religion (commonly called the *Thirty-nine Articles*), and that they were not binding. In any case the thirteenth canon did not purport to, and did not, exclusively set apart Ascension Day as a day of religious observance within the proviso of by-law 4, and the provisions of the Education Acts. It was also contended, on behalf of the respondent, that the statute 5 & 6 Edward 6, c. 3, must be interpreted in the light of the conditions which existed at the time when the Act was passed. Forming, as it did, part of a scheme for compelling uniformity of worship under the sanction of penalties, it could have no force in the altered conditions of religious freedom of the present day.

Lord Cecil, K.C. (for the appellants in both cases): The general effect of the statutes and canons was to impose a duty on members of the Church of England to attend church on Ascension Day, and that it was a day "exclusively set apart for religious observance" by the Church of England within the meaning of section 7 (1) of the Education Act 1870; and that, in any case, there was a "reasonable excuse" for not attending within the meaning of section 74 (1) of the Act.

Danckwerts, K. C.: (for the respondent) The Canons of 1603 *proprio vigore*, were not binding on the laity. The Education Act 1870, s. 7 (1), referred to Roman Catholics and Jews, who had days exclusively set apart for religious observance. That subsection only dealt with a case where a religious

1. The Act of Uniformity. For an extract of the relevant passage see the note to this case on page 184, *infra.*

observance was imposed by the religious body on its own members. The Church of England did not of itself impose religious observance upon its own members; that was done by statute.

DARLING J.: I thought that the Church of England was an ancient Church in which certain abuses had sprung up, which abuses were got rid of at the Reformation.

Danckwerts: Your Lordship is now entering upon very debatable ground. There are two schools of thought in the Church upon that question.

PHILLIMORE J.: I thought that there were two schools of thought about everything.

Danckwerts: The day must be exclusively set apart for religious observance—that is to say, the whole of the day must be set apart for religious observance.

PHILLIMORE J.: Can you mention any religious body in which a whole day is set apart for religious observance?

Danckwerts: Yes; the Jews.

PHILLIMORE J.: Can you mention any other?

Danckwerts: I think Roman Catholics also.

PHILLIMORE J.: Oh, no.

Danckwerts: The section was passed to prevent children being compelled to go to school, contrary to the convictions of their parents, during a day exclusively set apart for religious observance.

LORD ALVERSTONE C.J.: Why does not that apply with equal force where the religious service or religious observance takes place during the school hours?

DARLING J. The parents may have religious convictions that their children should go to church on certain days, and may wish to take them there, and yet you say that though the parents may go themselves, they cannot take their children with them.

Danckwerts: The enactment is intended to meet cases where parents thought it wrong for their children to go to school on any part of the day in question. Sir Hugh Owen, in his *Education Acts Manual*, 20th ed., p. 208, says that the latter part of section 7 (1) is specially intended to meet the cases of Jewish and Roman Catholic children. The point that there may have been a "reasonable excuse" for not sending the child to school on the day in question, within the meaning of section 74 (1) of the Act of 1870, was not taken before the justices, and is not open now. In any case it was a question of fact for the justices. There are twenty-six days mentioned in the statute 5 & 6 Edward 6, c. 3, and the number is so large that the adoption of the appellants' view would dislocate the whole educational system. It would also take away the parliamentary grant. If "exclusively set apart" does not refer to the whole day, at all events it refers to the whole school day.

Extracts from Judgments

LORD ALVERSTONE C.J.: In this case two parents were summoned for not sending their children to school on Ascension Day. In the case of Marshall, which I propose to deal with first, it appears that the boy, by the desire and direction of his father, who belongs to the religious body of the Church of England, attended church instead of going to school in the morning of Ascension Day, but went to school as usual in the afternoon of that day; and the question which we have to decide is whether a father who, being a member of the Church of England, thinks it right to send his boy to church on Ascension Day is entitled to keep him from school for that purpose. The question turns upon the meaning of certain words which occur in two sections of the Elementary Education Act 1870 and which are reproduced in the by-laws under which the appellants were convicted. The first of those sections is section 7, which, by subsection (1), provides that "It shall not be required as a condition of any child being admitted into or continuing in the school . . . that he shall, if withdrawn by his parent, attend the school on any day exclusively set apart for religious observance by the religious body to which his parent belongs." The other section is section 74, under which the education authority are empowered to make by-laws, and which provides that "no such by-law shall prevent the withdrawal of any child from any religious observance or instruction in religious subjects, or shall require any child to attend school on any day exclusively set apart for religious observance by the religious body to which his parent belongs." The question is whether Ascension Day is so exclusively set apart by the Church of England, and whether the Church of England is a religious body within the meaning of that section. It was pressed upon us by Mr Danckwerts in the first place that the words in question afford no protection unless the day be exclusively set apart in the literal sense of that term—that is to say, unless the whole twenty-four hours, or at all events the whole of the school hours, be so set apart, and that as there is no day which in the Church of England is set apart for religious observance to that extent, the exemption does not apply to members of the Church of England at all. It was said that it was intended only to meet the case of Jewish and Roman Catholic children, and a note in Owen's *Education Acts Manual* was referred to in suppport of that view. I do not myself think that there is any foundation for that contention. Mr Danckwerts, when pressed, could only mention one day, or at the most two days, which are exclusively set apart, in the sense for which he contended, by the Jewish community, and even as to those he produced no authority for his statement; and as to the Roman Catholic Church, I certainly know of no day which it sets apart in that sense. I cannot, therefore, construe the word "exclusively" as meaning that during the whole of the twenty-four hours, or even during the whole of the school hours, there must be some religious observance going on which is inconsistent with the child being at school. It would be a most unfortunate construction to put upon the words, and one which would certainly not promote the harmonious working of the Act. I myself am inclined to think that the word "exclusively" was inserted only for the purpose of preventing ordinary directions as to religious practices upon many days of the year being used as an excuse for not sending a child to school. We certainly ought not to give any such meaning to it as would prevent the exemption from applying to Christmas Day, Good Friday, and other well-known sacred days, days which are consecrated to God in the sense that religious observance upon them is to be a primary duty of members of the Church.

It was secondly contended that, even if Ascension Day is exclusively set apart for religious observance among members of the Church of England, it is not so set apart by the religious body of the Church itself. It was said that the obligation to keep this and other saints' days holy is imposed by statute alone, and that a setting apart by statute is not a setting apart by the Church. This contention, however, is wholly opposed to what is known of the history of the Church. The authorities of the Church had long before the statute of Edward 6 prescribed a certain number of days on which the people were to devote themselves to prayer and religious observance. The statute of Edward 6 no doubt recognised the existence of those days as being "sanctified and hallowed, separated from all profane uses, dedicated and appointed not unto any saint or creature, but only unto God and His true worship," and at the same time it reduced the number of such days, a larger number having been originally prescribed by the Church, but it did not for the first time set those days apart as holy days.

In my opinion when Parliament enacted sections 7 and 74 of the Elementary Education Act 1870, they meant to protect the consciences of those who believe that they ought to observe these saints' days and keep them sanctified, and to enable such persons to withdraw their children from school on those days. I therefore come to the conclusion that Ascension Day is a day "exclusively set apart for religious observance by the religious body" to which these appellants belong.

We were told that as there were twenty-seven holy days specified in the Act of Edward 4,[2] the effect of our so holding would be to disorganise the educational system. I may observe that, as was pointed out in the course of argument, that objection is largely cut down by the fact that many of those days occur in what are known to be school holidays, but I do not in any way rely upon that. I do not stop to consider how many such days there may be, for I do not think that we ought to allow any consideration of their number to prevent us from giving effect to the obvious intention of Parliament to respect and protect the consciences of religious-minded people.

I only wish to say a very few words with regard to the other points in the case. Speaking of Marshall's case, if I had not taken the view which I have, I should certainly have come to the conclusion that there was a "reasonable excuse" under by-law 2, and that we ought so to hold. Mr Danckwerts said that the point had never been taken in the court below, and that the question of reasonable excuse was one of fact for the justices. But upon the facts as stated—and it is not suggested that any additional evidence could materially alter these facts—it seems impossible to say that, so far as Marshall is concerned, there was not a reasonable excuse. In Bell's case, also, the judgment

2. *Sic.* The Act referred to is, of course, that of Edward 6.

which I have already delivered entitles the appellant to succeed. But I must point out that, if I had not taken the view which I have expressed as to the meaning of the words "exclusively set apart," I should have had a difficulty in saying that there was any reasonable excuse in his case, for the child did not go to church in the afternoon, but stayed at home.

The other finding of the justices upon which the conviction in Bell's case was based is to my mind a very extraordinary one. We have not heard any argument from Mr Danckwerts upon it. The man said he was a member of the Church of England; he had been baptised and confirmed according to the rites of that Church. He had previously to his marriage attended church regularly. Since 1895 he had only attended twice, once on his wedding day and once on the occasion of a funeral. Upon this evidence the justices said that they were not satisfied that the appellant bona fide belonged to the Church of England. I think it would be very improper to hold that, because a man had been irregular in his attendance at church, he did not honestly belong to the religious body of which he claimed to be a member. I think that in both these cases the appeals must be allowed.

PHILLIMORE J.: . . . I will only add one word more. There is to my mind a third matter which the justices ought to consider when it is sought to convict a parent of infringement of the by-laws under such circumstances as the present. I do not think that "reasonable excuse" is the right description to give of the defence for a child's absence from school that he was obliged by law to be elsewhere during the school hours. For instance, if the child's absence was due to his having to attend on a subpoena before a court of law, the ground of his absence could not be properly described as a "reasonable excuse." The word "excuse" implies that what is excused is prima facie unlawful, but there is prima facie nothing unlawful in the child's absence in the case put. So here I incline to think that, apart from any question of reasonable excuse, it is a sufficient answer for the child to say, "As I am not a nonconformist, and consequently am not within the protection of the statute 9 & 10 Victoria c. 59, I cannot obey this by-law because I am bound to obey another Act of Parliament, 5 & 6 Edward, c. 3, which requires me to attend church," for the latter Act is kept in force by the 9 & 10 Victoria c. 59, subject only to this limitation, that no pecuniary penalty is any longer to be imposed for disobedience. I agree that the appeal should be allowed, and I am very glad to be able to do so, because it seems to me that the cause of civil and religious liberty would suffer much if the judgment were otherwise.

Appeals allowed: convictions
quashed

[NOTE: This case is still good law. The Education Act 1944, s. 39 (2), provides: "In any proceedings for an offence against this section in respect of a child who is not a boarder at the school at which he is a registered pupil, the child shall not be deemed to have failed to attend regularly by reason of his absence therefrom with leave or . . . (b) on any day exclusively set apart for religious observance by the religious body to which his parent belongs."

The Act of Uniformity, 5 & 6 Edward 6, is still in force. The relevant extract reads:

"Forasmuch as at all times men be not so mindful to laud and praise God, so ready to resort and hear God's Holy Word, and to come to the Holy Communion and other laudable rites, which are to be observed in every Christian congregation, as their bounden duty doth require: Therefore, to call men to remembrance of their duty and to help their infirmity, it hath been wholesomely provided that there should be some certain times and days appointed, wherein the Christians should cease from all other kind of labours, and should apply themselves only and wholly unto the aforesaid holy works, properly pertaining unto true religion—that is, to hear, to learn, and to remember Almighty God's great benefits, His manifold mercies, His inestimable gracious goodness so plenteously poured upon all His creatures, and that of His infinite and unspeakable goodness, without any man's desert; and in remembrance hereof, to render unto Him most high and hearty thanks with prayers and supplications for the relief of all our daily necessities; and because these be the chief and principal works wherein man is commanded to worship God and to properly pertain unto the first table. Therefore, as these works are most commonly, and also may well be called God's service, so the times appointed specially for the same are called holy days; not for the matter and nature either of the time or day, nor for any of the Saints' sake whose memories are had on those days (for so all days and times considered are God's creatures, and all of like holiness), but for the nature and condition of these Godly and holy works, wherewith only God is to be honoured, and the congregation to be edified, whereunto such times and days are sanctified and hallowed—that is to say, separated from all profane uses, and dedicated and appointed not unto any Saint or creature, but only unto God and his true worship; neither is it to be thought that there is any certain time or definite number of days prescribed in Holy Scripture, but that the appointment both of the time and also of the number of the days is left by the authority of God's Word to the liberty of Christ's Church, to be determined and assigned orderly in every country, by the discretion of the rulers and Ministers thereof, as they shall judge most expedient to the true setting forth of God's glory, and the edification of their people. Be it therefore enacted by the King our Sovereign Lord, with the assent of the lords spiritual and temporal, and the Commons, in this present Parliament assembled, and by the authority of the same, that all the days hereafter mentioned shall be kept and commanded to be kept holy days, and none other—that is to say, all Sundays in the year, the days of the Feast of the Circumcision of our Lord Jesus Christ, of the Epiphany, of the Purification of the Blessed Virgin, of Saint Matthie the Apostle, of the Annunciation of the Blessed Virgin, of Saint Mark the Evangelist, of Saint Philip and Jacob the Apostles, of the Ascension of our Lord Jesus Christ, of the Nativity of Saint John Baptist, of Saint Peter the Apostle, of Saint James the Apostle, of Saint Bartholomew the Apostle, of Saint Matthew the Apostle, of Saint Michael the Archangel, of Saint Luke the Evangelist, of Saint Simon and Jude the Apostles, of All Saints, of Saint Andrew the Apostle, of Saint Thomas the Apostle, of the Nativity of our Lord, of Saint Stephen the Martyr, of Saint John the Evangelist, of the Holy Innocents, Monday and Tuesday in Easter week, and Monday and Tuesday in Whitsun week; and that none other day shall be kept and commanded to be kept holy day, or to abstain from lawful bodily labour."

The 13th Canon of the Canons of 1603 reads as follows:

"All manner of persons within the Church of England shall from henceforth celebrate and keep the Lord's Day, commonly called Sunday, and other holy days, according to God's holy will and pleasure, and the orders of the Church of England prescribed in that behalf—that is, in hearing the Word of God read and taught; in private and public prayers; in acknowledging their offences to God, and amendment of the same; in reconciling themselves charitably to their neighbours, where displeasure hath been, in oftentimes receiving the Communion of the Body and Blood of Christ; in visiting of the poor and sick; using all godly and sober conversation."]

(F) RELEASE OF CHILD: PARENTAL AUTHORITY

68 Price *v.* Wilkins (1888) 58 L.T. 680

QUEEN'S BENCH DIVISION

When a schoolmaster is asked to release a child, the parental authority must prevail, and the parent may have a habeas corpus if a master detains a child against his wish.

Facts: The plaintiff was the proprietor of a school for boys under fifteen at the Philberds, Maidenhead, and the defendant was a gentleman of independent means whose three sons were pupils at the school.

The plaintiff sued for £25 13s. 4d., being the balance of an account for a term's fees. The defendant paid £12 into court without admitting liability, and counterclaimed for damages amounting to £68 for the wrongful dismissal of his youngest son, Frederick, of which £50 was for the loss of the boy's education.

The facts are fully stated in the judgment.

Cur. adv. vult

Judgment

WILLS J.: The plaintiff in this case is a schoolmaster. He sues the defendant for £25 13s., one quarter's school fees in respect of the defendant's son, payable in advance on January 27, 1887. The defendant denies his liability, and with such denial pays £12 into court, and counter-claims for loss of board and lodging, which he says ought to have been supplied to his son, and for damages for loss of his son's education. The plaintiff further claimed a quarter's payment in lieu of notice to withdraw the defendant's son from the school; but, having discovered that notice had been duly given, abandoned that claim. The circumstances are as follows: The number of boys at the plaintiff's school was stated to be somewhere about a hundred. The defendant's son Frederick was the third of three sons whom he had placed successively with the plaintiff. The other two had left, and notice had been given for Frederick to leave at the end of the Easter term, which began on January 27 and ended on April 6, 1887. The defendant had had copies of the plaintiff's prospectus, and in particular one had been sent to him before the term which began in October 1886, and I cannot doubt that he was perfectly familiar with the rules of the school. The prospectus stated the amount of the school fees per annum, and that one-third was to be paid before the commencement of each school term. It was admitted that the amount due from the defendant in respect of his son Frederick, on January 27, 1887, when the Easter term began, was £25 13s. Appended to the prospectus was a list of "Rules and Regulations." The first of these was as follows: "*Exeats* are avoided as much as possible. No *exeats* are allowed during the Easter term."

During the Christmas holidays of 1886–87 the defendant, without consulting the plaintiff, had promised his son that he should come home during the Easter term. He attempted to show that he had between February 3 and 16 called upon the plaintiff and obtained his leave that Frederick should come home on February 16, which was his sister's birthday, in honour of which event there were to be some festivities and private theatricals. For reasons which I will give by-and-by, I am unable to accept this statement, and I am satisfied that no such permission was either asked or given. On February 13 the defendant wrote to the plaintiff—"Will you please let my son come over early next Wednesday morning, and he can stay the night. We will send him back first thing on Thursday." The plaintiff wrote back on the 14th, saying that what was proposed was against the rules of the school, and refusing permission. The defendant wrote on the 15th: "In answer to yours of yesterday it is my particular wish my son should come over, and I will send my servant with the cart for him about 10 o'clock. It will be his sister's birthday, and he has been promised a holiday." The plaintiff received this letter about 8.30 a.m., and at ten the cart came. The plaintiff sent the boy to his father's in the cart, and sent with him this letter: 'I allow your boy to go to you on the strict understanding that he returns, without fail, this evening." The boy's lessons would have gone on in the regular course till one o'clock that day, after which time there was a half-holiday. The defendant lives at Datchet, about seven or eight miles from the plaintiff's school. The boy reached home soon after eleven o'clock and the defendant telegraphed at 11.30 in answer to the plaintiff's letter: "Not convenient to send him back to-day. Return to-morrow, as stated in my letter." The plaintiff received this telegram between 12 and 12.30, and immediately telegraphed back: "Unless your son returns to-night, shall not receive him back." To which the defendant replied at 2.25 p.m.: "As you refuse to receive my son to-morrow, kindly send his trunk home," which was done.

Before proceeding further, I will give my reasons for saying that I cannot accept the statement that the defendant between February 3 and 16 called on the plaintiff, and asked for and received the permission for his boy to come home on the 16th, although a gentleman whom I do not so much as suspect of an intentional misrepresentation accompanied the defendant, and so far as he could recollect permission was given. I think it is impossible that, if such an incident had taken place, the defendant should not have alluded to it in the foregoing letters, which I have given in full. The expression "he has been promised one holiday" is one which could hardly have been used if, within a very few days, the plaintiff had promised that the boy should be free to return home, on this specific occasion. A long correspondence ensued, in which the defendant complained of the treatment he had received from the plaintiff, and in which the plaintiff pointed out the printed rules, and complained of the deliberate resolution of the defendant to have them set at nought, and the only matter insisted upon by the defendant to show that the treatment was harsh was a reference to "the years my three sons have been with you." The defendant

also made an affidavit, sworn on July 25, 1887, in which he set out at length
his version of the case, and to which no reference is made to the permission
now alleged to have been given between February 3 and 6, but an account is
given which is totally inconsistent with his having had then in remembrance
any such call and conversation as that spoken to by himself and his witness.
He was utterly unable to give any explanation of these facts, and I think he
and his witness must either have been dreaming of an interview which never
took place, or erroneously attributing to that period something which took
place on some totally different occasion. I therefore discard that piece of
evidence, to deal with the case as if it had not been given. The plaintiff was
entitled on January 27 to the £25 13s., now sued for, and had a cause of
action on the 28th, for its nonpayment. The defendant cannot be in a better
position because he had not performed his contract in this respect, and must
therefore, as it seems to me, in order to defeat that right of action, show a
state of things which would have entitled him, had he paid that sum on January
27, to recover back the whole or a portion of it after February 16. He cannot
do this unless the plaintiff has broken his contract. Now, what was his contract?
Mr Greene, on behalf of the defendant, contended that it was an absolute
one to board, lodge, and educate the defendant's son for the Easter term in all
events. I do not think this is a correct representation of the relations between
a schoolmaster and the parents of his pupils. The parent surrenders for the
time being a part of his otherwise exclusive right to direct or control the child,
and certainly undertakes that the master shall, so far as he or his action are
concerned, be at liberty to enforce with regard to his son the rules of the
school, or, to put it at the very lowest, at all events such rules as are known to
him and assented to by him. He cannot, without breaking the contract implied
by the very relation between them, require his son to disobey such a rule of
the school. And the contract of the master is, not at all hazards and in all
events to supply board, lodging, and tuition, but to supply them on the terms
that these rules are observed, so far at least as the action of the parent is
concerned. It seems to me that the very nature of school life imports such an
obligation on the part of the parent. If all fathers were to do as this defendant
did, the discipline without which a school could not be carried on would be
at an end; the authority and legitimate power of the schoolmaster would be
brought to nought; and incalculable mischief would be done to education
in the best and widest sense of the term. The contract of the plaintiff was, in
my opinion, that he would give to the defendant's son a term's education on
certain conditions, one of which was that the father would submit to his son
having no *exeat* during Easter term. An *exeat*, it appears, is understood at
this school—and the defendant did not affect to put any other construction
upon it—to mean leave to go and stay out the night. The defendant was
determined that this condition forbidding *exeats* during Easter term should
not be observed in his son's case. The plaintiff when he received the defendant's
letter of February 15, could not withhold the son from the father. The parental
authority in case of conflict must of course prevail, and the father might, no

doubt, have had a habeas corpus if the master detained his son against his wish. But the condition affected virtually the discipline of the school. Were it broken all round, or by any considerable number of parents, school teaching would be, if not impossible, at all events carried on under difficulties which would very seriously impair the efficacy of the training, and destroy the order and regularity by which it ought to be distinguished. The remedy which was suggested by cross-action would be cumbrous and impracticable. It seems to me to be one of those cases in which, from the very nature of the act to be done or forborne, the observance of the condition by the parent lies at the very root of the contract, so that when the defendant refused to be bound by it, and insisted on having and keeping his son at home for the night, in spite of the plaintiff's objections, the plaintiff was justified in refusing to keep the boy any longer upon terms which were not those upon which he had agreed to take him, and which he had a perfect right to regard as fatal to the discipline of his school. The plaintiff was willing to go on with the boy's schooling, if he were returned the same evening. It seems to me that, in refusing to go on with him if that rule were broken, he was breaking no part of his contract, and that, therefore, the defendant would have had no right to recover from him any part of the term's fees had he paid beforehand. By parity of reasoning, he cannot claim any deduction in the present action. In my opinion he has no cause of action of any kind against the plaintiff. It was admitted by the plaintiff that, under ordinary circumstances, if a boy were, for some just reason, removed in the middle of a term, an abatement of a guinea a week, for the unexpired portion of the term, would be allowed, and that this is the general custom. But such a custom cannot have any application where the father breaks the contract in a manner which justifies the schoolmaster in refusing to teach the boy any longer.

Judgment for plaintiff

(G) ADMINISTRATIVE NEGLIGENCE

69 Hollands *v.* Canterbury City Council and Hooke (1966)
Kentish Gazette, September 30 and October 28

CANTERBURY COUNTY COURT

Damages may be awarded to a student who suffers shock on learning that he has been officially, but wrongly, informed by his place of education that he has passed an examination.

Facts: The plaintiff was a nineteen-year-old girl, Miss Mavis Hollands, who had been a full-time student for the Ordinary level of the General Certificate of Education at Canterbury Technical College. She sat for the examination in English Language, English Literature, Geography and Biology in the summer of 1964. She hoped to become a nurse but, discovering that she could not start her training before the age of eighteen, she applied to Saint Augustine's Hospital, Canterbury, for appointment as a dispenser's assistant. She was asked about her examination results, and was asked to let the hospital know as soon as she received them.

In September she received a letter from the College saying that she had passed in all four subjects, and that her certificate would be sent on in due course. She told her friends and neighbours of her success, and informed the hospital. As the certificate did not arrive by the end of the year she made enquiries, and was told that the certificate had not been sent because she had failed in every subject. This was at the beginning of February. Claiming that the news made her ill, she sued the City Council and the principal of the College for £300 damages, saying that she had lost the opportunity to continue her studies to enable her to sit again immediately for the examination, and also that she had suffered from nervous shock.

After she received the letter telling her she had failed, she saw the Principal, who offered to let her return to continue her studies part-time, and who said he would waive the fees and provide special coaching. By this time she was already spending a day a week studying in London, and was also taking chemistry at the Technical College. She felt that she did not wish to add to her studies, and also said that she was unable to concentrate on her work. She agreed in court that she did not think she had much chance of passing except in English Language, particularly as she was suffering from tonsillitis when she took them. Had she been properly notified, however, she would have gone back to the College in September in order to sit again in the following year.

Some twelve days after being notified that she had failed, the plaintiff collapsed at work. This was on February 17. She was examined by Dr A. R. Fox who found she had a temperature of 102° and a cold in the throat. He thought neither was due to shock. Three days later she was seen by Dr D. J. E. Wood who said she complained of pains in the abdomen and vomiting, and that this was consistent with severe nervous shock. Dr Fox saw her again on February 26 when she was suffering from nasal catarrh. Dr Fox said she was not in bed for a fortnight at this time, and the plaintiff agreed that her collapse occurred twelve, not two, days after hearing she had failed.

Mr R. J. Hooke, the principal of the College, said that he would not have advised the plaintiff to return. She was an average student who had failed a two-year full-time course, and he thought she would have had very great difficulties with a part-time course. She had secured the bottom grade in three subjects, and had secured one grade below the pass mark in the other. He was doubtful, in any case, if she would have returned. He agreed that the second letter must have been a shock to her, and also that people arrange their lives accordingly after they have been told that they have passed an examination. The College dealt with some two thousand examination entries, and some hundreds of certificates, each year, and the system concerned with the notification of results had now been tightened up.

On behalf of the City Council it was pointed out that the plaintiff had managed to obtain particular employment on the assumption that she had managed to pass four subjects at "O" level. In spite of the fact that it was later discovered that she had not passed in any subject she had been allowed to retain that appointment; therefore she was better off than she should have been since, normally, she would never have been allowed to start that particular kind of work without a General Certificate of Education. Furthermore, it was not proved that she would have gone back if she had known from the beginning of her failure. Counsel asked: "Was physical damage foreseeable? In my opinion there is no action which was foreseeable on this claim for damages. Leaving aside causation, the present alleged damages were not recoverable."

On behalf of the plaintiff it was urged that her reports from Chartham Secondary School had indicated that she would benefit from further education, and her previous examination results had been satisfactory. Her G.C.E. results were below standard, but the examination coincided with her illness. "This," said Counsel, "is a horrible case. This is a young woman who thought she may not have stood a great chance of passing the examination, but was then told she had passed. Six months later she asks for her certificates, and she is told in a most brutal way in a two-line letter that she had not passed."

Extract from Judgment

JUDGE SUMNER: This is a most unfortunate case. I do not think anyone could fail to have a great deal of sympathy for Miss Hollands. Mr Hooke has said it was highly unlikely that she would have returned to sit for the examination again, and I accept that. We now know that she had only gained the lowest grades in three of the subjects, and in the fourth she missed passing by one grade.

I am quite satisfied that on the evidence as a whole she did get into an acute nervous state of shock in the medical sense, but I am not satisfied that it did require her to go to bed for two weeks. Still, it was a very unpleasant thing to happen to her.

Anyone who has children knows how they get worked up over their examination results. In this case she thought that she had passed, and a few months later she was told she had not.

The plaintiff's first claim fails because I do not think she would have gone straight back to college to take the examinations at the earliest opportunity. I do think, however, that she suffered nervous shock, and on this claim I award her £50 in damages.

Judgment for the plaintiff

(H) DISTANCE BETWEEN HOME AND SCHOOL

70 Hares *v.* Curtin [1913] 2 K.B. 328

KING'S BENCH DIVISION

In measuring the nearest available route between home and school the calculation is not confined to any particular class of road, and includes a cart track.

Facts: The appellant, George Hares of Wellington Farm, Cheddar, was convicted by the justices of unlawfully neglecting to cause his thirteen-year-old son to attend school.

The by-laws provided, *inter alia*, that it should be a reasonable excuse ". . . (c) That there is no elementary school open which the child can attend within three miles measured according to the nearest road from the residence of such a child, provided that, when a local education authority provides suitable means of conveyance for a child between a reasonable distance of its home and a public elementary school, such reason shall not be a reasonable excuse (7 Edw. 7, c. 43, s. 14 (1))."

The nearest public elementary school to the appellant's home was at Charterhouse, which was open on July 6, 1911, on which date the local education authority did not provide any suitable means of conveyance for the child between a reasonable distance of its home and any public elementary school.

The ordnance map of the district was exhibited before the justices and on it there were indicated three routes from the appellant's residence to the school, coloured respectively red, blue and green.

The distance from inside the porch of the appellant's residence to inside the porch of the school was three miles and thirteen and two-thirds yards measured along the red route, as indicated on the map along the north and east sides of the field in the appellant's occupation (No. 422 on the map), to the south-east corner of the field and thence along the centre of the public highway. By taking a direct route from the appellant's residence in the field (No. 459 on the map) into the field No. 22 there would be a saving in distance of thirteen yards. By not going into the acute angle in the north-east corner of the field, as shown by the red line, there would be a saving in distance of eight yards, and a yard could be saved at the gate at the south-east corner of the field by taking the shortest course. This would reduce the total distance by the red route to less than three miles. Inside the gate at the south-east corner of the field No. 422 there were for some distance signs of a roadway, such as wheel tracks and cart tracks, along the east wall of the field, but there were no signs of a made road along the north wall of the field except at one point. A tithe map showed a road from the gate at the south-east corner of the field No. 422 along the eastern side of the field to a gate at the north-east corner, but did not show any roadway along the northern side of such field nor across the field by the blue or green routes.

The distance from the appellant's residence to the school by the blue route through the field No. 422 towards the south-east corner and thence joining the red route along the highway was 317 yards under three miles. This blue route was clearly defined by cart tracks and a distinct sign of a footpath.

The distance by the green route in the field No. 422 and thence along the highway was 275 yards under three miles. This green route was clearly defined by cart tracks.

The field No. 422 was formerly an arable field and while under cultivation as such there was no road from the highway to the appellant's residence

except by the red route. For seventeen years and upwards the field had been
laid down as pasture and had so continued down to and including July 6, 1911.
During this period the blue and green routes had been regularly used as
approaches to the appellant's residence, the green route being used in bad
weather. Neither red, blue, nor green routes were public highways. The child
could on July 6, 1911, have walked from his residence to the school at
Charterhouse without any detriment to his health.

On behalf of the appellant it was contended that the nearest road within
the meaning of the by-laws and of section 74 of the Elementary Education
Act 1870 was according to the red route indicated on the map, and that
measured in this way the distance from the child's residence to the nearest
public elementary school exceeded three miles; and that the blue and green
routes were not roads within the meaning of the by-law or the Act.

It was contended on behalf of the respondent that both the blue and the
green routes were available on July 6, 1911, as roads within the meaning of
the by-law for the use of the child; and that the distance by the red route,
if not measured along the centre of the track and of the highway, but by the
shortest practicable route, did not exceed three miles.

The justices were of opinion and found and determined on the facts proved
and admitted that on July 6, 1911, there was a public elementary school open,
which the appellant's child could have attended, within three miles measured
according to the nearest road from the child's residence, and they accordingly
convicted the appellant.

On appeal, by way of case stated:

Sutherland Graeme (for the appellant): The word "road" in this by-law and
in section 74 of the Elementary Education Act 1870 means a defined and
recognised way along which traffic can go; it does not include a rough cart
track through a field. On the facts found by the justices none of the routes,
red, blue, or green, is a road within the by-law. A route is not the same thing
as a road.

Judgment

LORD ALVERSTONE C.J.: On the facts found by the justices it is impossible
to allow this appeal. They have found that for the last seventeen years the
routes coloured blue and green on the map have formed the approaches to the
appellant's house, and that the distance by either of these routes to the nearest
school is under three miles. It is true that these routes are not public highways,
but that is immaterial, for in my opinion the word "road" in this by-law is not
confined to highways or to roads constructed for the purpose of carrying
every class of traffic. It does not mean a road of any particular class, but simply
a route from the residence of a child to the nearest school. The justices were
therefore right in holding that there was a school within three miles measured
according to the nearest road which the child could have attended, and this
appeal must be dismissed.

Appeal dismissed

71 Shaxted v. Ward [1954] 1 All E.R. 336

QUEEN'S BENCH DIVISION
Distance, not safety, is the test for determining the "nearest available route" between home and school.

Facts: Bertie Herbert Shaxted of West Stourmouth was convicted by the Kent justices because his six-year-old child had failed to attend regularly at Preston County Primary School, which was less than two miles from his home.

The Education Act 1944, s. 39 (1), provides that a parent is guilty of an offence if his child fails to attend regularly at the school at which he is a registered pupil but, by section 39 (2):

"the child shall not be deemed to have failed to attend regularly at the school . . . (c) if the parent proves that the school at which the child is a registered pupil is not within walking distance of the child's home, and that no suitable arrangements have been made by the local education authority either for his transport to and from the school or for boarding accommodation.

The term "walking distance" is defined in section 39 (5):

". . . means in relation to a child who has not attained the age of eight years two miles, and in the case of any other child three miles, measured by the nearest available route.

The father appealed, contending that the route which measured less than two miles was not the "nearest available route" because part of it was unsafe for children who were not escorted.

Extract from Judgment
LORD GODDARD C.J.: . . . What the justices had to decide was whether or not the school was within walking distance, and it is said that the route which the child took, and which is under two miles, is not the nearest available route because part of it is said to be dangerous for children to walk along unescorted. I cannot read the word "available" as meaning necessarily safe, because we can see how that word got into the Act. By the Elementary Education Act 1870, s. 74 (3), it was a reasonable excuse: "that there is no public elementary school open which the child can attend within such distance, not exceeding three miles, measured according to the nearest road from the residence of such child, as the by-laws may prescribe. The Education Act 1921, section 49 (b), provided an identical "reasonable excuse." Before the Act of 1921, in *Hares* v. *Curtin*,[1] in which it was suggested that a cart track could not be a road and that the walking distance had not been measured according to, "the nearest road," Lord Alverstone C.J., giving judgment, said: "It does not mean a road of any particular class, but simply a route from the

1. [1913] 2 K.B. 328; see page 190, *supra*.

residence of a child to the nearest school." In the Act of 1944 the words used in section 39 (5) are "two miles . . . measured by the nearest available route." I do not think that they were meant to make any change in the law, except that a number of somewhat unnecessary words were cut out and there were substituted the expression which had been used in this court in *Hares* v. *Curtin*.[2]

To some extent I sympathise with the views of the appellant in the present case. It may be that parents would like to bring pressure on the Kent County Council to have someone to see that this "bit of road," as the justices call it, is safe for the children to cross—someone, for example, as is seen in London, wearing a white smock and holding a board with the words "Children Crossing, Stop." That, however, is a matter for the education authority to consider and put into operation if it thinks fit. I can only say, speaking for myself, that a route along which a child can walk and which measures not more than two miles is "the nearest available route." It may sometimes be unsafe. Sometimes the route might be flooded, and, if so, and the child could not walk along it, that might be a reasonable excuse for not using it on that particular day. We are not dealing with that sort of question. We are dealing with the question where the parents think it is not safe. Parliament has not substituted safety for distance as the test. Any question with regard to safety must, and I have no doubt, will, be taken into consideration by the education authority. I think in this case the justices came to a right decision and the appeal fails.

Appeal dismissed

(I) SAFETY OF PREMISES

72 Ching *v.* Surrey County Council [1910] 1 K.B. 736

COURT OF APPEAL

A local education authority has a statutory duty to keep the premises of a school in a state of repair, and is responsible for neglect of that duty by those actually managing the school.

Facts: The plaintiff, Alfred Ching, was a nine-year-old pupil at Maybury School, Woking, a maintained public elementary school. For about six months there had been large holes in the floor of the playing shed, and on July 9, 1908, the plaintiff caught his foot in one, fell, and broke his left arm. He claimed damages for negligence on the ground that under the Education Acts the defendants were liable to maintain the school and keep it efficient, and to preserve the premises safe for the use of pupils.

The action was tried at Guildford Assizes before Bucknill J. sitting with a jury, and the plaintiff was awarded damages amounting to £83 19s. 6d. The case was argued on further consideration in London, and judgment was given for the plaintiff.

The defendants appealed.

2. [1913] 2 K.B. 328; see page 190, *supra*.

Extract from Judgment

EARL OF HALSBURY L.J.: In this case a point of law arises upon facts which I think raise no serious question of fact. The plaintiff undoubtedly was injured, and, upon the finding of the jury, which we are not disposed to disturb, his injury was caused by that which with proper care might have been avoided. A hole was allowed to exist in the asphalt paving of the playground, upon which it was intended that the schoolboys, of whom the plaintiff was one, should amuse themselves by running and otherwise; and it has been found by the tribunal whose function it is to determine questions of fact that the accident which occurred was due to negligence on the part of those whose duty it was to keep the playground, which formed part of the school premises, in proper condition. It seems to me obvious that any one charged with that duty was bound to take care that the playground where boys were expected to play, it being intended for the purposes of their recreation, should be in such a condition that they should not be exposed to unnecessary danger while playing there. With regard to the question of fact, it is enough, I think, to say that it seems to me impossible for any one seriously to contend, upon the evidence with regard to the nature of this hole in the pavement, that it was reasonable to leave such a hole in a place where boys were expected to play and run, so that the accident might obviously occur which has occurred in this case.

But the substantial question which arises in this case is one, not of fact, but of law. Assuming that somebody or other is responsible for the negligence which I have described, the question arises, who are the persons so responsible? I do not think that there is really any doubt about the answer to that question, for in my opinion it is determined by statute. The persons once responsible for maintaining the schools provided by them were the school board. The powers which were in the first instance conferred upon the school board are now transferred to the county council, and the duties which were originally imposed upon the former are now imposed upon the latter body, which is therefore responsible for the performance of all those duties. I object very much, in dealing with this case, to go beyond the exigency of the particular case. Other cases may depend on different circumstances, and upon the nature of the particular duties which may be alleged in those cases respectively to exist, whether by virtue of the common law or by statutory enactment. With respect to this case, as I have said, I do not think there is any doubt. It does not appear to me to be really material to consider whether section 7 or section 5 of the Act is the section upon which the case depends. In my opinion, the words "maintain and keep efficient," as applied to a school, must necessarily include, not only what has been described as the "scholastic system" which is to be enforced, but also the place where the duty is to be performed by those who are under the main duty of keeping the school efficient for the scholars. Whatever may be necessary for the purpose of performing the main duty appears to me to be included in the general description of "keeping the school efficient." It is unnecessary to consider whether or not the word "maintain" in section 7 would, of itself, as applicable to the matter with which we are at present dealing, namely, keeping the school efficient, have necessarily included all the rest, that is to say, keeping the school premises in a proper condition as regards health and comfort, and all that is involved in saying that they shall be so kept as to be a proper place for the reception of the children, as regards the school for the purpose of teaching and as regards the playground for the purpose of exercise and recreation. Without going through all the matters which are necessarily involved in maintaining and keeping efficient the school, it is enough for the purposes of this case to say that the duty which I have mentioned, and which was obviously formerly imposed upon and performed by the school board, has by the statute been imposed upon the county council. I decline to go beyond that, and, having come to that conclusion, it is unnecessary for me to consider the question whether, without section 5, the word "maintain" as used in section 7 would, necessarily and in itself, include the duty which is here in question, because section 5 in my opinion clearly imposes that duty upon the county council. I therefore think that this action is well founded, and that it is brought against the persons who are by law made responsible as principals for the discharge of the statutory duty. I do not think it necessary to discuss the machinery provided by the statute with regard to the persons by whom the acts necessary for the performance of the statutory duty are to be actually performed. The body on whose behalf these acts are to be done is the county council; the duty is upon them and is one for the non-performance of which they are in my opinion responsible. There may possibly be some question, as between themselves and some other body or persons, who are responsible, and as to the means to be taken to compel those persons to perform their duty more efficiently, but that is altogether beside the present question. For these reasons I think the appeal must be dismissed.

Appeal dismissed

73 Morris *v.* Carnarvon County Council [1910] 1 K.B. 840

COURT OF APPEAL
A local education authority's duty to maintain the premises of a school in a state of repair extends to the discovery and remedying of defects on the transfer of a school from another body.

Facts: The plaintiff, Maggie Morris, was a six-year-old child. She attended a school provided by the defendants in which two rooms were connected by a heavy door which swung in both directions. On November 4, 1908, she was told by a mistress to leave the room. No one opened the door for her and, as she was going through, it swung back and injured one of her fingers, which was later amputated.

At Bangor County Court the jury found that the defendants were negligent in allowing the door to remain as it was, whereupon the judge asked: "Will you consider further whether it was negligent to construct this door in the first instance?" The jury replied that they did not think that the door as originally constructed was suitable for infants. Counsel for the defendants objected to this question on the ground that it amounted to an amendment of claim alleging that the defendants were negligent in 1903 and that such a claim would be out of time under the Public Authorities Act.[1] Judgment was given for the plaintiff.

The defendants appealed by way of case stated to the Divisional Court of the King's Bench Division. The appeal was dismissed on the ground that the answers to the questions amounted to a finding that the door as originally constructed was, with regard to a child like the plaintiff, a trap. Since it was a trap in the first instance, it was negligent to allow it to remain in the same condition and the defendants were liable.

The defendants appealed further to the Court of Appeal.

Extract from Judgment
VAUGHAN WILLIAMS L.J.: The injury to the plaintiff in this case was occasioned by a heavy door with a very strong spring. I do not think that it can be seriously argued that this door, as originally put up was not a very improperly constructed door for the purposes of this school. It was very likely, if used by a young child to occasion such an accident as happened in this case. It was urged for the defendants that this door was put up by their predecessors, the school board, and that, this being so, although the defendants permitted it to continue to be used in their time, they ought not to be held liable for negligence in respect of the accident which occurred through its existence. That argument amounts to saying that, if some structure of a dangerous character, like this door, was put up in the school at a time when the defendants' predecessors had the management of it, no duty rested on the defendants, after the school was transferred to them, to discover and remedy the dangerous nature of the structure. This is really the only way in which the defendants' case can now be put. Before the decision in *Ching* v. *Surrey County Council*[2] it might have been argued that the duty which would have rested on the school board in respect of such a matter was not transferred by the Education Act 1902 to the defendants, but they were only by that Act charged with the maintenance of the scholastic system in force in the school, and not with the maintenance and keeping efficient of the fabric of the school premises; but since the decision in that case it is impossible to put forward that contention. Under these circumstances the only question which we have to consider appears to me to be whether there was a duty on the part of the defendants to discover and remedy the danger occasioned by this door. I think that there clearly was such a duty imposed upon them. In my opinion there was evidence that this was obviously a dangerous door for the

1. See pages 63–65, *supra*.
2. [1910] 1 K.B. 736; see page 194, *supra*.

purposes of a school for young children, and, there being an obligation on the
defendants to remove such a door, and substitute for it a safe mode of entrance
into and egress from the class-room, the defendants failed to perform that
obligation. For these reasons I think the appeal must be dismissed.

Appeal dismissed

74 Lyes *v.* Middlesex County Council (1962) 61 L.G.R. 443

QUEEN'S BENCH DIVISION

*The common law duty of a schoolmaster to his pupils is that of a prudent parent
bound to take notice of boys and their tendency to do mischievous acts, not in the
context of the home but in the circumstances of school life, and extends not only
to how the pupils conduct themselves but also to the state and condition of the
school premises.*

Facts: The plaintiff, John Lyes, was a pupil at Northside Secondary Modern
School, Finchley, which was built about 1900.

On December 7, 1955, when the plaintiff was fifteen years old, a physical
training lesson took place in the school hall. After dismissal, the boys filed
out from the hall into a corridor leading to two swing doors. The doors were
seven feet in height, the upper halves consisting of four glass panels divided
by a glazing bar, so that each piece of glazing was about twelve inches in
width and eight or eight and a half inches in depth. The glass was twenty-
four-ounce glass, approximately one-eighth of an inch thick.

The plaintiff and some other pupils left the hall earlier than the rest.
Preceding the plaintiff was a boy named Lee who entered the changing room
by the first door, made around the changing room to the other door and to
keep somebody out "for a lark" put his foot near that door. He felt someone
trying to push the door, and the next thing he knew was that the plaintiff's
hand came in through the glass. According to the plaintiff, he put his hand
on the woodwork between the two lower glass panels, which was about five
inches wide, and pushed at the door. His hand slid off the framework and
went through the glass, causing serious injury to his right wrist.

The plaintiff sued for damages for personal injuries, alleging negligence
on the part of the defendants.

Extracts from Judgment

EDMUND DAVIES J.: . . . The claim, as originally framed, alleged that the
defendants were liable both at common law for negligence and also for a
breach of statutory duty. The duty which the defendants, as the education
authority, owed to the plaintiff is larger than it is in respect of one aspect of
the case. Mr Solomon,[1] who has admirably assisted the court, at one time said
that the duty of the defendants to the plaintiff was that of invitor to invitee,
and accordingly that they had to warn him of any unusual danger of which they

1. Counsel for the plaintiff.

knew or ought to have known. The duty, in my judgment, is higher than that. It is the duty enunciated in the classic passage of Lord Esher M.R. in *Williams v. Eady*,[2] who there said, approving the direction of the trial judge, that "the school master was bound to take such care of his boys as a careful father would take of his boys, and there could not be a better definition of the duty of a school master. Then he was bound to take notice of the ordinary nature of young boys, their tendency to do mischievous acts, and their propensity to meddle with anything that came in their way." That is a duty which, I think, extends not merely to how the pupils conduct themselves and how the staff discharge their duties but also extends to the state and condition of the school premises. But Mr O'Connor[3] was not disposed to dispute that in any way.

Accordingly, as far as negligence is concerned, that is the standard which has to be applied. The plaintiff additionally puts his case on the basis of a breach of statutory duty founded on section 10 (2) of the Education Act 1944,[4] which provides that: ". . . it shall be the duty of a local education authority to secure that the premises of every school maintained by them conform to the standards prescribed for schools of the description to which the school belongs." For the purpose of these proceedings there can be no doubt that the defendants are a local education authority within the meaning of that provision, and that this is a school maintained by them. I now turn to the regulations made under the powers conferred on the Minister by that Act in the Schools Grants Regulations 1951.[5] The plaintiff originally sought to rely upon regulation 6 (1) alone, which provides that "the premises of the school shall be . . . kept in a proper state of repair"—I omit the irrelevant words. I indicated to Mr Solomon at an early stage that the essence of this case was that the glass in that panel was dangerously thin and that the defendants ought to have known about it. Even though the plaintiff established both of those matters, could it be said that the door was not in a state of repair? I think Mr Solomon, without abandoning regulation 6, was at least a bit impressed by the question. He sought leave, without opposition by the defendants, to amend his statement of claim by invoking in addition the preceding regulation, regulation 5, which provides that "the school shall be kept on a satisfactory level of efficiency." Does "efficiency" embrace the state of the premises? Does it apply to the complaint made here on the plaintiff's behalf, that the door panel was far too thin and far too brittle? If that were established as a fact, then I would hold that the door was not an efficient door, and if authority were needed for that proposition, which is again I think not resisted by Mr O'Connor, it is to be found in *Morris v. Carnarvon County Council*,[6] where the decision in *Ching v. Surrey County Council*[7] was followed and applied. In that case the accident arose by reason of the fact that in the

2. (1893) 10 T.L.R. 41; see page 240, *infra.*
3. Counsel for the defendants.
4. 7 & 8 Geo. 6, c. 31.
5. S.I. 1951 No. 1743; now replaced by the Schools Regulations, S.I. 1959 No. 364.
6. [1910] 1 K.B. 840; see page 196, *supra.*
7. [1910] 1 K.B. 736; see page 194, *supra.*

school premises there was a heavy swing door with a powerful swing, and the plaintiff while leaving the class-room was injured through that door closing on her fingers. The door was in a good state of repair and in the same condition as it was when the school had been taken over by the defendants from their predecessors. The jury found that the door was not a suitable one for use by young children when put up in the first instance. The defendants were guilty of negligence in allowing it to remain in the school. The Court of Appeal held that, the duty of the defendants being to keep the school premises in proper condition for the purpose of a school—which I equate with keeping them on a satisfactory level of efficiency—they were responsible for a breach of duty in not discovering and remedying the unsatisfactory construction of the door in question and were accordingly liable.

Without more I shall hold accordingly, that, subject to what must here be said as to whether or not negligence has to be proved against the defendants, a door of this kind, if fitted with glass of a too fragile nature to stand up to the ordinary demands of school life, would be an inefficient door.

. . . This case therefore stands or falls by the plaintiff's allegation that that glass panel was too thin; that the defendants knew that it was too thin and that they ought to have done something about it. I have referred to the breach of statutory duty relied upon. The two cases cited, *Ching* v. *Surrey County Council*[8] and *Morris* v. *Carnarvon County Council*[9] established that a breach of that duty does give rise to an action for damages. What has been canvassed at greater length largely at my instigation is, what is the exact nature of the duty.

Mr Solomon at one stage contended that it was absolute in its nature and that, looking at a school, the test is whether the premises were kept on a satisfactory level of efficiency: Deciding that matter objectively, if the answer to that question were "No," then there must be liability. Later, however, he thought better of that, and he now concedes that, having regard to the wording of regulation 5, the school should be "kept on a satisfactory level of efficiency," it is incumbent upon him to establish that the defendants ought to have done something, their omission amounting to a failure in their duty of care in respect of the premises, before liability can be established.

Mr O'Connor on the other hand submits that this regulation adds nothing to the common law duty of care such as would be taken by a reasonably prudent parent. I hold that the standard is that of a reasonably prudent parent judged not in the context of his own home but in that of a school, in other words, a person exhibiting the responsible mental qualities of a prudent parent in the circumstances of school life. School life happily differs from home life. The more the merrier. A lot of pupils are apt to make much more noise even than a few children in a small home and there is, to use an expression of one of the witnesses, more skylarking, and a bit of rough play, but the reasonable parent in school premises would be mindful of such considerations as that.

Was this glass too thin? In my judgment it was. It may be that the conse-

8. [1910] 1 K.B. 736; see page 194, *supra*.
9. [1910] 1 K.B. 840; see page 196, *supra*.

quences of the decision I have arrived at in this case may be widespread. If they are widespread and lead to greater safety in the care of the young then no consummation could be more devoutly desired. I hold the glass to be too thin. I do not think that anybody who has heard the general body of evidence in this case can have any doubt about it. I am not of course unmindful of the fact that the size of the panes has much to do with it. The bigger the pane, the greater the need for tough glass. I have not forgotten that the pane of glass here was small, merely twelve inches by eight inches, but there can be no doubt in my mind that certainly by today the education authority is fully alive to the undesirability of having twenty-four-ounce, that is to say, one-eighth of an inch thick glass in door panels situate, as this one was, at about shoulder height. I dare say, though I have not heard any very satisfactory evidence about it, that the defendants are by today getting busy about the matter. If they are not, then I think they should be.

Mr O'Connor was not seriously disposed to contest that, even in such a panel, twelve inches by eight inches, as this one was, twenty-four-ounce glass was not the safest glass that could be put in. But the real comment about the matter has been this. He says that the statutory provision adds nothing to the common law. It is well established that whether a party was negligent has to be determined in the light of the knowledge prevailing at the time of the accident. If the state of knowledge, if the appreciation of circumstances by the general body of reasonably minded persons was such that they would not have regarded the risk as curable by the standard reasonable care involved, then no liability exists. He says it matters not that after an accident knowledge increases, there is a better appreciation of risks involved, and matters obviating the risk suggest themselves.

In this case, within a very short time, a matter of days, after the plaintiff's accident eight panes of glass in this door were taken out and the four horizontal glazing bars removed, and the panes were replaced with tougher glass. It appears that it was quite fortuitous and unrelated to this accident that the glazier was about to make a visit to the school and I accept what the borough surveyor says—that the fact that the glazier was going to the school in any event led him to give the instructions that this reglazing be performed. I direct myself also, as Bramwell B. did many years ago in *Hart* v. *The Lancashire & Yorkshire Railway Co.*,[10] that the fact that as people grow older they become wiser does not necessarily establish they were foolish or negligent before. It is true that accidents have a habit of teaching people many things of which hitherto they had not been aware. It would accordingly be dangerous to spell out from the fact that improvements were very rapidly effected on this door any sort of recognition of negligence on the defendants' part. Nor do I spell it out. All the same, the fact that they were effected only a few days after the accident demonstrates that it was a job very easy to accomplish.

The question arises, ought it to have been done before? Ought the defendants to have appreciated the need for it on the facts of this case—namely, with

10. (1869) 21 L.T. 261.

H

regard to a door leading to a changing room and having glass panels, glazed with such glass as this, at shoulder height? The glass could not have been thinner. It is the thinnest glass used for household purposes. You do sometimes find that eighteen-ounce glass is used for picture frames and leaded lights, but apart from that, twenty-four-ounce or one-eighth of an inch glass is the lightest normally used in houses. It is used in houses, I recall, not only in windows but also in doors. An experienced practical glazier who gave evidence for the plaintiff, said he would prefer glass three-sixteenths of an inch thick, preferably one quarter of an inch. He thought that twenty-four-ounce glass could in doors in houses be safely used for a panel twelve inches by eight inches but he also said that the situation was quite different when you came to glazing a door in a school. His objection was put in this way; that it is not sufficiently strong where there are children who are skylarking. He said that home hazards are not as great as at school. There are more hazards at school and more horseplay, facts which no one can deny, human nature and boys' youthful human nature being what it is. He says that any glass of this thickness in any school where there is any likelihood of an impact would be unsafe. He claims if he had gone to that school in 1955 before the accident and had ascertained the thickness of the glass in these panels, he would have advised their instant removal. I think that a reasonably careful person addressing his mind properly to these circumstances in 1955 would have been alerted to the risk of such an accident as this happening.

The plaintiff is content to adopt the view that he cannot succeed under regulation 5 unless he establishes negligence. "The school shall be kept on a satisfactory level of 'efficiency' involves, he concedes, that there was negligence by the defendants—in other words, that the defendants either knew or ought to have known that such glass should not have been used in such a place and that despite that knowledge or imputed knowledge they failed to take any steps to remedy the position. I desire to say no more about whether the regulation lays down an absolute duty or a qualified duty having regard to that concession, and I hold that, if it is incumbent upon the plaintiff to establish negligence in order to succeed under the regulation, that task he has discharged. I hold, for the reasons indicated, that the glass was too thin, that there should have been either thicker sheet glass or plate glass or some other kind of glass, maybe covered by meshing of some kind or another, and that the failure to take any steps of that kind amount to negligence by the education authority.

Judgment, with damages of £3,750
for the plaintiff

75 Reffell *v.* Surrey County Council [1964] 1 All E.R. 743

QUEEN'S BENCH DIVISION

An education authority which fails to maintain a school safely may be found negligent at common law in addition to being in breach of their duties under the Education Acts.

Facts: The plaintiff, Lynn Reffell, was a pupil at the County Grammar School, Godalming. On July 15, 1960, when she was about twelve, she was hurrying along a corridor between classes at about 3 p.m. As she neared a pair of partly glazed swing doors, one door swung towards her. She put out her right hand to stop the door, as a result of which the hand went right through a pane of obscured pin-head morocco glass, one-eighth of an inch thick and four feet from the ground. She suffered injuries which had still left two scars on her forearm four years later. She also suffered loss of movement of two fingers, one of which stuck out at an angle. The injuries would be a handicap in playing the piano or typing.

The plaintiff brought an action against the Surrey County Council for breach of statutory duty and negligence. The defendants denied liability, and pleaded contributory negligence.

Extract from Judgment

VEALE J.: . . . The school was built probably in or about 1919. The defendants had employed a reputable firm of architects, who were concerned in the building not only of this but also of other schools. Altogether, at the present time, the defendants are responsible for something over seven hundred educational establishments, which include 677 primary and secondary schools at which there are something under 190,000 pupils. . . . At no time since the school has been built had there been any accident at the girls' cloak-room door. However, the boys' section of the school had a similar cloak-room with similar doors and it appears that in 1937 one boy, when chasing another, did put his hand through the glass in that door. Fortunately, he was not seriously injured. . . . Since the war, the defendants have clearly appreciated the danger of thin glass in doors. Whatever may have been the position before the war, there is no doubt but that new schools have always had toughened glass installed in their doors; and, since the war, according to Mr Parkin the Assistant County Education Office, broken glass in places where danger is to be apprehended, such as the doors, has always been replaced by toughened glass.

. . . However, as I say, as from 1945 the defendants had clearly appreciated the danger of one-eighth inch glass in doors. Further, there have, since the war, been accidents at schools at doors containing glass. How many I do not know. The defendants have given no evidence about it at all and have called no witnesses with any knowledge of it. All I know is that in 1963 there were eleven reported accidents involving injury to scholars as a result of the breaking of glass in school doors. This case has proceeded on the basis that the 1963 figures are a fair picture of the actual number of such accidents, both after and before 1960, though, of course, the defendants point to the large number of school doors under their control and to the large number of pupils. If this is indeed so, there had been a substantial number of accidents at school glass doors before the accident with which I am concerned in July 1960. I do not know what type of glass it was that broke, nor do I know the circumstances of the other accidents. But, if the glass that broke was one-eighth inch glass, the defendants clearly had knowledge of the danger. If the glass that broke was in fact thicker than one-eighth inch, all the more did the defendants have knowledge of the danger of one-eighth inch thick glass. In any event, since 1945, all replacements have been of toughened glass.

. . . I do not think that there has been any express decision on section 10 of the Education Act 1944 and regulation 51,[1] and I confess that I have had some doubt about the matter. . . . Bearing in mind that no penalty is laid down by the statute for a breach, I think that an action, by a pupil or master at a school who can prove a breach of the regulation, does lie.

. . . I think that the duty to secure (that is the word in the section) that safety shall be reasonably assured (which are the words of the regulation) is an absolute duty and the test of breach or no breach is objective. Putting it another way, if safety is not reasonably assured in the premises in fact, then there is a breach.

That leads us to the third question. Were the premises on July 15, 1960, with this one-eighth inch glass in the cloak-room door, at a height of four feet, reasonably safe? I have no hesitation in saying that they were not. This one-eighth inch glass in a cloak-room door was, in my view, asking for trouble. True, there had been no previous accident at this door, but there had been accidents of some sort at such doors elsewhere, and there had been an accident at the boys' cloak-room door in 1937 and the boys' cloak-room door was altered because of the danger of unruly boys. Boys are more unruly than girls, or so Mr Wakefield told me. Boys will be boys; but, equally, I should have thought girls will be girls. Even if they do not fight like small boys and if they generally behave with more decorum, they, nevertheless, have been known to chase each other and to run in corridors. It is easy to visualise one girl following another, the one in front swinging the cloak-room door to and the following girl putting out a hand to arrest it, without any element of horse play at all. I cannot help thinking that the defendants have been lucky that there has been no previous accident at this door.

. . . I am not, I hope, being wise after the event, and I exclude, I hope, the wisdom of hindsight; but, if instead of considering whether there was a breach of regulation 51 on an objective basis, I was to approach the matter on a common law basis, I should still say, and indeed I find, that the defendants were negligent. This is not the case of an isolated hit for six out of a cricket ground as in *Bolton* v. *Stone*[2].

. . . If it is too much to ask an education authority confronted with this problem of glass in doors to change every door with one-eighth inch glass in it, it is not too much to ask them to do something more than merely wait for major adaptations or breakages. . . . Not only, in my judgment, was the risk of accident a real risk, but it was both a foreseeable risk and one which was in fact foreseen. If it had not been foreseen there would not have been the policy

1. Of the Standards for School Premises Regulations, 1959.
2. [1951] A.C. 850; [1951] 1 All E.R. 1078.

of replacing broken one-eighth inch glass with toughened glass. In the result, I find the defendants liable to the plaintiff both under the statute and regulation and at common law.

Judgment for plaintiff

76 Abbott *v*. Isham and others (1920) 90 L.J.K.B. 309

NORTHAMPTON ASSIZES

The managers of a voluntary school are liable to keep the schoolhouse in repair, whether required to do so by the local education authority or not. Notice given to the managers at one time will not operate as against managers subsequently appointed, but each manager is guilty of negligence if on appointment he does not ascertain and remedy defects.

Facts: The plaintiff, Mr William Lawson Abbott was the headmaster of the non-provided school of Hanging Houghton and Lamport, Northamptonshire. The defendants were the managers of the schools.

The plaintiff sued for damages for personal injuries following an explosion in the boiler of the school's heating apparatus, alleging that the managers were in breach of duty in allowing the apparatus to be out of repair, the pipes being old, worn-out and leaky; and repaired with sheet-iron instead of being replaced. Further, there was no safety-valve or exhaust on the boiler which, though it represented the best knowledge on the subject at the time of its construction, had not been modernised and would not have been considered safe at the time of the action.

The defendants denied negligence or that the apparatus was out of repair. They alleged that the explosion was due to an exceptional frost, and that the plaintiff was guilty of contributory negligence in not reporting the alleged disrepair, in not taking sufficient care to prevent the water from freezing, and in allowing a fire to be lighted while the water was frozen. The defendants also claimed that on the principle of *volenti non fit injuria* the plaintiff could not recover as he knew of the defect and the managers did not.

Cur. adv. vult

Judgment

HORRIDGE J.: This is an action brought by the plaintiff, who is employed by the defendants, the managers of a non-provided school at Hanging Houghton in the County of Northampton, for damages for personal injuries occasioned to him whilst in the discharge of his duties by the bursting of a boiler.

The boiler was connected with a heating apparatus which carried the hot water by means of pipes through the school; but there was not upon the boiler any safety-valve or any vent to allow the escape of excessive steam.

This heating apparatus had been put in about the year 1870 and its construction had never been altered since that time.

The plaintiff, on September 29, 1901, by an agreement in writing, was appointed schoolmaster by the then managers, and was still in the same position at the commencement of this action against the present defendants. Sir Vere Isham and Lady Millicent Isham have been managers since 1904, and the defendant Castell had been a manager since 1908, but the other defendants were appointed since that date.

In 1905 the boiler and heating apparatus were inspected by a Mr Crane, who warned the plaintiff that there was a danger of the boiler bursting on account of the obsolete arrangement of the whole thing, and the plaintiff duly reported this opinion very soon after to Mr Pitchford, who was acting on behalf of the then managers in looking after the school.

On September 16, 1908, the plaintiff obtained from a Mr Capell, an iron-monger, a report in which the following passage appears: "Should you retain the apparatus as it now exists, it will be necessary to have the boiler out and cleaned, and also to take out several lengths of the piping that are defective and insert new ones." This report was also shown to Mr Pitchford.

There were several documents put in, which were within the knowledge of Mr Pitchford, and in which the hot-water apparatus was specially referred to, and the latest of these was a letter from Mr Pitchford to Lord Ludlow in which the following occurred: "But after getting the best possible terms, our income will not exceed £63 or £63 10s. The repairs and maintenance have cost us, during the last few years, an average of over £20 per annum, and we have also to provide religious books. New flooring and heating apparatus will soon be required."

I find as a fact that the dangerous character of the heating apparatus was known to the plaintiff as far back as 1905, and that he on several occasions up to August 5, 1909, brought its dangerous condition to the knowledge of Mr Pitchford.

Shortly before the explosion occurred, the plaintiff informed Lady Frederick, one of the defendants, that there was difficulty in keeping the frost out of the pipes on account of the scarcity of coal, and she said that the plaintiff would have to burn wood but no wood was supplied to him. For several days prior to February 10, 1919, there was a frost of exceptional severity, with the result that the pipe of the heating apparatus got blocked; the flow of steam and water being interfered with, causing the pressure of steam on the boiler which eventually resulted in the bursting.

In these circumstances the plaintiff seeks to recover from the defendants as managers of the school.

The first question that I have to decide is what liability the managers are under, as regards the condition of the school premises. By section 7 (1) (d) of the Education Act 1902, it is enacted that "The managers of the school shall provide the school house free of any charge . . . and shall, out of funds provided by them, keep the school house in good repair, and make such altera-tions and improvements in the buildings as may be reasonably required by the local education authority. . . ."

I think the true construction of that clause is that although the managers are bound to make alterations and improvements as required by the local authority, they are nevertheless themselves under the liability to keep the school house in good repair, and, as they were in charge of the premises in which the plaintiff was bound to carry out his duties, they were, within the language of Lord Herschell in *Smith* v. *Baker*,[1] under the duty of taking reasonable care to provide proper appliances and to maintain them in a proper condition and so as not to subject those employed by them to unnecessary risk. I can find nothing in the Act of Parliament which shows that the managers are to be treated in any way as a legal body with succession, so that notice given to the managers at one time would operate as against managers subsequently appointed. In my view, the only managers who can be affected by the notice to Mr Pitchford are the defendants Sir Vere Isham, Lady Isham, and Mr Castell; but I consider that the managers subsequently appointed were bound, with the earlier managers, to see, on their appointment, when they became the employers of the plaintiff, that the premises and appliances in them were reasonably fit for the purposes of being used by the plaintiff as a school-room. It was said that there was no negligence on their part in not discovering the absence of a safety-valve or other vent. The evidence of Mr Crane was that anyone with any experience would have discovered that this heating apparatus had no such safety-valve or vent, and that for thirty or forty years past heating apparatuses have always been provided with these precautions. I further find as a fact that each of these managers on taking office was negligent in not ascertaining and remedying the condition of the heating apparatus and, in the case of Sir Vere Isham, Lady Isham, and Mr Castell, they were negligent after having notice from the plaintiff of its condition.

The next point taken was that the plaintiff was guilty of negligence himself in not seeing the matter attended to, and in using the school-room after the severe frost preceding February 10, knowing, as he did, that danger was to be apprehended in the case of a severe frost.

I do not think he was negligent, as, in my view, he did all he could in reporting the matter as he did, and he was not negligent in his position in opening the school and having the fire lighted on February 10. It was further said that he voluntarily incurred the risk, but the question whether he did so or not has been decided in *Smith* v. *Baker*[2] to be always a question of fact, and I find, as a fact, that he did not so voluntarily incur the risk.

The last point is a difficult one, namely, whether this case falls within the doctrine laid down in *Griffiths* v. *London and St Katharine Docks Company*.[3] It is quite true that the plaintiff knew of the risk which arose from the defective apparatus, and it is also clear that with the exception of the three defendants, Sir Vere Isham, Lady Isham, and Mr Castell, the defendants did not in fact know, either through themselves or through an agent, of the condition of the apparatus.

1. [1891] A.C. 325; 7 T.L.R. 679.
2. [1891] A.C. 325; 7 T.L.R. 679.
3. (1884) 13 Q.B.D. 259.

Does the decision in *Griffiths* v. *London and St Katharine Docks Company*[4] apply to a case where the negligence is in allowing an apparatus forming a portion of the premises upon which the plaintiff was originally engaged to work to be defective and dangerous? The matter was considered in the case of *Williams* v. *Birmingham Battery and Metal Company*,[5] in which the plaintiff was clearly aware of the absence of any proper ladder, and A. L. Smith L.J.,[6] in his judgment, says: "This is not the case where a master has provided proper appliances and done his best to maintain them in a state of efficiency, in which case the man has no action against his master if the appliances became unsafe, whereby the man has been injured unless he avers and proves that the master knew of their having become unsafe, and that the man was ignorant of it: *Griffiths* v. *London and St Katharine Docks Company*.[7] When proper appliances have been supplied by a master to a man they may well become unsafe to the knowledge of the man and without the knowledge of the master, and so it is that each issue must in such a case be established by the man when he sues his master. This is the case of no proper appliances having been supplied by the master at all, so that the man might carry on his operation in such a way as not to be exposed to unnecessary risk. The case is similar to that of *Mellors* v. *Shaw*.[8] If this case had stopped here it appears to me clear that there must have been judgment for the plaintiff, she having proved personal negligence in the defendants whereby the deceased man met with his death; and how do the defendants seek to get rid of this case so far successfully made and proved against them?"

The language used in the opinions of the House of Lords in *Smith* v. *Baker*[9] seems to me to show that that doctrine does not apply to a case where an employer has not provided proper appliances. Lord Halsbury L.C.[10] says: "I think the cases cited at your Lordships' bar of *Sword* v. *Cameron*[11] and *Bartonshill Coal Company* v. *McGuire*[12] established conclusively the point for which they were cited, that a negligent system or a negligent mode of using perfectly sound machinery may make the employer liable quite apart from any of the provisions of the Employers' Liability Act. In *Sword* v. *Cameron*[13] it could hardly be doubted that the quarryman who was injured by the explosion of the blast in the quarry was perfectly aware of the risk; but nevertheless he was held entitled to recover notwithstanding that knowledge." And Lord Herschell,[14] referring to the case of *Sword* v. *Cameron*[15]

4. (1884) 13 Q.B.D. 259.
5. [1899] 2 Q.B. 338; 15 T.L.R. 468.
6. [1899] 2 Q.B. 338, at 343.
7. (1884) 13 Q.B.D. 259.
8. (1861) 1 B. & S. 437.
9. [1891] A.C. 325; 7 T.L.R. 679.
10. [1891] A.C. 325, at 339.
11. (1839) 1 Sc. Sess. Cases, 2nd series, 493.
12. (1858) 3 Macq. 300.
13. (1839) 1 Sc. Sess. Cases, 2nd series, 493.
14. [1891] A.C. 325, at 364.
15. (1839) 1 Sc. Sess. Cases (2nd series) 493.

says: "This case appears to me to be analogous to the present, and the ground upon which Lord Cransworth bases the liability of the employer to be applicable to it. It will be noticed that in that case the defective system which created the risk, and from which the pursuer suffered, was known to him, and that he continued his work notwithstanding this knowledge; yet it never appears to have occurred, either to the Scotch Court or to Lord Cransworth, that this absolved the employer from liability."

In the recent case of *Monaghan* v. *Rhodes*,[16] although the plaintiff must clearly have known of the danger, it was held that he could recover—see the language of Lord Sterndale M.R.,[17] and Atkin L.J.[18] I do not think that the doctrine of *Griffiths* v. *London and St Katharine Docks Company*[19] applies to a case where the plaintiff establishes personal negligence on the part of the master in failing to provide proper premises or appliances, and where it is negligence on his part not to see that the premises and appliances are reasonably fit.

The out-of-pocket expenses in this case were agreed at £132 10s., and I assess the damages at £300, and give judgment for the plaintiff for that amount with costs.

Judgment for the plaintiff

77 Gillmore *v.* London County Council [1938] 4 All E.R. 331

KING'S BENCH DIVISION
It is the duty of a local education authority to provide a floor which is reasonably safe in all the circumstances. If a student is injured through falling on an unsuitable floor during the course of instruction the defence of volenti non fit injuria *is not available.*

Facts: The plaintiff, William Stephen Gillmore, registered for a course of physical exercises in January 1937 and paid a fee of five shillings. The course was held at the Porchester Hall, Paddington, and on June 22, 1937, the plaintiff fell and broke his leg.

On the basis that his registration concluded a contract with the local education authority, the plaintiff claimed damages for breach of warranty in that the floor of the hall was so highly polished as to be unsafe for instruction in physical exercises. Alternatively, he claimed damages in negligence.

The defendants denied breach of warranty or negligence. They claimed that the floor was not so slippery as to be unsafe, and that its condition was not the cause of the plaintiff's fall. Alternatively, they contended that if the floor was dangerous, this was obvious to the defendant and that he voluntarily undertook any risk by doing the exercises.

16. [1920] 1 K.B. 487.
17. [1920] 1 K.B. 487, at 496.
18. [1920] 1 K.B. 487, at 498.
19. (1884) 13 Q.B.D. 259.

Extract from Judgment

DU PARCQ L.J.: The plaintiff, having seen an advertisement of classes in physical training organised by the defendants, the London County Council, was interested, and eventually joined one of the classes. He paid a small fee for the privilege of admission, and attended for some time, no doubt with benefit to himself. When he first attended the classes, they were being held in the hall which during the summer months in a slightly altered form fulfils the purpose of the Paddington swimming bath. As commonly happens when the bathing season is over, such baths are floored over and used as halls. In the present case, when the bath was wanted again for its purpose as a swimming bath, the classes were transferred to the Porchester Hall, which is a very fine hall let out by the Paddington Borough Council. . . . The exercises were Swedish exercises. Some of them were of a rather formal character, but some were less formal and regulated. . . . The material form of exercise in this case was one which was performed by the young men in pairs, each one hopping on his right leg with his hands behind his back, endeavouring, by making lunges at the other, which the other sought to avoid, to compel the other to put his left foot down on to the ground.

On June 22, 1937, the plaintiff was engaged in that exercise with a Mr Ryan as his partner, when, according to his own account of the matter, he went to put his foot down and slipped. He was hopping on his right leg, and he says that, when he put down his left leg—or rather, when he went to put down his left leg, as he puts it—he just sat on it, and he was definite that he slipped. He had never slipped before, and it had never occurred to him that the floor was dangerous, even when he had run upon it. He was wearing, as I think certainly on this occasion all those participating in that exercise were wearing, rubber shoes. . . .

The case for the plaintiff is that the floor surface at Porchester Hall is really not suitable for exercises of this kind. It is a polished surface, because the hall is very largely used for dances. . . . However, the question is, I think, whether it is a reasonably safe floor to use when one is inviting people to come and make use of it for physical exercises of this kind. . . . I think that the proper way to put it is this. If any person or body of persons invite a man for reward to take part in physical training, and invite him to come for that purpose to premises which they have hired, or of which for the time being they are in possession, then, in those circumstances, that person or body of persons impliedly warrant that they have taken reasonable care to see that the premises are in all respects reasonably safe for the purpose. . . .

I have had evidence, of course, on each side here, and, if I summarise the evidence for the defendants, I think it comes to this, that, though nobody would choose a polished floor, polished as this one was so as to be suitable for dancers, for the purpose of physical exercises, still, the real reason for that is not so much any possibility of danger as the fact that, of course, it would be gratuitous and a little absurd to polish a floor when the polish at any rate would do no good. It would never occur to anybody to say that a gymnasium ought to have a polished floor. It does not follow that, if it has a polished floor, it becomes a dangerous place.

I think that one ought first of all to consider why there is any objection, if objection there be, to a polished floor. I am bound to say that the witnesses for the defendant council were extremely frank, and gave me every assistance. One of them, a gentleman of great experience, says that the reason why polish on a floor of this kind is not satisfactory—at any rate, not ideally satisfactory— is that polish on hard wood accentuates the tendency to slipperiness which you find in hard wood. He says, and I have no doubt quite rightly, that you cannot get the perfect floor. If you have a soft-wood floor, then, there is a tendency, not only to collect dust, but also to form splinters, and they, of course, have their dangers. Hard wood, no doubt, is better, but hard wood has a tendency towards slipperiness which soft wood has not. I imagine, however, that everyone would say that hard wood was to be preferred. Nobody could say, however, that you ought to accentuate that unfortunate tendency to slipperiness by polishing that floor, and it would make matters no better if it were polished rather more in some places than in others, which may have been the case here, when I recollect the evidence which was given by Mr Nunn, the attendant at Porchester Hall. There is also much evidence for the defendants by gentlemen who, I am sure, have been absolutely straight- forward, who told me that they had tested this floor and found that really it was very difficult to slip when you were wearing rubber shoes. They say that whatever danger there may be said to be in a polished hard-wood floor is entirely counteracted if you wear rubber shoes. What it comes to is that they said: "I wore rubber shoes, and I tried to slide, and tried to slip, and really could not do it." That appears valuable, though it may be that to a certain extent it must be discounted. I think that it is almost outside the powers of a human being who knows that a floor is under suspicion, and goes to test it himself, wearing rubber shoes, to see if he can slip on it, to make a perfectly fair test, however honest and however impartial he may be. The man who, be it only subconsciously, wants to say. "You can slip," probably will slip, and a man who hopes to say that there you cannot slip probably will not slip. It is hardly likely, in any case, that anybody who goes on to a floor in that state of mind will slip, because, when you know that there is some danger through slipping, all the muscles which counteract a tendency to slip auto- matically come into play. I think that I am bound to start here by finding that, on the facts, at any rate, I am persuaded by the evidence that the plaintiff did slip. He is an active young man, very well-built and compact, and, I should imagine from the look of him, accustomed to taking a good deal of exercise. He does not look clumsy, not the sort of man who would tumble over merely because he was hopping, even when he saw a much taller man, Mr Ryan, bearing down on him. I think that he did slip, and that he slipped on something. I have not seen his shoes, and have heard nothing about them except that they were rubber shoes, and I think I ought to assume that they were in reasonable order. When I find that this floor was polished, and when other people like Mr Ryan and Mr Taylor also said the same thing—namely, that they slipped on this floor when, apparently, they found no similar tendency to slip on the floor at the Paddington Baths—I think that I am bound to find that he slipped because of the condition of this floor.

If one looks to see what the condition was, it is not very difficult to find it, because what distinguished this floor from other floors was that it was a fairly highly-polished floor, suitable for dancing. I am bound to say, on the facts, that it does not seem to me to be very suitable for this sort of physical exercise. No doubt you might have people there day after day and week after week and nobody might fall and hurt himself. Nevertheless, it was a matter which obviously struck people from the first as one which needed consideration, because it was debated whether it would be wise to put down some sort of drugget or matting, and it was thought, and I think rightly, that it would be better not to do so. It was certainly felt by Mr Crane, the instructor actually in charge of this class, that this floor was wholly unsuitable—and, indeed, dangerous—for what he called gymnastic work, although he had come to the conclusion that it was safe for the particular exercise which was being performed at the time. I do not think that it was safe. I think that it was dangerous, and that this accident has certainly proved that it was dangerous. The question that remains is, therefore, whether there was a breach of the warranty that it should be reasonably safe. I should not say for a moment that, because many people might think that a soft-wood floor was better than a hard-wood floor, because a hard-wood floor was more slippery, therefore there was any negligence in having a hard-wood floor. It is a choice, I will not say of evils, but between two not perfect surfaces. However, where you get hard wood plus polish of this kind, I do not think that it is possible to say that it was reasonably safe. It certainly was not safe on the facts as I have found them, and I do not think that it is right to say that it was reasonably safe.

I regret, in some ways, having to give a decision which may make things a little difficult for the council, and which perhaps may make it less easy for them to provide suitable places for physical training; but, after all, people who accept their invitation are entitled to assume that they are to be provided with premises where they can safely conduct any activities which they are bidden to conduct by the instructor in charge. That leads me to the question whether anything can remain here of the defence *violenti non fit injuria*—that is, that the plaintiff cannot complain because he agreed to take the risk, and was willing to run any risk there was. It is plain, in my view, on the evidence, that he did nothing of the sort. He trusted to those who had invited him and to those who were, so to speak, in command. It never occurred to him that he was being asked to do anything dangerous in a dangerous place. Of course, he took certain risks. Anybody who plays a game which involves any bodily violence or is content to hop about on one leg lunging at somebody else takes certain risks, and, if he fell down in the normal way, he cannot complain, just as anybody who is unfortunate enough to break his collar-bone on the football field in the ordinary way has no right to claim damages at law against anybody else. Here, however, there was added danger, in my view. He did not assume the risk willingly. I think that it did not ocur to him that there was an added danger, and, with that added danger there, he was entitled to assume that it was safe. I do not think that it was safe, and, on that ground, the warranty being as I have stated it, I think that the plaintiff succeeds. I suppose that, by adopting the same reasoning, one might say that there was a failure on the part of the defendants or their agents to take reasonable care.

In those circumstances, fortunately, the damages are not very heavy, because there is no permanent injury at all, or, if there is, it is so slight that apparently the plaintiff will never notice it, so that I can disregard it. I do not think that a young man like this wants money for pain and suffering, and so on. I think that, if I give him a sum of £220 in all, that will adequately cover the injuries he has suffered. There will be judgment for that amount with costs.

Judgment for the plaintiff for £220, with costs

[NOTE: For a consideration of the standard of the schoolmaster's duty of care, see the note on *Williams* v. *Eady*, page 240, *infra*.]

(J) INDEPENDENT SCHOOLS:
DISQUALIFICATION TO MANAGE

78 Byrd *v.* Secretary of State for Education and Science; Secretary of State for Education and Science *v.* Byrd (1968) *The Times*, May 22

QUEEN'S BENCH DIVISION

The Independent Schools Tribunal has a discretion to disqualify a person from being a proprietor of an independent school without disqualifying that person from being a teacher in any school.

Facts: The appellant's husband, Mr William Michael Byrd, was headmaster of Cholderton College, an independent school near Salisbury. In May 1967 he was convicted on charges alleging assault and cruelty to pupils at the school, and was sentenced to five years' imprisonment. On appeal the sentence was reduced to two years.

Mr and Mrs Byrd were equal shareholders and directors in the company owning the school, but Mr Byrd automatically forfeited his directorship on conviction. Mrs Byrd is reported to have said (*Daily Mail*, May 10, 1967): "I will carry on the school, and I shall be principal. I have always been co-principal with my husband. Now I will advertise for a deputy headmaster to handle the boys."

The Secretary of State for Education and Science then served a notice of complaint upon Mrs Byrd in accordance with the Education Act 1944, section 71 (1), which provides:

"(1) If at any time the Minister is satisfied that any registered or provisionally registered school is objectionable upon all or any of the following grounds—

    (a) that the school premises or any parts thereof are unsuitable for a school;

    (b) that the accommodation provided at the school premises is inadequate or unsuitable having regard to the number, ages, and sex of the pupils attending the school;

    (c) that efficient and suitable instruction is not being provided at the school having regard to the ages and sex of the pupils attending thereat;

    (d) that the proprietor of the school or any teacher employed therein is not a proper person to be the proprietor of an independent school or to be a teacher in any school, as the case may be;

the Minister shall serve upon the proprietor of the school a notice of complaint stating the grounds of complaint together with full particulars of the matters complained of, and, unless any of such matters are stated in the notice to be in the opinion of the Minister irremediable, the notice shall specify the measures necessary in the opinion of the Minister to remedy the matters complained of, and shall specify the time, not being less than six months after the service of the notice, within such measures are thereby required to be taken."

The particulars relating to Mrs Byrd alleged that "as a director . . . she was responsible for the employment of [her husband] at the college and for his conduct as headmaster."

Mrs Byrd's appeal against the complaint was heard by the Independent Schools Tribunal, who disqualified her from being a proprietor of any independent school, but did not disqualify her from being a teacher.

Two appeals followed. Mrs Byrd appealed against the decision that she could not be a proprietor of any independent school, and the Secretary of State appealed against the decision not to disqualify her from being a teacher in any school. The appeals were heard together.

Extract from Judgment

WALLER J.: The tribunal was entitled to conclude that Mrs Byrd was an equal party in running the school, and responsible for what happened. She was one of two principals taking an active part in administration.

She had taken the younger boys to witness an incident in which a naked boy was thrown twice into the school swimming pool, and made to run round rough ground of a garden near by. She made no protest, did not withdraw the boys, and did not give evidence that there was any other explanation than that she assented.

If the Secretary of State had been strictly confined to the particulars, he would have been in considerable difficulty in establishing the case.

Had I thought that, by reason of the particulars of complaint, Mrs Byrd through her counsel had really been shut out from a proper consideration of her conduct, I would have taken a different view. It is clear from section 72 (2) (*e*)[1] that, once the tribunal was hearing the matter, it had power to disqualify if satisfied that the person was not proper to be the proprietor of an independent school. The order was proper.

The tribunal was entitled to conclude that the order should direct that she was not to be disqualified from being a teacher in any school, in accordance with section 72 (4).[2] There was evidence that she had contributed to the good academic record which, in some respects, the school had, and the tribunal had decided that it was unnecessary to bring her teaching career to an end provided that the management of any school in which she was a teacher was in other hands.

Fisher J. delivered a concurring judgment, and Lord Parker C.J. agreed.

Appeals dismissed

---

1. (2) Upon a complaint being referred to an Independent Schools Tribunal the tribunal shall, after affording to all parties concerned an opportunity of being heard, and after considering such evidence as may be tendered by them or on their behalf have power . . .

(*e*) if satisfied that any person alleged by the notice of complaint to be a person who is not proper to be the proprietor of an independent school or to be a teacher in any school is in fact such a person, by order to disqualify that person from being the proprietor of any independent school or from being a teacher in any school, as the case may be.

2. (4) Where by virtue of an order made by an Independent Schools Tribunal or by the Minister any person is disqualified either from being the proprietor of an independent school or from being a teacher in any school, then, unless the order otherwise directs, that person shall, by virtue of the order, be disqualified both from being the proprietor of an independent school and from being a teacher in any school.

V

PUNISHMENT

(A) GENERAL PRINCIPLES

79 Mansell v. Griffin [1908] 1 K.B. 160, 947

COURT OF APPEAL

An assistant teacher in a public elementary school has power to inflict corporal punishment which is moderate, not dictated by bad motive, such as is usual in the school, and such as the parent of the child might expect it to receive if it did wrong.

Facts: The plaintiff was a pupil in a public elementary school in Gloucester, and the defendant was an assistant mistress in the school. The action was brought for an alleged assault on the ground that the child had been struck on the arm with the edge of a boxwood ruler. It was proved at Gloucester County Court that the child had suffered from cartilaginous tumours, and that the swelling found on her arm after the punishment was due to one of these tumours.

The regulations of the City of Gloucester Education Committee provided that:

"Corporal punishment shall be inflicted only for grave offences, and shall forthwith be recorded in a register kept for the purpose. No corporal punishment shall be administered by anyone but the head teacher or by certain certificated teachers specially named by him from time to time in such register. . . . All other teachers than those specially authorised are hereby prohibited from inflicting such punishment. All such punishment shall be inflicted with a birch rod or cane; cuffs on the head, pulling or boxing the ears, blows with a book or slate, and other punishments causing bodily pain are strictly forbidden.

Certain questions were left to the jury by the judge. The jury found (1) that having regard to the facts, the punishment was moderate; (2) that the instrument used was an improper one, having regard to the fact that the rules provided for the use of a birch or cane, but that it was not so hurtful as those instruments; (3) that the exceptional constitution of the plaintiff was not known to the defendant; (4) that the defendant had exceeded her authority by striking the child without the sanction of the headmistress; but (5) that the

216

school regulations on this point had not been brought to the defendant's knowledge.

Judgment was entered for the defendant.

The plaintiff applied for a new trial on the grounds that the verdict of the jury was against the weight of the evidence, and that the plaintiff had not had a fair trial owing to the bias of the jury and the undue influence brought to bear on them. Affidavits were laid before the judge to the effect that attempts to influence the jury had been made by persons interested in the schools. The judge said that he would not have granted a new trial on either point but, as there was something to be said upon both, he would do so.

The defendant appealed against the decision to grant a new trial to the Divisional Court of the King's Bench Division (Phillimore and Walton JJ.).[1] The Court held that there was no evidence of bias on which the judge could act to grant a new trial. There was, however, another point which might make the verdict of the jury insensate as there must have been a trespass by the defendant and accordingly some damages, and probably substantial ones, were due to the plaintiff.

Extract from Judgment

PHILLIMORE J.: . . . It was contended before us that this teacher had no express authority under the regulations and had no implied authority by reason of the relation between herself and her pupil, which would justify her in administering any corporal punishment (even though that punishment was moderate and not so hurtful as that which might have been administered with either of the authorised instruments of correction), and that therefore she had no defence to an action for assault. It is no doubt true that as a matter of the internal government of the school the teacher, though she did not know it, was prohibited from administering corporal punishment, and it is also true that the only instruments of corporal punishment authorised by the school regulations are a cane or birch. But it did not, in our view, necessarily follow that, because as a matter of internal government the teacher was prohibited from administering corporal punishment herself, that she was necessarily without defence when it came to be a question of an action brought by the pupil against her for trespass to the person or of an indictment for assault. It seems to us that the question must go deeper and must rest on more general considerations. It was admitted that the question depended on the delega- tion by the parent of the parental authority to administer moderate corporal punishment to a child; but it was contended for the plaintiff that a parent could only be considered as delegating his or her authority to a head master or head mistress, and this contention was founded on the position that this kind of regulation as to the administration of corporal punishment by under-teachers is very common, and that in the great public schools and grammar schools of the country corporal punishment can be inflicted only by the head master. As a matter of history that is not absolutely correct. In the great public school of

1. [1908] 1 K.B. 160.

Westminster, and I think in the great public school of Winchester, and also at
Eton and probably in many of the great grammar schools of the country, there
were two statutory or foundation masters; the others are modern and all
assistants. I think it will be found—I know it to be so in the case of Westminster
—that where there were two such statutory officers the under, or second,
master had, at least with regard to those who were specially under his control,
the same powers of corporal chastisement as the head master had. But I do
not rest upon that; we have to consider the general relation of pupil and
teacher, and it has from the earliest times been the practice for teachers to
enforce discipline by some form of coercion. Even if a parent put a child
under the personal supervision of a tutor for that child alone, he must expect,
unless he specially restrains the tutor, that the tutor will on some occasions
administer some form of personal correction to the child; and the matter is
a fortiori, when there is a large class, in which example has to be considered
and discipline for a number of children has to be preserved. It is, I suppose,
false imprisonment to keep a child locked up in a classroom, or even to order
it to stop, under penalties, in a room for a longer period than the ordinary
school time without lawful authority. Could it be said that a teacher who
kept a child back during play hours to learn over and say his lesson again,
or who directed a child to stand up and kept him standing perhaps for an
hour, subjecting him thus to fatigue and to the derision of all his class-mates,
or who put upon him a dunce's cap, as was frequently done in earlier days
in the case of stupid or backward children—could it be said that such a
teacher would be liable in an action for trespass to the person? The cases I
have instanced are not cases of the infliction of blows, but they are cases of
interference with the liberty of the subject, and it seems to me that the
principle must be the same for all these cases. If that be so, there seems to me
no reason why the power of punishment should necessarily be confined to
the head master of the school. If there were regulations or there was a known
custom, confining the administration of corporal punishment to the head
master of the school, and if those regulations or that custom were known to
the parents, this would no doubt give rise to a strong argument to show that
the parent had only delegated to the under-teacher that authority which the
rules of the school gave, and that the parent, therefore, had no more reason
to expect his child to be struck by an assistant teacher than he would that the
child would be struck by the caretaker of the school. Here, however, there is
no reason to suppose that these regulations were brought to the knowledge
of the parents, or that this child was sent to school on the faith of any such
regulation or any such custom. The fact that the teacher herself did not know
of the restrictive regulation on this matter is probably immaterial, although
it does have its bearing on the question of the teacher's good faith. That being
the case, on what does the authority of the teacher rest? My brother,[2] and I
have considered this matter carefully, and I will read a sentence which he has
been good enough to compose: "The ordinary authority extends, not to the

2. Walton J.

head teacher only, but to the responsible teachers who have charge of classes." In other words, if I may add anything to what he has written, a teacher of a class has the ordinary means of preserving discipline, and as between the parent of the child and the teacher it is enough for the teacher to be able to say: "The punishment which I administered was moderate; it was not dictated by any bad motive, and it was such as is usual in the school and such as the parent of the child might expect it would receive if it did wrong." That being the case, if this punishment was moderate, and was not so hurtful as that which the regulations warranted, and was administered by a certificated assistant mistress who was in charge of this class, apparently some forty children, we think that she can in an action justify that which she did. I desire to add here that the position of a certificated mistress in a public elementary school is, as regards the head master or mistress of that school, a more independent one than the position of an assistant master in the great public schools, or the public grammar schools of this country. In those schools, for the most part, the masters other than the head master are merely his assistants, appointed by him and dismissed by him, subject possibly to the question of reasonable notice, at pleasure. A certificated assistant teacher in a public elementary school, such as the defendant, is not appointed by the head mistress and cannot be dismissed by her. She is appointed by the local education authority, and is removable by that body alone. In that respect, therefore, she has a more independent position than the assistant master at one of the higher grade schools.

We think, therefore, that, supposing the first and second findings of the jury are correct, the jury would be right in saying that there were no damages, and in finding a verdict for the defendant. But we think that the learned county court judge ought to have a further opportunity of considering whether he will or will not grant a new trial on the ground that the verdict was on a matter of fact contrary to the weight of evidence. We give no encouragement to the suggestion that this verdict ought to be set aside on that ground, but we think that the judge who has set it aside on two grounds may have thought one alone would be sufficient, and that he ought to have an opportunity *de novo* of considering whether he will say he so disagreed with the verdict of the jury in answer to question No. 1 that he thinks there ought to be a new trial. For that purpose the matter will be referred back to him.

Appeal allowed

The plaintiff appealed against the order of the Divisional Court.

The Court of Appeal (Lord Alverstone C.J., Farwell L.J., and Kennedy L.J.) dismissed the appeal and, under the circumstances did not think it necessary to express any opinion on the question of law with regard to the authority of an assistant teacher in a public elementary school to inflict corporal punishment on a pupil otherwise than in accordance with the school regulations, which had been dealt with in the court below.

Appeal dismissed

80 R. *v.* Hopley (1860) 2 F.& F. 202

LEWES ASSIZES

A parent or schoolmaster who inflicts immoderate and unreasonable corporal punishment is answerable to the law and, if death ensues, it will be manslaughter.

Facts: Thomas Hopley, aged forty-one and described by *The Times* as a "person of gentlemanly appearance," was indicted at Lewes Assizes on July 23, 1860, for the manslaughter of Reginald Channell Cancellor. The prisoner, who was a man of high attainments and previously good character, was the principal of a school at Eastbourne.

Reginald Cancellor was aged fifteen at the time of his death, and was a pupil at the prisoner's school at a fee of £180 per annum. He was the son of one of the Masters of the Court of Common Pleas; the godson of Channell B., previously leader of the Home Circuit; and his brother was curate of Send in Surrey. It was admitted by the prosecution that he was an obstinate boy, and the evidence given at the trial suggested that he was very retarded. At the end of his first term at the school, which was the autumn term, 1859, he was punished to some considerable extent, and his father complained to the headmaster.

About the middle of April 1860, the prisoner wrote to the boy's father, stating he had tried every means to conquer his obstinacy without avail. He added that the only course left would be strong measures of corporal punishment, and he asked for the father's consent, which was given.

Evidence given at the trial suggested that Cancellor had been in trouble on Saturday, April 21, 1860, and would not do the simplest sum, even though he knew how. The headmaster had spoken to him kindly and seriously but, as the boy still resisted, he made him remain in the pupil room while the other boys went to prayers. After this, the prisoner said that he went to him and prayed with him, and adjured him to submit, warning him what the alternative would be. As the boy was still obstinate he looked around for something with which to correct him, but he was so unused to chastising boys that he had not a cane in the house. He found an old skipping rope and beat him, so he thought, sufficiently, but the boy remained obstinate. This happened four or five times until the boy threw himself on the floor and refused to go to bed. He then dragged Cancellor upstairs to his room. According to a maid who slept next door, this was about a quarter of an hour before midnight. As the boy was still obstinate, Hopley fetched the rope from downstairs and beat him again. The maid heard him say: "Now do these as a dear good boy." The beating with the rope and a walking stick continued for about half an hour, and the boy shouted loudly enough "to be heard half over Eastbourne." The maid said that the screaming stopped suddenly, after which there was a good deal of movement up and down stairs, and the sound of a water tap.

On the Sunday morning the prisoner said that he had found Cancellor dead in bed. He sent for Mr Roberts, a surgeon practising at Eastbourne, who said he could not assign the cause of death. The prisoner went to register the death before church time on the Sunday, but was told that this was not possible until an inquest had been held. He also telegraphed Mr Cancellor to inform him of his son's death. On the Monday he visited Mr Roberts and asked for a certificate of the cause of death, but this was refused.

On Tuesday, April 24, Cancellor's brother visited the school with an undertaker. The boy's body was in a lead coffin in the bedroom and the brother inquired whether a mark on the cheek was not a bruise. Hopley replied that he believed it was only the discolouration that often took place after death, and added: "Heaven knows, I have done my duty by that poor boy." The body was removed to the deceased's home at Barnes with the brother's permission. On Friday, April 27, an inquest was held, and Hopley sent a report to Cancellor's brother. The report appeared to state that Hopley had left the boy at 10.30 p.m., and found him dead at 6.30 a.m. the following morning. There was no reference to the punishment. At the time that the brother received the report of the inquest he thought that only a rope had been used. Hopley told him that he had made a statement to the coroner which had purposely been kept out of the newspapers, and asked him to go with him to one of the jurors to hear what had actually taken place.

A post-mortem examination was held on Saturday, April 28, by Mr Prescott Hewett, Dr Willis, and Dr Holmes of St George's Hospital. The legs and arms were of a dark livid colour, and swollen from extravasated blood in large quantities. Under the skin of one palm the extravasated blood was three-quarters of an inch thick; and the cellular membranes under the skin of the thighs were reduced to a perfect jelly, torn to pieces and lacerated by the blows. The injuries must have been inflicted by a heavy blunt instrument. Mr Hewett thought the rope was calculated to make the bruises, and the stick to have produced the lacerations. On the right leg were two wounds about the size of a sixpence which might have been caused by jabbing with the pointed end of the stick. The boy's head was large, and exhibited the appearance of his having suffered from water on the brain, and this turned out to be the case when the head was opened. This condition would account for his defective intelligence. Considerable violence had been used, and death was caused by a shock to the nervous system and the large quantity of blood extravasated into the cellular membranes.

A second post mortem was held on May 11 at the prisoner's request.

In a statement made before the examining magistrates, the prisoner admitted using the stick and the rope, but said he only beat the deceased about the head and shoulders. He was not at all in a passion or in anger, but he felt he was doing his duty, and he repeatedly requested the deceased to give in, and spare him the pain of inflicting further punishment upon him.

Extract from Summing-up

LORD COCKBURN C.J.: By the law of England, a parent or a schoolmaster (who for this purpose represents the parent and has the parental authority delegated to him), may for the purpose of correcting what is evil in the child inflict moderate and reasonable corporal punishment, always, however, with this condition, that it is moderate and reasonable. If it be administered for the gratification of passion or of rage, or if it be immoderate and excessive in its nature or degree, or it it be protracted beyond the child's powers of endurance, or with an instrument unfitted for the purpose and calculated to produce danger to life or limb: in all such cases the punishment is excessive, the violence is unlawful, and if evil consequences to life or limb ensue, then the person inflicting it is answerable to the law, and if death ensues it will be manslaughter. . . .

It is true that the father authorised the chastisement, but he did not, and no law could, authorise an excessive chastisement.

Verdict: guilty

[NOTE: The prisoner was sentenced to four years' penal servitude. The reason for not preferring a charge of murder was given by Serjeant Parry in outlining the case for the prosecution: "I and my learned friend have attentively considered the evidence, and I feel it right to state that the only reason why a charge of wilful murder has not been preferred against the prisoner is that he stood in the position of a schoolmaster, and that the father of the deceased young gentleman had delegated his authority to him, and as the law of England sanctions the use of corporal punishment to a moderate extent in such a case, and in the present instance the death was alleged to have arisen solely from the excessive use of that power, it is thought the more advisable course to prefer a charge for the minor offence only against the prisoner."]

81 Herring *v.* Boyle (1834) 3 L.J. Ex. 344

COURT OF EXCHEQUER

An infant cannot maintain an action for assault and false imprisonment against a schoolmaster who has improperly refused to deliver him up to his mother without evidence that he knew of the refusal and of some actual restraint.

Facts: The ten-year-old plaintiff became a pupil at the defendant's school at Stockwell at Midsummer 1833. On December 24, when the mother went to fetch her child home, the defendant refused to allow him to leave until the bill was paid. At the time the mother was unable to pay, and the account was not due for settlement until the next day.

On December 30 the mother returned and paid the bill up to Christmas Day, but the defendant still refused to release the child unless another quarter was paid. A writ of habeas corpus* having been obtained, the defendant allowed the boy to go home.

In an action for false imprisonment it was contended for the defendant that the action was not maintainable. It did not appear that the boy had been detained against his will. He knew nothing of his mother's action, he was well looked after, and neither felt nor expressed any desire to go home. Gurney B. said he would have been glad to send the case to the jury, but the other members of the court had corroborated his opinion that the action should have been brought by the mother, not the son. The plaintiff was nonsuited.

An attempt was made to set aside the nonsuit on the ground that it was sufficient to show that the plaintiff had not consented to be kept at school, and that the will of the parent must be taken to be the will of the child. If the detention was by the plaintiff's permission, the defendant should have pleaded leave and licence, or that the plaintiff was left with him by his mother and did not wish to return.

Judgments

BOLLAND B.: This was an action of trespass and false imprisonment, brought by an infant, by his guardian. The facts of the case were these: the plaintiff had been placed by his mother at the school kept by the defendant, and it appeared that she had applied to take him away. The schoolmaster very improperly refused to give him up to his mother, unless she paid an amount which he claimed to be due. The question is, whether it appears upon the Judge's notes that there was any evidence to go to the jury of an assault and false imprisonment. In my opinion there was not, and, consequently, I think this rule must be discharged. The ground upon which the argument for the plaintiff was put was, that the misconduct of the defendant amounted to a false imprisonment; but I cannot find anything upon the notes of the learned Judge which shows that the plaintiff was at all cognisant of what was going on, or of any restraint. There are many cases which show that it is not necessary, to constitute an imprisonment, that the hand should be laid upon the person; but in no case has any conduct been held to amount to an imprisonment in the absence of the party supposed to be imprisoned. An officer may make an arrest without laying his hand on the party arrested; but in the present case, as far as we know, the boy may have been perfectly willing to stay; and there was no evidence of any restraint upon him, nor of any act whatsoever done by the defendant in his presence. I think that we cannot construe the refusal to the mother in the boy's absence, and without his being cognisant of any restraint, to be an imprisonment of him against his will; and therefore I am of opinion that the rule must be discharged.

ALDERSON B.: There was a total absence of any proof of consciousness of restraint on the part of the plaintiff. No act of restraint was committed in his presence; and I am of opinion that the refusal in his absence to deliver him up to his mother was not a false imprisonment. My Brother Parke, who heard the rule moved, but who was not present at the argument, concurs in the opinion of the Court.

GURNEY B.: This plaintiff complains of an assault and false imprisonment. There was no evidence of any restraint upon him. There was no evidence that he had any knowledge of his mother having desired that he should be permitted to go home, nor that anything passed between the plaintiff and defendant which showed that there was any compulsion upon the boy; and there was nothing to show that he was conscious that he was in any respect restrained.

LORD LYNDHURST C.B.: I did not hear the rule argued, but I was present when it was moved for, and I am of the same opinion.

Rule discharged

(B) CORPORAL PUNISHMENT
82 Gardner *v.* Bygrave (1889) 53 J.P. 743

QUEEN'S BENCH DIVISION
Caning on the hands is permitted by law.

Facts: The appellant was convicted of assault after he had given a boy four strokes of the cane on the hands. He appealed to the Divisional Court of the Queen's Bench Division, and the magistrate stated a case:

"(2) The appellant was the head master of the Church Street Board School, Hoxton, in the county of Middlesex, and the respondent was a pupil attending the said school. On the 1st day of March, 1889, the respondent committed a fault which properly called for corporal punishment by the appellant, who inflicted the same by giving the respondent four strokes with the cane on the hand. I was of opinion that, if caning the hand was a proper method of punishment to adopt in the circumstances of this case, the punishment was inflicted unobjectionably.

(3) But I was also of opinion that punishment by caning on the hand, however inflicted, was necessarily attended by risk of serious injury to the hand; that there were methods of corporal punishment quite as available, efficacious, and not necessarily attended by any risk, of which methods, if the appellant had used due caution, one or other would have been substituted by him for that which he adopted; and that for these reasons, caning on the hand was, in the circumstances of the case, improper, and ought not to have been inflicted.

The question of law submitted to the High Court is whether I was bound by the considerations stated in paragraph two, to dismiss the summons, notwithstanding the considerations stated in paragraph three. If yea, the conviction to be quashed; if nay to be affirmed, or the case to be otherwise dealt with as the Court may direct."

Robson (for the respondent): . . . School board masters must be taught to exercise due caution. They ought to make inquiry into the circumstances of the possible trade or occupation of the boy before caning on the hand. Such a punishment might seriously interfere with his occupation, and the punishment could just as well be inflicted elsewhere.

MATHEW J.: But suppose a sedentary occupation.

Robson: Now that education is made compulsory, parents must send their children to be under board schoolmasters. It is, therefore, doubtful whether the power of inflicting punishment which a parent has can be said to be delegated to the master. It is not the same as if the boy was sent to a school chosen by the parent.

Extract from Judgments

MATHEW J.: The conviction must be quashed. The point of law put to us is this: Is it, according to the law of England, criminal for a master to cane a boy by striking him on the hand? The magistrate states the boy deserved corporal punishment. He does not, as the counsel for the respondent apparently does, attack the right to inflict corporal punishment, when applied with a view to intellectual stimulation, for he states that there are other methods of corporal punishment "quite as available, efficacious, and not necessarily attended by any risk." However, he grounds his judgment on his opinion that caning on the hand, however inflicted, is necessarily attended by risk of serious injury to the hand, but he finds as a fact that in this case it was unobjectionably inflicted, and does not find that any serious injury was caused by it. The magistrate was wrong in thinking that under these circumstances the possible risk made it criminal for the master to cane on the hand.

WILLS J.: . . . When Parliament lays down a chart showing the particular region of the body to which corporal punishment in schools shall be confined, the Court will take care that those limits are not overstepped. At present there is no such chart. . . .

> *Appeal allowed. Case remitted to magistrate*
> *with direction to acquit*

83 Ryan *v.* Fildes and others [1938] 3 All E.R. 517

LIVERPOOL ASSIZES
A moderate blow may exceed reasonable and lawful correction.

Facts: The plaintiff, Patrick Ryan, was a ten-year-old pupil of St Austin's non-provided* Boys' School, Thatts Heath, St Helens.

Because of his lack of discipline, the plaintiff was punished by his school-mistress, Miss Ellen Fildes. It was said that, thinking it necessary to correct some of the forty-six children in the class, she gave Ryan a blow on the back of the head, and then struck him with her open hand on the face and over the ear. As a result the drumhead of the ear was ruptured, and the boy's hearing was permanently impaired. The mistress denied that what she did was anything more than reasonable correction, or that she struck Ryan on the face or ear.

An action for damages was brought against the managers and the mistress. It was proved that there was an agreement between the mistress and the managers, which was not proved to have been brought to the notice of the parents, whereby the mistress agreed to teach and conduct the school "in accordance with the requirements of the Board of Education and in accordance with the directions given from time to time by the managers." The only regulations dealing with corporal punishment which were proved in evidence were those of the borough education committee, made without the consent of the managers and not adopted by them.

Extract from Judgment

TUCKER J.: . . . With regard to Miss Fildes, I think that it is quite clear that he must succeed against her. What she did, in my view, undoubtedly exceeded reasonable and proper punishment. In the words of the headnote in *Mansell* v. *Griffin*,[1] I think that this was not punishment which could be described as moderate or such as is usual in a school, and such as the parent of the child might expect that the child would receive if it did wrong. The blow struck was moderate in the sense that it was not a very violent blow, but, as punishment, it was not moderate punishment, because I do not think that the proper way of punishing a child is to strike it on the head or the ear. Nor do I think it was, on the evidence, punishment which can be described as usual in this or in any other school. Nor is it such as the parent of a child might expect that the child would receive at a school in these days. I think that punishment of that kind cannot really be justified. No one can help having a considerable degree of sympathy with Miss Fildes in the fact that, dealing with a lot of unruly boys, she may have done something which was a natural thing to do, and something which in nine hundred and ninety-nine cases out of a thousand, probably would have produced no ill-consequences. Unfortunately, however, I think that she did do something which she was not really entitled to do by way of punishment, and that, as it cannot be justified in law, and as it has had these unfortunate consequences, she has rendered herself liable to pay damages to the plaintiff. . . .

Judgment for the plaintiff

(C) EXPULSION

84 Hutt and another *v.* the Governors of Haileybury College and others
(1888) 4 T.L.R. 623

QUEEN'S BENCH DIVISION
The power of expulsion must be exercised reasonably.

Facts: Two actions were tried together. In one the Reverend William Wayman Hutt J.P., rector of Hockwold-cum-Wilton, Norfolk, brought an action against the Governors of Haileybury College for damages for breach of contract by the expulsion of one of his sons from the school. In the other, the son, Henry Robert Mackenzie Hutt, claimed damages for assault and false imprisonment, and for libel and slander.

Henry Hutt became a pupil at Haileybury in 1883, and was in Mr Fenning's house. There was a good deal of theft in the school, and this state of affairs

1. [1908] 1 K.B. 947; see page 216, *supra.*

continued to the time of the trial. On Friday, March 11, 1887, there was a theft from study No. 17, and a marked coin which had been stolen was found in Hutt's box at 12.30 p.m. on the following day. Hutt denied having stolen the money, and could not account for its presence in his box. On the same day Mr Fenning wrote to Charles Hutt, an elder brother who had also been in his house as follows: "He has been caught stealing; suspicion has long been directed to him as guilty of a series of thefts from the studies." Hutt was locked up in a room in the infirmary, and saw no-one but the infirmary matron until he was visited again by his housemaster at 5.30 p.m. on Sunday, March 13. He was then refused permission to write home and, when he offered to account for his movements on the previous Thursday and Friday, he was told: "Oh, that would be no good whatsoever."

On the Monday, Charles Hutt visited the school and saw his brother for a short while. At about 3.45 p.m. Mr Robertson, the headmaster, who had been on a visit to Oxford, went to the infirmary and said to Hutt:

> "This is a very serious charge, and of course you must be guilty as no one else could have put the money there. Had you been one of the servants you would have been imprisoned with hard labour, as any jury in England would have convicted you; and, unless you think of confessing, I shall seriously entertain the idea of prosecuting you, and a nice disgrace that will be to your parents. I will give you a quarter of an hour to consider and, unless you confess, I shall seriously consider what I have said as to prosecuting you."

On Tuesday, March 15, the headmaster went to see Hutt at about 10 a.m., and said: "I have just come to tell you that you are expelled, and you will be branded with disgrace all your life because you have been expelled from one of England's public schools." Half an hour later Mr Fenning went to say good-bye to him, and said: "I am very sorry for you, Hutt, old fellow, and I think it is partly my fault that I was not stricter with you. Now, old man, you had better make a clean breast of it all and make reparation to your victims." Hutt replied that he could not confess what he had not done, to which Fenning replied: "I am very sorry for you, the evidence against you is overwhelming and conclusive." On the same morning, Hutt's father, who was in the north, received a letter from Charles Hutt, telling him of the affair. The same day, Charles Hutt also wrote to Mr Fenning telling him that suspicion might be directed towards another boy.

On March 16, Mr Robertson, the headmaster, wrote of Hutt: "He has lied to the last." On March 17, Mr Fenning replied to a letter from Mrs Hutt: "There is not a court of law that would have hesitated to convict him. Short of actually being caught in the act, no boy was ever convicted upon clearer evidence. You plead for him a character free from dishonesty. He holds among his companions here a quite different character. What would Harry's fate have been at the Assizes?"

On Thursday, March 17, the boy's father visited Haileybury and saw both the headmaster and the housemaster. The former expressed sorrow and regret, and said: "What a blessing it would be to this boy if he would break a limb, or have a severe fever or some other disease that it might remove from him that thick skin which he has around him." Mr Hutt asked the headmaster to remove the expulsion so that he might withdraw his son from the school. The headmaster replied that he could not, but he would—at the father's request—hand the boy over to the authorities and have the case investigated in a police court.

In evidence the headmaster said that fourteen boys had been expelled from Haileybury during the four years that he had been headmaster, including seven for theft. There had been six expulsions since Hutt left; two for stealing and four for indecency.

The defendants denied that the headmaster had expelled Hutt save in the discharge of his duty as headmaster, and upon reasonable suspicion of having stolen money, after a bona fide* investigation of the charge. Alternatively, the allegation of theft was true, and it was necessary to expel him for such an offence. They denied assault and false imprisonment, pleading alternatively that they had acted bona fide and with reasonable cause, to the best of their judgment, in separating Hutt from his companions, and had acted in the interests of school discipline. With regard to the alleged libels they pleaded privilege. The governors pleaded separately, in substance supporting the action of their masters.

Extract from Summing-up
FIELD J.: . . . I am prepared to hold that there is no such absolute discretion in masters of schools as that claimed in the governors' statement of defence as was originally pleaded. Such a power would be far too great and dangerous —*viz.*, that any boy at school should be liable to be branded for life by expulsion simply because a master on his sole authority and discretion— however distinguished he may be—had come to the conclusion that such a course was necessary for the well-being of his school. Such an absolute discretion could never be permitted. All large bodies must, of course, be governed in the public interest, and in some cases such absolute discretion is necessary, but not in such a case as this. . . . What is the authority of a master of a public school? There is very little, if any, authority upon the point. The only case has been referred to in the course of the trial.[1] It seems, however, clear that the master is the delegate of the parent. Then what is a parent's authority over his infant child? By Roman law it was absolute over life and death even. There is no such power in this land, but still he has a great power over his child. It is his duty if the child will not do what he advises it to do to take whatever steps he considers reasonably necessary for its correction. But he must act honestly in this course. There must be a cause which a reasonable father believes requires punishment. In the case of mere childish fault for a parent to use weapons would be, for instance, so unreasonable

1. *Fitzgerald* v. *Northcote* (1865) 4 F. & F. 656; see page 148, *supra*.

as to destroy a parent's right. The law therefore does justify a parent in a case where he honestly considers correction necessary in administering blows in a reasonable and proper manner. But then this power is not limited to corporal punishment, but extends to detention and restraint. I think that the father parts with all these powers and delegates them to the master under whose charge he places his child. We have all experienced, no doubt, a parent's punishments. Therefore, unless limited by special contract, I think that the master has the power of judging when a punishment is required, and also to what extent. . . . While the child remains in its own family its interests are synonymous with those of its fellows; but when the delegation I alluded to occurs, and the child enters a public school, these interests are greatly extended, and the master must take into consideration the interests, not only of the one boy, but those of the whole school. No doubt there are circumstances under which a master might be called upon to decide a case upon what at the time he considered to be facts, but which eventually turned out not to be so. Would he not in such a case be justified if the nature of the case required immediate action and he had acted honestly and his conclusions were under the circumstances reasonable? What amount of power is actually delegated by a parent to a master must depend upon the circumstances in each case. . . .

I have already said what the duties of the masters are to each pupil, and to the school as a whole, and have dealt with the question of expulsion. I will now deal with that of detention. I think, but that is for you, that a larger discretion must be given to masters on this than on the head of expulsion. For the consequences are not serious to the same extent, and there ought to be some such discretion of restraint given to masters in the interest of school order and discipline.

[The jury found that Henry Hutt was not guilty of theft, and there were not reasonable grounds for his expulsion. Further, the libels and slanders were false, but the masters had uttered them bona fide, believing them to be true. They believed that they had reasonable grounds for expelling Hutt, and were justified in suspecting him and in isolating him from his companions. Field J. ruled that the libels and slanders were uttered on privileged occasions.

The headmaster, as part of the settlement, agreed to append a note to all entries in any of the Haileybury school books relating to Hutt's expulsion, to the effect that the jury had found that Henry Hutt was not guilty of theft.]

Verdict and judgment for the Revd W. W. Hutt
against the Governors for £100 without costs;
verdict and judgment for the masters
against Charles Hutt without costs

85 Wood *v.* Prestwich (1911) 104 L.T. 388

KING'S BENCH DIVISION
Where a scheme provides that a headmaster shall have power to expel a boy no action will lie in the absence of mala fides.

Facts: The plaintiff, Mr W. Wood, brought an action against the headmaster of Richmond Grammar School, Yorkshire, for damages for breach of contract by the expulsion of Herbert Wood from the school.

Herbert Wood, the son of the plaintiff, entered the school as a Brackenbury scholar in September 1909. In May 1910 he was expelled by the headmaster after an investigation into an allegation that he had stolen some postage stamps belonging to another boy.

The school was an endowed school within the meaning of the Endowed Schools Acts 1868 and 1869, and was the subject of two schemes made in 1892 and 1909 respectively by the Charity Commissioners under the Endowed Schools Act 1869, such schemes having, by section 45 of the Endowed Schools Act 1869, the effect of statutes.

By section 39 of the scheme of 1892 it was provided that,

"Subject to any rules prescribed by or under authority of this scheme, the Headmaster shall have under his control the choice of books, the method of teaching, the arrangement of classes and school hours, and generally the whole internal organisation and management and discipline of the school, including the power of expelling boys from the school or suspending them from attendance thereat for any adequate cause to be judged by him; but on expelling or suspending any boy he shall forthwith report the case to the governors."

By section 44 the advantages of the school were stated to be open to all boys of good character and sufficient health residing within a certain specified district.

Section 52 provided for the institution of scholarships known as Brackenbury Scholarships, which exempted the holder wholly or partially from tuition fees.

The action was tried before a jury at Stockton-on-Tees County Court. The jury found (1) that the boy was expelled by the defendant; and (2) that the boy was not reasonably expelled, but that there was no gross unreasonableness. Damages were assessed at £50.

The defendant appealed to a Divisional Court of the Queen's Bench Division.

Extract from Judgment
RIDLEY J.: This action was brought by the parent of a boy who had been entered as a scholar at the Richmond Grammar School in Yorkshire in 1909, having previously gained what is known as a Brackenbury Scholarship under terms which are part of a scheme authorised under the Endowed Schools Act 1869. That scheme by virtue of section 45 of the Endowed Schools Act has the force of an Act of Parliament. I think that the effect of that enactment is that all persons who enter boys as scholars at the school are subject to the provisions of the scheme, and, if it were necessary to make any distinction

between different classes of boys, I think that it is abundantly so in the case
of boys who have gained scholarships. That being so, I think the plaintiff
cannot be heard to say that he had no notice of the terms of the scheme. The
present action was brought in respect of the boy having been expelled by the
headmaster, and the plaintiff framed his case for breach of a contract which
he alleged had been entered into between himself and the headmaster. If I
understand Mr Mortimer, the plaintiff's case is that this contract came in to
existence when the boy entered the school and took the benefit of the instruction provided there. . . . It is no doubt the fact that Cockburn C.J., in *Fitzgerald*
v. *Northcote*[1] used expressions which tended in that direction. He said that
there was as between a parent and a schoolmaster an implied contract that
the latter will continue to educate the child so long as his conduct does not
warrant his expulsion from the school. . . . But in *Fitzgerald* v. *Northcote*[1] it
was unnecessary for the decision in that case to hold that in all cases there was
necessarily such an implied contract as has been suggested here. . . . Had it
been necessary in the present case to decide this point, I should have had
considerable doubts about the matter, because I am not sure how far it is
wise to interfere with the discretion of the headmaster of a public school
in such a matter as this. As I have said, however, it is in my opinion unnecessary to decide that point in the present case, because I think the parent of this
boy was bound by the scheme, and consequently by clause 39 which formed
part of it. Accordingly, when the boy went to the school and began to reap
the advantages of the scheme, the arrangement between the parent, the boy,
and the headmaster was expressed by the scheme and, amongst other points,
by section 39 of it, and I do not think it is possible that there can be any
contract between the parties which is not in agreement with the terms of that
document. From the time, therefore, when the boy went to the school, the
position of affairs was that the headmaster had the power of expelling the boy
from the school or of suspending him from attendance thereat for any
adequate cause to be judged by him. We have had several cases cited to us by
plaintiff's counsel as to the meaning of such a phrase, but they do not afford
us much assistance. If anything, they go to show that so long as the authority
given to the master is properly and bona fide* exercised, it cannot be interfered with. The case of *Wright* v. *Marquis of Zetland*,[2] however, is an authority
more clearly in point for the purpose of assisting us as to the meaning of
clause 39 than the cases to which Mr Mortimer referred us. That was a decision upon section 40 of this same scheme, which, so far as is material, is as
follows: "The headmaster shall have the sole power of appointing and may at
pleasure dismiss all assistant masters in the school. . . ." Those words are not
absolutely the same as those of section 39, but it is a little difficult to see how
there could be a wider discretion given to a person who has power to dismiss
an assistant master than is given to a person who, as headmaster, has the power
to expel a boy for adequate cause to be judged by him. It was held that under

1. (1865) 4 F. & F. 656; see page 148, *supra.*
2. [1908] 1 K.B. 63.

section 40 the power given was an absolute one, and I think in the present case we ought to say that there was absolute power to expel a boy, subject to that power being exercised honestly. . . . I think that is a strong decision in favour of the defendant in this case, for I cannot distinguish the two cases except in this respect, that one was dealing with an assistant master and the other with a boy. In giving judgment Vaughan Williams L.J. said "that the pleasure must be exercised in good faith." With that I agree, and I think that the power given to the headmaster in the present case to expel a boy must also be exercised in good faith. If it were not, then I think the power would be wrongfully exercised and the master would be liable to be proceeded against. Now in this case what has happened? It was submitted to the learned judge and it was contended before us on behalf of the defendant that there was no cause of action, because there was no contract with the parent and, further, that under the scheme the headmaster had sole control, including the power to expel a boy for adequate cause. For the reasons I have given I think those contentions are right. It was submitted to us by Mr Mortimer that section 39 deals only with the internal management of the school and is not binding upon anyone outside the foundation. In my opinion the scheme binds all persons who are affected by it directly or indirectly. And consequently the parent of a boy at the school is bound by the scheme. That being so, what took place at the trial? As I understand it, it was admitted that there was no shred of mala fides in the conduct of the defendant. That was admitted at the trial and has been stated to us. The learned judge left two questions to the jury in which he did not sufficiently distinguish between the question of unreasonableness and the question of mala fides. He used language which indicates that he knew what the right question to leave to the jury was, but, in leaving it to them, he seems to have suggested that it might be sufficient to entitle the plaintiff to a verdict if there were gross unreasonableness upon the part of the defendant. Gross unreasonableness might be so gross as to amount to mala fides, but such a thing is not suggested here. I think perhaps some confusion arose from his not having sufficiently defined the meaning of the words he used to the jury, and the result was that the jury found as facts matters which were of no consequence. They found that the boy was expelled, and unreasonably expelled, and then being asked if there was gross unreasonableness they said no. I think that was immaterial. It was admitted that there was no evidence of mala fides, and, that being so, it seems to me that there ought to have been a verdict for the defendant. For the reasons I have given I think this appeal must be allowed and judgment entered for the defendant.

AVORY J.: . . . I am not expressing any opinion, and it would not be advisable to do so, as to whether any offence had actually been committed in this case or not. All I say is that there were ample grounds for the headmaster reasonably coming to the conclusion at which he arrived in this case.

Appeal allowed; judgment for the defendant

86 Hunt *v.* Damon (1930) 46 T.L.R. 579

KING'S BENCH DIVISION

Wrongful expulsion of a pupil does not of itself, without more, constitute an actionable tort.

Facts: The plaintiff, Miss Mollie Frances Hunt, who was nineteen years of age at the time of the hearing, claimed damages for alleged libel and breach of duty as a schoolmistress from Miss Kathleen M. Damon, the headmistress of a girls' school called Upper Chine, at Shanklin in the Isle of Wight.

The plaintiff became a pupil at Upper Chine in 1924, and remained there until she was expelled in May 1929. Except when the plaintiff had an operation in 1927, and the defendant was very kind to her, she did not get on well with her headmistress. The defendant tried to end a friendship between the plaintiff and the matron of the school. The matron showed the headmistress certain correspondence which had been received from the plaintiff during the Easter holidays in 1929, and the defendant rebuked the plaintiff about this and about her slackness in work. In the dormitory that night the plaintiff discussed her interview with the headmistress, and this was reported to the defendant who sent for her again on May 7.

Miss Damon said: "In view of this and of your extreme disloyalty, I cannot keep you here, and you are going home at once." Miss Hunt asked whether she might get her things, but Miss Damon said: "No. They will be sent on to you."

Miss Hunt was sent away from the school at a moment's notice in the charge of a mistress. She was dressed in her gymnasium clothes and had merely her night attire with her. On the train she was not allowed to speak to a friend. At Waterloo Station Miss Jackson, the mistress, handed her over to her aunt.

On May 6 Miss Damon had sent to Mrs Carre, Miss Hunt's mother, a telegram in which she said: "I regret I must ask you to remove Mollie from here at once."

In a letter sent on the same day, Miss Damon said that Mollie had written some very disloyal letters, but that she had offered the girl a fresh start. The letter continued:

> "I now hear that Mollie has been talking to the other girls on the subject [of her conduct at school] and speaking in a most disloyal way in the presence of a new girl. She told the new girl that I was unjust, etc., and ridiculed the interview that I had had with her, and the other girls in the dormitory were so disgusted that they felt bound to bring the matter to my notice.
>
> I have no alternative, therefore, than to tell you that I wish Mollie to leave this school immediately.
>
> I hope she will not make any attempt to come back to Upper Chine again and I forbid my other pupils to write to her or have any further dealings with her."

I

In reply, Mrs Carre described Miss Damon's action as unnecessarily cruel, in view of the fact that she (Mrs Carre) was ill, and she said that she had been advised that "Mollie's conduct, reprehensible though it be, does not justify such drastic treatment as her dismissal from school."

On May 9, Miss Damon wrote another letter to Mrs Carre, in which she said:

"I am now hearing on every side how disloyal she has been. It would be ridiculous for you to suppose that I sent her away for her last misdemeanour alone. It was the *culminating point of repeated disobedience* and she had broken her promise to ME OVER AND OVER AGAIN. The fact that she made fun of the promise she had just made and tried to unsettle a new girl by disloyal talk showed me that she had *not the smallest intention of behaving herself this term.* Her criticisms of my personality have no bearing on the case, and you have entirely misread my letter if you imagine that is so.

No one is more sorry than I that it was necessary to send Mollie away. I can only hope that she may even now from this episode learn a salutary lesson on the sacredness of keeping a promise and of the elementary principles of loyalty."

After she had left, the plaintiff wrote to one of her friends in the school:

"My dear old Alice,—What ho! I have been expelled!!! I do not suppose I ought to write to you as Miss Damon said I was not to correspond with any one at the school so don't, for the love of the Lord, say that you have heard from me.

The one point I will tell you is that Sister is at the bottom of all this and, anyhow, I do not deserve to be expelled. Mum is going to law about it. I have got to go up to London on Monday morning to see the lawyer, but I don't mind as he is an awfully nice man and very nice-looking and he said Miss Damon had no right to expel me on the grounds that she has done. . . .

What fun if I have to stand up in a witness-box against Miss Damon! One of the reasons that she gave was that I was disloyal to her. All my family are furious with her and I am having a ripping time down here with theatres, etc.!!!

By the bye, thanks most awfully for your letter and the pictures of Ronald Colman. They are topping."

The plaintiff claimed that the letters written by the headmistress to Mrs Carre, the plaintiff's mother, were defamatory in that they meant she was a girl of bad character and was unfit to associate with her fellow pupils. The defendant denied breach of duty, said that the words complained of were incapable of the defamatory sense alleged, and pleaded privilege and justification. Lord Hewart C.J. held that the occasions on which the letters alleged to constitute libels were written were privileged.

The jury found the words complained of were not defamatory and that they were not published maliciously. They found that the plaintiff had been expelled without reasonable cause, and assessed damages at one farthing.

Extract from Judgment

LORD HEWART C.J.: . . . The question for me is what is the appropriate judgment, having regard to the jury's finding that the defendant did not act upon reasonable grounds in expelling the plaintiff, bearing in mind that they awarded a farthing damages. There was no privity of contract between the parties, nor was this particular claim associated with defamation, false imprisonment, or any other head of recognised tort. On the contrary, the claims under those heads had been abandoned or negatived. It was said that the mere fact that the defendant in the circumstances refused to continue the girl's education involved a tort giving rise to a claim to damages on her part, but I do not think that any such claim is sustainable in law.

I am satisfied that there is no evidence entitling the jury to answer, in a sense adverse to the defendant, the question whether the defendant acted upon reasonable grounds in expelling the plaintiff, and I would have answered the question in the negative. Even if it had been otherwise, the jury having awarded a farthing damages, I would still have deprived the plaintiff of her costs, because that amount shows that the jury thought, as I myself think, that it is an action which ought not to have been brought. There must be judgment for the defendant, with costs.

Judgment for the defendant with costs

(D) OFFENCES AWAY FROM SCHOOL PREMISES

87 Cleary *v.* Booth [1893] 1 Q.B. 465

QUEEN'S BENCH DIVISION

The schoolmaster's authority to punish extends to offences by a pupil on his way to and from school.

Facts: The appellant was the headmaster of a board school in Southampton who had been convicted by the justices of assault on the respondent, Booth, a pupil at the school. The appeal was heard by the Divisional Court of the Queen's Bench Division by way of case stated.

On the day in question the respondent Booth was on his way to school with another pupil named Callaway. They met a third pupil named Godding. Callaway assaulted Godding, but there was no evidence before the magistrates that Booth also assaulted him. The appellant caned Callaway and Booth on the hand and back following a complaint by Godding's mother.

In the opinion of the justices the headmaster was not entitled to punish a pupil for anything done, although against another pupil, each being on his way to school; the act being committed off the school premises and unconnected with the school.

The appellant's solicitor informed the bench that he would not call witnesses, but would ask the justices to state a case. The justices convicted the appellant, but agreed to state a case.

Extracts from Judgments

LAWRANCE J.: The question in this case is not an easy one; there is no authority, and it is a case of first impression. The question for us is whether the headmaster of a board school is justified in inflicting corporal punishment upon one of his scholars for an act done outside the limits of the school, and the appellant's counsel has in his argument relied on what might happen if a boy were not punished by the master for such acts. The facts seem to be that a boy while coming to the appellant's school was assaulted by another boy belonging to the same school; that complaint was made to the appellant, who then and there punished the boy who had committed the assault and also the respondent, who was in his company. The first observation that occurs to one to make is that one of the greatest advantages of any punishment is that it should follow quickly on the offence. The cases cited to us show that the schoolmaster is in the position of the parent. What is to become of a boy between his school and his home? Is he not under the authority of his parent or of the schoolmaster? It cannot be doubted that he is; and in my opinion among the powers delegated by the parent to the schoolmaster, such a power as was exercised by the appellant in this case would be freely delegated. If we turn to the Code we find that there are several things for which a grant may be given, including discipline and organisation, and that the children are to be brought up in habits of good manners and language, and of consideration for others. Can it be reasonably argued that the only right of a schoolmaster to inflict punishment is in respect of acts done in the school, and that it is only while the boys are there that he is to see that they are well-mannered, but that he has exceeded all the authority delegated to him by the parent if he punishes a boy who within a yard of the school is guilty of gross mis-behaviour? It is difficult to express in words the extent of the schoolmaster's authority in respect to the punishment of his pupils; but in my opinion his authority extends, not only to acts done in school, but also to cases where a complaint of acts done out of school, at any rate while going to and from school, is made to the schoolmaster. In the present case I think that weight may properly be placed on the fact that the act for which the boy was punished was done to another pupil of the same school. I think, therefore, that the justices were wrong in convicting the appellant as they did, and that the case must be sent back to them to find as a fact whether the punishment was excessive.

COLLINS J.: I am of the same opinion. It is clear law that a father has the right to inflict reasonable personal chastisement on his son. It is equally the law, and it is in accordance with very ancient practice, that he may delegate this right to the schoolmaster. Such a right has always commended itself to the common sense of mankind. It is clear that the relation of master and pupil carries with it the right of reasonable corporal chastisement. As a matter of common sense, how far is this power delegated by the parent to the school-master? Is it limited to the time during which the boy is within the four walls of the school, or does it extend in any sense beyond that limit? In my opinion, the purpose with which the parental authority is delegated to the schoolmaster, who is entrusted with the bringing up and discipline of the child, must to some extent include an authority over the child while he is out-side the four walls. It may be a question of fact in each case whether the conduct of the master in inflicting corporal punishment is right. Very grave conse-quences would result if it were held that a parent's authority was exclusive up to the door of the school, and that then, and only then, the master's authority commenced; it would be a most anomalous result to hold that in such a case as the present the boy who had been assaulted had no remedy by complaint to his master, who could punish the assailant by thrashing, but must go before the magistrate to enforce a remedy between them as citizens. Not only would such a position be unworkable in itself, but the Code, which has the force of an Act of Parliament, clearly contemplates that the duties of the master to his pupils are not limited to teaching. A grant may be made for discipline and organisation, and it is clear that he is entrusted with the moral training and conduct of his pupils. It cannot be that such a duty or power ceases the moment that the pupil leaves school for home; there is not much opportunity for a boy to exhibit his moral conduct while in school under the eye of the master: the opportunity is while he is at play or outside the school; and if the schoolmaster has no control over the boys in their relation to each other except when they are within the school walls, this object of the Code would be defeated. In such a case as the present, it is obvious that the desired impression is best brought about by a summary and immediate punishment. In my opinion parents do contemplate such an exercise of authority by the schoolmaster. I should be sorry if I felt myself driven to come to the opposite conclusion, and am glad to be able to say that the principle shows that the authority delegated to the schoolmaster is not limited to the four walls of the school. It is always a question of fact whether the act was done outside the delegated authority; but in the present case I am satisfied, on the facts, that it was obviously within it. The question of excess is one for the magistrates.

Appeal allowed. Case remitted to justices

88 R. *v.* Newport (Salop) Justices, *ex p.* Wright [1929] 2 K.B. 416

KING'S BENCH DIVISION

Reasonable punishment may be inflicted for the breach of a reasonable school rule relating to the conduct of pupils when they are not on the school premises.

Facts: Frank Douglas Wright was a fifteen-year-old pupil at Newport Grammar School, who, with another boy named Williams, was reported to the headmaster for smoking in the street. Next morning the headmaster

called the two boys out in the presence of about seventy other boys, and said
he intended to cane them. Wright tried to escape, and was brought back by
masters who held him while the headmaster caned him. Williams was caned
without resistance.

On January 8, 1929, Frank Wright's father laid an information charging
the three masters with unlawfully assaulting and beating his son by administering corporal punishment. The justices dismissed the information and ordered
the father to pay five guineas costs.

The father asked the justices to state a case for the opinion of the Divisional
Court, but they certified the application as frivolous. The father then obtained
an order nisi on the grounds (*a*) that the justices were wrong in law in holding
that the defendants had authority to inflict corporal punishment on Frank
Douglas Wright; (*b*) that at the time of committing the act complained of the
boy was in the control and under the authority of his father; (*c*) that the act
complained of was committed by Frank Douglas Wright by permission of
his father and that therefore the defendants had no authority to inflict the
punishment.

Pratt (supporting the rule): if the justices were right, the cane was hanging
suspended over the poor boy not only while he was at school but after he had
returned home. His whole life was spent under the shadow of that threat.

LORD HEWART C.J.: That is merely a picturesque way of saying that he is
required to obey the school rules.

Extract from Judgment

LORD HEWART C.J.: . . . I am satisfied, therefore, that, if the case did involve
a question of law, this Court has power to direct the justices to state and sign
a case.

But is the question involved in this case a question of law? The complaint
of the present applicant was that the headmaster and the two assistant masters
did unlawfully assault and beat the applicant's son on December 7 last. The
justices have made a joint affidavit in which they state that they found the
facts to be as follows: That there was at the school a school rule prohibiting
smoking by pupils at the school during the school term on the school premises
and in public; that the rule was a reasonable rule; and that the boy was aware
of the rule and deliberately broke it. The justices add that they found that the
punishment administered was a reasonable punishment for the breach of the
rule; and that the father of the boy by sending him to the school authorised
the schoolmaster to administer reasonable punishment to the boy for breach of
a reasonable school rule. These being the findings of fact, what is the point
of law which is said to emerge? Apparently it is a question as to the authority
of the schoolmaster to make and to enforce the rule in question, which
contemplates acts done, not indeed beyond the school term, but beyond the
precincts of the school and in public. It is obvious that the justices in directing
their minds to the facts have taken a view of the law. Is there any ground for
saying that the view which they have taken is a wrong view? Mr Walker

referred us to *Mansell* v. *Griffin*,[1] in which an assistant teacher was charged with assault for inflicting corporal punishment upon a pupil for a breach of the school regulations. In the course of his judgment in that case Walton J. said: "There is no evidence in this case that the parents of the plaintiff had any knowledge of the regulations of the school, and therefore, it must be taken that the parents gave to the authorities of the school that ordinary authority which is presumed from the fact of a parent sending a child to a school." He also said: "It seems to me that the authority to administer moderate and reasonable corporal punishment, which any parent who sends a child to a school is presumed to give to the authorities of the school, extends to the mistress occupying the position which the defendant occupied in this school." That is a clear statement of the legal proposition that any parent who sends a child to school is presumed to give to the teacher authority to make reasonable regulations and to administer to the child reasonable corporal punishment for breach of those regulations. So far from holding a view contrary to that statement of the law, the justices have almost in terms expressed the same view of the law as is there set forth. . . . The justices appear to have rightly appreciated the law as there laid down, and the question was therefore only one of fact—namely, whether in the circumstances the conduct of the master in inflicting the punishment was reasonable. It has been suggested as a *reductio ad absurdum* that the schoolmaster might make one foolish rule and the father of the scholar a contrary foolish rule, and afterwards the boy whether he did the act to which the rules applied or not would equally suffer punishment under either the one rule or the other. The case so put seems to exemplify the saying of Horace: *Quidquid delirant reges, plectuntur Achivi.* . . .

There having been no misapprehension of the law or misdirection in point of law by the justices, the question was and remains a question of fact on which the decision of the justices is final. I see no ground for the statement of a case or a point of law, and in my opinion rule should be discharged.

AVORY J.: . . . As to the merits, I agree that the decision of the justices was right and that no question of law arises on which a case should be stated. As I was a member of the court which granted the rule, I should like however to add that it was granted upon an affidavit which declared that the boy was over sixteen when in fact he was under that age and therefore contravening the law by smoking in the street.[2]

The affidavit ought to have disclosed that fact. It was also alleged in the affidavit that the boy Wright had no knowledge of the rule of the school against smoking. But the justices have found that the boy had knowledge of the rule and deliberately broke it. In these two respects the affidavit was misleading. Apart, however, from what is shown on the affidavit there is, in my opinion, no ground on which the court should direct the justices to state and sign a case.

Order discharged

1. [1908] I K.B. 947; see page 216, *supra.*
2. Children Act 1908, s. 40; see also the Children and Young Persons Act 1933, s. 7.

VI

NEGLIGENCE

(A) DUTY OF CARE: GENERAL PRINCIPLES

89 Williams *v.* Eady (1893) 10 T.L.R. 41

COURT OF APPEAL

The duty of a schoolmaster is to take such care of his boys as a careful father would take of his boys.

Facts: The plaintiff's son, Kenneth Williams, was one of three brothers who were pupils at a school owned by the defendant at Kenley in Surrey.

There was at the school a conservatory in which were kept cricketing things, etc., and among some bottles was one containing phosphorus. The boys had access to the conservatory, but the defendant claimed that the boys had to get permission (which was readily granted) as the key was kept in the kitchen where they had no right to go.

On April 11, 1892, a pupil named Edgar Scypanski took the bottle containing the phosphorus, put a match to it, and shook it up. The bottle exploded as the plaintiff was passing, and he was burned in his face and hand.

The plaintiff claimed damages for negligence. There was a counter-claim for school charges for the plaintiff and his brothers, and the doctor's bill (which the defendant had paid) and also for removing the boys without a term's notice.

The action was tried in the Queen's Bench Division before Cave J. and a jury.

CAVE J.: What is negligence is a question of degree—*e.g.* to leave a knife about where a child of four could get at it would amount to negligence, but it would not if boys of eighteen had access to it. Again, there are some things that are necessary to leave about though they are dangerous to a certain extent, but it is different if dangerous articles are kept which are not necessary. I cannot understand how the defendant, having boys of varying ages under his care, should have kept the acids, having no further use for them after the chemical lectures were abandoned, as they were of trifling value; and, again, why having put them in the cupboard, the key should be put in the kitchen. It is beyond doubt that somehow the phosphorus had got among the bottles in the conservatory.

The jury found that the defendant had been negligent, and that his negligence had contributed to the plaintiff's injury. They awarded £75 damages; but also found that the plaintiff was aware that, if he removed his sons without notice, he would have to make an equivalent payment. They awarded £30 on the counter-claim.

The defendant appealed.

Extracts from Judgment

LORD ESHER M.R.: . . . As to the law on the subject there can be no doubt; and it was correctly laid down by the learned judge, that the schoolmaster was bound to take such care of his boys as a careful father would take of his boys, and there could not be a better definition of the duty of a schoolmaster. Then he was bound to take notice of the ordinary nature of young boys, their tendency to do mischievous acts, and their propensity to meddle with anything that came in their way. Then, having phosphorus in his house, he was bound not to leave it in any place in which they might get at it, and so if he left it in the conservatory he did not use due care, but otherwise if he kept it locked up. If, therefore, the defendant kept the bottle locked up there would be no evidence of negligence. But if the bottle was left in the conservatory for any time before the accident then there was evidence on which the jury might find negligence and a want of proper care for the safety of the boys. Was the twofold question left to the jury? I cannot say that it was not, and there was certainly evidence to support the verdict given by the jury. That being so there is no ground for a new trial. Even if the judge had not left the proper question to the jury there was evidence to support a verdict of negligence, and I would be surprised if a jury on the same evidence should find a different verdict. That being so there is no ground for a new trial, and the appeal must be dismissed.

LOPES L.J.: . . . It would be impossible to lay the law down more correctly than the learned judge has done. There was ample evidence to support the verdict, for there was the undoubted fact that the bottle was found by the boys in the conservatory. It is very improbable that if it had been kept locked up any boy could have got at it, and it is very improbable that any boy would have done so.

Appeal dismissed

[NOTE: Cave J.'s dictum on the duty of a schoolmaster, which was quoted with approval by the Master of the Rolls (a schoolmaster is bound to take such care of his boys as a careful father would take of his boys) has become the standard common law definition of the duty of care resting on a schoolmaster. Two recent cases, however, have implied that a higher duty of care may be required of a schoolmaster: *Lyes* v. *Middlesex County Council* (page 198, *supra*) and *Beaumont* v. *Surrey County Council* (page 246, *infra*). It should be noted, nevertheless, that the principle laid down in *Williams* v. *Eady* was approved by the Court of Appeal, whereas the recent judgments were given in the Queen's Bench Division. The effect had been to leave some uncertainty about the precise extent of the duty of care *in loco parentis* which is unlikely to be resolved until a further case comes before the Court of Appeal. The present tendency seems to be to consider the doctrine of the "careful parent" in relation to life at school, rather than at home, and to suggest that a prudent parent would take rather more care of his pupils if his family were as large as a school. No such suggestion was made by the Court of Appeal in 1893, and it is quite impossible at present to say whether that Court would today regard this view as coming within the principle then laid down.]

90 Jeffery v. London County Council (1954) 52 L.G.R. 521

QUEEN'S BENCH DIVISION

School authorities must strike some balance between the meticulous supervision of children at every moment when they are under their care, and the very desirable object of encouraging the sturdy independence of children as they grow up; such encouragement must start at quite an early age.

Facts: Raymond Jeffrey was a pupil at Middle Row School, North Kensington. It was the practice in the school, after classes had been dismissed for the day, to allow the pupils to disperse into the playground.

Shortly after 4 o'clock on June 27, 1952, Raymond Jeffery, then aged five years and ten months, was found lying unconscious and gravely injured in the lavatory in the school playground. He appeared to have climbed nine feet on to the glass roof of the lavatory to get a toy motor car thrown there, and died from the injuries he received when he fell through. There was nobody on the scene except other infants, and they all ran away but one, who fetched the boy's aunt from her home opposite the school. The aunt took Raymond to hospital, where he died at about 4.20 p.m. From the dismissal of the class until the boy's death no member of the staff was present or aware of the accident.

The father brought an action for damages for negligence against the London County Council. He complained that no adult was present, and that the school authorities ought to have had some person in authority until the children left the premises.

Extract from Judgment

MCNAIR J.: . . . The class in which this child was in the infants' school was one containing some thirty-six to forty small children of similar age; and, in accordance with the usual practice of the school, the mistress had dismissed the class at about four o'clock, and the children were allowed on dispersal to run out into the playground. The playground abuts on to the infants' school building, and round the corner, in a comparatively secluded position, there is the lavatory, which adjoins a covered play-shed. It would seem that this lavatory would not be under the actual observation of anyone standing in the infants' playground.

The case made against the London County Council, as the education authority, is twofold. It is said, first, that this lavatory was unsuitable and unsafe because it had a water-pipe which could be climbed, and because it had a glass roof through which a child could fall if he did climb the water-pipe. I can dispose of that matter quite shortly by saying that, in my view, there is no ground at all upon which any court could hold that a children's lavatory constructed in the way this lavatory was constructed in a playground such as this is unfit.

Secondly (and this is the main point in the attack against the London County Council), it is said, as the evidence shows, that no adult was present from the time when the child met with his injury until he was taken away to hospital; that there was lack of reasonable supervision in the playground, and that the school authorities, when they allowed these small children to disperse, ought to have stationed, either in the playground or, at any rate, in a position where they would observe what was going on in the playground, some person in authority who would see that the children at least left the school premises in safety. That, of course, is not a proposition of law, but is a conclusion of facts which I am asked to draw. I have applied what I understand to be the proper principles of law. There is no doubt about it that the school authorities, as has been said in some of the cases, were under a duty to exercise the same standard of care over children as would be exercised by a good parent with a large family.

The question whether the school authorities were at fault in this case can be decided by asking whether, on the facts here, there should have been any reasonable anticipation, if these children were allowed to disperse on their own without supervision, that they would meet this or some similar hurt if they were not supervised. It being conceded that it is not, and never has been, the law that at every moment of time the children have to be under the actual eye of a master or mistress, it seems to me that school authorities, when they are considering the care of children, must strike some balance between the meticulous supervision of children every moment of the time when they are under their care, and the very desirable object of encouraging the sturdy independence of children as they grow up; and I think encouragement of sturdy independence and the ability to get on without detailed supervision must start at quite an early age.

The evidence in this case as to the practice of the school was given almost entirely by Miss Allen, who has been the headmistress of this infant school for the last eight years. She gave me the impression that she took her responsibilities very seriously, as one would expect of a person in her position, and that in the evidence which she gave me she was trying to give an accurate picture of what went on in the school and in no way arguing the case defensively on behalf of the London County Council. One striking fact that emerged from her evidence is that, connected with the infant department, there is a nursery school for young children of before school age, namely, up to five. In the case of these children, the class broke up at about ten minutes to four, and she or the education authority thought it right that, in the case of children under five, there should be in attendance, until they actually were collected and taken from the premises by their mothers or other persons, somebody in actual supervision and contact the whole time. Miss Allen, however, told me that in the case of the five-year-olds and children over that age she did not think it necessary to have the same detailed supervision over the children after they had dispersed into the playground, as by the time they reached the school age of five they had learned that they were going to be collected from the playground by their mothers or others, and had learned that, if they were not collected within a minute or two, they should go in and report. She said that, in her experience, she had found that that is what they did. It seems to me that there a responsible decision has been taken as to detailed supervision; and I should require very strong evidence indeed to convince me that the decision was wrong.

Furthermore, she told me (and I accept it) that in the case of Raymond Jeffery, whose mother lived across the road and was out at work during the day time, she had made an arrangement with Mrs Jeffery that during the midday break she, Miss Allen, would keep Raymond in the school buildings until he was collected by the mother, because she might be late; but that she had also arranged with the mother that, as regards the dispersal at the end of the afternoon session, she, Mrs Jeffery, should collect the boy from the playground or arrange for him to be collected at the gate of the playground.

That arrangement worked perfectly satisfactorily until this day, when, as I find, Mrs Jeffery unfortunately must have been a few minutes late; because it is clear that by the time this accident happened all the other children had, with the exception of this one companion, either gone home on their own or had been collected.

Some evidence was given, not of a very precise nature, as to the climbing activities of some of the children in this school, going back ten years in one case, and more recently in another case; from which it was urged that I ought to find that the school authorities ought to have known that there was a particular risk of these small children climbing about generally, and, in particular, climbing on to this lavatory, and that they ought to have taken special precautions. I do not feel myself, as a judge of fact, that this evidence really amounted to more than illustrations of the general propensity of small children to climb, I cannot believe that it is the duty of the school authorities, in all circumstances, to keep the children under such detailed observation that they cannot climb. Miss Allen said that there were in the school spasms of these climbing activities, and from time to time she checked children who were found climbing and imposed a mild, but adequate, punishment upon them; and that that was part of the educational process.

That seems to me to be good sense and unobjectionable unless, of course, one could point to any particular danger or any particular allurement on the premises which would excite children to climb more than in accordance with the natural propensity of children so to do. I cannot find that there is anything in this case of that character at all.

My general conclusion, therefore, is that, without laying down any general proposition of law, on the facts of this particular case I do not find that there was any failure to exercise reasonable care for the children under the charge of this school.

[After a discussion regarding costs, in which it was disclosed that the plaintiff was in receipt of legal aid, and that his maximum contribution was nil:]

MCNAIR J.: I confess that it fills me with great alarm to know that an action of this kind (which I view merely as a way of claiming money representing a wholly artificial cause of action) should be supported by public funds; but I think that is probably irrelevant if the legal aid committee have taken the view that it is a proper form of action to support with public funds. There will be no order as to costs, except the usual order for taxation for the purposes of legal aid.

Judgment for defendants

91 Suckling *v.* Essex County Council (1955) *The Times,* January 27

QUEEN'S BENCH DIVISION
It is better that a boy should break his neck than allow other people to break his spirit.

Facts: The plaintiff, Roger Leslie Suckling, then aged eleven, was a pupil at William Torbitt School, Ilford. During handicraft lessons the pupils used four-inch scorer knives for modelling. These were handed out by the teacher. During the absence of the teacher from the room another boy went to a cupboard and took out a knife. Some horseplay ensued, and the plaintiff received injuries which resulted in the loss of his left eye. There were forty-eight pupils in the class.

The defendants were sued for damages in negligence.

Extract from Judgment
VAISEY J.: I have to consider whether keeping the knives locked up was a necessary and reasonable precaution to take or whether the precaution that was taken—putting the knives into the unlocked cupboard and telling the class not to take them out without permission—complied with the rules of safety. It seems to me that if I were to hold that every school with small children was committing an actionable wrong in leaving unlocked such implements as these scorer knives I would be putting an altogether excessive burden on educational establishments. Not only would it be difficult for them to be conducted in a successful and reasonable manner but it would run the serious risk of turning these children into votaries of the principle of safety first. It is better that a boy should break his neck than allow other people to break his spirit.

Judgment for defendants

92 Beaumont *v.* Surrey County Council (1968) 66 L.G.R. 580

QUEEN'S BENCH DIVISION

It is a headmaster's duty, bearing in mind the known propensities of boys and girls between the ages of eleven and eighteen, to take all reasonable and proper steps to prevent any of the pupils under his care from suffering injury from inanimate objects, from actions of their fellow pupils, or from a combination of both.

Facts: The plaintiff, William Arthur Albert Beaumont, suffered injury as the result of an incident at the De Burgh Secondary School, Tadworth, during morning break on February 10, 1965. The plaintiff, then aged fifteen, was eating a biscuit near the playground when he was hit in the right eye by a piece of elastic. He lost, to all intents and purposes, the vision of that eye.

The remaining facts are fully stated in the judgment. The plaintiff sued the Surrey County Council for damages for negligence resulting in personal injuries.

Extract from Judgment

GEOFFREY LANE J.: . . . The headmaster, Mr Mather, gave evidence before me, and he had described the system which operated during the mid-morning break. A bell goes at about ten minutes past eleven and the break then lasts for nearly twenty minutes until another bell goes at about twenty-eight minutes past eleven. Apart from the fifth and sixth form pupils who have the option to stay in their classrooms or not, it is compulsory for everyone else to go out, and to go out on to the playground or into the loggia, that is of course weather permitting. The playground on the far right comprises tennis courts and that is out of bounds, but the other two playgrounds are those which are frequented by the pupils when they emerge at ten minutes past eleven.

It will be appreciated that the efflux of a very large number of children between the ages of eleven and seventeen or eighteen in a very short space of time, particularly when they have come from the confines of the classroom, on to the broader acres of the playground may present some problems of discipline, and the system again described by the headmaster is as follows. There are two members of staff who, during the break, have the duty of supervision. In an agreed document before me that is described as duty No. 11 and reads as follows: "Break: in charge of playground and clearing the classrooms etc. with assistance of prefects, subprefects. On bell supervise re-entering."

The two members of the staff whose duty it was on this particular day to carry out the supervisory function were a Mr Clerke, whom I have seen in the witness box here today, and a Mr Colin Richard Chapman, who has emigrated to Canada, but whose affidavit sworn in Saskatchewan I have before me. The two members of the staff were in their turn assisted by a number of the more senior and responsible pupils of the school. There were four prefects, four subprefects and four monitors. They were intended to assist, as I say, in the maintenance of discipline and there were various forms of sanction which were open to the two members of the staff to institute. They could either institute them on their own initiative or be prompted thereto by a report from one of the prefects, subprefects or, I gather, monitors. They needed that assistance because before they themselves could emerge with a clear conscience into the playground to supervise there, they had to ensure that the buildings had been cleared of pupils otherwise than the privileged few in the fifth and sixth forms.

On the day in question Mr Clerke had described how things were particularly difficult and somewhat exceptional, so much so that the whole of his break-time in effect was taken up by clearing out the classrooms, and he never emerged on to the playground, at any rate before the time when the accident took place. Mr Chapman in his affidavit said that on the day in question the tour that he had made of the classrooms was uneventful until he was informed of the circumstances of the accident, but he does say that it took him as a rule about ten minutes to get along to the end of the building and back to the loggia again leaving only something under ten minutes for the supervision by him of the playground. He does add that from time to time as he went through the buildings of the school he would emerge from the doorways leading towards the playground, and take a look at what was going on in the playground and thereabouts before going back into the school to continue his tour there. So much for the particular system operated to keep order during the break.

So far as general standards of discipline are concerned in this particular school I have heard what the boys have to say and I have seen the headmaster himself. Also I have heard what the master, Mr Buckland, who was to some extent in charge of the physical education of this school, has said, and I accept entirely and there can be no doubt at all that the general standards of discipline at this school were extremely high.

The situation in short on this particular day so far as supervision was concerned up to the time of the accident was this. Somewhere presumably either on or near the playground were the twelve senior pupils charged with the assistance in keeping discipline. So far as staff were concerned no member of the staff was at the loggia or on the playground at any time from the commencement of the break until the time when the plaintiff suffered his injury.

I will now turn to the particular facts of this accident. Happily, and it is only right that I should say this, apart from one very comparatively minor matter there has been practically no dispute as to the sequence of events at all, and I am happy to be able to say that, whether they succeeded or not, each witness who gave evidence before me was doing his level best to tell the truth, which is not always the case. On February 10, 1965, when the bell which started off the break sounded, the plaintiff went straight from his classroom to the loggia. In the loggia was a table or stall from which it was possible for pupils to buy biscuits. He armed himself with some biscuits which he was eating at the same time as talking to some of his friends; indeed, I think they were some of his classmates. He had been there for about five minutes when he saw two friends of his, by name Baines and Callaghan, playing with a long piece of multi-stranded, fabric-covered, circular section elastic. That is a long phrase describing the sort of elastic which people use to keep suitcases down on roof racks on motor-cars.

He, that is to say the plaintiff, next saw Callaghan coming towards his group of friends. Callaghan put this elastic round the waist of another young man called Graham Giles. Giles resisted, pulled away, the elastic flew out and it either broke there and then or one end flew out of Callaghan's hand, it matters not which. The result was that one end of the elastic, either via the pillar or direct, hit the unfortunate plaintiff in the eye with the results which I have indicated already.

What was the history of that elastic? It was this: in the gymnasium there was an implement called a trampette which is apparently a sort of mini-trampoline used in gymnasium exercises. The base of the trampette is sprung and the springing system was provided by four strands of the type of elastic which I have just described. Mr Buckland, the head of the physical education department, who spent three days a week at this school and the rest of the week at various other educational establishments under the Surrey County Council, had visited the gymnasium and had discovered that this trampette was unserviceable and dangerous because one at least of the strands of elastic was worn to breaking point and clearly required replacement. So at one o'clock in the afternoon of February 9, that is the day before the accident, he set to work on the trampette in the gymnasium, which at that time was out of bounds to the pupils of the school. He took off the old bit of elastic, put in a new bit and then so far as the old bit was concerned he said he bound the elastic into a coil, wound one end of the elastic round the coil, put the end through as one does with a length of string making it into a neat little bundle, and then put it in a wastepaper bin in the loggia which I have just described. The type of wastepaper bin is simply the normal type of litter bin one sees in public parks, consisting of wooden slats enclosing a metal, opaque and removable interior wastepaper basket.

The way that Mr Buckland gave his evidence about his disposal of that elastic was perhaps illuminating. He said in chief that it looked fairly inconspicuous. He said he put it in the waste bin of the loggia at the bottom of the bin and "I thought it would be taken away." In cross-examination he said that, even in retrospect, he still would have put it in that bin because it would have been covered by litter and because he said he did not foresee the possibility of any danger. It did not occur to him, he said, that there was any more danger than if it had been a cricket ball or a stick. "I would not have left it lying on the playground. That would have invited people to play with it leading to boisterous behaviour and possibly to someone getting hurt, but I did not and could not have anticipated the fantastic chain of circumstances which in fact took place."

There is the elastic in the litter bin in the wastepaper basket shortly before mid-day on February 9.[1] What happened next? For that one turns to the evidence of the various lads who were in that loggia apart from the plaintiff himself. The first of those was Graham Giles. He, also, is now eighteen and a carpenter. He said that when the bell rang he went to the loggia, got his biscuits and he was standing round talking and eating. He then noticed a crowd of young boys—and by that he meant presumably eleven- or twelve-year olds—playing with some elastic, flicking it at each other's legs. The next thing he saw was the elastic hanging over the edge of the wastepaper bin in the loggia. He saw Baines take it out, chasing Callaghan, Callaghan getting the elastic, attacking Giles himself with it and finally the elastic flicking the plaintiff in the eye. The evidence that Giles gave about the young boys playing with the elastic is about the only matter in this case of fact which is in dispute. It is true that no other witness spoke of it, it is true that in the headmaster's report, an agreed document which is before me, there is no mention of any such incident although it is plain the headmaster must have interviewed Giles before making his report, and it is true that in one respect it does not coincide with what Baines says because Giles says it was hanging on the edge of the bin and Baines says he took it from the bottom of the bin. I do not believe that Giles was lying about that, indeed I am certain that he was not, because if he had the craftiness to lie about that matter I dare say we might have had some so-called supporting evidence from the lads and that has not been forthcoming. My impression of Giles on that point was that he was telling the truth and was accurate that the younger boys had taken the elastic from the bin before the older boys got it. I am supported in that view by the fact that Mr Buckland, whose evidence so far as the facts are concerned I accept entirely, said (and there is no reason to disbelieve him) that he wrapped this up into a careful bundle with the end tucked in so that it would not come adrift. If Baines is to be believed, by the time he got to it it had ceased to be a closely wrapped bundle and was in a looser coil at the bottom of the bin. Somebody had unwound the bundle, somebody had made it into a coil. It is conceivable that it happened by the inherent elasticity of the subject which was bundled, but I doubt it. The most likely solution seemed to be that somebody had interfered with it before Baines got there, and that somebody so far as I can see was the young people of whom Giles spoke.

The other witnesses simply bore out what I have already described. There was this horseplay. Undoubtedly Callaghan did wrap the elastic round Giles' waist, undoubtedly Giles struggled, undoubtedly the elastic either broke or was released, undoubtedly it hit the plaintiff in the eye. The only matter where there is any difference of opinion was the length of time which this accident took. It varies between moments on the one hand and five minutes on the other. The headmaster himself thought (of course he did not witness it), and said, that he could quite understand horseplay such as this taking about five minutes. Callaghan said it took about five minutes. Baines said it

1. *Sic.*

took about two minutes and so on. My own view for what it is worth, and estimates of time of course are always bound to be misleading, is that this scuffle with the elastic did take four or five minutes. It was quite a lengthy scuffle to and fro, and so far as the earlier incident is concerned with the little boys no time has been given as to that, but it seems to me quite possible, and indeed probable that the first seven or eight minutes of this break were taken up by various sorts of horseplay, first by the eleven- and twelve-year olds, and second by the fifteen-and-a-half-year olds with this piece of elastic.

Those being the facts, what is the law to which those facts must be applied? The duty of a headmaster towards his pupils is said to be to take such care of them as a reasonably careful and prudent father would take of his own children. That standard is a helpful one when considering, for example, individual instructions to individual children in a school. It would be very unwise to allow a six-year old child to carry a kettle of boiling water—that type of instruction. But that standard when applied to an incident of horseplay in a school of 900 pupils is somewhat unrealistic, if not unhelpful.

In the context of the present action it appears to me to be easier and preferable to use the ordinary language of the law of negligence. That is, it is a headmaster's duty, bearing in mind the known propensities of boys and indeed girls between the ages of eleven and seventeen or eighteen, to take all reasonable and proper steps to prevent any of the pupils under his care from suffering injury from inanimate objects, from the actions of their fellow pupils, or from a combination of the two. That is a high standard.

It is said against the defendants in the present case that the staff of the school failed in two main respects to achieve the necessary high degree of care, and it has been agreed most helpfully between counsel on each side that the allegations fall into those two convenient categories. First, that the elastic should not have been left in an open wastepaper basket by the loggia on what was really a highly frequented means of access to the school and, indeed, a place where at breaktime large numbers of pupils would have congregated for their biscuits. It should have been foreseen, it is said on behalf of the plaintiff, that by leaving it there some injury might be done to one of the pupils of the school. The second arm of the allegation is this, that even if such foresight is expecting too much, there was unfortunately insufficient supervision in and around the playground, and in particular on the loggia, on that morning of February 10, and that with proper supervision this horseplay would have been stopped before this accident had had a chance to happen.

Dealing with those matters separately: first leaving the elastic in that basket. I confess that at first blush in this case I was of the view that it was not unreasonable to put elastic into a wastepaper basket wherever it was. That view has gradually changed during the progress of this case. First, this was not ordinary elastic. It is a material of very considerable power, and one has only to observe it stretched or indeed flicked to realise that this is about as far removed from the ordinary idea of a rubber band as could be imagined. Secondly, the other matter that assisted to change my view about the elastic was the evidence of Mr Buckland, the physical education officer, and of one of the masters who was on duty at the time, Mr Clerke, a man obviously of very great experience.

I have already read the evidence in brief of Mr Buckland, and it seemed clear to me at any rate from that evidence, that when he wrapped that elastic up and when he was in his own mind pleased to see that it was inconspicuous, he knew, not subconsciously but at least in the back of his mind, that this was not a very satisfactory place in which to place that article, and if he had stopped to think he would have realised why it was not a very satisfactory place in which to leave that article, because it was an object which was a fatal attraction to any young man whose eye might light upon it and who might very easily realise what it was. It was much more attractive than damaged pens, ice cream cartons, cricket balls and other matters which have been adumbrated before me.

The other evidence, that of Mr Clerke, which impressed me was the fact that he said if he had seen this lying around upon the playground he would have immediately picked it up. It was plain that that action of his would not have been dictated solely by the desire not to leave litter lying around, but because he realised quite rightly that if that object fell into the hands of some youngster it might very well cause injury.

Instead of it being on the playground it was, certainly when Mr Buckland left it and it seems to me when discovered by the eleven-year olds, lying uncovered in a low wastepaper backet into which anyone who cared to peer could see quite easily within a matter of feet of the playground itself, and the distinction between the object lying on the playground where it would plainly have been a menace, albeit not a very great menace, to the children, and the distinction of it in this open wastepaper basket a yard or two away seems to be one which is a distinction scarcely without a difference.

Mr Clerke explained that he would not expect his charges to go routing round, as he put it, in a waste-paper basket, but there would have been no routing around to do. If the facts are as I take them to be, the elastic in the basket on the face of it was very nearly the same as leaving it on the playground. May I hasten to add that nobody for a moment suggests nor have they suggested throughout this case, that anyone, let alone Mr Buckland, or Giles or Callaghan, could possibly have foreseen that the injury which in fact was going to happen would have been such a tragic injury as this one. It is sufficient so far as the law is concerned for the possibility to be there—for the possibility to be foreseen that some physical injury might be caused by the extension or use of, or horseplay with, that piece of elastic. If such, even slight, injury is foreseeable,then the defendants must foot the bill if unforeseen and major injury occurred.

So far as the second head is concerned, that is to say supervision, I find here also that the defendants did not measure up to the high standard of care which was demanded of them through their servants. It may be that this was a particularly difficult day as Mr Clerke has indicated, it may be that the system of prefects, subprefects and monitors was not quite up to standard. It may be that on the one day when pupils were possibly reluctant to get out on to the playground insufficient staff were available to clear out the class-rooms which meant that insufficient staff were available in the playground and on the loggia to supervise. Suffice it to say, that had the system been working properly I have no doubt at all that either a prefect, subprefect, monitor or one of the staff on duty would have seen or would have been summoned to see what was going on with the elastic, and it is plain from the evidence of Mr Clerke and the headmaster and also Mr Buckland that horse-play of this sort was at this school not tolerated for one moment. A whistle would have been blown and the forces of law and order would have moved into action. The offenders would have been either put into what I am told is the supervising master's private detention or into the school detention or would have been reported to the headmaster, according to the view which the master took of the gravity of the offence. At all events it would have been stopped immediately, and had it been stopped immediately, or even within two or three minutes of this inception by the eleven-year olds, then this tragic matter would never have happened.

It is, as I say, a high standard of care, and in ordinary circumstances had it been an ordinary day at the school Mr Clerke, having been able to get out on to the playground, would have seen these things and the accident would never have happened. They, the defendants, in the manner which I have described, regrettably fall short of the standards which the law demands of them.

In the result, the plaintiff with his injured eye was taken off to hospital. . . . Taking all those matters into consideration I assess the general damages at £3,250 to which must be added the special damages, which have been agreed at £81. 6s.

Judgment for the plaintiff

[NOTE : This case should be read in sequence with *Williams* v. *Eady* (page 240, *supra*) and *Lyes* v. *Middlesex County Council* (page 198, *supra*). There is some reason to think that the courts are gradually raising the standard of care in all actions for negligence, and *Lyes's* case was the first educational action in which this trend was clearly discernible. The tendency was followed in this case, which may well prove to have established the standard which the courts will apply in the future.]

(B) CLASSROOM DANGERS: FALLING BLACKBOARD

93 Crisp v. Thomas (1890) 63 L.T. 756

COURT OF APPEAL
The mere fact of the fall of a blackboard is not evidence of negligence.

Facts: The plaintiff, Alice Crisp, was a pupil at St Michael's Church of England School, Wood Green. The defendant was the vicar of the parish, and also a manager and trustee of the school. The staff of the school consisted of the headmistress, an assistant mistress, and two pupil-teachers.

In September 1888, the pupil-teacher in charge of the plaintiff's class was away, and a senior scholar named Clara Rider was put in charge. During school the blackboard fell down and struck the plaintiff on the head. It was said, on behalf of the plaintiff, that paralysis set in, and her life was despaired of for three months. It was still, at the time of the hearing, doubtful whether she would even regain her health.

The plaintiff sued for damages for injuries due to negligence and the action was tried in the Queen's Bench Division before Charles J. and a common jury. Evidence was given that the blackboard had fallen several times before, and that the flooring was loose near to the spot where it stood. For the defence it was alleged that the blackboard was upset by another little girl who dropped her pencil and was going after it. Miss Godfree, the second mistress, said the plaintiff was a child of weak intellect, who dragged one leg and appeared in bad health. The headmistress, Mrs Turner, said the plaintiff was a healthy, rosy-looking girl, but very stupid.

The jury found for the plaintiff for £20, but Charles J. refused to give judgment until the point of law as to the defendant's liability and the evidence of negligence had been argued before him.

At a later date, after argument, Charles J. said he had originally thought that there was no evidence to go to the jury of negligence in the defendant, but he had thought it best to allow the case to go to them. But, because the jury disbelieved the two little girls called by the defendant, they had jumped to the wrong conclusion that they must find for the plaintiff. The thing done was nothing unusual or dangerous in itself. There was no case of negligence made against the defendant, for whom there would be judgment with costs.

The plaintiff appealed. The Court of Appeal (Lord Esher M.R., Lopes, and Kay L.JJ.) dismissed the appeal.

Extracts from Judgments

LORD ESHER M.R.: The case is perfectly clear against the plaintiff, both on the question of negligence and on the question of the liability of the defendant. The plaintiff says there is negligence in someone, but he must point out the person who has been guilty of it. The easel was put in position, and the black-board put on it by Clara Rider, and it is said that she did not see that the pegs were properly fixed; but is there any evidence that it was her duty to look at the pegs and see that they were put in safely? She was only bound to use ordinary care. There was no evidence that she put the pegs in, but only that she put the easel in its place and laid the blackboard upon it, and that she did just as any person with ordinary care would have done. Then it is argued that the mere fact of the board falling down shows want of care, and cases have been cited to show that such a mere fact as that is evidence of negligence. But in those cases the judges have always said that the question depends in each case on its own particular circumstances. The application of the maxim

Res ipsa loquitur depends upon whether the judge in each particular case can see that the mere fact of a thing happening is more consistent with there being negligence than not. The facts of the case here are not more consistent with negligence than with accident, and Charles J. was right in so holding. There was some suggestion that the accident was caused by the looseness of a board in the floor, but as there was no evidence that the looseness had any-thing to do with it, I leave out any further reference to that. Therefore I think that there was no evidence of negligence on the part of Clara Rider, nor on the part of the schoolmistress. That is of itself sufficient to decide the case in favour of the defendant. But I will go further and say that, even if there were any negligence either on the part of Rider or on the part of the schoolmistress, the defendant would not be liable. The defendant is the vicar of a parish, and as such he is one of a committee for the management of this school, but he is not a partner with his other committee men, they are not his servants or agents, and each of them is liable only for his own negligence. The defendant is only responsible for his agent and servant, and the school-mistress was not his servant. He did not pay her wages; she was not bound to obey any order he might give her; he could not appoint her alone, nor of himself could he dismiss her. It is true that he could with the rest of the committee appoint and dismiss her, but even then, supposing that they should dismiss her wrongfully, she could appeal to the bishop, and he could reappoint her. Neither the defendant nor the committee have power to direct the schoolmistress what to do, or what not to do in the daily management of the school. Therefore she was not in any sense a servant either of the defendant or the committee. Still less was Rider his servant; he could not appoint her as teacher, or dismiss or interfere with her in any way at all, and therefore, even if she were negligent, he was not responsible. I think, therefore, that judgment ought to be for the defendant on both points, and that there was no case for the jury at all.

LOPES L.J.: . . . This case is so much like an accident as to be more consistent with there being no negligence than not; there was no want of care in anyone, it was a pure accident. . . .

KAY L.J.: . . . To say that there must be negligence whenever an accident happened, is a contention quite untenable. It is not a dangerous thing to use a blackboard. It seems that the schoolmistress, in the absence of one of the teachers, employed a girl to give lessons; the girl put the blackboard on an easel, and the evidence is that soon after her leaving the easel the board fell. Whatever the cause of the board falling it could not be at the highest more than the negligence of the girl. It does not appear who put the pegs in, so that the only negligence on her part that could be possibly relied on would be the putting up of the board without first seeing that the pegs fitted tight. I do not think that she could be held liable for that; but, even if she were negligent, that would not make the defendant liable. Rider was clearly not his servant. The appeal must be dismissed.

Appeal dismissed

(C) INSTRUCTION TO UNDERTAKE DANGEROUS OPERATION

94 Foster *v.* London County Council (1928) *The Times*, March 2

COURT OF APPEAL
It is negligence for a teacher to order a child to undertake a dangerous operation.

Facts: The plaintiff, Gladys Gertrude Foster, a child of about ten years of age, was a pupil at Vernon Square Girls' School, King's Cross. In February 1926, the class of about forty children was in charge of a Miss Elsie Doris Perry, aged twenty, who was a student at Greystone Place Training College for Teachers.

During the scripture lesson the plaintiff was the book monitress and gave out the Bibles. At the end of that lesson, Miss Foster was giving out the books for the composition when one of the girls said her pen would not write. Miss Foster sent the girl to the front of the class where Lily Palumbo, a thirteen-year-old girl was acting as pen monitress. According to the plaintiff another girl said she could not get her nib out, and Miss Perry said to the plaintiff: "Let us see what you can do. Take the pincers out of my drawer." When she pulled the nib with the pincers it splintered, and the pieces flew into her eye.

Miss Perry denied that she told the plaintiff to take out the nib, and she did not see her do it. About ten or fifteen minutes later the plaintiff was standing between the desks giving out blotting paper, and Miss Perry noticed that she had a red eye. Miss Perry asked her if she had a cold in her eye, and she replied: "No I have got something in it." The plaintiff had said that the student removed the pieces with a handkerchief, but Miss Perry said she did not look into the eye as the child objected. She was sent to bathe her eye. On her return she was unable to see properly, and was told to clear out a stock cupboard. Miss Perry said that in the afternoon the child did not complain that she could not read, and she (Miss Perry) did not know of the accident until told by the principal of her college in April.

Lily Palumbo, the pen monitress, said that she had tried unsuccessfully to pull out the nib; then, having to go to her desk for a handkerchief, she put the pen on top of a cupboard, Gladys Foster was standing near, and was told not to touch the pen. When Lily returned she found Gladys trying to pull out the nib with the pincers, and she would not put the pen and pincers down. Returning again from her desk, she found Gladys Foster with her hand to her eye.

The plaintiff brought an action for damages for personal injuries against the London County Council, alleging negligence by the Council, their servants or agents. The defendants denied negligence, and pleaded contributory negligence by the plaintiff.

The action was tried before Avory J. and a common jury in the King's Bench Division. Dr David Vey said he saw the plaintiff at the Central London Ophthalmic Hospital on April 20, 1926. There was a scar on her left eyeball, and there would always be traces of the injury. He advised a seaside holiday. Mr William John Corbett, an ophthalmic surgeon, said he had examined the plaintiff on November 8, 1927. There was an injury above the pupil of the left eye which affected the sight. The injury was permanent.

The jury found for the plaintiff, awarding £100 damages to the child, and £27 13s. 6d. special damages to the father.

The defendants appealed, applying for a new trial on the grounds (1) that there was no evidence of negligence fit to be submitted to the jury; (2) that the verdict was against the weight of the evidence; and (3) misdirection.

Extract from Judgment
SCRUTTON L.J.: This is a case in which a little girl sues by her father for damages for injury sustained during school time. The first question then, is what in fact did happen. The plaintiff had told one story, and the teacher had given quite a different account of what happened. The case is one which has been tried before a jury and it was for them to decide which of the two versions was right, subject to this check, that the verdict must not be one which no twelve reasonable men could find or one which was so much against the weight of the evidence as to be unsatisfactory. The Court of Appeal must always bear in mind that the jury is put there to decide questions of fact. . . .

In my opinion, it is impossible to say that the jury were wrong in believing the plaintiff's story. If that story were true, was it negligence on the part of the teacher to order the child to remove the rusty nib with a pair of pincers? That, again, was a matter entirely for the jury. I think that no complaint could be made of the judge's very careful summing-up. In my opinion it is impossible to interfere with the verdict which the constitutional tribunal has found.

Appeal dismissed

(D) DANGEROUS SUBSTANCES AND OBJECTS

95 King *v.* Ford (1816) 1 Stark 421 N.P.

COURT OF KING'S BENCH
A schoolmaster who permits an infant pupil to use fireworks is responsible for the mischief which ensues.

Facts: The plaintiff, a stable-keeper, had placed his son as a pupil at an academy in Brixton kept by the defendant. The action was for an injury sustained by the boy on November 5, 1815, it being contended that the injury was due to the most imprudent and illegal conduct of the defendant.

For the plaintiff it was alleged that the headmaster had encouraged a fund for the purchase of squibs, crackers, rockets, etc., and had himself spent more than £10 on them. When the fireworks were distributed, a Mr Phillips gave the thirteen-year-old son of the plaintiff a number of squibs which the boy put in his breeches pocket. In the playground at night they were ignited, and discharged themselves without the possibility of relief before the injury was completed. The boy was put to bed and attended by a surgeon, but it was nearly a fortnight before the father was informed of the accident.

Thereupon the father took his son home on a feather bed in a spring cart, but it was many weeks before even a partial cure was effective. The plaintiff was poor and was arrested and compelled to pay sixteen guineas surgeon's fees, the school fees due to Christmas, and money for poultices and port wine ordered for the boy. The boy returned to school after his recovery. For the plaintiff it was contended that the defendant was liable to a penalty of £5 under the statute 9 & 10 William 3, c. 7, "to prevent the throwing and firing of squibs, serpents, and other fireworks."

Charles King, the plaintiff's son, said the fireworks were given by the headmaster to the head boy for distribution. As he had not subscribed, he did not receive any, but he later obtained a dozen squibs from Mr Phillips, a relation of the defendant. The defendant did not go out to see the fireworks discharged, and King did not know whether the headmaster knew that he had any. A boy named Gabriel put a light to all the squibs in King's pocket. King agreed that, three weeks before the accident, he had some cartridges and some gunpowder he had taken from his father. When the plaintiff visited him he said he had got the powder from his uncle, whereupon the father said: "You are a damned liar, and I wish it had blown your head off at once."

The plaintiff went to see Mr Gabriel, whereupon the boy Gabriel denied lighting the squibs and said that Charles King was a most notorious liar. The plaintiff agreed. The headmaster told the plaintiff that Charles King had been burnt by his own gunpowder.

ELLENBOROUGH L.C.: In all the three counts of the plaintiff's declaration it was laid that the defendant "delivered or caused to be delivered" these fireworks to the boy; whereas it appeared he was ignorant of the fact of the delivery by Phillips. The allegation, therefore, is not sustained by the proof. *Spankie* (for the plaintiff): If a school-master allowed these dangerous missiles to be employed, and the fact of his knowledge could be established, it would be sufficient to sustain the words "delivered or caused to be delivered."

ELLENBOROUGH L.C.: I cannot by any means accede to that proposition. I do not say that the action would not have been maintainable for permitting fireworks to be used; but as it is now charged, unless it can be shown that the defendant "delivered or caused to be delivered," the plaintiff must be non-suited.* . . . I am sorry there are no counts to meet this proof, and to justify damages where a schoolmaster has permitted the use of fireworks. Within a short time some accidents, we know, have occurred at great schools that have extended even to the life of the party injured.

Attorney-General (for the defendant): I hope that what your Lordship has just said will be widely disseminated: the masters of seminaries are in great want of an authority upon this subject, without which, in some cases, they did not dare to prohibit the discharge of fireworks on the 5th of November. It would henceforth be known that masters were liable if they permitted them without employing their utmost exertions to the contrary.

ELLENBOROUGH L.C.: . . . If a master of a school, knowing that fireworks would be used, were to be guilty of negligence in not preventing the use of them, he would be answerable for the consequences.

Plaintiff nonsuited

96 Baxter *v.* Barker and others (1903) *The Times*, April 24 and November 13

COURT OF APPEAL

The headmaster of a school may not be liable for the non-observance of a school rule.

Facts: The plaintiff, Herbert Baxter, was a pupil at St Marylebone Central Schools Higher Grade and Technical Departments for Boys.

On May 1, 1902, he was, with two other boys, in a cloister leading from the school to the headmaster's house. The cloister was sometimes used as a playground with the master's consent; occasionally the boys played there without permission. The plaintiff and two others were playing cap-touch at 4.30 p.m. after the end of school. At this time, two boys were carrying a flask of vitriol to a sink at the end of the cloister. While endeavouring to escape from one of his fellows, the plaintiff ran down the corridor, either backwards or laterally, and collided with the boy carrying the vitriol. The flask broke and some of its contents were scattered on the head and face of the plaintiff, causing painful injuries and permanent disfigurement.

In an action against Canon Barker, the chairman, and the other managers, and against Mr L. C. Brooke, the headmaster, the plaintiff sought to recover damages for negligence. It was contended that the negligence consisted in sending the vitriol in an unprotected glass flask held in the hand through the cloister at a time when it might reasonably be supposed that other boys would be there.

For the defendants it was established that the managers were an unpaid body carrying out a public duty; the headmaster and assistant masters were appointed by the managers and the headmaster had no power of appointment or dismissal; that the chemistry master was a competent and qualified man; that the boys carrying the vitriol were class monitors, well acquainted with the properties of the acid; and that the flask was not carried in the hand but affixed to a stand.

The acid was carried through the cloister at 4.45 p.m., at which time the plaintiff should have left the premises. The monitors endeavoured to avoid the injury by calling out. For the defendants it was alleged that the injury was entirely due to the plaintiff's negligence in running backwards.

The action was tried in the King's Bench Division before Kennedy J.

sitting with a jury. It was found that the headmaster was negligent because, although there was a school rule that boys should leave the premises when they were dismissed, no steps were taken on this occasion to see that it was carried out. There was also negligence on the part of the chemistry master in sending the acid across the cloister in so fragile a vessel without ascertaining that the way was clear. The rules made were sufficient, but they had not been carried out, and there was no contributory negligence on the part of the plaintiff. Damages were assessed at £50. Judgment was given for the plaintiff against the headmaster, and for the managers against the plaintiff, they to have such costs as had been incurred by making them parties to the action.

The headmaster appealed.

LORD ESHER M.R., after reviewing the evidence, came to the conclusion that there was no evidence of want of care on the part of the headmaster fit to be left to the jury.

Judgment for the appellant

97 Chilvers *v*. London County Council and others (1916) 80 J.P. 246

KING'S BENCH DIVISION

There is no negligence when a child is injured in an accident which might have happened in any nursery where children play with toy soldiers.

Facts: The plaintiff, Wilfred Chilvers, was a five-year-old pupil at St James' Norland School, North Kensington, at the time of the accident which gave rise to this action.

On January 29, 1915, a fellow pupil named Palmer brought some toy soldiers to school with the knowledge and approval of the teacher. One of these represented a lancer, whose lance moved up and down on a pivot, and the children played with it. The plaintiff fell, and it was found at the West London Eye Hospital that his eye had been pierced by something sharp. The eye was enucleated as its sight had been destroyed, and it was feared that the other might be affected.

The plaintiff claimed damages against the London County Council and the managers of the school, alleging negligence by the teacher in not exercising sufficient supervision over the children, and in permitting the introduction and use in the school of toys which were dangerous to young children.

The plaintiff's father said that Mrs Thomas, the class teacher had told him she was reading a book while the children were playing. One of the children drew her attention to what had happened through the plaintiff having fallen or having been pushed down, on the toy soldiers.

Shakespeare (for the managers): There is no evidence to go to the jury on any want of care on the part of the defendants. It had been said that permission given by the teacher to the children to play with toys was evidence of a want of care, but the duty of a schoolmistress to a child could not be put higher than that of a mother towards her child: for the purpose of the case he would assume it to be the same. There is evidence that the plaintiff's mother allowed her children to play with toy soldiers.

Turner (for the plaintiff): The case ought not to be looked at from the point of view of the toys which were allowed to be used at home, where there were only a few children to be looked after. The degree of attention required from a teacher in the supervision of the children under her care is greater than that which a mother is expected to show, as a teacher has very many more children to look after. Here the teacher was reading a book instead of looking after the children.

Extract from Summing-up

BAILHACHE J.: I have come to the conclusion that there is no evidence to go to the jury of negligence on the part of the defendants. Had the toy which caused the damage been a pistol from which pellets were fired the case might have been different. Here, however, the toy was similar to the toys with which children generally play. I cannot shut my eyes to the fact that children do play with toy soldiers. It is said that this was a toy "lancer"—the toy soldier carrying a sharp lance; but apart from that there was a sharp point on the cap which might injure a child falling upon it. The accident no doubt was deplorable; but it was for the plaintiff to show that the teacher was negligent. No such negligence had been proved. The accident might have happened in a nursery, where there were several nurses looking after the children. There must be judgment for the defendants.

Judgment for the defendants

98 Dixon *v.* Roper (1922) *The Times*, February 3

KING'S BENCH DIVISION

As children are commonly allowed to play with crackers it is not negligent to permit them to do so.

Facts: The plaintiff, Philip Dixon, was a pupil at Ladycross School, Seaford, which was owned by the defendant.

On November 24, 1920, the assistant matron gave the boy a box of crackers as a birthday present. There was a toy whistle in one of the crackers and during the afternoon, as he was running about on the football field, the plaintiff allowed the whistle to slip down his throat, where it stuck.

The plaintiff told the matron that he had swallowed a fly, or a wasp, or a bee. An hour or so later, when he was getting worse, he told her what had really happened. The school doctor recommended suitable food, but the boy could not swallow. He was X-rayed at the Sussex County Hospital at Brighton, and allowed by the surgeon to return to school the next day. About a week later, he complained of pain, and was sick. He was again X-rayed at Brighton, and then taken to London where the whistle was removed surgically on December 9.

The plaintiff brought an action against the headmaster for damages for personal injuries, alleging that the defendant was negligent. The defendant denied negligence on the ground that neither he nor his staff knew of the existence or size of the whistle. He further pleaded that it was not part of the assistant matron's duty to make a present or presents to the pupils, and that he was not responsible therefor.

Extract from Judgment
ROCHE J.: . . . I have arrived at a conclusion adverse to the plaintiffs. It was said that there was negligence in allowing the boy to have the whistle, and that in various ways the treatment of the boy afterwards was improper and negligent. It is purely a question of fact, and there is no dispute about the law. The first question is whether there was negligence in allowing the boy to have the whistle and, if so, whether it was in the course of the duty of the assistant matron to give him the crackers. I do not think that it was in the course of her duty as assistant matron to give the boy presents. With regard to the question of negligence, I cannot hold that there was any evidence of any negligence in the case. I am satisfied that ordinary prudent parents would themselves allow their children of seven or eight years of age to have crackers at Christmas and on birthdays. I am satisfied that there was no negligence in allowing this sharp little fellow to have this cracker on his birthday.

The other point is negligence with regard to the treatment. I do not propose to review that part of the case in any detail. One observation I will make is that from about 4 o'clock on that afternoon, the management and care of the boy passed from the defendant quite rightly to the medical gentlemen, whose directions were wholly carried out. Accordingly I find no negligence or breach of duty on the part of the defendant. The action fails and there must be judgment for the defendant.

Judgment for the defendant

99 Wray *v.* Essex County Council [1936] 3 All E.R. 97

COURT OF APPEAL
An oil-can is not an inherently dangerous thing, nor is it a dangerous thing in the special circumstances of a school for young children, and a master is under no duty to take special precautions in connection therewith.

Facts: The plaintiff, John Wray, was a twelve-year-old pupil at Halbutt Road School, Dagenham. On February 14, 1936, he was "trotting" ahead of the other boys in his class, from one classroom to another. At a blind corner with two steps he collided with Arthur Biggs, aged thirteen, who was carrying an oil-can which had a spout six inches long. The spout struck Wray in the eye, disabling him for some weeks and practically destroying the sight of that eye.

Biggs was carrying the oil-can to the handicraft room for a master, Mr Lawrence, who had said: "You are just the boy I want; you are a prefect; take this to Mr Sharpe." Boys were moving between classes at the time.

There was a school rule forbidding pupils to run on the school premises except at games, but the judge found that neither boy was negligent.

The plaintiff sued for damages for personal injuries, alleging that the local education authority were negligent in that their servant, Mr Lawrence, failed to give Biggs proper instructions how to carry the oil-can.

The case was heard at Ilford County Court, where Judge Beazley found for the defendants. In case his judgment should be reversed on appeal he assessed the damages at £450 general and £2 4s. 6d. special damage.

The plaintiff appealed.

Extracts from Judgment
LORD WRIGHT M.R.: . . . The learned county court judge has decided against the plaintiff. I can best sum up the effect of his careful judgment by reading a short passage. He said:

> "In my view there was no duty upon Mr Lawrence, as a reasonable man, to give directions to Biggs to hold the can in any particular way, or to anticipate that such an unfortunate event as this would result from his entrusting the can to Biggs to carry from one classroom to another, although at the time he entrusted it to him the boys were changing classes and Biggs was likely to encounter other boys whilst he was carrying the can."

Before that the learned judge had held that the oilcan was not a thing which was in itself dangerous. He goes on to say:

> "I really do not see how it could be. If the boy had been holding a pen with a nib in it the result would have been more or less the same. It is not a thing which is in itself dangerous, as a bottle containing phosphorus was held to be dangerous or a gun or pistol was held to be dangerous."

I agree with the learned county judge in both these respects. It is impossible not to feel a great sympathy with this poor boy who has suffered this serious injury at the outset of his life and who will be in future a one-eyed person; but in an action of this sort the onus is on the plaintiff to establish that he has a cause of action, and I really find it quite impossible here to hold that there is any such cause of action.

The case of things dangerous in themselves, or, as they are sometimes called, inherently dangerous, is a case separate and distinct and holds a special place in the law of negligence. Where you are dealing with a dangerous thing you are dealing with something which, if left, may at any moment and under modern circumstances cause damage. Such articles are things like a gun or a pistol. If a gun or pistol is left about loaded, in a condition in which it may go off if handled in a certain way, if anyone handles an instrument of that sort the risk of danger is obvious. Such a case is illustrated by *Dixon* v. *Bell*,[1] and in a very striking Irish case, *Sullivan* v. *Creed*,[2] where Gibson J. says this at page 325:

> "A hatchet, a bottle of poison labelled 'poison' the same bottle unlabelled, a loaded gun, gunpowder, or dynamite, all represent articles of varying degrees of danger, and the greater the danger the higher is the standard of the diligence which the law exacts."

And he gives further illustrations. Then Palles B. says this, on page 329:

> "I hold that anyone who is in possession of a dangerous instrument owes a duty to the public, or at least to such members of the public as are reasonably likely to be injured by its misuse, to keep it with reasonable care, so that it shall not be misused to the injury of others."

I need scarcely refer to other cases, but there is the case of a stick of phosphorus, which was considered in *Williams* v. *Eady*.[3] The Court of Appeal held, without much hesitation, that that was a dangerous article. As pointed out by Scrutton L.J. in *Langham* v. *Governors of Wellingborough School*,[4] there may be borderline cases; there may be cases which fall on the side of dangerous articles and cases which fall on the side of articles which are not dangerous, and Scrutton L.J. cites the interesting case of *Chilvers* v. *London County Council*,[5] where a child was unfortunately injured by the point of a toy lance which was part of a toy soldier. Bailhache J., whom Scrutton L.J. quotes with approval at page 515, said:

> "You cannot say that toy soldiers in themselves are dangerous; to play with them has been the right of every nursery in the kingdom for centuries, and the fact that the master or mistress had allowed a toy soldier to be in the room could not be treated as evidence of negligence or lack of proper supervision."

I need not quote other cases. It may not be possible precisely to say what article is inherently dangerous and what is not by any general definition, yet when you come to particular articles there is, I think, no difficulty in drawing the line you take as the standard in the one case. Things like a naked sword or a hatchet or a loaded gun or an explosive are clearly inherently dangerous— that is to say, they cannot be handled without a serious risk. On the other hand, you have things in ordinary use which are only what is called "potentially dangerous"; that is to say, if there is negligence or if there is some mischance or misadventure then the thing may be a source of danger; but that source of danger is something which is not essential to their ordinary character; it merely depends on the concurrence of certain circumstances—in particular,

1. (1816) 5 M. & S. 198.
2. [1904] 2 I.R. 317.
3. (1893) 10 T.L.R. 41; see page 240, *supra*.
4. (1932) 101 L.J.K.B. 513; see page 296, *infra*.
5. (1916) 80 J.P. 246; see page 259, *supra*.

generally, negligence on the part of someone. I feel, I am bound to say with no doubt at all, that this can does not come within the category of inherently dangerous articles. It is an ordinary article of domestic use; apart from something quite extraordinary, it is not likely to cause damage and is not calculated to cause damage to anybody.

There is, however, the further point: even if it is not inherently dangerous there may be circumstances in which it would be proper for the schoolmaster to exercise, as Lord Esher M.R. said in *Williams* v. *Eady*[6] he is bound to exercise, "such care of his boys as a careful father would take of his boys"; he would be: "bound to take notice of the ordinary nature of young boys, their tendency to do mischievous acts, and their propensity to meddle with anything that came in their way. Therefore the schoolmaster in this case, Mr Lawrence, has undoubtedly a special duty towards the boys of the school. But in every case when you consider the standard by which the duty is to be tested and according to which it has to be ascertained whether there has been any breach of duty, it is necessary to consider whether there is something which the schoolmaster ought to have anticipated, something reasonably foreseeable and something, therefore, which, because it is foreseeable, the master ought to have guarded against. I say "foreseeable" because the mere fact that he did not foresee a risk or a particular contingency would not excuse him if it was something which he ought to have foreseen. But when I look at the facts of this case, it seems to me to be a misadventure which could not have been reasonably foreseen by anybody; it happened by an unfortunate concurrence of circumstances. It is true that the master must have known, and did know, I suppose, that boys were moving about the school at that time, but he had no reason to foresee that the plaintiff (for whom I have every sympathy) would be trotting round the blind corner just at the time when he did and under such circumstances. But he came directly straight and in contact with this can. Biggs was carrying the can in the ordinary way, and no one is blaming him for anything he did; he was moving at an ordinary pace, and if anyone could be held responsible—I do not think anybody is responsible for this unfortunate mischance, which appears to me to be pure misadventure—it would be rather the poor boy himself, who was trotting round the corner. But even so there is no reason for anyone to foresee that this innocuous and ordinary commonplace oil-can carried in the ordinary way by Biggs would have caused the mischief which followed. If you get a foreseeable risk it is, of course, material to consider what are the chances against that risk eventuating; if there is a real risk there is a duty to guard against it, even though the precise damage which follows has not been carefully foreseen and contemplated. But here, as I think, there is nothing which the master could or ought to have foreseen; I think he committed no breach of duty towards the plaintiff. His employers, accordingly, are not responsible, and the action must fail. The appeal, therefore, will be dismissed.

Appeal dismissed with costs

6. (1893) 10 T.L.R. 41; see page 240, *supra*.

(E) WORKSHOPS AND MACHINERY

100 Smerkinich v. Newport Corporation (1912) 76 J.P. 454

KING'S BENCH DIVISION

Volenti non fit injuria. (No-one suffers damage through what he does of his free will.)

Facts: The plaintiff was a nineteen-year-old apprentice of four years' standing in a carpenter's shop. During the winters of 1910 and 1911 he attended classes at the Newport Technical Institute on payment of a fee of 5s. a session.

There was at the Institute a twelve-inch electrically-driven circular saw. The plaintiff was allowed to use this by himself during his first session, and he used it habitually during the second session. Mr Williams, the instructor, had shown the class of from twelve to twenty persons how to use the saw, and on October 3 the plaintiff received permission to cut a piece of wood with it. In so doing his left hand was drawn into the machine, and his thumb cut so that it had to be amputated.

The saw had no guard, and the plaintiff said that all such saws as he had seen in his own and other shops had guards. He was allowed to use the saw without permission, but he asked leave on the date of his injury because the machinery had stopped, and he did not know if anything had gone wrong. He knew the saw was dangerous, but he had not suggested to the instructor that it should be guarded.

The plaintiff sued the Newport Corporation, as the persons responsible for the management of the Institute, for damages arising from their negligence in not providing a sufficient guard or "sword," and/or in not warning him that the use of the saw was attended by great risk.

A second-term fellow pupil said he heard the plaintiff ask for permission, as he was supposed to do. The instructor replied: "Yes, be careful."

A foreman carpenter at the Alexandra Dock, with twenty years' experience of circular saws, said that he had never seen such a saw without some kind of protection. At the docks the back of the saw was protected by a "riving knife" and the side by Ford and Pickford's patent, but there was no protection for anyone guiding the timber at the front with his left hand. A builder with a similar length of experience said there were several devices for guarding the front of the saw. The plaintiff, recalled, said that he had got to the back of the saw when he was injured.

The instructor said that he could not remember the plaintiff asking for permission. The piece of wood was two feet long, and all but six inches had been cut through at the time of the accident. At that point the left hand might be partly over the saw, but it would not be at the back of it.

In the county court Judge Kelly held that there had been negligence in not providing a guard for a saw being used by boys of between seventeen and nineteen years of age. A guard could have been provided which would have

K

prevented the plaintiff from getting his fingers into contact with the cutting surface of the saw. *Volenti non fit injuria* did not apply, and there would be judgment for the plaintiff for £100.

The defendants appealed by way of case stated to the Divisional Court of the King's Bench Division.

Extracts from Judgments

RIDLEY J.: . . . The question is whether it was reasonable and proper, according to the experience of persons accustomed to saws, that such shields should be provided, and the evidence, so far as we can understand it, is that with such a saw there is no such protection usually provided. It does not follow from the fact that the accident could have been prevented by the use of a guard that therefore it was the duty of the corporation to provide such a guard.

The other point is as to whether the doctrine *volenti non fit injuria* applies. That of course is not a new question. In this case the man knew that there was a danger in using this machine and that if he brought his hand in contact with the saw he would be injured. He asked the instructor to allow him to use the saw without his assistance. It seems to me, therefore, that the question of whether or no he took the risk upon himself is not satisfactorily dealt with by the judge when he said,

> "It is impossible, as it seems to me, to say that there is any evidence that he consented to this danger. It is true that this lad did not say to the instructor that a guard ought to have been placed over the saw. But they perhaps did not know of the danger, or of the degree of danger, that they were exposed to. I do not see how it can be said that the plaintiff was *volens* in this case. I doubt very much, under the circumstances whether that doctrine is applicable, and I must decide against the defendants on that contention."

So far as I can understand it the evidence is the other way. I think that if the maxim is to be regarded as having any value at all this is just one of the cases in which it would apply to what has taken place. It must be remembered that in *Smith* v. *Baker*,[1] when the court laid down the doctrine which we have followed for so many years, it was there said that the maxim means that the workman must have taken upon himself the risk of operation he was told to conduct, and not merely that he did not withdraw from the labour because there was a risk connected with it. It means that he must be understood to have had his eyes open when he took on the job. The court there was dealing with the case of a workman who had done nothing immediately connected with the operation in consequence of which the injury was caused to him. He was generally about the work of the premises, and the stones that fell upon him fell as he was working a drill. As I understand the judgment in that case, after having stated what the facts were, the court said that

1. [1891] A.C. 325; 55 J.P. 660.

it was a question of fact in each case how far it was applicable to the particular circumstances, and that in some cases it might apply and in others not.

Lord Watson, in his judgment, gave an illustration which was nearer to the present case than any of the others mentioned. He said:

"On the other hand there are cases in which the work is not intrinsically dangerous, but is rendered dangerous by some defect which it was the duty of the master to remedy. In cases of that description the relations of the workman to the peril are so various that it is impossible to lay down any rule regarding the operation of the maxim which will apply to them all alike, and I shall refer to two instances only by way of illustration. The risk may arise from a defect in a machine which the servant has engaged to work of such a nature that his personal danger and consequent injury must be produced by his own act. If he clearly foresaw the likelihood of such a result and, notwithstanding, continued to work, I think that, according to the authorities, he ought to be regarded as *volens.* . . ."

Upon the whole I am of opinion that this judgment should be set aside and judgment entered for the defendants.

LUSH J.: I am of the same opinion, that this judgment must be set aside and judgment entered for the defendants.

The burden was on the plaintiff to establish his cause of action. To do so he had to prove (1) that the defendants broke some obligation which they owed to him—in other words in this case, they did not take that care of him which they were bound to take, and (2) that this negligence was the approximate and real cause of the injury which he suffered.

The defendants' case was that the plaintiff had not established either proposition. As to the first, they said: "We provided a proper saw, and in any case a saw with an instructor to assist these young men if they wanted to work it." On the second issue they said: "Whether there was any such breach of duty here or not, the plaintiff himself knew and appreciated the risk and voluntarily chose to incur it. He chose to work this saw, appreciating his danger."

I am far from satisfied that there was any real evidence of negligence. One witness did speak of a guard being placed in front of circular saws like these but he appears to have left it in some doubt as to whether this was a recognised thing to do. But the learned judge has found that there was negligence on the part of the defendants. In my opinion he did not really apply the proper principle by ascertaining whether this was such a regular and well-recognised method of working circular saws that the defendants ought to have employed it. He seems to me to have thought that since it was possible to devise a mode of protecting this saw, and the defendants had not done it that this constituted negligence in point of law. Assuming there was evidence of negligence, the other question is still in issue, and one has to see whether there was evidence that the negligence did in fact cause the injury. We have to see whether the plaintiff on his own case did not show that he was a volunteer, and that well appreciating the risk, he voluntarily incurred it. In my opinion that appears to be so from the plaintiff's own evidence.

Had the plaintiff been a child the case would have been different. But he was a youth of eighteen or nineteen years of age and for two years he had been using this saw. This was the second session of technical classes he had attended before the accident occurred. He was not permitted to touch this saw without asking leave of the instructor. Appreciating the danger he did ask for this leave. His own evidence was that appreciating the danger he did ask permission to use it. And having got leave he knew the risk he was running, and without the least necessity for running it, and entirely for his own purposes, he chose to bring about that state of things which he knew would expose him to this peril. He did so expose himself, and in the course of doing so this accident happened. No doubt the question of *volenti* is one of fact, but I think the plaintiff's own evidence shows beyond controversy that, even assuming there had been negligence on the part of the defendants, the danger was perfectly well known to the plaintiff.

For these reasons I am of opinion that this appeal must be allowed.

Appeal allowed. Judgment for
the defendants

[NOTE: This case should be carefully compared with that which follows (*Butt v Inner London Education Authority*). There is no indication in the report of the latter case that *Smerkinich* was considered.]

101 Butt *v.* Inner London Education Authority (1968) 66 L.G.R. 379

COURT OF APPEAL

While a college of further education is not a factory, so that the provisions of the Factories Acts do not apply, it is the duty of the local education authority to provide for the safety of their pupils.

Facts: The plaintiff, David Edward Butt, was a trainee student at Camberwell School of Arts and Crafts. On January 18, 1965, when he was almost seventeen, he was an apprentice at a factory dealing with printing machines and it was a condition of his employment that he should attend the college every other week.

While operating a Thomson-British auto platen machine for the first time, his hand was caught by the delivery bar. Three of his fingers were broken and, after healing, one was a quarter of an inch shorter than previously.

The plaintiff sued the Inner London Education Authority for damages for negligence resulting in personal injury. At Lambeth County Court Judge Barrington awarded him £150 in damages.

The defendant authority appealed.

Judgment

DANCKWERTS L.J.: This is an appeal by a trainee, who suffered an accident in the course of his instruction at the Camberwell School of Arts and Crafts, for which the defendants are responsible. It is the type of case with which one is very familiar in factories where the Factories Acts have application, but in this case the school of instruction is not a factory, and the Factories Acts do not come into it at all directly.

The plaintiff was a young man of sixteen and three-quarters, who was an apprentice in a factory dealing with printing machines, and one of the terms of his employment was that he was to attend the school, I think, every other week, and he had been doing that since 1964.

The accident happened on January 18, 1965. The plaintiff was operating an automatic letter-press machine, which is operated by sheets of paper being taken by a delivery bar and placed on to a platen, which then goes upwards to join the forme, as it is called, which is another sort of plate, and in the course of that operation an ink roller runs over the forme and inks it so as to produce the necessary result. At the top, the jaws are fixed, the platen coming up pressing with considerable force against the forme, and then coming back again as the printed sheet which has been transferred drops into a receptacle at the back of the table. There is, therefore, a considerable amount of moving machinery involved in the operation.

The case as put originally was that the plaintiff had got his hand caught between the platen and the forme. The result of the accident was that he had broken fingers, which, however, have healed up; the bones have joined, and the principal result is that one finger is a quarter of an inch shorter. As the case progressed, however, it seemed to be fairly clear that the cause of the accident could not be that he had caught his hand between the platen and the forme because, the pressure being several tons, or something of that sort, he would probably have had his hand very considerably smashed if that had been what happened. It seems more likely that in some way his hand was caught by the delivery bar and pressed against some part of the machinery, and therefore suffered the somewhat lesser injury which he has had in the present case.

The particulars of claim raise a number of complaints which it is suggested render the defendants liable. There was the question of supervision, but the judge quite properly, I think, rejected that because the plaintiff was acting under the supervision of an older pupil, a coloured man, who had some experience and therefore was able to provide supervision for this student, who on the day of the accident was operating this kind of machine for the first time.

The next point is the question of instruction. Two instructors are allowed for a class of sixteen, but, in fact, there were only fourteen students on this occasion and, therefore, the level of instructors to students was well observed. The two instructors were a Mr Lansdowne and a Mr Wright, and it is quite clear that, so far as warning was concerned, they gave repeated warnings that students were not to put their hands into the machinery in any way, and the plaintiff quite clearly, and the other students, had been sufficiently warned to protect them, unless they were careless or forgot, from an accident of this kind.

The really operative feature, however, was the question whether this machine should have been fenced. It was moving machinery, and it is quite plain that, if it had been a factory, there would have been a breach of section 14 of the Factories Act 1961, which requires such machinery to be effectively fenced. The evidence was that, although this type of machine had been in use at least since 1936 (and very generally in use), the practice in factories had not been, so far as the witnesses knew (and there were experts called on each side), to provide any fencing. One of the experts, I think, was the managing director of the manufacturers making these machines. The curious thing, however, is that, in the case of non-automatic machines of this type, the machine was fenced in practice, but the automatic one was not fenced; I suppose it was thought that, once you set it in motion, it looked after itself, and there was no need for the plaintiff or any other operator to put his hand in in any way. The plaintiff had apparently been warned about skylarking, which is liable to happen in a school of rather active young men, but I doubt whether that had anything to do with the accident because he received a warning after the occasion when he was said to have been skylarking.

The question is whether the defendants were liable, as the judge held, on the ground that they ought to have provided for the machine to be fenced. It is quite clear that, if this machine, or this type of machine, had been operated for thirty years in factories without being fenced, there must, I think, have been a breach of section 14 of the Factories Act. But, of course, the Factories Act does not apply to a machine in use in a training school of this kind, and the question is whether it was negligent at common law for the defendants not to have provided a fence or guard for this particular machine. It is argued that they were training these students to be able to work in the same way that they would be required to work in a factory, and it is said, therefore, that they were bound to teach the students the conditions which they would find in any factory to which they went. It is a point, of course, which does permit of argument.

The judge reached the conclusion that the defendants should have arranged for some kind of guard. The expert pointed out some difficulties in providing a guard for a machine of this type. The guard no doubt would have to cover a considerable space in width, and would have to provide sufficient clearance for the operation of the platen swinging up to join the forme. But they agreed that it was possible from the engineering point of view, and would present no great difficulty. Looking at the machine in the photographs, I myself cannot see that it was not possible to provide an effective guard with the necessary arrangement so that it could be let down in whole or in part when it was necessary to put paper in the appropriate place on the machine for the operation which was required. Apparently, factory inspectors had not required a guard.

The county court judge came to the conclusion, I think correctly, that the plaintiff did not suffer his injury by his hand being caught between the platen and the forme, and that the most likely cause of the accident was that his hand was caught by the delivery bar which moves across in taking the paper on to the platen and taking it off, and so forth, in the course of the operation. It is said, of course, that if no guard was provided in factories, a school of this kind could not be expected to go to the trouble, and the expense, I suppose, of obtaining a guard, which would have to be made specially for the purpose, from the manufacturers. It seems to me, however, that it is the duty of the school to provide for the safety of their pupils, and I think that the county court judge was perfectly right in reaching the conclusion that they did not adequately provide for the safety of their pupils in the circumstances of the case.

I, therefore, would dismiss the appeal.

DIPLOCK L.J.: To use the expression which has been mentioned in the course of the argument in this case, I found Mr Scrivener's[1] argument persuasive, but not in the end conclusive, and I accordingly agree that this appeal should be dismissed.

SACHS L.J.: This young man succumbed to the temptation of trying to move a misplaced sheet of paper, a temptation of an obvious type, and one from which, it is conceded by counsel for the appellants, workers in industrial premises should be protected by a guard. When once that has been conceded, I consider that the school was clearly not entitled to expose this young man to that obvious risk.

Appeal dismissed

[NOTE: This case should be compared carefully with *Smerkinich* v. *Newport Corporation* (page 265, *supra*). *Butt's* case would appear to overrule the previous judgment of the King's Bench Division. It is interesting to note that the common law duty of care bound on an educational establishment by this case appears to be higher than the factory inspector's interpretation of the statutory duty laid down in the Factories Act 1961.]

(F) DOMESTIC SCIENCE

102 Fryer *v*. Salford Corporation [1937] 1 All E.R. 617

COURT OF APPEAL

A local education authority should foresee the danger of an unguarded gas stove used for instruction in cookery, and should take steps to guard against that danger.

Facts: The plaintiff, Betty Fryer, was an eleven-year-old pupil at a school maintained by the Salford Corporation. She was undergoing instruction in cookery with eighteen other girls, when she sustained serious injury.

1. Counsel for the defendants.

In an action for damages for injuries through negligence Swift J. found for the plaintiff. The defendant corporation appealed. The facts are fully set out in the judgment of Slesser L.J.

Extracts from Judgments
SLESSER L.J.: In this case, a little girl named Fryer was seriously injured while attending a class at a domestic training centre in the city of Salford, in a school maintained by the corporation of Salford, under the Education Acts. It is its duty, under the Education Act 1918, section 48, to give to children of a certain age practical instruction in cookery. It was in accordance with that statutory power that the instruction was given in the present case, and this little girl, Fryer, was attending the class when she met with her injuries. She is a child of eleven—approaching twelve—and, for the purpose of this particular instruction in cookery, it is only at the age of eleven that children attend. The mistress, Miss Cox, who was engaged by the corporation of Salford, was, on the day when the accident happened, giving instructions to the little girl. and to some eighteen other young children of about the age of eleven or twelve years. The particular matter which they were being taught was the very useful science of making a pudding. It appears that the children bring to the class, normally, when these puddings are made, basins; they also bring a small sum of money, I think in this case 2½d., to cover the material in the puddings, and the puddings are duly cooked, under instruction, and the children are entitled each to take her pudding home with her when they leave the class. The practice is that the pudding is put into a steamer. The steamer is a cylindrical tin, which is put over a gas-fire, the water is allowed to boil, and subsequently to simmer, and then the puddings are duly taken out when they are ready.

On the afternoon in question, the puddings were duly cooked in the usual way. There were two stoves on which the steamers were put, and one was further from the open fire than the other. There seems to have been some difference of opinion as to the exact whereabouts of the lady who was conducting the class at the time when the accident happened. Speaking for myself, I do not know that it is very material. What the learned judge said is this:

> "Miss Cox proceeded to one of the steamers in order to extract the puddings, and, while she was doing that, the girls left their places and went towards the place where Miss Cox was, expecting her to give them a pudding or call their number. As their numbers were called, it was the practice for them to go up and receive the pudding appropriate to their particular number."

As regards this particular girl, Miss Fryer, who was injured, she, it appears, did not go up to the stove at which Miss Cox was, but stood alongside the other stove, the larger one, where a second steamer was boiling and some of the burners of that stove were alight. Again, to quote the learned judge:

"the girl stood beside the gas-table. It is not quite certain what happened, but the evidence of the little girl herself is that her apron caught fire. She says that, after they had been away from the room for some time, while the puddings were being prepared, they came back, and, when they had finished what they call their domestic duties, Miss Cox said: 'I will call out all those who have got puddings in the steamer to come and receive them.' Then Miss Betty Fryer says she went to the stove (that is, the stove other than that at which Miss Cox then was.) She was holding her apron (and she indicated how she was holding her apron out), and then a girl told her that her pinafore was on fire. She thought she had been standing round the gas-stove for about five minutes before she found that her apron was on fire."

In those circumstances, it is alleged now that the corporation was negligent in that it failed to have round this stove at which the plaintiff stood any guard or fence, so as to prevent the pinafore, or apron, or any other part of the clothing, getting into the gas flame and catching fire. Before Swift J. there was also an allegation of negligence against Miss Cox, the lady who was teaching cookery, but that allegation wholly failed. Therefore, so far as she is concerned, there is here no question on the appeal: there is no cross-appeal in this case. Therefore, the whole question now resolves itself into this, whether the only ground on which the learned judge said the corporation was negligent, that is to say, that it was its duty, in the circumstances, to have protected the children from the gas, and that it had failed to protect them by a sufficient guard, can or cannot be supported on the evidence in the case. The learned judge said this:

"The trouble about it, as it seems to me, is that, while people were passing, while children were passing, around this table, in order to go to where Miss Cox was serving out the puddings, they came near to the flaming gas and I think that that flaming gas ought to have been protected; there should have been a guard, which could so easily be provided . . . it is a simple guard, which our mothers put over the fireplace every day of our lives when we were young, to prevent us tumbling into the fire. The education authority, in my view, should have supplied such a guard. I do not think it was right to have nineteen or twenty little girls passing close to this burning gas-stove, as they must have passed, in order to get their puddings, full of their childish eagerness and anxiety to get the prize which they were going to take home in exchange for the 2½d. which they had brought, without guarding it."

In my view, the learned judge was fully entitled, on the evidence in this case, to come to the conclusion which he there states. It must be remembered that a distinction should be drawn, when the question, "What is the duty of a local authority to guard against possible dangers?" is being considered, between the case where the possiblity of danger emerging is reasonably apparent, in which case there is negligence if no precautions be taken, and the case where:

> "the possibility of danger emerging is only a mere possibility which would never occur to the mind of a reasonable man, then there is no negligence in not having taken extraordinary precautions."

I quote from a passage of Lord Dunedin, in the case of *Fardon* v. *Harcourt-Rivington*[1] at page 392. In my view, in the present case, having regard to all its circumstances, this was a case where the danger emerging was reasonably apparent.

Mr Lynskey has pointed out that the uncontradicted evidence in this case is, first, that no such guards have been placed upon gas-cookers of this kind, used by children, by other education authorities, or by the Salford authority, and, secondly, that no previous case is known of a child being injured in this way, and he draws our attention to a large number of authorities, to the effect that no man may reasonably be called upon to guard against dangers which he ought not reasonably to anticipate. The matter is put very clearly, from that point of view, in the case of *Hall* v. *Brooklands Auto-Racing Club*[2]; but really, in my view, it is a principle which goes back very much further, and may be discovered in the well known authority of *Readhead* v. *Midland Ry. Co.*,[3] where it was said, at pages 384, 385:

> "An obligation to use all due and proper care is founded on reasons obvious to all, but to impose on the carrier the burden of a warranty that everything he necessarily uses is absolutely free from defects likely to cause peril, when from the nature of things defects must exist which no skill can detect, and the effects of which no care or foresight can avert, would be to compel a man, by implication of law and not by his own will, to promise the performance of an impossible thing."

In the present case, I do not think that it can be said that what here happened was that which no reasonable person could anticipate, merely because such an accident had not happened before, or because there was no reason to suppose that it would happen. In my view, the very nature of the case is such as to render reasonably apparent the possibility of danger emerging. The situation is this: there is, first, this stove with a naked flame, which may be turned down in order that the water may simmer, but yet a flame which is not in any way guarded; secondly, young children, who are waiting to take their puddings from this or the other stove, and, although it may be that, as an ideal discipline, they would be expected to remain in their seats, yet, taking the nature of young children eleven years of age, I think there is a very reasonable probability, at any rate when the mistress's back is turned, that they will crowd around these unprotected stoves, in the way in which, in fact, they did

1. (1932) 146 L.T. 391.
2. [1933] 1 K.B. 205.
3. (1869) 4 Q.B. 379.

crowd around in this particular case. Various words have been used with regard to the temptations which may be set before young children. They have been referred to as allurements, enticements, and traps, and various phrases; but, whatever phrase you use, I think it is quite clear that for young children, witnessing the final transfiguration of their own puddings, it was a distinct allurement, and nothing was more natural than that children should crowd around this stove in order to receive their puddings. In that case, it appears to be clear that the danger which would, or might, arise was, if not self-evident, at any rate a danger which ought reasonably to have been anticipated; nor can it be said, on the evidence, that the guard which was suggested, to protect these children, was anything which was impossible. It cannot be said here that the local authority, in being called upon to perform its statutory duty of teaching cooking, was doing anything which necessarily required this danger to be incurred of allowing the children to get near the flame. Mr Cutter, it is true, in an official utterance, on being asked, "Is there any reason why the flame should not be guarded?" replied: "Well, sir, educational practice does not guard the stoves." That in itself seems to be an insufficient reason for not placing upon them a guard. But he is saying no more than he had said previously, that, in fact, the local authorities have not guarded these stoves. But Miss Margaret Weddell, who was called as a witness by the corporation, and is headmistress of the Training College of Domestic Economy, under the control of the Manchester Education Committee, was quite frank on this matter. When it was suggested to her that something like the old nursery guard, which we used to have round the fire to prevent the baby falling into the fire, might be used, on being asked, "Would there be any trouble in putting one around that?" she did say: "Well, we would have to stretch across it to reach the stove." She said they had got guards round the open fires in the centres, and that those guards could be taken away when the lessons were finished. She did say that she did not think it would be desirable to put a guard round the gas-stove when the children were cooking, but the reason she gave, as I understand her evidence, was that they would not have such a guard at home, and, therefore, it would not accustom them really to the conditions they would have to face in their own homes. As against that, it may well be said, and no doubt was urged, that the circumstances in which girls do cooking at home are quite different from those in this cookery centre. It may well be—I do not know—that the age of eleven years is a little early for them to manipulate a gas cooker. In their homes, it may be that there would not be the pressure of children round the stove that there would be in the cookery centre. At any rate, this lady does not suggest that it is not feasible for such a guard to be put round these stoves when the actual cooking operations are not proceeding, in the sense that it is necessary continuously to get to the gas itself. While the steamer is simmering, and while there is occasion to use the gas, there appears to have been no adequate reason why these guards should not be put round the stove.

If the learned judge had come to a contrary conclusion, upon a consideration of all the evidence, it may well have been that this court would not have thought fit to disturb his finding, but, having heard all the evidence in this case—I understand he saw the stove, which was an advantage we also had—he came to the conclusion, on the balance of consideration, first, that this was a danger which ought reasonably to have been anticipated, and, secondly, that it was a danger which could reasonably be guarded against. He has, therefore, come to the conclusion that the plaintiff succeeded in establishing a duty towards her, on the part of the local authority, and a failure to perform that duty. For these reasons I am of opinion that this appeal fails.

SCOTT L.J.: . . . I think that really the local education authority was in a logical dilemma: either there ought to have been two teachers, or a guard to the stove. There was no suggestion made of two teachers; the question was not discussed. We reach the position of the finding of the learned judge, that there ought, as a reasonable precaution, having regard to the ages of the little girls, and the proximity of the flames to their clothes, and the inflammable character of their clothes, to have been a guard; and that decision, in my view, is a decision of fact, pure and simple, upon which this court should be very slow to disagree with an experienced judge. I think, therefore, the appeal should be dismissed.

FARWELL J.: About this case, I have felt considerably more difficulty than the other members of the court. I am not, however, prepared to say there was no evidence upon which the learned judge could have come to the conclusion he did, and, therefore, I do not dissent from the order which it is proposed should be made.

Appeal dismissed with costs

(G) PHYSICAL EDUCATION

103 Harvey *v.* Newberry and others (1925) *Western Morning News,* February 4

EXETER COUNTY COURT
In considering claims for negligence arising from the use of unorthodox apparatus, the court will consider the facts in each case.

Facts: The plaintiff, Audrey Harvey, was a seven-year-old pupil at St Sidwell's Infants' School, Exeter. The defendants were the headmistress, Miss Ethel Mary Newberry, and the six managers of the school.

On June 24, 1924, the plaintiff took part in an organised game which consisted of jumping over an inverted wastepaper basket about fourteen inches high. The class consisted of both boys and girls. The plaintiff was the youngest pupil, and rather heavily built for her age. The headmistress, an assistant teacher, and a pupil-teacher were present but none was standing near the wastepaper basket. The room had a wooden block floor, and there was no mat on which the children could land.

The plaintiff was the last to jump. She did so from her right foot, cleared the basket with her left, and fell as her right foot caught the obstacle. She sustained a fracture of the left elbow, and underwent an operation.

For the plaintiff it was alleged that there was negligence in that the exercise was not suitable for her having regard to her age and size, that the basket was too large for her to jump over, and that no precautions were taken to prevent her from falling or from being injured in so falling. It was said that her elbow was permanently misshapen, and that there was a possibility that osteo-arthritis would develop after ten or fifteen years. The plaintiff's father, a policeman, said that the exercise had been discontinued since the accident. The girl wore iron protectors in her boots "or you would never keep your children shod going to school." The plaintiff was away from school for a week after the accident, and attended hospital for about five weeks.

The headmistress said that it was part of her orders under the Board of Education to have organised games and to give instruction in running and jumping. Questioned by counsel for the plaintiff whether the Board of Education's instructions suggested the children should jump over a rope, she agreed that the wastepaper basket was her own idea. The plaintiff had fallen before she reached the basket, and touched it with her head. A mat was unnecessary, and a loose mat might slip and cause an accident. Mr C. E. Bell, a surgeon for thirty-six years at the Royal Devon and Exeter Hospital said the plaintiff had completely recovered, and the idea of osteo-arthritis was far-fetched.

On evidence being given that the Reverend Lanyon Owen, one of the managers, had not been instituted as rector of St Sidwell's until July 22, 1924, a month after the accident, he was discharged from the suit.

Held: There had been no negligence.

Judgment for the defendants

104 Jones *v*. London County Council (1932) 96 J.P. 371

COURT OF APPEAL

When a game has been played without serious accident for many years, it is not, by reason of its dangers, negligent to order a boy to play it.

Facts: The plaintiff, Albert George Jones, was an unemployed lad of seventeen. Under the Unemployment Insurance Acts 1920–30, he was ordered to attend a juvenile instruction centre as a condition of receiving unemployment benefit. The centre was at Herold's Institute, Drummond Road, London, S.E., and on April 22, 1931, he wrote an essay on "Should hanging be abolished?" and received a lesson in the Morse code. He was then ordered to go to the gymnasium to take part in a game called riders and horses.

In that game the boy mounted the back of another, and endeavoured to bring to the ground the foot of the boy who was acting as rider in an opposing pair. During the game the plaintiff, who was taking the part of a horse,

fell on the floor and sustained a very serious injury to his right arm. There
was no evidence of undue roughness, and no suggestion that the floor was
defective. The only evidence of the accident was the boy's statement:
"Suddenly I went down."

The action was tried before Judge Moore and a jury at Southwark County
Court, judgment being entered for the infant plaintiff for £1,000, and for the
mother for £30. The defendants appealed by way of case stated to the King's
Bench Division.

AVORY J. (allowing the appeal): It has been stressed on behalf of the respondent that the game had been played on a wooden floor and that there was no
matting. If there had been matting it would have been said that there ought
to have been a mattress; and if there had been a mattress it would have been
said that there ought to have been a feather-bed; and if there had been a
feather-bed; that the boys ought to have been wrapped up in cotton-wool or
rubber. . . . Even if it is assumed that the game was one in which one or more
of the competitors was likely to fall, that would not be sufficient to establish
a case of negligence; otherwise it might be said that no instruction in physical
exercise or games could even be given in a school without the authorities
being liable if a boy fell and happened to hurt himself. . . .

The plaintiff appealed.

Extract from Judgment
SCRUTTON L.J.: . . . The plaintiff had undoubtedly suffered serious injury
but it does not follow that because he has suffered an injury that therefore
he can get compensation from anybody: he has to show some breach of a
legal duty which entitles him to recover compensation for his injury. Now the
circumstances under which the plaintiff met with his injuries were these.
He was a boy between sixteen and eighteen years of age and he was out of work,
and he applied, therefore, for what is popularly known as the dole. Now
Parliament has made some provision—possibly not as much as some people
think it ought to have done—that people shall not get the dole without doing
some work, and in the case of boys under eighteen the Unemployment
Insurance Act 1930 makes it by section 15 (2), the duty of the Minister of
Labour, if there is an approved cause of instruction at which the boy can
reasonably be required to attend . . . the Ministry is to tell the boy: "Here is
a course of instruction which you can take; if you do not take it you will not
get the dole." . . . I think we now understand that the Minister of Labour has
asked the London County Council, as the educational authority, to provide
classes of instruction for these boys. . . . Under these circumstances the educational authority submitted to the Minister of Labour a proposal that classes
should be held at Herold's Institute and that that course of instruction should
include three hours instruction weekly in physical exercises. That proposal
was approved, and consequently there is an approved course of instruction
in physical exercises. Neither the Minister of Labour nor the educational
authority did prescribe the exact details of the exercises, but they put the

course in charge of an instructor of twenty years' experience with a first-class Army certificate in physical exercises, and he and three other people of equally long experience who were called, said that one of the regular exercises in a course of physical exercises is a game called "riders and horses". . . .

Now a game of this sort which you can play for twenty years without any serious accident having happened before this is a game which it seems to me cannot be made the subject of an allegation of negligence on the part of the London County Council for allowing it to be played. . . . It really comes to this, that there is hardly any physical exercise which you can take in which an accident may not happen; you may always slip and fall, and on slipping and falling you always may suffer some muscular injury; but to say that the numerous physical exercises which you can generally undertake without any accident happening are dangerous because an accident may happen at some time, seems to me to be going beyond a reasonable finding which a jury can make. When the jury found in favour of the plaintiff in this case, they were, in my opinion, coming to a finding without any evidence which would support the plaintiff. That is the view which the very experienced judges in the Divisional Court, Avory and Talbot JJ. took, and I think it is the correct view. While, of course, everybody must be sorry for the boy who has met with this accident, you are not entitled to give him a legal remedy simply because you are sorry for him.

Under these circumstances the appeal must be dismissed with costs.

Appeal dismissed: judgment for the
defendants

105 Gibbs *v.* Barking Corporation [1936] 1 All E.R. 115

COURT OF APPEAL
A master in charge of gymnastic training is under an obligation to take reasonable care, and to act with promptitude.

Facts: The plaintiff, a pupil at a school in Barking, was required to vault over a horse in the course of gymnastic training. For some reason he landed "in a stumble." The master in charge did nothing to assist the boy, and an action was brought against the local education authority and the master.

At Ilford County Court, Judge Beazley held that the master had not taken reasonable care, and that the local education authority were liable in damages to the injured boy.[1]

The local education authority appealed.

Judgment
SLESSER L.J.: It is a question of fact that has been decided by the learned county court judge. The respondent was required to undergo gymnastic

1. In English law a master is liable for torts committed by his servants in the course of their duty.

training in the school which he was attending and, in company with other boys, was required to vault over a horse, and the learned county court judge finds that it is the duty of the games instructor to see that each boy, as he jumps over the horse and comes to the other side, does not fall. Whether this boy fell before he had completely finished his task of jumping over the horse or whether he fell just after he had jumped over the horse and before he had recovered his complete equilibrium, the learned judge found that he landed in a stumble and there is ample evidence, in my opinion, why he could come to that conclusion. He landed on the mat on the far side and stumbled and fell. The master and the boy agree on that. That might properly be held to be a fall or stumble during the process of the vaulting in which the master was under an obligation to take care and the learned county court judge has found that there was an absence of reasonable care. The games' master does not seem to have acted with that promptitude which the law requires. With regard to the local authority, everything against them was withdrawn before the case came on to be heard. Their only liability is as the employers of the master. The appeal fails and it will be dismissed.

Appeal dismissed

106 Cahill *v.* West Ham Corporation (1937) 81 S. J. 630

KING'S BENCH DIVISION
It is not negligence to allow children to play in a room surrounded by glass partitions if proper instructions are given.

Facts: The first plaintiff, William Cahill, attended continuation classes at the Arts and Crafts Technical School, West Ham.

On December 17, 1936, a master organised a relay race in one of the classrooms. The plaintiff, then aged thirteen, took part and, on reaching the end of the room, his arm was severely cut when it went through a glass partition. He was an in-patient at Poplar Hospital for some weeks.

He brought an action for damages, alleging that the defendants were negligent in allowing the race to take place in a room surrounded by glass partitions, with a slippery floor, and with the boys in their ordinary clothes and shoes.

The second plaintiff was the lad's father, William Patrick Cahill, a boilermaker, who claimed special damages.

The defendants denied negligence. Attendance at the centre and participation in the race were voluntary, and any clothing or shoes could be worn. They alleged contributory negligence, in that the plaintiff failed to obey the rule requiring him to touch the master, and not the partition. They relied on the maxim *volenti non fit injuria.*

Extract from Judgment
PORTER J.: . . . Those who organised the relay races owed a duty of care; the only question was how much care, and whether they fulfilled that duty.

The plaintiff said that he was told to run down the hall, touch what was in front of him, and run back. Even if that were the case I would have held that there was no negligence. It might have been otherwise if the plaintiff had been told to touch the glass. I accept the evidence of the masters that the instructions were to run up to and touch the master who stood at the far end of the room. I think that that was more likely than that they should have been told to touch what was in front of them. In those circumstances, I find no negligence and the action must fail.

Judgment for the defendants

107 Clarke v. Bethnal Green Borough Council (1939) 55 T.L.R. 519

KING'S BENCH DIVISION

It is not necessarily negligence if a swimming bath attendant fails to see a performance which affects two children out of fifty.[1]

Facts: The infant plaintiff, Marie Irene Clarke, sued the Bethnal Green Borough Council for damages for personal injuries which, she alleged, she suffered through negligence of the defendants or their servant. Her mother, Mrs Alice Gertrude Clarke, sought to recover £12 2s. 6d. expenses to which she had been put as the result of her daughter's injuries.

The accident happened on June 12, 1937, during a women's swimming session at the Bethnal Green baths. The infant plaintiff, a good swimmer, was standing on the springboard at the deep end, preparing to dive. Another child hung on to the board from below and, when she let go, the board sprang up, throwing the plaintiff on to the edge of the bath. She broke two of her front teeth. It was alleged that the attendant, Miss J. G. Bookthorpe, was standing near the door at the far end, and talking to a male attendant instead of supervising the children.

The defendants denied negligence. Miss Bookthorpe had seven years' experience as a bath attendant, and had never known a similar accident. There were about fifty children aged between ten and fourteen in the bath at the time. At the time of the accident she was standing outside the women's toilet watching the bathers, and was not talking to a male attendant. If she had seen anyone hanging on to the springboard she would have told them to get down as they might be hurt if someone jumped on them. It never occurred to her that such an accident as that particular one would occur.

Extract from Judgment

OLIVER J.: . . . I am clearly of opinion that the action fails. The negligence complained of by the plaintiffs was said to be that of the bath attendant, Miss Bookthorpe, and it was said that she was not properly supervising the

1. This is not, strictly, an educational case, but it is included since many schools now have swimming pools and, where this is not the case, most schools arrange swimming instruction for their pupils.

children and that, if she had been, she would have prevented the accident. In my judgment it is a case in which children should certainly have supervision. It is recognised as a duty by everyone keeping public swimming baths that an attendant should be provided. It must be quite obvious, however, to anyone who knows anything about public swimming baths at all well that to supervise every individual in the bath is quite impossible unless there is a swarm of attendants watching. No one can say that the duty of those keeping swimming baths extends so far as that. I am satisfied that the attendant provided by the defendants was a thoroughly competent young woman, and the question therefore arises whether she was on that occasion acting in a negligent manner.

It was alleged by the infant plaintiff that when the accident happened the attendant was talking to a man at the doorway of the bath. The child is a candid and intelligent child, and I was very much struck by the way in which she gave her evidence. When, however, I have to weigh her evidence against that of Miss Bookthorpe, without saying a word against the child I accept Miss Bookthorpe's statement that when the accident occurred she was standing in a position from which she had a general view of the bath. With regard to the suggestion that she had been talking to a man at the time I would merely observe that it is almost inconceivable to anyone who knows public swimming baths that a man would come walking in during a women's session at the baths. I accept without reservation Miss Bookthorpe's denial that any man was there.

Was the attendant committing a negligent act in standing where she did? It was alleged that she must have been wool-gathering. The facts are that there were about fifty children in the bath, making a very considerable noise. The attendant was said to have been negligent because she did not see something going on at the springboard which she ought to have stopped. I am of opinion that to say that she was acting negligently because she did not happen to see a performance which affected two children out of fifty is going farther than common sense should tolerate. Even if she had seen the girl about to jump from the springboard to which another girl was hanging, was it negligent in the attendant not to stop it? No such accident had ever been heard of before, and was not to be anticipated. It does not really matter whether I decide that point or not, as I have come to the conclusion that there was no negligence on the part of the attendant in not seeing what was happening. . . .

The action fails, and there must therefore, be judgment for the defendants.

Judgment for the defendants

108 Ralph *v.* London County Council (1947) 63 T.L.R. 239, 547

COURT OF APPEAL

A local education authority is liable if one of its servants, acting in the course of his duty, fails to contemplate an action which a prudent father would have foreseen.

Facts: The plaintiff, Ronald Daniel Ralph, was a fourteen-year-old pupil at the Central School, Mina Road, Walworth.

On March 19, 1945, he was taking part in a physical training lesson, under the supervision of one of the masters, in the assembly hall of the school which measured 61 feet by 29 feet. The assembly hall was divided from the dining hall by a partition which ran the length of one of the long sides, and which consisted of glass panes down to 3 feet $2\frac{1}{4}$ inches from the ground.

The boys were playing a game of "touch," in which a group of boys were required to chase another group in order to touch them upon any part of the body. Any boy so touched went out of circulation, and in due course the game began again with other groups of boys. About twenty-five or thirty boys were taking part.

While being chased the plaintiff ducked, jumped up, and swung round, unwittingly putting his hand through a glass pane in the partition. He sustained serious injuries to the little and ring fingers of the left hand, and sued the London County Council for damages for negligence. Byrne J. found for the plaintiff:

BYRNE J.: ... It is agreed that the question for decision is whether the accident was a matter which a reasonable and prudent father would have contemplated if he had allowed his children to take part in that game in that way.

The headmaster gave evidence as to the kind of games and exercises which take place in the hall. In the other games and exercises which he mentioned—which seem to me to be entirely different from the type of game which was taking place on this particular day—his descriptions showed that to a certain extent—I emphasise "to a certain extent"—the movements of the boys were circumscribed. In this game of "touch" there was no place in the hall to which any boy could make his way and then, as it were, be in safety; he was in play, so to speak, the whole time. He could be chased, from where he was to begin with, over every part of the floor space of the hall, and it must be a mere matter of common sense to realise that, without any limitation being put on the movements of the boys taking part in the game, they would be running about the hall, twisting and turning, slipping and sliding—I am not finding that the floor was slippery, or anything of that kind—but boys, many of them, owing to the shortage of plimsoles, would be wearing ordinary shoes and running about on a wood floor—they would be slipping and sliding about all over the place.

In those circumstances I bear in mind, as Mr Monier-Williams[1] has pointed out, that one must be careful not to be wise after the event. It is necessary to apply the principle of law to the circumstances as they existed at that time. Although since the accident happened forms have been placed along the length of the partition to prevent boys from running into it, Mr Monier-Williams has reminded me that that is not to be taken as being any indication that, at the time when the game was in progress, the master in charge should in any way have realised the danger. I entirely agree with counsel about that. But

1. Counsel for the defendants.

that makes no difference to the question whether a reasonable and prudent
father would have contemplated that such an accident might have happened
if he had seen his children playing that kind of game in the circumstances
which existed. The view which I take without any hesitation is that in a room
61 feet by 29 feet, one side of which is all glass above 3 feet 2¾ inches from
the ground, and with the boys playing "touch," any reasonable and prudent
person, having regard to the wild nature of the game while it lasted, must
have contemplated, or should have contemplated, that the accident which
happened might happen. In those circumstances I find that there was negligence
so far as the London County Council is concerned.

With regard to damages, in my view the appropriate figure is £500, and I
give judgment for the plaintiff for that sum.

The defendant council appealed to the Court of Appeal.

Extracts from Judgments
LORD GREEN M.R.: . . . The decision of Byrne J. is unassailable. There is
ample evidence on which I myself would have come to the same conclusion
without hesitation. That does not mean that the managers of the school
were consciously disregarding the safety of the pupils, but that they had
committed an error of judgment.

No question of principle whatsoever is involved; it is a question of evidence.
It was an unsuitable game for that particular place, it was the first time it
had been played in that particular place, and it is a case in which the appellants
have fallen short of the standard of care which is required. . . .

ASQUITH L.J.: . . . The question is one of fact, and the judge put the right
question to himself. It was just such an accident that a prudent parent would
have expected to happen in the circumstances. . . .

CROOM-JOHNSON J.: . . . The judge applied the right test and the right
standard of duty, and that standard of duty had manifestly not been reached.
Counsel for the appellants tried to persuade the court to reconsider the facts
with the idea that we could come to a different decision. If I had tried the
action I should have come to the same conclusion as the judge who has applied
the right test and the right law. . . .

Appeal dismissed

109 Wright *v.* Cheshire County Council [1952] 2 All E.R. 789

COURT OF APPEAL
*The test of what is reasonable in ordinary everyday affairs may well be answered
by experience arising from practices adopted generally and followed successfully
for many years.*

Facts: The plaintiff, Roger Neill Wright was a pupil at Grange Secondary
School, Ellesmere Port. On March 25, 1949, when twelve years old, he was
one of a group of ten boys taking part in physical exercises in the gymnasium.

In the course of the exercise he was required to vault over a buck and, as he did so, he fell and sustained serious injuries.

It was the practice in the school that the instructor stood beside the buck during the early stages of training in order to support any boy who was falling. After some proficiency had been gained, each boy who vaulted acted as the stand-by for the next, the intention being to teach co-operation and self-reliance. The method was generally adopted and recommended by the Ministry of Education, but an expert witness at the assizes said he considered it dangerous.

At the time of the accident the instructor was not standing by the buck. As the plaintiff vaulted, the bell rang for the beginning of break, and the boy who should have been standing by ran away.

The plaintiff brought an action for negligence against the local education authority. At Liverpool Assizes, McNair J. accepted the evidence of the expert witness that the practice was dangerous, and awarded £261 4s. 11d. in damages. The defendant appealed.

Extracts from Judgments

SINGLETON L.J.: . . . The plaintiff relied on the evidence of Mr Charles Lord, who was a fellow and also an examiner of the British Association of Physical Training, and an organiser of physical training for the Y.M.C.A. on Merseyside, and who had had a long experience of gymnastics and of physical drill. He was asked by counsel whether he considered that the system adopted at this school was a safe system, and his answer was: "In over fifty years' teaching I have never allowed a boy to stand in at the buck or the box. I think it is for an adult. It is a very precarious practice. I think the buck is the most useless piece of apparatus in the gymnasium." The learned judge then asked him how high the buck was, and he said: "Three feet roughly, but it can go to six." Then the learned judge said to him:

"*Q.* You say it is dangerous for boys to go over a buck three feet high?
A. Not having an adult to catch him, I do.
Q. What age of boy?
A. Any boy aged from nine upwards.
Q. A boy of eighteen?
A. Well, yes, I would not even allow boys of eighteen to go over a buck by themselves.
Q. Three feet high?
A. There is always a danger of a boy who is rather tight in the muscles not being able to do an astride position to get over and falling backwards, and then he goes on the floor, because there is no mat where he takes off.
Q. I suppose you have seen leapfrog played?
A. Yes. I teach leapfrog in my own classes.
Q. And I suppose you have seen it played in the playground?

A. Yes, but then they are doing it at their own risk.

Q. Do you think it is an unsafe sport?

A. I do really, but boys will be boys. In the gymnasium it is up to the teacher to see that there is no danger. If I have the buck I do not have the box. I do something else like a long jump, balance walking and mat work. I had one or two slips in my early teaching career on the buck and decided to abandon it."

When that witness was cross-examined he was asked by counsel for the defendants whether or not the exercise, as performed in the gymnasium in the school on the day in question, was a regular exercise, and he answered:

"Yes.

Q. And one of the purposes of it is to inspire the boys with a little self-confidence and courage, is it not?

A. Yes.

Q. And provided the boy stays and does his job there is no risk involved, is there?

A. I think there is. There are very few boys I would allow to stand in at a buck. There are only certain boys gifted with what I call the courage to grip that boy. I have seen them when I have gone round examining. The British Association. . . .

Q. I am not challenging what your personal view is, but the point is that right throughout the educational service there are thousands of teachers teaching P.T.?

A. Yes.

Q. And they all teach this method?

A. Yes.

Q. It is the recognised method?

[No reply].

MCNAIR J.: Do you agree with that?

A. I do not.

Q. Do you agree that it is the recognised method?

A. I have heard of it, but I myself do not approve of it. A lot of things the Board of Education recommend I do not stick up for.

Nelson: My Lord is asking you this: You know that is what they do?

A. They do, I know.

Q. But you say you do not approve of it, but you know from the reference books that is the recognised method?

A. They do. They recommend the boys for standing in."

In re-examination by counsel for the plaintiff the witness was asked:

"*Q.* Therefore what you are saying, as I understand it, is that you do not approve of it. You say an adult ought to be there, and you say the Board of Education allow lads to be there?

A. Yes, I know they do by the reference books."

Evidence was given by several of the boys, and there was a question of fact on that which had to be decided, and was decided, by the learned judge. Evidence was given, too, by the master, Mr George, a trained and experienced physical trainer and gymnastic instructor. He said he followed the ordinary practice, the practice in which he had been trained, and he considered it good practice after the boys had been under him and directly supervised by him for a while. They only had to clear a three foot buck lengthwise, and it was about one foot six inches, or, perhaps a shade more, long. It was good practice that they should be left to themselves, one of the ten in turn being at the receiving end of the buck where there was a mat. He said that, apart from the fact that it was found to be good in practice, it was good training for the boys that one should rely on the other, and that one should be there to help the other in case of need. That was the recognised practice followed everywhere so far as he could find, although the plaintiff's expert witness said he did not approve of it.

The class of forty, all boys about twelve years of age, was split up into four parts or squads. Each of the squads was on a different form of exercise from the others. The master in charge, Mr George, supervised the work. The members of the squad, of which the plaintiff was one, had to vault in turn over the buck three feet high and one foot six inches long. That would not appear to be a particularly hazardous operation, as there was a mat at the end at which the boy landed. The plaintiff himself had been some seven months at the school. He had done this exercise on many occasions before, and he had cleared the buck on four occasions on this very day without anything untoward happening. Mr George had had this squad under his care until they were accustomed to vaulting the buck, and when he thought they were fit to carry on without an adult in immediate proximity he left them to do that which they were doing on the day of this accident. One of the ten boys went to the receiving end, and the other nine were in a queue. The first of the queue went over the buck with the one waiting to receive him and to aid him if necessary. Then the receiver went to the end of the queue, and the remainder of the boys followed over the buck in turn, one always standing at the receiving end. As I have said, this was the regular and the recognised practice not only in this school, but in other such schools, as the expert witness called on behalf of the plaintiff admitted. The boys were all the time within the view of Mr George, though he himself was giving his first attention to a more advanced exercise in which the boys went over a higher and more difficult obstacle.

The case for the plaintiff alleging negligence was based almost wholly on the evidence of Mr Lord, who gave the answers to which I have referred already. The learned counsel were agreed on the law to be applied. The measure of duty owed by the defendants, as the education authority, is that which a reasonable parent should exercise towards his child. It is a duty to take reasonable care, no more and no less. McNair J. held that the defendants were responsible, and he said:

"Though I hope I am the last to express the view that boys of ten or twelve require mollycoddling or nursing, it does seem to me that this particular operation, which is admittedly unsafe for these boys unless there is someone to receive them, ought to have demanded that there should be some adult ready to receive the boys or support them on landing, and that it was not a proper discharge of the defendants' duty to exercise the care of a reasonably careful parent to allow that duty of supporting the boys on landing to be discharged solely by a small boy of the age of these boys. It seems to me that the circumstances of the case as disclosed to me in the evidence require that an adult should be physically present at any time when boys of this age are performing this particular operation."

With all respect, I do not think that that can be right on the evidence which was before the court. I recognise that this is largely a question of fact, but the proper test must be applied. The evidence on both sides showed that the ordinary and recognised practice was being followed, and the plaintiff's expert witness agreed that it was the practice recommended in books on the subject, and one which gave boys a sense of responsibility. He said, however, that he did not like it and would not recommend that even boys of eighteen should vault over a three foot buck without an adult to aid them. I find it difficult to appreciate the view of that witness. Entirely apart from that, I cannot see how it can be said that the defendants were negligent if they adopted the well-recognised practice in a matter of this kind. The view of the plaintiff's witness would seem to indicate the necessity of having four adult instructors in the gymnasium for a class of forty boys. I cannot accept that. There may well be some risk in everything one does or in every step one takes, but in ordinary everyday affairs the test of what is reasonable care may well be answered by experience from which arises a practice adopted generally, and followed successfully over the years so far as the evidence in this case goes. Indeed, it would appear from the judge's findings of fact that the cause, or a cause, of the accident to the plaintiff was that the boy who ought to have been standing by the mat left his post when the bell sounded. The bell was an indication of a break for play-time. In the ordinary course the boys, on the sound of the bell, would receive an order to go to the corner at which their squad paraded before being dismissed. Why should the defendants apprehend that on this, or on any, occasion the boy would run away when the plaintiff was in the act of vaulting? So far as we know, that sort of thing had never happened before. The boys all had experience, seven months, in this school, and the plaintiff (and no doubt the other boys) had been in a junior school before and had taken part in physical exercise and drill. In my opinion, the judgment in favour of the plaintiff cannot stand on the evidence which was before the court, and I would allow this appeal.

BIRKETT L.J.: ... The only difficulty in the case was the evidence of Mr Lord on the other side, and it would be quite wrong for me sitting here, not having seen Mr Lord, to make anything in the nature of any adverse comment on his evidence. He was a man of seventy-two years of age who had had very many years' experience, and his answers made it perfectly plain that he did not approve of the buck being there at all, to start with, and he would not have had any exercise performed with the buck if he had had his own way, but he made it abundantly plain also, when pressed in cross-examination, that there were thousands of physical training instructors carrying out similar duties to Mr George, who were adopting this self-same system, and when further pressed he said he knew that it was the recognised system. Indeed, the learned judge in his judgment goes the length of saying (although I do not think there is any precise evidence on this matter) that the training manual as put forward by the Ministry of Education recommended that the process be adopted. I mention that to emphasise what I think my Lord had already emphasised, and that is that the general rule that a defendant charged with negligence can clear himself if he has shown he has acted in accordance with the general and approved practice some has application at least. It is true that the general practice may not conform to the standard of care required by a reasonable and prudent man, but in the ordinary circumstances where you find a general standard in the medical profession followed by general practitioners, or a general standard in the educational profession followed by physical training instructors, and a defendant can come and say: "In all that I did I followed the approved practice generally adopted throughout the land," at any rate he is in a position of considerable strength to answer a charge of negligence.

On the second point, if it be said the general system does not accord with the standard of a reasonable and prudent man, all I desire to say is this, that when you have, as a fact in this case, a system in general use which had been adopted in this school and followed with perfect safety, so far as we know, until this day, it is a very strong thing indeed to say that the authorities were negligent. I observe that the learned judge, who attached some importance to this case, said:

> "If the authorities had really applied their minds to this problem, it ought to have been within the range of reasonable foreseeability that these small boys, however well trained and however obedient, might not adequately perform their function of supporting."

So the authorities are being blamed because they allowed this system, with the boys operating in the way they did, to be the system in vogue. For my own part, if I were asked what would a reasonable and prudent man do, I think, first of all, he would have regard to the nature of the exercise, and the nature of the exercise, as I see it, requires care, but it is not in itself a dangerous operation, and I think, further, that, if there had been a system in vogue, as there was here, whereby a boy waited to support the boy vaulting, a reasonable and prudent man would say: "If the boy has been made proficient by his training, there was no negligence in not having an adult there." It is, I think, impossible to avoid the conclusion that it was a most unfortunate, unforeseeable, and quite unpredictable thing which occasioned the accident on this day. There was, of course, a great contest about how the accident happened; it was said that the boy himself disobediently made the leap after the bell had sounded. The judge found conclusively against that, and so it goes out of this case, but it was the ringing of that bell which occasioned the trouble, because the supporting boy, answering the bell and the cry of "fall in," was not there. It appears that this was the first time such a thing had happened. In those circumstances, I feel it is impossible to say on the facts that any negligence was shown on the part of the defendants, and for these reasons, and for the reasons which have already been given by my Lord, I agree with the conclusion that this appeal ought to be allowed.

Appeal allowed

110 Webb *v.* Essex County Council (1954)
Times Educational Supplement, November 12

QUEEN'S BENCH DIVISION

An action for negligence cannot succeed if it is founded on an event which is simply an accident.

Facts: The plaintiff, Clifford John Webb, was a pupil at South Ockendon Primary School. In July 1951, when he was aged five-and-a-quarter, he fell while jumping from a stool which formed part of the agility apparatus. He fractured his left elbow, and was said at the hearing to have sustained permanent injury.

The apparatus consisted of a ramp leading up to a stool said to be 2 feet $4\frac{1}{2}$ inches high. There was a thick mat on the other side, and there were rubber mats under the apparatus.

The plaintiff sued for damages in negligence. As he could not remember, he was not called to give evidence. It was contended that, when he was required to jump down from nearly his own height, someone should have been nearer than twelve to fourteen feet away. The father said that the headmistress had told him that she was talking to the teachers at the time of the accident. When they turned round the boy was lying on the floor. He got up, but fell again.

The headmistress denied that she was talking to the teachers. The apparatus was installed in April 1951 and she had seen the plaintiff jumping from the stool. He had never shown that he had any difficulty. The children were told that they could have help if they needed it, but the whole point of the apparatus was to give them self-confidence.

An assistant teacher said Clifford seemed to like jumping from the stool. It was not too high for him.

Extract from Judgment

DEVLIN J.: . . . The apparatus itself and the way in which it was designed to be used were safe. It is clear that Miss Bush and Miss Evans were not personally negligent and I do not see what they could have done had they seen the boy jump. There is nothing to show that it was anything but an accident.

Judgment for the defendants

111 Conrad *v.* Inner London Education Authority (1967) *The Times* May 26[1]

COURT OF APPEAL

Where a course of action follows general and approved practice an action of negligence will not lie.

Facts: The plaintiff, a solo ballet dancer and choreographer was under contract to the Stadt Theatre in Ulm from 1960 to 1962 at a salary which after payment of tax was equivalent to about £25 a week. He had prospects of a higher salary. While on holiday in London in 1962 he enrolled for three courses in judo, dancing and German, arranged by the former London County Council at Woodberry Down School each at a fee of five shillings a session.

Evidence was given that there are two schools of thought as to initial instruction in judo. The older is slower and more cautious, and great importance is attached to beginning with the "breakfalls." These are methods of breaking the fall of the person to be thrown so as to minimise the risks of injury. After this, the various stages of a throw were taught and practised separately before a throw was attempted with a non-resisting partner. Competitive throwing did not commence until after a number of lessons.

Criticism in England of this method began in the mid-1950s, and was led by a Mr Gleeson, the national coach to the British Judo Association. It was said that the method took too long, that beginners got bored, and that it was difficult to link the various stages into a complete throw. Mr Gleeson advocated that students should attempt the whole throw from the beginning with a non-resisting partner, and then correct their faults by studying the parts. In this way a novice could attempt his first throw within fifteen minutes of the beginning of the first lesson without previously being taught "breakfalls."

In 1960–61 the London County Council, after consulting an ancient Japanese expert and Mr Gleeson, decided to introduce the newer method, with the modification that a pupil should not attempt a full throw in his first lesson until he had practised it in parts. Classes and tests were arranged for instructors, and in the spring of 1962 Mr Wing, who was to become the plaintiff's instructor, passed the test. His first class consisted of sixteen pupils, of whom all but two or three were novices, on September 27, 1962. The class warmed up, and practised "breakfalls" for about twenty minutes, after which Mr Wing demonstrated a modified *Ogoshi* (major hip throw). In this manoeuvre the aim of each contestant is to manoeuvre his opponent off

1. The report of the hearing in the Queen's Bench Division appeared in *The Times* of November 29, 1966.

balance by pushing or pulling while holding the left lapel of the opponent's tunic in the right hand, and the right sleeve below the elbow with the left hand. Finally the opponent is thrown to the floor with a circular motion.

There was a discrepancy in the evidence given as to the instructions which the candidates received. Mr Wing said that he told the class that, when a throw was being attempted, the opponent was not to resist, but to relax and do a decent "breakfall." According to the plaintiff, Mr Wing said: "Get your man down three times. Don't mind how you get him down, but get him down."

The plaintiff said that the practice was not limited to what had been taught. One witness was thrown over his opponent's head by what is variously called a "James Bond throw" or a "one-footed monkey climb." The plaintiff won his first two bouts, but in the third he felt a snap like a piece of wood, which was the sound of a spiral fracture of his right humerus.

Lyell J. sitting in the Queen's Bench Division to determine a claim by the plaintiff against the Inner London Education Authority (as successors to the London County Council) for damages for negligence, said that in the light of the evidence the practice went far beyond *Randori*, the free practice of what had been taught. Mr Wing told the performer of the one-footed monkey climb that it was not a fair throw; otherwise he allowed the contestants to do as they liked. "The risk of injury was a foreseeable one; it is a well-recognised warning that one should not try to run before one could walk, and that is a warning that Mr Wing had failed to heed. What he had initiated towards the end of the first class was not free practice but a competition which inevitably involved hazards with which a beginner could not be expected to cope. He did not sufficiently warn the class of the danger of opposing force with force. The plaintiff had suffered injury for which the defendants were responsible.

The plaintiff's fracture did not unite for nearly two years. There was a lengthy period of pain, and a loss of earnings of about £1,100 at the estimated rate of £30 to £35 a week after deduction of tax. Damages were assessed at £5,500.

The Court of Appeal (Sellers, Davies, and Salmon L.JJ.) reversed the decision, and refused leave to appeal to the House of Lords.

Extract from Judgment
SELLERS L.J.: Judo is a robust and manly sport which is somewhat dangerous because it involves throwing one's opponent about. There are two schools of thought about the correct mode of instruction, the main difference between them being the speed of progress at which pupils should face each other in combat.

The older method was to allow the pupils a number of lessons before they engaged in practical demonstrations, but the modern method is to let them indulge in *Randori*, or free practice, at the end of their first lesson. The defendants after careful consideration decided to adopt the modern method. It was accepted on appeal that that was not a ground of negligence.

The plaintiff, a man in good physique, decided to join the session beginning on September 17, 1962. His instructor, Mr Wing, was experienced and competent, and had been on a course in which the new method was taught. It was his first employment with the defendants, although he had been employed elsewhere as an instructor.

He taught the pupils the *Ogoshi* throw, and at the end of the first lesson invited the plaintiff and another member of the class to practise what they had been taught. The object was that by taking similar holds, the one should get the other down by putting him off his balance. It was in the course of the contest that the accident occurred.

The ground on which the instructor was said to have been negligent was that he was alleged to have told the class that each had to get the other down in language which indicated that it did not matter how it was done. There was a great conflict of evidence on that allegation; it was made by the plaintiff alone and unsupported by any other witness. It was not satisfactorily resolved by the judge, who did not say whether he accepted or rejected the plaintiff's evidence on that matter.

It might well be that the instructor had told the pupils that each should practise what he had been taught to get his man down. But even if the instructor had said that, it did not amount to negligence on the part of the instructor. Accordingly the appeal will be allowed.

Appeal allowed

(H) PLAYGROUNDS AND RECREATION

112 Jackson *v*. London County Council and Chappell
(1912) 76 J.P. 217

COURT OF APPEAL

Both the local education authority and a contractor may be liable if dangerous materials are left in a school playground.

Facts: The plaintiff was a pupil at Middle Row School, North Kensington. Mr Chappell was a contractor who was employed to carry out repairs at the school and who, on January 7, 1911, sent a truck of "rough stuff" (four parts of sand, one part of lime, and a little hair) which was left in the playground at the caretaker's suggestion.

The school reopened on Monday, January 9, and the headmaster immediately instructed the caretaker to have the truck removed. The caretaker telephoned the contractor who sent a man who, however, did nothing. The playground was supervised by teaching staff during the morning and afternoon breaks. At the end of afternoon school the truck, being unguarded, was tipped up and some boys played a game of "snowball' with the rough stuff. The plaintiff was hit in the left eye, injuring his sight and causing considerable pain and suffering.

In an action for damages it was contended that the defendants were negligent in not seeing that the building materials were safeguarded to prevent the
children from injuring themselves by meddling with the same. There was a
dispute as to whether the accident happened in the playground or the street.

The trial was before Bray J., sitting with a common jury, who found (1) that
the boys were on the school premises when the accident happened; (2) that
the London County Council were, by their servants, guilty of negligence
which was the cause of the accident; (3) that Mr Chappell, by himself or his
servants, was guilty of negligence which was the cause of the accident. They
found for £50 in damages apportioned equally against each defendant.
Judgment was given accordingly.

The defendants applied for judgment or a new trial.

Extract from Judgment

VAUGHAN WILLIAMS L.J.: The most difficult point in this case we have
not to deal with; that the jury had to deal with. Bray, J. in his judgment
says:

"I confess that I have very great doubts indeed about this case, as to
whether there was any evidence or not, but I felt bound to leave it to the
jury" (that means, I think there was some evidence) "and I told the jury that
the first thing they must be satisfied of before they could find for the plaintiff
was that the accident was one which might have been reasonably anticipated,
and should have been guarded against, and then I said, 'The next question you
have got to consider is if that be so whether the defendants, or either of them,
were guilty of negligence in not guarding against it.' " The jury to whom
Bray J. put those questions have in substance found, first, that the accident
was a consequence which might reasonably have been anticipated from leaving
the barrow of lime where it was; but that was not the only question for the
jury—that would not be enough—that only goes to the extent of saying that
the boys were very likely to play with anything of the sort which was left there.
But you must go a step further and find that that which they played with was
something which was in itself dangerous when left convenient as a plaything
for children. The jury found that the defendants were, both of them, guilty
of negligence. . . .

I do not know whether the jury were at all influenced by sentimental sympathy for the boy. It is not nowadays in the twentieth century an unknown
effect for juries and others who have to deal with a claim made on behalf of
a little child rather to strain the circumstances in order to find in favour of the
child; but I do not think that we can say it was so here; it was left to the jury
and I agree with the learned judge there was evidence against both defendants.
There was evidence against the schoolmaster because, on his own evidence, he
gave a sort of preliminary judgment against himself because he recognised the
barrow as a source of danger, and that made him send the messages he did to
the builder. And then when you come to the builder you find that he was told
he ought to send somebody, and he acted upon it; but he did not act efficiently

upon it, and he did not send, as he ought to have sent, if he had looked after his business. Under the circumstances I cannot say that there was no evidence to go to the jury. The appeals will, therefore, be dismissed with costs.

Appeals dismissed

113 Gow *v.* Glasgow Education Authority, 1922 S.C. 260

A schoolmaster is not liable for a sudden act which could not have been prevented by supervision.

Facts: The pursuer,[1] Andrew Gow, was the father of a seven-year-old blind boy, and claimed £500 damages in respect of injuries sustained by his son while an inmate of Woodburn House, a hostel provided by the defenders for the reception of blind children.

The boy resided in the hostel each week from Monday to Friday, and during the daytime he was conveyed to Oatlands Public School for his education. For some time it had been the practice for a few children not afflicted with blindness also to reside in the hostel.

During the evening of February 22, 1921, Donald Gow was playing in a room at the hostel with other children, some of whom were blind and others of whom had their full sight. Unexpectedly, a boy named Alexander Smith jumped suddenly on Donald Gow's back causing him to fall, and to sustain serious injuries, the chief of which was the fracture of an arm.

The pursuer alleged that the defenders had been negligent in their duty of supervision, which was all the more incumbent upon them when they permitted blind and sighted children to play together.

"It is well known to the defenders that children, and particularly those not afflicted as above, are prone to indulge in games involving violence, and that children afflicted by blindness are liable to be victims of any misconduct or roughness of other children not so afflicted, and are unable to protect themselves from such violence and roughness. . . . They ought accordingly to have made arrangements for some servant or teacher to be present when the mixed children were at play in the said room and the children ought not to have been left without supervision."

The defenders pleaded, *inter alia,** that the pursuer's averments being irrelevant and insufficient to support the conclusions of the summons, the action should be dismissed.

The Lord Ordinary, Lord Hunter, refused the issue, and dismissed the action.

The pursuer reclaimed.[2]

1. In Scottish law the plaintiff is called the *pursuer*, the defendant is the *defender*. The appellant is known as the *reclaimer*.
2. Appealed.

Extract from Advice

SCOTT DICKSON (Lord Justice-Clerk): ... The fact that, at the actual time of the accident, there was "no servant of the defenders left in charge of the said children" is the sole ground of fault alleged. It is not said—and, indeed, the contrary appears—that there were not an ample number of attendants provided for the hostel; but there was not one at the time in the room actually in charge of the children. The pursuer says that the children ought not to have been left without supervision. But then he goes on to say:

> "Had the defenders provided a servant or servants to watch over the conduct of the children in the said room on the said occasion the said Donald Gow would not have sustained the forementioned injuries, as such servant would have been able to control the children and prevent interference of one with another, and for their fault and negligence in not making such provision, or alternatively for that of those whom they have placed in the said hostel as superintendents, in not making such provision, the defenders are responsible."

It seems to me that that would be putting an impossible burden upon the Education Authority, because it would come to this, that the Education Authority would practically have to warrant the safety of the children against all accidents, however free from personal blame the officials of the hostel might be.

There is nothing alleged against the boy Alexander Smith, who was the cause of the unfortunate occurrence, further than that it was his jumping unexpectedly on to the back of Donald Gow that caused the latter to fall to the ground and suffer the injuries which ultimately led to this action. There is nothing said about the hostel being under-staffed, but only that at the time in question there was not actually in the playroom some servant who was to watch over the conduct of the children and safeguard them so as to ensure that no misfortune would happen to them. Strictly speaking, it is not legitimate to refer to the defenders' statement on a question of relevancy, but one may do so by way of illustration. One of the matrons, or one of her assistants, was moving about the rooms from time to time where the children were playing, taking a general supervision of what was going on. Therefore it was not a case where the children were put into the room, the door locked, and they were left alone. There was a general supervision being kept over them. What actually occurred was an unexpected, an unforeseen, and, I think, an almost unforeseeable misfortune, and even if there had been a matron or some other servant actually in the room where the children were playing, I do not see how that would have prevented the accident. The occurrence is described as one boy jumping unexpectedly on to the back of the boy who was injured. It was the thing of a moment. There was no prolonged struggle or fight or contest which could have been stopped by a servant or person in authority actually in the room. If there had been a struggle or fight going on for some time, one could have understood that there might have been room for complaint. But here was a boy who is not said to have been animated by ill-feeling towards the youngster who met with the accident. They were just playing as children will, and blame can hardly be attributed to him who caused the unfortunate results which happened. I do not think, moreover, that Gow's unfortunate affliction of blindness had any material bearing on the accident.

I think the case fails because the obligation which was sought to be imposed on the Education Authority was higher than the law imposes upon it, and also because I do not think that the fault which is alleged was a fault that conduced to the accident, or that the provisions which the pursuer says the defenders should have made by providing a servant or servants to watch over the conduct of the children would have succeeded in preventing this unfortunate accident.

I am, therefore, of opinion that the Lord Ordinary reached the right conclusion that this record discloses no ground for a claim against the Education Authority; and that the action was rightly dismissed.

Reclaiming note refused[3]

114 Langham *v.* Wellingborough School Governors and Fryer (1932)
101 L.J.K.B. 513

COURT OF APPEAL

Where there is no evidence of lack of supervision or that, assuming there was such supervision, it would have prevented an accident, there is no liability.

Facts: The plaintiff, Stephen François Langham, was a pupil at Wellingborough School.

In July 1931, he was going from one room to another during break, and had to pass an open door leading to the playground. As he did so, he was struck in the eye by a golf ball which had been hit with a stick by a boy in the playground. As a result he had practically lost the use of the eye.

The plaintiff brought an action for damages for negligence against the proprietors or governors of the school and the headmaster, alleging want of proper supervision. The governors denied negligence, and alleged that the whole internal organisation, management and discipline were the responsibility of the headmaster under the scheme governing the school.

At the Northampton Assizes Horridge J. ruled that there was no evidence against the governors, and they were dismissed from the action. Damages amounting to £295 were awarded against the headmaster, who appealed.

Healy K.C. (for the appellant): There was a rule in the school that no hard balls should be used and, unless there was a duty on the headmaster to put a guard over every boy under his charge to see that he did not use a golf ball, it is impossible to conceive any means by which the accident could have been prevented. It would be a different matter if the headmaster had allowed balls

3. Appeal dismissed.

L

to be knocked around in the playground without supervision, and one could conceive that a charge of negligence might be made if the headmaster allowed such a game as hockey to go on in the playground without permission.

GREER L.J.: I am not so sure of that. No schoolmaster in the world could prevent a naughty boy doing naughty things on some occasions.

ROMER L.J.: Unless one searches the boys every day when they come to school to see what they have in their pockets, I do not see how one can detect the presence of golf balls.

SCRUTTON L.J.: Was the ball hit with a golf club?

Healy K.C.: No, I believe it was only a stick.

GREER L.J.: I once heard golf described as hitting a white ball over the grass with an inverted walking stick.

Eales K.C. (for the respondents): The decision of the judge was right, and it was the only decision he could have come to on the facts. A golf ball plus a stick in the hands of a boy on a playground with an asphalt surface is a very dangerous combination.

SCRUTTON L.J.: I remember once when the Bar was playing, the actors had to leave by train. The train was late and they had a competition to see who could drive over a signal-box from the asphalt platform. The result was that the platform was filled with terrified passengers crouching for safety against whatever protection they could find.

Extracts from Judgments

SCRUTTON L.J.: . . . At the close of the plaintiff's case, the defendants counsel submitted that there was no evidence to go to the jury. The learned judge thought that there was some evidence, and he summed up to the jury, saying that they might infer, from the fact that the golf ball was hit from the playground and damaged somebody inside the house, negligence of the headmaster in not providing for proper supervision of the playground.

I personally have had some doubt in this matter; I think more than my brothers have had. I can see that it is possible to argue that this is one of the cases which come within the principles laid down by the majority of the Court in the Exchequer Chamber through the mouth of Erle C.J. in the well-known case of *Scott* v. *London and St Katharine Docks Company*.[1] In that case the defendants owned a warehouse. The plaintiff was passing underneath the warehouse when a bag from the second floor of the warehouse dropped on him and injured him. The judge at the trial, Martin B., had held that there was no evidence of negligence. The Court of Exchequer had differed in opinion. The Court of Exchequer Chamber differed in opinion, but Erle C.J., giving the judgment of the court, said this, which has been constantly cited in subsequent cases: "The majority of the court have come to the following conclusions: There must be reasonable evidence of negligence." I imagine that the whole court would have come to that conclusion. "But where the thing is shown to be under the management of the defendant or his servants,

1 (1865) 34 L.J.Ex. 220; 3 H. & C. 596.

and the accident is such as in the ordinary course of things does not happen if those who have the management use proper care, it affords reasonable evidence, in the absence of explanation by the defendants, that the accident arose from want of care."

It is sought to apply that to this case by saying: "The school is under the management of the headmaster. In ordinary circumstances you would not expect a golf ball from the playground to make its appearance inside the house and hit a person in the eye. If there had been proper supervision, the boy, Tony Briggs, would not have been playing with a golf ball and stick in the playground. The headmaster offers no evidence as to what amount of supervision he provided in the playground." That is the class of argument put forward to justify the finding of the jury that there was negligence on the part of the headmaster, coupled with a wide statement of Lord Esher's that the headmaster of a school has the same measure of duty as a careful parent would have to his boys—a statement which does not enlighten me very much, because I do not know that a father is liable to third persons for damage done by acts of his sons, and I find difficulty in imagining a case where a father is liable to his son because another of his sons has damaged the plaintiff.

. . . It seems to me that there must be evidence: (1) of lack of supervision; and (2) that the lack of supervision caused the accident. I put a case to counsel for the respondent which no doubt is stronger than the present case: Supposing that what happened was that a boy, in a sudden fit of temper, being called a name, hit out at the other boy and damaged his eye. It is difficult to see how one could say that any supervision would have prevented a sudden outburst like that. To that counsel assented. You have further facts, first, that the golf ball is not in itself a dangerous thing; a boy might carry a golf ball about in his pocket without the necessity of a master taking it away; and, secondly, the only evidence is, not that it was habitual to knock a golf ball about with a stick in an asphalt playground, but that the boy who gave the evidence said that he had never known of such a thing before. In all these circumstances I have come to the conclusion that there was no evidence which justified the jury in finding that the headmaster was negligent, because (1) there was no evidence that he had not provided supervision against this occurrence; and (2) there was no evidence that the supervision, if he had provided proper supervision, would have prevented the accident.

For these reasons, with some doubt because I say frankly that my mind has hesitated during the course of the argument, I have come to the conclusion that the learned judge ought not to have left the case to the jury and, therefore, the judgment must be set aside, and the appeal allowed with costs.

ROMER L.J.: I have arrived at the same conclusion. There is no direct evidence here of any act or omission on the part of the headmaster to show that he had been guilty of any negligence. There are cases, and it is said that this is one of them, where the mere narration of the event that has caused damage to the plaintiff is evidence from which the inference may be drawn that the defendant has been guilty of negligence, or, to use the words of

Greer L.J., where the narration of the event renders it probable or indicates a reasonable probability that there has been negligence giving rise to the accident. In the present case the narration of the fact of the accident is not, in my opinion, evidence from which any inference of negligence can be drawn. It does not indicate to me that the headmaster was probably guilty of negligence. It does not indicate to me that any master was guilty of negligence, least of all the headmaster. It does not suggest to me that there was no supervision provided by the headmaster in the playground, or that any supervision provided by him was not properly and adequately exercised. It does not suggest to me that, even if there had been supervision, the accident would have been prevented. . . .

Appeal allowed

115 Rawsthorne *v.* Ottley and others [1937] 3 All E.R. 902

MANCHESTER ASSIZES

A lorry, as such, is not an allurement to children and neither headmaster, managers, nor owners of the lorry are liable for an accident arising in an unsupervised playground through the presence of a lorry during break.

Facts: The plaintiff, on September 9, 1935, was a thirteen-year-old pupil attending Edenfield Church of England School. At about 10.45 a.m. the senior boys went into their playground accompanied by the headmaster. The headmaster then returned to the school, where he was brought a weight-note relating to the delivery of coke. As the notes were not always brought on the day of delivery he did not assume that a delivery was going on.

Meanwhile a lorry belonging to the Ramsbottom Gas Company had arrived with a load of coke which the driver, who was unaccompanied, intended to deliver down a chute under a window in a building on one side of the playground. The lorry was backed into position, the load tipped, and the tipping part of the lorry returned to the horizontal. The driver then got back into the cab and, as he started to move the lorry, there was a clatter of clogs, a bang, and a scream. The driver got down to find the plaintiff with his leg jammed between the tipper and the oil box, which is at the front.

The plaintiff sued the managers and Thomas Mansell, headmaster of the school, for damages for personal injuries, alleging that they permitted boys to ride upon and/or interfere with the lorry and/or its tipping gear; and that they allowed the lorry to enter the yard, where it constituted an allurement and/or trap to the plaintiff and/or other children. These defendants denied negligence. The plaintiff also brought an action against the Ramsbottom Gas Company, alleging negligence in that they sent a tipping lorry, that they sent the lorry without a "second man," and that they permitted the plaintiff to ride on the lorry. The Company set up a defence of contributory negligence by the plaintiff, the negligence of the other scholars, that the plaintiff was a trespasser, and that he had been warned.

Extracts from Judgment

HILBERY J.: . . . What had happened was, in my view, this: As the driver got back into his cab, no boys were on the wagon. They were, of course, about, and near, and they would be near, merely from the presence of the wagon in the playground, and, as boys, would be interested in the driver working the valve, and the like. As the driver began to move, the boys jumped on to the lorry, the plaintiff on to a part out of the sight of the driver, at the back of the cab, and other boys, at or about the same time, after running at the wagon, leapt on to the back in sufficient numbers to pull down the back of the tipping part and to pull up the front. Then they apparently let it go, frightened at what they had done, and it came down to crush the leg of the little boy, the plaintiff, at the front.

On the facts, one would never think, in this case, that a wrong had been done to the boy by the headmaster, or the managers, or the Gas Company. But children's cases have been fruitful of litigation, not unproductive of damages, and not unproductive, therefore, of costs. I consider a case of a very intelligent little boy with grave anxiety. This is such a case.

I consider first the case against the headmaster. The duty of care is that of a careful parent. So be it. In what is it suggested that the headmaster committed a breach of that duty? It is said that the lorries came to deliver coke, but he had no reason to anticipate that one might come that day. It is said that he would know that the lorry which would come would be a tipping lorry, and therefore—in a phrase now established in the law—an "allurement" to boys. The headmaster said he did not know a tipping lorry would come, and I believe him. He further says that, if he had known it would come at playtime, he would have stopped it, not because of any danger, but because it would interfere with games and proper recreation in the yard. As to the allegation of permitting, it is said that the headmaster allowed the boys to play without supervision when the lorry was there. Mr Mansell did not see it there; he had left the yard before it came, and, in my view, quite properly; he did not know the lorry was there. It is said that a person is not exercising proper supervision if he leaves a boy of nearly fourteen to play alone. Is a tipping lorry more attractive to the child mind than was the old-fashioned tip cart to us as boys? Suppose that this had been a horse-drawn vehicle: there are plenty of cases in the books to show that horse-drawn vehicles are interfered with by children— what parent would be held negligent if he left such a child to watch a horse and cart in operation? It is true that this is a mechanical contrivance, but what more common thing is there about today? I myself would not say that the headmaster was negligent in leaving boys in the playground when coke was being tipped. I think that these rules can be strained too far with a view to damages.

As to control, what supervision or control ought a headmaster to have exercised over boys in the senior class in a playground in playtime? He saw them start to play; then he went in. In my view, it is not the law, and never has been the law, that a schoolmaster should keep boys under supervision during every moment of their school lives. Having regard to the fact that the schoolmaster did not know that the lorry was there, I find that there is no negligence. It has been said that he knew it might have come. I still do not think that he should have stayed, lest such a possibility should have become the event. Should he have stopped its coming during playtime? I do not think that that is lack of supervision, and it would necessitate extra supervision. Apart from its being a tipping lorry, to know that an ordinary lorry comes, and not to prevent it during playtime, is not lack of supervision. It is said, on behalf of the other parties, that the headmaster and managers permitted the operation without supervision. I think I have sufficiently indicated the answer on the facts. They did not give an actual permission, and I think that there is no tacit permission. They did not take steps to prevent it, because (1) it had happened on rare occasions only, and (2) they anticipated no danger from the delivery of coke.

It is said that this vehicle was dangerous, an allurement or a trap. A lorry as such cannot be said to be an allurement to children today. As to a tipping lorry, it was not the tipping gear that brought about the accident. No permission was given to the plaintiff to interfere, or to other pupils to interfere. No one in authority anticipated that the pupils would interfere or were interfering. In my view, this disposes of the case against the headmaster, and that against the managers, who stand in the same position as did the headmaster. The case here is put against the managers, not as occupiers, but as superiors of the headmaster.

. . . I have listened carefully to the boys' evidence. I doubt if some of the little boys actually got into the cab and put their heads out. If they did, it was at the last second, and the driver could not get rid of them. In that last second, the plaintiff got on to the rear of the running-board, and a second later before the driver could become acquainted with that fact, the wagon tipped, the boys let go, the wagon collapsed and crushed the boy's leg. It is said that the driver should have taken care to see that the boys were off the wagon. The cause of the accident was not the driver's starting with the boy on the lorry. The cause was the rush of boys to the back, their leap on to it, and its tipping up when the plaintiff was in that dangerous position into which he had put himself. Did the fact that the driver knew of the wagon's attractiveness to boys raise a duty to look if it had attracted them to hang on? I am satisfied that till this happened, no reasonable being could have anticipated sufficient weight to tip it up. The rush of boys caused it to tip up. The allegation is a mere guess; I cannot accept it. The driver says that the boys had never hung on before, and the boys do not suggest that they had been in the habit of jumping on to the back. No former experience would prompt the driver to suppose that they were going to jump. Common experience teaches that boys may jump in this way, but I do not think it was negligent not to look. He could not anticipate that boys hanging on would cause danger.

In those circumstances, the plaintiff fails to make out that the accident was due to the negligence of the headmaster or of the managers or of the Gas Company.

Judgment for the defendants

116   Hudson *v.* Governors of Rotherham Grammar School and Johnson (1938) *Yorkshire Post*, March 24 and 25

WEST RIDING ASSIZES

The courts will not put on a headmaster any higher standard of care than that of a reasonably careful parent.

Facts: The plaintiff was the father of Ralph Hudson, a ten-year-old pupil at Rotherham Grammar School. On April 26, 1937, the boy joined two others who were pushing the roller on the cricket pitch. In some way Hudson went over the roller and underneath, with the result that he sustained two fractures of the skull and other injuries.

The boys had been told that the junior school playing field would be out of bounds for ten days or a fortnight. During break on the morning of the incident Mr Selby Johnson, the master-in-charge of the junior school, had made visits of supervision in various places and, before going back into school he was perfectly satisfied that no boys were out of bounds or that anything untoward was happening. He was in the staff room on school business for only four minutes, and was on the point of leaving when a boy came to tell him about the accident.

The plaintiff brought an action against the governors, the headmaster (Mr Frederick William Field), and the master-in-charge of the junior school, alleging negligence and claiming damages. It was said that after the accident the boy became very nervous, suffered from periodic headaches, and was unable to take part in games or gymnastics. It was contended that, if any sort of watch had been kept, the school authorities could not fail to have known that the boys were using the roller.

The action was tried at the West Riding Assizes at Leeds before Hilbery J., sitting with a jury. The claim against the headmaster was abandoned at the end of the plaintiff's case.

Extract from Summing-up

HILBERY J.: . . . It was not suggested for the plaintiff that anybody could reasonably say that a master must watch boys, not merely in classes, but throughout every moment of their school lives.

What has a reasonably careful parent to do? Supposing a boy of yours has some other little boys, who are friends of his, coming to tea on a Saturday afternoon, and you see them all playing in the garden.

Suppose your garden roller happened to be there—would you consider you had been neglectful of your duty to the parents of those other boys, because for five minutes you had gone into the house and two of them managed to pull the roller over the third?

Would you think that, in those circumstances, you had failed to exercise reasonable supervision as a parent? These things have got to be treated as matters of common sense not to put on Mr Johnson any higher standard of care than that of a reasonably careful parent.

If boys were kept in cotton wool some of them would choke themselves with it. They would manage to have accidents. We always did, members of the jury—we did not always have actions at law afterwards.

You have to consider whether or not you would expect a headmaster to exercise such a degree of care that boys could never get into mischief. Has any reasonable parent yet succeeded in exercising such care as to prevent a boy getting into mischief, and, if he did, what sort of boys should we produce?

Judgment for the defendants

117 Ricketts *v.* Erith Borough Council and Browne [1943]
2 All E.R. 629

KING'S BENCH DIVISION
It is not incumbent upon a local education authority to have a teacher continuously present in a playground during a break.

Facts: The plaintiff, Anne Elizabeth Ricketts, was a pupil at St Fidelis Roman Catholic School, Erith. During the midday break on June 9, 1942, the plaintiff then being aged six, about fifty children were playing in the playground. There was an unlocked gate and, if given permission, the children could leave the playground to go home for lunch or to buy sweets and toys. From time to time one of the teachers went into the playground, but there was no continuous supervision.

A ten-year-old boy left the playground, went across to a nearby shop, and bought some blunted pieces of bamboo made up as a bow and arrow. On his return, unseen by the teachers, he discharged the arrow close to the plaintiff. The arrow splintered the glass of the plaintiff's spectacles, and a piece of the glass penetrated her eye. It was necessary to enucleate the eye.

In an action for damages for negligence against the Borough Council and the shopkeeper, the latter contended that he did not know, and ought not to have known that the child would take the bow and arrow to the playground, nor that he had come from the playground, and he denied that the toy was dangerous.

Extracts from Judgment
TUCKER J.: . . . The facts are these. This is a Roman Catholic School. There were in all at this school some seventy pupils of ages ranging between five and ten. The staff, at the material time, who were dealing with these children, were Sister Bailey, a certificated teacher, Sister Murphy, the headmistress, and another younger uncertificated teacher. This accident happened during the midday break. At twelve o'clock the lessons end, and a number of the children

have lunch at the canteen on the school premises. On the day in question some forty of these children, including Anne Ricketts, the infant plaintiff, had their lunch at the canteen. After that, she and a number of others, went and got their second bottle of milk in a classroom where Sister Bailey supervised the distribution, and as each child finished its milk it went out into the playground to play with the other children, and it would be about one o'clock by the time this batch of children had finished having their milk and had gone out into the playground. There, they would be playing for another half an hour or so, and then it would be time to resume school. Not all children of the school stayed for lunch; some went home. Some children, with permission, who lived nearby, stayed for lunch and went home after lunch for a few minutes and did not play in the playground. Of the children that did play in the playground, some, from time to time, were given permission, if they asked for it, in suitable cases, to leave the playground and go out and purchase sweets or things of that kind; but, of course, they had to ask for permission.

The playground was situate in a lane off the main road, West Street. The entrance to the playground was up the lane off that street—about the length of this court was the description of the headmistress. During this time, after the children had had their milk, and before school was resumed, that is to say, during this period of about half an hour, with the staff that I have described, the practice at this school was for one of these teachers from time to time to go out into the playground to see that all was well; but there was no teacher continuously in the playground throughout the whole period of time, and the gate to the playground was not locked; these children could get out if they were so minded, and, as I have already said, some of them actually went home and others were allowed to go out into the street and buy sweets. Thus they were not locked into this playground, nor was there a teacher continuously present throughout the whole time while these children were playing about in the playground.

During the time when Sister Bailey was not actually present in the play-ground, this little boy, Thomas Fitzgerald, got out and went across the road to Browne's shop, Browne having a shop at which he sells confectionery, tobacco, toys, medicines, and fruit. He is much patronised by the little children who go to this school and a number of other children who go to other schools in the locality; and Thomas Fitzgerald purchased there, for the sum of one penny, two pieces of bamboo—for that is what they are. One of them serves the purpose of an arrow; it is a blunted piece of bamboo; it is not sharpened at either end; it is about fourteen inches in length. The bow is another piece of bamboo, one of the ends of which is rather sharp, at any rate, the ends of the bow are considerably sharper than the end of the arrow; and with a bit of string attached to each end of this pliable piece of bamboo, it constitutes a bow and arrow. Armed with this toy—for that is what it is—he went into the playground, and unfortunately discharged it in very close proximity to this little girl, and broke her spectacles. He says that it went off because he slipped as he was pointing it to the ground. However that may be, he shot it off very close to the little girl, and broke her spectacles.

It is agreed by the teachers that, if they had seen this little boy armed with this bow and arrow and about to discharge it in this rather congested playground, where at any rate there were some fifty children playing about, no doubt all running about in all directions, they would not have allowed him to go on playing with it or using it in those circumstances at that particular time. But there was nobody there who saw him use it, and the whole thing was over and done before they became aware that he had got it.

The infant plaintiff was brought to school and fetched away again by her parents; she was very young, and she stayed to lunch; but a number of the other children, as I have already said, found their way backwards and forwards to the school, and some of them went home to their lunch during the break.

Those are the facts with regard to the school, and it is said that they indicate negligence, and that this accident was the result of that negligence—that lack of supervision enabled the small boy to get out of the playground, to arm himself with something which it is said was dangerous or might be dangerous if he used it in that particular place, and that as a result this accident happened.

The duty of the defendants is that of a reasonably careful parent, and I have come to the conclusion that they were not guilty of any failure to exercise that degree of care which may be expected from a reasonably careful parent. Incidentally, in considering the facts of a case like this, one has to visualise a parent with a very large family, because fifty children playing about in a yard is, of course, a different thing from four or five children playing about together in a garden. That is perfectly true, and it has to be remembered. None the less, I find it impossible to hold that it was incumbent to have a teacher, even tender as were the years of these children and bearing in mind the locality of this school, continuously present in that yard throughout the whole of this break; and nothing short of that would suffice. Unless that is their duty, nothing less is any good, because small children, or any child, can get up to mischief if the parents or teacher's back is turned for a short period of time. I think the evidence in this case shows that the system which prevailed at this school, and that the degree of supervision which was exercised, was in fact reasonably sufficient and adequate, having regard to all the circumstances of the case. I, therefore, hold that the claim against the corporation of Erith as the education authority (whose responsibility, if there was negligence, is not in issue in this case) fails.

With regard to the claim against Browne, I am satisfied that, when he sold this toy to this little boy, he did not apply his mind to the question, and had not got it in his mind whether or not this little boy came from this particular school or from any other school; nor had he got it in mind that the little boy was going back to play in a congested playground. He simply sold this toy to a little boy aged ten, without knowing or thinking whether he was on the way home or on the way to school or where he was going or what he was doing. He sold it to an intelligent, bright looking little boy, ten years old, for a penny. In those circumstances is he liable for the consequences which followed? Incidentally, the evidence before me is that these bamboo sticks, which are called bows and arrows, have been sold by him for a number of years in considerable quantities to children of all ages, and I have had evidence from the wholesalers that they also have supplied great quantities of them for some years, without any ill effects brought to their knowledge, at any rate.

Of course, any article can be a danger handled by young children in close proximity to other young children, and there can be no doubt, as the teachers have said, that they would not have allowed one of these little boys or girls to go shooting this thing near a whole lot of other little children running hither and thither. But I have to consider whether it is an article of such a nature that this shopkeeper was failing in his duty to the public at large in putting such a thing into the hands of an ordinary intelligent little boy of ten years without knowing the particular use that he was going to make of it or where he was going to take it in the immediate future.

The case that has been much relied on is a decision of Atkinson J., *Burfitt v. A. and E. Kille.*[1] In that case the defendants were the proprietors of a shop and they sold to a little boy aged twelve, what was called a "safety pistol" with fifty blank cartridges; and, in dealing with the evidence in the course of his judgment, Atkinson J. described, at page 750, the nature of this pistol and ammunition. He pointed out that it did not come within the prohibition contained in the Fire Arms Act 1937. He said, at page 749:

> "This pistol is designed so as to be outside the definition of these pro-hibited firearms. They are real firearms specially adapted to be used with blank cartridges and so designed that no ready-made bulleted ammunition can be used in them. Despite this, they are dangerous and capable of inflicting serious injuries at close quarters. To describe them as 'safety' pistols is to mislead and to encourage ignorant users to regard them as toys, which they are not."

Then he dealt with the expert evidence that had been called, of a Major Pollard, with regard to this pistol, and he said, at page 750:

> "I think that Major Pollard's summary is well-founded, and I find that the pistol is very dangerous, that the accumulation of fouling in an in-accessible horizontal chamber means a cumulative increase of danger invisible to the owner, that it becomes more dangerous with wear, and that serious wounds can be caused with such a pistol, even when new and in perfect order. Major Pollard added that it was totally unsuitable for sale to schoolboys or young people; that no boy would be aware that the pistol was not functioning normally; and that instructions ought to be given that the fouling should be cleaned out after every five shots. He pointed out that there is no cleansing apparatus supplied with the pistol at all. Therefore, in my view, the pistol sold along with the ammunition did constitute a thing dangerous in itself in the hands of Alexander, a boy of twelve."

1. [1939] 2 K.B. 743; [1939] 2 All E.R. 372.

Those are the facts that Atkinson J. found with regard to the instrument that had caused the damage in that particular case; and dealing with the law which, of course, I accept, he states it as follows, at page 746:

"The question when a seller of a chattel owes a duty of care to persons other than the purchaser has been repeatedly debated, and no one can pretend that the law is clearly settled. It is clear in the present case that there was no duty based on contract, but, in my opinion, the cases establish the following propositions. Firstly, if A places in the hands of B a chattel which belongs to a class of things dangerous in themselves in the hands of such a person as B, as distinguished from a chattel which is dangerous only because of some defect peculiar to the particular chattel handed over, a duty of care rests on A not only towards the recipient, but also towards all such persons as may reasonably be contemplated as likely to be endangered."

That being the law and those being the facts in the case cited to me, I respectfully accept the law, and the question is whether the facts in the present case are anything like the facts in that case, and I think they are not. I think that these two pieces of bamboo, with the piece of string attached, cannot possibly be put into the same category as the pistol and ammunition which were there described by Atkinson J. I find it quite impossible to say that this is a thing dangerous in itself in the hands of this particular purchaser. Of course, anything is capable, as I have already said, of becoming dangerous in certain circumstances in the hands of children, and this is certainly not a thing that a parent would allow his child to discharge all over the place in a confined space where there were a number of children together; but it might be a very suitable toy to use in a garden where there were only a few children about. I find it quite impossible to say that it is a thing dangerous in itself, even in the hands of a child of ten, so as to bring it within the class of article with which Atkinson J. was dealing in that case, and for these reasons, regretting as one does this lamentable accident, I find it quite impossible to say that it has been established that either of these defendants is responsible, in law, for what happened. Therefore there will be judgment with costs for both defendants.

Judgment with costs for the defendants

118 Rich and another *v.* London County Council [1953] 2 All E.R. 376

COURT OF APPEAL

A local education authority is under no obligation to prevent boys having access to a heap of coke in a playground.

Facts: The plaintiff, Derek Anthony Rich, was a pupil at Montem School, Tollington Park. On February 16, 1950, when he was about seven years of age, a very young boy hurled a lump of coke at him, causing injuries leading to the enucleation of his left eye. The coke had been obtained from a heap lying unfenced on a part of the senior school playground.

The plaintiff sued the London County Council for damages for negligence in the management of the school, alleging that the defendants had failed to provide adequate supervision, or to fence or safeguard the heaps of coke though they knew well that the children were in the habit of playing on them and using lumps of coke as missiles.

The case was heard by Slade J., who found that the council had adequate reasons for storing the coke where they did. There had been adequate supervision, exhortation, and instruction; but, with the knowledge which they had, or ought to have had, they should have removed the coke or put up some form of fence or wooden structure which would have prevented the boys, for all practical purposes, from having access to the coke. He awarded £1,750 damages and £348 3s. 9d. special damages.

The defendants appealed.

Extract from Judgment

SINGLETON L.J. . . . . Counsel for the defendants has submitted that the judgment of Slade J. is wrong, that it goes too far, and it places too high a duty on those who manage and conduct such a school as this was. Counsel on behalf of the plaintiffs has submitted that this was a question of fact for the decision of the learned judge, and that there was evidence on which he could come to the conclusion at which he arrived. I need hardly say that a finding of fact by the judge of first instance based on the evidence of witnesses whom he sees and hears will always receive full consideration in this court, and it is only if this court is satisfied that the conclusion of the judge is wrong that it will interfere. Counsel is right to a large extent in describing this question as a question of fact, but before a proper decision can be reached on that question of fact it is necessary to ascertain the measure of duty owed to a child by those responsible for the management of a school.

The learned judge was of the opinion that the defendants were obliged to store additional coke somewhere, and, as there was no place under cover in which they could put it, they put it in the senior boys' playground. The fact that there was this heap of coke in the senior boys' playground was an anxiety and a burden to the teachers and to the school authorities. The headmistress had complained and reports had been made from time to time. It was known that children often throw missiles at one another. The little boy who lost his eye was asked about it, and he said that he knew that things should not be thrown and that he would be punished if he did throw things. The schoolkeeper said, in his evidence, that whenever he found boys playing on the coke he chased them away. They were a little out of hand until January 1950, when a new headmaster came.

As I have said, Slade J. found that there was no practical alternative for the county council to adopt. They had to have a heap of coke in the yard. Further, he found that the infants were supposed to keep to their own part of the playground, and not to go into the playground which was for older children. He found that there was adequate supervision, and he accepted the evidence of

the headmistress and of the other mistresses and helpers who were called that
there was adequate supervision and that no supervision would have prevented
this accident, for children will do some things at a time when the teacher's
back is turned. He found, further, that the boys knew that they would be
punished if they threw missiles, and he said: "The question resolves itself into
whether something ought to have been done physically to prevent access to
these dumps of coke so long as they remained in playgrounds accessible to
children, and to as many as two hundred and seventy children in the infants'
school alone. . . ."

We have to consider whether or not the judgment of Slade J. can be supported on the facts proved before him and accepted by him. Perhaps the most
important of his findings is that there was adequate supervision. There was a
large number of pupils in the infants' side of this school, but there were plenty
of people to supervise them, and they were properly supervised during their
playtime. That is the finding of the learned judge. Having considered the
authorities, he adopted the test stated by Lord Esher M.R. in *Williams* v.
Eady.[1] That was an action by a boy against a schoolmaster for an injury
alleged to have been caused by his negligence in leaving a bottle of phosphorus
about. Lord Esher M.R. said: " . . . as to the law on the subject there could be
no doubt; and it was correctly laid down by the learned judge, that the schoolmaster was bound to take such care of his boys as a careful father would take
of his boys, and there could not be a better definition of the duty of a schoolmaster." That test has been the one adopted ever since. Slade J. continued:

> "I feel sympathy with the London County Council for the position in
> which they found themselves, with adequate reasons for storing the coke
> where they did, no practical or practicable alternative, adequate supervision
> (as I have found), adequate exhortation and instructions (as I have found).
> But with the knowledge that they had, and, if they did not have it, with the
> knowledge that they ought to have had (and I am satisfied that they did
> have it), what should they have done, bearing in mind their duty to which
> I have already referred? It seems to me that there were only one of two
> things that they could have done to discharge that duty, and that is: (i) re-
> move the coke from the playgrounds, or (ii) take steps to ensure that it was
> no longer accessible to the boys. If they could not do (i), then they could
> have done (ii). They need not have put up a wire fence in case it had the
> risk which Dr Topping envisaged. What they could have done was to put
> up some form of fence or wooden structure which would have, for all prac-
> tical purposes, prevented the boys from having access to the coke. . . . Posing
> the question to myself: What would a careful father have done towards his
> own son, with knowledge of that risk which his son was running being
> pointed out to him over and over again; would such a father have left the
> coke there unprotected, with the consequences which the father knew might
> ensue and which, in due course, did ensue? I answer the question by saying

1. (1893) 10 T.L.R. 41; see page 240, *supra*.

that no careful parent would so have acted, and I accordingly find that the defendants were negligent in not taking steps to protect the coke or prevent the boys from having access to the coke."

I cannot accept that. It seems to me that it is putting much too high a burden on the education authority, and, in my view, it is stating the way in which a father would approach the duty to his children in too general a way. I wonder how many yards in private houses or attached to public buildings have been without some fuel in the yard or yards in recent years. One who looks from a window in this building can see coke or some other fuel in the yard. It has to be kept there, I assume, because of the difficulty in getting regular supplies. That difficulty may be resolved. As the learned judge pointed out, it is regarded as a temporary difficulty, but he says that a careful father, looking on a matter of this kind, would say: "I must have this fenced for the safety of my children." What expense would be incurred in the small back yard of a private house or what it would be in the case of one school in the London County Council area I do not know. I do know, however, from the evidence that no one said that an accident of this kind, arising from the throwing of coke, had ever happened before, and no one said that any infant was known to have taken a piece of coke and thrown it at another child in this school before. Yet it is said that the duty of the education authority is either not to have the heap of coke there or to put up some form of fence or wooden structure which would, for all practical purposes, have prevented the boys from having access to the coke. That would mean putting up some structure over which boys could not climb, for, if it were something over which boys could climb, it would not, for all practical purposes, prevent the boys from having access to the coke. I cannot accept that as the duty in these circumstances.

Slade J. found that the supervision at this school was adequate. The school-keeper said that there had been no trouble in regard to the coke since the new headmaster came in or about January 1950, approximately a month before this accident. An accident of a most unfortunate kind occurred, but I do not see that the defendants can be blamed for it. If this be a question of fact, I am bound to say that I take a different view from that of the learned judge, but I am not sure that it is wholly a question of fact. It is necessary to look at the test which Slade J. laid down. He found that in the circumstances the duty on the London County Council was to do one of two things: either to remove the coke or to take steps to ensure that it was no longer accessible to the boys. I do not agree with that. If their supervision was adequate, it was not necessary that they should take steps to ensure that the coke was no longer accessible to the boys. Their duty was to exercise the care which a careful parent would exercise in the like circumstances. On the evidence in this case I do not find that they failed in that duty. For those reasons I am of opinion that this appeal should be allowed and that judgment should be entered for the defendants.

Appeal allowed

119 Clarke v. Monmouthshire County Council (1954) 52 L.G.R. 246

COURT OF APPEAL

The duty of a schoolmaster does not extend to the constant supervision of all the boys in his care all the time; only reasonable supervision is required.

Facts: The plaintiff, Stuart Clark, was a pupil at Tredegar Grammar School, Monmouthshire. During the course of a morning break in July 1951 there was a scuffle in the school yard. The plaintiff and another boy got hold of a third boy, Roger Thomas, of about the same age, in order to take his knife. Thomas drew a sheath knife from his belt and lunged with it, not deliberately or intentionally. The knife struck a very vulnerable part of the plaintiff's left leg, which had to be amputated.

The plaintiff brought an action for damages arising from injuries due to negligence. Mr Commissioner Goodman Roberts, sitting at Newport, Monmouthshire, found for the plaintiff. The defendant authority appealed.

Extract from Judgment

DENNING L.J.: . . . One can well understand the feelings of parents when a child comes from school injured in this way; they feel that there must have been some negligence somewhere. Indeed the Commissioner so found. The question for us is whether there is any evidence on which he could so find. It is not suggested that any of the masters knew that Roger Thomas had this knife on that day. But it is said that they ought to have known it: they ought to have seen him with it, and they ought to have taken it from him. Alternatively, it is said there was no proper supervision on that day in the playground, and if there had been the scuffle would have been stopped. There is evidence to show that some of the boys had on a few occasions taken sheath knives to school—some of the boys said so themselves—but I cannot find any evidence that the staff knew or ought to have known of any danger from it. The headmaster had not seen any boys coming to school with knives, nor had any others of the staff, except Mr James, the senior master. He said: "Prior to their going to camp it was quite the thing for them to bring their equipment to school, including a sheath knife, and under those circumstances I have seen them. . . . A few of them brought them to me down in the workshop for me to polish them up." He said that they used to bring them to him in the workshop, not on their belts, but in their hands, so that he might polish them. He used to wrap them up in paper and give them to the boys to take back again. That is the sum total of the evidence that the staff knew about the knives. It shows that knives were brought for an innocent purpose not likely to result in danger. It does not show that the staff knew that boys brought knives to this school simply to play with them, or to take pride in them, or for any purpose likely to result in danger. It was suggested that knives should have been banned altogether, but I think that the headmaster and Miss James, the form mistress, took quite a proper standpoint. Their evidence was to this effect: "If I had seen a boy with a sheath knife in his belt I would ask him what he had it for. If he was a boy of sixteen or seventeen and had a good reason for it, such as that he was going to camp, I would let him keep it; but if he was a young boy and there was no good reason or explanation of it, then I would take it away." In other words, it would depend on the circumstances what action was taken by the staff. This I think was right.

I do not think that the staff could be expected to have seen this knife on Roger Thomas. He had come to school with a lumber jacket on, and the sheath of the knife might protrude just below the jacket; but he sat at the back of the class and it is quite likely that he kept it concealed. It was an isolated action which was not observed by the staff and of which they had no reason to be aware. They were not negligent in not observing it.

The second point was that there ought to have been more supervision on that day. This was a day towards the end of term when the boys were collecting their books, and there was not the same routine as during the rest of the term. It was said that in the playground on this occasion there was no prefect, whereas usually there were two prefects. Apparently, the two prefects had been sent out to mark points on a cross-country run. I do not think that was negligence. The master on duty passed through the yard twice during the break. The duty of a school does not extend to constant supervision of all the boys all the time, that is not practicable. Only reasonable supervision is required. I do not think it can be said that the school was negligent in not having a master on duty all the time. Furthermore, the incident happened in a flash. There was just a scuffle between two boys trying to get a knife from a third boy. It was the sort of scuffle which would pass unnoticed in a play-ground in the ordinary way. The incident would take place in the fraction of a second which the presence of prefects, or indeed of a master, would not have done anything to prevent at all.

It seems to me that the allegation that there was negligence on the part of the school authorities is not well founded, indeed there is no evidence of it. In my opinion the decision of the Commissioner was in error and should be reversed.

Appeal allowed

120 Price v. Caernarvonshire County Council (1960) *The Times*, February 11

COURT OF APPEAL

Even if there has been a failure of supervision, the question arises whether the best of supervision could have prevented an accident.

Facts: The plaintiff, David Conrad Price, was a pupil at St Mary's Primary School, Garth Road, Bangor.

On April 30, 1956, the plaintiff was playing rounders in the boys' play-ground during the midday luncheon break. The game had been arranged by the boys themselves. It started with the use of a stick, then the boys played with their hands, and finally one boy in breach of instructions took the rounders bat from the dining room and the boys played with that. While one boy was receiving the bowling he missed two services, took a swipe at the third service and missed again, but the bat flew out of his hand and struck the plaintiff's right eye. The plaintiff was standing in the queue of boys waiting to bat.

The plaintiff lost the sight of his right eye as a result of the accident, and brought an action against the Caernarvonshire County Council for damages for injuries. It was alleged that the bat was defective in not having a proper handle with twine but, at Chester Assizes, Barry J. found that that case had not been made out and that the bat was not defective. The plaintiff was awarded £2,500 damages.

The defendants appealed.

Extracts from Judgments
SELLERS L.J.: . . . The school had limited playground accommodation. Because of its restricted nature and not because of any danger of the bat flying out from the batsman's hand, the use of a stick or bat had been prohibited by the headmaster, and the boys were required to play with their hands. It might be said that the prohibition of a bat was setting a high standard, but having imposed it, the headmaster was held to have been negligent in failing to prevent the use of the bat by having adequate supervision of the midday break games. The headmaster did not know of the use of a stick or bat, but the judge held that he ought to have known of it. The judge applied the right standard when he said that it would be a disservice to the community if schools were required to exercise permanent or continuous supervision of normal games played by schoolboys.

It was accepted that supervision of midday games consisted of one tour of inspection of the school building and the playground by a member of staff. On the day in question the headmaster himself went round, but he did not see the boys playing with a bat or stick. The judge found that that was because the headmaster was not vigilant enough when he went on his tour of inspection. But when the headmaster paid his visit the evidence was consistent with the game being played by the boys with their hands. It was not established that the bat was used at that time.

The judge formed a favourable view of the headmaster and his staff, and said that they were careful and experienced schoolmasters. It would therefore be wrong to hold that there was a failure of supervision when there was no evidence to justify the finding that the relevant inspection was cursory and inadequate. Even if there had been a failure of supervision, the difficult question would arise whether the best of supervision could have prevented this type of accident.

Although it was a very careful judgment and I feel great sympathy for the boy, the appeal must be allowed.

ORMEROD L.J.: . . . The standard to be applied is that of the reasonably careful parent, which involves a reasonable amount of supervision. The case really turns on the supervision exercised during the midday break and the judge's finding that it was insufficient could not be supported by the evidence.

HARMAN L.J.: . . . The judge had reasoned that owing to lack of supervision the boys had made a habit of using a stick; that as a result on this occasion they were emboldened enough to use a forbidden bat; and that without the bat the accident would never have happened. So stated, there were several leaps in the air. It was not any lack of supervision which caused this accident. It was just as probable in an open field when a group of boys were playing an organized and supervised game. The peril of the bat slipping from the batsman's hand was not one anticipated by any of the experts who gave evidence. It follows that unless rounders is to be treated as so dangerous as not to be allowed, the appeal must succeed.

Appeal allowed

121 Newton *v.* Mayor and Corporation of West Ham (1963)
The Guardian, July 11

QUEEN'S BENCH DIVISION
An education authority is not liable for injury suffered by a pupil in the course of rough play in the playground merely because there are insufficient supervisors to watch all parts of the yard all the time.

Facts: The plaintiff, Graham Newton, was a pupil at the Central Park Infants' School, East Ham. On December 30, 1960, when the plaintiff was about four-and-a-half years old, an older boy threw a piece of coke at another boy, and inadvertently hit the plaintiff in the right eye. He was said at the hearing to have permanently reduced vision in that eye.

An action for damages was brought against the Mayor and Corporation, as local education authority, alleging negligence by want of adequate supervision.

Extract from Judgment
LORD PARKER C.J.: . . . The accident happened at lunch-time on December 30, 1960, when the plaintiff was in the playground talking to some other boys. Mrs Glading, the welfare supervisor, was in charge of the playground and was aware of nothing unusual until the plaintiff and some other boys ran up to her and said that he had been hurt.

The plaintiff's father sued on his son's behalf, alleging that the school authorities were negligent in providing insufficient supervision in the playground. The court is satisfied that Mrs Glading was not personally negligent, and the case narrows down to the proposition that she should have had some assistance. There were some thirty-five small boys in the playground and they had all been told that they were not to meddle with the coke.

The boys have given evidence that there was a fracas going on for about ten minutes during which boys spat at one another, and threw missiles. The court is satisfied that this account was exaggerated, and the suggestion that Mrs Glading should have seen this disturbance and dealt with it is not well founded. Quite clearly, the throwing that did take place occurred when Mrs Glading was looking at other children in another part of the playground. The court is quite unable to say that the authorities had been negligent. The case will be dismissed, with no order as to costs.

Judgment for the defendants

122   Martin *v*. Middlesbrough Corporation (1965) 63 L.G.R. 385

COURT OF APPEAL

A local education authority may be liable for damages in negligence if there is a failure to make and enforce suitable arrangements against foreseeable risks in connexion with the use of milk bottles in schools.

Facts: The plaintiff, Juliet Martin, was a pupil at Archibald School, Middlesbrough. On December 9, 1960, when she was eleven years old, she slipped on the icy surface of the playground, and cut her hand on a piece of broken glass lying on a drainpipe grating. The flexor tendons of the middle and ring fingers of her right hand were severed. After three operations the flexion of these fingers was still severely limited, and the little finger was also affected.

In an action against the Corporation, as local education authority, at York Assizes, McKenna J. dismissed the claim. Invited to say what damages he would have assessed had he found for the plaintiff, he fixed the sum at £1,250.

The plaintiff appealed against the judgment, and also asked the Court of Appeal to say that the sum stated was, in any case, too low.

Extracts from Judgments

WILLMER L.J.: . . . On December 9, 1960, when she [the plaintiff] was a girl of eleven years of age, she was unfortunate enough to meet with an accident while playing in the school playground during the midday break, when she slipped on the icy surface of the ground and fell, cutting her hand on a piece of broken glass. The glass was lying on a grating over a drainhole outside the girls' latrine, which is across the playground and roughly opposite the senior girls' entrance to the school, and something less than twenty yards therefrom.

Unhappily, the plaintiff's injury proved to be somewhat more serious than might have been expected and has resulted in some degree of permanent disability. It is not suggested that the plaintiff was in any way at fault herself. The question is whether the defendants are shown to have been guilty of negligence causing the accident.

The defendants, of course, are not insurers, but they do owe a duty to exercise care for the safety of their pupils. Under the Occupiers' Liability Act 1957[1] they owe a common duty of care, but the Act provided (perhaps some-

1. 5 & 6 Eliz. 2, c. 31.

what unnecessarily) that they must be prepared for children to be less careful than adults. So far as the standard of care is concerned, I am prepared to accept the submission made to us by Mr Campbell, that what is required is that which would be expected of a prudent parent in relation to his own children. It is alleged that the defendants fell short of this standard in allowing broken glass to be present on this playground or, alternatively, in allowing children to play there when there was broken glass on the ground. In that connection much reliance has been placed on an admission made by the school caretaker that there were quite often pieces of broken glass in the playground, sometimes as often as twice a week. In those circumstances, it has been contended for the plaintiff that this is almost a case of *res ipsa loquitur*. It seems to me that on any view it must be accepted that the plaintiff makes out a strong prima facie case.

It is necessary, therefore, to look closely at the precautions which the defendants have taken to minimise the risk of accident through broken glass. It is accepted, I think, on both sides that the broken glass which caused this injury was probably part of a broken milk bottle, and that it probably came from one of the milk bottles consumed at the school. The school milk, which is contained in one-third pint bottles, was delivered to the school in crates first thing in the morning before the children arrived, and the crates were left in a small recess against the wall just to the left of the senior girls' entrance. In addition to the school milk there were usually a few loose pint bottles for the use of the staff, which were delivered at the same time and left in the same place. The routine was that when the children arrived the crates and loose bottles were carried indoors by senior boys or girls, and the crates were taken to a landing on the upper floor, which is the floor on which the senior girls' classrooms are. From there the milk was distributed to the classrooms by senior girls or monitresses for consumption by the girls immediately before the mid-morning break, which was between 10.30 and 10.45. The girls drank their milk in the classrooms and were supposed to replace their empty bottles in the crates, after which the crates were then collected by monitresses and taken back to the landing at the beginning of the mid-morning break.

According to the plaintiff's evidence, the normal routine was for the crates then to be taken by monitresses straight downstairs back to the recess by the side of the entrance in the playground and stacked there. There they would remain until collected by the milkman on his afternoon round somewhere between 1 o'clock and 3 o'clock. The plaintiff said that there were always some girls who were slow drinkers, and who consequently did not finish their drinking before the crates were collected. Those girls had to carry their own bottles downstairs, and would then put them in a crate if there was space, otherwise they would stand them loose on the ground alongside the stack of crates. Sometimes, she said, one girl might bring down an armful of loose bottles. If this evidence from the plaintiff is right, it is obvious that with hundreds of children playing on the playground, both during the mid-morning break and

later during the midday break, there would necessarily be abundant opportunity for the occasional breakage of a milk bottle.

But the evidence of the headmistress (whom the judge said that he found an
impressive witness) was rather different from that of the plaintiff. She said
that the crates of empties were not taken downstairs until the midday break
(that is, after 12 o'clock), and, if that be so, it is clear that opportunities for
breakages would be somewhat reduced. Further, she said that it was exceptional for there to be any loose bottles, as the girls mostly replaced their bottles
in the crates, as they were supposed to do. This conflict of evidence between
the plaintiff and the headmistress was never in terms resolved by the judge.
But there was evidence from the school caretaker, which corroborated the
plaintiff's evidence to the extent of showing that quite often there were loose
bottles standing on the ground alongside the crates in the playground, and this
he regarded as dangerous. I am quite sure that the headmistress was correctly
describing what was supposed to be the routine, but notwithstanding that I am
left with the impression that the plaintiff probably knew more about what
usually happened in practice. The collection of the empty milk bottles into
crates, according to the headmistress, was supposed to be supervised by a
mistress, but no other mistress, apart from the headmistress, was called as
a witness in this case.

It is complained on behalf of the plaintiff that this system of disposing of
the empty milk bottles was a source of danger particularly on occasions when
there were loose bottles which had not been put into the crates. With children
in large numbers playing in the playground, both during the mid-morning
break and during the midday break, there must always have been the risk of
a bottle being broken through a child being careless or even mischievous. If
this did occur, it would, of course, be easy enough for a piece of broken glass
to be kicked almost anywhere on the playground. Against this the headmistress said that in the eighteen years during which she had been at the
school before the accident she had never known of an accident taking place
through this cause. That circumstance is much relied on by the defendants as
showing that the risk of accident through breakage of a milk bottle was really
extremely small.

One of the duties of the caretaker employed by the defendants was to keep
the playground well swept and tidy at all times. He said in evidence that he
regularly swept the playground twice a day, once in the early morning before
the children arrived and again in the afternoon after afternoon play. The
judge, having heard his evidence, said that he was satisfied that the caretaker
carried out his duties faithfully and well. But, as has been pointed out to us
by Mr Campbell, if there was a risk of broken glass occurring through milk
bottles being stacked out of doors during the mid-morning break, this sweeping
would be of no value for the purpose of obviating any such risk. . . .

In this court we have been invited to consider various other alternative
methods which, it is said, could have been adopted for disposing of empty milk
bottles so as to eliminate or reduce the risk of accidents occurring through

breakages. . . . These all sound very attractive suggestions, but for my part I should have been happier if they had all been fully canvassed in the court below when the witnesses were giving their evidence, so that the defendants could have had a proper opportunity to deal with them.

There are however, as I think, two respects in which the evidence actually given was sufficient to enable this court to form a conclusion. First, the head-mistress described the place where the full crates of bottles were stacked at the top of the stairs as "a very convenient corner" where there was "plenty of room." If that is so, then it must have been an equally convenient place for stacking the empties and keeping them until such time as the children had finished playing in the playground. Had this been done, I am satisfied that there would have been less risk of breakages, and this at least would have reduced the possibility of broken glass from milk bottles finding its way on to the playground. Secondly, the headmistress said that when the empties were carried down by the girls and stacked outside, there were always two mistresses on duty, and they would see that the girls did it. This answer at least recognised the need for supervision if and when the bottles were brought downstairs and stacked outside. I have no doubt that there ought to be such supervision. But the evidence given by the plaintiff as to the prevailing routine for bringing the bottles down seems to show that in actual practice there was in fact no such supervision. Moreover, as I have said, the defendants did not see fit to call any mistress to prove that such supervision was in fact exercised. These are two respects in which, as it seems to me, the defendant's arrangements for disposing of the empty milk bottles could have been improved. Had either of these procedures been adopted, the risk of broken glass finding its way on to the playground could have been much reduced.

I am, of course, reluctant to differ from the conclusion reached by the judge on what is basically a question of fact, especially where he has had the oppor-tunity of seeing and hearing the witnesses. I recognise how easy it is to succumb to the temptation of being wise after the event, and how easily one's judgment may be swayed by the fact of the plaintiff having sustained such serious injuries. But in the end I have felt driven to the conclusion that the plaintiff did make out a case against the defendants, which the defendants have not succeeded in answering. I feel satisfied that Mr Campbell was right in submitting that the judge never really appreciated just how dangerous to children milk bottles can be. In my judgment, on the evidence, the risk of an accident such as this occurring was a reasonably foreseeable risk against which the defendants could and should have guarded by making better arrangements for the disposal of empty milk bottles. I do not think that the arrangements which they in fact made were such as would commend themselves to any reasonably prudent parent.

Accordingly, in my view the judge came to a wrong conclusion so far as liability is concerned, and should have found in favour of the plaintiff.

That makes it necessary to go on to consider the question of damages. The judge, at the request of counsel for the plaintiff, did proceed to express his

view as to what the damages should be, in the event of the defendants being
held liable. He arrived at a figure of £1,250, and we are now invited on behalf
of the plaintiff to say that this figure is much too low. . . .

The result of the accident, in a sentence, was that the flexor tendons of the
middle and ring fingers of the plaintiff's right hand were severed. Since the
accident she has had to undergo three operations, but unhappily these have
been only partially successful. She is left with the flexion of these two fingers
severely limited, and it appears that the little finger is also indirectly
affected. . . .

The plaintiff has now reached the age of sixteen and what the future holds
in store for her is largely a matter of conjecture. She may, of course, marry and
spend the rest of her life as a housewife, and if that should happen then clearly
the loss of dexterity in her right hand will be a severe handicap in the performance of ordinary household duties. If on the other hand, she seeks to earn
her living as a wage-earner, it is manifest that her earning capacity will be
seriously and probably permanently affected. The condition of her right hand
is something with which she has to live for the rest of her life.

In those circumstances, without elaborating the matter any further, I am
satisfied that counsel for the plaintiff was well-founded in submitting that an
award of £1,250 is too low, and so much too low that this court ought to
interfere. I would substitute an award of £2,000. . . .

DAVIES L.J.: I agree. . . . I think that on the evidence the risk was a serious
one, a risk which the defendants should have seriously considered, and a risk
which called for the taking of reasonable precautions by the defendants. . . .

In my judgment, however, there were two steps which the defendants could
have taken which would have gone a long way to protect the children from the
possibility of danger from broken glass. In the first place, it should have been
a strict rule that all empties should be placed in crates inside the building; that
the empties should be carried down in crates only; that no child should carry
a bottle down in her hand, and that in no circumstances should loose bottles,
other than crated bottles, be left in the recess. . . . Another and even better
system (which as Willmer L.J. has said, was not apparently investigated at the
trial) would be to add to the rules which I have above suggested the provision
of a large cupboard, bin, or locker in which the crates could be deposited to
await removal by the milkman. . . .

My conclusion, therefore, on the evidence in this case of the frequent
presence of broken bottles in the playground and the frequent standing of
loose bottles by the crates in the recess, is that the defendants knew, or ought
to have known, that there was an obvious and serious risk of injury to the
children, and that they took no steps whatever to prevent or lessen that risk.
They were, therefore, negligent. . . .

SALMON L.J.: . . . To my mind the most salient fact in this case is that prior
to the accident broken milk bottles were quite often found on this playground. . . . It is self-evident, I should have thought, that broken milk bottles
on playgrounds are dangerous. . . . It is true that for a period of eighteen years

(I will assume that milk was being delivered at the school all the time) no accident occurred. All I can say is that the school and the pupils were indeed very fortunate. It is remarkable if during the whole of that time there were broken milk bottles lying about with the frequency to which the defendants deposed that no accident did in fact occur. I do not think that any prudent parent or any prudent schoolmaster would in any circumstances have accepted broken milk bottles on a playground with anything like the frequency that they were on the playground in this case. To my mind, once the authorities knew about the frequent presence of broken milk bottles (and it is quite plain that they knew, or ought to have known this fact) they should have said to themselves: How did they get there? I do not think that one would need the deductive faculties of a Sherlock Holmes or even any high degree of academic distinction immediately to appreciate how the broken milk bottles did get on to this playground. . . .

I am unable to accept the finding of the judge that there was no serious risk. I think that there was a very serious risk of serious injury to the children; indeed, it was perhaps a miracle that an accident of this nature had not happened before.

Appeal allowed

[NOTE: This case stresses the need not only to provide that there is a satisfactory system designed to provide for the safety of the pupils of a school, but also the necessity to ensure that the system is strictly enforced.]

(I) PERSONAL ERRANDS FOR TEACHERS

123 Smith *v*. Martin and Kingston-upon-Hull Corporation
[1911] 2 K.B. 775

COURT OF APPEAL

Education includes the inculcation of habits of order, obedience and courtesy and orders directed to this purpose are within the scope of the teacher's employment.

Facts: The plaintiff, Amy Smith, was a thirteen-year-old pupil at Mersey Street Elementary School, Hull, where she had reached the sixth standard. She had completed two courses in cookery, and was undertaking a third; she had also had two courses in laundry work. The defendant, Miss Emily Martin, was the plaintiff's teacher. On the day of the accident Miss Martin did not feel well, and intended to have her lunch in the teachers' common room. Just before the recreation break she sent the plaintiff to poke the fire and draw the damper in that room. While so doing the plaintiff's pinafore caught fire and she sustained serious burns. She sued the Kingston-upon-Hull Corporation and Miss Martin, alleging that the latter had acted "negligently and improperly and in violation of her duties for the safeguarding of the plaintiff."

The action was tried at Leeds by Lawrance J. sitting with a special jury who awarded the plaintiff £300 damages. Judgment was entered against Miss Martin, the learned judge holding that her act was not done by her as a part of the work of carrying on the school, but was done for her own private purposes; the Corporation—having discharged their duty in appointing a competent teacher—not being liable for acts of the teacher which had no relation to the actual educational work of the school.

Miss Martin's appeal against judgment was dismissed, it being held that it was impossible to say that there was no evidence of negligence fit for the consideration of the jury.

The plaintiff also appealed against judgment in favour of the Kingston-upon-Hull Corporation.

Cur. adv. vult

Extracts from Judgments on the Plaintiff's Appeal
VAUGHAN WILLIAMS L.J.: I think that this appeal should be allowed. I have read the judgments of Fletcher Moulton L.J. and Farwell L.J. and agree in the results of them and in their reasoning. I only wish to add that in the case of *Ching* v. *Surrey County Council*,[1] which was, as this is, a case of a provided school, the argument was put forward, and overruled, that the managers were an independent statutory body which is not as a whole appointed by the county council, being partly appointed by the minor local authority, and therefore could not be considered as their agents or servants, and that such bodies, who in point of fact deal with the matters connected with the management of a school, do so as independent statutory bodies, by virtue of the provisions of the statute, and not as the delegates or agents of the county council; so that the principle *qui facit per alium facit per se*, by reason of which a principal or master is made responsible for the act or omission of his agent or servant, is not applicable. A similar, although not identical, argument was put before us, and is really disposed of by that case, as well as by *Shrimpton* v. *Hertfordshire County Council*[2] in the House of Lords. I think that the decision of Lawrance J. was wrong, and that this appeal should be allowed.

FLETCHER MOULTON L.J.: . . . I wish to refer explicitly to the decision of the House of Lords in *Shrimpton* v. *Hertfordshire County Council*, as it appears to me on further consideration that their decision has a direct bearing on the present case. In *Shrimpton's* case the House of Lords held that a jury was entitled to hold it to be negligence to allow a country girl of twelve years of age to ride to school in an ordinary brake without a conductor to help her in and out, even though she had been accustomed to ride in that way and in that brake for some months. Accepting this, I must, as indicating the standard of care with regard to children of this age that the tribunal of final appeal holds it reasonable for a jury to adopt, I think it impossible to say that a jury was perverse in holding it to be negligent to send a child of about the same age

1. [1910] 1 K.B. 736; see page 194, *supra*.
2. (1911) 104 L.T. 145; see page 53, *supra*.

wearing a print pinafore to poke the fire and draw out the damper in a grate of this construction with which she was not familiar.

The main contention on behalf of the education authority, and that to which the judge of first instance gave effect, was that it was not liable for the act of the teacher, first, because the relation of the education authority to the teacher was not that of master and servant, and, secondly, that even if the teacher must be held to be under a contract of service with the education authority, this particular act was so completely outside the scope of the teacher's employment that the employer was not liable in respect of it. With regard to the first point I confess that I am quite unable to follow the argument in favour of the education authority. The school was a provided school under the control of the defendant corporation as education authority. They had with regard to it all the powers and duties of a school board and school attendance committee under the Elementary Education Acts 1870–1900, and thus had the entire control of the school. It is true that they exercised this control and management through an education committee, but that would not alter their responsibility. It was contended that we ought to hold that the employment of a teacher is *in pari materia* with the employment of a physician, and that this case therefore came under the class of cases where it has been held that a person whose duty it is to provide medical attendance has discharged that duty when he was appointed a competent medical man, and that he is not responsible for the negligence of the doctor so appointed. The analogy, in my opinion, is a false one. The position of a medical man is in such matters a very special one and bears no resemblance to that of a teacher of an elementary school. The layman is presumably incapable of judging of the right treatment to be adopted by the medical man, and accordingly he is not required to interfere with it or even warranted in doing so. But the education authority can and ought to take cognisance of the way in which the teaching is given, and, although it is rightly guided to a great extent by the advice of the teacher, it can direct the teacher what to do and what not to do, and it is clear that he must obey. Speaking for myself, I can see nothing in the position of an elementary teacher, appointed by an education authority to carry out its statutory duties of providing education for the children under its care, which distinguishes the teacher, in respect of his being under a contract of service, from any other official, and the ordinary consequences as regards liability for the acts of a servant must attach in such a case.

But there remains the further question: was the direction given by the teacher to the plaintiff so completely outside the scope of the employment that the education authority is not liable for the consequences? There is no doubt that the facts of the case go some way to support this contention. They seem to be as follows. In the schoolhouse there was a room appropriated to the use of the teachers. It had a fire in it, and on the present occasion the teacher, who had been unwell for a few days, was minded to take her meal in that room instead of going to her home for the purpose. Accordingly during the lesson and shortly before recreation time (when she would take her meal) she sent the plaintiff to the teacher's room to poke the fire and to draw out the damper in order that she might be able to heat her food, and it was in obeying this command that the child's pinafore caught fire and she was injured. It was strongly contended on behalf of the education authority that such an order as this was not within her duty as teacher, and that her employer was no more liable in respect of it than if she had asked the child to run an errand for her in the street and the child had been injured in so doing. Notwithstanding the skilful argument of Mr Scott Fox I am of opinion that in this case the education authority is liable. We must recognise that the position of a teacher is peculiar in this respect, that immediate obedience is expected on the part of the children, as otherwise it would be impossible to maintain that discipline which is so indispensable to effective teaching. It would not be reasonable to hold that children ought to be able to draw the line between what is within the intended ambit of the teacher's authority and that which is just outside of it, and to limit the liability of the education authority to orders given by the teacher which are such as she was intended to give. . . . In my opinion, the teacher was put in a position in which it was intended that her commands should be obeyed by the children, and the education authority is responsible for orders given by her in that position, such as the one we have to consider. It does not seem to me to have been an order which in its nature differed essentially from such an order as to shut the door of the schoolroom or to open the window. It is true that it related directly to a matter personal to the teacher, but she may well have thought that it was in the interests of her teaching that the act should be done, and that it was better that she should send one of the scholars to do it than that she should leave the class unattended to while she did it herself. A wide discretion in small matters such as this is in my opinion inseparable from the quasi-parental position of a teacher towards her class in such a school, and, without discussing what are the exact limits of such an authority as is thus given to her, I am of opinion that in the present case the act was one for which the education authority is liable, and that this appeal should be allowed.

FARWELL L.J.: . . . In my opinion, the Education Acts are intended to provide for education in its truest and widest sense. Such education includes the inculcation of habits of order and obedience and courtesy; such habits are taught by giving orders, and if such orders are reasonable and proper under the circumstances of the case, they are within the scope of the teacher's authority, even although they are not confined to bidding the child to read or write, to sit down or to stand up in school, or the like. It would be extravagant to say that a teacher has no business to ask a child to perform small acts of courtesy to herself or others, such as to fetch her pocket handkerchief from upstairs, to poke the fire in the teachers' room, to open the door for a visitor, or the like: it is said that these are for the teacher's own benefit and to save herself trouble, and not for the child's benefit, but I do not agree: not only is it good for the child to be taught to be unselfish and obliging, but the opportunity of running upstairs may often avoid punishment: the wise teacher, who sees a volatile child becoming fidgety, may well make the excuse of an errand for herself an outlet for the child's exuberance of spirits very much to the benefit of the child. Teachers must use their common sense, and it would be disastrous to hold that they can do nothing but teach. . . . Here, in addition to the considerations that I have already stated, and which are in my opinion quite sufficient, the corporation supply a common room in which the teachers sit, fitted with fireplace and oven so that they can cook and eat their dinners there if convenient, but they supply no one to look after the fires or the room; it is therefore necessary for the teachers to do it themselves: in the present case, the teacher might have gone herself, but if she had, she would have left her class unattended: it cannot be said that she chose an alternative beyond the scope of her employment in sending the child; such sending was within such employment, but she did it in a negligent manner: the corporation are therefore liable for her negligence. I am therefore of opinion that this appeal must be allowed.

Plaintiff's appeal allowed

124 Cooper *v.* Manchester Corporation (1959) *The Times,* February 13

COURT OF APPEAL

The making of tea by children for the staff is an ordinary domestic duty, and does not impose on the school a higher standard of care than that of a reasonably careful parent.

Facts: The plaintiff, Sandra Cooper, was a pupil at St Margaret's Church of England School, Moss Side. One of her duties was to carry a pot of tea to the staff-room just before break, when the passages and stairways were empty of children.

As she rounded a corner on one occasion she collided with a small boy charging out of a room, and was scalded by tea from the pot which had a capacity of sixteen cups. In an action against the local education authority in the Manchester County Court, Judge Raleigh Blatt awarded her £275 damages.

The defendants appealed.

Fenton Atkinson, Q.C. for the appellants: It is quite impossible to say that this was a dangerous operation. The school was a mixed school with boys and girls whose ages ranged from eight to fifteen. The older girls were trained in domestic science and, as part of their training, and possibly also for the convenience of the staff, were required to carry out certain domestic duties, one of them being that two girls were required every day to make tea for members of the staff. The county court judge possibly disapproved of pupils being required to brew tea for the staff when they might have been studying English literature; but the justification was that it was a good part of their general training for life.

Council then described the tea-making operation.

WYNN PARRY J.: A cold tea-pot! Then they were not being taught domestic science.

Fenton Atkinson, Q.C.: Then I am a very bad tea-maker. The judge's view against the defendants was based on the idea firmly fixed in his mind that at the time of this accident children were thronging out of the classrooms; and if that had been so there would be a foreseeable risk of its happening; but the evidence was plain that this took place before the break began. It is wrong to approach these cases on the basis that children of fourteen years old should be guarded against the least physical injury. If that were to be the basis, cricket would be played with soft balls, gymnastics would be abandoned, and cooking classes would cease.

Summerfield, for the respondent: If the school desired free labour a greater burden of case was placed on it. The girl had to pass twenty-five yards along a narrow corridor and staircase containing a number of rooms from which anyone might properly emerge, and containing three blind corners. To require a girl to carry about half-a-gallon of hot tea on such a route when there were over two hundred children in the building constituted a bad system. The kettle had two handles, and the girl could not hold it in one hand. An adult might have been able to do so, and would have been better able to control the kettle.

Extract from Judgment

HODGSON L.J.: . . . The standard of care imposed on the school is that of a reasonably careful parent. The carrying of a pot of tea is an ordinary domestic duty; a great many domestic operations carry danger with them, but the judge considered there was exceptional danger here, because there were crowds of children thronging the corridors. There is no evidence of that, and it was not contended to have been the case.

The incident occurred five minutes before the break and there was no reason to foresee at that time that a single boy would be out of his classroom. On the facts of the case there is nothing to justify a finding of negligence, and the appeal will be allowed.

Appeal allowed: judgment for the defendants

(J) STRAYING CHILDREN

125 Carmarthenshire County Council *v.* Lewis [1955] A.C. 549

HOUSE OF LORDS

The presence of a child of four years wandering along outside the school premises when he is in the care of the local education authority indicates a lack of reasonable precautions.

Facts: On April 19, 1952, the mistress in charge of a nursery school decided to take David Morgan, a four-year-old boy, and a little girl for a walk during the midday break. The two children were made ready and left in a classroom while the mistress went to the lavatory. On her way back, she met a child who had fallen down and cut himself. She washed and bandaged him, and then returned to the children she was taking out. In all she was away about ten minutes.

Meanwhile, the two children had left the classroom, and had reached the highway. David Morgan attempted to cross the road in the path of a laden lorry driven by a Mr Lewis. The driver swerved to avoid the child, and was killed when the lorry hit a telegraph pole.

The widow, Mrs Dilys Eileen Lewis brought an action against the Carmarthenshire County Council for damages arising from her husband's death, alleging that the Council were liable to her. At the hearing at Cardiff Assizes Devlin J. awarded damages amounting to £3,037 19s. 6d. to the plaintiff and her three children. The defendants appealed.

The Court of Appeal (Somervell, Denning, and Romer L.JJ.) affirmed the judgment of Devlin J.[1] The defendants now appealed to the House of Lords (Lord Goddard, Lord Reid, Lord Tucker, and Lord Keith of Avonholm; Lord Oaksey dissenting) who dismissed the appeal.

Extracts from Speeches

LORD OAKSEY (*dissenting*): . . . My Lords, in these circumstances, Devlin J. and the Court of Appeal have held that Miss Morgan was negligent in leaving David and that her negligence caused the accident to the respondent's husband. I should agree that, if Miss Morgan was negligent, her negligence was causally connected with the accident. If a child of under four years, who is in the charge of a schoolmistress, is negligently allowed by the schoolmistress to stray into a crowded street, I am of opinion that the negligence is causally connected with an accident caused by the child. But I do not think that Miss Morgan's conduct was negligent. . . .

I think, therefore, that the case ought to stand or fall upon the issue of Miss Morgan's conduct, and, in my opinion, it cannot be decided in favour of the respondent without inferentially holding that education authorities are bound to keep children under constant supervision throughout every moment of their attendance at school, which, in my opinion, is to demand a higher standard of care than the ordinary prudent schoolmaster or mistress observes.

. . . I would allow the appeal.

LORD GODDARD: . . . The question of general importance that is raised is whether there is a duty on the occupiers of premises adjoining a highway to prevent young children from escaping on to the highway so as to endanger other persons lawfully passing upon it. By "young" children I mean those of such tender years that they may be presumed to be unable to take any care for their own safety and whom a prudent parent would not allow to go into a street unaccompanied. A long series of cases, culminating in *Searle* v.

1. [1953] 2 All E.R. 1403; *sub nom. Lewis* v. *Carmarthenshire County Council*; [1953] 1 W.L.R. 1439.

Wallbank,[2] have established, now beyond controversy, that an occupier is under no duty to fence his fields, yards or other premises so as to prevent his cattle or other domestic animals from escaping on to the highway, though by so doing danger, and it may be disaster, is caused to passers-by. If, then, an occupier is not liable for the escape of an animal, is he to be held liable for that of an infant, who from the standpoint of reasoning powers is much the same as a sheep or any other domestic animal? Now, once a doctrine has become a rule of law it is the duty of the courts to apply and follow it without regard to its origin, but if to follow it would be to extend it, in my opinion it is not only legitimate but essential to examine the origin and reason for it if it be known. How some rules of law arose is not always known. . . . But how the rule your Lordships have to consider arose is, I think, known, its origin having been explained particularly by Viscount Maugham L.C. in *Searle* v. *Wallbank*[2] and in *Heath's Garage Ltd.* v. *Hodges*[3] in the judgment of Neville J. It arose because at least most of the roads in this country originated over unenclosed country when the open field system of farming prevailed and long before fencing became usual, and to this day hundreds of miles of roads run through unenclosed land, so cattle, sheep and all domestic animals could and still do wander on and over such roads, and the presence of domestic animals was not regarded, to use the words of Neville J., as inconsistent "with the reasonable safety of the public using the road." Whether this doctrine should prevail in these days of swift-moving motor traffic, at least in the case of roads in enclosed country, is for the Legislature to consider, but it has never been applied to the presence on the roads of human beings of whatever age, nor to an inanimate object. Perhaps the simplest way of accounting for the rule is that dedication of roads, at least in country districts, must be presumed to have been *sub modo*, subject, that is, to the possible presence of domestic animals upon them. How far the doctrine applies in towns or populous places may, I think, still be considered a debatable question. Having regard, then, to its origin, it would, in my opinion, be unwarrantable to extend it to the facts of the present case.

The position, then, is that the appellants maintain a nursery and infant school in premises adjoining a highway in a town and are, in my opinion, under a duty to take care that the children themselves neither become involved in nor cause a traffic accident. . . . The learned trial judge thought it a borderline case, as did Somervell L.J., but on the whole found the teacher was negligent. This is an inference drawn from the facts found by the learned judge and, in my opinion, is open to review by your Lordships, who, accepting the facts so found, are in as good a position as the courts below to determine whether they justify holding Miss Morgan guilty of a want of care. Reluctant as I must be and am to differ on such a matter, I cannot hold than an inference of negligence on her part should be sustained. Her duty was that of a careful parent. I cannot think that it could be considered negligent in a mother to leave a child

2. [1947] A.C. 341.
3. [1916] 2 K.B. 370; 32 T.L.R. 570.

dressed ready to go out with her for a few moments and then, if she found another of her children hurt and in need of immediate attention, she could be blamed for giving it, without thinking that the child who was waiting to go out with her might wander off into the street. It is very easy to be wise after the event and argue that she might have done this or that; but it seems to me that she acted just as one would expect her to do, that is to attend to the injured child first, never thinking that the one waiting for her would go off on his own. The utmost length of time she was out of the room was ten minutes, but it is plain that the child must have gone off very soon and I should think almost immediately after Miss Morgan had gone to the lavatory. He had to go from the room, across the playground, out into the side lane, down to the main road and then some way along the latter, cause the accident and be brought back to the place from which he started, there to be seen by Miss Morgan, all within this short space of time. And this was a child described as obedient and who had never before left the school by himself as he was always fetched by his mother. I cannot bring myself to lay the blame for this tragic accident on Miss Morgan.

But this does not conclude the matter as far as the appellants are concerned. They maintain a nursery school and an infant school on these premises. In the former they accept the care of children from three to five years and in the latter those of five to seven. During the time when this child was in their care he is found outside the school premises, wandering in the street. That, in my opinion, clearly calls for an explanation from the appellants. They have only shown that the child left the room in the temporary absence of the teacher and so got into the playground. In the playground he would have been safe at least from traffic risks. All we know is that the gates must have been open or so easy to open that a child of three or four could open them. True the nursery children are put, when out of school into the playpen, but infants from five to seven play in the playground. If it is possible for children of that age, when a teacher's back may be turned for a moment, to get out into a busy street this does seem to indicate some lack of care or of precautions which might reasonably be required. There is no analogy between a school playground and the home in this respect. At any rate no satisfactory explanation has been given for this child being found in the street at a time when he was in the care of the appellants, and for this reason I would dismiss the appeal.

Appeal dismissed

[NOTE: Devlin J., at first instance, and Somervell L.J. in the Court of Appeal both thought that the teacher was negligent. This appears from Lord Goddard's speech. The teacher was at no time joined in the action, but her interests were watched by the solicitor to the National Union of Teachers as the plaintiff had imputed negligence to her. It was the National Union of Teachers which pressed for an appeal to the House of Lords in a final endeavour to vindicate the teacher. The appeal was unsuccessful so far as the local education authority was concerned, but it is interesting to observe that both the majority speeches and Lord Oaksey's dissenting speech expressly cleared the mistress in charge of any imputation of negligence.]

M

(K) SCHOOL BUS: SUPERVISION BY PREFECTS

126 Jacques *v.* Oxfordshire County Council and another (1968)
66 L.G.R. 440

OXFORD ASSIZES

Bearing in mind the duty to make reasonable provision for the safety of school-children, and that the standard of care is that of a reasonably prudent parent applying his mind to school life where there is a greater risk of skylarking, it is not negligent to leave the supervision of well-disciplined children of secondary school age in the hands of prefects.

Facts: The plaintiff, Roland Herbert Jacques, was a fourteen-year old pupil at the time of the accident giving rise to the action. On December 9, 1964, he was travelling to school on a bus which collected children for a number of schools in Bicester. There were about forty-two pupils on the bus, and the supervision was in the hands of two prefects. Unruly conduct was usually stopped by the prefects. On the date in question the plaintiff was hit in the right eye by a paper or lead pellet. There was no evidence to prove that any particular pupil had fired the pellet which injured the plaintiff.

The plaintiff brought an action for damages for negligence against the local education authority for damages for negligence for personal injury, and against a fellow pupil, John Merry, alleging negligence and/or trespass.

Extracts from Judgment
WALLER J.: This is a claim by Roland Herbert Jacques, who was at the time of the accident in 1964 fourteen years old, against the Oxfordshire County Council as the local education authority and John Merry, another boy of roughly the same age as him, for personal injuries which he suffered when his eye was struck by some object on December 9, 1964, causing injury to that eye.

The background of the case is this: at Bicester buses are operated by the local education authority to the various schools in Bicester from the outlying areas. Each bus is not restricted to pupils of one school, but collects from a particular district taking pupils from more than one school from the district to those schools. The bus with which this case is concerned collects for, among other schools, Bicester Grammar School and Highfield Secondary Modern School, as they were in 1964, and collects from Merton, Charlton and other places. The system which is operated by the authority is that prefects are appointed to be in charge on the bus, a senior girl and a senior boy, because there is not any adult supervision on the bus other than the driver. On this particular bus a girl, Lois Wilshire, had been appointed as bus prefect and she had been a prefect for more than a year; and a boy, Alan Bunce, had been appointed as the boy prefect, at the beginning of the term.

On December 9, 1964, the bus had a number of pupils on it, probably about forty-two, and Roland Jacques, the plaintiff, was on the bus. He was in the fourth seat from the back on the driver's side and Alan Bunce, the boy prefect, was on the same seat and he had another boy sitting on his knee. There was quite a lot of noise in the bus. Some flicking of paper pellets was going on between boys at the back and between the plaintiff, and I think others. Among the boys on the back seat was the second defendant, John Merry. The boys on the back seat were in fact firing at the back of the head of the prefect Bunce. According to the plaintiff, he said: "I stopped flicking and I turned round and knelt on the seat. As soon as I looked round Merry hit me in the eye with a pellet and afterwards said: 'I got him, he's crying. I'll try and do it again,' whereupon one of the other boys said, 'No'."

It is quite clear that on that day the plaintiff was hit in the right eye and his right eye was seen to be watering afterwards by others on the bus, although it was not appreciated at the time that the injury was a serious one. As a result of what has happened from that accident his right eye has got worse and has lost a considerable amount of its sight. It is problematical as to how much of it can be restored. The situation has not yet become static. It may be that if he can be fitted with a contact lens he may have some sight, but if he cannot, all he can distinguish with his right eye are the outlines of shapes.

The first question I have to consider is whether or not the second defendant, Merry, did cause this injury, because if he did he will be liable to the plaintiff for damages, whether or not the education authority are. There is no dispute that he was flicking pellets in the direction of Bunce and Jacques, no dispute because Jacques said so and because he himself says so. But so were others; this was not just one person flicking, there were others on the back seat who were flicking pellets also. But it follows from the fact that there is no dispute that Merry was flicking pellets with others that it is quite possible that he did hit Jacques in the eye. It is said that it was a metal pellet that hit Jacques in the eye. The evidence for that is very shadowy, perhaps principally resting on the fact that there was an injury to the eye.

Merry gave evidence. He was the last witness to be called and I am bound to say I thought he gave a good impression in the witness box, trying to recall events which took place as near as makes no matter three years ago. And he made an admission, which might be a significant admission one way or the other, that he did in fact have on him lead in his pocket which he had taken from home that morning in order to make pellets and fire them when at school, but he said he would not and did not fire any lead pellets on the bus and that all he fired were paper pellets. I just do not know and am unable to make a specific finding as to whether or not this injury was caused by a lead pellet or by a paper pellet. The fact that there was an injury rather indicates that it was something harder than paper. On the other hand, the fact of the matter was that neither Jacques nor his father apparently thought it was very serious at the time and that therefore rather indicates it was perhaps only a paper pellet. . . .

I realise that it is quite possible that Merry did fire the pellet which hit the plaintiff in the eye, but I am not satisfied on the balance of probabilities that it was his pellet that hit the plaintiff in the eye; I am not prepared to say there is any greater probability that it was Merry who fired it than one of the other boys on the back seat of the bus. Accordingly I am not prepared to find that Merry was responsible.

The next question is, Can it be said that the local education authority was responsible? In order to consider that, it is necessary to go a little more into the facts as they existed on the bus at the time. Lois Wilshire was called. She was the girl prefect and she gave as I thought a fair account of the general situation on the bus. I do not think she could give any account of the particular situation because she did not remember it, but she did give an account of the general situation. She had never seen a metal pellet fired nor had any reason to suspect it. She had seen pellets being fired but she thought that generally they were stopped. She thought that both Jacques and Merry were rather noisy and probably if there was any trouble they would probably both be involved, but she thought that on the whole the boys answered to control fairly well. It was sought by Mr Butter to show that Alan Bunce, the senior boy prefect, was ineffective and that he was young and inexperienced and did sometimes have difficulty in maintaining order among his friends, but Lois Wilshire said that she did not think that he did and that by this time, that is the time of this incident, Bunce had been a prefect for some two months. She was also asked about the amount of flicking of paper pellets and she said that things were sometimes thrown, paper was flicked by a ruler or elastic, but she had sometimes intervened and Bunce had sometimes intervened. The general picture I got from her was that there was nothing seriously wrong with the way pupils on this bus behaved. There had been occasions apparently when Bunce had some difficulty in controlling pupils who were running up and down, but that is not something with which this case is concerned.

Bunce himself said that nothing unusual happened on this journey, there was paper thrown for a while, pieces of paper folded up. He said they were projected by elastic bands and he told them to stop it. He did not know of the suggestion that they were metal pellets until he made a statement in October 1965. And he said that night nobody appreciated that anything serious had happened.

In my view this group of pupils were reasonably well controlled, there was nothing exceptional in their behaviour and there was no particular reason why the behaviour of the pupils on this bus should be regarded as other than the normal behaviour of pupils of that sort of age. There may have been occasions from time to time when paper pellets were being flicked by elastic bands but there is no evidence, and I have in mind that Price[1] gave evidence of one occasion, but in my view there is no accepted evidence that metal pellets were ever used. I do not think there was any situation which could be regarded as requiring further drastic action arising from the flicking of paper pellets. There may have been occasions when pupils did not desist at once, particularly

1. Another boy.

probably when Bunce was first appointed and was acquiring control, but I am unable to find that there was any occasion when he ought to have reported the matter to the master in charge.

What is the duty of the local authority in these circumstances? They owe a duty to see that the bus is reasonably safe and that includes a duty to see that it is reasonably safe for the children who are going on the bus including the provision of supervision if it is necessary. I think that the standard which is to be adopted is that of the reasonable parent, and I adopt the words of Edmund Davies J. in *Lyes* v. *Middlesex County Council*[2] that it is the reasonable parent applying his mind to school life where there is a greater risk of skylarking, and it may be that it is a reasonable parent of a rather large family. Did the authority perform that duty in this case properly? Mr Dorrell, the deputy director of education, gave evidence. He said that this question of supervision on school buses had been specifically considered by the education sub-committee, and I think by the education committee, on several occasions, the last one being in 1962, when it had been decided that the policy then was that buses wholly occupied by young children or buses occupied by sub-normal children should have an adult as a supervisor in addition to the driver, but that apart from those the supervision of an adult was not considered necessary. Mr Dorrell was of the opinion that while there are arguments both ways about this it really is part of the growing up process of the young that they should learn their own discipline, and it must be remembered that the two boys principally concerned in this case were shortly going to leave school, that is at the end of the year. He thought that the system of a prefect on the bus was a proper system, both from the point of view that the prefect should learn to exercise control himself but also from the point of view that the other boys and girls should learn to accept that control.

Mr Symms, who was at that time the deputy headmaster of Highfield Secondary Modern School, thought the prefect system had worked perfectly well and he saw no reason to suspect that this prefect, that is Bunce, was not doing his job. It is true that Mr Symms in cross-examination said that probably if he had an adult available he might put that adult on the bus, but I do not think that Mr Symms was then attempting in any way to go back on his general view that this system worked reasonably well; I think he was giving a balanced opinion about it.

So I come to the conclusion that since there was no evidence in this case that the bus passengers were particularly boisterous and undisciplined it was perfectly reasonable on the part of the local education authority to leave the supervision of the buses to the children, that is to say senior children appointed as bus prefects. As I have already indicated I do not think there was any evidence here that this bus had abnormally boisterous or undisciplined passengers. In fact Lois Wilshire said that she thought they were quite reasonable, she certainly had been on worse buses. Therefore I can find no ground on which it could be right to hold the local education authority as

2. (1962) 61 L.G.R. 443; see page 198, *supra.*

being guilty of negligence in the respects alleged. Accordingly this claim must fail against both defendants.

Judgment for the defendants

(L) SUPERVISION ON HALF-HOLIDAY ACTIVITIES

127   Camkin *v.* Bishop and another [1941] 2 All E.R. 713

COURT OF APPEAL

A headmaster owes no duty to a pupil or his father to provide for the supervision of boys working on a farm on their half-holiday.

Facts: The infant plaintiff was a boarder at King's School, Warwick, where the defendant was headmaster.

On July 6, 1940, a party of twenty-two pupils volunteered to spend their half-day that afternoon working on a farm a few miles from the school. They were accompanied by a senior boy, but no master was with the group. It was the habit of the school authorities to allow their pupils to go anywhere they liked within eight miles of the school on half-holidays.

On this occasion the pupils were to receive sixpence an hour for their work. During the absence of the farmer some of the boys began to throw potatoes at each other. One boy shouted something opprobrious to another, who retaliated by throwing a lump of earth at his insulter. This boy ducked to escape the missile, which hit the plaintiff, who was hoeing beet, on the side of the forehead. His eye was so gravely injured that it had to be enucleated the next day.

The father brought an action against the headmaster for damages for personal injuries alleging:

    (1) that it was the duty of the headmaster to send a master in charge of the boys to prevent them from indulging in such horseplay;

    (2) that his failure to do so was negligence; and

    (3) that the negligence was the cause of the injury suffered.

Cassels J. awarded £750 general damages to the infant plaintiff, and £64 special damages to his father.

The defendant appealed.

Extracts from Judgments

SCOTT L.J.: . . . I entirely agree with the defence. The whole action is misconceived and ought never to have been brought. I cannot understand how the judge came to think that either the statement of claim or the plaintiff's evidence disclosed any cause of action. The defendant's counsel might have submitted at the close of the plaintiff's case that no case had been made out, and have asked the judge to rule accordingly. As he did not, the unfortunate headmaster was put into the position of having to go into the witness box and justify his action when it needed no justification. The defendant, as headmaster, owed no duty to the boys to refuse to let them go to help the farmer in his need of labour without an under-master, or an under-nurse for that matter, in charge. The incident might have happened just as easily on a natural history expedition, or on any other country outing on which the boys were regularly allowed to go without supervision. Indeed, it might have happened even if a master had gone, for he might have been temporarily absent and the two boys who quarrelled might have done so during his absence.

The first witness called for the plaintiffs was the assistant executive officer of the Warwickshire War Agricultural Executive Committee, whose evidence was tendered for the purpose of putting in a document which had no direct relevance to the allegations in the statement of claim, but part of which had been read by counsel for the plaintiffs in his opening speech. The document was a long communication from the Ministry of Agriculture to all county war agricultural executive committees. It related mainly to the scheme for holiday camps, but contained a paragraph about local half-holiday assistance by schoolboys to farmers in the neighbourhood, in which it was said that in most cases small parties of boys should be sent on to farms in charge of a master or a prefect in each case. This expression of opinion by the Ministry of Agriculture was obviously concerned only with the agricultural efficiency and usefulness of the boys' labour, and had nothing whatever to do with any possible danger to the boys in the absence of control. It could not be evidence of any duty owed by the headmaster to the boys concerning their safety, but it seems to have affected the mind of the judge. In truth, there was no evidence that the document was shown to the defendant or that the sentence in question was read to him, or even to the two assistant masters to whom the defendant had delegated the duty of carrying out the plan of allowing the boys to volunteer for agricultural work. There is nothing, therefore, in the point made before us by counsel for the respondents that the assistant masters had not been called in spite of the threat of counsel that he would comment severely if they were not called.

The reality of the whole position was that the boys volunteered for the work, that the farmers were glad to have them, and did not ask for masters to supervise them, that the boys knew that they were to be under the farmers' orders, and that, in general, they gave satisfaction. No duty at common law of the kind alleged ever arose. The judgment below must be set aside with costs here and below. . . .

GODDARD L.J.: I agree that this appeal should be allowed. The question we have to determine is whether there was any breach of duty by the headmaster, his duty being that of an ordinary careful parent. I ask myself whether any ordinary parent would think for a moment that he was exposing his boy to risk in allowing him to go to a field with others to weed beet or lift potatoes, occupations far safer than bicycling about on the roads in these days.

I confess that I have some difficulty in appreciating the view taken by the judge. He found that the defendant failed in his duty by reason of a lack of supervision. If this means anything, it must mean that it is the duty of a head-master to see that boys are always under supervision, not only while at work, but also at play, or when they are free, because at any time they may get into mischief. I should like to hear the views of the boys themselves on this proposition. Would any reasonable parent forbid his boy of fourteen to go out with his school-fellows because they might possibly get up to mischief, as all boys will at times? Here at this school on free afternoons the boys are allowed out, their bounds being some eight miles, and they are left to themselves, provided they are back by a certain hour. No complaint is made of this free-dom. If there is nothing wrong in that, how can it be wrong to let a boy go with others to such a harmless occupation as doing some farm work of the most innocuous character? As Clauson L.J. put it during the argument, if the headmaster is not guilty of any breach of duty in allowing the boys to go off for walks and so on by themselves, how can he become liable because during the walk they go and work in a field and meet with some accident while thus engaged? If he is liable in this case, so will he be if some boy does a mis-chievous act in the playing field which injures another while a master or prefect does not happen to be present, or while out for a walk climbs a tree and breaks his legs.

The judge seems to have paid great attention to the circular from the Ministry of Agriculture about schoolboys working on farms. Apart from the fact that it was never proved to have been brought to the notice of the head-master, I cannot see the relevancy of it. Officials of the Ministry of Agriculture are not the persons to tell headmasters how to run their schools. It is obvious that all the passage so often referred to was dealing with was that it might be as well to have some responsible person present to see that the boys did the job for which they were being paid, a task which one would suppose would also be undertaken, at least to some extent by the farmer who was paying them. Indeed, the evidence of the boy Ives shows that that is just what did happen on one occasion at least at Hobbs' farm. The views of some gentleman at the Ministry of Agriculture who may well be anxious that farmers should get value for their money cannot have any bearing whatsoever on the duty a master owes to his pupils. Nor was there any duty on the master to ask the farmer to supervise the boys for their safety. How could it occur to anyone that there was any danger in the occupation? If every master is to take pre-cautions to see that there is never ragging or horseplay among his pupils, his school would indeed be too awful a place to contemplate. Of course there was no supervision on this occasion. Nor was there any duty to provide it, having regard to the innocuous nature of the occupation. This case bears no anology to those in which boys have been allowed to handle dangerous chemicals or to be in proximity to dangerous machinery. There was no evidence, in my opinion, of any breach of duty whatever.

It was not objected at the trial that the plaintiffs had made no case, I dare say, because it was thought desirable to put the defendant into the box. His answers showed him to be transparently frank. Boys of fourteen and sixteen at a public school are not to be treated as if they were infants at crèches, and no headmaster is obliged to arrange for constant and perpetual watching out of school hours. For one boy to throw something at another is an ordinary event of school life, but the fact that there was in this particular case a disastrous and wholly unexpected result is no reason for throwing responsibility on the master. I agree with Scott L.J. that this is an action which ought never to have been brought.

Appeal allowed, with costs in both courts

(M) TIMES OF SCHOOL SESSIONS: VARIATIONS

128   Barnes *v.* Hampshire County Council (1969)
See Appendix, *infra*.

VII

DEFAMATION OF TEACHERS

(A) BY THE SECOND MASTER OF A SCHOOL

129 Hume *v.* Marshall (1877) *The Times*, **August 2, 3, 4 and 6,**
November 26, and December 22

CROYDON ASSIZES

*A communication about one of his colleagues made by the second master of a
school to the headmaster is privileged if made bona fide* and without malice, but
if there is exaggeration and ill-feeling an action for defamation may lie.*

Facts: The plaintiff, Mr Hume was an assistant master at Dulwich School. He
brought an action for slander and libel against the under master (*i.e.* the
second master), the Reverend Mr Marshall, alleging that he had been defamed
by an imputation that he was addicted to habits of drinking. The defendant
pleaded the truth of the statements and that, at all events, they were
privileged.

There appeared to have been some disharmony among the staff of the
school concerning plans for reorganisation. In the middle of 1876 rumours
concerning the plaintiff's drinking habits reached the headmaster, Dr Carver,
but they were denied by the plaintiff and the headmaster could find no one
who had ever seen the plaintiff under the influence of liquor. In February
1877, the defendant told the headmaster that at a large dinner party he had
been told by a guest that the plaintiff was addicted to drinking, and had been
seen drunk at the railway station. On the following day the headmaster made
the defendant sign a minute of what he had said. The headmaster said that he
had sometimes seen the plaintiff unsteady in his gait, but he attributed this to
a knee injury.

Extracts from Summing-up
LORD COCKBURN C.J.: .... There can be no doubt that habits of drunkenness
are an absolute disqualification for that business or life to which the plaintiff
has devoted himself, and therefore it is of importance to him to vindicate
himself, if he can, from the imputation of drunkenness. But we must not
forget that it is equally important to a scholastic institution that a man who
has these habits should be prevented from contaminating by the evil example
of such habits those over whom he is called, more or less to preside. There is
not only the evil example of one of those vices which produces the most fatal
consequence to the individual and to mankind, but there must necessarily be,

338

if the scholars know that any of their masters indulge in such a vice, a great decline of that reverence and respect with which it is desirable they should regard their tutors. We must not, therefore, be in a hurry to condemn those who have thought it their duty to the institution to make an inquiry into the charges which may have been rife against the plaintiff.

It is rather hard upon the defendant that he should be made to bear the brunt of the plaintiff's attack, because one thing is quite clear—that it was not the defendant who invented or first put into circulation statements derogatory to the plaintiff's character in this respect. These reports were, beyond all question, circulated a long time before the defendant came on the scene. They may be true or they may be untrue; but he was not the inventor of them, and there is this most undoubted fact in his favour—that, though he may have lied or exaggerated, on both the occasions on which he made these statements the defendant was called upon, imperatively called upon, to bring these matters under the knowledge of the headmaster . . . in the first instance, and afterwards of the Governors, who most properly instituted an inquiry. When, therefore, the plaintiff is advised to anticipate the decision of the committee to whom he had submitted the inquiry, he has brought his action, not against those who had asserted that they had seen him drunk, but against the person who was bound to bring these statements forward. Every man is liable to be the object of slander; no position can protect a man against wholesale slanders which have no foundation in anything but the diabolical malice of those who utter them. But if the man who is the object of such slander desires to vindicate himself, the party against whom to do so is surely the person who has uttered those slanders, and not a person who may in the course of his duty have been called upon to repeat what has been originated by another. . . .

Now, as to the law on the subject—no doubt defamatory words are actionable unless they can be substantially justified as true, or unless the statements were made in circumstances which would protect them by reason of privilege. The first question, therefore, is whether these statements were true; that is whether the plaintiff was a man of drunken habits, for that, in substance, is the effect of the statements made; and the next is whether, if not true, they are covered by privilege. When a man has a duty to make a communication to another, and makes it with good faith, and with an honest desire to discharge his duty, and with a belief in the truth of the statements he makes, the occasion protects the statements made, and an action cannot be maintained against a person who has made a statement in these circumstances. The business of life could not go on if communications made in such circumstances were not protected. You may believe in the existence of a fact, and may feel it to be, and it may be, your duty to communicate the fact to some one who has an interest in it. You may be mistaken—it may turn out—when the matter comes to be inquired into—that the statement cannot be substantiated; nevertheless, you are protected, because if it were not so, and if in every instance, before you could warn a person of a fact it is all important to him to know, you had to enter into a careful inquiry into the truth of the statement, these communications would be withheld from a fear of consequences, which it may be essential should be communicated. That being so, if the communication is made in good faith it is protected, and therefore if you should be of opinion that these statements were not true, you would still have to consider whether they are protected by the privilege the law affords to statements so made.

The first question is whether the defendant has succeeded in showing that the plaintiff was a person of drunken habits. Now, it has never been asserted that he is an habitual drunkard—that is, that he is drunk (so to speak) "in season and out of season"; that he is a man who not only allows himself to indulge in convivial habits, but who cannot control his habit of drunkenness. But on the other hand, in the case of the master of a public school coming home night after night to a place like Dulwich visibly the worse for liquor, you are entitled, if you think that is established, to consider that he is a man of drunken habits and unfit to be in the position of a master in such a school. Now a body of testimony, which I cannot help thinking is of a most formidable character, has been accumulated upon this question which I will call your attention to minutely.

The burden of proof on the question is on the defendant. The plaintiff, by bringing the action instead of submitting himself to the inquiry, has changed places with those who were his accusers; he has turned the tables upon them, and makes them the accused, and he has thus thrown upon them the burden of proof. That he had the power of doing so there is no doubt, and therefore it is for the defendant to make out the truth of his statements. Some of the witnesses are mixed up with what had been called "Dulwich politics," and others are not; and as to those who are, of course, their evidence will have to be more closely looked at.

It has been suggested that the defendant has been actuated by malice, arising out of those college quarrels, and no doubt there were two parties strongly opposed to each other. Some years ago it was proposed to divide the school into a classical school and a modern school—Dr Carver to be at the head of the one and Mr Marshall of the other. Dr Carver and most of the masters opposed the scheme, while Mr Marshall supported it; and some heats and animosities arising out of this discussion may have insinuated themselves into these matters, though I should hope that such feelings would not influence the minds of educated and honourable men. Still, it is possible that some such feelings may have influenced the minds of some of those who have been before you; but that is for you to consider. Certainly some nine or ten respectable persons have deposed to having seen Mr Hume in a state of drunkenness, and it is for you to consider whether they can have invented these statements or whether they can all have been mistaken. . . .

Verdict for the plaintiff, judgment for the plaintiff for 40s.
with costs

[NOTE: This case is sometimes cited as (1878) 42 J.P. 136. That report, however, merely deals with the judgment of Lord Cockburn C.J. as to costs. The trial of the action itself was reported only in the press.]

(B) BY THE HEAD OF A SCHOOL

130 Reeve v. Widderson (1929) *The Times*, April 24

HOUSE OF LORDS

A report on a teacher made by the head of the school to the Chief Education Officer of the local education authority in whose area the school is, is privileged in the absence of malice.

Facts: The plaintiff, Miss E. Reeve was formerly a teacher on the staff of the Willesden Education Committee, and in 1924 was an assistant mistress of the girls' department of Carlton Vale Council School, Willesden. The defendant was the headmistress of that department.

The plaintiff brought an action against the respondent for damages for an alleged libel contained in a letter written by the defendant to Dr Samuel Joseph Bridges, Chief Education Officer for Willesden, on May 19, 1924. The words complained of were as follows: "Miss E. Reeve does not fit in with the organisation of this department and I most earnestly request that she may be transferred elsewhere as speedily as possible, as I consider her presence on the staff is detrimental to the well-being and happiness of this school."

The plaintiff, by her statement of claim, alleged that the defendant meant, and was understood to mean, that the plaintiff was unfit for her work as a teacher in the defendant's school and that by reason of the alleged libel the plaintiff had been injured in her credit and reputation as a teacher, and had been deprived of her appointment as a teacher on the staff of the Willesden Education Committee.

The defendant, among other defences, alleged that the letter was written in discharge of her duty as headmistress and without malice, and the occasion was, therefore, privileged.

The action was tried before Acton J. and a common jury. At the close of the plaintiff's case the judge ruled that the occasion was privileged and, in answer to a request by the foreman of the jury, directed the jury as to the meaning of privilege and malice, and the law relating thereto. On receiving these directions the jury consulted together, and the foreman then intimated to the judge that in the opinion of the jury there was no evidence of malice. They, therefore, returned a verdict for the defendant and judgment was entered for her accordingly.

The plaintiff appealed to the Court of Appeal (Scrutton, Greer and Sargent L.JJ.), who dismissed the appeal, whereupon the plaintiff appealed further to the House of Lords.

Extract from Speech

LORD BUCKMASTER: . . . Counsel for the appellant has done all that counsel could do to place before the House an appeal for which there is no possible ground. I cannot help regretting that these proceedings have gone so far. The plaintiff is clearly a very sensitive person who has a feeling that she had been suffering from a very grievous wrong, but I think she should have been content to accept the decision of the Court of Appeal, who upheld the verdict and judgment of two courts in favour of the defendant. That the letter complained of as a libel was written on a privileged occasion could not be disputed. The only question is whether from the terms of the letter or from other evidence it would be possible to show that the letter was written not to advance the interests of the school, but from a feeling of personal spite to the plaintiff.

At the end of the plaintiff's cross-examination the jury asked to be directed on the question of malice, and on receiving that direction they gave a verdict for the defendant. The judge's direction on the question of privilege and malice has never been challenged. All that is said is that he ought to have dissected the evidence in greater detail, and that certain matters ought to have been put before the jury which had not been put. I think that there was no such duty. The jury, as plain sensible men, were perfectly able to decide for themselves whether the letter was written from ill-feeling.

Appeal dismissed

(C) BY A SUBSCRIBER TO A SCHOOL

131 Ripper *v.* Rate (1919) *The Times*, January 17

KING'S BENCH DIVISION
Statements made by a subscriber to a school are privileged if they are made to the person who has jurisdiction over the headmaster in matters of misconduct.

Facts: The plaintiff, Mr S. C. Ripper, was headmaster of the Church of England School at Dorking. He claimed damages for libel against Mrs Alice Rate, of Milton Court, Dorking, on the ground that she had made charges against him of having inflicted great cruelty on the schoolboys under his control.

At the end of September 1917, a boy named Friday had to be caned for insubordination, and some days later Friday was found bullying a smaller boy, and he was again ordered to be punished. The vicar, who was chairman of the school managers, then came into the school and privately forbade the headmaster to punish the boy. On October 5 there was a managers' meeting at which it was said that the local education committee had asked Ripper to resign.

The first libel alleged was a letter written by the defendant on October 8 to the secretary of the Surrey Education Committee, charging Ripper with showing great cruelty to one of the boys, and stating that the local committee had asked him to resign. The defendant added that if he resigned he might get an appointment at another school "which would be most undesirable." The secretary of the Education Committee replied that the managers were satisfied that the punishment inflicted was not so exceptional as to need further comment.

On October 15, a boy named Pullinger refused to sing in the school. He said that he had sung enough in the previous week. He was then ordered to hold out his hand for the cane. He refused and the headmaster gave him several strokes of the cane on the back. Pullinger's father summoned Ripper for assault and battery. The magistrates at the Dorking Petty Sessions found that the punishment was excessive, and that the cane was too short and too rigid for corporal punishment. Ripper was fined 10s.

On October 30 the defendant wrote to the secretary of the Surrey Education Committee, saying that the headmaster's excuses were quite beside the real facts of the case, and that the fine of 10s. was absurd. The defendant also said that there were other cases of cruelty. In other letters allegations were made that the boys from the school had cried so bitterly at home that they were unable to sleep. In one case, it was said, a boy's hand had to be surgically treated after a caning. The effect of the libels was that the defendant asserted that the plaintiff was unfit to hold a responsible position as a school teacher. On January 28, 1917, the managers of the school had given the plaintiff a high testimonial.

The plaintiff had no knowledge of the letters until he went before the managers. He agreed in court that Friday's guardian had complained about her ward's harsh treatment, and that possibly four or five boys were caned each day. Punishments for minor offences were not entered in the punishment book although the rules required it: this, said the plaintiff, was a rule more honoured in the breach than the observance.

Extract from Judgment

LUSH J.: The occasion was privileged. It is enough to say that the defendant had subscribed to the school, and that the letters were all written to the secretary of the Education Committee who had jurisdiction over the headmaster in matters of misconduct. That being so, the plaintiff has to prove express malice on the part of the defendant. It is not sufficient to show that there might have been some sinister motive in the defendant: the plaintiff must prove that there actually was such a motive. It is clear that there is no extrinsic evidence of malice. There is none outside the letters themselves. Indeed, the contrary is shown by the letter which the defendant had written to the plaintiff himself. That tends to show that there was anything but malice. There is not a particle of evidence that the defendant had any desire to do anything but help towards the truth. Evidence that the letters contained untruths is not evidence of malice. There is no evidence of express malice— none that calls upon the defendant for an explanation. . . .

Judgment for the defendant

(D) SLANDER RELATING TO PROFESSIONAL CONDUCT

132 Jones *v.* Jones and another [1916] 2 A.C. 481

HOUSE OF LORDS

An action of slander will not lie for words imputing adultery to a schoolmaster, in the absence of proof of special damage, unless the words are spoken of him touching or in the way of his calling.

Facts: The appellant, Mr David Jones, was the headmaster of the Llidiardau Council School, Rhoshirwaen, Pwllheli. He was a bachelor, and lived with his aunt. The school was looked after by his aunt, as caretaker, and she was in the habit of employing a Mr Roberts to do some of the cleaning.

In May 1914, Mrs Ellen Jones, the wife of a farmer, told Elizabeth Jones and, it was alleged, Eliza Roberts, that the plaintiff had committed adultery with Mrs Ellen Roberts, the cleaner's wife. She added that Mrs Roberts herself had told her so.

The plaintiff brought an action against Mrs Jones, and joined her husband in the action as being liable for his wife's tort. The complaint alleged that the slander concerned the plaintiff in relation to his profession as a headmaster.

The action was tried at the Carnarvon Assizes, where Elizabeth Jones stated in cross-examination that the words were not spoken at all in reference to the plaintiff as a schoolmaster.

Lush J. left three questions to the jury which, with their answers, were as follows:

(1) Were words spoken by the defendants of the plaintiff imputing moral misconduct between the plaintiff and Mrs Ellen Roberts?—Yes.

(2) Were they spoken of him in the way of his calling, *i.e.* in such a way as to imperil the retention of his office?—Yes.

(3) Did they impute that he was unfit to hold his office?—Yes.

The jury fixed the damages at £10. Lush J. adjourned the case for further argument in London, during which counsel for the defendant again admitted that the county council would naturally not allow a master who was carrying on an immoral intercourse to stop in the school and teach children, but stated that this admission would be equally true of any other person holding a public position. Lush J., after hearing the arguments, entered judgment for the plaintiff.

The defendants appealed. The Court of Appeal (Swinfen Eady L.J., Warrington L.J., and Bray J.) set aside the judgment on the ground that words imputing adultery or immoral conduct, even when spoken of a man holding an office or carrying on a profession or business, were not actionable without special damage* unless the words related to his conduct in the office, profession, or business, or the imputation was connected with his professional duties, except in the case of a clergyman holding clerical preferment or employment, and that the imputation upon the plaintiff was not connected with his occupation or employment.[1]

The plaintiff appealed to the House of Lords.

Cur. adv. vult

Extracts from Speeches

VISCOUNT HALDANE (read by Lord Wrenbury): My Lords, the question in this appeal is whether the appellant, who was plaintiff in the action, can recover general damages for an untrue verbal imputation of immoral conduct with a married woman. He is a certificated teacher and is the senior master of a council school in Wales. It is not in dispute that the imputation of such conduct, if believed, would be seriously prejudicial to a person in his position, and might lead to the loss of an appointment which, concerned as it is with the teaching of the young, implies in the person who holds it freedom from reproach of this kind. At the same time it must be remembered that the position of a certificated teacher is not unique in this respect, for there are many other appointments that are held on a similar condition, express or implied.

The school in which the appellant was employed was looked after by his aunt, as caretaker, and she was in the habit of employing the husband of a Mrs Ellen Roberts to do some of the cleaning. The respondent, Mrs Jones, is found by the jury before which the action was tried to have spoken words imputing moral misconduct between the appellant and Mrs Roberts. Mrs Jones was the defendant in the action, and her husband was joined as being liable for his wife's tort. The jury found further, in response to questions from Lush J., who tried the case, that the words "were spoken of him in the way of his calling, that is in such a way as to imperil the retention of his office," and further that "the words imputed that he was unfit to hold his office." It is, however, clear that there was no evidence that any words were used which referred to his office or his conduct in it, and the first part of the finding cannot be relied on as anything more than an inference. Nor was there any evidence of the use of words which could, by the terms used, bear out the second part of the finding. It was, moreover, not alleged that the appellant had been dismissed or otherwise pecuniarily injured in his calling, and indeed there was no evidence whatever of special damage. The jury, however, assessed general damages at £10. . . .

The Court of Appeal reversed the judgment of Lush J. and entered judgment for the respondents.

After examining the authorities, I have come to the conclusion that the Court of Appeal were right, and that the judgment of Lush J., notwithstanding the care which he had obviously bestowed on it, cannot be supported. He seems to have regarded the decided cases as having laid down a broad principle, which could be legitimately extended to a case like the present. My Lords, I think that is not so. The action for slander has been evolved by the courts of common law in a fashion different from that which obtains elsewhere. As one of the consequences the scope of the remedy is in an unusual

1. [1916] 1 K.B. 351.

degree confined by exactness of precedent. It is not for reasons of mere timidity that the courts have shown themselves indisposed to widen that scope, nor do I think your Lordships are free to regard the question in this case as one in which a clear principle may be freely extended. . . . There is a difference between slander and libel which has been established by the authorities, and which is not the less real and far-reaching because of the fact that it is explicable almost exclusively by the different histories of the remedies for two wrongs that are in other respects analogous in their characters. The greater importance and scope of the action for libel was mainly attributable to the appearance of the printing press. The Court of Star Chamber quickly took special cognisance of libel, regarding it not merely as a crime punishable as such, but as a wrong carrying the penalty of general damages. After the Star Chamber was abolished by the Long Parliament much of the jurisdiction which its decisions had established and developed in cases of libel survived, and was carried on by the courts of common law to whom it passed.

The history of the action for slander is radically different. Slander never became punishable in the civil courts as a crime. In early days the old local courts took cognisance of it as giving rise to claims for compensation. When these courts decayed, the entire jurisdiction in cases of defamation appears to have passed, not to the courts of the King, but, at first at all events, to the courts of the Church. However, after the Statute of Westminster the Second had enabled novel writs *in consimili casu** to be issued, the action on the case for spoken words began to appear as one which the courts of the King might entertain. Subsequently to the Reformation, when the authority of the courts of the Church received a heavy blow and began to wane, the courts of the King commenced the full assertion of a jurisdiction in claims arising out of spoken defamation concurrent with that of the spiritual tribunals. As might have been expected of civil courts, whose concern had been primarily with material rights and not with discipline as such, the new jurisdiction in claims based on slander appears to have been directed to the ascertainment of actual damage suffered and to a remedy limited to such damage. This explains the restricted character of the development of the remedy and the tendency to confine its scope by the assertion that actual damage was the gist of the action. The observations of Pollock C.B. in the course of his judgment in *Gallwey* v. *Marshall*[2] illustrate the importance of these considerations. The rule thus established was to some extent relaxed in its form by decisions which in certain nominate cases treated particular types of slander as so injurious by their very nature that the suffering of actual damage might be presumed and need not be proved. These exceptional types of slander comprised imputations of the commission of serious criminal offences, imputations of suffering from certain noxious diseases, and imputations of special forms of misconduct which would manifestly prejudice a man in his calling. But, as a general principle, as to the actionable character of words spoken of a man to his disparagement in his calling the courts, with an exception to which I will refer later, appear on the

2. (1853) 9 Ex. 294.

balance of authority to have laid down the limitation that the words must have been actually spoken of him "touching" or "in the way" of that calling. . . . Subject to the carefully-guarded exceptions to which I have referred, the rule is that laid down in Comyns' Digest, *Action upon the Case for Defamation* (D. 27): "But words not actionable in themselves, are not actionable, when spoken of one in an office, profession or trade, unless they touch him in his office, etc." In *Doyley* v. *Roberts*[3] Tindal C.J. applied the law as laid down in this passage by refusing relief to an attorney of whom it was falsely said that he had defrauded his creditors and been horsewhipped off the course at Doncaster. That this is the basic principle which limits the cases in which the common law permits general damages to be awarded was laid down in striking language in the judgment of the Court of King's Bench in *Ayre* v. *Craven*[4] delivered by Lord Denman C.J. "Some of the cases," he said, "have proceeded to a length which can hardly fail to excite surprise; a clergyman having failed to obtain redress for the imputation of adultery; and a schoolmistress having been declared incompetent to maintain an action for a charge of prostitution. Such words were undeniably calculated to injure the success of the plaintiffs in their several professions; but not being applicable to their conduct therein, no action lay." . . .

My Lords, I think that these authorities and others which were referred to in the arguments at the Bar have settled the law too firmly to admit of our extending the exceptions which have been made further than the decided cases go. I agree with what was said by Lord Herschell in the judgment in *Alexander* v. *Jenkins*,[5] which I have already quoted, and with the carefully-guarded judgment of Swinfen Eady L.J. in the present case. If we were to admit that an action for slander can lie in the case of a schoolmaster who has not proved either that the words were spoken of him "touching or in the way of his calling," or that he has suffered the actual damage which is the historical foundation of the action, and is even now its normal requisite, I think we should be overruling *Ayre* v. *Craven*[6] and other decisions of great authority, and should be doing what only the Legislature can do today. It required an Act of Parliament, the Slander of Women Act 1891, to enable a woman to recover general damages for an imputation of unchastity. In my opinion it would require an analogous Act to enable the present appellant to recover such damages for an imputation of adultery which was not obviously directed to his reputation as a schoolmaster. I am therefore of opinion that we have no option to do anything but dismiss this appeal with costs.

LORD WRENBURY: . . . Damage includes, but is not confined to, pecuniary damage. Slander by imputation of contagious disease, such as leprosy, is actionable. The damage in such case is the exclusion of the plaintiff from society. Slander by imputation of misconduct in an office which is not an

3. (1837) 3 Bing. N.C. 835.
4. (1834) 2 Ad. & E. 2.
5. [1892] 1 Q.B. 797.
6. (1834) 2 Ad. & E. 2.

office of profit is actionable. The reason for this is not very clear, but would seem to be that the slander might, if true, show that the man ought to be deprived of his office: see Lord Herschell in *Alexander* v. *Jenkins*.[7] At any rate it is not pecuniary damage. The damage need not be (although in most cases it is) pecuniary, but there must be damage proved or as matter of law presumed.

The fact that the imputation is a gross and grievous attack upon personal character is not of itself enough. For otherwise a statute would not have been necessary to enable a woman or a girl to sue for slander upon her chastity. The imputation must be such and the state of facts such, *not* as that a judge would necessarily or reasonably presume or infer damage, but as that judges in the past have presumed or inferred damage. This involves a confession which I fear must be made that the law of slander rests not upon any principle whose elasticity will admit new cases, but upon artificial distinctions. An artificial and arbitrary rule is not a principle. The plaintiff must for success bring his case within the very limited class of cases in which slander has been held actionable. He must show that the imputation is such and the state of facts is such as that a presumption of damage as matter of law has been made in the past under like circumstances. I am of course here speaking, and throughout this opinion I am speaking, of cases in which damage is not proved.

Setting aside the case of slander actionable by statute under the Slander of Women Act 1891, there are only three heads within some one of which the plaintiff must bring his case; they are:

1. Imputation of crime.
2. Imputation of a contagious disease tending to exclude the plaintiff from society.
3. Imputation against the plaintiff in the way of his office, profession, or trade, or which will touch him in the way of his office, profession, or trade.

The present case is sought to be brought under the third head. . . .

The case before your Lordships' House is that of a schoolmaster and the imputation is one of moral misconduct with a married woman. The calling was not mentioned in the conversation. The jury found that the words were spoken of the plaintiff in the way of his calling, but the Court of Appeal held (and I agree) that there was no evidence to support that finding. The question put to the jury, however, goes on this: "In the way of his calling, that is, in such a way as to imperil the retention of his office." I am unable to follow the intention of this paraphrase, or to see that it is a paraphrase. The jury answered the question in the affirmative, and further found that the words imputed that he was unfit to hold his office. What has most pressed me in the case is that Mr Artemus Jones, who appeared for the defendants, admitted at the trial that the imputation would endanger the plaintiff's position. He admitted (to use his own expression, on further consideration) that "undoubtedly a public authority would remove him just as it would remove any other of its servants."

7. [1892] 1 Q.B. 797.

His point was not that the imputation would not injure him, but that it was not said of him in his profession of a schoolmaster. In consequence of his admission the plaintiff abstained from calling evidence upon this point. I feel great doubt whether under these circumstances it was not open to the jury to find as they did, and whether the only point left was not whether the absence of the colloquium was necessarily fatal. This, I think, would be a point which would require careful consideration. However, as your Lordships do not attach the importance which I do to this aspect of the case, I shall not press my view to the extent of differing from the motion proposed by the noble and learned Lord on the woolsack.

Order of the Court of Appeal affirmed and appeal dismissed with costs

(E) BY THE SECRETARY OF AN OLD BOYS' ASSOCIATION

133 M'Carogher *v.* Franks (1964) *The Times*, November 25

QUEEN'S BENCH DIVISION

There may be circumstances in which the secretary of an Old Boys Association has a duty to speak to pupils of the school about a member of the teaching staff of the school, in which case malice must be proved if an action for defamation is to lie.

Facts: The plaintiff, Miss Averil Ernestine Sanctuary M'Carogher, formerly a teacher at Christ Church Cathedral Choir Oxford, claimed damages for slander against Mr Leslie Franks. The defendant, a justice of the peace, a former city councillor, and church warden of the university church of St Mary the Virgin, founded the school's Old Boys Association in 1933, and had been its secretary ever since.

The plaintiff alleged that the defendant, on July 10, 1958, said of her to six pupils aged about thirteen: "She is abnormal. She has been like that for three years. Women of her age are often like that. She is a rotten teacher." The defendant denied speaking the words and that they were defamatory and claimed qualified privilege.* His son had told him Miss M'Carogher had criticised the headmaster, and he spoke to the boys about to leave at a meeting at his house when he talked about the Old Boys Association, so that they could use their influence in the school. His son who was among the leavers had told him that Miss M'Carogher had said to the boys that the headmaster, whose wife had died six months previously, should have waited twelve months before becoming engaged to a young under-matron.

A month before the meeting, Miss M'Carogher, who had been at the school for ten years, had been given notice of dismissal in a note sent up by a boy while she was coaching pupils in her room. She was promised, but not given an opportunity of speaking at a meeting of the Dean and Chapter as the governing body of the school. One of the boys referred to her dismissal in a Sunday letter home which she had the duty of reading.

Extract from Summing-up

PAULL J.: . . . There is not much difference between what the boys and Mr Franks had said in evidence. At the time the boys were thirteen, and no more: that was six and a half years ago, and the writ was not issued until March 1961. There is no doubt that the words were spoken about Miss M'Carogher, but did they make those who heard them spoken think the worse of her because they were uttered? If you do not think that those boys did think any the worse of her, Mr Franks is entitled to the verdict.

However, even if you come to the opposite conclusion, there are occasions when a person ought to speak out about what he really thinks and I have held that this is a proper case for Mr Franks to say what he really believed, provided that what he said was reasonable. If you find that Miss M'Carogher has not proved that Mr Franks acted maliciously, and not for the good of the boys and the school you should find for him. Unless you think that Mr Franks was speaking because, for some reason, he had a down on her, he is entitled to the verdict.

Verdict for the defendant

(F) BY THE PUBLIC AT LARGE

134 Baraclough *v.* Bellamy and others (1928) *The Times*, July 18

KING'S BENCH DIVISION
The defence of fair comment is not available if an alleged libel consists only of statements of fact.

Facts: The plaintiff, Mr Alfred Valentine Baraclough, was the headmaster of Goodall Road Borough Council School for Boys, Leyton, from 1926. He had been in the service of the Leyton local education authority from 1900 until the time of the action, save for his service during the First World War.

In 1926 he celebrated Empire Day in the school by addressing the boys on the Empire, and arranging for special lessons. Some councillors thought he should not have dropped the practice of forming the boys up in the playground to salute the flag, but it was decided that the observance was in accordance with the regulations. In 1927 Empire Day was observed in the same form as in the previous year, and in July a protest containing eighteen signatures was handed to the Council:

> "We, the undersigned, wish to protest to the education authorities against the action of the headmaster and the headmistress of Goodall Road Borough of Leyton School, in preventing on Empire Day, May 1927, the saluting of our national flag and by their general conduct leading the children to believe our national flag not to be worth saluting.
>
> We, the undersigned, beg the educational authorities to take measures to

prevent and punish disloyal conduct on the part of teachers and that the authorities will at once make inquiry into the above matter."

Some of the signatories were neither ratepayers nor the parents of pupils at the school. Five apologised, and the plaintiff brought an action for damages for alleged libel against the remaining thirteen. The action was tried before Swift J. and a special jury.

The plaintiff said he saw no necessity for the boys to salute the Union Jack. Never, when he had been on parade, had he seen the Union Jack saluted. He had not removed a Union Jack from the hall: he thought it was there on Empire Day, 1926, and it was shown and saluted in 1928 in accordance with the new regulations. Portraits of the King and of Queen Victoria had been removed from the hall because they had got into a bad condition, but he could not remember if he had the frames cleaned for other pictures. He had removed a wooden model of the Cenotaph because it got in the way of the school war memorial. He knew of no movement in Leyton to prevent all the Empire Day celebrations, especially saluting the flag and singing the National Anthem.

The senior master, Mr Henry Parsons, said the headmaster instructed him to give lessons on imperial subjects on Empire Day, 1927. He displayed a Union Jack, showed how it had been built up, and explained its symbolism. He dealt with the colonies, their history and their value to the Empire. He gave about half an hour to Canada and a quarter of an hour to India. [Laughter.] The pictures of the King and of Queen Victoria had given way to pictures of a more decorative and instructional character more in accordance with the everyday life of the boys.

SWIFT J. (looking at a photograph): I see that a camel on the bank of the Suez Canal is in one of the pictures. [Laughter.]

Under the previous headmaster the Union Jack was, on Empire Day, unfurled in the centre of the playground by the captain of the school. The flag was saluted and patriotic and folk-songs were sung. One of the songs was *Rocked in the Cradle of the Deep*. [Laughter.] On one occasion his class had sung *Rule Britannia*, but a number of the boys who had attended the Socialist Sunday School objected. There was a kind of meeting. The character of the Empire Day celebrations had now changed. The headmaster took no part other than giving instructions to teachers, but in 1928 he told them that it was a regulation of the education authority that they should salute the flag. They had to give lectures on the League of Nations: "We have to take great care not to stir up war-like passions in the coming generation."

Another master, Mr Thomas Henry Moore said that on Empire Day he told his class that the British Empire stood for freedom, equality and justice. The whole idea of an Empire Day celebration had been given up, the headmaster stood entirely aloof, and they were now stressing the educational side of the school; whereas previously they had stressed the "showy side."

The defendants pleaded privilege and fair comment. Mrs Emily Alice

Bunting said that on Empire Day, 1927, she went to the school to see the usual parade. It did not take place, and she was one of a hundred disappointed mothers. She had nothing against any of the teachers.

Mr Thomas Bellamy said that in 1927 he had three children at school. The matter of Empire Day was discussed all over the neighbourhood, and he wrote a letter to the local paper about it. He agreed that the lecture given to his son's class was excellent, except that it did not conclude with saluting the flag and singing *God save the King*. He did not approach Mr Baraclough, because the headmaster would not see anybody. He agreed that he had never called to see him.

Mr Edward James Costain, the licensee of the Birkbeck Tavern, was a pupil at Goodall Road School between 1900 and 1908. Signatures to the protest about Empire Day, 1927, were obtained in the Birkbeck Tavern one Sunday morning, but only for about an hour and a quarter. He realised he was making about as serious a charge as could be made against a schoolmaster: he did not want him removed, but thought he ought to be censured and made to come into line with loyal headmasters. He did not tell people that the protest was because the headmaster had punished boys for being Boy Scouts. All but four of the signatures were obtained on his premises.

Mr Compton, another defendant, said that if he had known of the headmaster's war service he would not have credited the charges of disloyalty.

Mr Francis George Magnus, formerly of the 12th Lancers agreed that there was nothing more serious than a charge of disloyalty. He still agreed with the protest.

Mrs Amy Wall, who lost her husband in the war, thought the Empire Day proceedings were disgusting.

Mrs Florence Victoria Jordan said that on Empire Day, 1927, she saw a small boy leaving the playground in a Boy Scout's uniform. The boy made a statement to her, and she said to Mr Magnus: "That's all right, isn't it? That poor little chap has been sent to change out of his Scout uniform."

Councillor Mrs Mary Alice Read said that in 1927 the education committee had directed that the National Anthem should be sung at all school functions.

At the conclusion of the evidence, Swift J. ruled that the defence of fair comment was not open to the defendants as the protest consisted only of statements of fact.

Extract from Summing-up

SWIFT J.: . . . You have not got to decide what is the best way of celebrating Empire Day. Some of you may think—as I myself think—that some ceremony such as marching the children round the playground, singing patriotic songs, and saluting the Union Jack is a better way of celebrating Empire Day than by merely putting the children into classrooms and giving them lessons on the history and produce of the Dominions. I cannot help thinking how much better it would have been in the present case if those lessons had been followed by some ceremony in which the children saluted the flag and sang patriotic songs. On the other hand, many persons think it wiser if the Empire Day celebrations are confined to lectures on the Empire. The question is whether the defendants used the occasion on which the libel complained of was published for the reasons for which that occasion was privileged, if it were privileged, or for some indirect and improper motive.

Verdict for the plaintiff. Damages assessed at £50

VIII

MISCELLANEOUS

(A) CHARITIES

135 Attorney-General *v.* Whiteley (1805) 11 Ves. 241[1]

COURT OF CHANCERY

The nature of a charity can be changed by an application to objects different from those intended by the founder only where it is clear that, by a strict adherence to the plan, his general object will be destroyed.

Facts: An application was made to convert the Leeds Free Grammar School into a commercial academy in which French, German and Mathematics would be taught on the ground that this would be of greater utility in a developing commercial town; and also to increase the number of the teaching staff.

It was objected that the founders did not intend more than one master and one usher to be appointed, and that the revenue from the estates, which were chiefly copyhold, would not be sufficient to pay more than two men of learning who received nothing else from the school but their salaries. Further, it was objected that the utility of French and German must depend upon accident and political and commercial circumstances, and could not therefore properly be made a permanent part of such an institution. It was contended that this was the first attempt to divert a charitable foundation from its original design, and that it was of the utmost importance to keep up foundations of this nature, and to secure to the master a respectable situation.

Judgment

LORD ELDON L.C.: This case appears under singular circumstances. The object of the information is to convert this old school into a commercial academy; and the court, instead of declaring by the decree the nature of the charity, has sent that to the Master who has decided that question. That creates a difficulty of form. Strictly the cause ought to be re-heard; and the court ought to declare what is the charity. But in a charity case I may do that now. Upon the principle that, the information praying wrong relief, the court will, as it ought, give such relief as will do justice to the defendants, I may in

1. This is sometimes referred to as the *Leeds Grammar School* case.

a charity case take so much liberty with the record as now to examine, and declare, what is the charity; and proceed upon that.[2]

The question then is, whether the court had any power to do this: what right this court had to alter the establishment of the charity by the instruments of foundation. Without going the length of saying the court has no such right if a case should arise in which the application of the whole fund would destroy the charitable purpose, in order to preserve that purpose, yet upon all authorities, to warrant the court in assuming that power, the case must be very clear; and the alteration of the nature of a charity is a proposition as serious as can be offered to the judgment of the court. The question is, not what are the qualifications most suitable to the rising generation of the place where the charitable foundation subsists, but, what are the qualifications intended. If upon the instruments of donation the charity intended was for the purpose of carrying on free teaching in what is called a Free Grammar School, I am not aware, nor can I recollect from any case, what authority this court has to say the conversion of that institution, by filling a school, intended for that mode of education, with scholars learning the German and French languages, mathematics, and anything except Greek and Latin, is within the power of this court. The proposition is quite different where the directions prayed are founded in a purpose to promote the direct object of the charity; and where boys are to go to this school, who are not to learn Greek and Latin, but are to have a particular part of the school set apart, and the funds applied for a different purpose from that intended by the donors; which may be very useful to the rising generation of Leeds; but cannot possibly be represented as useful to this charity. The difficulty is insuperable.

As to the salary, and the gratuity in addition to it, the actual dealing with the funds belonging to this charity has hitherto been upon a principle, which I do not say is incorrect: that is, supposing a competent master may be found to teach for this salary, that it is within the power of the trustees, if he conducts himself well in the execution of his duty, to give him a gratuity almost as large as the certain salary. It is much more consistent with the principles of this court from time to time to reward the master out of the fund, and very largely, perhaps in proportion to the number of years he has held the office, or to the number of boys, than to apply any part of the fund to a purpose the donors did not look to. As to the usher, some of the instruments expressly found an usher. It is more agreeable in principle to increase the emoluments of both the master and usher for carrying on the purpose of the foundation, than to bring in masters, to whom the object of it does not point.

At the date of the decree the number of boys at this school was forty-nine; and for some time previous had been forty-four; and it is supposed, that for that reason this court is at liberty to lay down a permanent plan for education in other studies, not the learned languages. Experience justifies the observation, that, where there is a school with a large establishment, and the scholars

2. *Att.-Gen.* v. *Parker*; *Att.-Gen.* v. *Smart*; *Att.-Gen.* v. *Scott* (1747) 1 Ves. 43, 72, 413.

go to it *gratis*, there is a strong temptation not to struggle to obtain many scholars; and therefore the amount of the salary sometimes defeats the purpose. But does that give the court power to apply the revenue of the foundation to other purposes than those, to which the author of the charity has devoted it; and, acting upon the ground, that at present the number of scholars is not as great as was intended by the founder, vary the nature of the establishment, at the hazard of preventing hereafter under another master an increase to the number, that was intended? Much less is that right, if there can be such a management of the fund, consistent with the object of the foundation, as can provide for the due execution of the master's duty; always securing to him a respectable, independent, situation; and as to the excess giving him a little beyond what will secure that respectable, independent situation, he ought to have.

The report states that there is nothing in the nature of this foundation, that excludes an application of the fund to any kind of useful learning; and that it will be very beneficial to the inhabitants of Leeds to add masters to teach the German and French languages, algebra, and mathematics; excepting expressly writing and arithmetic; as there are other seminaries in the town to which such an establishment will be prejudicial. Upon what principle does the master set off the prejudice those other seminaries would sustain against the benefit to the inhabitants of Leeds? If according to the plan every boy to be brought to the school was to be taught the learned languages, and the circumstance, that these other sciences were to be taught, would induce persons to send boys to the school to learn Greek and Latin also, that purpose might have a tendency to promote the object of the foundation. But, if these plans are to be distinct, the institution will be singular; hazarding the destruction of all utility whatsoever. This is a scheme to promote the benefit of the merchants of Leeds. It is not that the poor inhabitants are to be taught reading and writing English; but the clerks and riders of the merchants are to be taught French and German, to enable them to carry on trade. I fear the effect would be to turn out the poor Latin and Greek scholars altogether. To make this school, as a Greek and Latin school, useful, you must have there, what the authors of the charity express, a learned man, capable by his life and doctrine of giving the most useful information. If persons, inclined to place themselves in that situation, are told their emoluments are to depend upon the number of scholars in a school, to be founded upon the principle, that it is not for the benefit of the inhabitants of the town to learn Latin and Greek, you propose terms most calculated to repel candidates; for connecting the increase and decrease of emolument with the actual decrease of the scholars, who are to learn Latin and Greek, the necessary effect of this plan must be such, that very little hope can remain to the master and usher of an increase of their salaries. I doubt therefore, whether the plan which the master has adopted, is the most useful; if the principle can be represented as resulting from all these instruments.

Taking upon me now to correct the omission of this decree, and to declare, what this foundation is, I am of opinion upon the evidence now before me, that the free school in Leeds is a free grammar school, for teaching grammatically the learned languages, according to Dr Johnson's definition; upon circumstances, without variation in fact since the year 1553; to which I cling, as better interpreters of the real nature of the charity than any criticism I can form, or construction upon the instruments; for, with the exception of the highway, the original founder proposed to the inhabitants the benefit of this donation by his will for a free school: it appears that there has been a free school in Leeds: and to this time every charity, given by these instruments, has been by inquisitions and decrees upon them applied in fact for the benefit of the free school in Leeds; in which nothing has been taught but the learned languages; and under such facts the result of the evidence is that the free-school in Leeds is a free grammar school for teaching grammatically the learned languages. The reason of my opinion is, that I do not apprehend, it is competent to this court, as long as it can find any means of applying the charitable fund to the charity, as created by the founder, upon any general notion, that any other application would be more beneficial to the inhabitants of the place, to change the nature of the charity. A case may arise, in which the will cannot be obeyed: but then the fund will not go to the heir; upon the principle that an application is to be made as near as may be[3]; growing out of another principle, that you are to apply it to the object intended, if you can. It must therefore appear by the Master's report, that the court must despair of attaining that object: or the court cannot enter into the question in what other way the fund is to be applied.

Declare, that the charity intended to be established by the first donation, mentioned in the Master's report, is the sustentation and maintenance of a free grammar school for the teaching the learned languages: that the free school in Leeds is a free grammar school for the teaching grammatically the learned languages; and that it appears to the court that the free teaching thereof is the charity intended to be established by the several donations, mentioned in the report, so far as the same relate to the school. With that declaration let the Master review his report as to any plan they may think proper to lay before him; and it will be open to him to consider, what is proper and necessary, not for the benefit of the inhabitants of Leeds, but for the benefit of the charity, declared to be such upon this record. I send it to the Master in that large way; for, though it is determined, that the charity is a charity for the purpose of teaching the learned languages, yet it is open to consideration, what arrangement as to the management and the salaries and gratutities to the masters may, upon the whole, be proper for promoting that charity. But it goes much farther; for it is right to make that declaration in the decree.

[NOTE: Between 1791 and 1796 the number of pupils had dropped to forty-four, and the Committee of Charitable Uses (which acted as the governing body of the school)

3. *The Bishop of Hereford* v. *Adams*, Vol. VII, 324.

blamed an inadequate curriculum (Latin, Greek, and Divinity, only), poor teaching and a deterioration in discipline. Mr Whiteley was appointed as head master in 1789, and neither he nor the usher supported the introduction of modern subjects. Of Lord Eldon's judgment, Leach wrote: "This decision carried dismay to all interested in the advancement of education and nearly killed half the schools in the country. The case is fully discussed by S. J. Curtis in his *History of Education in Great Britain* (University of London Press, sixth ed., 1965, pp. 122–126). Curtis adds: "In justice to Lord Eldon, it may be said that he had before him numerous examples of grammar schools which were no longer grammar schools, but which had in fact become primary schools. He also showed respect to the declared intentions of the founder and brushed aside the plea that had the founder lived in modern times his bequest would have been worded differently. Lord Eldon's attitude presents a striking contrast to many education authorities, central and local, who seem sometimes to ride roughshod over the intentions of founders as expressed in the foundation deeds of schools." See also *R.* v. *Cockerton* (page 30, *supra*); *Lee* v. *Secretary of State* (page 23, *supra*); *Lee* v. *Enfield* (page 46, *supra*); *Bradbury* v. *Enfield* (page 39, *supra*) and *Wood* v. *Ealing* (page 143, *supra*).]

136 Attorney-General *v.* The Earl of Mansfield and others (1827)
2 Russ. 501

COURT OF CHANCERY

Where a school ought to be a grammar school for instruction in the classics, the trustees will not be permitted to convert it into a school for teaching merely English, writing and arithmetic.

Facts: Highgate Grammar School was established on April 6, 1565, by Sir Roger Cholmeley for the good education and instruction of the boys and young men in that place. The royal letters-patent provided that the instruction was to be in the knowledge of grammar. There was to be a master, who must be an ordained graduate.

In the same year the Bishop of London confirmed to Sir Roger Cholmeley the chapel called Highgate Chapel to be conveyed to the wardens and governors of the school.

The information charged that the wardens and governors of the school, thus established and endowed by Sir Roger Cholmeley, had permitted it to be converted, from a free grammar school, into a mere charity school, in which the children of the poor were taught to read English, and to write, upon the plan adopted in the national schools; that the master, though he received a salary of £250, did not devote his time to the business of the school, but employed for that purpose an illiterate person as usher; that, instead of considering the school as the primary object of the charitable fund, to which the performance of divine service in the chapel was to be auxiliary and secondary, the wardens and governors had treated the support of the chapel and the performance of divine service in it, for the general use of the inhabitants of Highgate, as the principal object of the charity; that, while they applied only small sums for the benefit of the school, they had expended the greater portion of the revenues of the property in repairing and enlarging the chapel and the adjacent burial-ground; and that the chapel was, in fact, treated as a mere parochial place of public worship, unconnected with the school, while the master devoted his time not to the business of the school, but to the discharge of the duties of pastor of the hamlet and clergyman of the chapel. There were, also, various other charges of misconduct against the wardens and governors. The prayer was, that the trusts of the charity might be declared and carried into execution; that certain accounts might be taken; and that the wardens and governors might be removed.

The evidence in the case proved that the hamlet of Highgate was situated in three different parishes, the churches of each of which were at a considerable distance from it; that the inhabitants of Highgate had no sittings in any of the three churches; that there was no other parochial chapel within the hamlet; that the chapel in its present state was capable of containing from 700 to 800 persons; that there were a considerable number of free sittings in it for the poor; that the master of the school performed service in the chapel, and discharged other pastoral duties, which were of great advantage to the inhabitants; that many of the inhabitants were in the practice of attending the chapel on Sunday, and several of them, on Wednesday and Friday; that the system of education adopted in the national schools, and known by the name of "Bell's system," or the "Madras system," had been introduced; and that the school was attended by about 110 boys.

Three questions were discussed:

First, Whether the wardens and governors executed their trust duly by permitting the school to be conducted, not as a grammar school for instruction in the classical languages, but as a place for teaching English, writing, and arithmetic?

Secondly, Whether they executed their trust properly by permitting the master to devote his time chiefly to the discharge of clerical duties, while he left to an usher the actual labour of teaching, and exercised only an occasional and general personal superintendence over the business of the school?

Thirdly, Whether the chapel was to be considered a chapel of ease, to be enlarged and repaired out of the revenues of the charity for the general accommodation of the inhabitants of Highgate, according as the increase of their number might require; or whether it was to be considered as a chapel annexed and belonging to the school?

Observations on Conclusion of Argument (January 1824)
LORD ELDON L.C.: The question as to the school may be subdivided into two branches: What is the sort of school which the court, if applied to immediately on the institution of the charity, would have established in the execution of the trusts?—and what is the sort of school which the court will be obliged now to insist on having carried on at Highgate, regard being had to what has taken place between the middle of the sixteenth century and the present period? Now, notwithstanding the peculiarity in the statutes as to reading and writing, it appears tolerably clear, taking the whole together, that this was intended to be a free grammar school, in which persons were to be

liberally educated; and that, according to the construction of the phrase free grammar school, and attending to what were to be the qualifications of the person who was to conduct the school, this school was to be carried on in such a manner, that, at least, there might be an opportunity for the specified number of boys (a number which the court would, perhaps, have power to increase, if it were necessary) to be taught, not merely the English grammar, but the elements of the learned languages.

If it can be made out, that this originally must have been a school in which boys were to be taught the elements of the learned languages, the next question would be, attending to all that has passed from the time of its institution down to this moment, and particularly to the statutes, and to the practice of the wardens and governors, whether the constitution and nature of the school has been legally and effectually changed.

Now, that view of the case will turn entirely on this,—Whether, by positive statute, the wardens and governors could, as trustees of this charitable institution alter the nature of the school? There have been a great many cases in this court, undoubtedly, in which, when the particular things prescribed to be done could no longer be carried into effect, a change has been made; a change approaching as nearly as might be, in what can be expected, to that which can no longer be executed; and such change has been sanctioned by the court: but if the original trusts are as capable of being executed at this day as at the time of their original creation, the only question is, Whether there was authority to change the nature of the trust? Now, looking at the instruments, it appears to me extremely clear, that it was the express intention of Sir Roger Cholmeley that the original nature of this institution should be preserved for ever. . . .

Extracts from Judgment (*November* 13, 1826)
LORD ELDON L.C.: . . . Much evidence has been given to what I may call the comparative utility of carrying on the charity according to the original foundation, and of carrying it on according to the changes which have taken place, and which may be represented as aberrations from the original foundation of the charity—to the comparative utility of a school, as it should seem to have been proposed by the founder to be established, and of the school as it is now carried on—and to the benefit which the inhabitants of this district might receive from the enlarging of the chapel, and from other circumstances which have been stated as part of the plan adopted on one side. But, in giving my judgment, I have no right to look at the propositions, on the one side or the other, as propositions, one of which promises to be more useful to the public than the other; because this court has no jurisdiction to substitute a better proposition for a less useful one, but is bound to carry into execution the trusts of the property, as it finds those trusts to exist. If the court is obliged to say that this school is, in the sense in which these words have always been used here, "a free grammar school,"—the individual who holds the Great Seal, even if he were perfectly convinced that a free grammar school could be

of no use or of little use, would be bound to carry on the foundation as the author of the foundation meant it should be administered; and there is no power, at least none here, to alter that foundation, with a view to any superior benefit which might arise from an institution of a different nature, however desirable it might be, if it were within the scope of my authority, to substitute the one for the other. Neither can I enter into the consideration, whether the labours of the present master of the school, as a minister exercising spiritual duties in the place or in the neighbourhood, are more beneficial to the public than the exercise of his duties, such as, it is asserted, they have been prescribed by the nature of this foundation. If the foundation of this charity requires from him different duties from those which are now discharged by him, the comparative utility of what he now does, and of what would be so required of him, is a matter to which, in this Court, I cannot pay any attention. My duty is to enforce the trusts as they stand. The founder was the person who was to judge, how far his institution was likely to be useful to the public. . . .

It appears, that the Highgate school was founded about the year 1565, by Sir Roger Cholmeley. Prior decisions on the subject would authorise and require me to say, that, when a free grammar school is instituted, it does not mean a school for teaching merely reading and writing, but it is to be a school for grammar in this sense, that boys are there to be taught those languages which, we know, are taught in almost all of what are called grammar schools in the kingdom; and let it be observed, that it was a great part of the policy of the times in which this school was founded, that grammar schools should be instituted over almost the whole of the kingdom. . . . If it be asked, what those grammar schools were?—nobody can doubt that they were not schools for the purposes of teaching merely reading and writing; but they were schools for the purpose of carrying on that species of learning, which, to this hour and to this day, is taught in most of those schools. That there have been changes made in many of them, and made without due authority, under the notion that education might be more usefully conducted upon another plan, is unquestionable: but if the time shall come when this court shall be asked, whether these changes have been properly made and by due authority—perhaps there are in this country individuals who may then be of opinion, that the persons, who have made changes in such establishments, would have acted more wisely, if they had not acted on their own authority. . . .

Is it then possible to say, that, if there is in Highgate a school, such as what are called the national schools, where boys are taught to read and write in the manner usual in those schools, the master of such school is a master doing the duty, which the master, appointed under the authority I have read, is required to do? Is a master, who appoints an usher to teach the boys to read and write, and goes into the school, if you please, twice a day, to see that the usher does his duty, a master who, according to the language of the statutes, "teaches and instructs young children in their A, B, C, and other English books, and to write, and also in their grammar, as they grow ripe"? If he is not, though he may be doing something which is infinitely more useful, this court cannot

N

authorise such a change of duty; and, if applied to, it must enforce the per-formance of the duty which was originally imposed. It is obvious, that, in a long series of years, there may have been such a departure from the original nature of the trust as to cause much difficulty in restoring it; but, whatever the difficulty is, the court must struggle through it: and the court can no more say that a school, which was originally a grammar school, shall not be restored, than it can say that a school, which was originally a grammar school, shall be turned into a national school. . . .

I observe that the number of boys is limited by the statutes, and it may perhaps be made a question, whether, if there are forty boys who are taught English, the master is obliged to take any more boys than those forty, although not one of them may intend ever to be taught Latin? Now I have no difficulty in saying, that such a mode of getting out of the effect of these statutes will not do; because, if it were the object of the founder, that boys who came there should be taught the learned languages after they had gone through the elementary process, then, if two boys were to come, with a declaration on the part of the parents of one of them, that he was meant to be taught the elementary knowledge only, and then to quit the school, this court would say, that the object of the founder must be enforced, and would compel the master to take the boy who was meant to acquire the learned languages in preference to the other boy. . . .

Decree

. . . "Declare that the charity founded by Sir Roger Cholmeley is a charity for the sustentation and maintenance of a free grammar school for teaching the learned languages.

. . . And refer it to the Master also to inquire and report whether any good and valid appointment of a master of the said free grammar school now exists, and if such appointment hath been made, whether such master has fulfilled the duties of his office agreeably to the statutes, rules, and ordinances of the said charity, as far as the same respect the master of the said school, but this is under the circumstances of this case to be without prejudice to any allowances to be made in account, with respect to any payments already made, or to be made, as has been usual to the master of the school, before such scheme, as aforesaid, is made and adopted by the court. And the wardens and governors are to be at liberty to allow the boys now educating at the school to continue to be educated therein, upon the present system, until such scheme is adopted.

As To The Petition

I can do nothing with it consistently with the rules and powers of the court but dismiss it, if the parties won't come to some agreement; but not with costs, because it seems that nothing can be done as usefully without an act of parliament as with an act of parliament, if parliament will grant it.

Decree accordingly

137 *Re* Manchester Free Grammar School (1867) 2 Ch. App. 497

COURT OF CHANCERY

Where a scheme for the management of a charity has become impracticable in any of its details, it is the positive duty of the trustees to apply to the court for new directions.

Facts: The Manchester Free Grammar School was founded in the reign of Henry VIII by Hugh Oldham, Bishop of Exeter. A high master and usher were to be appointed, "having sufficient literature and learning to be a schoolmaster, and to teach children grammar after the school use, form and manner of the School of Banbury . . . to teach freely and indifferently every child and scholar coming to the same school without any money or other rewards taken therefor, except only the stipend." The high master's stipend was fixed at £10 a year, and the usher's at £5. No scholar was to be refused admission "of what country or shire soever he be, being man child, except he have some horrible or contagious infirmity infective." "When it shall happen the chest to be at surplusage the sum of £40 sterling, the rest to be given to the exhibition of scholars yearly at Oxford or Cambridge, which hath been brought up in the said school of Manchester."

The income of the school's property increased over the years, amounting to as much as £5,000 a year, and in 1833 a new scheme provided for gratuitous instruction in modern languages and other subjects beyond grammar. The expenditure of £10,000 was sanctioned for rebuilding the high master's house and the schoolhouse, and the high master, usher, and assistants were permitted to receive boarders. A further attempt at amendment began in 1835 on the ground that the Attorney-General had been absent from the 1833 proceedings. This led to a further scheme, approved by Shadwell V.-C. in 1849, which prohibited boarders and provided for gratuitous instruction in mathematics, modern languages, and other subjects. Meanwhile, the income from the corn mills conveyed to the school by the founder had fallen from £2,500 in 1833 to £749 in 1849. By 1862 it had fallen further to £372.

In 1865 the trustees alleged before Wood V.-C. that they could no longer carry out the 1849 scheme, and proposed that, in addition to the 250 free scholars, up to 100 pupils should be admitted at a capitation fee of twelve guineas a year. The Vice-Chancellor made an order accordingly, together with provision for an entrance examination. The Attorney-General objected on the ground that the introduction of fee-paying pupils was contrary to the founder's intention. He further objected that the introduction of a competitive entrance examination would favour the children of the rich and that, as the statutes provided for the admission of boys as young as five years of age, a competitive examination would be absurd.

Cur. adv. vult

Extract from Judgment (*The Times, May 14, 1867*)

TURNER L.J.: . . . As far as I can judge from the foundation deeds, the school was originally intended for the children of rich and poor alike. I think that the trustees were not only fully justified in making the present application to the court, but that it was their bounden duty to come to the court for its direction, inasmuch as the provisions of the scheme settled in 1849 could not be all carried out in consequence of the falling off of the income of the charity. Two objections have been taken by the Attorney-General to the introduction into the school of a class of boys who should pay for their education. The first is that it would be an alteration of the constitution of the foundation which is a free school. The answer to that objection is that all the boys whom the funds of the charity would suffice to educate freely were to continue at the school. All the income was still to be applied in free education. No more boys could be educated freely, except by cutting off some part of the enlarged course of education which was sanctioned by the scheme of 1849. Nobody had suggested, or could suggest that to do this would be for the benefit of the free scholars. Therefore this first objection could not, I think be maintained. The second objection made was that the introduction of a class of paying boys would be prejudicial to the free boys. Without going the length of saying that in no case would there be any likelihood of danger resulting from the education of different classes of society in the same school, I think that in a case like the present the introduction of a higher class would tend to raise the character of the lower class. Considering the position of Manchester and the character of its large population I feel no doubt of the expediency of the introduction of 100 boys who should pay for their education. There are many men in a great manufacturing town, engaged either as clerks or in other responsible situations, in the large industrial establishments, who are in receipt of considerable salaries, and who would naturally desire that their children should have the benefit of a good and substantial education. Why should they, because of a deficiency of funds be excluded from the benefit of the school—a school which was founded originally for the benefit of all classes? If this scheme were not adopted the scale of education would have to be lowered. It would not be possible to provide for such things as the teaching of German, chemistry, and mechanics—all most important in a place like Manchester. Even if some evil might result from the plan, I think that it would be far outweighed by the benefits which would be produced. I therefore quite concur in the general provisions of the scheme which has been settled by the Vice-Chancellor. However, I think that some of the details require alteration. The provision for a competitive examination for admission to the school would tend to the admission of only clever boys. This provision must be altered and it must be left to the trustees to determine what boys should be admitted, having regard to the qualifications of the candidates and the purpose of the foundation as a free school. I also think that all the boys ought to be on the same footing. There ought to be no distinction of foundationers and non-foundationers. They should all be called foundation boys. The object must be

to promote good feelings between the boys, and not jealousy and ill-feeling. . . .
It might be better that the charge for paying boys should be more than
£12 12s. I think that £16 16s. would not be too large a sum.

Appeal dismissed. Order of Wood V.-C.
approved with amendments

(B) FOUNDERS OF A SCHOOL

138 *Re* St Leonard, Shoreditch, Parochial Schools (1884) 10 App. Cas. 304

JUDICIAL COMMITTEE OF THE PRIVY COUNCIL
Only the original subscribers are founders of a school.

Facts: In 1705 a boys' school was founded in the parish of St Leonard,
Shoreditch, and a girls' school in 1709. The schools had, from their foundation, been denominational and attached to the parish church, and the teaching
had been always religious. Baptism was required, and the Church catechism
was taught. Attendance at church was insisted upon, and the children were
publicly catechised from time to time.

In 1882 the Charity Commissioners submitted to the trustees of the girls'
school a scheme for their consideration.

The basis of the scheme of the Commissioners was the principle of con-
verting the schools into a system of exhibitions for public elementary scholars,
and the reasons which had moved the Commissioners to propound it were
briefly as follows:

> The space occupied by the schools was cramped and incapable of
> adequate expansion, except at an undue cost to the endowment. The ele-
> mentary education of the neighbourhood was sufficiently guaranteed by the
> existing supply of board and other schools, a condition of things under
> which it was proper that educational endowments should be utilised for the
> promotion of more advanced education. The united endowments would not
> suffice for the establishment and maintenance of a suitably equipped
> secondary school, whether for boys or girls; still less would they support
> such a school for children of each sex, and it was clear that in that case
> the claims of neither sex could be disregarded. On the other hand, a system
> of exhibitions such as that proposed in the draft would be of very great
> value as supplying to meritorious children of the poorer class an opportunity
> of carrying their education beyond the ordinary limit, and so entering upon
> a successful career. There was in the neighbourhood itself no lack of places
> of higher than elementary education at which the exhibitions might
> conveniently be held.

The trustees in reply, argued that in any scheme for the amalgamation of
the charities the schools must be held to be denominational of the Church of

N2

England in connexion with the parish church of St Leonard, Shoreditch, and that by section 19, the school was exempted from the provisions of the Endowed Schools Act 1869.

The Commissioners intimated their opinion that none of the endowments were entitled to special treatment as being denominational within the view of the Act, and their scheme had since then been approved by the Committee of the Council for Education. By that scheme no provisions were made—in the establishment of either senior or the junior exhibitions—for religious education in the principles of the Church of England, or for attendance at the public worship at the services of the church of St Leonard, Shoreditch.

The petitioners were Dr Burchell, Mr Alabaster and Mr Joseph Wilkinson, three of the trustees of the schools and the Reverend Septimus Buss, the vicar of the parish. They stated in their petition that section 19 of the Endowed Schools Act 1869, provided that:

"a scheme relating to any educational endowment, the scholars educated by which are, in the opinion of the Commissioners (subject to appeal to Her Majesty in Council), required by the express terms of the original instrument of foundation, of the statutes or regulations made by the founder or under his authority in his lifetime, or within fifty years after his death (which terms have been observed down to the commencement of this Act), to learn or to be instructed to the doctrines or formularies of any particular church, sect, or denomination, is excepted from the foregoing provisions respecting religious instruction and attendance at religious worship (other than the provisions for the exemption of day scholars from attending prayer or religious worship, or lessons on a religious subject, when such exemption has been claimed on their behalf), and respecting the qualification of the governing body and masters (unless the governing body constituted as it would have been if no scheme under this Act had been made assents to such scheme)."

The provision for the expenditure of £20 in prizes for religious knowledge was not, the petitioners urged, a due or sufficient compliance with the spirit and wishes of the founders and early supporters of the school. They also contended that clauses which provided that religious opinion or attendance or non-attendance at any particular form of religious worship, or exemption from attending prayer or religious worship, in either the qualification of the governors or the holders of the exhibitions, were not in accordance with section 19 of the Endowed Schools Act with regard to such endowments, and that no provision was made for the religious education of the holders of the exhibitions at schools in connexion with the Church of England, or for attendance at public worship at the parish church on the Lord's day, or for further religious and catechetical training, except in the granting of prizes of the value of £20, which provision did not extend to the learning and study of the catechism and teaching of the Church of England. For these reasons, among others, the petitioners prayed Her Majesty in Council to withhold approval from the scheme, or in any case from those parts of it which were inconsistent with their contentions, or which injuriously affected the petitioners and their vested interests.

Extract from Judgment

EARL OF SELBORNE L.C.: . . . the Commissioners, for whatever reason, have thought that those endowments may be made useful if they are not any longer applied in carrying on the particular schools in the parish of St Leonard, Shoreditch, but are applied in exhibitions for the benefit of a larger area of schools for boys and for girls. Their Lordships are unable to find any solid reason for saying that this was not within the power of the Commissioners. Taking it to have been within their powers, no question is or can be raised as to the way in which they have exercised them; and that is not a proper subject of appeal if the scheme was not in that respect unauthorised by the Act. . . .

Now it is impossible to read the 19th clause of the Act of 1869 without being struck by the care and anxiety which the Legislature has exhibited there to prevent denominational restrictions from being applied to any school as to which there was not demonstrative evidence that the original founders of the school had not only formed, but expressed, an intention that the children should be instructed according to the doctrines or formularies of a particular church, sect, or denomination, or, in the added words of the later Act, should be members of a particular church, sect, or denomination. It is impossible not to be struck by the anxiety which the Legislature has displayed to exclude, not only every uncertain, but also every merely probable, implication from practice alone of such an intention; for it is required, first of all, that the denominational purpose should be manifested by the express terms, either of the original instrument of foundation, or of some statutes or regulations. Perhaps it is not absolutely necessary to say that regulations within the meaning of the clause could not have been oral, but it is tolerably plain that there would be great difficulty in the proof of any such oral regulations, even if binding; and certainly the other words, "instrument of foundation or statutes," point with great distinctness to written instruments. The Legislature, by requiring "express terms," going for the present no further, has manifested a clear intention to exclude mere implication. It is not that only. Not only must it be done by the express terms of that which, in two cases at all events, must necessarily be an instrument in writing, and in the third case could scarcely be otherwise; but the instrument of foundation, statutes, or regulations, must in the next place have been made by the founder or by his authority, and if by the founder of course in his lifetime. What is meant by founder, and what is meant by authority? Now, in the ordinary case of a foundation by one or more individual persons who created the endowment, there is of course no difficulty in the application of those words. But their Lordships have here to deal with a charity not so founded, but which was commenced by subscriptions at Michaelmas 1705. The Bishop of Oxford was asked at that time to preach a

charity sermon for the school; and in the list of benefactions the first benefac-
tion appears to have been given in 1706, and it goes on at different dates; a
collection being made for building in 1722.

Now let us consider what is the reasonable manner of applying to such a
charity the word "founder." It is reasonably clear that not every subscriber or
contributor could be a founder having control over the school, or capable
within the meaning of the Act of Parliament of impressing on it, by his own
act or by his own authority a denominational character. It is also reasonably
plain, when you have once started with a foundation in 1705, though by small
beginnings, yet that everything afterwards added, every accretion to the
original subscriptions, which was not an endowment for any new and special
purpose, must be taken to be upon the footing of the original foundation; not
a new foundation, but something contributed for the purpose of the original
foundation. You are carried back, therefore, in considering who ought to be
regarded as the founder or founders, to the very inception of the charity, to the
very first subscriptions, in this case to the years 1705 or 1706. Now it is quite
conceivable that a number of persons might have met at that time, and might
have come to a common agreement as to the purposes for which they should
subscribe and solicit subscriptions; and if that had been embodied in writing,
and if they had solicited subscriptions on the footing that either they them-
serves were to make a law for the charity and give it statutes, or that this was
to be done by others in a particular manner, or if in any original documents
soliciting subscriptions there had been a written law laid down for the charity
expressing the purposes for which it was to be founded, those persons so
initiating the subscriptions, and so declaring the purpose for which they were
made and solicited, might be regarded as founders within the meaning of this
clause. But it appears to their Lordships to be quite impossible to attribute
that character to those who come after them—whether they contributed to the
building fund or any other fund in aid of the existing charity or not. They did
not found the charity; they found it existing; they merely aided and assisted it.

The question in this case is, whether the conditions of this clause of the
statute are shown to have been fulfilled as to the charity which had its foundation or inception in the only sense which can bring the words of the clause into
play at all—as early as 1705 or 1706. The clause says that there must be express
terms. Here it is admitted there is no original instrument of foundation at all;
there are no statutes, therefore they may be laid aside. Then we come to the
other word "regulations," and we must find by proper evidence the express
terms of some regulations which were made by the founder or by his
authority; and it is clear that there are no regulations of which the express
terms appear, directly or indirectly, made by the original founder, or by his
authority; and that last term, "by his authority," is not without any limit of
time, but must be either in his lifetime or within fifty years after his death.

If it is sound reason that the original founders must be taken to be those
persons who first subscribed to and collected subscriptions for this charity in
the years 1705 and 1706, what is there upon which the conclusion can possibly

be founded, that any regulations requiring in express terms that the scholars should be instructed according to the doctrine or formularies of the Church of England, or should be members of that Church, what is there from which it can be inferred that any such regulations were ever made, and still more that they were made within fifty years after the death of the original founders, and by their authority? The only thing brought forward in support of the conclusion that there were any such regulations consists of certain entries in books, which show that as a matter of fact the children were taken to church, and probably that they were instructed in the catechism. Suppose it to be so, there is all the difference in the world between a practice for the time being and statutes or regulations expressly requiring that such a practice should always be observed. The clause in the Act would not be satisfied without statutes or regulations in express terms; and the manifest purpose of the clause would be defeated as to almost every school in the kingdom, not of very recent origin indeed, if it were held that mere practice should be taken as sufficient evidence of there having been at some time or other regulations made under the authority of the founder expressly requiring that practice always to be observed.

That disposes of everything except the regulations of 1774. Now, if their Lordships had thought it necessary to hear counsel from the Commissioners, it is probable that some argument might have been addressed to them as to the effect of those regulations and whether they would be sufficient, even if made within fifty years, or by the founder, to establish the denominational character of these schools. But, not having heard the counsel on the other side, their Lordships are ready to assume, for the present purpose, that what appears upon the face of those regulations, if they had been made by the original founders, might have been enough. They do not, of course, decide that it would have been so. But what is the evidence that those regulations were made by the authority of the original founders, or were made within fifty years after their deaths, which may also be assumed for this purpose to mean the death of the last survivor. The original foundation was nearly seventy years before the date of those regulations—of those orders. It is more probable than not, at all events, that the original founders were in 1705 at least persons of full age—twenty-one years of age. They might have been living within the fifty years before 1774. The burden of proof as to this is upon those who allege that the case is brought within the clause of the statute, and no attempt has been made to prove that any one of the original founders was living within fifty years before 1774, which would be necessary to make it come within the limit of time, unless we are to assume that Mr Collman was one of the original founders. All, however, that we know about Mr Collman is, that at a date considerably later than the original foundation, 1718, he appears as a trustee and as *de facto* treasurer, and taking an active part in the management of the charity. His name does not appear in the list of benefactors as an original contributor; and if he was not, he was not a founder who could himself have made statutes or given any authority to do so. Then there is an equal defect of the necessary evidence of authority, even if it were known that some of the original founders were living within fifty years of 1774. What is the evidence that the rules and orders of that date were made by the authority of those original founders? The authority of some of those original founders might not have been enough—it must have been that of all the original founders. Is the mere fact that the management of the charity was carried on by certain trustees enough to lead to an inference of law that they might at any time make rules impressing a new character, a more definitely denominational character than it had before, upon the foundation? They might, if that doctrine were tenable, have in many other respects altered the conditions of the charity, and might have made it more or less beneficial according to their mere will and pleasure. It was admitted—no other answer could have been given to the question—that if they had changed its character, and made it denominational in any new or different way, as, for instance, a Roman Catholic school or a Jews' school, in 1774, they would have been guilty of a gross breach of trust, for which no authority whatever could have been presumed, and which the Court of Chancery of that day would most undoubtedly have corrected. If they could not impress upon it any new denominational character, could they impress upon it any denominational character of a binding nature different from that which it originally had? Could they do that which this clause contemplates— exclude from the school, if otherwise admissible to it, any persons who were not willing to learn or to be instructed according to the doctrine or formularies of any particular church, sect, or denomination—not merely exclude them by way of management or discipline from year to year, but as by statute and regulation for ever?—

It would be impossible to infer that the original founders intended, under mere ordinary powers of management, to give any such authority to the managers for the time being. The result is, that the case is not brought within this clause of the statute, either by the orders of 1774 or by any other means; and that the petition fails.

Their Lordships will therefore humbly recommend Her Majesty that the Scheme of the Charity Commissioners relating to these foundations should be approved.

Petition dismissed

(C) WHAT IS A UNIVERSITY?

139 St David's College, Lampeter *v.* Ministry of Education [1951]
1 All E.R. 559

CHANCERY DIVISION
A college is not a university unless this is expressly or impliedly declared in its charters, especially if its power to confer degrees be limited.

Facts: The plaintiff college sought a declaration that they were a university, and were providing a university education; and further they were a university within the meaning of the regulations relating to university supplemental awards, and were entitled to have their claim for the recognition of their scholarships for supplementation under the regulations considered by the Ministry of Education on its merits.

The college was founded as the result of a scheme put forward to found a college in Wales for the training of candidates for Holy Orders who could not afford to proceed to Oxford or Cambridge, and was opened in 1827. It was incorporated by royal charter in 1829. The first charter conferred no power to grant degrees.

Further royal charters were granted in 1853, 1865 and 1896, as a result of which the plaintiff college was authorised to confer on its students the degrees of B.D. and B.A. In addition to a pass course for the degree of B.A., the plaintiff college provided honours courses in classics, mathematics, history, English, Welsh, philosophy, and theology. Graduates of the college were granted by other universities a status equal to that of their own graduates.

In March 1949, the college applied to the Ministry of Education for recognition of its scholarships as ranking for supplementation under the regulations relating to university supplemental awards. That request was refused by the Ministry, which stated that such supplemental awards could be awarded only to students of an institution coming within the definition of a university or university college, and that the plaintiff college was not so recognised by the Ministry.

Evidence was given by Mr Douglas Veale, the Registrar of Oxford University to the effect that the college was affiliated to the University and had the privilege of sending its graduates to Oxford where they were entitled to take a degree without preliminary examinations and without the usual three years' residence. He agreed that St David's College and the University College of North Staffordshire[1] were the only colleges in the country restricted to awarding bachelors' degrees. The Registrar of Cambridge University, Dr Walter Grave, said that St David's College was affiliated to his university with effects similar to those at Oxford.

Mr Hedley Pickbourne, the Registrar of Nottingham University, said he thought that what was meant by a university was a power to confer degrees and frame its own course of instruction. Mr J. T. Christie, the principal of Jesus College, Oxford, considered a university to be a place of higher education with power to confer degrees. He thought the distinction between a university and a university college was the power to confer degrees.

Dr Leonard Hodgson, the Regius Professor of Divinity at Oxford said that St David's had a good university standard, parallel to that of other institutions. Similar evidence was given by Professor A. G. Dickens, Professor of History at University College Hull, and chairman of the board of external examiners at St David's College.

Canon H. K. Archdall, the Principal of St David's College, said its purpose

1. The University College of North Staffordshire received its charter of incorporation as the University of Keele in 1962, and may now award a full range of degrees.

was to give a general education, and it was no longer restricted to persons destined for Holy Orders. It had always existed to help poor people, and its fees were about £130, as against £300 at Oxford. The number of students had dropped from 200 to 170 because, although the College had funds for building, they had not been able to get a builder's licence. He regarded the power to confer degrees and the possession of a charter as the marks which distinguished a university from a university college.

On behalf of the Ministry of Education, Mr G. N. Flemming, a deputy secretary, said that it was the established practice to treat as universities institutions named as such in royal charters.

Buckley (for the defendants): St David's College could not become a university until the status of university was conferred on it by the Crown. Unless it is true that a university is a body accorded that status by the Crown, the term "university" is as indefinite and equivocal as, for example, the term "public school." The word "university" has never been judicially considered. There is no statutory definition of it. Dr Johnson, in the eighteenth century, thought that it was a place where all the arts and faculties were taught. But it is doubtful whether that would apply today. Wharton defined it as a body "having power to grant degrees such as Masters of Arts and Doctors of Divinity." In the older universities the right to a voice in Convocation is restricted to Masters of Arts and to Bachelors of certain selected faculties. The right to give bachelors' degrees only could not give a body conferring them the right to call itself a university.

Sir Andrew Clark K.C.: There is no ground on which it could properly be suggested that St David's College is not a university. The matter is not a trivial one. The question whether the college is or is not a university is one of considerable interest and importance.

Extract from Judgment

VAISEY J.: . . . In my judgment, the word "university" is not a word of art, and, although for the most part one can identify a university when one sees it, it is, perhaps not easy to define it in precise and accurate language. There are obviously universities which are such by common consent, the status of which as such no man could deny. That applies not only to the two ancient universities—Oxford and Cambridge—but to others which have since been founded (I think nearly all of them not earlier than the nineteenth century). There is no question that such institutions as the universities of London, Durham, Manchester and so forth, are universities in the fullest and most proper sense. St David's College, Lampeter, is admittedly a borderline institution. One of the witnesses described it as in its nature unique, and I ventured to use a phrase of, perhaps, identical meaning and to call it *sui generis*, *i.e.* it is an institution which stands in a class by itself. The question which falls for me to decide is: Is that class within the ambit of the definition and proper understanding of the word "university" or is it not?

Counsel for the plaintiffs has enumerated what he regards as the essential qualities which justify an institution being described as a university, and I do not think that there is much doubt that essentially, with exceptions which I will mention, St David's possesses those qualifications. He said, in the first place, that it must be incorporated by the highest authority, *i.e.* by the sovereign power, succeeding, no doubt, to the Papal privilege which was exercised in Christendom in the middle ages by the proper, and indeed, only, body which could incorporate and give authority to a great teaching institution. There is no doubt that St David's College was incorporated and re-incorporated and that its incorporation was confirmed and strengthened by acts of the sovereign power, that is to say, by royal charter. Secondly, it is suggested that, to be a university, an institution must be open to receive students from any part of the world. There, again, there is no suggestion that there is any kind of bar to students from any locality at St David's College. It is said further that there must be a plurality of masters, *i.e.*, that there cannot be a university with only one teacher. It is clear from the charters that those who teach in this college are numerous. Again, it was suggested that a university, to be such, must be an institution in which at least one of the higher faculties is taught, those higher faculties being, of course, theology—the queen of sciences—law or philosophy, which in some definitions are regarded as identical, and, thirdly, medicine. Then it is said that there cannot be a university without residents either in its own buildings or near at hand. It is said that residence is a necessary qualification. I have left until last what is stated to be the most obvious and most essential quality of a university, that is, that it must have power to grant its own degrees. Here we find the very curious situation that the royal prerogative of granting degrees in the various faculties and branches of knowledge has been granted to this particular institution subject to a very strict limitation. It is only entitled to grant the degrees of bachelor of arts and bachelor of divinity. It has not of its own essential power any right to grant degrees, but to that limited extent the royal privilege has been acceded to it by royal concession.

That being the position, I have no doubt that St David's College possesses (I will come back to the question of degrees) most of the necessary ingredients that go to make a foundation or institution a university, but, if the word "university" is not one of art, I have to try to see what it means, regard being had to those particular qualities which I have enumerated. I have to see whether or not, in accordance with the ordinary language of mankind, this small college, doing admirable work, is properly to be described as and ought to be regarded as a university. I think that it is very difficult, when you are dealing with a word of general import like this, to lay down the precise criteria, but I ask myself what the ordinary man would say if he were asked whether this college was a university. I am not referring to the man in the street—a man who, perhaps, has had no university education or no experience of what a university is—but to the ordinary man who does know what a university is or who has received his education at a university. I cannot bring myself to believe that such a man would say that St David's College, Lampeter, was a university. It does not, I think, follow that, if it possesses all or most of the qualities of a university, it necessarily follows that it is a university. I am inclined to think that the onus must lie on this institution, which has never been called a university in any of its charters. It is true it is included among the universities in, for instance, such a well known reference book as *Crockford's Clerical Directory*, and it may for some purposes count as a university or be considered as equivalent to a university, or, to use another phrase, to rank as a university or to provide instruction of university standard. I cannot bring myself to think that that is enough. I cannot help feeling that this extraordinarily limited power of granting degrees, which has throughout been regarded during the arguments as being really the test for the solution of this problem, is an indication that this institution falls short of a university properly so called. It was suggested to me that weight must be given to the fact that, in the charters on which its existence depends and by which it was founded, though there are possible slight indications the other way, care is taken not to call this institution a university. It was never incorporated as a university, and, although the word may not have any technical significance and one can imagine a case in which a teaching institution is given such plenary powers of instruction and so forth as would lead irresistibly to the conclusion that the Crown intended to make it a university, I do not think that this is such an institution. Although I must not be supposed for one moment to think that a university has to be judged by its size or the number of its pupils or by the range of instruction which it gives, still, size is a matter of some consideration. I cannot believe that this one single college, this one single educational establishment, with all its merits and the good work which it does and all the advantages which it gives to those who resort to it for instruction, in any ordinary sense of the word could properly be described as a university.

I agree that since the foundation of the University of Wales with its four constituent colleges there has been some confusion. A great many people, I think, might ignorantly be led to believe that St David's College was part of the University of Wales. It is nothing of the kind; it is an entirely separate and older foundation. In a sense it might be regarded as a rival and complement of the University of Wales, but the question which I have to decide is whether or not it stands on the same footing and is of the same character and quality as the University of Wales which was incorporated as a university. It has never called itself a university and, although included with the universities in certain books of reference, I have had no evidence to show that anybody has ever referred to it as a university. It may in certain ways be said to give a university education, that its standards are those of a university, and that its teaching is of the quality which is to be found in a university, but there still remains the gap to be bridged, the doubt whether, however closely it approximates in its aims, character, activities and merits to a university, this college can properly be described as a university. Judging the matter both on broad principles and on the narrow principles of its limited powers and the absence of any express intention of making it a university by the sovereign power, I think that the plaintiffs have not discharged the onus of satisfying me that the college ought to be called and to be considered, in accordance with the proper meaning of the English language, a university.

I am also asked to declare that the foundation is providing university education. I do not propose to do that, but I would like to say, though I do not think it is a matter to be put in the form of an order, that it is providing education of the same type and class as is to be found in universities and the teaching is of the highest class, and that I do not wish anything that I have said to limit in any way the high reputation which this college is enjoying.

Declaration that St David's College,
Lampeter, is not a university

[NOTE: After this judgment the University Grants Committee examined various ways in which the College might be helped and, in 1957, reported that assistance could be given only if it entered into an organic relationship with an existing university institution. A suggested association with the University College of Wales at Aberystwyth was not acceptable to Lampeter but, in December 1960, a sponsorship scheme acceptable to the University Grants Committee was agreed. The College is now sponsored by the University College of South Wales and Monmouthshire, Cardiff, but candidates for the degree of Bachelor of Divinity are still examined under the charter of 1852. The College was enabled to receive a grant for its temporary building scheme, to expand to 250 Arts students, and to increase its tutorial staff.]

(D) UNIVERSITY EXAMINATIONS: POWER OF COURTS TO INTERFERE

140 Thorne *v.* University of London [1966] 2 Q.B. 237

QUEEN'S BENCH DIVISION

All questions affecting the construction and the carrying into effect of the regulations of a university relating to degrees are exclusively justiciable by the Visitor, and cannot be determined by the Courts.

Facts: Dr Carl Thorne was a candidate in three subjects at the examination for the degree of Bachelor of Laws of the University of London. He alleged that his failure was due to the negligence of the examiners in marking his papers, and claimed damages for negligence, the writ being endorsed: "The plaintiff's claim is for damages for negligently misjudging the plaintiff's examination papers for the intermediate and final LL.B., and for a mandamus* commanding the defendants to award the plaintiff the grade at least justified."

The University entered an unconditional appearance to the writ, and applied to strike out the plaintiff's claim as frivolous, and disclosing no reasonable cause of action. The master struck out the writ and statement of claim accordingly, and this decision was upheld in chambers by John Stephenson J.

The plaintiff made an *ex parte** application for leave to appeal. Notice of the application had not been given to the defendants, and the Court (Wilmer, Dankwerts, and Salmon L.JJ.) adjourned the application.

At the adjourned hearing (before Diplock and Salmon L.JJ.) the plaintiff maintained that he did not need leave to appeal, since leave was necessary only in the case of an interlocutory order,* and an order striking out a writ was a final order. He also claimed that by entering an unconditional appearance, the defendants had submitted themselves to the jurisdiction of the High Court, thereby waiving any objection to the jurisdiction of the court. Finally, he maintained that a dispute arising from an implication of negligence in the marking of examinations was a matter which might be determined by the High Court, and was not simply a dispute between members of the University.

Extract from Judgment

DIPLOCK L.J.: . . . The plaintiff has set out a good deal of praise of his ability as a lawyer . . . and he claims that [his failure] was a result of negligence on the part of the examiners. There is clear and recent authority in *R. v. Dunsheath, ex p. Meredith*[1] that actions of this kind relating to domestic disputes between members of the University of London (as is the case with other universities) are matters which are to be dealt with by the Visitor,* and the court has no jurisdiction to deal with them. In that case which was a decision of the Divisional Court, Lord Goddard C.J. referred with approval to *Thomson v. London University*.[2] That was another case in which a budding lawyer complained about what had happened to him in the examinations held by the university, and there is a passage in the judgment of Kindersley V.-C.

1. [1951] 1 K.B. 127. In this case 50 members of the university had signed a requisition to summon a special meeting of Convocation to discuss, *inter alia*,* the refusal of a school of the university to re-employ one of its teachers. The chairman of Convocation refused on the ground that the matter was not one which related to the university, or one on which Convocation could properly declare its opinion because it related to a matter within the discretion of the council of the school in question. The 50 members sought an order of mandamus,* which was refused on the ground that the question whether an officer of the university had refused to perform a duty placed upon him by the statutes of the university was a domestic matter and, therefore, one essentially for the Visitor.*

2. (1864) 33 L.J. Ch. 625. The university had awarded the plaintiff a gold medal as being the candidate who had obtained the highest marks in the 1861 examination for the LL.D. degree. Two years later the senate discovered that, according to the senate's construction of the regulations, the examiners had miscarried in the mode they had adopted in ascertaining the highest number of marks. The senate then gave a second gold medal to the candidate who, in their view should have received the award in the first place. The plaintiff alleged that, before becoming a candidate, he had been informed by the registrar that the examination would be conducted, and the marks ascertained in the way in which they subsequently were. He maintained that he had become a candidate and had paid his fee upon that footing, and he asked that the university might be restrained from awarding such other medal. It was held that the court had no jurisdiction, since the matter was entirely for the Visitor, and, even had jurisdiction been established, the plaintiff had not alleged any sufficient ground of equity.

which covers exactly the sort of claim which the plaintiff has put forward in the present case. Kindersley V.-C. said this:

"The holding of examinations and the conferring of degrees being one, if not the main or only object of this university, all the regulations, that is, the construction of all the regulations and the carrying into effect of all those regulations as among persons who are either actually members of the university or who come in and subject themselves to be at least *pro hac vice* members of the university—I mean with respect to the degrees which they seek to have conferred upon them—all those are regulations of the domus: they are regulations clearly in my mind within the jurisdiction, and the exclusive jurisdiction, of the Visitor."

Those words, which were approved in *R* v. *Dunsheath, ex p. Meredith*,[3] cover precisely the sort of claim which the plaintiff seeks to bring before the High Court in this action. The High Court does not act as a court of appeal from university examiners; and, speaking for my own part, I am very glad that it declines this jurisdiction. Clearly, it does decline the jurisdiction.

The action is wholly misconceived, and the decision of the judge to strike out the indorsement on the writ and the statement of claim and to dismiss the action was clearly right.

Application dismissed with costs

(E) EXTRANEOUS DUTIES: COLLECTION OF MEALS MONEY

141 Price *v.* Sunderland Corporation [1956] 3 All E.R. 153

QUEEN'S BENCH DIVISION

It is ultra vires *for a local education authority to require teachers to collect money for the purposes of the schools meals service.*

Facts: The plaintiffs, Mr P. P. Price, headmaster of Thomas Street Junior Mixed School, Sunderland, and five other schoolmasters were members of the Sunderland and District Association of Schoolmasters, a division of the National Association of Schoolmasters.

From the coming into force of the School Meals Act 1906, the provision of meals during school hours was regulated by supervision of meals by teachers and the collection of money by teachers. During the war the provision of school meals was national policy, and teachers voluntarily undertook supervisory duties and, in most places, the collection of money.

Section 49 of the Education Act 1944 empowered the Minister of Education to make regulations for the provision of meals " . . . so, however, that such regulations shall not impose upon teachers at any school . . . duties in respect of meals other than the supervision of pupils. . . . " Some authorities provided clerical assistance for the collection of the money; in other places the teachers went on doing it.

3. [1951] 1 K.B. 127.

In the mid-1950s there was considerable feeling in the teaching profession about increases in salaries, and this was heightened by a decision to raise the superannuation contributions deducted from teachers' salaries from 5 to 6 per cent. The National Association of Schoolmasters, in order to draw public attention to the situation, instructed members in a number of its branches to stop collecting money for school meals from the beginning of the summer term, 1956.

All local education authorities concerned, with the exception of Sunderland, accepted the situation. The Sunderland County Borough Council said that the collection was a term of employment of the teachers. Thereupon the Association's branch in Sunderland, consisting of about 350 schoolmasters, asked the court for a declaration whether the authority's claim was right or not. The local education authority then dismissed five of the plaintiffs. The six plaintiffs now moved for (1) a declaration that a resolution of the council that those teachers employed by the defendants who were members of the association and refused to collect money for school meals in school hours be given notice to terminate their engagement on August 31, 1956, was *ultra vires** and in breach of the defendants' statutory duty to the plaintiffs under section 49 of the Education Act 1944; and that the defendants were not entitled to impose on the teachers in their employment any school duties in respect of meals other than the supervision of pupils, namely the duties of clerks and cashiers; and (2) an injunction restraining the defendants from giving effect to their resolution to dismiss the plaintiffs.

Extract from Judgment

BARRY J.: . . . Two questions arise and require consideration. The first is whether, on the true construction of section 49 of the Education Act 1944, these plaintiffs could be required by the defendant council, as a term of their employment, to carry out the particular duty of collecting money from the children when brought to the school as payment for meals. If section 49 of the Act does not prohibit the defendant council from making any such requirements, then clearly the resolution of the council was warranted by the facts and is a valid resolution. Counsel for the plaintiffs did not seek to argue the contrary. If, on the other hand, the correct interpretation of section 49 of the Act is that it prohibits local education authorities from requiring their teachers to take any part in the administration of the school meals service other than the mere supervision of the children at the time when they are having their meals, then there arises a further question whether the resolution of the defendant council was *ultra vires*?

Counsel for the defendant council contends that, even if he is wrong in his submission as to the true effect of section 49, none the less the defendant council were perfectly entitled to dispense with the services of these six teachers by giving them the appropriate period of notice in accordance with their contract of service. . . .

Counsel for the plaintiffs puts his case very simply. He says that section 49 of the Education Act 1944 means what it says, namely, that a local education authority or borough council may not impose on teachers at any school duties in respect of meals other than the supervision of pupils. He says that the collection of money paid by parents for meals provided is quite clearly a duty in respect of meals and, on the clear wording of the section, no teacher can be required, as part of his conditions of service, to undertake that duty. That is how he puts the plaintiffs' case; and I am bound to say that it has a simplicity and a clarity which, at first sight at least, adds considerable conviction to his argument.

The argument of counsel for the defendant council, as I understood it, was based on the submission that the words "duties in respect of meals" mean merely duties in respect of meals understood in the narrow sense, that is to say duties in respect of the period during which the children are actually consuming the food which is placed before them by the local authority. He refers, of course, to the wording of the earlier Acts, particularly section 85 of the Education Act 1921, and points to the phrase contained in that section "supervising or assisting in the provision of meals or in the collection of the cost thereof." He says, as I understand his argument, that this expression "duties in respect of meals" means something different from duties connected with the provision of meals, and that, on the true construction of the section, such duties as the collection of the cost of the meal, which was separately dealt with by section 85 of the Education Act 1921 can still be imposed on the teachers as not being a duty in respect of a meal in the narrow sense for which he contends, but possibly a duty in connection with the service of the meal or the provision of the meal. He points out, with some force, that it is, on the face of it, strange that the section does not place any similar limitation on the powers of the authority in relation to their duties connected with the provision of milk or other refreshment and is confined to the question of meals alone. His argument is reinforced by the fact that, at the time the Act was passed (and, incidentally at the time when the regulations under section 49 were made) a charge was made for the provision of milk, and the regulations do in fact deal with the charges to be made both for milk and for other refreshments.

It is not for me to explore the motives which may have actuated the Legislature in framing the Act in the widest terms; but I am bound to say that I find it quite impossible to place such a narrow construction on the words "in respect of meals." If section 49 of the Education Act 1944 had repeated the words "assisting in the provision of meals" I think it might well have been right to say that those words would not cover the work of collecting the cost of the meals, which was, of course, treated by the Education Act 1921 as an entirely separate duty and not as part of the service of assisting in the provision of meals.

It is on account of the very much wider words, namely, "in respect of meals," used in the Act of 1944, that I do not think I can cut down the meaning of those duties in respect of meals to say that they exclude the collection of money held by the children or their parents for those meals. I feel bound to accept the submission that the collection of that money is beyond argument a duty in respect of meals. The money is payable for the meals. It would not be if the meals were not provided or if the children did not partake of them, but on any reasonable construction the words "duties in respect of meals" must include the collection of money payable for the meals.

I have therefore come to the conclusion, not without some hesitation, that the plaintiff's contention as regards section 49 is the correct one, and that under that section the local education authority may require their teachers to supervise the pupils during meals. That does not mean the defendant council cannot, with the teachers' consent, carry out the full scheme which is at present being carried out; but it does mean that the services rendered by the teachers in the carrying out of that full scheme are voluntary, and that the defendant council cannot require the teachers, as a condition of their employment, to undertake them.

Teachers, as everyone knows, do undertake a number of voluntary services, and I for one sincerely hope that nothing in the present decision of the court will prevent that happy state of affairs from continuing. None the less, I am quite satisfied that under the clear provisions of section 49 of the Education Act 1944, any services rendered by teachers in connection with what the Minister in the Provision of Milk and Meals Regulations 1945[1] described as the school meals service, other than that of supervision, are services voluntarily undertaken. That is the view of the Act for which these plaintiffs and their association have always contended, and it is a correct view.

Having reached that conclusion, I have to consider the second question which requires consideration in view of the fact that teachers cannot be required to give services to the school meals service other than the work of supervision of the pupils during meal time, namely, have the authority power to pass the resolution which is now called in question?

It has long been held that the courts will not inquire into or interfere with the decisions and actions of local authorities and other statutory bodies so long as their decisions are reached bona fide and within their statutory powers. It is conceded by counsel for the defendant council, and indeed it is abundantly clear on the authorities, that, in relation to the dismissal of servants, a statutory body such as a borough council stands in a somewhat different position from that of a private individual. Under the law of this country a private individual can engage and dismiss servants at his will, and if he engages a servant on terms that that servant's employment can be terminated at a month's notice, the master, if he be a private individual, can give a month's notice and no court can inquire into the motive for his doing so.

The position is somewhat different in the case of statutory bodies. A local authority or any statutory body cannot either employ or dismiss servants except under statutory authority: their powers are derived from the statute or statutes under which they are created. And it is a very well-known principle of law that statutory powers can only be exercised for the purpose for which

1. S.R. & O. 1945, No. 698.

they are granted. Therefore there may be cases where a local authority in resolving to dismiss a servant or to take any other action, can have its decision called into question in the courts if those who call it into question can establish that that decision was taken either *mala fide* or that it was a decision which did not lie within the local authority's statutory powers.

The burden rests on those who call into question any decision of a local authority, and it is a heavy burden. I have not here to decide whether it was right or wrong that the local authority in this case should have decided to dismiss these six teachers and the other members of the association. What I have to inquire into is whether it was within their statutory powers to do so in the particular circumstances now under consideration. . . .

It is abundantly clear that the defendant council were saying that unless the teachers withdrew their refusal to collect the children's money, they had got to go. That seems to me, without any shadow of doubt, to be a requirement that the teachers shall undertake a duty in respect of meals other than the supervision of pupils. If that be so, I find it very difficult to attribute any other meaning to the resolution—either read alone or in conjunction with the letters preceding it and following it—than one which indicates that it is *ultra vires*. It cannot be within the powers of the local authority to resolve to take an action which the Act of Parliament under which their powers are derived clearly prohibits.

There can be no doubt that this resolution does require the teachers to collect the school meals money under pain of dismissal. That is the only way in which such a requirement can be enforced; and a threat of dismissal unless a teacher carries out that duty is the clearest possible contravention of the express wording of section 49 of the Education Act 1944.

In those circumstances I have come to the conclusion, that, although no one suggests that the defendant council were not acting in a sense bona fide, or that they were actuated by a malicious motive, their decision to dismiss the plaintiffs merely because they decided to withhold voluntary service, when the Act of Parliament expressly prohibits the defendant council from requiring that service, was *ultra vires*. The plaintiffs are therefore entitled in substance to the relief claimed.

[After discussion the declaration was made in a form declaring that the duties of collecting and recording the cost of school meals were duties in respect of meals other than supervision within the meaning of section 49 of the Education Act 1944 and that the defendant council were not entitled to impose such duties on teachers in their employ.]

Declaration and injunction with costs

[NOTE: Barry J.'s judgment was delivered on July 13, 1956. On July 20 the association lifted the ban on the collection of money and requested the authority to receive a deputation with a view to making suitable arrangements "whereby teachers shall be freed from such tasks and, in particular, from the collection and recording of school meals money." At a special meeting of the Council on August 15, 1956, the notices of dismissal were withdrawn following a resolution not to appeal against the decision of

Barry J. It was suggested that the school health and welfare sub-committee be instructed to consider future arrangements. All references to the notices of dismissal were to be expunged from the records.

For a discussion of further developments following this case see G. R. Barrell, *Teachers and the Law* (Methuen, 3rd ed., 1966) pages 206–210.]

(F) SUPPLY OF CLOTHING TO PUPILS

142 Clements *v.* Williams (1837) 8 C. & P. 58

COURT OF COMMON PLEAS

No schoolmaster has the right to charge for clothing which he has caused to be supplied without the sanction, expressed or implied, of the parent.

Facts: The plaintiff was a schoolmaster at Turnham Green, and the defendant was an attorney living at Sawbridgeworth in Hertfordshire.

In about 1832 William Lewis was admitted as a pupil of the school. The boy inherited some property from one of his mother's relatives but, the father having turned out badly, the Chancellor gave the lad's custody to the defendant. The defendant allowed the boy to remain at the school. Having regard to the fact that the sum allowed by the court for the boy's education and maintenance was £50 per annum, the defendant objected to the inclusion of several items in the half-yearly school bills, although he had paid them regularly at first.

An agreement was signed by the plaintiff by which he undertook the whole charge, except for "coach-hire, letters, and parcels" for the sum of thirty guineas per annum.

Shortly afterwards the parties fell out, and the defendant called to take away the boy and to pay the half-yearly bill. The plaintiff offered to release the pupil to the defendant on the production of a proper order from the Chancellor authorising him to do so. This was obtained, and the plaintiff then returned the boy to his guardian, having previously permitted him to visit his father. With the boy was sent a bill in which he charged not only for a half-year's board, but also for a quantity of sundries, far exceeding the amount agreed upon. These items consisted chiefly of a cloak, a suit of clothes, stockings, handkerchiefs, and a quarter's drawing lessons in 1832. The account was for £28 7s. 7d., of which the defendant paid £16 13s. 6d. into court, leaving a disputed balance of £11 14s. 1d.

The plaintiff claimed that the items were reasonable and usual, the boy having been very badly provided by his guardian, and having been kept away from church because of the shabbiness of his clothes. He had a new suit of clothes in June 1834, but these things were not given him by the plaintiff until September 1835.

The boy said that he had told his guardian in August 1835 that he did not need anything, and the clothes were not provided until just before the Christmas vacation, after notice of intended removal had been given. The cloak was actually sent to him while he was staying with his father during the holidays. For the defendant it was claimed that the charge for the drawing lessons had been paid in 1833.

Extract from Summing-up

WILLIAMS J.: . . No schoolmaster has any authority to cause his pupil to be supplied with articles of wearing apparel without the sanction, express or implied, of the parent or guardian, and it is the duty of the schoolmaster, if he observes his pupil to be in want of such articles, to communicate that fact to the boy's friends, and not to furnish him with such things without their authority. However, there is a distinction to be drawn between providing new clothes and the expenditure necessary to repair the clothes in use, which you will no doubt pay attention to in returning your verdict. The sum of £16 13s. 6d. has been paid into court, and the question is, whether the plaintiff is entitled to anything beyond that sum.

Verdict for the plaintiff for the sum paid in, together with 17s. 6d. for reparation

(G) ASSAULT ON A TEACHER

143 M'Carogher *v.* Hodgson (1964) *The Times*, November 24

QUEEN'S BENCH DIVISION
Running on to the hand of another does not constitute an assault by that other person.

Facts: The plaintiff, Miss Averil Ernestine Sanctuary M'Carogher was, for ten years, French mistress at the Christ Church Cathedral Choir School, Oxford. She claimed that she had been assaulted by the Reverend Canon Leonard Hodgson, Regius Professor of Divinity at Oxford on July 19, 1958.

The plaintiff said that she had taught French at the school for ten years, and was giving evening private coaching in her room on June 12, 1958, when a boy delivered a letter to her from the headmaster stating that, having made several unsuccessful attempts to see her, he was writing what he would have said, that he had for some time been worried about the progress of "the less gifted in French," and had decided in spite of her knowledge of the language and efforts in teaching, that he had to give her a half-term's notice, and that, if she required a testimonial, she should let him know.

She made arrangements to see the Governors, and wrote a letter to the headmaster saying that she did not accept her dismissal. On July 19, after class, the headmaster came to her room, telling her that Professor Hodgson—he was then acting Dean—wished to see her, but she said that it was not worth while talking to the Professor. The headmaster left, and she started writing a letter to the Professor, but had not written much when there was a knock at the door and, in response to her invitation to enter, the Professor came into the room, shutting the door and standing with his back to it. She was not expecting to see him, and rose from her seat. He then said that her influence in this school, or house had been, or was, so bad—without giving any idea of what it was—and the accumulated evidence against her so great—without giving her any idea of it—that she had to leave the school within six hours, or the police would come. She was so shocked, and felt so ill, that she just looked at him.

He repeated the words, adding "with all your possessions." She remembered wondering how she could get out in six hours with all her possessions accumulated in ten years. He wore his clerical collar with a tweed pepper-and-salt suit. She then asked him to leave her room, but he repeated that she had six hours to get out. As he did not move, she went to where he stood with his back to the door, in order to get hold of the door handle and to pass out of the room, thinking that he would move aside. He did not, but she did not push him.

Then he took her by the upper arms and shook her, saying: "You get out within six hours, or the police will come." He went away, muttering under his breath about having done his part.

Later, she was allowed to remain over the weekend on undertaking in writing not to interfere with the school life. On December 16, 1960, a letter was written by her then solicitors to Professor Hodgson complaining about the assault.

The defendant said that he retired in 1958. He was a member of the governing body of the school. On July 19, 1958, the Dean was ill and unable to act, and he (the defendant) as senior Canon, was chairman of a meeting of the Chapter; it fell to him to convey to Miss M'Carogher the Chapter's decision. He asked the headmaster to request her to see him. She did not come, and, as it was a disagreeable job that he had to do, he decided not to bother about his dignity; he went up to her room. She was in a very disturbed, emotional condition, and he felt that he had to make it quite clear what the Chapter had told him to say, that she had to leave that day.

Before he had time to say anything she said that she did not want to see him or hear anything that he had to say. He stood there, determined that he had to do his task and see that she clearly understood what he had been charged to say. She told him to go out of her room. He said that he must make clear what he had to say, and she said that if he would not go out she would. She came to push past him to the door. He may have put out his hand to try to stop her, but he was quite sure that he never shook her. She was in such a distressed, emotional state that, he thought, it was quite possible that she may have felt shaking that really came from herself. He felt that, in spite of her emotional condition, he had got to make quite clear what he had been told to say, and, as soon as he had done that, he came away feeling thankful that the job was over. He had no precise recollection of what he said. He may have spoken—apparently he did, regretfully—rather brutally, because when one had a disagreeable job to do one had to be clear.

Later he allowed Miss M'Carogher to remain at school over the weekend on her undertaking not to participate in school life. A solicitor acting for her made no complaint on her behalf of any assault, and it was a surprise to hear of it two and a half years later.

Extract from Summing-up

PAULL J.: . . . The evidence is of events which took place a very long time ago. It was once said that for every moment that elapses after an incident memory grows weaker and imagination grows stronger. If you are in doubt whether to believe Miss M'Carogher or Professor Hodgson, then Miss M'Carogher, having brought this action, has to prove that it is more probable that she is right than that Professor Hodgson is right. If you say that you just do not know, you have to find for the Professor.

There is no doubt that he had a right to visit her to inform her of the Chapter's decision. If she chose to rush at the door to try to get out, and all he did when she was a little distance away from him was to say: "No, just wait until I tell you something," and she chose to run on to his hand, then that was not an assault by him, if he did nothing more than stand there in the way and—possibly, as he said—put out his hand.

You are not concerned with any other action that Miss M'Carogher may be bringing. There is no question here of either of them trying to make up a story.

Verdict for the defendant

(H) CORRESPONDENCE SCHOOLS' RIGHT TO BALANCE OF FEES

144 International Correspondence Schools Ltd. *v.* Ayres (1912) 106 L.T. 845

KING'S BENCH DIVISION

A correspondence college is entitled to receive the instalments for which a student has bargained, whether the student refuses to receive the instruction or not.

Facts: The plaintiffs carried on a course of tuition by correspondence in telephone engineering. On October 28, 1910, the defendant entered into a contract with them by which it was provided (1) that the fee to be paid was to cover all instruction until the defendant obtained a diploma, provided he did so within five years; (2) that the fee of £14 10s. should be paid by a deposit of 10s. at the time of signing the application, and 10s. every month thereafter until the fee was paid. The defendant paid the deposit, and an instalment of 10s. on December 2, 1910. Shortly afterwards he informed the plaintiffs that he would not continue with the course.

The plaintiffs brought an action in the Derby and Long Eaton County Court to recover £5 10s., being the balance, less £1, of the instalments in arrear at the time of bringing the action. The county court judge held that the plaintiffs were entitled to recover, as damages for breach of contract, only such instalments as had accrued at the time when the defendant broke the contract and refused to continue. He found that the contract was broken after the instalment had fallen due, and gave judgment for the plaintiffs for 10s.

The plaintiffs appealed by way of case stated to the Divisional Court of the King's Bench Division contending that upon the terms of the contract they were entitled to recover all the instalments due at the commencement of the action.

Extract from Judgment

BRAY J.: This case turns upon what is the true construction of the contract between the parties. The plaintiffs claim that they are entitled to recover the instalments agreed to be paid by the defendant under the arrangement between them, and the answer which was made in the county court and which was accepted by the learned judge, was that the plaintiffs were only entitled to bring an action for damages for breach of contract because the instruction contracted for had not in fact been given. . . . What we have to see is whether it was intended in the present case, that the money should be paid by the defendant, even though he refused to receive the instruction. It is very much like the case of rent payable in advance, or a water rate payable in advance, where the consideration for the payment is the right to have the occupation of the house or the right to receive a supply of water.

We have to look at the contract in order to gather its meaning. The course of instruction was to extend over five years if necessary, and the instalments were to be spread over a period of a little less than two and a half years. That seems an indication that the money was to be paid before the whole of the instruction had been received. The plaintiffs had always been ready and willing to give the instruction, and consequently the defendant has had the consideration for which he bargained, namely, the right to receive the instruction, and if he does not choose to avail himself of it, so much the worse for him. It seems to me that the plaintiffs are entitled to sue for the instalments as they become due, whether the defendant refuses to receive the instruction or not, and that their remedy is not merely an action for damages for breach of contract. The appeal must therefore be allowed.

Appeal allowed; judgment for the plaintiffs

[NOTE: The decision in such a case turns on the exact terms of the contract. Many correspondence colleges state explicitly that, if a student abandons a course, no more fees are due. This was not so in the case instanced above, and the student was liable for all fees which had accrued up to the time of the commencement of the action.]

(I) USE OF UNION FUNDS TO SUPPORT OFFICIALS' LITIGATION

145 Hill *v.* Archbold [1967] 2 Q.B. 418

QUEEN'S BENCH DIVISION

The right of a master to support his servants' litigation is an exception to the general rule prohibiting the maintenance of other men's actions, and there must be implied in a master a power to do whatever a good employer would reasonably do for the benefit of his servants, having regard, among other things, to his own interest.

Facts: The facts are fully set out in the judgment.

Judgment

MACKENNA J.: The plaintiff, Mr Hill, a member of the National Union of Teachers, brings this action against the union's treasurer to restrain him from using the union's funds to pay the costs incurred by two officials of the union, Sir Ronald Gould and Dr Barnes, in unsuccessful libel actions brought by them against Mr Hill.

I shall state the relevant facts as briefly as I can. In 1963 and 1964 Dr Barnes was the secretary of the union's Superannuation and Salaries Committee, and Sir Ronald Gould was the union's General Secretary. Both were whole-time salaried servants of the union. They had been, but were no longer, subscribing members of the union. In those two years Mr Hill wrote letters to Dr Barnes in his official capacity raising points on the working of the Teachers (Superannuation) Act 1956, which had imposed a liability on teachers to contribute an extra 1 per cent. of their salaries to a superannuation fund established by an earlier Act. Dr Barnes, with Sir Ronald Gould's approval, given by him as General Secretary of the union, replied to Mr Hill's letters expressing the view that the teachers had not been treated unjustly. Mr Hill thereupon published to several members of the union a circular accusing Dr Barnes of having knowingly made false statements with intent to deceive in his replies to Mr Hill's letters, and accusing Sir Ronald Gould of having been a party to the deceptions. The circular meant that both officials were unfit to be employed by the union. Mr Hill threatened to repeat these statements. The defamed officials applied to their employer, the union, for assistance in defending their reputations against Mr Hill's attack.

On November 6, 1964, the Law and Tenure Committee of the executive passed the following resolution: (1) That authority be given for legal assistance to be extended to the General Secretary and Dr Barnes, as employees of the union and when so acting in the course of their duties, in any action to be taken against Mr Hill. (2) That approval be given to such legal assistance being rendered to the General Secretary and Dr Barnes by an outside firm of solicitors.

Before passing this resolution the committee had been referred to an opinion of counsel dated October 22, 1964, advising as follows:

"(a) That the statements made by Mr Hill in the circular in question are defamatory both of Sir Ronald Gould and Dr Barnes; (b) that it would be impossible for Mr Hill to justify such defamatory allegations; (c) that there is ample evidence of malice on his part to defeat any defence of qualified privilege that might be raised."

On December 5, 1964, this resolution was confirmed by the executive.

In seeking to protect their servants' reputations which had been attacked because of letters written by them in the course of their employment, these committees acted in good faith, reasonably believing that their servants had been unjustly defamed, and as good employers they believed that what they were doing was in their union's interest. The success of Mr Hill's campaign, if it were successful, might have made it impossible for the union to retain the services of Dr Barnes and Sir Ronald Gould.

On December 10, 1964, a writ was issued by Dr Barnes against Mr Hill, claiming damages for libel and an injunction. On December 16, 1964, a writ making similar claims was issued by Sir Ronald Gould. The purpose of these actions was to vindicate the reputations of these two gentlemen and to stop the threatened further publication of the circular. Mr Hill was in no position to pay substantial damages. The union did not instigate this litigation. They supported actions which both they and the two officers reasonably thought were necessary to vindicate the officers' reputation and to protect them against further attacks.

Outside solicitors were instructed in accordance with the resolution, and the union did not intermeddle in the litigation which followed the issue of the writs.

Mr Hill defended each of the actions pleading justification and later, by amendment, privilege.

In June 1966, the two actions were tried before Milmo J. and a jury, who returned a general verdict in Mr Hill's favour. At the instance of counsel for Dr Barnes and Sir Ronald Gould, the judge asked the jury whether they had found for Mr Hill on the ground of privilege or because the defamatory statements were justified. The foreman answered: on the ground of justification. The unsuccessful plaintiffs appealed to the Court of Appeal, complaining that the jury's verdict was perverse. There was (it was said) no evidence on which justification could properly be found. Their appeal was dismissed.[1] As I understand the judgment of the Court of Appeal, the reason was that the jury ought not to have been asked to give the grounds of their verdict. The foreman's answer should, therefore, be ignored, and without that answer the verdict could as well be supported by Mr Hill's plea of privilege, which was not assailable, as by the more questionable ground of justification.

1. *Barnes* v. *Hill* [1967] 1 Q.B. 579; [1967] 2 W.L.R. 632; [1967] 1 All E.R. 347, C.A.

The costs in question here are those incurred by Dr Barnes and Sir Ronald Gould in these unsuccessful actions and appeals. Mr Hill did not ask for any costs in either court and was awarded none.

There are two questions to be considered by me. (i) Is it the offence of maintenance for an employer to support his servant's action for libel brought in the circumstances of this case, where the defamed servants were accused of misconduct in the course of their employment by the union, where the defamatory statements had been circulated to many members of the union and were likely to be circulated to many more, and where the purpose of the action was to vindicate the reputation of the defamed servants and to protect them against further attacks of the same kind? If not, (ii) can the power to give such support be implied in the union's constitution as one reasonably necessary for the attainment of the union's objects?

If it is to be held that the union's funds are expendable for this purpose, the first question must be answered negatively and the second affirmatively; first, because there can be no power to spend the funds for an illegal purpose and, secondly, because, as I shall show, there are not express powers to spend the union funds in supporting a servant's action, because the power if it exists at all, must be implied, and, because no power can be implied unless it is reasonably necessary for the attainment of the union's objects. I would answer the first question negatively and the second affirmatively.

On the first question, I have read all the cases to which I have been referred by Mr Hill and by counsel for the defendant, as well as the passage in Winfield's *Present Law of Abuse of Legal Procedure*, 8th ed. (1921) at pages 34–39, and *Hickman* v. *Kent* or *Romney Marsh Sheepbreeders' Association*.[2] I do not propose to discuss these many cases at length. Most of them were considered in the judgment of Jenkins L.J. in *Martell* v. *Consett Iron Co. Ltd.*[3] I summarise my conclusions on this part of the case in two propositions:

(i) The right of a master to support his servant's litigation is an exception to the general rule prohibiting the maintenance of other men's actions.

(ii) No modern case decides that this exception is obsolete or that it is inapplicable to an action for libel whose object is to protect a servant's reputation attacked by reason of acts done by him in the course of his employment.

The exception was applied in *Hickman's* case,[4] which was one of libel. Bray J. had refused to apply the exception to the master's maintenance of his servant's action for slander in *Scott* v. *National Society for the Prevention of Cruelty to Children*[5] for reasons which are inapplicable to the present case. The judgment of Bray J. apparently assumed that the exception was still alive and that it applied to actions for slander. *Oram* v. *Hutt*[6] is not against my second

2. (1920) 37 T.L.R. 163, C.A.
3. [1955] Ch. 363, at 396; [1955] 2 W.L.R. 463; [1955] 1 All E.R. 481, C.A.
4. (1920) 37 T.L.R. 163, C.A.
5. (1909) 25 T.L.R. 789.
6. [1914] 1 Ch. 98; 30 T.L.R. 55, C.A.

proposition. Although it was argued in that case that it fell within the exception of master and servant, and although the indemnity given to the union's
official was held to be obnoxious to the law of maintenance and therefore *ultra
vires*, Lord Sumner, one of the three judges of the Court of Appeal, stated[7]
that the relations between a maintained official and the union excluded the
application of any of the recognised exceptions of the rule as to maintenance,
notably those relating to master and servant. He gave no reasons for the view
that the maintained official was not a servant of the union. A possible explanation is that the union's officials in that case were unpaid. This may also be the
reason why in *Baker* v. *Jones*[8] the union's claim to support its officials was not
based on the relation of master and servant. Lynskey J.'s dictum,[9] so far as it
relates to servants, is not, in my opinion, supported by the two cases which he
cites, *Oram* v. *Hutt*[10] and *Alfin* v. *Hewlett*.[11] I have already mentioned *Oram*
v. *Hutt*.[12] As to *Alfin* v. *Hewlett*,[13] it does not appear from the report that the
relation between the official and the union which maintained him was that of
master and servant. Furthermore, the maintained official alleged in his defence
that he was acting on his own behalf at the material time, and his defence was
supported by his union only because they wished to prove that he was not
acting on their behalf.

Another case relied on by Mr Hill was *Greig* v. *National Amalgamated Union
of Shop Assistants*.[14] There, too, there was no relation of master and servant
between the union and the maintained litigant.

As it seems to me reasonable that a master should be allowed to support
such litigation as that between Dr Barnes, Sir Ronald Gould and Mr Hill, and
as there is, in my opinion, no authority deciding that he may not do so, I shall
hold that a master does not commit the offence of maintenance by supporting
such litigation.

The question remains whether the power to give such support to a servant
can be implied in the union's constitution. Before considering this question
I shall state those provisions of the rules to which I have been referred as
bearing upon this question. Rule 2 sets out the objects of the union, including
under "*L*" "To afford advice and assistance to individual members in educational and professional matters, and in legal cases of a professional nature."
Rule 3 provides that "Conference is the supreme authority of the union," and
rule 4 that the affairs of the union shall be managed by the executive, and that
all decisions of the executive involving the salary policy of the union as
approved by conference must be in accord with that policy, subject to an
exception which I need not mention. Rule 5 deals with the qualifications for

7. [1914] 1 Ch. 98 at 108.
8. [1954] 1 W.L.R. 1005; [1955] 2 All E.R. 553.
9. [1954] 1 W.L.R. 1005 at 1011.
10. [1914] 1 Ch. 98.
11. (1902) 18 T.L.R. 664.
12. [1914] 1 Ch. 98.
13. (1902) 18 T.L.R. 664.
14. (1906) 22 T.L.R. 274, C.A.

membership of the union: no one can be a member of the union who is not a teacher with the necessary qualifications. Rule 18 provides that the officials of the union shall be the General Secretary and all other officials whose offices have been sanctioned by the annual conference, and that the power to appoint or dismiss any official of the union shall be vested in the executive. Rule 39 provides that there shall be established a number of funds, including a General Fund, and that those funds shall be applicable for the purposes of attaining the objects of the union as defined by, and subject to, the provisions of the rules. Rule 40 provides that annual subscriptions shall be paid into this fund and that all expenditure other than expenditure on account of sustentation or of disbursements chargeable to the Building Fund shall be made from the General Fund. I am told that this fund is not treated as covered by the provisions of rule 43 relating to trustees, and Mr Hill has not contended that this practice is wrong.

Rule 46 is, for present purposes, an important rule. I shall quote verbatim the provisions of that part of the rule lettered (*a*):

"46.—Administration of Legal Assistance.—(*a*) GENERAL,— No payments shall be made out of the funds of the union except for the purposes of cases of professional conduct, cases under sections (*f*) and (*o*), and for the purposes of affording legal assistance or support to members, in accordance with the resolution of the Newcastle conference."

There follow the provisions of that resolution which stipulate for legal assistance to members involved in cases affecting the rights and interests of teachers, and the support of teachers who may have suffered through legitimate action taken in defence of professional objects. Section (*f*) deals with cases not involving proceedings in court, and (*o*) with arbitration. It is clear from these and other provisions of the rule that it deals only with the giving of legal assistance to subscribing members of the union. As I said earlier in this judgment, neither Sir Ronald Gould nor Dr Barnes was, at any time material to these proceedings, a subscribing member of the union.

Other provisions of rule 46, notably sections (*i*) and (*j*), regulate the manner in which this legal assistance shall be given.

The defendant concedes that there is no express provision conferring the necessary power, but argues that it is to be implied. His argument may be summarised in these five propositions: (i) The union has express power to employ servants such as Sir Ronald Gould and Dr Barnes for the purpose of attaining the union's objects. (ii) As incidental to this power, there must be implied a further power to do such things as a good employer would reasonably do for the benefit of his servants, having regard, among other things, to his own interest. (iii) This general implied power includes the power to support the servant's litigation in cases like the present. (iv) Such an implied power is not inconsistent with the express provisions of rule 46. If it were, the implication would of course be impossible. Rule 46 (*a*), read literally, would forbid the use of the union's funds for any purpose except the provision of legal assistance in accordance with the rule, which would be absurd. The provision of legal assistance is only one of the union's many objects, and its funds must be expendable for other purposes. It follows that rule 46 must be read with some limitation. There are three conceivable limitations. One is to read the rule as dealing exclusively with the matter of legal expenses: "No payments shall be made out of the funds of the union except for the purposes of cases of professional conduct," etc. But that would preclude the union from litigating in protection of its property or interests either as plaintiff or as defendant, which would be equally absurd. An alternative is to read the rule as dealing exclusively with the matter of legal assistance to persons or bodies other than the union itself. The third and—it is argued—the more reasonable alternative is to read it as dealing with the matter of providing legal assistance in performance of the objects described in rule 2 (1), *viz.*, to afford advice and assistance to individual members in educational and professional matters, and in legal cases of a professional nature. Read in this way, there is, it is said, no inconsistency between the implication of a power to support the union's servant's action in a proper case and an express power to provide legal assistance to its members in accordance with the provisions of rule 46. (v) If it is within the union's power to support a servant's litigation, expense incurred in exercising the power can be defrayed out of the General Fund, which is available for that and any other expenditure for attaining the union's objects.

In my opinion, the argument succeeds. I do not consider that the observations of Lord Parker in *Oram* v. *Hutt*[15] are inconsistent with this argument. He was dealing with the possibility of implying a power to give legal assistance to a union's members. Because it is impossible to imply a power of that kind, it does not follow that it is impossible to imply a power to give legal assistance to a union's servants in any case where a good employer would give that assistance, acting reasonably and having regard to his own interests. I have found some difficulty in accepting the fourth step of the argument, which seeks to reconcile the implied power with the express provisions of rule 46, but in the end I was convinced by Mr Stable's argument.

The action fails. There will be judgment for the defendant.

It seems to me, Mr Stable, subject to anything you have to say, that it would be reasonable to make no order as to costs in this case. Mr Hill has raised an important and difficult question affecting himself and the other members of the union, and it seems to me that it was very reasonable that the opinion of the court should be taken upon the matter.

Judgment for the defendant, who did not
ask for costs

15. [1914] 1 Ch. 98 at 105.

APPENDIX

CHAPTER II

(H) REORGANISATION OF SCHOOLS: SAFEGUARDING AND REDUNDANCY

26 Stott v. Oldham Corporation (1969) 67 L.G.R. 520

COURT OF APPEAL

A teacher whose appointment is temporary pending the reorganisation of his school is entitled to safeguarding of his salary under section Q of the Scales for Teachers in Primary and Secondary Schools, England and Wales 1967, but only with effect from July 1, 1967.

Facts: The respondent, Mr H. Stott, was appointed as deputy head of Robin Hill Secondary School, Oldham on May 4, 1960. When the post was advertised the local education authority had stated:

"The position will be reviewed in four or five years time when it is expected that the second instalment of the Breezehill School building will be ready. At that stage the school will be regarded as reorganised and in view of the extent of the enlargement the committee will obviously have to reconsider all senior appointments at that stage. The appointment therefore will be regarded only as a temporary one until such time as this reorganisation takes place."

The resolution appointing Mr Stott was worded as follows:

"Resolved—That Mr H. Stott be appointed as deputy head teacher at Breezehill County Secondary School with respect from September 1, 1960. The appointment, initially on a temporary basis, to be reviewed together with all other senior posts when the reorganisation of the school takes place on completion of the project."

The respondent, who had been in the authority's service for some years, continued to receive his salary as a qualified teacher, together with the appropriate deputy head's allowance for the school. On September 9, 1964, the Director of Education informed him:

"that the school will be regarded as reorganised on September 1, 1965, and that, under the terms approved by the education committee, your appointment as deputy head-teacher at that school will cease on August 21,[1] 1965."

1. *Sic*—As the standard terms of service provide for notice to expire on April 30, August 31, or December 31, this is presumably an error either in the letter or the Report.

The Scales of Salaries for Teachers then in force provided:

"The local education authority may, in its discretion, pay an allowance to mitigate or prevent hardship to a teacher whose post is lost or whose salary is diminished as a result of the reorganisation or closure of a school."

Mr Stott was not offered another appointment at the same grade and, since the authority did not exercise the discretion referred to above in his favour, he lost his allowance and reverted to his basic salary as a qualified teacher.

Section Q of the Scales of Salaries for Teachers negotiated in 1967 altered the provisions for safeguarding, making it mandatory and retrospective:

"Where a teacher whose post is lost or whose salary would otherwise be diminished as a result of the closure or reorganisation of a school or department continues as a full-time teacher in a primary or secondary school maintained by the same authority the teacher shall be deemed, for salary purposes, to continue to hold the post he/she held immediately prior to the closure or reorganisation, provided that, if at any time, the teacher unreasonably refuses to accept an alternative post in a primary or secondary school maintained by the authority the safeguarding under this section shall cease.

"The provisions of this section shall apply from the date of the closure or reorganisation of the school or department except where that occurred before July 1, 1967, in which case the teacher shall receive the benefits of this section with effect from July 1, 1967, provided that he/she has not, at any time, unreasonably refused to accept an alternative post offered by the authority."

On the assumption that the terms of the respondent's appointment provided that his post should cease when the school was reorganised, and that the dismissal was in accordance with the terms of the contract rather than as a result of the reorganisation, the local education authority did not reinstate Mr Stott's allowance as a deputy head from July 1, 1967.

The plaintiff claimed against the authority for arrears of salary from that date, maintaining that he had fulfilled all the conditions prescribed by section Q of the 1967 scales. On July 18, 1968, Judge Addleshaw, sitting at Oldham Court, allowed his claim.

The authority appealed.

Extracts from Judgments
LORD DENNING M.R.: . . . The last sentence[2] shows clearly that the provision is retrospective. It applies to teachers whose posts were lost before 1967, but the additional payment only dates back to July 1, 1967. So it applies to Mr Stott, if—and this is the real point of the case—if he was "a teacher whose post is lost . . . as a result of the closure or reorganisation of a school." If he was, this provision entitles him to be paid a deputy head-teacher's allowance.

2. Section Q of the Scales of Salaries (1957) for Teachers, quoted *supra*.

I think it plain that in 1965 Mr Stott was a teacher "whose post is lost." His post at Breezehill was that of a deputy head-teacher. It was so described in the advertisement and in the resolution. It was the duty of the local education authority to establish that post, and they did. They appointed him to fill it. I think it equally plain that the post was lost "as a result of the closure or reorganisation of a school." In 1965, on the reorganisation taking place, his post as deputy head-teacher was lost, and it was lost as a result of the reorganisation.

The local education authority suggest that the provision does not apply to Mr Stott, because his post was not permanent but temporary. I see no reason for distinguishing between the two. In any case it was lost. The local authority next suggest that it was not lost as a result of the closure, but as a result of the terms on which he was appointed. I think it was lost for both reasons: and one is enough. His post was lost as a result of the closure or the reorganisation. The local education authority then took a point on the later words:

"Where a teacher whose post is lost . . . the teacher shall be deemed to continue to hold the post he/she held immediately prior to the closure or reorganisation."

It was said that Mr Stott could not be deemed to "continue" to hold the post, seeing it was only a temporary post which had come to an end. But there is a simple answer. He is deemed to continue as a deputy head-teacher only for salary purposes: and he can be so deemed, even though the post has come to an end.

I think this is a plain case. Mr Stott was appointed to the post of deputy head-teacher. The post was lost as a result of the closure or reorganisation of the school. He is entitled to be safeguarded for salary purposes. He is entitled to receive a deputy head-teacher's allowance even though he is not himself a deputy head-teacher any more, but is now only doing the duties of a qualified teacher. The back payment, however, only goes back to July 1, 1967.

It was said that this was unreasonable. I do not think so. It seems to me that when a man has filled the post of deputy head-teacher for five years, it is only right that he should be safeguarded. He should not, so to speak, be thrown out as redundant without having some financial compensation. But reasonableness is not for the court. The only question is the interpretation of the Scale. Upon the true interpretation of it I find myself in agreement with the county court judge, and I would dismiss the appeal.

SACHS L. J.: I agree. In May, 1960, Mr Stott was appointed to a post which has been created by virtue of the provisions of the Burnham "Scales of Salaries" Report of 1959. Section K, paragraph 1, provides: "The local education authority shall"—and I emphasise the word "shall"—"for the purposes of this Report establish a post of deputy head-teacher." The post was one which by 1960 was known would, on the then current educational scheme, cease to exist when a reorganisation took place at a date estimated to be between four and five years from May, 1960. On September 9, 1964, the anticipated reorganisation was brought into effect and Mr Stott's post ceased to exist.

I now turn to the relevant retrospective provisions of the Scales of Salaries for Teachers in Primary and Secondary Schools, England and Wales, of 1967. There one finds a cross heading to section Q which reads "Safeguarding of salary on reorganisation or closure of a school." In it there are to be found the relevant words: "Where a teacher whose post is lost . . . as a result of the closure or reorganisation of a school"—and the question is whether Mr Stott was such a teacher. To my mind the answer is clear: the post was lost. I doubt if it is necessary to decide whether the word "post" should be read as if preceded by the word "permanent" in contradistinction to "temporary." I would rather have said it was a post within the meaning of section K of the 1959 scale or its successors. But if it were necessary to read the word "permanent" as being placed before the word "post," then to my mind it was none the less a permanent post despite it being one which under current decisions would be, subject to alterations in educational schemes, at some future date abolished.

The only difficulties in this case are in reality purely verbal—stemming first from a possible confusion between, on the one hand, the word "post," and, on the other, the words "appointment to a post"; and, secondly, as to what is meant in the particular context of the advertisement for the post and the subsequent documents by the word "temporary." So far as the first of those two points is concerned, I have already made clear my views. As to the second one, when one considers it in connexion with the words "appointment to a post," the word "temporary" has to my mind in the present case one of two connotations. The first and the most usual is in the context that while the permanent incumbent is away through illness or other causes, then one makes a temporary appointment. That view is fully exemplified when one looks at section N of the 1959 scale of salaries and finds under paragraph 4 of the "Temporary Allowances":

> "Where a teacher holding a post of deputy head teacher, head of department, second master or second mistress in a mixed school, or a graded post, is absent for a prolonged period, a temporary (acting) allowance may be granted, in the discretion of the local education authority, to the teacher who undertakes the duties of the post during such absence, provided that the rate of such allowance is not in excess of the allowance of additional payment which would be payable to the teacher if appointed to the post."

Clearly, of course, Mr Stott's appointment was in no way temporary within the meaning of that paragraph. There is also another possible meaning of the word "temporary" which equally cannot be applied to Mr Stott. That is where one finds a post created to meet some passing special need, such as on the occasion of a centenary or other such matter.

When one comes to the facts of this particular case it is, as already indicated, clear that Mr Stott's appointment (incidentally subject to the terms usual for established posts as to giving notice on either side) could not within the framework of the Burnham scales be said to be temporary.

It has been submitted by Mr Bingham that strange results may follow from this ruling; but to my mind there is nothing strange, in an era when staff is very often only obtainable on terms as to present holders being compensated in one form or another upon a post becoming redundant, for this particular teacher to have been compensated in the way contemplated by section Q. Indeed I would add that to my mind there might be definite detriment to the educational system as a whole if the appellants' suggestions were correct. There must be at present a great number of cases where it has been decided under some scheme as currently envisaged that a school is going to be merged in a comprehensive school or to cease to exist but the date has either not been determined or has been determined at some years ahead. Alterations in educational schemes or lack of availability of finance are matters which are always liable to defer the implementation of such schemes to something which those keen upon them are apt to regard as the Greek kalends. What then would be the effect on the recruiting in such cases of a deputy head-teacher if no certainty existed (for Burnham purposes) that the appointees would be treated as deputy head-teachers afterwards. That is a question to which there may perhaps be more than one answer, but to my mind it is one which would lead to the detriment of the educational service.

I have only added these comments because of the way in which the case was presented by Mr Bingham. The court is simply concerned with the interpretation of certain words, and, that interpretation being to my mind manifest, this appeal should be dismissed.

PHILLIMORE L.J.: I agree, and I only add a few sentences in deference to the argument of Mr Bingham. Mr Stott's claim for compensation depended upon his bringing himself within the words of section Q of the Scales of Salaries for Teachers in Primary and Secondary Schools, England and Wales, 1967. The vital words are: "Where a teacher whose post is lost or whose salary would otherwise be diminished as a result of the closure or reorganisation of a school"—and there follows provision for compensation. What is said by Mr Bingham is that when the plaintiff was appointed to this post in 1960 he was told that it would only be temporary until the school was reorganised, when the whole position, and, in particular, his position of deputy head-teacher would be reviewed; and he says that therefore this is[3] a post which he has lost and his salary thereunder diminished as a result of the reorganisation of the school. It is said that the post was only temporary pending the reorganisation. What the words mean in this context I confess I find some difficulty in appreciating. Mr Bax has told us that any school master in the position of the plaintiff was in any event subject to a two-months' notice in

3. *Sic*—The word "not" appears to have been omitted.

the winter and a three-months' notice during summer; so that if you are told your appointment is only temporary for four or five years, it is in fact more permanent than most. However that may be, it seems to be plain that this post was not lost and the salary diminished solely as a result of the fact that he had been told his appointment was temporary. At the very least these events also resulted from the reorganisation of the school. In my judgment this appeal is virtually unarguable, and I entirely agree with the county court judge and with the views expressed by my Lords.

Appeal dismissed

27 Taylor v. Kent County Council (1969) 67 L.G.R. 483

QUEEN'S BENCH DIVISION

In making an offer of suitable alternative employment to a displaced teacher, a local education authority must have regard to the teacher's age, qualifications, and experience, and must offer conditions of employment reasonably equivalent to those under the previous employment notwithstanding the fact that the teacher's salary may be safeguarded.

Facts: The appellant, Mr Vernon Stephen Taylor, then aged forty-three, was appointed headmaster of Deal Secondary School for Boys on January 1, 1958. In 1968 the local education authority decided to amalgamate the school with a girls' school, to make the new school co-educational, and to double the number of pupils. The appellant was not appointed as headmaster of the new school, and on February 21, 1968 the Kent local education authority informed him that his appointment would be terminated on the reorganisation taking place at the beginning of the following September. The local education authority confirmed that Mr Taylor's salary would be safeguarded under the terms of section Q of the Scales of Salaries for Teachers, England and Wales, 1967.

The appellant was offered appointment to the county mobile staff by which he could be required to serve in schools in the county, generally for one or two terms and not normally for longer than a year, under the direction of the headmaster of the school to which he was sent.

The appellant refused the offer, and applied for a redundancy payment under the Redundancy Payments Act 1965, section 1 (2) of which provides:

". . . an employee who is dismissed shall be taken to be dismissed by reason of redundancy if the dismissal is attributable wholly or mainly to—(a) the fact that his employer has ceased, or intends to cease, to carry on the business for the purposes of which the employee was employed by him. . . ."

The London Industrial Tribunal, sitting under the chairmanship of Sir Richard le Gallais, held that the appellant had been dismissed by reason of redundancy and that, since the proposed new contract differed from the old, section 2 (4) of the Act applied:

"An employee shall not be entitled to a redundancy payment by reason of dismissal if before the relevant date the employer has made to him an offer in writing to renew his contract of employment or to re-engage him under a new contract, so that in accordance with the particulars specified in the offer the provisions of the contract as renewed, or of the new contract, as the case may be, as to the capacity and place in which he would be employed, and as to the other terms and conditions of his employment, would differ (wholly or in part) from the corresponding conditions of the contract as in force immediately before his dismissal, but—(a) the offer constitutes an offer of suitable employment in relation to the employee . . . and the employee has unreasonably refused that offer."

The tribunal considered the applicant's age, qualifications, and experience, and also the protection afforded by his contract, and the loss of status which would ensue. They found that the loss of status could not be considered without reference to the fact that his salary was safeguarded, and found that the offer of employment in the mobile pool of teachers was an offer of suitable employment which the applicant had unreasonably refused.

The applicant appealed.

Extract from Judgments

LORD PARKER OF WADDINGTON C.J.: . . . when this reorganisation was about to take place, the appellant was apparently considered for the appointment as headmaster of the new co-educational school. For one reason or another he was not chosen. The tribunal drew attention to the fact that the circumstances of this case were charged with emotion, and it may be that there was strong feeling in Deal about it. I do not propose to say anything about that; I will assume, and will assume only, that what was thought to be the case was that this man, who had done apparently ten years as headmaster of the boys' school, would not be able to cope with a school run on co-educational lines with double the number of children.

On February 21, a letter was written to him in these terms:

"The Secretary of State has, as you know, now approved the establishment of a new co-educational secondary school in Deal from September 1, 1968. This means that with the closure of the Boys' secondary school your post will cease to exist and it is therefore formally necessary to give you notice of the termination of your present appointment on August 31, 1968."

Pausing there that is why, as I said earlier, this man became prima facie entitled to a redundancy payment. The letter continues:

"This I now do."

That is giving him notice.

"Your salary will be safeguarded, of course, in accordance with section Q of the Scales of Salaries for Teachers in Primary and Secondary Schools,

England and Wales, 1967. The committee will give you all the help in their power to obtain a suitable alternative appointment. A post in the new school to be established has been offered to you, but this you do not wish to accept."

Nothing turns on that because it was not in writing.

"The committee are prepared as an alternative to offer you a post in the Mobile Pool of teachers (of which I enclose particulars) in category III from September, 1968. This post appears to give you the best opportunity to move into a permanent appointment while at the same time being in the position of waiting for the appearance of a permanent post which you may find especially suitable to you. A member of the mobile pool must go, of course, to schools where his services are needed but, within this obvious requirement, we should naturally try to arrange your duties in a way making the best use of your qualifications and therefore, I hope, most congenial to you. This offer would apply whether you remained at your present address or whether you moved to another part of the county."

The particulars concerning the mobile pool of teachers were enclosed, and it is necessary I think to read passages from that. It is headed:

"Appointment to the County Pool of 'Mobile' Staff. Kent Education Committee invite applications from qualified and experienced teachers, able to give effective assistance in a variety of teaching situations, for appointment to the county's pool of mobile staff. The teachers appointed will be asked to serve in primary or secondary schools as may be required for short periods, generally one or two terms but not normally longer than a year."

Then having referred to the highest category, which was the appointment he was being offered, namely as a head teacher category III, the particulars go on as follows:

"Appointment to the pool offers opportunities to suitably qualified teachers to help the committee in the present difficult staffing situation and to broaden their experience in different kinds of schools. Teachers may be assured that the committee will do what they can to ensure a variety of experience. A teacher serving under these arrangements will perform such duties as are assigned to him by the head of the school to which he is attached for the time being. In normal circumstances travelling expenses in excess of 5s. a week will be paid at public transport rates (second-class rail and/or bus fares). If public transport facilities cannot conveniently be used, the committee are prepared to consider applications for car mileage allowances. Members of the pool will, in normal circumstances, be allocated each term to secondary schools in the areas of special shortage, which for this purpose are the Medway Towns, Gravesend, Dartford, Maidstone and Sheerness, and as a consequence it is a condition of appointment that the teacher should reside in the north-west Kent area; this is defined as extending not farther south than the Maidstone area and not farther east than Sittingbourne.

Pausing there, it will be seen that that last sentence that I have read, namely that he would have to reside in the north-west Kent area, was treated by the tribunal and I think rightly, as having been superseded by the words in the letter itself, which said: "This offer would apply whether you remain at your present address or whether you move to another part of the county." The only observation I would make is that it is conceded that he could not possibly have done this going from Deal, and therefore whatever the offer said, it necessitated his moving his house.

It is important to see what that means. This headmaster of ten years' experience was being offered an appointment, and I would like to make it clear that I accept that it is a permanent appointment, in category III in this pool. But it is to be observed that when in the pool he can be sent anywhere in the county, though normally in this north-west area of Kent; he can be sent to one place for one term or two terms, and then to another place for one term or two terms, sometimes a year; he can be told to go round from place to place, and when he does that he has to undertake the duties which are assigned to him by the headmaster of the school to which he is sent. The question which arises is whether that was an offer of suitable employment within section 2 (4).

The tribunal said:

"The suitability of the offer must be considered in all the surrounding circumstances not just one to wit: status. Taking into account not only the applicant's age, qualifications, experience, loss of status, but also the protection afforded by his contract,"

Pausing there, that means that his salary as headmaster is going to continue pursuant to section Q of the Burnham Award—

"and not forgetting the unfortunate showing at the interview, we have come to the conclusion that in all the circumstances the offer of appointment to the mobile pool was one of suitable employment in relation to the applicant. Of course another headmastership would have been more suitable, but his employers were not in a position to make a written offer of such a post. However the fact that the offer that was made was less suitable does not necessarily make it unsuitable."

Let me say at once, suitability is almost entirely a matter of degree and fact for the tribunal, and not a matter with which this court would wish or could interfere, unless it was plain that they had misdirected themselves in some way in law, or had taken into consideration matters which were not relevant for the purpose. It is to be observed that so far as age was concerned, so far as qualifications were concerned, so far as experience was concerned, they negative the suitability of this offer, because he is going to be put into a

O

position where he has to go where he is told at any time for short periods, to any place, and be put under a headmaster and assigned duties by him.

The only matter which can be put against that as making this offer suitable is the guarantee of salary under scale Q. One would think, speaking for myself, that for a headmaster of this experience, he would think an offer which, while guaranteeing him the same salary, reduced his status was quite unsuitable. To go to a quite different sphere of activity, a director under a service agreement of a company is offered on dismissal a job as a navvy, and it is said: but we will guarantee you the same salary as you have been getting. I should have thought such an offer was plainly unsuitable. Here one wonders whether one of the matters which affected the tribunal was this reference to the words "Not forgetting the unfortunate showing at the interview." That is a reference to when he was interviewed, not by the Kent County Council, but by the governors of the school with a view to taking on the headmastership of the new school. One really wonders what the relevance of that was unless it be that the tribunal felt from what they had heard that he was not up to a head-mastership at all. But at once one says to oneself: if that was in their mind, it was not evidence upon which they could properly act, having regard to the fact that the appellant had given satisfaction for some ten years, and if he was not up to his job he could have been dismissed for that reason, and no question of redundancy would have arisen.

But for my part I feel that the tribunal have here misdirected themselves in law as to the meaning of "suitable employment." I accept, of course, that suitable employment is as is said: suitable employment in relation to the employee in question. But it does seem to me here that by the words "suitable employment," suitability means employment which is substantially equivalent to the employment which has ceased. Section 2 (3) which I read at the begin-ning, is dealing with the case where the fundamental terms are the same, and then no offer in writing is needed, but when they differ, then it has to be put in writing, and must be suitable. I for my part think that what is meant by "suitable" in relation to the employee means conditions of employment which are reasonably equivalent to those under the previous employment, not the same, because then subsection (2) would apply, but it does not seem to me that by "suitable employment" is meant employment of an entirely different nature, but in respect of which the salary is going to be the same. Looked at in that way, it seems to me that there could be only one answer in this case, and that is that the appellant was being asked to do something utterly different; as I have said just as if a director under a service agreement with a company was being asked to do a workman's job, albeit at the same salary.

In those circumstances, I find it unnecessary to go on and consider what I think is the more difficult question, as to whether the offer, if of suitable employment, was one which the appellant here unreasonably refused. There are two rival interpretations which one day will have to be resolved, though I find it unnecessary today. In *Carron Co.* v. *Robertson*[1] a somewhat similar

1. (1967) 2 I.T.R. 484

matter came before the Court of Session; it is clear from that that the Lord President took the view that the consideration governing the reasonableness of the refusal was quite different from those governing the question of suitability. His approach was to say that you consider the terms of the offer to see whether it is suitable employment looked at objectively, but that when you come on to reasonableness you consider personal factors affecting the particular applicant, such as that his doctors told him to live in the south of England and he cannot go to the north, that for domestic and family reasons he has to stay in the south, the fact that the slightly different machine in a factory in connexion with which he is being offered work is one which for reason of some physical deformity he cannot do, all those matters. But when one goes on to read the judgments of Lord Guthrie and Lord Migdale, they take the view that there is an overlapping here, and that in considering reasonableness you can consider in addition to the personal factors all the matters which have been considered in regard to suitability. As I have said, I find it unnecessary to come to a firm conclusion in the matter, though I confess as at present advised I prefer the view taken by the Lord President.

In these circumstances I would allow the appeal and send the case back to the tribunal with a direction that, in default of agreement, they should assess the redundancy payment.

MELFORD STEVENSON J.: I agree.

WILLIS J.: I agree.

Appeal allowed. Remitted to
London Industrial Tribunal

CHAPTER VI

(M) TIMES OF SCHOOL SESSIONS: VARIATIONS

128 Barnes v. Hampshire County Council (1969) The Times, October 9[1]

HOUSE OF LORDS

To release a small child, who is normally met by his parent, before the time appointed for the end of school could forseeably cause an accident and, if it does, it amounts to negligence.

Facts: At the time of the incident which gave rise to this action the plaintiff, Sandra Lesley Barnes, was a five year old pupil at the annexe of King's Road Infants' School, Chandlers Ford, Hampshire.

1. At the time of going to press the only report of this important case which was generally available was that printed in *The Times*. The speeches in the House of Lords printed below are taken from the transcript by permission of the Controller of H.M. Stationery Office.

It was the system at the school that children who were met by their parents at the end of the day were escorted by a teacher to the gate. The pupils were instructed that if no one was waiting to collect them they were to return to their teachers. They were also given kerb drill. The school was 170 yards from a very busy main road, where a traffic warden was on duty at appropriate times.

On the last day of term in the summer of 1962 the plaintiff, who had been at school for a month, left the school premises while her mother was still on her way to meet her. The child set out on her own, and made her way to the main road which she attempted to cross some 80 yards from its junction with the lane in which the school was situated. She was knocked down by a lorry and severely injured, sustaining partial paralysis of the left arm and foot.

Park J., sitting at Winchester Assizes, dismissed a claim for damages for negligence, and his judgement was upheld by the Court of Appeal (Diplock L.J. and Goff J., Lord Denning M.R. dissenting). Lord Diplock said that the school system was reasonable, and that the case was borderline and a matter of degree. If the school had been situated immediately on a busy highway, it might have been negligent. "Ordinary prople in ordinary life do not carry a chronometer; and I do not think that the three to five minutes in the present case constituted a breach of duty." In his dissenting judgment the Master of the Rolls said that the school's system of transfer of children to parents depended on two factors: (1) the parents being there to meet them at 3.30, and (2) the school not letting them out till 3.30. To let them out before the mothers were due to arrive was to release them into a situation of potential danger and, in his view, a breach of duty.

The plaintiff appealed to the House of Lords.

Speeches

LORD REID: For the reasons given by my noble and learned friend, Lord Pearson, I would allow this appeal.

LORD GUEST: My Lords, I have very little to add to the dissenting opinion of the Master of the Rolls expressed with his usual lucidity and in terms with which I entirely agree.

The attack on the respondents' system of dealing with the infant children at the close of the afternoon session at Chandlers Ford Infant School necessarily failed. The system suggested of "pairing off" individual children with their respective parents, before they were released outside the school gates, while no doubt an ideal procedure was quite impracticable in the circumstances. Moreover, it was not adopted in any other schools. The system in vogue at Chandlers Ford, which was for those mothers who wished to collect their children to wait outside the school gates at 3.30 p.m. when the children were let out of school, was reasonably safe provided it was operated properly. But this system did of necessity require fairly close timing on the part of both the mothers, or their deputies, and the school authority. If a mother who wished to accompany her child home was late, she ran the risk of the child wandering off unattended. On the other hand, if the school "closed" early there was a similar risk to the child. The standard of care for the school authorities was to take such care of the children as a reasonably careful parent would do. Most parents showed their standard by appearing at the school gates promptly at or before 3.30 p.m. to collect their children.

On the occasion in question the accident to Sandra happened at 3.29 p.m., on the main A.33 Winchester road, a distance of 250 yards from the school gates. I see no reason to differ from the learned judge's finding that Sandra was released from school at 3.25 p.m. The trial judge did not regard this as negligence on the part of the teachers. This seems, with respect, to be in conflict with Mr Potter's evidence—he was the respondents' deputy education officer—that breaking point, when the children might become bored and wander away, would come after five or six minutes' waiting. He also said that if the children were released five or six minutes early they were placing a far greater strain on the parents than they ought to. The school gates were only 170 yards distant from the main road and a child walking at the slow speed of two miles per hour would reach the main road in just under three minutes. The main road carried a heavy volume of traffic. In my view, having regard to all the circumstances, particularly the age (five years and two months) and the disposition of the child, which was said to be unpredictable, and the proximity to the main road, it was not an acceptable risk to release the children at 3.25 p.m. when the parents knew that the time for release was 3.30 p.m.

Where I find myself in disagreement with the views of the majority of the Court of Appeal is with Diplock L.J. (as he then was) when he said that the time of the release was a question of degree. If the release had come at 3.28 or perhaps 3.29 p.m., it may be that this could be characterised as a question of degree; but a matter of five minutes does not, in my view, fall within that ambit.

Broadly for the reasons expressed by the Master of the Rolls, I would allow the appeal and deal with the case in the way suggested by my noble and learned friend, Lord Pearson.

VISCOUNT DILHORNE: My Lords, The facts in this case have been fully stated by my noble and learned friend, Lord Pearson, and there is no need for me to repeat them. In the statement of claim negligence on the part of the respondents was alleged on two grounds: (1) in failing to ensure that the pupils at the Annexe, of whom Sandra was one, were not allowed to leave the school "unless and until they were collected therefrom by parents or other responsible persons" and (2) in failing to prevent Sandra from leaving the Annexe when it was known or ought to have been known that neither her mother nor any other responsible person was there to collect her. School was supposed to end at 3.30 p.m., and it was alleged that she was released from school by her teacher at or about 3.15 p.m.

In the defence delivered on the 16th June, 1964, the defendants alleged that she had been let out of school at or very shortly after 3.30 p.m., and said that they would deliver particulars of the arrangements maintained by them for the children leaving the Annexe after school.

Those particulars were delivered on the 25th November, 1964.
The material parts read as follows:

"(b) The principal teacher at the said school made the arrangements for the children leaving school which are set out at (c) below. . . .

(c) The arrangements made were as follows:

As school ended, of the two teachers at the Annexe, one took such children as were to go on the school bus to the main school while the other remained in the playground to supervise the rest of the children.

Certain of such children were by their parents' wish allowed to leave school on their own, the remainder were required to remain in the playground until the persons who were to take them home arrived.

Under these arrangements Sandra should have remained in the playground until her mother arrived to take her home. There was thus on the pleadings no issue as to arrangements the respondent should have made.

At the hearing the principal teacher of the school in examination in chief said that the children remained in the playground until their parents arrived. "They were," she said, "not allowed through the gate until the parent is just outside." She was followed in the witness box by the two teachers at the Annexe. They said that a different system from that stated in the particulars and deposed to by the principal teacher had been followed; that the children who were to be met were allowed out of the playground to meet their parents and that they were told that, if their parents were not there, they were to return to and wait in the playground. The next day the principal teacher was recalled. She said that she had been confused when she gave her evidence, that she had nine years' experience in a nursery school, and that the practice there was to hand over each child to a parent, "pairing off" as it was called. She also said that she had never given instructions to the two teachers to do that.

A considerable number of witnesses, headmasters and others, were called by the respondents. They said that the system which the two teachers said was followed was a satisfactory one. It was said that a pairing-off system was "just impossible" and "not feasible," though why a system feasible at a nursery school for children under five should become not feasible and impossible when a child reaches five and goes to an infant school, and why the respondents should have given particulars of arrangements which at the trial it was asserted were not feasible or possible, is not clear to me.

The system which the two teachers said was followed involved the risk that a child let out of school and who was not met would disobey or forget the instructions given to her, and not return to the playground but seek to make her way home on her own.

Nevertheless, in the light of the evidence called by the respondents, Park J. held that the system which the two teachers said was followed was satisfactory.

Lord Denning M.R., in the Court of Appeal, said that he did not think that they could upset that finding, and in this House it was not sought to challenge it. Lord Denning said that speaking for himself he could not think the system satisfactory. I am inclined to agree with him, for I doubt very much whether a system which permits the release of a five year old from school without supervision while looking for a parent, with the risk that the child will try to go home on its own can be described as satisfactory. It should not, I think, be assumed that Park J's finding is necessarily one which will be followed should this system again come under consideration.

The main contest in relation to the second ground on which negligence was alleged was as to the time when Sandra was released from school. The two teachers swore positively that the children did not leave until 3.30 p.m., when it was the parents' responsibility to meet them and the responsibility of the school authorities ceased. Mr Potter, the deputy education officer for Hampshire, was asked whether, if it were the fact that the children were released before the appropriate time that day, he would seek to excuse the teachers responsible. He said, "No, I should say we should not release children before the appointed time."

At the end of the hearing on the 6th July Park J. said that on the evidence he was not satisfied that the children were let out early "and if they were, it was nothing more than a minute."

Then evidence was found which established the time of the accident, and on the 14th July this evidence was called. A Mr Proctor working in his garden heard a noise from the road, so he went down his drive, saw that a girl was hurt, and ran back and telephoned for an ambulance. His telephone call was recorded in the telephone exchange as received at 3.30 p.m. In the light of this evidence Park J. held it was probable that Sandra was knocked down at 3.29 p.m.

The place where the accident happened was 253 yards from the gate to the Annexe. If she was knocked down at 3.29 p.m., she must have left the school appreciably before that time. She passed a bus stop on the corner of King's Road and the main road, where a Mrs Munro was standing with her young child whom she had collected from the school. Park J. thought it was probable that Mrs Munro had walked quickly to the bus stop, and estimated that it had taken two and a half minutes to do so, and that Sandra had passed her half a minute later. He said that it would indicate "that the children were released from the Annexe, at the earliest, at about 3.25 p.m."

I do not understand why he said "at the earliest." It would seem to me that Sandra cannot have been released from school later than that time. If Mrs Munro walked slower than the judge held probable, she must have been released earlier.

But whether Sandra was released at about 3.25 p.m., or before then does not, in my opinion, matter.

At the hearing it was accepted that the school was responsible for her until 3.30 p.m. It was accepted that it was extremely unsafe for a little girl of five to go alone to the main road and, in my view, once it was established that she must have been released in sufficient time before 3.30 p.m. for her not only to get to the main road, but also eighty-one yards along it, it followed that the respondents were guilty of negligence.

As Lord Denning said: "You would have thought that at this point the case of the school authority broke down completely." I think it did, despite the evidence given by Mr Potter, when he was recalled after the evidence as to the time of the telephone call for the ambulance had been given, to the effect that it was permissible for the school authorities to release the children up to five minutes before the school was supposed to end.

Throughout the hearing the respondents' evidence showed the importance attached to release at 3.30 p.m., and not before, and recognition of the fact that it was not until that time that their responsibility came to an end. No doubt they would not be held to blame for an error in releasing the children a few seconds, or even a minute or so, before that time, but to release them five minutes or, as I think, possibly more than that, before the school was supposed to end and before parents would expect their children to be released cannot, I think, be regarded otherwise than as a breach of duty on their part in consequence of which Sandra sustained serious injuries.

For these reasons, in my opinion, the appeal should be allowed, and judgment entered for the appellant for £10,000, the sum now agreed as damages, with costs as agreed.

LORD DONOVAN: My Lords, I need not repeat the facts. They are set out in detail in the Opinion of my noble and learned friend, Lord Pearson, with which I agree, and to which I need add but little.

In the matter of handing these five years old children over to their parents or some other responsible adult at the close of the day, I think a reasonably safe system was in force at this school. Its situation did not call for confining the children in the playground, or in the school, until each one was collected. That being so, I do not see how one teacher, in charge of forty children, could cope with the physical task of properly pairing off each one, and preventing each child leaving until she had done so. The situation was dealt with by fixing the end of school hours at 3.30 p.m., telling the mothers they must be there at the school to meet their children at that hour or make some arrangement for someone else to do so, and telling the child to return to the teacher if it were not met.

But since children of this age are admittedly unpredictable, so that a five year old might well disobey or forget this injunction to return to teacher, and instead begin to toddle off home on its own, it was essential to stick to the timetable. Here, on this day, this was not done.

It is now admitted that the children were let out of school four to five minutes early, and that the appellant was knocked down and injured on the main road at a point some 250 yards from the school gate at a time still within school hours, i.e. at about 3.29 p.m.

Because the children were let out only a few minutes early, it is contended by the respondent that this is all a matter of degree, that teachers cannot be expected to carry chronometers, and that in the circumstances the decision of the trial judge in their favour ought not to be disturbed.

It seems on the evidence that considerable care was taken in the school to ensure that proceedings were ordered according to the right time. The school caretaker testified that he kept the school clock to time every morning and afternoon, checking it against his watch, which he checked in turn against the "pips" on the radio, which he listened for. There was also a clock in the annexe to the school (where the infant plaintiff was) and this, too, was "always" checked. The clock in the school governed the time when a bell was rung at the end of the school session. One of the two school teachers concerned said that she and her colleague compared their watches and released the children when it was 3.30 p.m. School never stopped before that time. The headmistress of this infants' school also insisted that school never closed early, and in fact closed a few minutes late on the day of the accident. The school caretaker supported this evidence.

When these witnesses were confounded by the subsequent testimony which proved that the children were let out at least four minutes too soon, no suggestion was made that this resulted through the school clocks or the teachers' watches, being less accurate than chronometers, were unfortunately fast that day; and the conclusion seems inevitable that the children were released at a time which the teachers knew, or could have known, was before 3.30 p.m. There may have been an understandable inclination to grant this indulgence on what was the last day before the Whitsun break.

Unfortunately the few minutes in question were enough to allow this child to proceed alone 170 yards to the main road, walk up it for a further 80 yards, and then dart across the road into the side of a moving lorry. Presenting the child with the opportunity of doing this destroys the argument about its premature release being a matter of degree. I agree with the Master of the Rolls that it establishes negligence: and I would therefore allow the appeal and give judgment for the appellant for the damages and costs which the parties have now agreed.

LORD PEARSON: My Lords, The infant plaintiff, Sandra Barnes, was seriously injured in a road accident which occurred at Chandlers Ford, Hampshire, when she attempted to run across a narrow and busy main road and ran into a lorry. The driver of the lorry was in no way to blame for the accident. On behalf of the plaintiff it is claimed that the accident was caused by negligence on the part of the defendants, the Hampshire County Council, as the education authority responsible for the school concerned. At the trial there were two main contentions on behalf of the plaintiff, namely, (1) that the defendants had a defective system for releasing the children at the end of the afternoon session, in that the children were allowed to walk out of the school gate without having been first "paired-off" with their waiting mothers or other persons coming to meet them, and this defect in the system caused the accident, and (2) that there was negligence on this occasion by allowing the children to leave the school premises before 3.30 p.m., which was the proper finishing time for the afternoon session, and this premature release of the children caused the accident. As to the first contention, there was evidence from a number of witnesses at the trial that it would have been impracticable to operate a "pairing-off" system in the manner suggested, and the judge so decided, and his decision on this point has not been attacked in this appeal. Accordingly, the first contention has been abandoned, and it is only the second contention that is now relied upon. The evidence relating to the way in which the children were released at the end of the afternoon session is now relevant only in so far as it bears on the second contention, which is that the premature release constituted negligence and caused the accident.

The main road on which the accident happened is the A.33 running between Winchester and Southampton. When it passes through Chandlers Ford it is on the average only a little over twenty feet in width, there is a pavement on either side, and the speed limit is thirty miles an hour. It carries a heavy volume of traffic, and is a dangerous road for young schoolchildren.

Sandra, the plaintiff, was only five years and two and a half months old at the time of the accident. She had gone to school for the first time on the 8th May, 1962, one month before the accident. She lived at Fryern Close, where she would not have much experience of traffic. That is east of the main road, and the school is west of the main road. The main part of the school, where children who are six years old or over are taught, is between King's Road and Kingsway, and the Annexe, where five year old children are taught, is at the far end of Kingsway. King's Road is a made-up road, but Kingsway is a lane and not made-up. Exact distances have been agreed, expressed in feet, and for convenience I will convert them into distances in yards to the nearest yard. A person walking from the Annexe, where Sandra went to school to Sandra's home in Fryern Close would, on coming out of the gate of the Annexe, turn left and walk down Kingsway past the main school, and along a short stretch of King's Road to the main road. The distance from the gate of the Annexe to the junction of King's Road with the main road is 172 yards. Then the person would have to turn left and walk along the main road for more than a quarter of a mile (472 yards) to the junction of the main road with Oak Mount Road, and then turn right and walk for a distance of 402 yards via Oak Mount Road to Fryern Close. The total distance is well over half a mile (about 1,046 yards). The main road would have to be crossed.

At the Annexe there were two teachers, and the number of the children, all of whom were five years of age, would normally be about eighty, though on the day of the accident an outbreak of measles had reduced the number to about sixty-five. There was a usual procedure for the release of the children at the end of the afternoon session. According to the evidence of some of the parents, there might be deviations from this procedure, but such deviations, if they occurred, would not be material to the issue in this appeal. When the children were ready to go home, the door of the school building would be opened, and the children would be led across the playground to the gate, which would be opened by one of the teachers. About twenty of the children were to be taken home in the school bus: these children would form up in a "crocodile" and be led by one of the teachers down Kingsway to the gate of the main school, where the bus would be waiting. The remainder of the children would pass out through the gate of the Annexe under the supervision of the other teacher. Most of these children would be met by their mothers outside the gates of the Annexe. In speaking of "mothers" I mean to include other persons coming to collect the children. A few of the children, say five or six, would habitually not be met and would go home on their own. Also some mothers waited at the end of Kingsway or in cars in King's Road. The teacher standing at the gate of the Annexe did not try to operate any "pairing-off" system; a child would not be kept in the playground until it was ascertained that the mother had come to collect the child. As I have said above, it is not contended in this appeal that there should have been a "pairing-off" system. The children had been duly instructed in matters of road safety. Also they had been told that, if a child was expecting to be met but could not find the mother, the child was to come back to the teacher in the playground, and children did sometimes come back accordingly. There would be on every afternoon at the school-leaving time a school crossing patrol warden on duty in the main road at the point where it was joined by King's Road. He would collect a group of mothers and children and "shepherd" them across the main road.

In the ordinary course of events, the children being released at the end of the afternoon session at the official time, which was 3.30 p.m., there would be a risk that a child expecting to be met would not be met because the mother was late or unexpectedly prevented from coming; and the child, having walked along Kingsway, would, instead of obeying the instructions to report back to the teacher, decide to continue on the homeward journey and would enter the main road; and then the child, not knowing or forgetting that the safe place to cross was at the school crossing under the supervision of the crossing patrol warden, would go further along the main road and try to dart across it and be knocked down and injured. There would be that risk, but in all the circumstances it would not be a great risk, and it can be assumed for the purpose of this appeal that it was a necessary risk and could reasonably be taken.

The complaint against the defendants is that to the necessary risk they added on this occasion an unnecessary risk by releasing the children too early, and it was the additional and unnecessary risk which caused the accident. A simple illustration will show the nature of the additional risk. Be it assumed that the average speed of a five years old child—when running and skipping and dawdling are taken into account as well as walking—is about two miles per hour, and that the average speed of a mother bringing a younger child with her would be about the same. Then a child released from the Annexe at 3.30 p.m. would be met before covering the distance of 172 yards and entering the dangerous main road, if the mother was on time, or not more than about two and a half minutes late. But a child released from the Annexe at 3.25 p.m. would not be met before entering the dangerous main road, if the mother was on time but not so much as two and a half minutes early.

The judge considered very carefully the evidence as to the times, and his main findings, fully justified by the evidence, were that (i) the children were released from the Annexe at or very shortly after 3.25 p.m.; (ii) the time at which Sandra, having made the journey from the Annexe to the main road and passed the school crossing place and walked about eighty yards up the main road, attempted to run across the main road and ran into the lorry and was knocked down and injured was about 3.29 p.m.; (iii) the mother arrived at the scene of the accident at about 3.31 p.m. and therefore probably she would have met Sandra before Sandra entered the main road, if Sandra had been released from the Annexe at 3.30 p.m., the official time. It follows that on a balance of probabilities the premature release of the children by the defendants was a cause of the accident.

There remains the question whether the premature release of the children constituted negligence on the part of the defendants. As a matter of first impression I would say that of course it was negligent, because it added an unnecessary risk, and was unfair to the mothers and the children. The mothers might fairly be held responsible for the safety of the children after 3.30 p.m., when the school's responsibility would, for most purposes, subject to emergencies and special arrangements, come to an end. But why should a mother, who had so timed her journey that she would reach the school gates at 3.30 p.m. (or shortly before or shortly after that time), have to find her child already on the dangerous main road? The difference in time between about 3.25 p.m. and 3.30 p.m. is not trivial: it cannot be regarded under the *de minimis* principle.

I should, however, refer to the evidence and the curious course of events at the trial, which was in two stages. The first stage took place on the 4th, 5th and 6th July, 1967. Although there was some evidence from the plaintiff's witnesses of the children being released too early on the day of the accident, the defendants' witnesses believed that the children were in fact released at 3.30 p.m. on that day, and gave evidence on that basis.

A witness who was one of the teachers at the Annexe on that day said that the children emerged just a second before half-past three from the doorway. She agreed that the main road is a very dangerous road, particularly on a Friday; and that it would be quite unsafe to let a child of five on that road by itself, even if the child had had instruction in road safety; and it would still be unsafe to let the child on the road alone even if it had been told that it ought only to cross where the crossing keeper was on duty, because a child of that age cannot be trusted to cross only where the crossing keeper is; and that Sandra was a normal spirited child and as unpredictable as any other five year old. She said, referring to Sandra: "She is my responsibility until half past three . . . by half past three I expect the mother to be there." She said:

"We never left before half past three, ever." She was asked in re-examination: "Had you any instructions what was your duty about dismissing the children?" She replied: "I was to make sure it was half past three." She was then asked: "Does that mean that if you had dismissed them and turned them out before half past three you would have been disobeying your instructions?" She said: "Yes."

The witness who was the other teacher at the Annexe on the day of the accident said that the school went out at 3.30 p.m. She agreed that the main road "could be a death trap" for little children, and no five year old child of the Annexe should be allowed on that road by herself, and such a child could not be trusted, if it did get on that road alone, to cross only where the crossing keeper was, and that such a child is unpredictable. She said: "School finishes at half past three, and my responsibility finishes at half past three." She said that some parents waited at the end of the lane for their children, and some of them in cars. She said: "School never stopped before three-thirty," and "I always looked at my watch before releasing the children at the end of the day. I was most particular." In re-examination she said: "I think the duty of every parent is to be at the school gate at half past three to meet the child. . . . They knew the school finishes at half past three, and it is their duty to be there."

Four parents were called as witnesses for the defence. They thought the children had not been released early on the day of the accident. Some of them expressed opinions as to the extent of the teachers' responsibility. One said: "They had a duty to see that they walked across and out of the gate at a reasonable time. If you personally asked a teacher to look after a child on a specific day, I am sure they would have done this, but I did not feel they had any duty at all to see to the child after school hours." Another said: "Well, of course, these things do happen, as it did happen, but I still cannot see that the teacher should be blamed at all since they came out at the right time."

Evidence was given also by three headmasters and a former headmistress. Their evidence was directed mainly to the question whether a "pairing-off" system would be practicable, and they concurred in saying that there was no such system in their experience, and it would not be practicable. They were asked about children being let out early from school. One of them said: "I think it is a very good thing that the children should be encouraged to become independent as soon as is reasonable." Another said: "In my experience there has never been any doubt that it has been the parents' responsibility to see either that the child was accompanied or that the child went home alone, and that the parents made that decision."

The last witness for the defence at this stage was the deputy education officer for Hampshire. He also said that pairing-off would be impracticable. He said: "It is accepted by parents that they have two responsibilities, both to see the child to and from school, and I think to make arrangements that if anything detains them the child knows what to do—rather to arrange for the child to go to and from school, not necessarily to conduct them. This is their decision." He was asked the question: "If it be the fact that those children were released before the appropriate time on this particular day, would you seek to excuse the teachers responsible?" He answered: "No, I should say we should not release children before the appointed time."

At the end of the evidence the judge said he was not satisfied on the evidence he had heard that the children were let out early. After the speeches he reserved judgement. But then enquiries were made, and witnesses were found whose evidence would show with some exactness when the accident happened. On application their evidence was allowed to be adduced. One of them was a young man who was working in a garden, heard the thud of an accident, went to the gate and saw the child lying on the road, and then went back to the house, dialled 999 and asked for the ambulance service. Other witnesses, speaking of the times when the call was received and put through, were a supervisor at the telephone exchange and the chief controller of the ambulance service. In consequence of their evidence the judge made his findings as to the material times, to which I have referred, putting the time of the accident at 3.29 and the time of the release of the children from the Annexe at or very shortly after 3.25 p.m.

The deputy education officer for Hampshire was then recalled. With regard to his previous answer to the effect that he would not defend letting the children out early, he explained that he was thinking of the allegation on behalf of the plaintiff that they were let out a quarter of an hour early. He felt that the school authorities would be at fault if the children were let out so early that the period would be too long for the children to wait, and breaking point would come certainly after five minutes, but a waiting period of up to five minutes would not be unreasonable. In cross-examination he was asked to consider release at 3.25 or two or three minutes earlier, and he answered: "I should consider that we were at fault in releasing the child as early as that, and the degree of fault depends on the degree of earliness." It was then put to him that, if the child is released as much as five or six minutes early, the parents' arrangements cannot be expected to function properly, and he said: "We are placing a much heavier strain on them than I think we ought to."

The judge held that the two mistresses were not negligent in letting the children out of the Annexe at or soon after 3.25 p.m., but he did not explain why this breach of the system should not be considered to be negligence. The majority of the Court of Appeal held that it was a question of degree whether the early release of the children was sufficiently early to constitute negligence, and that in this case it was not.

The Master of the Rolls, dissenting, held that the school authorities were at fault in letting the children out too early. He said: "In this case the appointed time was 3.30 p.m. The evidence of the teachers themselves was explicit. They said it was the responsibility of the school to look after the children up to that time, and it was the parents' responsibility after that time . . . the parents cannot be expected to be there before the appointed time and if the school release them [*i.e.* the children] early, five minutes early, they are releasing them into a situation of potential danger."

I agree with the Master of the Rolls. The system proved by the evidence was as he stated it. It was the duty of the school authorities not to release the children before the closing time. Although a premature release would very seldom cause an accident, it forseeably could, and in this case it did cause the accident to the plaintiff.

I would allow the appeal and direct that judgment be entered for the plaintiff for damages and costs in accordance with the terms of settlement which have now been agreed between the parties on the basis of the appeal being allowed. Those terms are as follows:

(1) That the respondents will pay damages in the sum of £10,000.

(2) That the respondents will pay the appellant's costs to be taxed on Solicitor and own Client basis from the commencement of the action by writ of summons in the Winchester District Registry of the High Court of Justice 1964 B. N. 60 dated the 17th April 1964, to include second leading Counsel in the House of Lords.

Judgment accordingly

GLOSSARY

A Fortiori. All the more so

Ab Initio. From the beginning

Articles of Government. An order relating to a secondary school, made under the Education Act 1944, s. 17, defining the respective powers of the local education authority, the governors, and the head master. See also *Governors*

Assault. "An attempt or offer to beat another, without touching him" (Blackstone). Even though no suffering be proved, the person injured may have redress by action for damages as compensation for the injury. **Battery** is the unlawful beating of another, and includes any touching of another wilfully or in anger, however slight

Board School. A public elementary school established by a school board (*q.v.*)

Bona Fides. Good faith. (*Bona fide*—in good faith)

British School. A school provided by the British and Foreign Schools Society, an undenominational body with strong nonconformist leanings founded by Joseph Lancaster

Certiorari. See *Prerogative Writs*

Code. The name popularly used for the Code of Regulations for the Conduct of Public Elementary Schools, setting out in detail the requirements for grant-aid. First issued in 1860, the Code was frequently revised, and disappeared finally (with the public elementary schools) on 31 March, 1945

Contributory Negligence. Culpable negligence whereby a person has contributed to an injury to himself for which others are partly or mainly responsible. Until the passage of the Law Reform (Contributory Negligence) Act 1945, proof of contributory negligence was an absolute bar to the success of any action for damages for negligence. The effect of the Act of 1945 is to reduce the damages awarded proportionately to the contribution of the plaintiff to his own injury. See also *Negligence*

Cur. Adv. Vult (*curia advisari vult*). The court reserved judgment. The term is used to indicate that, instead of giving judgment immediately after the conclusion of arguments, the court gave a considered judgment after an interval

Damages. The pecuniary award made in a civil action in satisfaction of the wrong suffered by the plaintiff. *Unliquidated damages* are assessed by the court in each case, and take into account such matters as the plaintiff's loss of earning power (whether by death or injury) and its effect on his dependants, loss of expectation of marriage, and so forth. *Liquidated damages* or *special damages* represent the amounts ascertained to have been lost by the plaintiff, as for example, fees for medical treatment or the repair of a motor car. *Exemplary damages* are damages on a considerable scale, designed to make an example of the defendant and to deter others, where there has been malice or other aggravating circumstance. In recent years the courts have tended not to award exemplary damages, the current view being that damages should serve only to compensate the plaintiff, and not to enrich him by imposing a penalty on the plaintiff. *Nominal damages* takes the form of a trifling sum awarded when the plaintiff has made out his case, but it is the opinion of the court that he has not suffered considerable damage

De Facto. In fact. The expression describes the actual state of affairs, regardless of any question of legal right (*de jure*)

De Novo. Anew

Declaration. A decision by a court which declares the legal rights of the parties without ordering anything to be done

Defamation. Published matter which tends to bring upon the person defamed the hatred, ridicule, or contempt of his fellows. In general, if the publication is in permanent form it is *libel* (*q.v.*), if transitory, slander (*q.v.*)

Divisional Education Executive. The committee for a part of the area of a county (but not a county borough) local education authority to which certain powers in respect of education have been delegated by the authority in pursuance of a scheme of divisional administration prepared in accordance with the Education Act 1944, Sched. I, Part III. See also *Excepted District*

Ex officio. By virtue of office

Ex Parte. (1) In the heading of a reported case the term is used to mean "at the request of. . . ." (2) Of the one part; one-sided

Excepted District. A borough or urban district with a population of sixty thousand (or where, in a smaller district, there are special circumstances) which has been permitted by the Secretary of State to prepare its own scheme of divisional administration in accordance with the Education Act 1944, Sched. I, Part III, paras. 4–5 and the Local Government Act 1958, s. 52. See also *Divisional Education Executive*

Exemplary Damages. See *Damages*

Foundation Governors/Managers. Managers or Governors of a *voluntary school* (*q.v.*) appointed otherwise than by a public authority. The bodies or persons having power to appoint are specified in the Instrument of Management or Government for the school, and may include, *e.g.* a religious denomination, the bishop of a diocese, a body of educational trustees, or a City livery company. See also *Governors*; *Managers*

Governors. The body of persons appointed to conduct a secondary school under the terms of an Instrument of Government made in pursuance of the Education Act 1944, s. 17. See also *Articles of Government*; *Foundation Governors/Managers*

Habeas Corpus. See *Prerogative Writs*

In Banco. A sitting of one of the superior courts at Westminster for the purpose of determining matters of law and giving judgment. Matters heard at *Nisi Prius* (*q.v.*) by the itinerant justices were frequently sent for judgment *in banco* prior to 1873, when such sittings were discontinued under the Judicature Act

In consimili casu. Before 1285 a plaintiff might be refused a legal right because it was impossible to frame his cause within the rigid structure of the writs available. By the Statute of Westminster II in this year it was provided that actions similar to those (*in consimili casu*) available through the existing forms of action should have similar remedies. Thus it became possible to vary the old writs, but not to invent new rights or remedies

In Pari Materia. In an analagous case

In Statu Pupillari. In the status of a pupil

Injunction. An order of the Supreme Court of Judicature ordering the person to whom it is addressed not to do (or to cease from doing) a specified act which does not amount to a crime. Legal proceedings may not be restrained by injunction. An *interim* or *interlocutory injunction* may be granted until a cause has been heard or determined if it appears just or convenient. This has the effect of preventing the party restrained from doing any act which may so affect the issues before the court that it will be impossible or grossly inconvenient to enforce the legal rights of a party to an action when these have been settled. The purpose of an interlocutory injunction is, thus, so far as possible, to maintain the *status quo* (*q.v.*) until the court sees what should be done. An injunction which is not interlocutory is said to be *perpetual*

Instrument of Government. An order made under the Education Act 1944, s. 17, constituting the body of governors of a secondary school. See also *Foundation Governors/Managers*; *Governors*

Instrument of Management. An order made under the Education Act 1944, s. 17, constituting the body of managers of a primary school. See also *Foundation Governors/Managers*; *Managers*

Inter Alia. Among other things

Interim Injunction. See *Injunction*

Interlocutory Injunction. See *Injunction*

Intra Vires. Within their powers

Letters Patent. An authority under the Great Seal of England by which a subject is allowed to do or enjoy something which otherwise he could not. Letters patent are open (*patentes*) so that they may be readily displayed in support of the right allowed

Libel. A publication in permanent form (*e.g.* by writing, pictures, or the like,) which will tend to degrade the subject of the libel in the opinion of his neighbours or make him look ridiculous. By the Defamation Act 1952 defamatory broadcast statements are regarded as libellous. In addition to the civil remedies available, a person publishing a gross libel may be amenable to the criminal law

Local Education Authority. Local education authorities were first established by the Education Act 1902, *inter alia*, to take over the powers of the school boards (*q.v.*). Until 1944 they consisted of county councils and county boroughs (for all purposes) and of certain non-county boroughs and urban district councils for the purpose of elementary education. The Education Act 1944 abolished the powers of non-county boroughs with regard to education, although some became excepted districts within the area of their county. The London Government Act 1963 established the Inner London Education Authority as the *ad hoc* education authority for the area of the former London County Council, and the outer London boroughs (comprising the remainder of Greater London) as education authorities in their own right

Locus Standi (*lit.* a place of standing). The right to appear before a court or before Parliament in any given matter. A person with no such right is said to have no *locus* (*standi*)

Mala Fides. Bad faith. (*Mala fide*—in bad faith, *i.e.* maliciously)

Malfeasance. The doing of an unlawful act. See also *Misfeasance*; *Nonfeasance*

Managers. The body of persons appointed to conduct a primary school under the terms of an Instrument of Management made in pursuance of the Education Act 1944, s. 17. Before 1945 the term was used to describe those responsible for the management of a Public Elementary School. See also *Foundation Governors/Managers*; *Rules of Management*

Mandamus. See *Prerogative Writs*

Misfeasance. The improper performance of a legal act. See also *Malfeasance*; *Nonfeasance*

Negligence. A culpable failure to perform a positive duty. Where the plaintiff has suffered injury which can be assessed in pecuniary terms, an action for damages for negligence will lie if three matters are established: (1) that the defendant owed a duty of care to the plaintiff; (2) that, by something which he did, or failed to do, the defendant failed in that duty; (3) that thereby the plaintiff suffered the injury for which he claims damages. It is for the jury to decide whether, in fact, there has been negligence, once the judge has held that there is evidence from which it may be inferred. Damages (*q.v.*) are assessed by the judge. An appellate court will not interfere with the findings of the jury unless their verdict is perverse or against the weight of the evidence. See also *Contributory Negligence*

Nisi. Unless. The term is used to indicate a provisional state of affairs. Thus a degree nisi is a decree unless good cause be shown why it should not be made absolute

Nisi Prius. (1) Writ commanding the sheriff to bring the men empanelled as jurors in any outstanding civil action in the country to Westminster on a certain date, unless first (*nisi prius*) the royal justices of assize had visited the county. In this case the jurors were to be brought to the assize. (2) The Statute (1285) under the authority of which the writ of Nisi Prius is sent. (3) By analogy, the civil business of the assizes

Nominal Damages. See *Damages*

Nonfeasance. Failure to perform an act required by law. See also *Malfeasance*; *Misfeasance*

Non-provided School. This term was used between 1870 and 1944 for a public elementary school when the building was not provided by the local education authority but by a voluntary body. These schools are now known as voluntary schools

Non-suit. (1) The renunciation of a suit by the plaintiff, usually on discovering an error or defect. (2) Failure of the plaintiff to appear. (3) Declaration by the court that the plaintiff has not made out his cause of action

Obiter. By the way. See page 13.

Obiter Dictum (pl. *obiter dicta*). Saying by the way. See page 13.

Overseer. Officer appointed to provide for the poor of a parish under the Poor Relief Act 1601. The office has fallen into desuetude by the transfer of powers to local authorities by the National Assistance Acts

Per Se. Of itself; taken alone

Pleadings. The written statements of cause in an action

Prerogative Writs. These were the means by which the Court of King's Bench exercised a supervision over the executive and the inferior courts. *Certiorari* lay to remove the decision of an official or an inferior court into the King's Bench, so that it might be quashed if improper. *Prohibition* lay to prevent an official or an inferior court from acting improperly, and could be employed before a decision had been reached below. *Mandamus* lay to direct an official or an inferior court to carry out a duty imposed by law if this could be secured in no other way. *Habeas Corpus* could be used to direct any person having the custody of some other person to show good cause for the detention. All four remedies are still available through the Divisional Court of the Queen's Bench Division but the first three are now exercised through orders of the court instead of by writs

Prima Facie. Something which requires an answer. A prima facie case is one established by sufficient evidence, and capable of being overthrown only by rebuttal. The term arises from the use of the front, or face, of a document to establish a case, the reply being written on the back

Privilege. Because it is necessary, on certain occasions, that a person should be able to speak frankly what is in his mind without fear of condemnation by the law, certain communications are said to be privileged, and the protection of privilege may be pleaded as a defence to an action for defamation. *Absolute privilege* applies to communications between great officers of state, to words spoken by a member of either house of Parliament in that house, and to any remarks made by a judge, counsel, or witnesses during a trial. Absolute privilege is not destroyed by proof of malice although, of course, a false witness may be prosecuted for perjury. *Qualified privilege* extends to communications honestly made in pursuance of a public or private duty, *e.g.*, character references by one employer to another. Qualified privilege is destroyed by proof that a statement was made maliciously

Prohibition. See *Prerogative Writs*

Provided School. This term was used between 1870 and 1944 for a public elementary school when, in addition to maintenance of the school as a school, the building itself was provided by a school board (1870–1902) or local education authority (1902–44)

Public Elementary School. The term used between 1870 and 1945 to describe a maintained school or department of a school "at which elementary education is the principal part of the education there given." The term was applied both to board (1870–1902) or council (1902–44) schools and to voluntary schools. For a description of the function of such schools see the statement of facts at the beginning of *R.* v. *Cockerton*, pages 30–32, *supra*

Puisne judge. A junior judge of the High Court, *i.e.* one who is not, by virtue of his office, a member of the appellate courts.

Quasi-judicial. This term has not been precisely defined. It is commonly used of the discretion exercised by a Minister following his own procedure while subject to the rules of natural justice; as distinct from a judicial decision by the courts in accordance with strict legal procedure

Qui Facit Per Alium Facit Per Se. He who does a thing by another does it himself. This saying summarises the general legal doctrine concerning the rights and liabilities of a principal and his agent, including those of master and servant: (1) if a servant does what his master should do, it is as though the master had done it himself; (2) even if such an act be done without the consent of the master, it is sufficient if the master ratify it; (3) the doctrine applies to all acts done by a servant within the scope of his authority, but not to those outside that scope; (4) the doctrine does not apply to the acts of an agent of an agent. It is from this doctrine that is derived the maxim that "An employer is liable for the torts of his servant committed within the scope of his employment"

Re. In the matter of . . .

Reductio Ad Absurdum. Proof that an argument is fallacious by showing that its logical result would be an absurdity

Res Integra. A matter in which no action has been taken

Res Ipsa Loquitur. The thing speaks for itself. In actions concerned with negligence the expression suggests that no further proof is needed once it is established that the mishap occurred; *i.e.* it could not have happened if there had been no negligence

Rule Nisi. A superior court may make an order upon motion in a matter in which it has summary jurisdiction. Instead of making a rule absolute in the first instance, the court may grant a rule nisi (or rule to show cause) by which the rule requested is granted unless the opposite party show sufficient cause against it by a specified day

Rules of Management. An order relating to a primary school, made under the Education Act 1944, s. 17, defining the respective powers of the local education authority, the managers, and the head master. See also *Managers*

School Board. A statutory *ad hoc* local body established under the Education Acts to provide schools for the purpose of elementary education in areas where there were insufficient places provided otherwise. The school boards were abolished, and their powers transferred to local education authorities by the Education Act 1902

Slander. Material published in an impermanent form (*e.g.* spoken words or gestures) which will tend to bring the person defamed into the hatred, ridicule, or contempt of his fellows. Unlike *libel* (*q.v.*) slander is never a criminal matter unless an immediate breach of the peace is to be apprehended. Defamatory broadcast material is, by the Defamation Act 1952, libellous and not slanderous. Subject to the following exceptions, slander (as distinct from libel) is not actionable without proof of *special damages* (*q.v.*): (1) an implication that a woman is unchaste; (2) an assertion that a person has committed a crime for which he could be imprisoned; (3) a statement that a person is suffering from an infectious or contagious disease which would make him unfit for decent society; (4) words which would disparage a person in his trade, business, profession or calling (see *Jones* v. *Jones*, pages 344, 349, *supra*)

Special Damages. See *Damages*

Status Quo. The state in which things are

Status Quo Ante. The state in which things were before

Sub Modo. Conditionally; subject to a restriction

Sub Nom. (*sub nomine*). Under the name

Sui Generis. Of its own kind

Tale Quale. In its existing state

Tort. A civil wrong arising otherwise than exclusively by breach of contract, the infringement of a purely equitable right, or a crime. Examples are *libel, assault,* and *trespass* (*q.v.*). Negligence (*q.v.*) is considered by some authorities as a separate tort

Trespass. Formerly a term used for any offence against the law, the word trespass is now usually confined to acts by which another is injured as touching his person (*e.g.* assault or false imprisonment) or property (*e.g.* by illegal entry). At one time violence was an essential ingredient of trespass, and an action was always brought for trespass *vi et armis* (by force and arms)

Ultra Vires. Beyond their powers

Vis-à-Vis. With regard to. (*lit.:* face to face)

Visitor. A person appointed to visit, inquire into, and correct abuses and irregularities in a society or corporation

Viva Voce. Orally

Volens. Consenting. See *Volenti Non Fit Injuria*

Volenti Non Fit Injuria. That to which a man consents cannot be an injury

Voluntary School. A maintained school the buildings of which are not provided by the local education authority but by a voluntary body, *e.g.* a religious denomination, a City company. or an educational foundation. Since 1944 voluntary schools have been divided into three groups— (a) aided schools; (b) controlled schools; (c) special agreement schools. A description of the differences in their administration may be found in G. R. Barrell, *Teachers and the Law* (Methuen, 3rd ed., 1966)

INDEX